# THE A. F. OF L.
# FROM THE DEATH OF GOMPERS
# TO THE MERGER

# THE A. F. OF L.
# FROM THE DEATH OF GOMPERS
# TO THE MERGER

---

by PHILIP TAFT

1970
## OCTAGON BOOKS
*New York*

*Reprinted 1970*
*by special arrangement with Harper & Row, Publishers, Incorporated*

**OCTAGON BOOKS**
A DIVISION OF FARRAR, STRAUS & GIROUX, INC.
19 Union Square West
New York, N. Y. 10003

AM

LIBRARY OF CONGRESS CATALOG CARD NUMBER: 75-96193

*Printed in U.S.A. by*
TAYLOR PUBLISHING COMPANY
DALLAS, TEXAS

to
E. R. and Nora
Piore

# Contents

# Preface

THE PRESENT work follows largely the same general approach as the first volume of this study, *The A. F. of L. in the Time of Gompers*. I have reduced to a minimum social and economic history not directly related to the issues covered. Of course the Federation did not operate in a vacuum, and its policies and actions were greatly affected by events. It would not have been difficult to meander down the well-traveled highways of economic and social history and pluck a few statistics and facts to embroider the record. That road as far as possible has been avoided, because I wanted to delineate more sharply the activities of the organization itself, and this could be done more effectively by a narrowed vision. This self-denying ordinance has not always been strictly observed, but I have tried to limit myself to examining the A. F. of L. as an institution and as the preeminent labor Federation of the United States and Canada in its time.

This volume, like its predecessor, is based largely on A. F. of L. records, public and private, letters of officials both incoming and outgoing, memoranda, minutes of meetings and conventions, including all the meetings of the Executive Council, government reports, and some secondary sources. It is not my purpose to review the reviewers of my first volume. On the whole, they have been more than kind. Several of them called attention to failures to deal thoroughly with specific events or problems. No one can complain of such criticism, and it is often well taken. Knowledge, judgment, and the availability of materials must influence the selection of subject matter, however, and I repeat that I am not preparing a general labor history but a study of the American Federation of Labor. Unless events or individuals directly affected the work or policies of the A. F. of L. they would not fall within my vision regardless of their merit.

This volume completes a work begun in 1949. It would not have been possible without the aid of the Executive Council, and especially of President George Meany and Secretary-Treasurer William F. Schnitzler. President Meany was also good enough to set aside time to discuss with me a number of questions covered in the study. Vice President George M. Harrison gave me the benefit of his extended knowledge of the A. F. of L., and Vice President David Dubinsky helped me to understand a number of important issues concerning the A F. of L. and the C. I. O.

President James Brownlow of the Metal Trades Department allowed me to examine documents in his files; President Michael Fox of the Railway Employees Department cooperated, and George Cuchic of that Department was generous with both time and materials and clarified a number of points I had not appreciated adequately. President Richard Gray was kind enough to discuss a number of issues relating to the Building and Construction Trades Department. The staff of the A. F. of L.-C.I.O. was always kind and helpful. Logan Kimmel of the records department, Bernard Greene of supplies, S. B. Wolls and Edwin Schmidt of the mail room, Stanley Ruttenberg and Peter Henle in research, Mrs. Eloise Giles of the library, Courtland Szell and the late Andrew Blanch, who have been in charge of the A.F.L.-C.I.O. building, Jay Lovestone and Henry Rutz of the International Relations Department, Nelson Cruikshank of the Social Security Division, Andrew Biemiller of the Legislative Committee, John L. McDevitt of the Political Department, Boris Shishkin of Fair Employment Practice, Mary Erb, Miss Virginia Teas in President Meany's office, and Albert Whitehouse of the Industrial Union Department were all of help, as were their staffs. To all the heads of the departments, officers, and staff members, I want to express my gratitude for the many kindnesses which made my work easier and more pleasant.

Professor Jack Barbash of the University of Wisconsin made a number of useful suggestions; Professor Maurice Neufeld of the Industrial and Labor Relations School at Cornell University read several chapters; and E. Taylor Parks of the Advisory and Review Section, Department of State, directed me to some of his files. My sincerest thanks to all these scholars.

Mr. Edward Tobin of the Union Labor Life Insurance Company was good enough to allow me to examine some of the late Matthew Woll's correspondence and records; Marx Lewis, Miss Ida Bilchick, and Jack Rich of the United Hatters, Cap and Millinery Workers' Union made available some of the C.I.O. material. Dr. Nathan Reingold, Walter Weinstein, Albert Winthrop, and Leonard Rapport of the National Archives aided me in examining some records. Edward De Roma of the Economics Division of the Main Branch of the New York Public Library was very helpful, especially in finding some scarce items. Miss Margaret Brickett of the Library of the United States Department of Labor took considerable pains to make several of my tasks easier. Helen Kurtz, in charge of government documents at the John Hay Library of Brown University, was of constant aid in running down government sources. Claire Brown of the Collective Bargaining Library of the Littauer Center in Harvard University was helpful on this and many other occasions. I also want to thank Dr. Herman Kahn, the head of the Franklin Delano Roosevelt Library in Hyde Park, and Robert L. Jacoby, William J.

Nicholas, and Jerome V. Deyo, members of the staff, for their assistance. Dr. J. Joseph Huttmacher of Georgetown University was kind enough to direct me through the papers of the late Senator Robert F. Wagner and gave me the benefit of his knowledge of the work of the late Senator.

In the first volume of this study I neglected to mention the aid of Miss Florence Thorne. It was an oversight which I regret and for which I alone must be blamed. Miss Thorne was the administrative assistant of Presidents Gompers and William Green for more than forty years. Although she always kept herself in the background, she played an important and vital role in the presentation of the ideas and policies of the A. F. of L.

My colleagues at Brown University, Professors Merton P. Stoltz, Deane Carson, and George Borts were kind enough to advise me on several topics. Dr. Carlin Kindilien's editorial advice saved me from many errors, and his assistance was extremely helpful. Theresa Taft acted as an editorial assistant and aided with some of the research. To all who have generously given of their time and patience, my sincerest thanks. A Ford Foundation Fellowship and a grant from the American Philosophical Society aided me to conduct my investigations. My thanks to the officers and directors of both groups. The American Federation of Labor, the American Philosophical Society, and the Ford Foundation are not responsible for any opinions, statements, or conclusions expressed in this work. Of course, all shortcomings, commissions, and omissions are the responsibility of the author.

PHILIP TAFT

*Providence, R.I.*

# I

## Inactivity

AN era ended with the death of Gompers. For more than four decades he had led the largest trade union federation fashioned on the North American continent. And his last years were not destined to be tranquil. He witnessed the great expansion in trade union membership influence during World War I, and he helped to ward off the challenge from more militant labor groups to the ideas and vision by which he and those around him had steered the labor movement since 1886. He was not spared the furious assault upon organized labor unleashed by business under the slogan of the American Plan, the concerted attack which led to large membership losses. The effect of his passing upon the thinking and feeling of those around him was summarized by a loyal follower with the declaration that "the stars by which we guided our ship have suddenly been blotted out."[1]

Gompers' death coincided with another crisis. The wartime gains had been slowly chipped away by the employer offensive. The unions' attempt to reestablish themselves in the open-shop citadel, the steel industry, and to retain nearly conquered positions in other sectors of the economy had been repelled with serious weakening of morale. Despite the widespread prosperity, labor organizations were not gaining in membership; in fact, they were failing to hold their own. One of the older and experienced leaders, James O'Connell, the head of the Metal Trades Department, noted in 1926 that never before had the metal trades' unions had "to contend with a situation of affairs as prevailed during the present year: that of having accomplished not one striking big thing. Our work has been largely routine."[2]

The same note of pessimism pervades the report to the convention of the following years. O'Connell was compelled to declare: "No matter how hard we may work or how conscientiously we may try, our efforts are not rewarded to the degree that we might expect, but I am confident that a return to the state for organization, on the part of workmen, cannot be far distant, and when that time is reached we will enjoy a phenomenal growth in membership throughout our entire labor movement."[3] O'Connell's hopes for a more favorable response to the organizing efforts of the metal trades were not soon to be realized. In 1928

1

another tack—establishing better relations with industry—was tried, but there were no important consequences. The report of the president of the Metal Trades Department to the convention of 1929 is critical of the indifference of the local membership, which had failed to cooperate in the organizing efforts of the international union. Despite the efforts of several international unions which launched organizing campaigns, few members were recruited to compensate for the money and energy expended. In O'Connell's view, a contributing reason "which made successful organizing work most difficult during recent years, has been an attitude of seming indifference on the part of the members locally, an indifference which led non-members to doubt if they were truly welcome if they applied for membership."4 In addition, O'Connell believed that if organizing methods were to be successful, they would have to be adapted to the changes that had occurred in the size of the firm.

The unions in the metal trades were among those which suffered severe membership losses in the postwar period. While unions in the building trades managed to hold most of their wartime gains, the metal trades, which faced severe opposition in many of the newly organized metal and machinery plants as well as on the railroads, could recoup none of their postwar losses. Although the membership of the A. F. of L. actually declined only in 1922, and was slightly higher in 1927, and by

MEMBERSHIP OF THE AMERICAN FEDERATION OF LABOR, 1925–1929

| Year | Membership (in thousands) |
| --- | --- |
| 1925 | 2,877 |
| 1926 | 2,803 |
| 1927 | 2,812 |
| 1928 | 2,896 |
| 1929 | 2,933 |

the standards of the time appreciably greater in the next two years, the movement seemed listless and without drive. In a period of high employment during the 1920's the trade union movement appeared static and unable to arouse enthusiasm within or generate a new following from without. Along with the failure of the metal trades, the membership losses suffered by the United Mine Workers of America were a great threat to the future of the movement. The coal miners of the North had been among the most dependable trade unionists; they had supported the A. F. of L. for three decades and had always rallied to pleas for help from other organizations. Now the union was fighting for survival in the northern fields which it had long held as its own. Yet the A. F. of L. was not entirely inactive.

## CHILD LABOR

From the beginning of its history, the A. F. of L. had sought legislative restriction on the employment of children. In 1916 it had helped to enact public statute No. 249 of the 64th Congress. This statute prohibited a producer from shipping or delivering for shipment in interstate or foreign commerce any article or product of any mine or quarry in which children under the age of sixteen years had been employed. The statute also barred the product of any mill, cannery, workshop, factory, or manufacturing establishment in which children under fourteen years had been employed or in which children over the age of fourteen years had been permitted to work more than eight hours in any one day, more than six days in any week, or after seven in the evening or before six in the morning. On June 3, 1918 the United States Supreme Court, by a vote of 5 to 4, declared that Congress had gone beyond its powers in attempting to exclude from interstate commerce a product not in itself evil.

A conference was called by Gompers to discuss permanent child-labor legislation, and it was finally agreed to sponsor a bill to levy an excise tax upon the product of any mill, cannery, workshop, factory, or manufacturing establishment in which children under the age of fourteen years had been employed. This was signed by President Wilson on May 2, 1919. The Supreme Court held, on May 16, 1923, that "Congress had not levied an excise tax but a regulative and prohibitive tax and therefore Congress acted outside its constitutional authority as a legislative body."

Immediately after the announcement of the decision, Gompers consulted the Executive Council and was authorized to issue a statement to the effect that the A. F. of L. would begin a campaign to secure a constitutional amendment to abolish child labor. The Council instructed Gompers to summon a conference to which all organizations interested in the abolition of child labor were invited.[5] The meeting was held in the Executive Council office of the A. F. of L. and was opened by Gompers on May 16, 1922. He was chosen chairman of the Permanent Conference for the Abolition of Child Labor. Eight of the sixteen members of the steering committee were officers of the Federation or of one of its affiliated organizations. Gompers actively participated in the work of the subcommittee which prepared the amendment. It was introduced by Senator Medil McCormick, and in 1924 the Congress passed by joint resolution an amendment to the Constitution of the United States which would give that body power to enact legislation for the protection of children engaged in gainful occupations.

The A. F. of L. carried on a continual campaign for the ratification of the amendment by the legislatures of the states.[6] But the opposition to ratification was too powerful. Manufacturing interests were joined by philosophical critics who opposed the transfer of state authority to the Federal government and by religious groups that feared the amendment would give the Federal government power to control the relationship between children and parents. Although the Federation continued the fight against the exploitation of children, the amendment never received enough votes. Not until the 1930's was child labor in factories dealt a mortal blow as a result of the change in constitutional interpretation by the United States Supreme Court.

### CONVICT LABOR

From its formation in 1881, the A. F. of L. sought a restriction upon the competition of prison-made goods. Over the years, conventions of the A. F. of L. had recommended that prisoners be paid the same wages, minus costs of maintenance, that were paid to free labor for the same kind of work. The Federation agreed that prisoners should be required to work—for their own reformation and for the benefit of their dependents—but not for the private profit of contractors, nor even for the financial advantage of the state. Throughout its history, the Federation sought the enactment of legislation on both state and Federal levels to abolish, or at least curtail, the competition of prison-made goods with those produced by free labor.

Experience had shown that after the enactment of a state law to prohibit the sale within the state of convict-made goods in competition with goods produced by free labor, convict goods were shipped in from other states and were sold in the open market. In 1928 the A. F. of L. sponsored the Hawes-Cooper Act, which made goods produced by prison labor in one state subject to the laws of the state to which they were shipped to the same extent and in the same manner as if they had been produced in that state. In other words, prison-made goods were, in fact, taken out of interstate commerce and made subject to the rules of the state to which they were consigned. Consequently, states could prohibit the sale of prison-made goods produced by other states if they themselves had outlawed the sale of such goods on the open market. Convict-made goods could, therefore, not be imported after January 19, 1934, when the Hawes-Cooper Act went into effect.

In answering the letter of thanks from President Green, Congressman John G. Cooper, one of the authors of the bill, summed up the contribution of the Federation in the enactment of this legislation. He declared: "I realize, however, that the many long years of labor by the A. F. of L. is the one outstanding thing responsible in placing this measure on our statute books."[7]

The victory on the national level was only a first step, and the

A. F. of L. continued its efforts to outlaw the competition of prison-made goods with those produced by free labor by continually urging its affiliates to seek the adoption of the state-use system of prison labor where such systems did not already exist. Under this system the use of prison-made goods is limited to state institutions.[8]

### Refusal to Allow President Green to Address YMCA

Despite occasional legislative victories, the status of organized labor in the latter part of the 1920's cannot be regarded as high. Perhaps the experience of the president of the A. F. of L. in Detroit during the convention in that city illustrates the attitude—at least of certain sections of the business and religious community—towards organized labor. It had been the custom for a number of years to invite trade unionists to address Protestant churches in the convention city on Labor Sunday, the Sunday of the week the convention met. Following this practice, the Protestant churches of Detroit invited the leaders of the Federation to address them during the convention of 1926 in that city. The Detroit Chamber of Commerce immediately launched a campaign against the speakers, and in an open letter to Detroit churchmen charged that the offer to labor speakers was part of a program to "make Detroit a closed shop city." While declaring against a desire to interfere with free discussion, the Chamber of Commerce expressed the view that if the "ministers of Detroit open their pulpits to men who are admittedly attacking our government and our American plan of employment, it is certain that they will submit to our request to furnish speakers on the following Sunday—Detroit speakers who will be happy to show that our city has outstripped all of her rivals simply because she has been unfettered by labor organizations."[9]

Green had been invited to address the Detroit YMCA, but the board of directors canceled the invitation that had been extended to him. The president of the local YMCA, M. R. VanDusen did not tell Green that the Detroit YMCA, then in the midst of a campaign to raise 5 million dollars, obviously feared that the appearance of a leader of labor at its forum might adversely affect contributions. Mr. VanDusen explained the unprecedented insult with the assertion that the YMCA was not willing to take sides in the closed-shop controversy.[10] A stormy denunciation of the Detroit churches and particularly the YMCA darkened the labor convention. The attempt to stigmatize as disloyal the leaders of the labor movement was particularly resented. Some of the resentment against the Protestant churches was allayed when the Rev. James Myers, Industrial Secretary of the Federal Council of Churches, intervened and arranged a mass meeting at the First Congregational Church. Green addressed this meeting. Eighteen Protestant ministers out of 225 in Detroit "stood firm and welcomed labor men to their pulpits."[11] The episode readily illustrates the low esteem in which organized labor was held among the industrialists of the leading unorganized community of the period, and perhaps points up even more the arrogance of the business community which was then enjoying a great wave of prosperity.

Perhaps politicians, especially those out of office, are more sensitive to events and have a better understanding of the drift of history than do men of business. In the winter of 1925, when Franklin D. Roosevelt learned that the Executive Council was to meet in Miami, he invited the members to lunch on his houseboat *Larooco*. The arrangements had been made by Louis Howe, and after the acceptance of the invitation, Roosevelt assured the Council, "I would come to see you myself but as you know, I am still on crutches."[12]

### WAGE POLICY

Although the second half of the decade of the 1920's was not attended by widespread organizing activity, the A. F. of L. defined its views on a number of issues, some of them of more than current importance. Wage policy came before the Federation as a result of a statement opposing wage reductions on the grounds that such reductions lowered standards of living and adversely affected the economy by reducing purchasing power. The statement was broadened, and the convention of 1925 recommended the elimination of waste in industry as a means of raising wages and reducing hours. A more detailed statement was worked out by the Executive Council.

In February 1926 the Executive Council issued a declaration in which high wages were related to high productivity. The payment of high wages, fair earnings to owners, and the management and the maintenance of a widespread, high, national, purchasing and consuming power could only be maintained if productivity continued to rise. Furthermore, the Executive Council expressed the view "that the wages paid all working people should be the highest which industry can afford and that it should represent an equitable participation on the part of the working people in the earnings of industry." The wage, moreover, should be large enough to enable the worker and his family to live decently and to save sufficiently during his working life to support himself in reasonable comfort during his old age and retirement.[13] The convention of 1926 added to this view by declaring that the "industry that cannot pay high wages is an industry self-convicted of inefficient management and wasteful methods. Organized labor may help to indicate the sources of waste and inefficient management so that the management may make the necessary changes."[14] The view presented was that rises in wages were largely a function of productivity and that the trade unions were to serve as a goad to exert pressure upon the inefficient producer to raise the level of output. In 1931 the Executive Council repeated the high-wage argument in another context. Confronted by widespread wage cutting, the Council insisted that to lower wages was to destroy the home market and cut down demand.[15]

### LABOR BANKING

From the beginning the A. F. of L. was not enthusiastic about labor banking. It was, however, powerless to withstand the belief that unions could strengthen their positions and enlarge their assets by entering the banking business. In 1925 the Council warned those who were thinking of embarking on this venture that they were assuming a "grave responsibility." It pointed to the risks to union funds which were "the sinews of organization maintenance and advancement." In the following year, the Council warned that "there is inherent in the development of labor banks the potential and real danger that interests not concerned either in the welfare of employers or employees, but prompted wholly for speculative gains, will seek entrance into this field and by methods not beyond criticism attempt to mislead well-intentioned workers and unions into banking ventures and security or investment enterprise that will spell ruin to themselves and cast discredit upon the organized labor movement."[16]

### ALIENS AND POLITICAL PRISONERS

In line with the historic policy of the Federation, the Executive Council opposed a bill for registering of aliens. The convention of 1926 commended the Council

for having so sharply and pertinently called public attention to this highly obnoxious measure which would, if enacted into law, mean the adoption by our government of the spying practices of private detective agencies. . . . It is inconceivable that the American Congress will seriously consider legalizing an elaborate system of espionage such as this measure contemplates; nevertheless, we earnestly urge upon the Executive Council a continuation of its opposition so that this dangerous proposition, anti-union and anti-American in principle, will not be written into law.[17]

At the A. F. of L. convention of 1929, Green reiterated the opposition to fingerprinting and compulsory reporting of aliens. This view, he declared, was in harmony with the historic policy enunciated by Gompers.

### SACCO AND VANZETTI

Inevitably, the Sacco and Vanzetti case came before the conventions of the A. F. of L. A resolution urging the granting of a new trial to Sacco and Vanzetti (charged with the murder of a paymaster in Braintree, Massachusetts) was passed by the convention of 1924. The delegates believed that the conviction of the two admitted anarchists had been based upon inadequate evidence and influenced by the heterodox social views of the defendants. Both the International Federation of Trade Unions and the secretary of the British Trades Union Congress appealed to Green to use his influence on behalf of the convicted men. After the conviction was upheld, Green refused to make a statement, but he believed it was necessary for the Executive Council to offer its views on the case.

The Council issued a statement pointing to the danger of a miscarriage of justice and to the widespread belief in the innocence of Sacco and Vanzetti and urged that a commission of inquiry be appointed to examine the evidence. Subsequently, Green, on behalf of the Council, telegraphed Governor Alvin Fuller, urging him "in behalf of millions of working men and women asking for commutation of sentence of Sacco and Vanzetti so that there may be time to develop facts which may establish their guilt or innocence."[18] The efforts of the A. F. of L. had as little effect as the campaigns for the commutation of the sentences carried on by hundreds of other organizations and individuals. Sacco and Vanzetti were executed, and the conviction that it was a grave miscarriage of justice has never been erased from the consciousness of those who asked for another chance to prove the innocence of the Italian shoemaker and fish peddler.

### ORGANIZING

Not many important organizing drives were initiated by unions or the general labor movement in the latter part of the 1920's. At the convention of 1924, a proposal was made to set up an organizing department for women. Instead, a special committee was suggested by the convention. At its meeting on July 29, 1925, the Executive Council authorized the launching of the campaign. To a conference on April 6, 1926, called for the purpose of mobilizing the unions with actual or potential women members, only four internationals sent representatives.[19] Several other unions were, however, willing to donate men and money for the purpose. Reflecting the general atmosphere of the time, the local unions in New Jersey, where the initial campaign was launched, were largely indifferent to the appeals of the Federation.

Edward McGrady, who was placed in charge, found the task difficult and likely to fail. Few unions cooperated, and some which agreed to participate provided only nominal aid. Green appreciated the difficulties, but he argued that the campaign was a necessary experiment and one that was needed to demonstrate to the women working in industry that the labor movement wanted to help them to improve their economic condition.[20]

### PASSAIC STRIKE

In the meantime a spontaneous strike in the woolen industry began. It was led by a Communist Textile Workers' Union. The strike lasted several months, and the hardship and suffering of the strikers made a deep impression upon the public. The employers, however, were in a strong position, for their refusal to deal with the Communist leadership had widespread public support. Convinced that the Communist union would not end the strike, several public-spirited persons negotiated a transfer of leadership to the United Textile Workers of América—an unusual procedure. The United Textile Workers soon thereafter appealed to the convention of 1926 for financial help for the strikers. The convention was deeply moved and responded by authorizing the Executive Council to issue an appeal for financial help. The A. F. of L. collected $34,414.99 for the help of the Passaic strikers, and while the sum was not great, it was donated in behalf of workers not until now affiliated with organized labor.[21]

### SOUTHERN CAMPAIGN

Despite the failures of the major organizing efforts and the indifferent support they received, many members and leaders felt that greater and more strenuous efforts were imperative on the part of the Federation in order to rally American workers into trade unions. In response to this feeling the convention of 1928 requested the initiation of a campaign to double the membership of the affiliates. In reporting on the problem of carrying out this instruction, President Green noted that Federation organizers could lend assistance in areas where organization activity was already under way, but "the initiative must come from the local group who must take responsibility for planning and carrying it through."[22]

Interest in organization had been increasing in the Southern areas. The Piedmont Organizing Council sponsored by the labor unions in the Piedmont communities of North Carolina was one of the manifestations of greater interest in unionism. The Council had been organized at the time the textile mills in that area were increasing their work loads. Charges that the stretch-out system was being introduced were widespread, and the pent-up discontent soon led to a spontaneous walkout at the American Bemberg and American Glanzstoff plants in Elizabethton, Tennessee, on March 13, 1929. The United Textile Workers of America and the Women's Trade Union League sent organizers into the field. The National Guard soon followed. The intervention of Federal mediators helped to achieve a temporary settlement favorable to the strikers. They were, under the terms of the agreement, to be rehired without prejudice and to receive a pay increase.

The forced peace was not long-lasting. On April 4, 1929 Edward McGrady, the representative of the A. F. of L. and later Assistant Secretary of Labor and Vice President of the Radio Corporation of America, and Alfred Hoffman, an organizer of the United Textile Workers of America, were seized by a mob at two o'clock in the morning, taken out of

the city, and warned not to return if they valued their lives. McGrady
was forcibly brought to Bristol, Tennessee, and Hoffman was led to the
North Carolina state line where he was threatened and cursed. As soon
as Green learned of these events, he vehemently protested to Governor
Henry H. Horton.[23] Sensing that the possibilities of a successful organizing campaign in the South were good, Green asked the Executive Council
for authorization to issue an appeal for financial aid for those on strike;
he also called the Council's attention to the widespread discontent in other
Southern textile communities. The Council authorized the issuance of an
appeal.

The strike at Elizabethton was not of long duration. With the aid of
Federal conciliators, an agreement was reached for the reinstatement of
all on strike, and those not reinstated were allowed to carry their cases
to an impartial arbitrator. Management also agreed to deal with a grievance committee selected by the workers through their union. The agreement was ratified by the strikers on May 25, 1929. McGrady believed that
"this agreement allow[ed] the United Textile Workers to remain intact.
There will be no discrimination against anyone belonging to the Union
and members of the Union can pursue their organizing activities outside
of the plant and outside of working hours."[24] But McGrady's confidence
was not realized. The companies introduced some changes in policy,
avoided for a time the more flagrant types of discrimination, and waited
for the sentiment for the union to decline. These Fabian policies were
successful.

Other parts of the Southern textile industry were also stirring. Strikes
against wage reductions and the stretch-out were spontaneously started
in a number of Southern communities. Millowners at Thomaston, Georgia,
and at Greenville and Woodruff, South Carolina, faced strikes. Most of
these were protest walkouts against grievances or wage reductions, but the
United Textile Workers and the A. F. of L. sought to channel this dissatisfaction into organized action. In this endeavor the Federation was
only partially successful. Nevertheless, the interest in organization shown
by Southern textile workers influenced the convention of the Federation
of 1929 to embark upon a more general and more vigorous effort to recruit
the Southern workers into union organizations. A preliminary conference
was held in Washington on November 14, 1929, and a statement was
issued in which the growing unrest of the workers of the South was
emphasized.

A conference of organizers met at Charlotte, North Carolina, on January 6, 1930, to plan the campaign. Two hundred and twenty-nine delegates attended the meeting; they represented twenty-six internationals,
seven state federations and central labor unions, the local unions, and the
A. F. of L. A committee of three—Francis Gorman of the United Textile

Workers, W. C. Birthright of the Tennessee Federation of Labor, and Chairman Paul Smith of the A. F. of L.—was appointed to handle the campaign. Thomas McMahon, the head of the United Textile Workers, asked the A. F. of L. to levy an assessment for the drive, but the A. F. of L. regarded this step as unwise. Green, Morrison, and Woll addressed the conference.

Despite the large attendance, the conference fell far short of expectations. Most of the organizations which sent delegates were not represented by their executive officers; the burden fell upon the A. F. of L. An appeal for finances was issued, but Green regarded the response as "most discouraging." He thought that the $14,000 contributed by different organizations was completely inadequate to finance the campaign projected.[25] Nevertheless, a headquarters was set up in Birmingham and the internationals were asked to assign organizers. Following Green's plea, twenty-four internationals assigned thirty-eight organizers to the Southern campaign. These, together with the four appointed by the Federation, made a total of forty-two organizers working to enroll Southern workers.[26] Following the adjournment of the meeting of January 6, Green toured the Southern areas. The organizers, working under the direction of the Southern campaign headquarters in Birmingham or cooperating through their own internationals, were spread over North and South Carolina, Georgia, Alabama, Mississippi, Tennessee, and Virginia. Less vigorous efforts were made in Arkansas and Kentucky. The textile industry was surveyed and a publicity man was hired to work for the committee.

At the end of the first four months, organizer Paul J. Smith, who headed the drive, reported that the response to the A. F. of L. efforts had been good "despite the shortage of organizers and industrial depression." He pointed to the organizing of a number of Negro molders in Birmingham as one of the results of the campaign. By the end of August, Smith reported that 112 locals of different crafts had been established, and he claimed that he could use many more organizers effectively. Some representatives of international unions had, Smith noted, not cooperated as closely with the Southern campaign as they might have.[27]

The Southern drive was increasingly hampered by growing unemployment. Before the campaign lost its force, the workers employed in the Riverside and Dan River cotton mills at Danville, Virginia, revolted against the discharge of union members and the announcement of a wage cut. The company had established the industrial-democracy type of company union, and when the workers joined the United Textile Workers of America, the company discharged some of those who joined. Four thousand workers were involved in the walkout that began on September 29, 1930. The A. F. of L. convention of 1930 endorsed the strike and authorized President Green to provide all possible aid. The Federation appointed three organizers, including Edward McGrady, and issued an appeal for financial assistance. In the meantime, the United Textile Workers informed Green that it had spent $32,000 from its national treasury and was unable to give any greater support; it asked the A. F. of L. for more help.[28]

Green was sympathetic to the strikers, but he was not altogether satisfied with the management of the strike by the United Textile Workers. He informed McMahon, president of that union, that complaints against the management of the walkout had come to him, and he suggested that some important officer of the United Textile Workers be on hand to advise the strikers. "There is a general feeling," McMahon was told, "that your best representative should be assigned to Danville and that he should remain there permanently as the leader of the strike."[29]

An effort was made to enlist the aid of a number of public men in the hope that they could settle the strike. At the suggestion of Green, McGrady approached Senator Swanson of Virginia. Swanson believed the strike was an error because the mill was overloaded with inventory and the market was sluggish. With the plant shut down, the mill had been able to shave its surplus stock considerably.[30] Finally, W. H. Morgan, a millowner who was not unfriendly to organized labor, quietly sought a settlement. After several conferences he advised the union that the company would not sign a contract. He was, however, able to get the head of the mills, H. R. Fitzgerald, to agree to a policy of no discrimination against union members. It was finally agreed that an employment office would be opened under joint control of the union and management and that strikers would register for employment. No discrimination would be practiced and a grievance committee would be recognized.[31]

There was considerable suffering among the strikers. More than 15,000 persons needed help, almost half of them children. An Emergency Committee for Strikers' Relief was organized and it collected some funds. The A. F. of L. raised over $28,000 in aid, and the Textile Workers' Union contributed a substantial amount. The total expenditures by Local Union 1685 of the United Textile Workers was $297,345.24.[32]

### Communist Efforts in the Ladies' Garment Workers' Union

In 1926 the Communists, after gaining control of the New York Joint Board of the International Ladies' Garment Workers' Union, precipitated a disastrous strike in the New York market. When the International finally intervened, the union's treasury was exhausted and its membership dispersed and dispirited. Hugh Frayne and Matthew Woll were appointed by the Executive Council to seek financial assistance and to cooperate in other ways toward restoring the health of the union. Appeals for funds for the Ladies' Garment Workers' Union were made. The most substantial aid came from the United Mine Workers' Union which loaned the union $75,000. The generosity of the Miners' Union, headed by John Lewis, was deeply appreciated, and when it was again suggested that the Garment Workers seek aid from the Miners' organization, Abraham Baroff, the Secretary-Treasurer of the Garment Workers, told Green that the Garment Workers "did not have the heart to go again to Mr. Lewis for help when Mr. Lewis had already been so good to them." Green called on Lewis and arranged, after explaining the reluctance of the Garment Workers, for more help.[33]

The A. F. of L. directly raised a small amount (about $25,000) and in addition tried to get some of the internationals to lend money to the Ladies' Garment Workers' Union.[34] The Executive Council assigned Edward McGrady, Frayne, and Woll to help the Garment Workers' Union. In the strike of the summer of 1929, McGrady actively worked with the heads of the union, and Green was present in the negotiations with the employers which ended in the gaining of a favorable agreement.[35]

#### References

1. John Frey to W. A. Appleton, September 23, 1924, in folders 1–9 of Frey Papers in the Manuscript Division of the Library of Congress.
2. *Proceedings of the Seventeenth Annual Convention of the Metal Trades Department of the American Federation of Labor*, 1925, pp.2–3.
3. *Proceedings of the Eighteenth Annual Convention of the Metal Trades Department of the American Federation of Labor*, 1926, pp. 8–9.
4. *Proceedings of the Twenty-first Annual Convention of the Metal Trades Department of the American Federation of Labor*, 1929, p. 26.
5. Press release in the archives of the A. F. of L., May 17, 1922.
6. Memorandum in archives of A. F. of L., November 22, 1924; Green to Father John Ryan, January 12, 1925; circular letter to state federations of labor and city centrals, by Green and Morrison, March 12, 1928.
7. John G. Cooper to Green, January 29, 1929.
8. Circular letter to state federations of labor, November 7, 1929.
9. Quoted in *Report of the Proceedings of the Forty-sixth Annual Convention of the American Federation of Labor*, 1926, p. 144.
10. M. R. VanDusen to Green, October 7, 1926.
11. *The Christian Leader*, October 16, 1926.
12. Franklin D. Roosevelt to Green, January 27, 1925; Minutes of Executive Council, February 4, 1925.
13. Minutes of Executive Council, February 18, 1926.
14. *Report of Proceedings of the Forty-sixth Annual Convention of the American Federation of Labor*, 1926, p. 317.
15. *Report of Proceedings of the Fifty-first Annual Convention of the American Federation of Labor*, 1931, p. 87.

16. *Report of Proceedings of the Forty-fifth Annual Convention of the American Federation of Labor*, 1925, p. 231; *ibid.*, 1927, p. 49.

17. *Report of Proceedings of the Forty-fifth Annual Convention of the American Federation of Labor*, 1925, pp. 48, 169.

18. Walter Citrine to Green, April 14, 1927; Minutes of Executive Council, May 10, 1927; Green to Governor Alvin T. Fuller, May 19, 1927 and August 9, 1927.

19. Memorandum of meeting to organize women workers into unions, July 29, 1925; Henry Hilfers to Green, April 6, 1926.

20. Edward McGrady to Green, July 22, 1926; Green to McGrady, August 10, 1926; Green to Henry Hilfers, June 11, 1926; Green to C. C. Coulter, June 14, 1926.

21. *Report of Proceedings of the Forty-sixth Annual Convention of the American Federation of Labor*, 1926, pp. 256–260; *Forty-seventh*, pp. 23; Green to Officers and Members of Organized Labor, October 18, 1926.

22. Report of President Green to Executive Council, November 12, 1928.

23. Green to Governor Horton, April 4, 1929 (telegram).

24. Edward F. McGrady and Paul J. Aymon to Green, May 26, 1929.

25. Minutes of Executive Council, January 9, 1929.

26. Organizers assigned by the American Federation of Labor and National Unions to Southern Campaign (Memorandum in files of A. F. of L.).

27. Paul J. Smith to Green, May 6, 1930; September 5, 1930.

28. Minutes of Executive Council, January 14, 1931; T. F. McMahon to Green, January 13, 1931.

29. Green to T. F. McMahon, November 24, 1930.

30. McGrady to Green, December 9, 1931.

31. H. W. Morgan to Green, January 22, 1931. Memorandum in files of A. F. of L., undated.

32. Statement from Mary Shumate, secretary-treasurer of Local Union 1685, Danville, Virginia, in files of A. F. of L.

33. Memorandum in the files of A. F. of L., December 16, 1926.

34. Green to James P. Noonan, March 14, 1927; Minutes of Executive Council, January 11, 1927; *Report of Proceedings of the Forty-seventh Annual Convention of the American Federation of Labor*, 1927, p. 23.

35. McGrady to Green, July 5, 1929; Raymond V. Ingersol to Green, July 22, 1929; David Dubinsky to Green, July 6, 1929; Minutes of Executive Council, February 20, 1929.

# II

## Inactivity

### TROUBLE IN COAL

The largest union in the Federation, the United Mine Workers of America, faced a different problem. In 1925 the miners in the anthracite fields were engaged in a serious strike. The A. F. of L. convention of 1925 endorsed the strike and Green issued two appeals for help. Lewis was appreciative, and he wrote Green: "On behalf of our organization I desire to thank you very sincerely for this manifestation of the principles of practical and helpful trade unionism. It will go a long way in assisting the Anthracite Mine Workers to win their struggle and win an agreement upon an honorable and satisfactory basis." Green reported that the two appeals had netted donations from A. F. of L. unions of almost $200,000.[1]

Almost as soon as the ink dried on the Jacksonville Agreement in February 1924, the contract between the Mine Workers' Union and the Northern bituminous coal producers came under attack. Strikes were called against operators who refused to comply with the terms of the agreement. At the same time, the union was beginning a serious and long-drawn-out strike in the anthracite fields. The convention of 1925 directed the Executive Council to cooperate with the officers of the United Mine Workers of America in their efforts to win the strikes. Soon after the convention adjourned, the Council approved another appeal, and Green in a statement declared:

The United Mine Workers' organization is doing its best, exhausting every resource at its command, to meet the urgent needs of the anthracite miners who are on strike and their families dependent upon them. For many months, yes, for more than a year the United Mine Workers of America has been spending many thousands of dollars each month in supplying relief in the way of food, clothing and shelter to members of the organization who have been on strike or who have been forced into idleness in West Virginia, Kentucky, and Pennsylvania and other sections. The situation has been bravely faced by the United Mine Workers of America. It is giving of its full resources to the members of its organization in both the anthracite and bituminous fields who are in need of assistance.

But the burden is too great for one organization and the cry for help reaches beyond the United Mine Workers of America. Organized labor in America must hear the cry, hearing it, must respond to the needs of men, women and children in the anthracite region who are suffering from hunger and who need our help. The attitude of the anthracite coal operators constitutes a challenge to the membership of the American Federation of Labor.[2]

As a result of the appeal, the A. F. of L. collected $200,710.67, which was sent to the Miners' Union.

The Miners' Union was able to maintain its position in the anthracite fields, but far more serious was the drive to undermine its power in the bituminous coal industry. In 1927 the bituminous coal miners confronted a fierce assault in the coal fields of central and western Pennsylvania and Ohio. A shift in the convention of 1927 from Los Angeles to Pittsburgh, Pennsylvania, was suggested as a means of directing attention to the plight of the strikers. This move was not found feasible. At a conference between Lewis, Philip Murray, Thomas Kennedy, and the Executive Council, the Miners' officers suggested a drive to organize the industries in the coal areas of western and central Pennsylvania. The meeting discussed proposals to present to President Coolidge when the Executive Council called upon him. Lewis' suggested that President Coolidge be asked to "include in his message to the forthcoming Congress a request that Congress make an investigation into the charges which we make that there is a conspiracy on the part of the large railroads of the country and certain coal interests to beat down wages in the coal industry and degrade labor in that industry; that the coal operators aided by railroads are importing and carrying on interstate commerce with gunmen."[3]

After the conference with President Coolidge, the view was expressed that he had been evasive and that Green would issue a statement if the President's report to Congress was not satisfactory. Lewis "stated that he desired to express his personal appreciation collectively and individually to the members of the Executive Council for their splendid cooperation and support, as well as to express the thanks of the United Mine Workers of America."[4]

A meeting of international unions was called by the Executive Council in November 1927 to consider the hardships of the bituminous coal miners. The intervention of the state and Federal governments was requested.

The conference also called upon all national organizations to help the miners with organizers and money. International unions were urged to "give every possible cooperation and support to this work by delegating organizers or representatives to this field of activity, and especially to aid the striking miners in Pennsylvania." The A. F. of L. assigned William Collins to head the work of the organizers from other unions.[5] A number of unions assigned organizers to aid the miners, and others appealed for financial assistance for the miners.[6]

In May 1928 a committee from the Mine Workers' Union appeared before the Executive Council and asked for the issuance of another appeal for help for the striking miners. The Executive Council responded with another appeal. It urged the international unions to levy an assessment "upon their membership, equal to one day's pay." Where this was not possible, the unions were urged to call for voluntary contributions equal to one day's pay.[7] Both Murray and Lewis expressed their satisfaction for the aid given. Murray appreciated "the very kind interest," and Lewis described the appeal as a "very fine and sympathetic action."[8] In addition to money contributions, a number of unions also shipped clothing and other goods to mining communities. It is obvious that affiliation with the A. F. of L. was of great value. The membership of the A. F. of L., under 3 million at that time, was also answering appeals for financial aid from the clothing and textile workers.[9]

Commenting upon the strikers in the coal-mining industries, the Executive Council, in its report to the convention of 1928, stated: "It is to the credit of the affiliated organizations that the Executive Council is enabled to report that 'within the space of two years the American Federation of Labor received, through appeals for relief to aid the United Mine Workers of America who were on strike, the sum of $689,235.15.' In addition to this, the Council reports, the value of food, clothing, and supplies which were included and distributed amounted to hundreds of thousands of dollars, there being no accurate information as to their exact value."[10]

Secretary-Treasurer Thomas Kennedy of the Miners' Union answered: "The amount contributed by the American Federation of Labor and its affiliated unions has been such as to help out materially in our great battle, and I want to say to you that in due time the formal thanks of our organization will be sent out supplementary to the verbal thanks which I am now conveying to the various international organizations."[11]

A request of a different kind, exoneration of per capita payments, was also made, and this request aroused some opposition. Secretary-Treasurer Kennedy appeared before the Executive Council and asked that the Miners' Union be exonerated from paying on 150,000 members. The Miners, owing per capita for the entire year, were willing to pay on a membership of 250,000. Kennedy called the Council's attention to the "life and death struggle, not only with non-union operators but with a number of union operators. Up until a year ago we had approximately five or six hundred thousand people depending upon us for support. The American Federation of Labor issued appeals to help us out and their help was of material aid and asistance. During the past year we have endeavored to so map out a policy and husband our resources as to enable our organization to get through the crisis and at the same time to build for the future." For strategy reasons Kennedy wanted the United Mine Workers of America to appear as if it were paying on 400,000 members, even though it was prepared to pay on only 250,000. The Executive Council granted the request.[12]

The Carpenters' Union was dissatisfied with the decision. Secretary Duffy, a member of both the Carpenters' Union and the Executive Council, was directed by the General Executive Board of his union to protest the use of fictitious and incorrect membership claims. Moreover, the Carpenters' Union wanted 150,000 of its members exempted on the ground that it was entitled to the same treatment that was being accorded the miners. Green explained that only *unemployed* miners were exempted from paying dues in the Miners' Union, that the latter had just lost a serious strike in Ohio and Pennsylvania, and as a consequence were unable to pay full per capita dues. Green claimed that the unemployed miners were members of the union. Duffy accepted the explanation and agreed to remit per capita on an additional 150,000 members of the Carpenters' Union.[13]

The A. F. of L. also helped Lewis to repel a secession movement which had started in the union as a result of the membership losses and the deterioration of standards in the industry. As conditions declined, the administration of John L. Lewis was subjected to increasing attack. In fact, from the time he had assumed the office of president in 1919, groups within the union regarded his office with mistrust and misgivings. Some opposed him on purely political and personal grounds; others looked with suspicion upon his policies. As the position of the union deteriorated, the chorus of criticism grew louder and Lewis did not accept it with resignation. He was able to take every blow of his opponents and even to repay them with powerful retaliatory smashes. The most serious challenge to his leadership came in one of the strongholds of anti-Lewis sentiment, Illinois District 12—his home district.

Charges of financial irregularity on the part of officers of one of the subdistricts in Illinois District 12 and the support given to them by the district officials led Lewis to revoke the charter of District 12. The suspended officers countered by securing an injunction against Lewis on the grounds that he lacked the authority to intervene because the constitution of the Miners' Union was no longer in force. The basis of the argument was that Lewis had failed to convene a convention at the regular date. The insurgents' call for a convention was signed by John H. Walker, president of the Illinois Federation of Labor and a former officer of the United Mine Workers of America. The executive board of the United Mine Workers of America, upon learning of the call for a convention by the insurgents, demanded the removal of Walker from his job of president of the Illinois Federation.

Green placed the issue before the Executive Council and all members except Arthur Wharton voted to ask for Walker's resignation. Wharton believed that Walker should first be tried by his union, and Frank Morrison, long-time secretary of the A. F. of L., summed up the Federation's historic position on this issue:

The history of the American Federation of Labor is continuous opposition to dualism in every form. Regardless of reasons for such divisions, the A. F. of L. has unwaveringly held that where a controversy exists within a national or international affiliate the only party to such controversy that can be recognized shall be the party that holds a charter issued by the A. F. of L. If we would vary from this historic policy we logically set ourselves up as judges of an internal dispute. This automatically annuls the assurance that autonomy is guaranteed to national and international affiliates when they are chartered by the American Federation of Labor. This principle is of the first importance to the A. F. of L. It transcends individuals and because of its far-reaching effect and its creation of a new rule of action, its application goes beyond the complaining affiliate in the present case.[14]

Green asked Walker to resign. Walker told Green he was acting as a member of the Miners' Union and not as an officer of the Illinois Federation of Labor. Walker sent Green a list of grievances against the action of the officers of the Miners' Union, especially Lewis.

Green answered:

in all the correspondence I have had with you regarding this particular matter I have scrupulously refrained from expressing my judgment or my opinion regarding the merits of the controversy which exists in the United Mine Workers of America. I have simply followed the course of regularity, of conformity to law and procedure in all matters affecting the relationship of the American Federation of Labor to the United Mine Workers of America. In advising you that it was the judgment of the Executive Council that your resignation as President of the Illinois Federation of Labor was necessary and inevitable, there was nothing stated or implied that the American Federation of Labor passed judgment upon complaints which you and your associates made against the policy pursued in the United Mine Workers of America or that either approved or disapproved the actions of any of the officers of the United Mine Workers of America. . . .

The Executive Council of the American Federation of Labor deplores the situation which has arisen in the United Mine Workers, and as I have repeatedly stated, we wish to be helpful and serviceable in any and every possible way in trying to bring about a settlement of the controversy.[15]

When Lewis called a convention to correct his initial error, the Federation threw its support behind him.

In addressing the convention called by Lewis's group, Green proclaimed that the Federation did not attempt to interfere with the autonomy of affiliates. He stressed the fact that the United Mine Workers of America had been given jurisdiction over workers in and around the coal mines and that there was no room in this jurisdiction for more than one union. Green declared: "When a charter of affiliation is granted to an organization by the A. F. of L., giving that organization jurisdiction over men and women employed in a trade or calling, the A. F. of L. enters into a solemn covenant with that organization to which the charter is granted. It gives it jurisdiction; it recognizes its authority; it clothes it with the power of absolute autonomy. And having granted these rights to a chartered organization, the A. F. of L. is under obligation to support that organization in the exercise of its jurisdictional and autonomous rights."[16] It is of course not possible to measure the effect of the A. F. of L.'s position on the ability of a factional group to survive, but the insistence of the Federation that irregular groups would not be recognized undoubtedly contributed to the willingness of the insurgents to compromise and disband.

### BROOKWOOD COLLEGE

One of the actions of the Executive Council which aroused the criticism of educators and liberals was its attack upon Brookwood College, at Katonah, N. Y., operated under the direction of A. J. Muste, a former Protestant minister active in textile unionism and supported by various organizations of labor. The social and political views of the faculty of Brookwood were, on the whole, left of the members of the Executive Council. In the spring of 1927 Matthew Woll, a vice president of the A. F. of L., was asked by Green to make an investigation of the teaching at Brookwood College. The College was not asked to present testimony, and upon Woll's recommendation the Exectuive Council urged international unions to withhold their support. Upon learning of the Council's decision in the press, Muste, on behalf of the Board of Directors, asked that the recommendation be withdrawn pending a hearing of the charges. The request was supported by Robert Fechner, a vice president of the International Association of Machinists and subsequently head of the Civilian Conservation Corps; Timothy Healy, head of the Firemen's and Oilers' Union; Julius Hochman and Fania Cohn, vice presidents of the Ladies' Garment Workers' Union; the Grand Council of the Brotherhood of Railway and Steamship Clerks; the president and three vice presidents of the Massachusetts Federation of Labor; E. A. Johnson, secretary of the Boston Building Trades Council; and several dozen officers of local unions. All those protesting urged the Executive Council to give Brookwood College a hearing so that it could defend itself against the charges. The Council refused on the ground that it had made "no charges against Brookwood College and inasmuch as Brookwood College is not a part of the American Labor Movement the Executive Council deems it unnecessary to conduct a hearing and upholds it as a right to make an investigation where Brookwood scholarships are supported by national and international unions affiliated with the American Federation of Labor. As a result of said investigation we are of the opinion that national and international unions should withhold financial support to Brookwood College."[17]

Of course, attempting to cut off the source of funds is a serious interference with an educational institution, whether it be one supported by labor, the community, or citizens at large. The Executive Council in advising its affiliates not to support Brookwood was interfering with its right to carry on its educational duties and was trying to stifle its activities. In arguing that the A. F. of L. was making no charges against Brookwood, the Council was being disingenuous, because obviously it was seeking to prevent the college, by destroying its support, from carrying on its activities. Woll, in a letter on the question, described the protest as "presumptuous." It was Woll's opinion that Brookwood ought to be repudiated. On the other hand, Morrison and James Noonan, president of the International Brotherhood of Electrical Workers and members of the Executive Council, believed that a hearing on the charges should be held.[18] The question aroused considerable debate on the floor of the convention of 1928 and the action of the Council was endorsed.

### INJUNCTIONS IN LABOR DISPUTES

The power of judges in the Federal courts to issue injunctions in labor disputes and the decisions of the Supreme and inferior Federal courts in labor cases made the A. F. of L. very sensitive to the social and economic views of judicial appointees. In the spring of 1929, the Executive Council visited President Hoover and emphasized its interest and concern in the kind of men who were appointed to the Supreme Court and other Federal courts. The Council commented favorably on the appointment of Senator William S. Kenyon of Iowa to the Circuit Court of Appeals and expressed the view that men of that kind would be good material for the Supreme Court. "The President referred to the difficulty of having men appointed confirmed by the Senate; that had to be taken into consideration." When William Howard Taft resigned from the Supreme Court, Green strongly recommended Justice Kenyon, and informed Hoover: "If you cannot select him because of geographical or other reasons we hope you can select a man of his type." Green also informed Hoover that Learned Hand would be acceptable for the post on the Supreme Court. When, instead, Hoover nominated Charles Evans Hughes, Green said, "I thought we would stand a fair chance with Hughes and I did not protest."[19]

When Justice John Parker of the Fifth Circuit Court of Appeals was nominated to the Supreme Court, Green decided to fight the nomination. He communicated his intentions to the Executive Conncil and to John L. Lewis, but Lewis doubted whether the A. F. of L. could successfully oppose. Green, nevertheless, decided to go ahead with his opposition. In opposing confirmation, Green cited Parker's decision in the Red Jacket Consolidated Coal case. Basing his opinion on the decision of the United States Supreme Court in the Hitchman Coal Company case in 1917, Parker had held that it was illegal for a union to seek to organize workers who were parties to a yellow-dog contract, i.e., one in which they agreed not to join a union during their employment with the particular company. Green charged that Parker's decision in the Red Jacket case meant that he was in sympathy with the Hitchman Company decision, and "that another injunction judge will become a member of the Supreme Court of the United States."[20]

President Hoover informed Green that he was misled, "and [was] doing a great injustice." Hoover also enclosed a memorandum from the Department of Justice which argued that Justice Parker's decision in the Red Jacket case "was dealing with points which had been settled by the Supreme Court which he was bound, under his oath of office, to follow. He and his two associates put their decision upon the controlling authority of the Hitchman case as they were constrained to do, but even in this they were careful not to go beyond the dictates of that decision." Green refused to be convinced and said, in a letter to President Hoover, that Justice Parker would "carry the point of view he expressed in the Red Jacket Consolidated Coal and Coke Company case to the Supreme Court if his appointment would finally be confirmed."[21]

The Federation and its affiliates strongly opposed the nomination and they contributed to the unfavorable vote on confirmation by the Senate Judiciary Committee and to the ultimate rejection of the nomination by the Senate by a vote of 41 to 39. In retrospect it cannot be said that the opposition to the nomination of Justice Parker was either wise or just. Subsequent evidence showed him to have been an enlightened, fair, and honorable judge, learned and understanding of the function of law in a changing society. In almost three decades of service on the Circuit Court of Appeals, after the rejection of his nomination to the Supreme Court, there was no evidence that Justice Parker was influenced in the slightest by what must have been regarded as a cruel and undeserved disappointment.

Opposition to the appointment to the Federal judiciary of persons hostile to organized labor was not an effective method of eliminating the indiscriminate use of the injunction in labor disputes. The greater readiness of courts to issue these orders, and their limitation upon an increasing number of trade union activities made legislative relief imperative. The Executive Council sought some means to limit the powers of the Federal courts to issue injunctions in labor disputes. Andrew Furuseth, the head of the International Seamen's Union, presented a ready remedy to the convention of 1926. It was to deny the Federal courts power to intervene in labor disputes by limiting their equity power to property defined as something "tangible and transferable." Furuseth's views were embodied in the following clause of the bill introduced by Senator Henrik Shipstead in March 1927: "Equity courts shall have jurisdiction to protect property when there is no remedy at law, and for the purpose of determining such jurisdiction nothing shall be held to be property unless it is tangible and transferable." This method of gaining relief was approved by the convention of 1927.

The Shipstead bill was sent to the Senate Judiciary Committee, and a subcommittee of Senators John Blaine, George Norris, and Thomas Walsh was appointed to hold hearings on the legislation. Woll, Victor Olander, secretary of the Illinois Federation of Labor, and John Frey, secretary-treasurer of the Metal Trades Department, were appointed by Green to help in the drafting of legislation. The Federation canvassed the legal profession and obtained the views of leading members of the bar on the necessity for relief from the use of the injunction in labor disputes by the Federal courts. Silas Strawn, president of the American Bar Association, favored a "practical plan for legislation which will relieve labor of the burden placed upon it by the interpretation given by the courts to the Clayton Act and to the Sherman Anti-Trust Act."[22] John W. Davis offered the view that "the writ of injunction has been greatly abused in connection with labor disputes. Through its use equity courts have been frequently called on to assume duties that belong to the police officers of the state. Orders have been issued that come dangerously close to a denial of constitutional rights to the defendants."[23] Many other lawyers expressed similar views.

The subcommittee rejected the Shipstead bill and reported a substitute measure. Weeks of hearings had been held, and the substitute was approved by Attorney Donald Richberg, Professors Francis Sayre and Ernest Freund, and by Roscoe Pound, who declared the "measure . . . exceptionally well drawn and certain to achieve whatever can be achieved in this connection by legislation." The same view was expressed by Professors Thomas Reed Powell and Felix Frankfurter.[24] Nevertheless, Furuseth had enough influence to have the Shipstead bill endorsed by the A. F. of L. convention of 1928,[25] and he informed the three Senators who had labored to produce a bill acceptable to organized labor that it was opposed by the unions of the country. The Senators felt that their work "should not be treated that way." Green believed that in view of the approval of the Shipstead bill by the convention of 1928 and the refusal of that convention to endorse the work of the senatorial subcommittee, he was in a serious dilemma with respect to the anti-injunction bill. The Executive Council then decided: "Inasmuch as the New Orleans

convention [1928] delegated to the Executive Council the power to determine the nature and character of legislation on the subject of injunction
relief, the Executive Council delegates that authority to the resident officers with authority to offer either amendments to the substitute for the
Shipstead Bill or offer a substitute measure, or to take such other action
as in their judgment may seem necessary to meet the situation."[26]

Green, acting with Woll, Olander, and Frey, then conferred with Senator Norris, who was chairman of the subcommittee handling the legislation. It was agreed that the Federation would examine the substitute and
submit it to critical examination. The Federation committee suggested
certain amendments and then submitted the bill to Attorney James Easby
Smith "and he gave the criticism careful study. He drafted the bill in the
light of these criticisms and in the light of the bill submitted by the
sub-committee of the Judiciary Committee. We had a meeting here this
week to consider the finished bill as proposed by Attorney Easby Smith.
He was here with us and we had the benefit of his legal advice. We
arrived at a conclusion on the measure. We have arrived at the draft of a
bill which is acceptable to the Committee with the exception of a few
things they have authorized me to take out."[27]

When the bill was considered on the floor of the convention in 1929,
Furuseth led an attack upon it. But the Executive Council was no longer
willing to support the Shipstead bill. In fact, Green told Furuseth that
"enough time had been wasted." The A. F. of L. had put forth great
effort in support of the Shipstead bill, and it was now anxious to obtain
relief through the bill approved by its lawyers. Despite virtually complete
approval for the substitute, the anti-injunction bill faced a number of legislative hurdles. The Senate Judiciary Committee by a vote of 10 to 7 voted
to report the bill unfavorably. When the bill was not enacted in 1930,
the A. F. of L. sent, during the congressional elections of 1930, to every
candidate for Congress a questionnaire which asked: "Will you support
the anti-injunction bill introduced by members of the Senate Judiciary
Committee and recommended in the minority report of the Senate Judiciary Committee?"

Before the opening of the 75th Congress, the Executive Council tried
to get Hatton V. Summers, the head of the Judiciary Committee of the
House, to introduce the bill, but he suggested that someone else do it.[28]
The task was undertaken by Congressman Fiorello La Guardia in the
House; Senator Norris directed the legislation in the Senate.

When the 75th Congress met, the A. F. of L. succeeded in prevailing
upon the leaders to consider the anti-injunction bill. It passed the House
by 363 to 13, the Senate by 75 to 5, and was approved by President
Hoover on March 23, 1932. The Executive Council was convinced that
the legislation represented the "outstanding legal accomplishment of the

American Federation of Labor. It marks a great step forward, reflecting as it does the culmination of years of effort to secure the enactment of injunction relief legislation."[29] Time has demonstrated the accuracy of this statement, and the legislation was enacted at the most opportune juncture, on the eve of the great organizing drives of the 1930's. Enacted in the midst of the depression, this law has been largely responsible for preventing interference with the activities of unions; it contributed greatly to the expansion of labor organization in the 1930's and to their growth to the present time.

## APPOINTMENT OF SECRETARY OF LABOR

Although the Federation was able to gain, in the enactment of the Railroad Labor Act of 1926 and the Norris-La Guardia Act in 1932, considerable concessions from Congress, it was not successful in having its candidates appointed to the Cabinet office which it regarded as its own. Secretary of Labor James Davis was not actively connected with the labor movement; and when he resigned, the A. F. of L. hoped that one of its members would be appointed. Green expressed the view "that he who serves as Secretary of Labor should understand labor and labor problems, and, in a very large way, should know the mind and thoughts of labor." Green suggested William Hutcheson, John L. Lewis, Woll, John Frey, and John R. Alpine as those who would be acceptable to the A. F. of L.[30]

The newspapers carried the story that Green had demanded that a representative of the A. F. of L. be appointed as Secretary of Labor. President Hoover then announced that the demand he appoint from one group necessitated his going outside the group to demonstrate the principle of equal opportunity and freedom of appointment in public office. Green was upset by the charge and in a letter to Hoover denied giving the impression to newspaper men that he had made such a demand upon the President. And he held his ground, insisting that William Doak, a member of the Brotherhood of Railroad Trainmen, was unacceptable to the A. F. of L. because he was unaffiliated with the Federation.[31] Hoover refused to retreat and Doak, a nonmember of the A. F. of L., became Secretary of Labor.

In September 1928 James Duncan, a member of the original old guard which had surrounded Gompers, died. Duncan had first been elected to the Executive Council in 1894 and had become first vice president upon the retirement of Peter McGuire. He was an out-and-out trade unionist and contributed greatly to hammering out the views of the Federation over the years. Duncan had been anxious to succeed Gompers, if only to complete his term, but this honor had been denied him by the Executive Council. He served for four years after the passing of Gompers, and in his last illness he was destitute and without funds. His friends in the labor movement raised $15,000 to cover the costs of his last illness, and the unspent portion was the only money left by Duncan who had served the labor movement in some official capacity for almost fifty years.[32]

The withdrawal of Daniel Tobin, Treasurer of the A. F. of L., in 1928, was voluntary and was the result of differences over the endorsement of the presidential candidacy of Alfred Smith. When the A. F. of L. Non-Partisan Committee reported on its experiences at the conventions of the two major political parties, Tobin moved that "the Executive Council endorse the Democratic Platform and the Democratic Candidates for President and Vice President of the United States, because of the fact that the Democratic Platform promises much more to labor than the Republican Platform, and because of the further fact that the Democratic Candidate for President was during his four terms as Governor of the great state of New York consistently the champion of the cause of labor and has placed more favorable labor laws on the statute books of the State of New York than any Governor that has preceded him." The motion was seconded by Jacob Fisher.[33]

Green objected to the proposal and cited the criticisms that had been made against the Executive Council when it endorsed the candidacy of Senator La Follette, even though the latter had worked for labor's legislative program over the years. At the meeting of the Council the following day, Green presented the following substitute for Tobin's proposal: "The American Federation of Labor has found from experience that the best interests of its entire membership have been protected and conserved through a strict adherence to a Non-Partisan Political Policy. . . . The wisdom of such action is clearly apparent when it is considered that the American Federation of Labor is composed of men and women who entertain different political opinions. They are not required to become identified with or to support any political party when they become members of the American Federation of Labor."

Tobin protested that the submission of Green's proposal was not in accordance with regular parliamentary procedure, and he appealed the ruling. When his point of order was rejected by the Council and the Green proposal was adopted, Tobin angrily declared:

I think the ruling of the Council is entirely wrong, parliamentarily wrong. . . . When a motion is properly presented and duly seconded by any member of the Council and that is destroyed by a substitute that does not deal with the original motion, I hold that such a procedure prevents the initiative of a member of the Council and destroys his usefulness as a member of the Council. . . . I repeat that my rights were set aside, and I say to you now that under such procedure I cannot and will not serve from today as a member of the Council.[34]

Tobin withdrew from the room and despite the pleas of the other members would not return; nor would he withdraw his resignation as Treasurer and member of the Council. There was, for a short time, fear that Tobin might induce his union to withdraw its affiliation to the A. F. of L., but he soon assured the Council that he had no such intention. Martin Ryan of the Brotherhood of Railway Carmen, the sixth vice president of the A. F. of L., was elected to fill Tobin's post; and John Coefield of the Plumbers' Union was elected to the post of seventh vice president, and Arthur O. Wharton to the eighth vice presidency.

## REFERENCES

1. Lewis to Green, January 23, 1926; Minutes of Executive Council, March 23, 1926.

2. From circular letter from Green to Organized Labor, December 21, 1925; Vote Book, December 18, 1925; Minutes of Executive Council, June 26, 1926.

3. Minutes of Executive Council, November 21, 1927.

4. *Ibid.*

5. Green to the Presidents of National and International Unions, November 18, 1927, and February 28, 1928. Two appeals were made.

6. Thirteen unions wrote to Green that they had assigned organizers, and a number of unions appealed to their members to help the miners. Street Car Men, Operating Engineers, Paper Makers, and Glass Bottle Blowers were among those who issued special appeals.

7. Green to the Presidents of National and International Unions, May 15, 1928.

8. Murray to Green, May 31, 1928; Lewis to Green, May 17, 1928.

9. In connection with an appeal for clothing for the West Virginia miners, Van A. Bittner, the head of the district wrote, "I desire to say that the clothing and shoes coming in as a result of the appeal you [Green on behalf of the A. F. of L.] issued is taking care of the situation in northern West Virginia and you can rest assured that the miners and their wives and children appreciate this wonderful assistance." Van A. Bittner to Green, January 12, 1925.

10. *Report of the Proceedings of the Forty-eighth Annual Convention of the American Federation of Labor,* 1928, p. 238.

11. *Ibid.,* p. 238.

12. Minutes of Executive Council, August 8, 1929.

13. Minutes of Executive Council, October 6, 1929.

14. Vote Book, March 3, 1930, for quote of Morrison's statement. Green to Executive Council, March 3, 1930.

15. Quote in Green to John H. Walker, April 14, 1930; Green to Walker, April 10, 1930; Walker to Green, April 12, 1930.

16. Quote in *American Federation of Labor Weekly News Service,* March 22, 1930.

17. Minutes of Executive Council, October 24, 1928.

18. Vote Book of Executive Council, September 3, 1928.

19. Minutes of the Executive Council, May 6, 1930.

20. Typescript of statement of Green to the Senate Judiciary Committee on the nomination of Justice John Parker to the Supreme Court of the United States: undated in files of A. F. of L. archives. Also Green to President Herbert Hoover, April 11, 1930.

21. Hoover to Green, April 14, 1930; Green to Hoover, April 16, 1930.

22. Silas Strawn to Green, December 7, 1927.

23. John W. Davis to Green, February 14, 1928.

24. Roscoe Pound to Green, July 9, 1938; T. R. Powell to Green, July 30, 1930; Felix Frankfurter to Green, July 30, 1930; Ernest Freund to Green, July 14, 1930; Francis B. Sayre to Green, July 16, 1930.

25. *Report of the Proceedings of the Forty-eighth Annual Convention of the American Federation of Labor*, 1928, pp. 250–252.

26. Minutes of Executive Council, February 19, 1929.

27. Minutes of Executive Council, August 8, 1929.

28. W. C. Roberts to Roger Baldwin, January 13, 1932.

29. *Report of Proceedings of the Fifty-second Annual Convention of the American Federation of Labor*, 1932, p. 65.

30. Green to President Herbert Hoover, April 24, 1930.

31. Hoover to Green, November 26, 1930; Green to Hoover, December 4, 1930.

32. Frank Duffy to Green, September 7, 1928.

33. Minutes of Executive Council, August 6, 1928.

34. Minutes of the Executive Council, August 7, 1928.

# III

## Unemployment

THE position of organized labor became even more serious when the high prosperity of the 1920's gave way to the deep depression of the early 1930's. The industrial production index which stood at 57 (based on 1947–1949 = 100.0) slid to a low point of 30 by 1932. Gross national product declined from 104 billion dollars in 1929 to 56 billion dollars in 1933, before it began rising again. More alarming from the point of view of the trade unions was the precipitous drop in the value of new construction, because it affected an industry with a large concentration of union members. New construction which amounted to 10.8 billion dollars in 1929 was only 2.9 billion dollars by 1933. In that four-year interval the value of new construction dropped during each succeeding year. In view of the great importance of union organization in the construction industry, the falling off in new construction had unfortunate effects upon union membership. The decline in production and gross national product was reflected in continually rising unemployment. In 1929, out of a civilian labor force of over 49 million, 1,550,000 or 3.2 per cent of the workers could not find employment. Unemployment rose steadily and, at its peak in 1933, the 12,800,000 idle workers represented 24.9 per cent of the civilian labor force of over 51 million wage earners and self-employed.

The Federation was aware of the danger of unemployment before it had become a serious economic problem on a nationwide scale. In September 1927 the A. F. of L. published its first survey of unemployment among union members. The survey covered twenty-three cities scattered through the United States. The *American Federation of Labor Survey of Business*, seeking to discover the ratio of all union men unemployed, used a sample that included all workers belonging to unions. Although this was a crude sample, it was, nevertheless, a contribution to economic knowledge because there were no statistics of unemployment regularly published, and no private or government organization was showing interest in compiling such data.[1] The information was collected and the survey continued for twelve years. Over the years, more than 2,500 local unions cooperated. The information gathered and organized contributed to an increasing awareness of the extent and severity of unemployment and encouraged the development of more extensive information by the United States Department of Labor.

Unemployment among organized building trades' workers and metal workers was high in 1928. According to the A. F. of L. survey, the lowest ratio of unemployment among organized building trades' workers in 1928 was 18 per cent in November. A 7 per cent unemployment among organized metal trades' workers in November was the lowest for the year; the unemployment high in this trade—13 per cent—had been reached in July. Unemployment in the printing trades ranged between 4 and 5 per cent through 1928. The survey was continued until the Federal government began to publish more inclusive figures on unemployment.

As unemployment among union members rose, the Federation became even more concerned with the problem. A report from the research department called Green's attention to the views of international officers that unemployment among organized workers was becoming acute. The report warned that "if unemployment continues to increase and the wage earners exhaust their resources, a crisis will have been reached equal to that of 1893–1894."[2] The Executive Council discussed the question for the first time at its meeting of February 19, 1929. The members expressed their concern at the growth in the volume of idleness and observed that "every man willing to work must have employment without regard to age."[3]

In the light of subsequent events, the program suggested by Green and approved by the Council was inadequate. The Council accepted the following plan for meeting unemployment: (1) establishment of a national employment service by Congress; (2) census of unemployment to be included in the decennial census to be taken in 1930; and (3) regularization of employment by management to provide stable work.[4] Here was a case in which recognition of a problem was not sufficient to bring forth even the suggestion of a remedy to meet it. Establishment of a national employment service had to wait for a new administration; and the stabilizing of employment became increasingly difficult as business activity declined. Congress agreed, after considerable opposition, to have a census of the unemployed taken in 1930. The Federation supported its program before Congress, and Green testified in behalf of the Economic Stabilization Act. This bill sought the establishment of an Economic Stabilization Board, a sort of Council of Economic Advisors, to advise the President of the existence or possibility of substantial unemployment. The President would thereupon request a special appropriation for public works. In Green's opinion, such bills were very conservative and represented a first step in handling the mounting problem of involuntary idleness. Green also pleaded for a system of national employment offices which he believed would increase the mobility of workers and make jobs more easily available to them.[5]

The report of the Executive Council to the 1930 convention gave more attention to unemployment than had been customary in former years. The report stressed the interdependence of businesses and the tendency of a decline in business activity in one industry to transmit itself to others. The Council recognized society's responsibility to provide work for all who wanted employment. It represented the following program as a means for relieving unemployment:

1. Shorter work hours to be introduced in industry, with the five-day week and vacations with pay.
2. Stabilization of employment.

The Federation stressed that prevention was more important than relief of unemployment.

In working out a program to maintain regularity of production, shorter work days and work weeks should synchronize with technical progress. . . . While individual production establishments must work out the problem of stabilization for themselves, there is needed in addition team work by the whole industry and team work between all industries. To accomplish this there should be comprehensive planning by an advisory body, representative of all production and consumer groups. Such a national economic council should plan the machinery for achieving economic equilibrium, and undertake to secure the cooperation of voluntary associations and governmental agencies in a coordinated undertaking.[6]

The Council also suggested that industry utilize more efficient policies in production and sales and urged the Federal government to establish a system of public employment offices, to initiate a system of public works, and to promote more effective vocational guidance. It also recommended that the President of the United States appoint a commission to analyze technological unemployment. A suggestion was also made for a study of the relief that should be provided for the unemployed.

A number of resolutions advocating an unemployment insurance plan were rejected in 1930 by the resolutions committee, whose members believed that such a system would require workers to carry passports. The committee did not want its rejection of the resolutions to be regarded as a "criticism against workers of European or other countries who have accepted the 'dole' by whatever name it is called."[7] Green defended the report of the resolutions committee, but presented no cogent argument against the suggested proposals. In fact, in discussing earlier that year the proposals of Governor Franklin D. Roosevelt for establishing a state system of unemployment insurance, Green expressed the view that unemployment insurance was "paternalistic: it is one system of the dole, [which] demoralizes ambition, stultifies initiative and blights hope." He did not believe that such a program would cure unemployment; "the real cure," he said, "is employment."[8]

The continued opposition to unemployment insurance by the A. F. of L. was based upon more than a desire to maintain a historic policy. At the meeting of the Executive Council in January 1931, the problem was canvassed. In reporting on this question, Green stated that the alternate policies were cure or relief. Prevention of unemployment was held to be the "constructive course." The problem was regarded from the same point of view as the maintenance of reserves for the payment of dividends and interest. The Federation believed that an application of the reserve principle to labor would assure workers either stable employment or income over the business cycle. "By allotting some of the income to a wage reserve, wages could be taken care of in business depressions in the same way as dividends and interest. We believe that the practice of wage reserves can be established in much the same way as were other reserves. There is involved the development of intangible rights, the acceptance of the right of a wage earner to his job, the obligation of industry to conserve and advance the investment the wage earner makes in the industry."[9]

This proposal is not far from the supplementary unemployment benefit plan of the Automobile Workers' Union. Not all members of the Executive Council were opposed to unemployment insurance. Arthur Wharton expressed a preference for employment at decent wages, but said if workers were denied employment then some means of providing for their needs must be devised.

As the depression continued to spread, the Federation sharply criticised the increasing reduction in wages. This policy, the Exectutive Council declared, was in violation of the promise made by business, at the conference called by President Hoover in the fall of 1930, that no widespread campaign to reduce wages would be undertaken. The assurance was regarded by the Council as a "constructive achievement. It meant a definite effort to maintain standards and to prevent the foundations of buying power from being completely undermined. It added a new element of security to wage earners' status. It was a recognition of the principle that the misfortunes of business are not to be handed over to wage earners in the form of wage reductions."[10]

The Council found one year later that many firms had resorted to wage cuts. The Council saw the tendency to reduce wages as

a public violation of the understanding reached at the President's Conference. The Council holds that the action of these employing interests is indefensible both from an ethical and economic point of view. Everyone knows that what we need is a restoration of buying power and the preservation of the

American standard of living. Apparently, those employers who would attempt to enforce reductions in wages think only in terms of increased production. . . . The Executive Council of the American Federation of Labor is of the opinion that the serious unemployment situation which now prevails calls for drastic consideration and drastic action. It firmly believes that the wage-cutting policy urged by certain banking interests and certain employers should be effectively stopped.[11]

When the United States Steel Corporation announced a reduction in wages on September 23, 1931 Green denounced the action as a "blow . . . struck against the forces which have been and are now serving to bring about the return of prosperity." The wage cut, Green charged, was a violation of the pledge given to President Hoover and was "morally wrong and economically unsound."[12]

The Council continued its demand for the employment of the idle through a reduction of the hours of labor of those employed. At its summer meeting in 1931, the Council urged federal, state, and community groups to begin immediate preparations for the relief of the needy. The statement criticised the failure of industry to devise a program to meet the economic catastrophe engulfing the country. The Council claimed that its program of reducing the working week to five days and the daily hours of labor to six was the only remedy at hand. The Council also proposed a meeting of representatives of labor and industry to

deal with the subject in a direct way. It could [the proposal stated] do more to assist and remedy the distressing unemployment situation than legislative bodies could hope to accomplish. . . . A National Conference, such as the Council recommends, should be called. It would stimulate buying power, restore confidence, overcome, in a very large degree, the psychological conditions which seem to have frozen the purchasing power of millions of people. . . . The Council sums up the situation as a choice between employment, work for all willing workers, or the development of an irresistible demand for unemployment relief legislation. Industry cannot prevent unemployment relief legislation if it refuses to supply work.[13]

The Federation was not ready in 1931 to endorse a system of unemployment insurance. Reporting to the convention of that year, the Executive Council had found that management practices had become rigid. Arguing that unemployment insurance might encourage workers to continue in declining industries and in obsolete trades, the Council reasoned, "unemployment insurance may be the crutch that permanently weakens industry and keeps it from solving a problem whose solution is essential."[14] The Council did not believe that the experiences of Germany and England with unemployment insurance could serve as a guide for the workers of the United States, because the percentage of workers organized in those countries was much higher and because those countries did not have aggregations of organized employers seeking continually to break down the labor organizations. Instead of unemployment insurance, the Council encouraged the creation and enlargement of work opportunities. Shorter hours and planned production were the methods, they believed, which could be and should be used to meet the curse of widespread unemployment.

The Council concluded that the "American working people want work. They demand work. They abhor charity and they resent the imposition of the dole. They are proud in spirit and resolute in purpose. They must not and will not become the victims of a paternalistic policy. Work must be supplied to all who are willing and able to work. Managers and owners of industry must meet this social obligation and discharge this responsibility."[15]

But not all affiliated groups were equally anxious to maintain the traditional position of the A. F. of L. Three resolutions endorsing unemployment insurance were submitted to the convention of 1931. The resolutions committee recommended nonconcurrence and the defense by the committee's spokesmen can scarcely be regarded as an impressive performance. Matthew Woll, the chairman of the resolutions committee, blandly, and incorrectly, announced that the "British trade union movement does not favor unemployment insurance." He repeated the traditional Federation view that "industry is responsible for work opportunity"; the adoption of unemployment insurance, he urged, would remove "the responsibility of industry and place . . . it upon Government."

Charles Howard, president of the International Typographical Union and future secretary for the Committee for Industrial Organization, feared that in the United States, where the trade unions were still fighting for their right to exist in some industries, a system of unemployment insurance might be used as an argument against organized labor. An important defection from the controlling group took place when Daniel Tobin criticised the report of the resolutions committee. Tobin brushed aside the argument that unemployment insurance was a dole; he reminded his listeners of the poverty and need abounding in every community and the paltry methods used to help those without means. Pointing to the Indiana villages inhabited by Green's organization, the United Mine Workers of America, he declared: "You can travel from village to village and from town to town and see starving men, children and mothers suffering from the loss of every kind of necessity, sickness predominating everywhere. No one can exaggerate the pictures, and I am not playing to prejudice." He went on to describe the suffering among the members of his own union and of other unions as well. Tobin's views were supported by William Mahon, the head of the Street Car Men's Union.

But Green still regarded the advocacy of unemployment insurance in

1931 as a sign that the A. F. of L. was being asked to act like "young men in a hurry." He informed the delegates that they were "the guardians of our movement. . . . There is imposed upon us an obligation to protect it, and surely when we consider a fundamental principle, such as is now being considered by this convention, involving the very life and existence of our movement, our duty is plain, and that is, first of all, to protect the movement that we love and represent." Green conceded that the labor movement would eventually support some form of unemployment insurance, or "permanent relief," as he called it, but, according to his view, the time had not yet arrived. The report of the resolutions committee was adopted; unemployment insurance was not approved.[16]

Economic conditions continued to deteriorate. Unemployment increased steadily in 1932, and the Executive Council reluctantly changed its position. In a statement on July 20, 1932, the Council reiterated its view that industry had the primary responsibility for supplying wage earners with jobs. "Labor cannot apply economic and industrial policies or adopt industrial remedies because it does not own or manage industry. Labor can urge and advise the acceptance of economic and social remedies." The Council offered again the prescription it had presented many times since the beginning of serious unemployment: the reduction of the work day and the work week. The Federation assumed that

industry as now mechanized cannot supply work for more than fifty million working men and women in the United States six days per week and long hours per day. The Nation must either give up machinery or give up the long work-week and the long work-day. If we are to do the work of the Nation through the operation of mechanical processes and the substitution of power for human toil we must adjust the work-time, the number of days worked per week and the number of hours worked per day, so as to conform to the increased productivity of individual workers and of industry. No thinking person would willingly see the human race deprived of the great benefits of machinery and power nor would he be willing to retrace his steps over the path of progress which the Nation has made.[17]

At the same session, the Council instructed Green to draw up legislation on unemployment insurance for the approval of the Council at its October meeting. Vice President Wharton favored Federal legislation.[18]

Green sought the advice of a number of experts on unemployment insurance and its legal aspects. Justice Brandeis expressed a willingness to see him at his summer home at Chatham, Massachusetts, but Green was unable to visit him there because of other commitments. Miss Florence Thorne, President Green's administrative assistant, was informed by Justice Brandeis's daughter, "Father assures me that he will be glad to counsel with President Green."[19] The Federation was anxious to have a Federal bill enacted, but it was assured by eminent legal advisors that such an aim was unrealizable. Felix Frankfurter, then a professor at the Harvard Law School, told the A. F. of L. that "an enactment Federal in scope appears clearly unattainable." In Frankfurter's opinion, the

settled doctrine of the Supreme Court precludes Federal legislation wider in scope than the protection of interstate transportation workers, etc., and even then such workers only when engaged in interstate business. In other words, there can be no constitutional federal legislation as to employees engaged in manufacture, construction, and the like activities. By no legal hocus-pocus, by no legal phrasing, is it possible to escape the conclusive body of the Supreme Court decisions differentiating between commerce on one hand and the manufacture, mining, and the construction of things that subsequently enter the stream of commerce. It is really idle to waste time on this hope for Federal legislation. If I speak dogmatically, it is because the Supreme Court decisions leave no escape.[20]

Frankfurter advised that laws be drafted for the states. He recognized that such state laws would be attacked on the ground of the denial of due process guaranteed by the Fourteenth Amendment to the Constitution, but he was "confident that . . . [owing to] the liberalizing education which the depression must be working even in the minds of conservative judges, [he thought] an appropriately devised state law will successfully run the gauntlet of objections based upon the due process clause."[21]

A group of experts on unemployment insurance were called into session to aid the Federation in drafting legislation. The report of the Executive Council to the convention of 1932 was more than the presentation of legislation on unemployment insurance. For the leaders of the A. F. of L., unemployment insurance was still regarded as far less desirable than steady work at good wages, and they tried to refrain on both philosophical and emotional grounds from endorsing a program which was not "industry-centered." The report to the convention contained a sharp criticism "of our institutions and practices . . . that precipitated the disaster." The report pointed to unlimited competition and attributed many of the existing economic difficulties to improper income distribution and the lack of adequate planning.

The Executive Council recommended a program that included steeply graduated income and inheritance taxes, constructive credit control, recognition of the workers' equities in the industries employing them, protection of their jobs to the same degree that investors are protected, creation of a Federal agency to collect information on wages and hours and income so as to develop better information on economic balance, Federal licensing of corporations, and organization of wage earners to advance their interests. In a marked reversal of historic policy, the Council also presented a plan for unemployment insurance.

In the section dealing with unemployment insurance, the Council presented a view that in principle favored a national law applicable throughout the United States.

But, due to the provisions and limitations of the United States Constitution as interpreted by the courts, since the regulation of manufacture and industry lies primarily within the province of state rather than federal activity, it is practically impossible to enact constitutional federal legislation adequately providing for unemployment insurance covering employees engaged in work in the different states. The American Federation of Labor, therefore, advocates the passage of unemployment insurance legislation in each separate state, and the supplementing of such state legislation by federal enactments; such, for instance, as bills covering employees engaged in interstate commerce or employed in federal territories.[22]

The Council sought the type of bill that would help to stimulate regular employment as well as to provide for compensation payments. The Council believed that the cost of unemployment insurance should be borne exclusively by the employer through a contribution to a state fund. They held, further, that workers should be protected in their rights to benefits by not being required to accept employment when a job was vacant as a result of a labor dispute, if wages and other conditions of employment were inferior to those prevailing for similar work in the locality, and if workers as a condition of employment would have to agree not to belong to a union or to refrain from joining a union during their tenure.

In addition to the report endorsing unemployment insurance by the Council, the delegation from the United Mine Workers of America submitted a comprehensive report in support of such a program. John Frey, the head of the Metal Trades Department, feared that this step, the endorsement of unemployment insurance, represented a significant change in Federation policy and he insisted that the surest unemployment insurance was a shortened work day. Charles P. Howard, the head of the Typographical Union, thought that in order to qualify for unemployment insurance workers would have to sacrifice their rights.[23] The convention, however, finally endorsed unemployment insurance over these objections.

UNEMPLOYMENT RELIEF

From the beginning of the depression, the A. F. of L. encouraged adequate appropriations for the relief of the unemployed. When the Costigan-La Follette bill for a Federal appropriation for the unemployed was pending in Congress, Green asked the Council to take a position on the legislation. He differentiated between the attitude to be taken toward a relief measure and one toward compulsory unemployment insurance which he described in January 1932 as "a union-wrecking measure." He asked the Council to approve the Costigan-La Follette bill and to order Edward McGrady, the A. F. of L. legislative representative, to testify on behalf of the measure.[24] Green also sought to gain the support of the Railway Labor Executives for this measure.

With the change of national administrations in 1933, the Federation submitted to Congress a program for unemployment relief. It urged that an appropriation of an "amount of money sufficient to meet the urgent relief needs caused by continuous unemployment" be set aside. "Feeding of the hungry, distressed men, women and children constitutes an emergency as great as the financial situation." In addition, the Federation requested the launching of a public works program as quickly as possible. Public buildings could, in the opinion of the A. F. of L., be constructed, and these could be supplemented by road construction, elimination of railroad grade crossings, reclamation, and other governmental projects. Along with this public work program, self-liquidating projects, such as slum clearances, new housing, and tunnel and bridge construction were to be encouraged wherever practical and feasible.

The main emphasis in this statement was again on the necessity for shortening of work hours for permanent relief of unemployment. Convinced that technical progress had made the five-day week and the six-hour day imperative, the Federation regarded relief and unemployment insurances as stopgaps and not as methods for curing the basic disease. Moreover, the A. F. of L. continued to think in terms of employment and income rather than in terms of relief and aid. Setting its sights upon shorter hours, it advocated the Black-Connery bill which was designed to achieve this end. In approving this legislation, the A. F. of L. was modifying its historical opposition to legislating on hours for men, but the Federation was convinced that only by reducing hours of labor without a reduction in wages could the widespread unemployment be overcome. The statement therefore urged the enactment of the Black-Connery bill to establish the six-hour, five-day work week. It concluded that "unemployment insurance offers a partial remedy for the suffering and distress caused by unemployment. Special efforts should be made to secure the enactment of adequate, practical unemployment insurance legislation both by the Federal government and by the different state legislatures."[25]

The A. F. of L. recognized that the wages paid on emergency relief projects, instituted by the first Roosevelt Administration in 1933, represented an improvement over the wages that were being paid on work-relief jobs by many local authorities.

On relief work organized by the Federal government, the Works Progress Administration, the Federation asked that prevailing wage rates be maintained on all such programs. In the view of the Council, it was not possible to maintain two wage rates, one in private industry and a lower one in relief projects. The Council believed that unless the prevailing rate was maintained, there would be a steady decline in rates until the relief wage was the prevailing one.[26]

In the relief appropriations, the Federation always sought to have a generous amount allocated to the Public Works Administration, which was used for building construction. These projects employed building trades' men and paid the going rates of wages. The Federation was not enthusiastic about the Civilian Conservation Corps organized by the Administration to aid the unemployed of younger age. On behalf of the Federation, Green wrote that "regimentation of labor through enlistment in the Civilian Conservation Corps, under military discipline and military control, will . . . waken feelings of grave apprehension in the hearts and minds of Labor. Military control and military domination, with its segregation plans, transgresses in a very large degree upon the free exercise of Labor, and, in itself, is repugnant to those who are earnestly endeavoring to bring about the restoration of normal economic and industrial conditions." In addition, Green criticised Army control and Army rates of pay, although he approved the reclamation and reforestation programs launched under the Civilian Conservation Corps program.[27] The Federation changed its views and was satisfied that the Civilian Conservation Corps would not be militarized after Robert Fechner, a vice-president of the International Association of Machinists, had been appointed to carry out its program.

REFERENCES

1. *American Federationist,* March 1929, pp. 328–329.
2. Memorandum to President Green, February 9, 1928, in files of A. F. of L.
3. Minutes of the Executive Council, February 19, 1929.
4. Minutes of Executive Council, May 21, 1929.
5. *Hearings before the Committee on the Judiciary, House of Representatives, 71st Congress, 2d Session, on S. S. 3059, 3060 H. R. 8374, etc.,* June 11 and 12, 1930, pp. 22–50.
6. *Report of Proceedings of the Fiftieth Annual Convention of the American Federation of Labor,* 1930, pp. 59–63.
7. *Ibid.,* p. 312.
8. Minutes of Executive Council, September 12, 1930.
9. Minutes of the Executive Council, January 13, 1931.
10. *Report of the Proceedings of the Fiftieth Annual Convention of the American Federation of Labor,* 1930, p. 59.
11. Minutes of the Executive Council, May 13, 1931.
12. *American Federation of Labor Weekly News Service,* September 26, 1931.
13. Minutes of Executive Council, August 12, 1931.
14. *Report of the Proceedings of the Fifty-second Annual Convention of the American Federation of Labor,* 1932, p. 162.
15. *Ibid.,* p. 163.

16. The discussions quoted are found in *Ibid.*, pp. 371–398.

17. Minutes of Executive Council, July 20, 1932.

18. *Ibid.*, July 12, 1932.

19. Elizabeth Brandeis to Florence Thorne, August 3, 1932.

20. Frankfurter to Green, September 29, 1932.

21. *Ibid.*

22. *Report of Proceedings of the Fifty-second Annual Convention of the American Federation of Labor*, 1932, p. 41.

23. *Ibid.*, pp. 325–360.

24. Minutes of Executive Council, February 4, 1932; *Hearings before a Subcommittee on Labor, House of Representatives, 72d Congress, 1st Session on H. R. 206, 6011, and 8088*, February 1, 1932 (Washington, D. C.: Government Printing Office, 1932), pp. 15–18.

25. Recommendations Submitted by Representatives of the American Federation of Labor, March 30, 1933.

26. *Ibid.*, February 16, 1935.

27. *American Federation of Labor News Service*, March 25, 1933.

# IV

## The National Industrial Recovery Act

To meet the serious and widespread unemployment, the newly elected administration of Franklin Delano Roosevelt considered a multitude of suggestions. The reduction of the hours of labor seemed a simple and direct method for spreading work and thereby reducing the number of those without employment and income, and a bill to establish the five-day, thirty-hour week was introduced into the Congress by Senator Hugo L. Black and Congressman William Connery. The Black-Connery bill, strongly supported by the A. F. of L., passed the United States Senate on May 17, 1933. While the bill was pending in the House, President Roosevelt submitted a substitute which proposed a more revolutionary approach to the problem of unemployment.

The National Industrial Recovery amendment sought to stimulate industrial recovery by a program of reemployment and to introduce permanent changes in the economy that would make a depression of the then current magnitude unlikely or impossible in the future. The National Industrial Recovery amendment provided for the promulgation of "codes of fair competition" by single industries which had for their purpose the elimination of forms of competition described as harmful. These codes of fair competition were to be drawn up by single trades or industries or by associations representing such groups. There were to be no formal restrictions upon admission. Such codes were to be approved by the President of the United States or his representative. As a condition for approving a code, the President had to find that the codes were designed to carry out the purposes of the recovery program and not to promote monopoly or oppression of the small producer. "Approved codes were to become standards of fair competition for the entire industry within the meaning of the Federal Trade Commission Act, and enforceable by proceedings in equity in the Federal Courts to restrain violations and by the imposition of a fine for any violation."[1]

The proposals for regulating industry through codes of fair competition were approved by leading businessmen and their organizations, and they sought the support of the A. F. of L. for this program. President Green "advised the members of the Executive Council that Mr. [Henry] Harriman, president of the United States Chamber of Commerce, said he would like to present his views to the Council in behalf of the production plan that has been discussed in the newspapers. He thought it might be helpful if we knew his point of view and that we might look with favor upon the principles of this character of legislation." Some members of the Council expressed a willingness to hear Harriman, but others felt that a meeting between the Council and representatives of the Chamber of Commerce might be misinterpreted by the public and members of organized labor. Harriman did not appear, and the members of the Council discussed "the control of production plan and the position was emphasized that we would not favor it unless there is included in the legislation a section guaranteeing the right of workers to organize in labor unions and be represented by persons of their own choosing; a section similar to the one enacted in the Bankruptcy Act declaring the public policy of the United States guaranteeing the right of labor to organize."[2]

Credit for the origination of Section 7 (a), which gave labor the right to organize and to bargain collectively, has been claimed by many, including John L. Lewis. The statement at the meeting of the Executive Council, however, was made without the prompting of Lewis, who was not then one of its members. Edward Keating, the editor of *Labor*, the newspaper published by the railroad unions, had called the attention of Arthur Wharton, the head of the International Association of Machinists, to the need for including protection of labor's right to organize in the Bankruptcy Act, which was enacted in the last days of the Hoover Administration. During a discussion between Wharton and Keating on the pending Bankruptcy Act to reorganize the railroads, Keating suggested the following proposal:

No judge or trustee acting under this Act shall deny or in any way question the right of employees under his jurisdiction to join the labor organization of their choice, and it shall be unlawful for any judge, trustee, or receiver to interfere in any way with the organizations of employees, or to use the funds of the railroad under his jurisdiction, in maintaining so-called company unions, or to influence or coerce employees in an effort to induce them to join or remain members of such company unions.

No judge, trustee, or receiver acting under this Act shall require any person seeking any contract or agreement on the property under his jurisdiction to sign any contract or agreement promising to join or to refuse to join a labor organization; and if such contract has been enforced on their property prior to the property coming under the jurisdiction of said judge, trustee, or receiver, the said judge, trustee, or receiver, as soon as the matter is called to his attention, shall notify the employees by an appropriate order that said contract has been discarded and is no longer binding on them in any way.

The provision had been drafted in rough form by Edward Keating with

Wharton's help. Keating asked Representative Hatton Summers to introduce the amendment, and the congressman, although in favor of the
amendment, refused, because he believed the legislation ought to be
sponsored by others. Summers suggested a "harmless" amendment be
attached which could be strengthened in the Senate. When the bill
reached the Senate, Keating discussed the matter with Senator Samuel
Bratton of New Mexico, who was opposed to the bill. According to
Keating the opposition to the legislation was gaining strength and some
of the advisors of President-elect Roosevelt were lobbying on its behalf.
In the meantime, Keating had submitted to Senator Norris a rough draft
of an amendment to protect the workers' right to organize.

Senator Norris's amendment, incorporated in the adopted bill, was
opposed by Senator Daniel Hastings in charge of the measure on the
Senate floor. Arguing that Norris's proposal was a new kind of legislation,
he offered an amendment to the amendment which would have diluted
the effect of the proposal. The Senate rejected Hastings' amendment, and
Hastings immediately sought a reconsideration of the vote. The Senate
then became entangled in a parliamentary wrangle which threatened to
postpone a vote on the bill. Hastings thereupon withdrew his amendment
"so that we may proceed" to a vote. The bill passed by a vote of 48 to 8,
with forty-four Senators abstaining from voting.[3]

Keating believed that the acceptance of the amendment to the Bankruptcy Act protecting the right to organize was an attempt to placate the
growing opposition to the bill.[4] In fact, the railroad unions and the A. F.
of L. had sponsored such a provision in the Railway Labor Act of 1926.
Certainly the evidence in the files of the Executive Council and the obvious determination of the unions of the Federation to press for the inclusion of a clause protecting the right of workers to organize in industries
subject to Federal bankruptcy legislation preclude any view that John L.
Lewis was the chief architect of the clause in the National Recovery Act
protecting the right to organize.[5]

Green appeared before the House Ways and Means Committee and
made the first extended defense of Section 7 (a) of the National Industrial
Recovery bill. This section originally stated that "employees shall have
the right to organize and bargain collectively through representatives of
their own choosing." Green at once urged an addition to this clause: "And
shall be free from the interference, restraint, or coercion of employers of
labor, or their agents, in the designation of such representatives or in
self-organization or in other concerted activities for the purpose of collective bargaining or other mutual aid or protection."

A second suggestion submitted by Green asked that the term *company
union* be substituted for the word *organization* so that the amended clause
read: "That no employee and no one seeking employment shall be re-

quired as a condition of employment to join a company union, or to refrain from joining a labor organization of his own choosing."

Green thought that the incorporation of these changes in the amendment would make clear the real meaning and purpose of this section of the act and would express the purpose of the committee which had drafted the legislation. The acceptance of his suggestions, he said, would bring the A. F. of L. behind the measure.[6]

The bill passed the House as amended and was sent to the Senate Committee on Finance which had begun hearings on its own bill. James A. Emery, the counsel and representative of the National Association of Manufacturers, vigorously opposed Section 7 (a). He wanted it replaced by the following amendment:

"1. Employers and employees shall have the right to organize and bargain collectively in any way mutually satisfactory to them through representatives of their own choosing.

"2. No employee and no one seeking employment shall be required, as a condition of employment, to join any legitimate organization, nor shall any person be precluded from bargaining individually for employment."

Another employer representative, L. E. Michael, representing the Virginia Manufacturers' Association, said that Section 7 (a) was likely to disturb the satisfactory relationships between labor and management wherever they existed. He asked that the section either be eliminated or rewritten to give employers and labor equal rights. This view was in general supported by Charles R. Hook of the American Rolling Mill Company. In order to make clear industry's position, Robert P. Lamont, representing the American Iron and Steel Institute, the voice of about 95 per cent of the industry, declared that his industry favored the open shop. John L. Lewis, appearing on behalf of the United Mine Workers of America and the A. F. of L., announced "we stand squarely behind Section 7 (a), as reported to the Senate in the House bill, as amended by the Ways and Means Committee."[7]

As finally reported, the version of the Senate Finance Committee contained a clause which would have allowed "existing satisfactory relationships between employers and employees of any particular plant, firm, or corporation" to continue undisturbed. An attack upon that provision was led by Senator George Norris, and was supported by Senators Edward Costigan, Robert Wagner, Burton Wheeler, Huey Long, Homer Bone, and Arthur Robinson. This clause was struck from the bill by a vote of 46 to 31, with nineteen Senators not voting, and the House version was incorporated into the law.[8] The law was signed by President Roosevelt on June 16, and the first code, the Cotton Textile Code, was approved on July 9, 1933.

The National Industrial Recovery Act was to be in effect for two years.

General Hugh Johnson was appointed Administrator. He appointed a number of boards, among them the Industrial Advisory Board and the Labor Advisory Board.

The codes were an experiment in industrial organization initiated and sponsored by the Federal government. Section 7 (a) represented a revolution in the law regulating labor relations. It is true that precedents existed in the nonbinding recommendations of government arbitration boards and investigatory commissions and the requirements governing labor organization embodied in the Bankruptcy Act. However, the recommendations would inevitably be of only limited importance, for they were not binding upon any one. The Railway Labor Act of 1926 and the Bankruptcy law of 1932 applied only to specific industries. Section 7 (a) was meant to apply to all industries, and for the first time the government sought, by imperfect means, it is true, to protect the right to organize.

While the National Industrial Recovery Act was still being considered, Green called the presidents of the international unions to a conference in Washington on June 6, 1933. In his call, Green emphasized that the meeting would seek to secure some of the benefits of the new legislation for the workers of the country. "The president of the American Federation of Labor will recommend that an organizing campaign be launched so that the unorganized workers of the country through organization may participate in the benefits of the bill and may demand that employers negotiate with their chosen representatives in the establishment of decent wages, shorter hours, and improved conditions of employment." Green expressed the hope that the machinery of organization would be started quickly so that "the message of organization [could] be carried to the unorganized workers of the Nation and through such a campaign they will be advised of their rights under the provisions of this act and the necessity for united action in order to secure for themselves the economic and social benefits, as well as the enjoyment of all the rights to which they are entitled under the provisions of the Industrial Recovery Act."[9]

Representatives of international unions, meeting in Washington on June 6, 1933, suggested the launching of organization drives, and Green reported that an "intensive organizing drive will begin in Detroit. Organizer William Collins will be in charge of that campaign."[10]

The unprecedented enthusiasm with which workers responded to the appeals of union organizers startled many of the leaders of labor unions. The Federation waived the old requirement of organization along strictly craft lines. "The Federation," according to its officers, "is meeting the emergency by enrolling the workers in entire industries in direct affiliation. In the last three weeks, says Mr. Morrison, [the A. F. of L.'s Secretary-Treasurer] charters were issued to 38 federal and trade unions by the American Federation of Labor." These charters naturally did not include the ones that had been issued by the international unions.[11] Thousands of steel workers in Pennsylvania and auto workers in Michigan and Ohio, factory workers scattered throughout the United States, and coal miners in West Virginia, Kentucky, and Tennessee were flocking into the organizations of labor. Secretary-Treasurer Morrison pointed to the large number of workers who had organized for the first time as of great significance in the expansion of unionization.[12]

Describing the effect of the National Industrial Recovery Act, Lewis declared:

mine workers in Kentucky, with the exception of the County of Harlan, have been made free. They enjoy now the right of public assemblage at will, the right to exercise their suffrage independent of their employers or other influences. . . . President Roosevelt recommended to the Congress the enactment of the National Industrial Recovery Act, which gave to the submerged and exploited workers everywhere the right to organize and to bargain collectively wherever they choose to exercise it. . . . President Roosevelt wrought mightly and through his farseeing vision and unswerving devotion to commendable objectives has achieved other great accomplishments.[13]

The importance of Section 7 (a) in stimulating organizing activity among workers can scarcely be overestimated. *Coal Age* reported that, citing the authority of Section 7 (a), organizers for Lewis's Coal Miners' Union pressed organization work in every coal-producing state in the Union. The Federation issued a circular which included the statement: "Here is the law. It was recently passed by Congress and signed by the President,"[14] in an effort to convince workers that the right to organize was protected by law and that workers need no longer fear reprisals for joining unions.

Employers, awakening to the danger that the organization drives held for their customary labor relations, took steps to curb the spread of unionization. Industry and labor did not agree on the meaning of Section 7 (a), and some employers, unaccustomed to bargaining with outside unions, believed that they could deal with employee representation plans. The spokesmen for the automobile industry promulgated the merit principle in which they insisted that management had the right to employ or advance workers on the basis of merit irrespective of union membership.

The NIRA had established code boards attached to specific industries and the A. F. of L. sought to have labor represented on all boards which might handle labor problems. Complaint departments for the settlement of disputes were set up in some industries. These boards were, however, not fitted to handle general problems involving the right of workers to organize. During this time the A. F. of L. tried to provide technical help for unions that were unaccustomed to dealing with government agencies.

At the recommendation of the Labor Advisory Board and the Industrial

Advisory Board of the National Recovery Administration, President Roosevelt created on August 5, 1933, the National Labor Board "as an agency to investigate and pass upon the merits of controversies concerning or arising out of labor relations, which may operate to impede the efforts of the government to effectuate the policy of that Act."[15] Green, Lewis, and George L. Berry were the labor members and Senator Robert Wagner was appointed chairman. This Board was succeeded by the National Labor Relations Board, established under an Executive Order in June 1934. A number of special labor boards, such as the Steel Labor Relations Board and the Textile Labor Relations Board, were set up in a number of industries to handle special problems.

The National Labor Board and its successors, as well as the special boards, attempted to settle strikes, including those over the recognition of a union, and to interpret Section 7 (a). The Board, in its interpretation of its duties and the rights of workers to organize, ran into employer opposition and was attacked by the National Association of Manufacturers. On June 19, 1934 President Roosevelt signed Public Resolution No. 44, which authorized him to set up a board, or boards, to investigate any controversies arising under Section 7 (a) that obstructed commerce. Under this authority Roosevelt established on June 29, 1934 the National Labor Relations Board of three full-time members. Like its predecessor it heard cases affecting the right of workers to organize into unions that were not controlled by employers and to hold elections to determine bargaining representatives. The board functioned through regional boards which had been organized by the preceding board. Lloyd Garrison was appointed chairman of the National Labor Relations Board, with Professor Harry A. Millis and Edwin S. Smith as the other two members.

Although the unions were making substantial gains, in many instances they were opposed by employers, especially in the traditionally unorganized industries. Green protested to the President the refusal of employers to cooperate with labor, and he cited the objections of the automotive industry to public hearings before the expiration of the automobile code. President Roosevelt commented favorably on Green's reaction, and to Donald Richberg, he wrote: "Every time we order an election, the Company takes it to court."[16]

Roosevelt was less sympathetic to the demands of the A. F. of L. for the removal of S. Clay Williams as chairman of the Administrative Division of the National Industrial Recovery Act. Williams was opposed to recognizing the union in his plant, and the Federation believed that someone more favorable to organized labor should occupy such a strategic position. When the request for Williams' removal was transmitted to President Roosevelt, he rejected it. On the motion of Matthew Woll, the Executive Council asked for the reopening of the issue and declared "that if inaccuracies are contained in either the preamble of the resolution [to remove Williams] or both, the Executive Council will appreciate being advised of such inaccuracies."[17]

Nevertheless, the Federation favored the National Recovery Administration. When the Senate Finance Committee approved a resolution extending the NRA for ten months only, the Council interpreted such action as an abandonment of the Administration's recovery program. It was the opinion of the Council that, through the application of the provisions of the National Recovery Act, "plans have been followed and practical methods have been employed in all the heroic efforts which have been put forth to overcome unemployment." Green and the Council believed that the NRA should be extended for at least two years; and the extension of the program for only ten months was regarded as an abandonment of it. The Council held "that the adoption of this Joint Resolution will represent a complete retreat and surrender to reactionary forces. Such action at this critical period of the Nation's history is unthinkable. Instead, we must go forward, attacking vigorously the problem of unemployment until we achieve success."[18]

The A. F. of L.'s desire for the extension of the National Recovery Act (NRA) did not mean that it was completely satisfied with its administration. One of the targets for its criticism was Donald Richberg, the head of the agency administering this law. Richberg, formerly an attorney for the Railway Botherhoods whose officers actively sponsored his appointment as attorney general in the first Roosevelt administration, had become disillusioned with the continuing demands of organized labor. In a memorandum to the President, Richberg wrote: "Nothing but absolute submission will ever content unionism or the A. F. of L. No matter how far the Government goes in acceding to its 'Demands,' for it always 'Demands,' it will turn upon the Government and rend it unless it yields to any and all its ukases."[19]

Richberg appeared before Congress and recommended the establishment of nonpartisan boards to deal with employer-employee problems under the National Industrial Recovery Act. Finally, the A. F. of L. denounced him for his role in the renewal of the automobile industry's code, which the Federation regarded as highly objectionable. When the code was renewed without a public hearing, the Council announced that "Mr. Richberg stands stripped of all pretenses. He can no longer parade as a sympathetic friend of labor." The Council pointed to his employment by a number of unions and observed that if "it had not been for Organized Labor who paid him thousands of dollars, he would still be serving somewhere as an inconspicuous attorney. He capitalized upon his association with labor and his sympathies for labor and for that reason largely he was brought by General Johnson into the National Recovery Administration. Labor has a right to expect, not favors, but at least fair treatment and a square deal from him."[20]

The Federation continued to support the National Recovery Act, and when the Supreme Court declared the law unconstitutional in the spring, Green regarded this action as serious enough to summon a special meeting of the Executive Council. He informed the Council by telegram that "the workers of the nation are expecting the American Federation of Labor through the Executive Council to weigh carefully and consider seriously the direct effect as well as the implications involved in the Supreme Court decision."[21]

At the meeting of the Council on June 6, Green submitted a sharp criticism of the Schechter decision which outlawed the National Industrial Recovery Act. He argued that the Wagner bill, then under consideration, was the piece of legislation most important for the labor movement. A number of suggestions for meeting the problems created by the Schechter decision were presented. After a prolonged discussion, the Council adopted a statement by a vote of 8 to 7; one member of the Council, Joseph Weber, was not present.

The declaration held that the Supreme Court's decision invalidating the National Industrial Recovery Act created an "emergency affecting Labor which calls for solemn consideration by the Executive Council of the American Federation of Labor." It called attention to the effect of the decision on the increase of child labor. Most concern was shown with the effect of the decision upon the right of workers to organize. Moreover, the abolition of the code-making authority, which created a greater need for the organization of workers for their own protection, made imperative the enactment of the Wagner Labor Disputes Act. The Executive Council declared that the people of the United States will demand that if the Constitution cannot be interpreted in the light of present-day facts, at least it be amended so as to suit the needs of present-day economic and social conditions.

Labor firmly believed that if the will of the people as expressed by Congress were made the supreme law of the land, the nation could find a solution for economic and social problems which were peculiar to each generation.

It was "the opinion of the Executive Council that the American Federation of Labor should assume leadership in a movement to secure the adoption of a constitutional amendment necessary to meet and overcome the objections to the enactment of social and economic legislation by the Congress of the United States, as set forth by the Supreme Court in its decision holding the Railroad Retirement Act and the National Recovery

Act invalid. Our great Labor Movement can most appropriately serve as a spearhead in the furtherance of such a most commendable social and economic enterprise."

In July 1935 the Federation supported in Congress a bill licensing business in interstate commerce and giving power to an administrative commission to determine minimum wages, maximum hours of work, and business practice. The bill did not get out of committee.

REFERENCES

1. *The National Recovery Administration, A Message from the President of the United States Transmitting A Report on the Operation of the National Recovery Administration, Which Has Been Prepared by Those Members of the Committee of Industrial Analysis Who Have No Official Relationship to the Government* (Washington, D. C.: Government Printing Office, 1937), p. 8.

2. Minutes of Executive Council, May 1, 1933.

3. *Congressional Record*, February 27, 1933, pp. 5122, 5136.

4. Interview over the telephone with Edward Keating, June 28, 1957; Minutes of Executive Council, May 2, 1933.

5. Lewis's claims are set out in Saul Alinsky, *John L. Lewis* (New York: G. P. Putnam's Sons, 1949), pp. 63–72. It should be noted that the right to bargain is protected in the Davis-Kelly Coal Stabilization bill sponsored by the United Mine Workers of America in 1932, but this bill was never enacted into law.

6. "National Industrial Recovery Act," *Hearings on H. R. 5064 before House Committee on Ways and Means*, 73rd Congress, 1st Session, pp. 117–142.

7. *National Industrial Recovery Hearings on S. 1712 and H. R. 5755, before Senate Committee on Finance*, 73rd Congress, 1st Session, p. 388.

8. *Congressional Record*, Vol. 77, part 6, pp. 5279–5284.

9. Circular letter appearing in *American Federation of Labor Weekly New Service*, June 3, 1933.

10. Green to members of Executive Council, June 21, 1933.

11. *American Federation of Labor Weekly News Service*, July 22, 1933.

12. *Coal Age*, July 1933, p. 249.

13. Quotation from an address by John L. Lewis delivered at Pikeville, Kentucky, October 28, 1935. Official File 142, Box 1, Franklin Delano Roosevelt Library.

14. Circular letter issued to Wage Earners and Salaried Workers by the A. F. of L., June 17, 1933.

15. President Franklin Roosevelt to Senator Robert Wagner, August 5, 1933.

16. Memorandum from President Roosevelt to Donald Richberg, Official File 142, Box 1, Franklin Delano Roosevelt Library.

17. Minutes of Executive Council, January 14, 1934.

18. Green to President Roosevelt, May 3, 1935.

19. Memorandum from Donald Richberg to President Roosevelt, February 11, 1935, Official File 142, Box 1, Franklin Delano Roosevelt Library.

20. Minutes of Executive Council, February 4, 1935.

21. Green to members of Executive Council, May 29, 1935.

# V

## Expansion

THE unexpected expansion in the membership of existing trade unions, as well as the widespread growth of organization sentiment among workers in traditionally unorganized industries, stimulated a desire for change within the general labor movement. As a result of the code in the clothing industry, the Amalgamated Clothing Workers of America was ready to cooperate with the A. F. of L. The Amalgamated, with the encouragement of John L. Lewis and George L. Berry, president of the Printing Pressmen's Union and an officer of the National Recovery Administration, sought to affiliate with the A. F. of L. In September 1933 Green and Thomas Rickert, president of the United Garment Workers of America, conferred with Sidney Hillman of the Amalgamated Clothing Workers. Following this meeting, the Amalgamated applied for affiliation.[1]

The Amalgamated, which had been established in 1914 as a secession from the United Garment Workers of America, had succeded in organizing a large part of the industry despite its inability to retain affiliation with the A. F. of L. In discussing the application of the Amalgamated with the Executive Council, Rickert, who had conferred with Hillman on this question, stated "the agreement was . . . to comply with the National Recovery Act policies in dealing with the clothing industry." He, however, denied that the agreement complied with the rules of the A. F. of L., which the Amalgamated would have to meet. He argued that the Amalgamated would have to define its jurisdiction before the charter could be acted upon by the Executive Council.[2]

The requirement that a union seeking affiliation with the A. F. of L. would have to submit a statement of its jurisdiction so that its claim would not conflict with those of existing affiliates was based upon Section 11 of the A. F. of L. constitution. Green informed Hillman that although the Council was sympathetic to his application, it wanted Rickert and Hillman to work out the details and submit them to the Council for study before a charter was issued. Hillman believed that a basis for agreement existed and that the Amalgamated and the United Garment Workers both should be allowed to retain all of their present membership, and that the "rights of both organizations in the industry should be recognized, maintained, and not injured by either side or members, or firms taken from one by the other." The Amalgamated also agreed not to organize any firms or workers in all kinds of play- and work-clothing production. These were left entirely to the United Garment Workers.

Despite the agreement reached between Rickert and Hillman, the Executive Council at first refused to grant a charter because the two organizations would be covering the same territory. Lewis and Berry attended the meeting of the Executive Council on October 5, 1933, and they argued that since Rickert and Hillman had reached an agreement, the Council should grant a charter. Rickert, however, denied that an agreement had been reached. The Council thereupon instructed Green to have Hillman meet with the Council to clear up the question of possible jurisdictional conflicts in the men's clothing industry. In discussing the issues with the Council, Hillman was willing to give up some craftsmen, but he was reluctant to surrender 25,000 newly organized shirtmakers to the United.[3]

The Amalgamated agreed to purchase labels from the United Garment Workers so that the firms dealing with the Amalgamated would be able to use the labels on the same terms as all firms dealing with the United Garment Workers. The Amalgamated was admitted to affiliation, and this act thereby temporarily ended almost twenty years of separation from the A. F. of L.

EXECUTIVE COUNCIL

The several resolutions seeking an increase in the size of the Executive Council were another manifestation of the desire for change. The significance of these requests was accentuated by their sponsorship. At the convention of 1933, the delegation from the United Mine Workers of America sought an enlargement of the Council from eight to twenty-five members. The resolutions committee's recommendation of nonconcurrence was based on the argument that whenever situations arose that seriously affected the labor movement, conferences of the internationals were called. The committee cited, as an example, the conference to consider the National Industrial Recovery Act. In addition, the resolutions committee observed that an Executive Council made up of twenty-five members would represent primarily the largest unions. This would "preclude any effective participation in any proposal by the delegates to the annual convention who are not directly represented on such an enlarged council, thus affecting our democratic procedure."[4] The resolutions committee also called attention to the decentralizing tendencies within the A. F. of L., and noted the establishment of departments in which the affiliated unions had direct representation and were able to deal with matters of "immediate trade and occupational issue."[5]

Thomas Kennedy, secretary-treasurer of the United Mine Workers of

America, sharply attacked the views of the resolutions committee. He ridiculed the fear of this proposal except by those "who perhaps would not want any more intelligence or the exercise of any more judgment on the Executive Council than that which obtains at the present time." Kennedy pointed to the increase in trade union membership by a million in the previous six months, and expressed the hope that 20 million more would soon be organized. His views were supported by George L. Berry of the Printing Pressmen and Charles Howard, the president of the International Typographical Union, who had introduced a similar resolution in the convention of 1932. Daniel Tobin, head of the Teamsters' Union, opposed the increase in the size of the Council. Going to the heart of the argument, Tobin said that he doubted the permanence of the membership expansion. In his view, "this great mushroom growth that is now coming to our labor movement will, perhaps, be frittered away, as the great membership we gained during the war was, and we are also confronted by enemies within the organization."[6] The resolution was defeated, 14,125 to 6,410, but the size of the vote in favor of a proposal opposed by the Council and those accustomed to dominating the convention and policies of the Federation was an augur of things to come.

The resolutions for enlarging the Executive Council were submitted to the convention of 1934. The one offered by the delegation from the United Mine Workers sought a Council of twenty-five; the Hotel and Restaurant Employees asked for an enlargement of the Council but did not specify the number of additions. The committee on laws recommended a Council of fifteen vice presidents, plus a secretary and a treasurer. Some delegates expressed fear that a council might be chosen exclusively from unions controlling the majority of A. F. of L. members. Other delegates sought to prevent, by amendment, more than one member of a union from serving on the Council, but they were only able to muster a few more than one-fifth of the total vote. The recommendation of the law committee was overwhelmingly adopted, and a Council of seventeen was established.[7]

### FIRST COMPLAINTS ON STRUCTURE

Expansion of union organization into new industries raised some serious problems which were almost from the beginning a source of contention within the labor movement. The difficulties in interpreting jurisdictional boundaries between unions in mass-production industries were long recognized by some of the leaders of the metal trades. The division into crafts and callings typical of industries such as building construction and printing were largely absent in the mass-production industries, the majority of workers being engaged mainly on semiskilled repetitive tasks. A discussion of policies to be pursued in the organizing of mass-production industries took place at the convention of the Metal Trades Department in 1929. The Chicago Metal Trades Council had asked for permission to organize a radio plant into a federal labor union, so that all workers regardless of the task they performed would be mustered into a single organization. A large majority of the international presidents of the unions affiliated with that Department agreed "to the organization of the semi-skilled or the unskilled workers into a federal labor union, but [insisted] that the tradesmen should become members of their respective trade unions."[8] This was the first time the leaders of the unions in the Metal Trades Department had agreed upon a workable program for organizing the workers in the mass-production industries. As a matter of fact, it had been recognized in 1929, that "where workmen were organized into a federal labor union and then segregation attempted, the result had been that the organization was destroyed."[9]

John Frey, the head of the Metal Trades Department, recognized in 1933, that there "is something brewing and stewing in the labor ranks."[10] Frey was suspicious of what he saw and showed some concern over the new forms of organization that were taking shape in the Federation. More charters were issued during the summer and fall of 1933 than at any other time in the history of the A. F. of L. In its report to the convention of that year, the Executive Council noted that "we have concentrated our efforts more especially upon the workers in the basic industries; that is, automobiles, textiles, oil and rubber. To the fullest extent of the Federation's financial ability, organizing campaigns in these centers have been aggressively carried on."[11]

In organizing workers in the mass-production industries, the Federation recruited them in federal labor unions; and Green felt obliged to state that

federal labor unions have been formed by the American Federation of Labor for many years. . . . In considering industrial codes applicable to these mass production industries the workers will be represented by the American Federation of Labor and will be given the benefit of such expert, technical and trained service as the American Federation of Labor can supply. There is no way by which these workers may engage in collective bargaining except through the establishment of federal labor unions affiliated with the American Federation of Labor.[12]

In the meantime, the first stirrings of dissatisfaction among older unions appeared. The metal trades' unions which had been gaining members were urged to set up metal trades' councils wherever possible.[13] The largest union in the metal trades, whose president, Arthur Wharton, was a member of the Executive Council of the A. F. of L., called attention to the difficulties encountered by the metal trades' unions as a result of the formation of federal unions. Wharton charged that statements had been made by Federation organizers that the A. F. of L. was organizing on an industrial basis. He asked the Executive Council to instruct its organizers to make clear that workers in the jurisdiction of metal trades' unions must be placed in their respective organizations. Green answered that upon the enactment of the National Industrial Recovery Act, the spirit of organization was aroused everywhere "and came on us like a rising tide, appeals to come here, appeals to come there. . . . It was a problem we had to meet quickly and the matter of meeting it in a judicious way was apparent. We met here sometime ago and we discussed the problem of organizing mass production industries, particularly the automobile industry, and as I recall we agreed that we would proceed to organize these workers in Federal Labor Unions."[14]

But the complaints of Wharton were echoed by the convention of the Metal Trades Department. A resolution protesting against the issuance of charters to federal labor unions in disregard of the jurisdictional rights of affiliates was introduced by the Chicago Metal Trades Council. The convention decided that "where prospective members are eligible for membership in any certain International Organization, in accordance with the jurisdiction of the organization already definitely established," organizers should be instructed "to place in their proper International Organization all such prospective members, unless the consent of the respective International Organization which would have jurisdiction over such prospective members has been secured to place them into an organization under a Federal charter."[15]

Wharton requested that a resolution on the subject be introduced at the next convention of the A. F. of L. He wanted "to have positive instructions sent out by the American Federation of Labor which will prevent any poaching upon our International Unions." He agreed that the A. F. of L. had promised to transfer mechanics into the respective unions having jurisdiction in the trade. He feared, however, that such transfers might be postponed a long time and that those who joined the trade union movement on a basis of low initiation fees and low dues might not be enthusiastic about being transferred. He also objected to the initiation of mechanics into federal labor unions on the grounds that the requirement that workers from federal labor unions be transferred without payment of additional initiation fees meant a loss of revenue to the craft unions.[16] Wharton's views were supported by the presidents of the Blacksmiths', Metal Polishers', and Sheet Metal Workers' Unions.

The A. F. of L. convention of 1933 was the first since the Scranton convention of 1901 to consider as a practical question the problem of the structure of new unions. The resolutions on industrial unionism which had been periodically submitted to the delegates of the Federation conventions had approached the problems abstractly. Whatever decisions might have been made, they could not significantly have affected the relations between unions or the kinds of organizations established. For the first time in three decades, the question of structure involved important practical relations and interests. On behalf of the Metal Trades Department, John Frey asked the convention "to take such immediate action as is necessary to prevent the inclusion in Federal Labor Unions of any mechanic or laborer [over] whom the International Unions have jurisdiction through charter given to them by the American Federation of Labor." Another resolution took the opposite point of view. Claiming that the old methods had failed, this resolution asked for the appointment of a strategy board to handle organizing in new industries.

The majority of the resolutions committee sought to straddle the issue. Pointing to the Scranton declaration, which allowed a union to adopt any form of organization suitable to its needs, the committee qualified that position with the warning that no structural changes could take place in organizations without the consent of all the unions involved. The committee recognized that changes in industrial techniques had presented new problems to organized labor and that these must be met "so that the rights and interests of affiliated national and international unions may be fully safeguarded and also [that] there [may] be provided an immediate basis for the tentative organizing of these wage earners."[17] Federal labor unions, it said, may serve for temporary purposes of organizing workers in the mass-production industries "when the affiliated national and international unions give consent to the granting of such charters, and in plants in small communities where it may prove difficult for affiliated unions to give the question of organizing their immediate attention."[18]

Charles Howard, the president of the International Typographical Union and a member of the resolutions committee, was dissatisfied with the report and submitted a minority view. The systems of mass production, he argued, were operated by companies which had heretofore resisted unionization. It was Section 7 (a) of the National Industrial Recovery Act, which, in Howard's opinion, "had the effect of freeing the flood of organization sentiment existing in the breasts of millions of workers who have been prevented by employer opposition from satisfying their desire for organization."[19] Howard was aware that "in many of the industries in which thousands of workers are employed a new condition exists requiring organization upon a different basis to be most effective." He presented a ten-point program aimed at coordinating the organizing efforts more closely and allowing workers to be organized into one union in industries where adherence to jurisdictional lines would interfere with continuity of employment. His proposals sought to protect the jurisdictional rights of the national and international unions, but Howard also acknowledged the need for experimenting with new methods in the mass-production industries. Both the minority and majority reports of the resolutions committee were referred to the Executive Council, on the motion of Frey, with instructions to call a conference of international unions to develop a program.[20]

A conference of international unions was held in Washington on January 24 and 25, 1934, with seventy-five representatives in attendance. The meeting declared its inability to alter the fundamental rules of the A. F. of L. or to interefere with the autonomous rights of affiliates; and it emphasized that the Federation, "contrary to common belief, does not desire to dictate the form of organization that shall prevail among wage earners. Its policy has been that of encouraging whatever form of organization in any trade, calling or industry [which] seems best to meet the situation and the requirements of the workers." Recognizing that, in periods of rapid and widespread expansion in the power of organized labor, conflicts over jurisdiction are inevitable, the representatives counseled forbearance and tolerance for the unions and their officers.

The report made the following recommendations:

1. The organizing work of the international unions should proceed with the utmost vigor and be supplemented by A. F. of L. activity. Moreover, "the fullest possible latitude should be exercised by the Executive Council in the granting of federal charters and . . . where and whenever a temporary infraction of the rights of National and International Unions may be involved, . . . the Executive Council [should] adjust such difficulties in the spirit of taking full advantage of the immediate situation and with the ultimate recognition of the rights of all concerned."[21]

2. The Executive Council should arrange conferences of organizers of different unions in various areas for the purpose of establishing harmonious relations and arranging for cooperation wherever possible.

3. In the future the Executive Council should consult the executive officers or representatives of the various divisions and departments of organized labor affiliated with the A. F. of L. for the purpose of deciding upon the organizing methods to be employed.

4. The A. F. of L. should call mass meetings of wage earners, and local unions should be asked to cooperate in making these meetings a means for promoting organization.[22]

As the committee which drew up the report recognized, the conference was without power to change the relationships between unions. Arthur Wharton, a member of the committee, was disturbed by the jurisdictional invasions of the metal trades by newly chartered federal unions. Another committee member, Charles Howard, believed that the older unions had to make concessions to the demands of the workers in the mass-production industries. Neither member could present a formula which the other would accept. At an Executive Council meeting in February 1934, Wharton complained of the infringement of the jurisdiction of the craft unions

in the metal trades by the federal labor unions. Green agreed on the
desirability of placing craftsmen employed in the mass-production industries in the unions having jurisdiction in those trades. At the same time
he reported that he had "tried to the limit and beyond the limit to
persuade them to go into their craft organization and take their place
with their fellow craftsmen in the craft unions, and they finally [said] to
us 'We won't organize in that way.' Is it to be the position of the American Federation of Labor to say you cannot be organized?" Green was
willing to make every possible effort to have craftsmen affiliate with the
organizations in their trades, but if the workers insisted upon joining a
federal union or no union, he thought the A. F. of L. should meet that
demand.[23] Green was instructed to send out a circular to voluntary and
full-time organizers directing them to take cognizance of the jurisdictional
rights of the craft unions.

At the May meeting of the Council, Wharton claimed that the Machinists' Union had not been able to get the cooperation of the A. F. of L. in
curbing invasion of its jurisdiction. Green defended himself by pointing
to the circular sent out by him advising organizers to protect the rights
of craft unions. Nevertheless, Green "expressed himself as being thoroughly convinced that it [was] impossible to organize mass production
workers in the automobile industry unless we organize them in Federal
Labor Unions. He cited the instance in Cleveland where complaints had
been made about taking in the Machinists employed in the Fisher body
plants 1 and 2. . . . The machinists were not admitted in the Automobile
Workers Federal Labor Union. As a result they went with the rump
organization known as the 'Mechanics Educational Society.' "[24]

Green went on to state that, if the A. F. of L. refused to organize
workers into federal labor unions, they would go into nonaffiliated organizations. "We do not get them, the Machinists do not get them." Green
had told the Council that workers in General Electric and in utility plants
in Massachusetts had been imploring organization, and he had refused
to issue federal charters. Pointing to the increase in the number of company and independent unions, he pleaded with the Council to remember
that there was "no question as to the machine shop, pattern making, boiler
making shop, but when in mass production plants they are all thrown
together and we try beyond the limit to separate them and they refuse,
are we to stop and say, you cannot come in?"[25]

To these arguments the members of the craft unions would make no
concessions. John Frey, the president of the Metal Trades Department,
saw in the conflict over jurisdiction a sufficient reason for greater cooperation among the metal trades and building trades. Looking upon the
industrial union as a threat, he believed that industrial organization would
lead to the dismemberment of the craft groups which had developed the

policies of the Federation.[26] In his report to his Department, Frey labeled the activities of the newly formed federal unions "a campaign to reconstruct the form of organization within the American Federation of Labor." Instead of industrial organization, he urged the utilization of the federated method.

> Our form of organization through federation does not keep the members of the several crafts employed in a metal manufacturing establishment or an industry separated and apart, forced to deal with employers as individual organizations. Instead, it enables these International Unions, with all of the experience they have passed through, and the knowledge they have gained, to join their efforts with other International Unions so that their strength is greatly increased, and the elements of weakness in the vertical union eliminated.[27]

The attempt to establish vertical or industrial unions was, Frey said, an attempt to wipe out the unions of skilled workers which "have been successful in protecting the skilled workers' legitimate right to secure terms of employment based upon the skill which workers have acquired as mechanics."[28]

Protests and warnings against attempts to usurp the rights of its unions also came from the Building Trades Department. The report of the officers to the convention of 1934 made its view clear: "Industrial plants in the country employ many thousands of building trades mechanics in the operations, repair and maintenance of their plants. Many of these men are members of our organization and those who are not, and are eligible, should be organized into their respective craft organizations. . . ."[29] Joint meetings between the Metal Trades Department and the Building Trades Department were held, and the head of the latter department expressed his belief "that through joint action by both Departments, much can be accomplished in eradicating the industrial form of organization, which is a growing menace to our craft organizations."[30]

REFERENCES

1. Sidney Hillman to Green, September 9, 1933.
2. Minutes of Executive Council, September 15, 1933.
3. "Hillman insisted that the purpose of his application was cooperation with the American Federation of Labor and if there was any question of causing friction with other organizations, he would be misleading his own organization in advising them to affiliate. He could ignore the jurisdiction of affiliated organizations on the outside better than he could in the American Federation of Labor. His purpose in affiliating is for cooperation."—Minutes of Executive Council, October 8, 1933.
4. *Report of Proceedings of the Fifty-third Annual Convention of the American Federation of Labor,* 1933, p. 386.

5. *Ibid.*

6. *Ibid.*, pp. 401–402.

7. *Report of Proceedings of the Fifty-fourth Annual Convention of the American Federation of Labor,* 1934, pp. 649–668.

8. *Proceedings of the Twenty-first Annual Convention of the Metal Trades Department of the American Federation of Labor,* 1929, p. 27.

9. *Ibid.*, p. 27.

10. John Frey to W. A. Appleton, March 13, 1933, Folder 6 of Frey Papers in Manuscript Division of Library of Congress.

11. *Report of Proceedings of the Fifty-third Annual Convention of the American Federation of Labor,* 1933, p. 33.

12. *American Federation of Labor Weekly News Service,* July 29, 1933.

13. *Report of Officers to the Twenty-fifth Annual Convention of the Metal Trades Department of the American Federation of Labor,* 1933, p. 3.

14. Minutes of Executive Council, September 7, 1933.

15. *Report of Proceedings of the Twenty-fifth Annual Convention of the Metal Trades Department of the American Federation of Labor,* 1933, p. 43.

16. The quotes are from *Ibid.*, p. 44.

17. *Report of Proceedings of the Fifty-third Annual Convention of the American Federation of Labor,* 1933, p. 501.

18. *Ibid.*, p. 501.

19. *Ibid.*, p. 502.

20. *Ibid.*, pp. 503–504.

21. *Report of Proceedings of the Fifty-fourth Annual Convention of the American Federation of Labor,* 1934, p. 42.

22. *Ibid.*, p. 42.

23. Minutes of Executive Council, February 7, 1934.

24. Minutes of Executive Council, May 10, 1934.

25. Minutes of Executive Council, January 6, 1934.

26. Frey to W. A. Appleton, July 20, 1934.

27. *Report of Proceedings of the Twenty-sixth Annual Convention of the Metal Trades Department of the American Federation of Labor,* 1934, p. 29.

28. *Ibid.*, p. 29.

29. *Report of Proceedings of the Twenty-eighth Annual Convention of the Building Trades Department of the American Federation of Labor,* 1934, p. 83.

30. *Ibid.*, p. 89.

# VI

## The Major Departments

### The Metal Trades Department

The Metal and Building Trades Departments were in the center of the industrial union controversy. They regarded the industrial union activity as an attack upon their jurisdictions. The Metal Trades Department was made up of fourteen international unions. The Hod Carriers', Electricians', Operating Engineers', Iron Workers' and Sheet Metal Workers' Unions were members of both the Metal and Building Trades Departments. The Metal Trades unions had always claimed, though never organizing them on any large scale, the thousands of craftsmen and machine operators employed in the mass-production industries. The Department established in 1908 was a loose form of federation of unions in the metalworking industry. In the early years joint organizing campaigns were discussed, and occasionally such campaigns were started. In 1911 several unions in the Metal Trades Department, and in 1913, all the unions, except the Stove Mounters and the International Union of Steam Engineers, agreed to assign an organizer to work under the Department's direction.[1] Before that time, the unions had tried to devise cooperative organizing campaigns and had given the president of the Department authority to direct these campaigns in the interest of all unions in the Department.[2] The first effort in 1914 to establish unions in the automobile industry was undertaken under a joint program to be directed by the Metal Trades Department.[3]

Attempts had been occasionally made to work out closer arrangements with the unions in the building trades, and in 1909 representatives of the executive councils of the Building Trades and Metal Trades Departments met in a new effort. The Building Trades Department approved in principle of these efforts, but no agreement upon a program was ever reached.[4]

In addition to encouraging common organizing programs, whose acceptance was optional with the affiliates, the Metal Trades Department chartered local metal trades councils. These were the organizations through which the membership of the affiliated local unions jointly worked out their local problems. The local councils, however, were not given authority to interfere in the affairs of affiliated local unions. They could not decide questions of jurisdiction or strikes, nor could they initiate action which violated the constitution of any of the affiliated organizations. The purpose of the local councils was to assist each affiliated local union in organizing the members in its jurisdiction, to help establish uniform terms of employment in its locality, and to assist in the negotiating of joint agreements of the several unions belonging to the local council. Whenever several local metal trades' councils cooperated in the negotiating of a joint agreement, approval of a majority of councils required the acceptance of the terms by all participants.

Following the decline in union membership in the metal trades after World War I, the local metal trades' councils became inactive and many ceased to function. During the expansion of membership in the period of the National Recovery Administration, the local councils were revived in many areas. The convention of the Metal Trades Department in 1933 approved the formation of district councils which allowed all unions whose members were employed in one division or subdivision of manufacturing to adopt common policies and negotiate jointly with the employers in that branch of industry. Under this provision a Marine Workers' Metal Trades District Council was organized in the Port of New York in 1934. The jurisdiction of this District Council covered all shipyard workers, so that "the District Council was in a position to represent the interests of all workmen in shipyards, from the masthead to the keel and from the stem to the stern of a seagoing vessel."[5] A district council organized in the office-equipment industry included all local unions whose internationals were affiliated with the Metal Trades Department.

Because the newly formed industrial unions were for the most part in the metal trades, this Department developed a very high sensitivity to the problem. It constantly tried to devise methods which would enable its workers to cooperate and at the same time would allow for the maintenance of the jurisdictions of the older craft organizations. At the Department convention of 1934, the delegates were warned of "widespread attempts by some groups to organize so-called vertical unions. This effort, which is now in full swing in some communities, provides for the organization of all employees of a shop or factory, or of an industry, into one union." The report called attention to the danger which such a program held for the affiliated unions. "Draftsmen; pattern makers; molders; machinists; boilermakers; sheet metal workers; blacksmiths; electrical workers; plumbers and steam fitters; engineers; in fact all of the skilled mechanics would be divided among the vertical unions which are now, or which may be, organized."[6] The report argued that skilled mechanics going from place to place in search of work would have to join several vertical unions.

The problems created by the rise of vertical or industrial unionism led the officers of the Metal Trades Department and the Building Trades

Department to try to set up a common program. It was agreed that in certain instances, the affiliated international unions acting through one or both departments would seek "to negotiate agreements with manufacturing corporations and other employers, which would cover all of the memberships represented by one or both Departments. So that this policy would be thorough-going in certain instances, it was agreed, where the memberships of both Departments were employed in a specific industry, that the two Departments acting jointly would endeavor to negotiate agreements and underwrite them when they were entered into."[7] In spite of their efforts to develop a policy of joint action—as an answer to the demands for industrial organization—the two departments were unable to devise a program of effective cooperation. The single significant example of their cooperation was the joint agreement negotiated with the Anaconda Copper Company in Butte, Montana.

The Metal Trades Department, although it was in the forefront in the attack upon the proponents of industrial organization, was forced as a matter of defense to develop closer cooperation among its own affiliates. At the beginning of the expansion of employment in the shipping industry during the defense period, beginning in 1939, the international presidents met in Cincinnati, Ohio, to establish a program of organization among the shipyard workers. The Machinists', Boilermakers', Electrical Workers', Sheet Metal Workers', Molders', and Operating Engineers' Unions agreed to assign several organizers to this joint campaign. Cooperation was also aided by the creation of district councils which aimed at establishing wage uniformity in the shipyards on the several coasts.[8] The Inter-Mountain District Metal Trades Council operated in the metal mining industry.

### THE RAILWAY EMPLOYEES' DEPARTMENT

To a greater extent than any other group of unions in the A. F. of L., the organizations of skilled workers in the railroad shops had developed an effective system of cooperation in collective bargaining which allowed the autonomous internationals to control their jurisdictions and manage their own affairs. Informal cooperation among the skilled mechanics employed on the railroads was the first step in the development of the federated system of negotiations and contract administration which has existed for almost sixty years.

In 1908 the A. F. of L. had chartered the Railroad Employees' Department, with Henry B. Perham, a telegrapher, president. The Department was designed to include all unions of railroad workers affiliated with the A. F. of L., but it failed to meet the needs of the mechanical trades, the most important and stable group of unionists among the nonoperating railroad workers. Agitation for an organization that would federate the activities of the unions of the shop crafts led to the formation of the

Southeastern Consolidated Federation of Railway Shop Employees in 1910.

In response to this demand, the Machinists' Union convention in 1911 instructed its president to explore with the executive officers of the other shop craft unions the possibility of organizing a federated organization to embrace all the mechanical trades. Another stimulus to federation was the shopmen's strike on the Harriman and Illinois Central lines which started in 1911, when these carriers refused to deal with a joint committee of all the shop crafts. The strike aroused bitter feeling among railroad men. The conference which met in Kansas City in April 1911 was designed to achieve two purposes: (1) to set up a viable federated organization; and (2) to devise a program of aid for the strikers on the Harriman and Illinois Central lines. Representatives from thirty-five western roads and the national officers from a number of nonoperating railroad unions met in April 1912 and established the Federation of Federations of Railway Employees of the American Federation of Labor.[9]

In November 1912 the Railroad Employees' Department adopted the laws and constitution of the Federation with minor changes. Arthur Wharton, who had been a leader in the federated movement, became the president of the now transformed Railway Employees' Department. A number of the unions which had affiliated with the old Department withdrew, although some sought to return later.

In contrast to the Building and Metal Trades Departments, the Railway Employees' Department became the agency through which the mechanical trades on the railroads carried on collective bargaining with the carriers. Control rested with the International unions, but the reorganized Department was from the beginning authorized to negotiate with the roads, although approval of the majority of the unions involved was necessary. The single trades had found themselves at a disadvantage when carrying on collective-bargaining negotiations and the federated program was designed to overcome it.[10] With the withdrawal of other nonoperating railroad unions, the Department increasingly became the agency of the unions in the mechanical trades which negotiated joint contracts with the carriers. The International Brotherhood of Blacksmiths, Iron Ship Builders and Helpers, which in 1951 absorbed the Blacksmiths' Union, the Brotherhood of Railway Carmen, the International Brotherhood of Electrical Workers, International Brotherhood of Firemen and Oilers, International Association of Machinists, and the Sheet Metal Workers' International Association have over the years been the basic organizations in the Department. The unions have been members also of the Railway Labor Executives' Association, organized in 1926, to promote "cooperative action to obtain and develop consistent interpretations and utilization of the Railway Labor Act, and for other purposes affecting the labor activities of the associated organizations." The Railway Employees' Department has cooperated with the other railway unions in making joint demands upon the carriers for changes in wages and working conditions.

Unions which did not represent basic trades in the industry were denied affiliation with the Department. Under the constitution of the A. F. of L., each Department had the authority to determine eligibility for admission. The Railway Employees' Department believed that acceptance of the membership of organizations which were not basic trades on the railroads would lead to an increase in jurisdictional disputes and would compel radical readjustments of work assignments. Consequently, they were ruled ineligible to join.[11] The interests of the pattern makers, molders, steam fitters, plumbers, and other craftsmen have been represented by one of the other trades, usually the Sheet Metal Workers or the Carmen.

From the beginning of its history, the Department was active in the settling of jurisdictional disputes which never took on the virulence they acquired in the building-construction industry.

In the event of a dispute, past practice governed until the dispute was settled by a committee composed of the general chairman of each craft on the system where it arose. A decision was made by a majority vote, but the decision was not effective until approved by the president of the Department.[12] He, however, was required to submit all facts to the chief executives of the organizations involved, who were allowed to accept the decision or ask for a conference. If the officers of the unions involved did not agree ultimately, the president of the Department had the authority to render a decision. Technically, decisions could be appealed to the Executive Council and conventions of the A. F. of L., but the rule has been to accept the verdict of the Department.

Joint negotiations were always conducted under the aegis of the Department. The president and the Executive Council had "authority to call a meeting of designated System Federation Representatives for the purpose of determining matters of interest and giving proper directions to any such negotiations with the carriers . . . irrespective of location, regions, or subdivision thereof."[13] Whenever necessary the component international unions conducted strike votes among their members in accordance with their laws. "Returns of a strike vote shall be forwarded immediately to the President of the Department by the respective Grand Lodge officers of the component organizations, or officers of the subordinate organizations. A legal strike vote of the Department shall be based upon an average total of the total vote cast, equalizing the constitutional requirements of the organizations involved. A sanction to strike shall be issued by the President and Executive Council of the Department."[14] The Department was also charged with the distribution of strike relief in the event of a strike, although levying of strike assessments fell upon the component organizations.

Up to World War I the unions on the railroads had succeeded in gaining recognition and agreements "on over fifty per cent of the railroads in the United States."[15] The unions were able to expand their membership on the railroads as soon as the government took over their operation in December 1917. Under General Order No. 8, no discrimination in hiring or tenure against workers who belonged or who had indicated a desire to join a union could be practiced. Under the rule of the Federal government, railroad unions were recognized and national agreements standardizing wages and working conditions were negotiated with them by the Federal Railroad Administration.

Federal control was ended in March 1920. The Transportation (Esch-Cummins) Act laid down the conditions under which they were returned to private ownership. The Railroad Labor Board, set up under the Transportation Act to handle disputes over the terms of employment, aroused strong opposition within the ranks of the railroad unions.[16] According to the unions, the Board had at the same time failed to rule on numerous grievances presented to them by representatives of their workers. It was a period of general dissatisfaction, and the mood of the railroad workers harmonized with the general feeling. Against the advice of the leaders, the 1922 convention of the Department ordered a strike vote. It was overwhelmingly approved. Strike sanction was given for a strike on July 1, 1922. It was a blunder and a costly failure, and the unions lost thousands of members. Company unions were established on many roads.[17] The Railroad Labor Board's outlaw resolution of July 3 declared that the members of "the six organizations comprising the six Federated Shop Crafts . . . having left the service of the carriers . . . are no longer employees of the railways under the jurisdiction of the Railroad Labor Board or subject to the application of the Transportation Act." It was deeply resented by the entire labor movement.

### THE RAILWAY LABOR ACT OF 1926

In July 1923 Gompers had suggested to the railway labor organizations, both those affiliated and unaffiliated with the Federation, the desirability of appointing a committee to draft a bill abolishing the Railroad Labor Board and providing the settlement of railroad labor disputes through conferences, agreements, board of adjustments, decisions in grievances, government mediation, and voluntary arbitration when necessary. A committee of nine, three from the A. F. of L., three from the Railway Employees' Department, and three from the railway operating unions, was appointed to draft this legislation.[18] The draft of a bill was submitted to Gompers and in general he approved of its contents. D. B. Robertson, who represented the operating railway crafts, asked Gompers to help push the bill through Congress. Vice President Matthew Woll and Secretary-Treasurer Morrison were appointed to work out methods of procedure with the railway unions.[19] Opposition to some of the provisions of the legislation quickly appeared. Daniel Tobin, the head of the Teamsters' Union and the Treasurer of the A. F. of L., objected to the compulsory-arbitration provisions of the bill. Similar objections were raised by Edward McGrady and Edgar Wallace, legislative agents for the Federation.

Despite the fears expressed by officers of the A. F. of L., Gompers joined in a statement endorsing the proposed legislation. The objections to the bill were based upon the requirement that grievances had to be submitted to a board of adjustment and that changes in wages and working conditions could be put into effect only after the machinery provided under the law had been employed to bring about an agreement. Another objection was made to the requirement that an agreement to arbitrate required acceptance of the award. Even though this was the practice followed generally by organizations of labor, the critics feared that giving the courts authority to enforce the arbitration award might be an entering wedge for compulsory arbitration.[20] When a number of union officers expressed concern with this provision, a conference was arranged between Gompers, Morrison, and Woll, the Federation's legislative representatives, and delegates from the railway unions. Gompers emphasized the urgent need of making a clear demarcation between the areas where compulsory action was to be permissive and where no compulsion could be used. In Gompers' view, any confusion on this point would serve as a pretext for the courts to intervene. On February 11, 1924 the Executive Council discussed the bill, and several members were suspicious of the compulsory provisions. The Council, in the end, approved the bill.

Gompers and Morrison were requested to help in arranging for the introduction of the bill in both houses of Congress. In addition, Gompers had to allay the fears of several unions which were determined to oppose the bill independently. He assured the Amalgamated Association of Street and Electric Railway Employees that "this bill is really a good bill and provides for a private conciliation policy to adjust matters of wages, hours, and conditions of empoyment of the railroad workers."[21] Gompers, the legislative representatives of the A. F. of L., and several members of the railroad unions' committee approached Senator Howell and asked him to introduce the bill in the Senate. The Senator was willing, but he expressed the belief that the clause guaranteeing labor the right to organize would run into formidable opposition from employers.[22]

Speaking for the labor representatives, Gompers led another group to Congressman Alben Barkley's office and urged him to take charge of the bill in the House and press it to a successful passage. He noted that the proponents of the bill wanted to avoid all rivalry and partisan advantage. Gompers went on to explain that the "bill is the result of thirty years of experience in legislation bearing on the transportation of the United States. It is the first time that the representatives of workers in the transportation service have offered a constructive proposition. Formerly they were always on the defensive, seeking either to defeat, modify, or amend a bill which had been introduced into Congress. This bill is the best yet devised to maintain the largest degree of good relations. It is not a cureall, but it does undertake to bring disputes to a minimum. The principle of the bill is that of freedom, maintaining it to the fullest extent." Gompers assured Barkley that the bill was supported by all railroad men, "the shopmen, the signalmen, the transportation men, the building tradesmen, metal, and the miscellaneous crafts. In that united spirit and in that confidence, we ask you to take charge of the bill."[23]

When the bill was strongly opposed in the House of Representatives, Robertson appealed to Gompers for additional assistance. Robertson expressed "the highest appreciation of the executives of the railway labor organization . . . for the earnest and effective support you have rendered in carrying out our legislative program to secure the enactment of our Railway Labor Bill. The legislative representatives of the American Federation of Labor have also rendered effective support in the Halls of Congress and we believe that a concentrated effort at this time directed towards the members of the Rules Committee, will bring the desired results." Gompers met with Robertson and Bert Jewell to determine the most effective method of getting the bill out of committee where it was bottled up. Every uncertain senator and congressman was sent a letter signed by Gompers urging support of the legislation, and the Executive Council assured hesitant legislators that all labor favored the bill. The opposition of the committee was overcome but the bill failed to pass.[24]

The railroad unions learned that the carriers were willing to try to work out an agreement upon railroad labor legislation. Joint committees from the railway labor unions and the railroads reached an agreement on a bill unanimously endorsed by the railway labor executives in December 1925. Some opposition existed among the members of the American Railway Executives' Association, but the report of the committee on labor representing the draft of the bill for the adjustment of labor disputes was that it was "hereby accepted and approved in principle, and the labor committee is continued for the purpose of having the same enacted into law with such changes in expression and details as it may approve." It was adopted by a vote of 52 to 20.[25]

On January 5, 1926, at a conference in which the unions were represented by Donald R. Richberg, counsel for a number of unions; D. R. Robertson, head of the Brotherhood of Locomotive Firemen and Enginemen; and

William B. Doak, of the Brotherhood of Railroad Trainmen, met with a committee of the carriers to iron out differences. James A. Emery, counsel for the National Association of Manufacturers, was allowed to address the conference. He assailed the bill. His advice was rejected, and the bill was presented to Senator James Watson, chairman of the Senate Interstate Commerce Committee, and Congressman James S. Parker, chairman of the House Committee on Interstate and Foreign Commerce, and their support was solicited. President Coolidge had been informed of the possibilities of an agreement between the carriers and the unions, and in his annual message he referred to the "substantial agreement" existing between railroad management and labor on the kind of legislation governing their relationships and advocated that a mutually acceptable bill be enacted. The President felt that whenever labor and management "bring forward such proposals which seem sufficient also to protect the interests of the public, they should be enacted into law."

The unions would have liked to have had the legislation sponsored by Congressman Barkley and Senator Howell, but they feared that their sponsorship might arouse needless antagonism because Barkley and Howell had introduced the earlier legislation opposed by the railroads. It was also felt that sponsorship of the proposed bill by the heads of the committees to which they would be referred would facilitate passage. During its consideration by congressional committees, James A. Emery of the National Association of Manufacturers asked for changes so as to weaken some of the labor protective provisions. Emery also favored granting the Interstate Commerce Commission power to suspend any agreement which would have the effect of necessitating rate increases for the carriers. Spokesmen for farm organizations also appeared in opposition. The bill had the full support of organized labor, and Edward McGrady appeared in its behalf as a representative of the A. F. of L. The Amalgamated Association of Street and Electric Railway Employees asked for the exclusion of urban and interurban street railways from coverage, and the request was granted. The final passage of the bill was largely due to the untiring efforts of the chiefs of the railroad unions, who were ably assisted by Donald R. Richberg, their counsel. After the passage of the legislation, the railroad unions thanked the Federation for its cooperation and held that Green's letter to congressmen endorsing the legislation convinced its opponents "that there was no doubt about the position of organized labor with respect to this Bill."[26]

The Railway Labor Act of 1926 abolished the much-hated Railroad Labor Board and in addition provided that representatives "shall be designated by the respective parties in such manner as may be provided in their corporate organization or unincorporated association; or by other means of collective action, without interference, influence, or coercion exercised by either party over the self-organization or designation of representatives by the other." Representatives so selected had the right to confer with the employer upon matters appropriate for consideration between employer and employee. Employers were required to recognize the union of their employees, and if no agreement could be reached, the services of a board of mediation, set up under the law, could be obtained. If the parties were unable to agree and a dispute threatened "substantially to interrupt interstate commerce," the President of the United States was authorized to appoint an emergency board to investigate and to report back in thirty days. Pending the report, neither party was permitted to change the terms of employment. If arbitration were agreed to by the parties, the decision could be enforced in Federal courts. The law provided for boards of adjustment to settle disputes under the contract, but no agreement upon the make-up of the boards to carry out this provision was ever reached. The law, by recognizing the right of railroad workers to organize, marked an important forward step, but it was not regarded as altogether satisfactory from the point of view of railroad labor.[27]

## UNION-MANAGEMENT COOPERATION

After the strike of 1922 the shopcrafts, jointly with the Baltimore and Ohio Railroad, began their experiment of union-management cooperation. Under an arrangement between the International Association of Machinists and the carrier, the Glenwood shops outside of Pittsburgh, Pennsylvania, were selected as the site for trial of the program. It was directed by Otto Beyer, an engineer and advocate of a new approach to labor-management relations. The following principles were accepted by the Machinists' Union and later by all the shopcraft organizations:

1. Recognition of the unions in the shops, and the extension of collective bargaining from the purely protective issues to questions dealing with efficient production.

2. Acceptance by the carriers of written contracts dealing with wages and other terms of employment.

3. Systematic cooperation between management and workers for the attainment of higher efficiency and the elimination of waste.

4. Elimination as far as practicable of instability of employment.

5. The development of methods for measuring the gains from this kind of cooperation and the devising of a procedure for sharing them between the carriers and labor.

6. The setting up of joint labor and management committees for periodic discussion of production problems so that methods of better

scheduling, saving of time and materials, routing of work, and stabilizing production might be devised.

From the point of view of the Railway Employees' Department, the new type of labor-management cooperation appeared satisfactory. It would appear that the willingness of the leadership to engage in such an experiment was to some extent due to the weakened position of the shopcraft unions. Such a program, the leaders hoped, might enable them to regain some of their lost ground and would perhaps lessen the appeal the company union held for many carriers.[28] Not many roads adopted the program; the Baltimore and Ohio Railroad and the Canadian National Railway systems were the more important carriers which tried it.[29]

### RAILWAY LABOR ACT OF 1934

In common with other organizations of labor, the railway unions suffered severely from declining employment during the Great Depression. With the change in the national administration in 1933, they sought an improvement in the law governing their relations to the railroads. The Railway Labor Act of 1926 had been a compromise dictated by the need to gain the support of the carriers. For this reason, a real method of enforcement had not been provided, and the acceptance of the provisions depended "solely upon the faith, good will and integrity of the parties."[30] The law did not provide a method for determining representation in cases where this issue was disputed, nor could coercion of employees be easily and directly prevented. In contrast, the Railway Labor Act of 1934 set up a procedure for determining representation; a union was certified under the law and it had to be accepted as the collective-bargaining agent by the carriers. Company unions were outlawed; coercion or influence by employers in the area of union organization was prohibited; and a National Board of Adjustment for the settling of disputes under the contract was established. Willful violations of the law were made punishable.

The enactment of this legislation was soon followed by the reestablishment of the standard railway unions on virtually every railroad in the country. In this expansion the Department played an important role. Organizers were not employed directly but were assigned to the Department for special purposes by the several international unions. Organizers on Department assignments concerned themselves with the interests of all the crafts; and they were not agents of their own International. Local lodges of particular crafts were organized at virtually all important railroad points, and these lodges selected their local grievance committees. General chairmen were then selected by each craft to represent their particular group over an entire railroad system. Negotiations between the carrier and the shop crafts were conducted through the System Federations to which the shop crafts affiliated. Wherever three or more of the following unions—Machinists', Boilermakers', Electricians', Carmen's, Sheet Metal Workers', and Firemen and Oilers' Unions—established system craft organizations, a system federation was established. Locals of the various craft unions were required to join a system federation. System craft organizations were delegate bodies, elected in accordance with the rules of the particular organization in question. Delegates to system federations were given one vote each, except in voting on a roll call when each craft organization had one vote, a majority vote of each system craft organization determined the vote of its delegation. "No individual system craft organization on a railway system where a System Federation is organized shall, without the consent of the President and Executive Council of the Department, negotiate a separate craft agreement with the management of the railway, but all such crafts shall be a party to the System Federation agreement negotiations for the section of the System Federation of which they are a part."[31]

Negotiations were conducted by the executive boards of the system federations with their respective carriers. If no agreement was reached by the officers of the system federation and the railroad, the president of the Department was called to assist. Only the president and the Executive Council of the Department were authorized "to invoke the services of the National Mediation Board, or to enter into an arbitration affecting any of the organizations, or members . . . comprising this Department."[32] The Department also had an important role in the settlement of grievances arising under the contract. Under the Railway Labor Act, differences which could not be settled directly could be taken to the National Railroad Adjustment Board Division No. 2. The rules of the Department required the handling of grievances by the local committee in the first instance. The general chairman was next in line, and if no settlement was reached, the issue was referred to the international executives of the union involved. Cases which were to be submitted to the Railroad Adjustment Board were sent to the Railway Employees' Department for handling. Whenever more than one craft was involved in a case, the issue had to be submitted directly to the Department for handling before the Board.

The Railway Employees' Department has had the responsibility for managing negotiations for revisions of wages and working conditions of its member unions. The number of organizations participating in national movements has varied, with fourteen to seventeen nonoperating organizations normally cooperating. Procedures for such changes are outlined in the Railway Labor Act, and it was customary for requests of this kind to be ultimately settled through the emergency-board proceedings. Such proceedings followed a necessary sequence required by law. Refusal to grant demands was normally followed by a strike vote, which, because of the possibility that it might lead to a substantial interference with interstate commerce, made necessary the appointment of an emergency board by the President of the United States. Preparation of materials incident to such a case was the responsibility of the Department in cooperation with other nonoperating labor organizations of the railroad industry.

The Railway Employees' Department evolved a satisfactory method by which autonomous unions cooperated in collective bargaining. In fact, from the point of view of collective bargaining, several railway mechanical unions have acted as one organization. Beginning with the turn of the century, Arthur Wharton, the president of the International Association of Machinists and a leader of the craft unionists in the 1930's, had played an important role in developing cooperation among the railway shop crafts. He had always been an exponent of the "federated idea," and believed it could be effective for mobilizing the combined strength of a number of unions without impairing their autonomy or invading their craft prerogatives. The attempt of the industrialists in the early 1930's to erase craft boundaries and muster the mass-production workers into industrial unions appeared to him unnecessary and an attack upon the rights of the skilled workers who were in his view the mainstay of the labor movement. Wharton believed that workers in different crafts and callings employed in the same industry should and could cooperate, but he saw no reason for the erasure of craft distinctions or autonomy. He failed to recognize, however, that the mass-production industries were made up of masses of production workers and a relatively small number of craftsmen and that the federated principle might not be feasible or effective. Moreover, the long trade union experience, which made it possible to administer a federated program, was absent in the mass-production industries.

### THE BUILDING TRADES DEPARTMENT

Strong opposition to the emerging industrial organizations was shown by the Building Trades Department, even though this Department was itself embroiled in a serious internal dispute among its affiliates. Like the Metal Trades Department, the Building Trades Department had been organized in 1908. The unions in the building trades were highly stable, and the continual involvement in jurisdictional disputes led some of the organizations to disaffiliate with the Department when decisions were not in their favor. Although disaffiliation was not usually for long periods of time, the refusal of a union as powerful as the United Brotherhood of Carpenters and Joiners to abide by decisions impaired the ability of the Building Trades Department to settle differences.

The Carpenters' Union, which had joined the Department in 1908, was suspended in 1910 when it refused to comply with a decision awarding work on hollow-metal trim to the Sheet Metal Workers' Union. The Carpenters reaffiliated in 1912 and withdrew the following year when the Department insisted upon enforcing the decision on hollow metal trim. In 1915 the Carpenters' Union rejoined the Department and again withdrew in 1921 after refusing to accept a decision of the National Board for Jurisdictional Awards. The Carpenters' Union reaffiliated in 1927 and withdrew again in 1929, when its proposal to reduce the per capita tax was rejected.

The Bricklayers' Union had joined the Building Trades Department when the Union affiliated with the A. F. of L. in 1916. Disputes between the Bricklayers' and the Plasterers' Unions were of long duration. The 1911 dispute, which involved the jurisdiction over artificial stone, ended in an agreement between the two unions, but this broke down in time and led to the tying up of a number of jobs. Green was able to bring about a truce and to set up a tribunal for settling disputes.[33] Elihu Root was chosen chairman of this tribunal. Later Green met with the executive boards of both unions, and it was agreed that the A. F. of L. would call another conference after the tribunal made its first decision. The conference was to direct its efforts toward restoring peace and understanding between the two organizations and to reestablishing the agreement of 1911.[34]

The first question before the Root arbitration tribunal was whether the Operative Plasterers' Union was justified in setting up locals in Florida after the Bricklayers' Union had abrogated the agreement between the two unions governing work on artificial stone and the plastering of walls to receive tile. Root held that the Operative Plasterers' Union was required to dissolve its local unions in all communities in Florida outside Daytona, Jacksonville, and Pensacola, and that the members of these locals were to transfer to the locals of the Bricklayers' Union.[35] Although the Operative Plasterers' Union at first agreed to accept this decision, it subsequently insisted that acceptance of this decision was dependent upon the full restoration of the 1911 agreement.[36]

To prevent the breakdown of the agreement, Green intervened and urged a meeting between the presidents of the two unions. When Green tried to attend the meeting of the two unions, President Bowen of the Bricklayers at first objected on the ground that Green was attending at the invitation of the employers. Bowen regarded it as unusual for Green to be invited by employers to a meeting which was "to consider and adjust differences which have been dealt with entirely within the trade union movement." While Bowen saw no necessity for Green's attendance, he finally extended him an invitation to attend so as to remove any appearance of employer influence at the conference.[37]

Green presided over the meeting of the representatives of the two trowel trades on August 17, 1927. They reached an agreement for an interchange of cards and took action against violators of rules laid down against work on unfair jobs by members of either organization. The agreement was destined to last only a short time.[38] A dispute over the right to work on artificial stone was started by the Baltimore local of the Operative Plasterers' Union against the Bricklayers' organization. The local building trades council supported the Plasterers and called strikes against the bricklayers on forty-two other jobs in Baltimore.[39] When the convention of the Department upheld the decision of the Executive Council, the Bricklayers withdrew. The International Brotherhood of Electrical Workers, an original member of the Department, withdrew in 1930 because of objections to a tribunal that had been set up to settle jurisdictional disputes. After the withdrawal of the Bricklayers' Union, the International Brotherhood of Teamsters was admitted to membership in the Department. The Department, despite the jurisdictional differences among its affiliates, was active in suppressing dual organizations in the industry.

### THE CONSTRUCTION CODE

The Building Trades Department devoted almost its entire meeting on June 28, 1933 to a discussion of the policies to pursue in view of the new labor legislation. To assure unanimity of action, a meeting of all building trades' unions, including the three organizations not affiliated with the Department, was held on July 10, 1933. The unions presented a request that the construction code incorporate a provision for a thirty-hour week and six-hour day, with the recognition of Saturday, Sunday, and holidays as no-work days and the same wage scales as prevailed in 1929. The code encountered serious opposition from employer groups, but with the assistance of Green, the industry was able to work out an acceptable code.[40]

In view of the desirability of close cooperation among the unions of the Department, Green undertook to have the three building trades' unions outside the Department reaffiliate.

The development of solidarity and cooperation among building trades organizations, [Green wrote] is to me a matter of supreme concern. . . . It is a matter of personal conviction at this important moment, following the adoption of industrial codes applicable to the building industry, that the United

Brotherhood of Carpenters and Joiners of America, the International Brotherhood of Electrical Workers of America, and the Bricklayers, Masons, and Plasterers International Union of America should become affiliated with the American Federation of Labor.

In conformity, therefore, with these expressed opinions and because of my deep practical interest, I am requesting your organization to make application for affiliation with the Building Trades Department of the American Federation of Labor. In making this request I wish to state that the affiliation of your International Union with the Building Trades Department would mean that your organization would be entitled to all the rights and privileges of an affiliated organization with the Building Trades Department and entitled to representation with all its rights and privileges in Conventions of the Building Trades Department.[41]

Following Green's letter, the three unions submitted applications for reaffiliation with the Building Trades Department, and their applications were accepted by the Executive Council of the Department. Opposition to the affiliation of these three unions immediately arose and was great enough that the credentials committee of the convention of the Building Trades Department in 1934 recommended "that such monies that they have paid to this Department be returned and their affiliation be denied."[42] The recommendation, finally approved by the convention meant that the three unions were denied affiliation with the Department. Green, who had urged the three unions to reaffiliate, now sought to have the Department reverse its decision. Addressing the delegates, he emphasized that if a reasonable basis for settling jurisdictional disputes were to be devised, all the building trades unions would have to be members of the Department. Michael J. McDonough, the president of the Department, declared that the Department and its unions had at first greeted the reaffiliation of the three unions with enthusiasm but had subsequently discovered that their reaffiliation would not "result in a harmonizing of the industry as you anticipated."[43]

The underlying and unexpressed reason for the reversal, according to McDonough, was a letter sent by William Hutcheson to his local unions on June 25, 1934, in which he informed his members that in affiliating with the Department, "it was agreed by the three organizations that the Tri-Party Agreement existing between the Electricians, Bricklayers, and our Brotherhood would continue in existence."[44] Green did not accept this as a valid reason for not allowing the three unions to affiliate. He argued that they had done nothing to violate the rules of the Department or labor solidarity and that they could not legitimately be denied affiliation with the Department. Nevertheless, the convention would not retreat from its position, and the fight between the unions employed by general contractors and specialty contractors[44a] continued. The members of the Electricians' Union were, however, employed by specialty contractors, and their alliance with the Bricklayers and Carpenters was for reasons of their own.

Failing to have the three unions admitted, Green called a special meeting of the Executive Council of the A. F. of L. to consider the dispute. He argued that the "rank and file of the building trades are represented in these organizations. The political situation is not a question for this Council to consider. The question . . . is whether this convention kept their solemn and binding promise to these three organizations when they sought the affiliation of those organizations."[45] McDonough answered the statement by questioning the good faith of the three barred organizations. He charged that the membership claims of the three barred unions had been padded so as to control the Department "to suit their own selfish ends." He accused "at least two of these organizations [of never] in their history having given true cooperation in any way to the building up of a solid sound Building Trades Department."[46]

The Executive Council of the A. F. of L. decided that the exclusion of legally affiliated organizations from representation in the convention of the Building Trades Department had made all the action taken by that convention illegal and void, and therefore, it could not be recognized by the Federation.

The Executive Council recommended that efforts to work out an agreement be continued, but if none were reached forty-five days after the adjournment of the Federation convention, the Executive Council would call a convention of the Department and invite all building trades' unions. Green was to preside and the action taken was to be regarded as the action of the convention of the Building Trades Department of 1934. The issue was hotly debated at the convention of the A. F. of L. in 1934. W. J. McSorely of the Lathers' Union charged that the three organizations aimed to control the Department and thereby determine jurisdictional disputes. Bates of the Bricklayers challenged the view. He said that an effort to reunite the building trades' unions started with the hearings on the construction code. According to Bates, "President Green asked . . . [the three unions] on several occasions to come back into the Department in the interests of the building trades' workers, to make it possible to present a solid front to the employers and if possible to secure provisions in the Code that would be protection to the industry."[47] After a long debate, the recommendations, with an amendment to give the Council unlimited time to adjust the differences, were enacted.

Green called a convention in Washington, D. C., on November 26, 1934. Although most of the unions which had been affiliated with the Building Trades Department refused to send delegates, the convention elected officers who claimed to represent the legitimate Building Trades

Department of the A. F. of L. Following the adjournment of the convention, the newly elected officers sought to gain possession of the records and books in the possession of their opponents. On June 6, 1935 Judge Adkins of the District Court of the District of Columbia ruled that the action of the Building Trades Department at its convention of 1934 was illegal and that the Executive Council of the A. F. of L. lacked authority to call the convention. Judge Adkins held, however, that the terms of the officers of the Department had expired on December 31, 1934, and that none had been legally elected. When the decision of the court became known, Hutcheson wanted the Executive Council of the A. F. of L. to call a convention of the Department. John L. Lewis suggested that mediation be tried first. George Harrison proposed that a committee be appointed by Green to mediate the differences, and in the event of failure, the committee would report back to the Executive Council. This suggestion was defeated by a vote of 9 to 4.[48]

In the discussion before the Executive Council, several building tradesmen were present. The presidents of the Carpenters' and the Plumbers' Unions, who held opposing sides in this dispute, were members of the Council. John Coefield charged that the A. F. of L. had not sought to heal the breach in the department and that the chairman of the committee to work out an agreement between the factions, T. A. Rickert, had been biased in favor of the three unions—the Carpenters', Electricians', and Bricklayers' Unions. The Council appointed another committee with George Harrison as chairman and Rickert and George Berry as the other members. An effort was made to bring the two factions together, and when it failed, the A. F. of L. called a convention of the Building Trades Department for August 1, 1935. The unions which had controlled the Department refused to attend, but the other unions met and elected officers. The case was carried to the convention of the A. F. of L. in 1935, and the issue was postponed until a committee from the two factions, aided by George Harrison, was able to reach an agreement on unifying the two factions. Harrison was authorized to decide any differences and to allocate the offices among the two groups.[49] Under the agreement a convention was held in March 1936, when officers were elected and the changes, including a board to settle jurisdictional disputes, were established.[50]

The dispute in the Building Trades Department was at last settled through the efforts of the A. F. of L. More difficult were the jurisdictional differences which were almost daily threatening to divide the movement into hostile factions. At the convention of the A. F. of L. in 1934, fourteen separate resolutions, either protesting invasions of jurisdiction by industrial unions or requesting recognition of industrial organization, were submitted. The one submitted by John Frey of the Metal Trades Department summarized the objections of the older unions to the encroachments of the newly formed organizations in the mass-production industries. Frey charged that the efforts of the industrial or vertical unions, as he called them, to invade the jurisdictions of the unions of the metal trades were causing serious confusion. He argued that a charter given to an international union by the Federation constituted a contract defining and guaranteeing its jurisdiction and that wage earners should not be organized except in the unions which had been granted such jurisdiction under these charters. On the other hand, several resolutions proposed industrial organization as the form suited for mustering workers in mass-production industries into unions. After six days of argument, a compromise proposal drawn by Charles Howard was submitted to the convention by the resolutions committee.

The resolutions committee gave "extended and most profound consideration to one of the most important problems with which our American Trade Union Movement is confronted. . . . The evidence presented to the hearings before the committee conclusively indicates that to deal effectively with the question of organization and with the fundamental questions involved there should be a clear and definite policy outlined by this convention that will adequately meet the new and growing condition with which our American Labor Movement is confronted."[51] The report called attention to the changed methods of work, to the existence of systems of mass production, and to the ability of the large aggregations of capital which control the mass-production industries to frustrate the organization of their workers. "The provision of the National Industrial Recovery Act protecting the right of employees to organize and select representatives of their own choice without interference on the part of employers, or their agents, has had the effect of freeing the flood of organization sentiment existing in the breasts of millions of workers who have been prevented by employer opposition from satisfying their desire for oganization."[52]

The report recognized the duty of the convention "to formulate policies which will fully protect the jurisdictional rights of all trade unions organized upon craft lines and afford every opportunity for development and accession of those workers engaged upon work over which these organizations exercise jurisdiction." It then argued that craft organizations were effective in protecting the interests of workers in industries where the "lines of demarcation between crafts are distinguishable." However, in "many of the industries in which thousands of workers are employed a new condition exists requiring organization upon a different basis to be most effective."[53] The Executive Council was directed to issue national and international union charters in the automobile, cement, aluminum, and such other mass-production and miscellaneous industries as the Executive Council might regard as necessary to meet the situation. In addition the Executive Council was to inaugurate at the earliest possible date a campaign of organization in the iron and steel industry.

Some obvious, although unexpressed, misgivings were manifested by Arthur Wharton of the Machinists' Union, who asked the committee to define the "automotive industry." Green called upon John L. Lewis, a member of the resolutions committee, for an answer. Lewis was unable to give a precise answer, stating that "we are unable to say as a committee where the line of demarcation upon jurisdiction should be, or if there should be a line of demarcation as between the several parts of the automotive industry." Lewis added that "under the policy recommended by the committee, the Executive Council now, as heretofore, will be clothed with the authority to decide the question of jurisdiction." Wharton then quoted Section 11 of the constitution of the A. F. of L. which prohibits the granting of a charter by the Federation to any union without a positive and clear definition of the jurisdiction claimed by the applicant union. Lewis saw no conflict between the clause quoted by Wharton and the power given to the Council, for "no matter what jurisdiction may be claimed by a national or international union," he said, "it still remains that before that question is settled the Executive Council of the American Federation of Labor will have to render a finding."[54]

Wharton remained unsatisfied that the craft unions were adequately protected, but subsequently he appeared less concerned when he was assured by Frey, who was also the secretary of the resolutions committee, that craft unions had little to fear from the proposals and that the report was designed to cover industries which "come strictly under the classification of mass production."[55]

Charles Howard, president of the International Typographical Union and also a member of the resolutions committee, said that his union wanted to see the unorganized workers marshaled under the banner of the A. F. of L. Howard pointed to the efforts of the employers in the mass-production industries and independent unions to win the suffrage of the unorganized; he argued that the greatest obstacle was the fear of the workers in the mass-production industries that they would be divided among "various organizations and thereby their economic strength will be destroyed," and secondly that in drawing "strict jurisdictional lines, the opportunity for continuous employment will be affected; because of the nature of their work they may be considered composite mechanics. One day they may be engaged upon work that would come rightfully under the jurisdiction of one organization and, in order to be continuously employed, at other times they are engaged upon work that would rightfully be considered under the jurisdiction of another organization."[56]

The report eliminated, according to Howard, these fears, and he believed that it would be possible to win the workers in mass-production industries to the A. F. of L.

William Hutcheson of the Carpenters' Union then pointed to the employment of building tradesmen by the mass-production industries to keep their buildings in repair. He wanted to know if the report protected the jurisdiction of the building trades' unions over these workers. The chairman of the resolutions committee, Matthew Woll, thought that it clearly did:

It goes further and says: "Experience has shown that craft organization is most effective in protecting the welfare and advancing the interests of the workers where the nature of the industry is such that the lines of demarcation between crafts are distinguishable." I want to confirm statements made by previous speakers that the subject deals more with the unorganized, and perhaps unorganizable, than it does with questions of craft, or industrial organization, horizontal or vertical. In that regard it does not change the policy of the American Federation of Labor, but it does realize that there is a situation existing that requires immediate, distinctive and effective work in the organizing in one form or another.

Woll sought to assure the leaders of the craft organizations that while the resolution directed the issuance of charters, it stated that "the jurisdiction is to be defined by the Executive Council, and no committee can render a decision upon it."[57]

Although the resolution was unanimously adopted, the question was not to be resolved, for the Executive Council felt free to interpret the directions given to it by the convention. Moreover, to avoid a floor fight, the resolution was made ambiguous and unclear enough to reassure the heads of the craft unions that their jurisdictional rights would not be sacrificed. As the Executive Council was dominated by men who were officers of unions whose jurisdictions might be cut into by the extension of the rights of the new unions, the heads of the craft unions felt reassured that their jurisdictions were safe as long as the Executive Council had to approve any new charter.

### REFERENCES

1. Minutes of Executive Council of the Metal Trades Department, June 23, 1910.
2. *Ibid.*, January 17, 1913.
3. *Ibid.*, January 16, 1914.
4. W. J. Spencer to A. J. Berres, July 7, 1910.
5. *Report of Proceedings of the Twenty-sixth Annual Convention of the Metal Trades Department of the American Federation of Labor*, 1934, pp. 7–8.
6. "Report of Officers," *Ibid.*, p. 30.

7. *Ibid.*, p. 30.

8. Minutes of the Executive Council of the Metal Trades Department, February 24, 1944.

9. *Official Proceedings of Convention of Federation of Federations of Railway Employees of the American Federation of Labor*, 1912, p. 32.

10. *Constitution and By-Laws of Federation of Federations of Railway Employees of the American Federation of Labor*, 1912, Section 8 (a).

11. *Official Proceedings of Third Biennial Convention of Railway Employees' Department*, 1916, pp. 73–77.

12. *Constitution and By-Laws of the Railway Employees' Department, American Federation of Labor*, 1926, pp. 23–24.

13. *Constitution and By-Laws of the Railway Employees' Department of the American Federation of Labor*, 1926, p. 18.

14. *Ibid.*, p. 19.

15. *A Brief Statement of the Facts concerning the Organization, Activities, and Accomplishments of the Federated Trades* (Chicago: Railway Employees' Department, 1933), p. 16.

16. *Official Proceedings of the Seventh Convention Railway Employees' Department of the American Federation of Labor*, 1926, p. 1.

17. *Ibid.*, pp. 35–69.

18. Gompers to Bert Jewell, July 16, 1923.

19. D. B. Robertson to Gompers, December 12, 1923; Gompers to Robertson, December 18, 1923; Gompers to Executive Council, December 24, 1923.

20. Daniel Tobin to Morrison, January 6, 1924; Tobin to Gompers, March 31, 1934; Edward McGrady and Edgar Wallace to Gompers, January 25, 1924; M. W. Warfield to Gompers, March 31, 1924.

21. Memorandum in archives of American Federation of Labor, February 16, 1924; Memorandum, March 24, 1924.

22. Memorandum in the archives of the American Federation of Labor, February 25, 1924.

23. Memorandum of a conference in the office of Congressman Barkley, February 24, 1924. Attending were Gompers, Frank Morrison, W. C. Roberts, E. F. McGrady, members of the A. F. of L. legislative committee; J. Paul Stevens of the Trainmen; W. N. Clark, Conductors; E. H. Kruse, Engineers; A. J. Lovell, Firemen; D. B. Robertson, president of the Firemen; and Congressman Barkley.

24. Robertson to Gompers, May 22, 1924; Gompers to Congressman Frank D. Scott, May 23, 1924; memorandum in archives of A. F. of L., May 23, 1924.

25. *Official Proceedings of the Seventh Convention of the Railway Employees' Department of the American Federation of Labor*, 1926, pp. 77–78.

26. Green to B. M. Jewell, January 25, 1926; Jewell to Green, June 23, 1926; Minutes of the Executive Council, March 23, 1926.

27. *Official Proceedings of the Eighth Convention of the Railway Employees' Department of the American Federation of Labor*, 1930, p. 41.

28. *Ibid.*, pp. 74–75; *Official Proceedings of the Eighth Convention of the Railway Employees of the American Federation of Labor*, 1930, pp. 13–22.

29. *Official Proceedings of the Eighth Convention of the Railway Employees' Department of the American Federation of Labor*, 1930, pp. 13–22.

30. *Official Proceedings of the Ninth Convention of the Railway Employees' Department of the American Federation of Labor*, 1938, p. 122.

31. *Constitution and By-Laws of the Railway Employees' Department of the American Federation of Labor*, 1938, p. 28.

32. *Ibid.*, p. 30.

33. William J. Bowen to Green, November 16, 1927. Bowen was president of the Bricklayers' Union. An agreement to this effect was signed by Bowen and E. J. McGivern, December 21, 1926.

34. Minutes of Executive Council, June 10, 1927.

35. In the Matter of Arbitration between the Bricklayers', Masons', and Plasterers' International Union and the Operative Plasterers' and Cement Finishers' International Association under the Agreement Made at Atlantic City, October 2, 1925. Decision of February 1, 1927.

36. Edward J. McGivern to Green, February 25, 1927.

37. W. J. Bowen to Green, August 11, 1927.

38. The agreement was signed for the Bricklayers' Union by George T. Thornton, Harry C. Bates, Walter V. Price, James T. Cavanaugh, and John Gill; for the Operative Plasterers by Edward J. McGivern, John M. Donlin, W. A. O'Keefe, T. A. Scully; for the A. F. of L. by Green.

39. *Report of Proceedings of the Twenty-first Annual Convention of the Building Trades Department of the American Federation of Labor*, 1927, pp. 85–88; quote on p. 85.

40. *Report of Proceedings of the Twenty-eighth Annual Convention of the Building Trades Department of the American Federation of Labor*, 1934, pp. 79–82.

41. Green to Harry Bates, Daniel Tracy, and William Hutcheson, June 14, 1934.

42. *Report of Proceedings of the Twenty-eighth Annual Convention of the Building Trades Department of the American Federation of Labor*, 1934, p. 104.

43. *Ibid.*, p. 127.

44. Quote in M. J. McDonough and W. C. O'Neil to the Executive Council of the A. F. of L., September 30, 1934.

44a. General contractors have chief responsibility for a job, and nominally supervise the carpentry and bricklaying. Specialty contractors are usually subcontractors who do plumbing, electrical work, etc.

45. Statement of Daniel Tobin in Minutes of Executive Council of A. F. of L., September 28, 1934.

46. Minutes of Executive Council of A. F. of L., September 28. 1934.

47. *Report of Proceedings of the Fifty-fourth Annual Convention of the American Federation of Labor*, 1934, p. 519.

48. Minutes of Executive Council, June 6, 1935.

49. *Report of Proceedings of the Fifty-fifth Annual Convention of the American Federation of Labor*, 1935, pp. 435–437; George Harrison to Daniel Tracy, January 2, 1936.

50. *Report of Proceedings of the Special Convention, Building Trades Department,* March, 1936, pp. 1–7.

51. *Report of Proceedings of the Fifty-fourth Annual Convention of the American Federation of Labor,* 1934, p. 586.

52. *Ibid.,* p. 586.

53. The last two quotes are in *Ibid.,* p. 586.

54. *Ibid.,* p. 589.

55. *Ibid.,* p. 590.

56. *Ibid.,* p. 593.

57. *Ibid.,* p. 593.

# VII

## The Dispute over Structure

THE problem of industrial organization and the jurisdictional rights of the craft unions which it involved was not solved by the decision of the 1934 convention. The vagueness of the declaration was the price paid for its enactment without a fight on the floor of the convention. John Frey, the leading intellectual spokesman for the point of view of the craft unions, was "confident that the declaration of policy [was] fully protective of the craft unions and of their interests."[1] Frey and other leaders of the craft unions were convinced that the method of "joint negotiation and joint agreement reached through the [Metal Trades] Department forms the most effective answer to those who have been advocating the vertical or the so-called industrial form of trade union organization. . . . It is carrying collective bargaining to a new plane, and enabling an employer to negotiate but one agreement which will cover all his employees, an agreement under such terms as makes the International Unions and the Department responsible for carrying out all of the labor responsibilities and duties provided for in the agreement."[2]

The metal trades' unions, whose nominal jurisdictions were being invaded by the new industrial organizations operating as Federal labor unions, were ready to concede the control of the emerging industrial unions over the semiskilled and unskilled workers in the mass-production industries; but they were not disposed to grant the industrial unions the right to organize the skilled craftsmen nominally in their jurisdictions. At the Executive Council meeting in February 1935, Arthur Wharton complained that the Machinists' Union had been encountering serious difficulties "because of demands of Federal Labor Unions with reference to classifications of work."[3] At the same meeting, a request for chartering a union in the public utilities was presented, but no action was taken by the Council.

### MINE, MILL, AND SMELTER WORKERS

A complaint from the Mine, Mill, and Smelter Workers' Union against the craft groups operating in the metalliferous mining industry was also discussed. Thomas H. Brown, the head of the union, appeared before the Executive Council and charged that representatives of the building and metal trades' unions had arrived in Butte "under sealed orders" and had negotiated a contract with the Anaconda Copper Mining Company while 8,000 members of his union in Butte and Great Falls, Montana, were out on strike. Brown said that negotiations between the unions of the Metal Trades Department and the company had been conducted in secret. The Mine, Mill, and Smelter Workers' Union had learned of the meeting only after the agreement had been consummated.

Wharton answered by arguing that the craft unions had never conceded the jurisdiction of the Mine, Mill, and Smelter Workers over craftsmen employed in the copper mines. Moreover, he explained that the agreement signed by his and other unions of the metal trades with the copper companies was "tentative in every respect and stated specifically therein that no settlement should be reached until a satisfactory settlement was reached with the Mine, Mill, and Smelter Workers." The issue was temporarily postponed, pending the arrival of the officers of the craft unions.[4]

In the discussion between the officers of the Mine, Mill, and Smelter Workers and the representatives of the unions of the metal trades, the Mine, Mill, and Smelter Workers' representatives claimed jurisdiction over the craftsmen employed in metalliferous mining if the union chose to exercise it. Both William Hutcheson and Wharton, refusing to accept that contention, pointed to the craftsmen who belonged to their organizations. Hutcheson claimed that members of the Carpenters' Union had been employed in the Butte mines for thirty-five years.

According to Frey, the Secretary of Labor had called a conference in Washington during the Anaconda strike, but Frey denied that their were any "sealed orders" involved. An agreement had been negotiated jointly by the unions of the Building and Metal Trades Departments, with the understanding that the settlement would not be effective until terms had been accepted by the Mine, Mill, and Smelter Workers. After hearing the discussion, John L. Lewis proposed that the Executive Council reaffirm the jurisdiction of the Mine, Mill, and Smelter Workers "as decided by the Atlanta convention and explained by President Gompers in a message to the United Mine Workers of America: that all International and National Unions participating or parties to the so-called Anaconda Agreement of 1934 be directed to respect the aforesaid jurisdiction of the International Union of Mine, Mill and Smelter men and retire from said jurisdiction upon the expiration of the existing agreements with the Anaconda Copper Mining Company."[5]

Daniel Tracy of the Electricians' Union answered Lewis by insisting that "craft organizations have a perfect right to negotiate agreements regarding employment conditions of their members." He said that invitations had been extended to the Mine, Mill, and Smelter Workers to send representatives to the meeting held by the craft unions, but the union had insisted on sending sixty-two delegates, a number deemed too large by Senator Wagner who was acting for the Secretary of Labor. When the Mine, Mill, and Smelter Workers refused to send a smaller committee, the craft unions decided to negotiate an agreement. "President Tracy emphasized the fact that the crafts did not go back, and the agreement so stipulated, until the Mine, Mill, and Smelter Workers case was settled. The Electrical Workers have had a local union in Anaconda for thirty-four years and have had a relationship with the company concerning employment conditions. There has been an [electrical] union in Great Falls for thirty-five years and Butte for thirty-nine years."[6]

Lewis again presented his proposal that the Mine, Mill, and Smelter Workers be given the jurisdiction voted to it by the Atlanta convention. He charged that the Anaconda agreement was

an intrusion of the jurisdiction of the Mine, Mill and Smelter Workers and a thrust, cold-blooded, at the jurisdiction of the United Mine Workers of America. The United Mine Workers has contractual relations with the Anaconda Company. It has no assurance that had the Anaconda Company been so minded there would not have been expounded the same type of agreement to cover the crafts employed in the coal mines of that company. The International Union of Mine, Mill and Smelter Workers . . . has suffered with inadequate leadership. Because of that fact it has not been able to protect its jurisdiction[,] but inability to protect jurisdiction is no waiver of the jurisdiction in the councils of the American Federation of Labor. The non-existence of jurisdiction in no manner impairs the principle involved or the right to enjoy the privileges of jurisdiction. . . . The Mine Workers have an interest in that organization. The day may come when this organization may affiliate with the United Mine Workers.[7]

Subsequently, in the debate on the industrial union issue at the convention of 1935, Lewis insisted that the failure of a union to establish itself in a part of its nominal jurisdiction gave other organizations the right to invade it so as to muster the workers into an organization of labor.

Lewis's motion to grant the Mine, Mill, and Smelter Workers jurisdiction over all employees in the metalliferous mines was seconded by George Berry. The motion was rejected, and a declaration proposed by Hutcheson that there had been no infringement of that union's jurisdiction was adopted by a vote of 12 to 2. Dubinsky and Edward Gainor were absent and did not vote.

### RUBBER WORKERS

The controversy in the metalliferous industries was really a revival of a long-existing dispute which had remained quiescent because of the serious losses suffered by the Mine, Mill, and Smelter Workers' Union in the recent decades. The question of union jurisdiction in the mass-production industries involved somewhat different issues. The craft unions had never established any locals in the mass-production industries, and their claims were based largely on the jurisdictional grants allotted to them in their charters by the A. F. of L. When the question of chartering a union for the rubber industry arose at the Executive Council meeting, Lewis proposed that "jurisdiction be granted to the organization to cover all workers employed throughout the rubber industry."

Matthew Woll then noted that the resolutions committee of the 1934 convention initially had not been able to agree upon the proposals on industrial unionism. A subcommittee had been named, and Charles Howard drafted the report which originally included the rubber industry among those whose workers were to be granted an industrial charter. Several members of the resolutions committee had called attention to the existence of a National Council of Rubber Workers and argued that the rubber workers should be allowed to work their problems out on an industrial basis. Although the rubber workers had not been included among those who were to be given industrial union charters, the authority given to the Executive Council by the convention included the phrase "and such other mass production and miscellaneous industries as in the judgment of the Executive Council may be necessary to meet the situation." According to Woll, that phrase gave the Council blanket authority to include any industry it saw fit.[8] Lewis thereupon withdrew his motion, declaring that he did not want to break faith. Wharton wanted to help the rubber workers organize, but he insisted on upholding the jurisdiction of the Machinists' Union.

At this point, Lewis reviewed the action of the San Francisco convention:

The report sustains the efficiency and virtue of craft organizations but . . . in certain industries in order to meet the requirements of those industries and the psychology of the workers[,] it gave authority to this Council to issue a charter of this kind to three industries and to other industries. . . . President Wharton feels that I am trying to strike a blow at the existence of his organization. In all my statements I sustain the right of craft organizations to live and render service. There was no desire to destroy the existing relations of these organizations but it was incumbent upon us to recognize [that] our procedure had not been successful and to follow the policy outlined. I understood that [it] was by the action of the San Francisco convention that we were authorized to follow that policy of organization in the automotive, aluminum, cement, and other industries of that type. . . . There has been no execution of the San Francisco policy and under the principle laid down by Vice President Wharton there will be no execution of this policy.[9]

Lewis warned that "the failure of the American Federation of Labor to organize the workers in these mass production industries creates a hazardous situation as far as the future of the Federation is concerned. If the Wagner bill is enacted there is going to be increasing organization and if workers are organized in independent unions we are facing the merging of these independent unions in some form of national organization."[10]

When the Council was unable to agree, a committee made up of Wharton, Lewis, and Frank Morrison was appointed to bring in a recommendation on the kind of charter to be given to the rubber workers. The committee failed to reach a decision. Morrison then proposed that a union in the rubber industry be established and that it submit its constitution and projected jurisdiction to the Council. The proposal was not accepted, and Wharton wanted the Executive Council to call a conference of delegates of locals in the industry who were to be advised that the issuance of a charter was contingent upon their willingness "to establish a rate of dues estimated to be sufficient to insure reasonable financial stability of the organization." In addition he asked that all rubber workers in Federal labor unions who were eligible for membership in craft unions be transferred before the charter was issued. Neither Morrison's nor Wharton's proposals were formally submitted. Lewis asked that the president of the A. F. of L. be instructed to "organize, in due form, a national union of Rubber Workers with jurisdiction over all workers employed in the rubber industry except those engaged in new construction work." Rickert went further and requested that the charter for the rubber workers exclude not only those who worked on new building construction but also those who engaged in manufacturing or installing machinery or in maintenance work. In Lewis's view Rickert's proposal would only continue "the trouble."

He insisted that the San Francisco convention had given the Council a mandate to organize the workers industrially. This brought forth a statement from Hutcheson, who disagreed with Lewis:

The declaration of the San Francisco convention clearly sets forth and maintains the jurisdiction of craft organizations. The proposal of Vice President Rickert maintains that but gives opportunity to organize those employed in the rubber industry. Vice President Lewis makes references to the United Mine Workers' jurisdiction. There is a vast difference between the Mine Workers in the manner [in which] they are employed and the rubber workers. The rubber workers and the automobile workers work in factories and buildings and these buildings have to be kept in condition. There is a big difference between these buildings and the mine buildings and I think there is a vast difference between the two groups of workers. Vice President Rickert said he thought his proposal would give to the rubber workers 95 percent of the men in the industry, although I admit I know little about how many are employed in these plants;

the men employed in maintenance would be a comparatively small number as compared to the total number employed in the rubber industry. I believe we can adopt that and still maintain the decision of the San Francisco convention because by doing that we will maintain the jurisdiction of the crafts and give the opportunity to organize the rubber industry.[11]

Green said that he would carry out the policies adopted by the convention and the Executive Council even if they were in conflict with his own views. He called attention to the unanimous vote of the San Francisco convention on the industrial union resolution. He thought that it was "impossible for us to organize these mass-production industries by adhering strictly and immovably to our old lines of organization. It cannot be done, but I think we can follow a policy that will to a large extent preserve the rights of the national unions."[12] Green did not want to transgress upon the jurisdictional rights of unions doing maintenance work or contract work, and he advocated organizing the workers in the mass-production industries "as best we can, then after they are organized if the question [arises] on the jurisdiction of an international union, perhaps by education we can bring about respect among these workers for the jurisdiction of the national and international unions." Green was convinced that, if the Wagner Act was enacted, the mass-production industries would be organized.[13]

At the conclusion of the debate, Rickert's motion to exclude maintenance men and those engaged in the installation of machinery from coverage in the rubber workers' charter passed by a vote of 12 to 2, with Dubinsky and Lewis opposed. Dubinsky, in casting his vote, declared that the resolution enacted at the 1934 convention was "quite clear. The general membership and the public at large took it for granted that it was a change of policy in organizing mass-production industries. I believe if the Executive Council does not act in the spirit as considered and accepted we will be severely criticized. . . . There are workers in the rubber industry who come under the jurisdiction of the Ladies Garment Workers. I do not intend to claim them."[14]

## LUMBER WORKERS

At the same meeting, Hutcheson asked that the Carpenters' Union be given jurisdiction over lumber and sawmill workers. According to Frank Duffy, secretary-treasurer of the Carpenters' organization, the lumber workers had always been regarded as coming within the jurisdiction of the Carpenters. Because conditions had been unpropitious in the past, the Carpenters' Union had not believed it could help the lumbermen. But the times had changed, and now Hutcheson insisted on control of these workers. He said that the lumber workers could either obtain a special membership with lower dues and per capita or a beneficial membership. The Council decided to grant the Carpenters' Union jurisdiction over the lumber and sawmill workers and to order the directly affiliated federal labor unions to transfer to that organization. Lewis seconded the proposal, which was unanimously adopted without any discussion.[15]

### ELECTRICAL WORKERS

The workers engaged in electrical manufacturing also sought an industrial charter, but the Executive Council refused their request. Virtually no union organization existed in this industry prior to 1933, and after the enactment of the National Industrial Recovery Act, the workers in the Philadelphia plant of the Philco Radio Company were given a charter for Radio and Television Workers Federal Labor Union No. 18368. In December a group of unions in the electrical and radio manufacturing industries established the Radio and Allied National Trades Council. At first the Federation refused to recognize the Council because it had allowed non-Federation unions to affiliate with it. Subsequently, these unions were excluded, and in December 1934, eleven locals with about 8,000 members met in Buffalo, New York, and voted to ask the Executive Council for a charter covering the electrical manufacturing industry.[16]

On February 12, 1935 James Carey, who had been elected to lead the National Radio and Allied Trades Council, appeared before the Executive Council and asked that his organization be granted a national charter covering the electrical manufacturing and allied industries. The request immediately encountered opposition from Hutcheson, who claimed that the Carpenters' Union had jurisdiction over the making of wooden cabinets, and from Bugniazet, who argued that his union, the International Brotherhood of Electrical Workers, had jurisdiction over the workers claimed by Carey's organization. Lewis disagreed "with the attitude of the Council in refusing to consider charter applications of workers in these mass-production industries." Wharton insisted that the craft unions would not support an organization campaign if their jurisdiction were invaded. He argued, moreover, that the crafts had evolved methods of cooperation, such as the one then in effect in the plants of the Remington-Rand Company, which were adequate to meet the needs of organizing the mass-production industries.

Green suggested that each application for an industrial charter should be judged on its own merits and that a general policy should be avoided. He called attention to the organization of the Federation.

It is made up of 109 national and international unions. They have been given charters and jurisdictions over their particular trades and callings. That is what the Federation is made of, but in the development of organization we are big enough to know while we shall protect and observe the autonomous rights and jurisdictional rights of each international union we will endeavor to meet extraordinary situations such as arise in mass production industries. We started on that at the Scranton convention of the American Federation of Labor when we recognized the existing facts in the coal mining industry and I think that the jurisdiction granted to the Miners was that they be given jurisdiction over all engineers in and around the mines.[17]

When Hutcheson wanted to know if Green meant that the industrial unions would be given jurisdiction over all workers employed by the companies, Green answered that the men employed in the machine shops of a mine belonged to the United Mine Workers of America. As Green saw it, "we will have to take each case without making a decision on industrial unions or vertical unions, but deal with each case." If workers in a given industry could not be organized in one way, Green said that common sense dictated that another method be tried.[18] Hutcheson felt that if unions sought to claim workers irrespective of the work they were performing, there would be considerable difficulty. He was "willing to help organize any group of workers along reasonable lines so long as it does not infringe on our organization that has helped to build up the labor movement to what it is today." The application of the radio workers was referred to Green with instructions that he seek to work out an understanding and report the results to the next meeting of the Council.[19]

No agreement could be reached, and at the meeting of locals of radio and allied workers in December 1935, it was decided to renew the request for a national charter. At a subsequent conference in February 1936, Daniel Tracy, president of the International Brotherhood of Electrical Workers, addressed the delegates. His proposals were not accepted.[20] In answer to the request of the radio and allied locals for a charter, Green, at the direction of the Council, wired:

Executive Council decided that the best interests of Radio Workers including those you represent would be served through their affiliation with the International Brotherhood of Electrical Workers. This is a strong existing international union and is ready and willing to accept radio workers into membership without additional initiation fee or additional cost. Full protection and service of international organization will be accorded radio workers. I urge you and your associates to confer with President Tracy and his associates for the purpose of arranging for affiliation of all members of federal radio workers' local organizations to be transferred to International Brotherhood of Electrical Workers. Executive Council is of the opinion that this course should be pursued rather than to create a new national union of radio workers.[21]

The Council's suggestion was rejected, and the radio allied workers remained outside the Federation.

REFERENCES

1. Frey to W. A. Appleton, February 21, 1935, in Frey Papers, Folder 6, Manuscript Division, Library of Congress.
2. *Ibid.*
3. Minutes of Executive Council, February 1, 1935.
4. *Ibid.*
5. Minutes of Executive Council, February 7, 1935.
6. Minutes of Executive Council, May 1, 1935.
7. *Ibid.*
8. Minutes of Executive Council, May 5, 1935.
9. *Ibid.*
10. *Ibid.*
11. *Ibid.*
12. *Ibid.*
13. *Ibid.*
14. *Ibid.*
15. Minutes of Executive Council, February 4, 1935.
16. Memorandum in files of A. F. of L.
17. Minutes of the Executive Council, February 12, 1935.
18. *Ibid.*
19. *Ibid.*
20. Report to Executive Council of American Federation of Labor by Lewis Hines, December 30, 1935; Minutes of Executive Council, January 27, 1935.
21. *Ibid.*

# VIII

## Automobile Industry

IN contrast to its activity in the electrical manufacturing industry, the A. F. of L. had sought to organize the automobile workers in the 1920's without any success. In 1925 James O'Connell, the president of the Metal Trades Department, had suggested that an effort be made to organize the workers in the automotive industry, but he questioned whether a campaign could be launched in this industry if traditional jurisdictional claims were insisted upon by the craft unions. He said that the "automobile industry [was] so highly and scientifically specialized as to produce a jumble of jurisdictional claims and disputes that would be almost impossible of unraveling."[1] The convention committee, after considering O'Connell's report, informed the Department convention that President O'Connell thought that the workers in the automobile plants should be organized along industrial lines. The committee was "in hearty accord" with the views of the President and recommended that the incoming Executive Council of the Department devise a program for organizing the automobile industry.[2]

The Metal Trades Department took no action during 1925, and at its 1926 convention, O'Connell renewed his discussion of the desirability of organizing the automotive workers. He now believed that because there were unions which were not affiliated with the Metal Trades Department that had an interest in the automobile industry, the proper body to initiate the campaign of organization was the A. F. of L. He thereupon requested the convention to instruct its delegates to the A. F. of L. convention to propose an organization campaign in the automobile industry. O'Connell's proposal was endorsed both by the convention of the Metal Trades Department and by the 1926 convention of the A. F. of L.[3]

O'Connell, a former president of the Machinists' Union, recognized the jurisdictional problems and the obstacles facing any campaign. He argued that

an industry, so highly specialized, so tremendously developed, requires, not the efforts of an individual organization nor the efforts of an individual department of an organization, but the tremendous strength and influence of this great body to approach this undertaking. It cannot be done in any other way and the question of how they shall be organized, whether in our regular trades organizations or in some other kind of organization . . . is a matter that must be worked out and decided by the men that may be called together by the President of the American Federation of Labor to sit down and give the matter careful consideration and work out some plan to bring this great industry into a state of organization.[4]

Green had been directed by the convention delegates to call a conference of unions that had an interest in the automotive industry. He proceeded to assemble data on the automobile industry and to arrange the conference.[5] The Metal Trades Department and sixteen unions, among them the Carpenters', Electricians', Plumbers', Machinists', Operating Engineers', and Sheet Metal Workers' Unions, were represented at the meeting. In opening the conference, Green pointed out that if the task of organizing was to be seriously undertaken, the representatives would have "to waive jurisdiction and the men organized in accordance with whatever means and methods may best suit the situation. After they are organized and we have established organization in the automobile factories we can then consider the jurisdictional question and through some educational process arrange to have the men thus organized transferred to the jurisdiction to which they belong." Noting the changes in the position of the skilled worker in industry, Green thought that "it would be difficult to distinguish craftsmen from other workers."[6]

The representatives of the unions refused, nevertheless, to agree to allow the workers in the automobile industry to be organized into federal labor unions as O'Connell had suggested. Green and O'Connell were convinced that the automobile workers were "so intermingled and so inseparably associated in the method of mass-production that it is practically impossible to draw trade union jurisdiction lines." The heads of the unions in the metal trades did not share these views.[7]

O'Connell invited representatives of the Machinists', Electricians', and Blacksmiths' Unions to discuss the organization of the workers in the automotive industry with the Executive Council of the Metal Trades Department. P. J. Conlon of the Machinists' Union claimed "that successful organization in this industry could only be brought about by mass organization." Thomas Keogh of the Molders' Union agreed with this view, but Roy Horn, a vice-president of the Blacksmiths' Union "questioned the wisdom of organizing these employees into one big union."[8]

Although Green was unable to report agreement by the unions on jurisdiction, he drafted a plan which he presented for approval to the Executive Council of the A. F. of L. Tentatively, the program called for the waiving of jurisdiction by all national and international unions in the automobile industry, which was defined as "all plants engaged in the manufacture of automobile parts, bodies, wheels, hardware and accessories, tops and trimmings, and the assembling of parts into completed automobiles." The campaign was to be directed by the A. F. of L. with the unions providing organizers.[9]

The Carpenters', Firemen and Oilers', and Sheet Metal Workers' Unions withdrew and refused to attend the second conference called for March 24, 1927. This meeting agreed that international unions having jurisdiction over work done in the automobile industry would suspend "jurisdiction in all plants where the conveyor or assembly line prevails or some method of mass-production under which specialization has subdivided the craft into repetitive operations." The A. F. of L. was charged with directing the campaign and appointing a director to lead it.

Workers in the automobile industry, except those engaged in the construction and maintenance of plants, equipment, parts or tools, shall be organized into local unions directly affiliated with the A. F. of L. A local union shall include all workers employed in one plant unless the size of the plant requires division into smaller units, or unless it is desirable to combine workers in a number of plants into one local union. The members of directly affiliated automobile workers unions shall be recognized by all national and international unions of the A. F. of L. and shall be given exchange privileges when changing their work from one automobile plant to another, and where possible shall be given membership in international unions without further cost, where such unions hold jurisdiction.[10]

It was also agreed that $2 of the $5 initiation fee, and 50 cents out of $2 dues were to be placed into the Automobile Organizing Campaign Fund for the purpose of aiding in the effort to bring the workers in the industry into the union. The Fund was to be under the control of Federation officers.

Another conference was held on June 24, 1927, and fewer unions were represented. Nevertheless, Green assigned Paul K. Smith to head the campaign, and several of the unions—Pattern Makers, Molders, Machinists, and Electricians—assigned organizers.[11] Green directed Smith to confer with the head of the United Automobile, Aircraft, and Vehicle Workers of America, an unaffiliated union, on the tactics to be pursued.[12] Temporary headquarters were established in Detroit. Smith soon reported that he was disappointed with the cooperation he received from the international unions and the responses from the workers in the industry. After several months Smith left Detroit and devoted himself to organizing some of the automobile plants around Milwaukee, Wisconsin. Although he found a more favorable attitude toward organization among the workers in the Nash plant, Smith feared that organizing openly "would simply result in the discharge of those active which would . . . precipitate a wild-cat strike."[13] Smith advised that strikes be avoided and that the organizing activity be carried on without too much publicity. No employers were willing to meet with the A. F. of L. or its affiliated unions. The Federation was unable to overcome the indifference of the workers, the hostility of the industry, and the mounting unemployment which made organizing even more difficult. Quietly the Federation withdrew from a campaign which had at best halfhearted support.[14]

As a result of the depression, which seriously affected their industry, the auto workers radically changed their attitude toward organization. Soon after the enactment of the National Industrial Recovery Act, the A. F. of L. sent William Collins to Detroit. A number of Federal unions were established, and almost immediately the craft unions raised objections to the method of organizing. The most vigorous complaints came from Wharton, who almost from the beginning of the NIRA had called the attention of Morrison and Green to the invasion of the jurisdiction of the Machinists' Union, which he headed. He particularly objected to the claim that the "plan of organization that was agreed to in Detroit in 1928" countenanced the industrial form of organization in the automobile plants. He charged that this plan had "been twisted around . . . as [a] change of policy of the American Federation of Labor [so] that we are now organizing on an industrial basis."[15] Wharton conceded, however, that the Machinists' Union had agreed in 1926 to organize all classes of workers in the automobile industry, except tool and diemakers, diesinkers, and maintenance men into Federal labor unions; but he pointed to differences in dues and initiation fees charged by the Federal labor unions and the craft organizations as constituting a major problem. Green, defending his actions, told of the many requests for organization from the mass-production industries and reminded Wharton that in the discussion of the "organizing of mass-production industries, particularly the automobile industry . . . we agreed that we would proceed to organize these workers in Federal Labor Unions."[16]

Green was, however, directed by the Executive Council to instruct the organizers of the Federation to show greater concern for the jurisdictional rights of the affiliates. In a directive to A. F. of L. organizers, Green wrote:

In the organization of federal unions it is important and highly necessary that the workers who become organized should be advised of the necessity of becoming affiliated with organizations granted jurisdiction over the trade and calling with which they are associated. Great patience should be exercised in advising workers of the organization plans of the American Federation of Labor and of the organized status which they would occupy through membership in a local union chartered by an International organization exercising jurisdiction in the industry, trade, or calling in which they may be employed and which international union has been duly chartered by the American Federation of Labor. In organizing workers in the mass production industries where it is difficult to define the lines of jurisdiction of each national and international union, we urge that all organizers exercise sound discretion and avoid in every possible way a transgression of the clearly defined jurisdictional rights of National and International Unions.[17]

Not a single union of automobile workers was affiliated with the Federation in June 1933. When the code of fair competition of the automobile industry was being considered by the National Recovery Administration, Green, on behalf of the Federation, submitted a brief and appeared in its behalf. The Federation asked that the code incorporate a requirement that weekly hours of work should be limited, normally, to thirty. In addition to the provisions on wages, the code signed by President Roosevelt on August 26, 1933 covered other conditions of work and included a merit clause (sharply attacked by Green) which read: "Without in any way attempting to qualify or modify, by interpretation, the foregoing requirements [those governing collective bargaining] of the National Industrial Recovery Act, employers in this Industry may exercise their right to select, retain, or advance employees on the basis of individual merit, without regard to their membership in any organization." The code was to expire on December 31, 1933.[18] Workers were to be employed an average of thirty-five hours per week, but they could, if necessary, be employed up to forty-eight hours in any week and for six days. Employment of minors below the age of sixteen was prohibited.

Green carried his concern about the merit clause in the automobile code to President Roosevelt. The President, agreeing that such a provision would not be included in any other code, declared:

Because it is evident that the insertion of any interpretation of Section 7 (a) in a code of fair competition leads only to further controversy, no such interpretation should be incorporated in any code. While there is nothing in the provisions of Section 7 (a) to interfere with the bona fide exercise of the right of an employer to select, retain or advance employees on the basis of individual merit, Section 7 (a) does clearly prohibit the pretended exercise of this right by an employer simply as a device for compelling employees to refrain from exercising the rights of self-organization, designation of representatives and collective bargaining, which are guaranteed to all employees in said Section 7 (a).[19]

In the meantime unionization spread, and the code for the automobile manufacturing industry was extended to September 5, 1934, although labor received no public opportunity to present its recommendations for changes. Labor was also not allowed to see the information submitted by the individual automobile companies. "This action on the part of the Administration," Green informed the automobile workers, "without consulting the employees concerned, is conclusive evidence that we must realize that, after all, it is not alone the law which is going to help us. We must depend upon our own efforts."[20]

Dissatisfaction with conditions and the attitude of the automobile companies toward the newly established unions led to serious consideration of a strike call during March 1934. The National Labor Board intervened and considered the demands of the unions. The unions asked that they be recognized and that the National Labor Board conduct bargaining elections to determine the right of the union to represent workers employed in particular plants. General Motors, speaking through its executive vice-president, William Knudsen, announced that it would not recognize the A. F. of L. unions nor agree to the holding of plant elections. The issue was taken to President Roosevelt, and after five days of negotiations, participated in by Green, William Collins, a committee of delegates from the Federal locals of auto workers, and the National Automobile Chamber of Commerce, an agreement was reached on March 25. It set up the Automobile Labor Board.

Employers were to bargain collectively with chosen representatives of their employees and not to discriminate against their employees on the grounds of union affiliation. If more than one union sought to represent a particular group of workers, "each bargaining committee [should] have a total membership pro rata to the number of men each group represents." This was the proportional representation clause which was to become a serious source of dissension between the Automobile Labor Board, appointed by the National Recovery Administration under the agreement, and the A. F. of L. The tripartite board, whose decision was to be final and binding on the parties, was to be given access to payrolls if that step were necessary to carry out its task. Dr. Leo Wolman was named chairman of the board; Nicholas Kelley, an attorney for the Chrysler Corporation, represented industry; and Richard L. Byrd, an officer of the Pontiac Automobile Workers Federal Labor Union No. 18941, represented labor.

President Roosevelt saw

in the settlement . . . a framework for a new structure of industrial relations—a new basis of understanding between employers and employees. I would like you to know [the President said] that in the settlement just reached in the automobile industry we have charted a new course in social engineering in the United States. It is my hope that out of this will come a new realization of the opportunities of capital and labor not only to compose their differences at the conference table and to recognize their respective rights and responsibilities but also to establish a foundation on which they can cooperate in bettering the human relationships involved in any large industrial enterprise. . . . In the settlement just accomplished two outstanding advances have been achieved. In the first place we have set forth a basis on which, for the first time in any large industry, a more comprehensive, a more adequate, and a more equitable system of industrial relations may be built than ever before. It is my hope that this system may develop into a kind of works council in industry in which all groups of employees, whatever may be their choice of organization or form of representation, may participate in joint conference with their employers and I am assured by the industry that such is also their goal and wish.[21]

Green expressed relief that the strike in the auto industry had been averted. He felt that if the unions in the automobile industry

could secure a settlement which provided for recognition of the right to collective bargaining and for a settlement of the grievances of the automobile workers, it would be far better to accept such a settlement than to run the risk of [a] strike in the automobile industry at the present time. We did not secure an ideal agreement or one that represents the full hopes and aspirations of the workers. The President intervened, urged acceptance of the settlement, and in order to avoid the conflict, the agreement proposed was accepted.[22]

Dissatisfaction with the conduct of the Automobile Labor Board appeared almost as soon as it was named. On April 9, 1934 a conference of representatives from sixty Federal labor unions in the automotive industry requested President Roosevelt to replace the chairman of the Automobile Labor Board unless he "is willing to carry out immediately your settlement of March twenty-fifth."[23] On the other hand, Walter Teagle, the head of the Standard Oil Company of New Jersey and a member of the National Labor Board, felt that Roosevelt had "removed a basic cause of industrial strife and made an obligation of industry and labor to compromise their difficulties in a spirit of fair play for each. This should prove a landmark in the development of cooperative industrial relationship."[24]

By June 1934 the automobile workers' unions reached their first milestone. In a period of one year their number of locals had grown to 106, and considering that in June of the preceding year there had not been a single local union in the industry, the Federation might have regarded its progress with at least limited satisfaction. On June 23 and 24, 1934, delegates from the federal locals of automobile workers met in Detroit and formed the National Council of Automobile Workers' Unions. The Executive Council of the A. F. of L. reported that a local union had been established by this time in "every major plant in the country as well as in many of the most important parts' plants."[25]

The Automobile Labor Board performed unsatisfactorily from the labor point of view in formulating the principles for layoffs and rehiring. Where the settlement had laid down the rule that seniority and marital status should be considered as well as individual merit,

the Board's formula was apparently based on a complete acceptance of the automobile code's "individual merit" clause. Both seniority and marital status gave way before employees whose work was deemed "essential by the management," or who had "special training" or "exceptional ability." Where seniority and marital status were equal, preference was determined by the "skill and efficiency of the individual employee," again "as determined in the judgment of the management." It is easy to understand, therefore, why these regulations . . . aroused vigorous resentment against and lively distrust of the Board among trade union workers.[26]

In December 1934 the Automobile Labor Board announced its procedure for determining representation. It provided for two elections in each automobile plant, one to nominate candidates and a second to elect representatives. At the nominating election, the employee or voter could write in the name of anyone he wished to have as representative in dealings with the employer. Employment with the company was not a requisite for nomination. The two names receiving the highest vote in the nominating election were placed on the ballot in the final election, and the one receiving the highest vote was chosen to represent the particular voting group. Even before the elections were held, the labor movement became suspicious of the members of the Automobile Labor Board. In fact, President Green sought the removal of the labor member of the Board, Richard Byrd, on the grounds that he was working against the interests of the A. F. of L.; but Secretary of Labor Perkins informed him that she could not comply with the request because Byrd was a presidential appointee.[27]

The A. F. of L. at this point protested the conduct of the Automobile Labor Board to President Roosevelt. Charlton Ogburn, the Federation's attorney, wrote the President that the unwarranted ordering of the elections by the Automobile Labor Board "without the consent and against the wishes of organized labor render it completely unacceptable."[28] The A. F. of L. sought to have the Automobile Labor Board change its policy; and the unwillingness of the Board to comply even in part with the protests led Green to announce that "in order to protect the interests of the American Federation of Labor and respond to what seems to be the universal wish of the automobile workers identified with the American Federation of Labor, [we wish] to officially advise you that the American Federation of Labor must now withdraw from participation in the work and decisions of the Automobile Labor Board."[29]

In a letter to President Roosevelt, Green claimed that "the fundamental difficulty in the relationships between automobile manufacturers and automobile workers lies in the refusal on the part of the manufacturers to acknowledge the rights of their workers to form self-governing unions." Green charged that

the Board lost the confidence of labor very shortly after it was established in March 1934. This loss of confidence came because (1) the labor member of the board completely failed to represent labor and . . . (2) the chairman of the Board made it clear to the unions that he looked upon the functions of his board as those of conciliation and mediation only. In no case has the board ever actually ordered reinstated or rehired a man discriminated against for union membership, and in no case where reinstatement was recommended was a time limit fixed for such reinstatement. Many whose reinstatement was recommended were forced to return to work on inferior jobs. The board's rules of seniority have not been satisfactorily enforced to protect workers in lay-offs and rehiring.

Since, according to Green, the agreement of March 25 was for no fixed duration of time and "since no plan of proportional representation had up to September 11, 1934 been announced by the Wolman Board, the American Federation of Labor upon that date notified you and the manufacturers of their withdrawal from the agreement."[30]

Despite the withdrawal of the A. F. of L., the Automobile Labor Board announced on December 7, 1934 that it would continue to hold elections. The Federation leaders were irked because these elections were being held in plants where employees had not requested them, and the elections were taking place on company property under the eyes of the employer or his agents. The Federation announced that the statements of the Automobile Labor Board on the strength of the A. F. of L. in the automobile industry were wrong, inasmuch as the A. F. of L. had directed its members not to participate in the elections. Moreover, "in only 4 per cent of the 10 plants in which elections [have] so far been held are there United Automobile Workers Federal Labor Unions affiliated with the American Federation of Labor." The charge was made that the Board had avoided elections in which the Federation unions had a majority.[31]

When the automobile code was extended for four and a half months to June 16, 1935, Green again denounced the extension "without the consent or approval of labor and without consulting responsible labor officials." Singled out for denunciation were Donald R. Richberg and Leo Wolman. The attacks upon the Automobile Labor Board led to its abolition; and in its final report it sought to answer the charges made against it by the A. F. of L.: "Discrimination because of union membership, in the opinion of the Board, was not by June, 1935 a problem of any magnitude in the automobile manufacturing industry, and has not been for some months previously. Employees in the industry knew that all cases of discharge were subject to review by the Board." The hearings of the La Follette Committee of the United States Senate are an adequate commentary upon the claims of the Board.[32]

While the A. F. of L. and its affiliated locals in the automobile industry were opposing the program of proportional elections or works councils, the demands for the chartering of an international industrial union in the industry were increasing in intensity. A committee of auto workers appeared before the Executive Council on February 1, 1935, and the majority asked that an international charter be issued in the industry. Michael Manning, a member of the committee, did not believe that the time for issuing a national charter had yet arrived. His views were shared by Francis Dillion, the Federation's organizer in the automobile industry. Green thought that the Council had been directed by the convention to establish an international union and he reported that the A. F. of L. had "organized 176 local unions of automobile workers. We have established splendid organizations in some of the automobile manufacturing plants and automobile parts plants . . . a fine nucleus for an international union has already been established, and an international union of automobile workers can be launched, and if launched I have every reason to believe if officered properly and supervised and helped by the American Federation of Labor it can be a success."[33]

Lewis was dissatisfied with the conduct of the A. F. of L. He charged that the failure to establish an international union in the automobile industry was a basic weakness which reflected itself in the attitude of the national administration. This failure, Lewis held, made

it possible for the Recovery Administration and the White House to make decisions with impunity or without fear of any successful challenge from the American Federation of Labor. . . . I would have the Executive Council set up an international union at once, by the issuance of a charter, by the selection of temporary officers by the President of the American Federation of Labor from the material you obviously have there. . . . As near as I can make out from Organizer Dillion he is not afraid of creating an international union but opposed to calling a convention on account of the political skirmishing that would take place there. A convention could be called in three months or six months or whenever in the judgment of this Council they are qualified.[34]

Lewis's proposal was not approved by Wharton, who was concerned about the effect upon his own organization of the chartering of an international union in the automobile industry. Wharton again referred to the original agreement accepted by his organization and other unions of the metal and building trades in 1926. They had expected the Federation to carry out a campaign. But, Wharton continued, there really was no campaign instituted following the action of the Detroit convention. I think there was an effort on the part of President Green to hold a conference with Ford but it fell through. There are a substantial number of workers who are an important factor in our organization that are connected with the automobile industry. There are a considerable number of tool and die workers who do not work for the automobile industry except at a certain period of the year. At the present time about 45 percent of the tool and die work [is done] in the automobile manufacturing plants operated by the companies themselves. In these plants the tool and die work is separate and distinct from all other operations of the plant. Fifty-five percent of the work is done by contract . . . our organization is not willing to relinquish jurisdiction over our men in the automobile plants and the automobile parts manufacturing plants. The skilled maintenance men, all plants employ a number of these men, tool and die workers, set-up men, as they call them under various names, belong to our organization.[35]

Green replied that he was satisfied from his experience during the organizing campaign of the 1920's "that it was absolutely impossible to organize these workers into unions where you draw the line of craft distinction. We cannot organize them that way. They are mass minded. They ask me over and over again. 'Are you going to divide us up?' I cannot change that state of mind; it is there. We cannot organize them on any other basis."[36] Lewis then submitted the following seven-point program:

(1) That a charter for a national or international union of automobile workers be issued at once. (2) That for a temporary period determined by the Executive Council the officers to function under the charter thus issued be designated by the President of the American Federation. (3) That an active organizing campaign be inaugurated by this international in the automobile industry under the direction of the American Federation of Labor. (4) That facilities be provided the new union for necessary publicity and even the publication of a paper if it is deemed advisable. (5) That organizing assistance and finances within the proper limitations of the American Federation of Labor be provided. (6) That every effort be made to expedite the complete organization of the automobile industry at the earliest possible time. (7) That all questions of overlapping jurisdiction on the automobile parts and special crafts organizations encountered in the administration policy be referred to the Executive Council for consideration at such time as the Council may elect to give these questions consideration.[37]

When Lewis's program was discussed the following week, the question of control over the maintenance men was raised by the secretary of the International Brotherhood of Electrical Workers, who claimed that many of those workers were within the jurisdiction of this organization. Green said that

the automobile industry presents the most perfect and highest development
in mass production. . . . The workers are brought into this industry in large
numbers en masse, they are employed en masse, they work together as cogs
in a great machine. There can be no private skill because no man begins
and completes an operation other than the skilled tool and diemakers. Even
pattern makers now are not required to perfect the pattern, begin it, construct
it and complete it. The facts are that the pattern maker does not know what
the finished pattern will be because each one is assigned a special part of
the pattern. . . . Is it not reasonable to conclude that as a matter of fact men
who are not regarded as skilled workers, men who are not required to
exercise skill, but are required to perform a repetitive operation day in and
day out would begin to think in mass terms? They become mass minded.
I have found that out in my experience with these automobile workers in
the production end particularly and I am convinced because of that psychological, economic and industrial condition established in the automobile industry, it is impossible for us to attempt to organize along our old lines in
the automobile industry. So long as I am president of the American Federation of Labor . . . I am going to conform to the decisions of the Executive
Council and the convention but I have been confronted with the difficult
task to execute the policies of the Executive Council and protect the rights
of every affiliated national and international union, and I have sent out
official communications, both to the steadily employed and volunteer organizers, instructing them to cooperate fully with the national and international unions in organizing the workers of the country. To that extent I
have endeavored to meet every complaint that has been filed but I must
confess that I have come, you will come, and all of us will always come face
to face with the fact, not a theory but a situation actual existing, that if
organization is to be established in the auomobile industry it will be upon
a basis that the workers employed in this mass production industry must
join an organization en masse. We cannot separate them.[38]

After Bugniazet reminded the Council that there were many maintenance men in the automotive industry who belonged to the Electrical
Workers' Union, Green expressed the view that the automobile parts industry was too closely related to the auto production for the workers in
the two industries to be separated. Hutcheson, intervening in the discussion, noted that "the American Federation of Labor has been brought up
to its present strength as a result of craft organizations. If it is an admitted
fact that the American Federation of Labor has been brought up to the
point it has, following the lines of craftsmanship, I think we should adhere
to that with the thought in mind of protecting these craftsmen and at
the same time giving these men the opportunity to organize."[39] He
thought it could be done, but not by giving the automobile workers a
charter so broad that they could claim any worker employed by an
automotive firm.

Lewis countered this argument with the claim that this program gave the Executive Council a final decision on all questions of overlapping jurisdiction. For Lewis "the fundamental obligation is to organize these people. If an injury would be done in the estimation of any organization they would have the right to take it up with the Executive Council after we had accomplished organization and not before, after the fact or organization has been accomplished[,] not tie on reservations that will in themselves deter an effective campaign."

Tobin agreed in part with Lewis's views, but he was opposed to industrial organization in general. Industrial organization, according to Tobin, "had been tried . . . and was found to be a complete failure with the exception of the Miners. It was successful there because the industry was isolated and men worked underground, and because of conditions peculiar to this industry, [the miners] were given special privileges not given to any other organization."[40] Nevertheless, Tobin favored a temporary relaxation of jurisdiction. Wharton thereupon declared that the basic problem was not the structure of the union to be formed but the conflict over the size of dues and initiation fees. He believed that an adequate income was necessary so that the automobile workers would be able to finance their organization once it was established.

George Harrison then moved an amendment that would give the auto workers jurisdiction over the automobile-parts plants but would deny them the right to organize workers engaged in the making of tools and dies and all others empoyed in and around automobile plants engaged in the maintenance of tools and buildings. Lewis pleaded that "cavilling be deferred until in the light of what accomplishment is made in the objective we can take up the question of dividing the members, that contention over the fruits of victory be deferred until we have some of the fruits in our possession."[41] Lewis was convinced that the labor movement faced a crisis unless steps were taken to organize these mass-production workers. Green supported Lewis's view: "If we lay down here a policy of organization and charge the President and his associates to organize people I do not want you to blame us for failure. I know their state of mind. The moment you attempt to segregate them you will never get anywhere. If you tell them to go here, you here and you there, you will never get anywhere. They are so closely related and inextricably interwoven they are mass minded. Whatever you do I will try to carry out but I will be the target of criticism and I know we will fail."[42] Despite Green's and Lewis's arguments, Harrison's amendment was passed by a vote of 12 to 2. Lewis and Dubinsky voted against the amendment.

On August 26, 1935, the A. F. of L. chartered an international union of auto workers. It did not include in the jurisdiction job and contract shops or workers engaged in the manufacture of dies, tools, and machinery. The officers—F. J. Dillion, president, Edward Hall, secretary-treasurer, and Homer Martin, vice president—were temporarily appointed by the Federation. A committee from the Automobile Workers protested the limited jurisdiction as well as the appointment of officers. The protest was rejected by the Council. All Federal labor unions in the automobile industry were directed to affiliate with the newly chartered International Union of United Automobile Workers of America. The automobile workers were dissatisfied with the solution provided by the Executive Council, but for the moment they had no alternative to accepting the decision.[43]

### REFERENCES

1. *Proceedings of the Seventeenth Annual Convention of the Metal Trades Department of the American Federation of Labor*, 1925, p. 23. See also Sidney Fine, "President Roosevelt and the Automobile Code," *The Mississippi Valley Historical Review*, June, 1958.

2. *Ibid.*, p. 54.

3. *Proceedings of the Eighteenth Annual Convention of the Metal Trades Department of the American Federation of Labor*, 1926, pp. 12, 46.

4. *Report of Proceedings of the Fifty-sixth Annual Convention of the American Federation of Labor*, 1926, pp. 171–172.

5. Green to William Collins, November 16, 1926.

6. Minutes on the Meeting on the Automobile Industry, December 2, 1926.

7. Minutes of Executive Council of American Federation of Labor, January 11, 1927.

8. Minutes of the Executive Council of the Metal Trades Department of the American Federation of Labor, January 25, 1927.

9. Minutes of Executive Council of the A. F. of L., January 17, 1927.

10. Conference of National and International Union Representatives, March 24, 1927.

11. Minutes of Executive Council of A. F. of L., May 10, 1927. Conference of Unions Held in Executive Council Room of the American Federation of Labor, June 24, 1927.

12. Green to Arthur E. Rohan, June 3, 1927.

13. Paul J. Smith to Green, February 27, 1928.

14. Minutes of Executive Council of the A. F. of L., April 24, 1929.

15. Minutes of Executive Council of the A. F. of L., September 7, 1933.

16. *Ibid.*

17. Green to State Branches, City Centrals, and Organizers, September 18, 1933.

18. National Recovery Administration, *Code of Fair Competition for the Automobile Industry* (Washington, D. C.: Government Printing Office, 1933).

19. *American Federation of Labor Weekly News Service*, December 9, 1933.

20. Green to locals of automobile workers, December 23, 1933.

21. Statement by the President of the United States, March 25, 1934, in A. F. of L. files.

22. Green to Executive Council, March 27, 1934.

23. William Collins to the President of the United States, April 9, 1934, signed on behalf of officers of Federal Labor Unions in conference at Detroit, Michigan, April 8, 1934.

24. W. C. Teagle to President F. D. Roosevelt, March 27, 1934, in Official File 716, Box 1, Franklin Delano Roosevelt Library.

25. *Report of the Proceedings of the Fifty-fourth Annual Convention of the American Federation of Labor,* 1934, p. 45.

26. Louis L. Lorwin and Arthur Wubnig, *Labor Relations Boards* (Washington, D. C.: The Brookings Institution, 1935), p. 363.

27. Minutes of Executive Council, August 6, 1934.

28. Charlton Ogburn to President Franklin Roosevelt, January 28, 1935, in File 716, Box 2, Franklin Delano Roosevelt Library. The notation on the letter signed DR (obviously Donald Richberg) was not to answer but only to acknowledge the letter.

29. Green to Alfred Reeves (Executive Secretary of National Automobile Chamber of Commerce), January 8, 1935.

30. Green to President Roosevelt, February 2, 1935, in Official File 142, Box 1, Franklin Delano Roosevelt Library.

31. *Ibid.*

32. *Final Report of the Automobile Labor Board* (signed by Leo Wolman, Nicholas Kelley, and Richard L. Byrd), not issued publicly and dated October 22, 1935, in National Archives.

33. Minutes of Executive Council, February 1, 1935.

34. *Ibid.*

35. *Ibid.*

36. Minutes of Executive Council, February 4, 1935.

37. *Ibid.*

38. Minutes of Executive Council, February 12, 1935.

39. *Ibid.*

40. *Ibid.*

41. *Ibid.*

42. *Ibid.*

43. To the officers and members of all local unions affiliated with the International Union, United Automobile Workers of America, from William Green, October 1, 1935; Minutes of Executive Council, October 5, 1935.

# IX

## The Steel Industry

DURING the hearing on the National Industrial Recovery bill, R. P. Lamont, who represented the American Iron and Steel Institute and claimed he spoke for about 95 per cent of the steel industry, stated that the industry opposed the closed shop.

For many years, [according to Lamont] the steel industry has been and now is prepared to deal directly with its employees collectively on all matters relating to their employment. It is opposed to conducting negotiations regarding such matters otherwise than with its employees; it is unwilling to conduct them with outside organizations of labor or with individuals not its employees. The industry accordingly most strongly objects to the inclusion in the pending bill of any provisions which will be in conflict with this position of the industry, or of any language which implies that such is the intent of the legislation. If this position is not protected in the bill, the industry is positive in the belief that the intent and purpose of the bill cannot be accomplished.[1]

In the discussion of the code for the iron and steel industry, Lamont appeared again and indicated that the industry held the same general views on collective bargaining. Green, who presented a proposal for a code at the same hearing, suggested that the government discover the preference of the workers in the matter of collective bargaining by holding free and secret elections. In addition Green sought appointment of an advisory Council of Industrial Relationships in the Iron and Steel Industry, which was to include labor representatives.

Under the stimulus of the code, the Amalgamated Association of Iron, Steel, and Tin Workers revived. The Amalgamated had steadily declined in membership and influence in the industry. Following the strike of 1919, the union continued to lose the support of the few steelworkers who were loyal to it. As soon as the National Industrial Recovery Act was passed, the Amalgamated started a campaign, and according to Secretary Louis Leonard, about 150,000 workers signed application cards or joined the union by paying full initiation fees.[2] But the gains made were not held.

The officers of the Amalgamated had long been in service and were not able to meet the new demands that the changed circumstances imposed upon them. They thought in terms of gaining a few additional members; they feared every manifestation of protest and novelty. The

110

leaders had tasted defeat many times, and they had great respect for and fear of the power of the steel industry. Unaware that drastic changes were in the making, they wanted to follow a policy of caution. On the other hand, the thousands of workers who had joined the union looked upon it as a means of gaining relief from the difficulties facing labor. As a result, conflicts and losses of membership followed, and there were increasing demands for change. In the meantime, action against the refusal of the steel companies to deal with the newly organized locals became imperative. The Amalgamated Association convention of April 1934 decided to demand recognition and threatened a strike call for June. As expected, the steel industry was unwilling to change its policies and deal with an outside union; the demand for recognition was rejected. When a strike appeared imminent, President Roosevelt took steps to avert it. On May 30, 1934 the President announced the extension of the code in the iron and steel industry and promised that the exercise of the right to organize by the employees in the steel industry would be respected and that the government would hold free elections to determine the wishes of the workers of the industry in this matter. The Iron and Steel Institute entered the fight by insisting that the Amalgamated Association represented only a small minority of employees in the iron and steel industry, and that the great mass of steelworkers were content to be represented by the employee representation plans widespread in the industry at the time.

The desire to test the sentiment of the workers by a strike increased, and the officers of the union, as well as President Green, vigorously opposed such action at the special convention of June 1934. In the meantime, Congress enacted Joint Resolution No. 44, authorizing the President to establish boards to investigate labor disputes and conduct elections to determine the desires of workers in the matter of union representation. It was Public Resolution No. 44 which subsequently served as a basis for the appointment of the National Steel Labor Relations Board by the President on June 28, 1934.[3]

The special convention presented several proposals as a means for avoiding the strike and settling differences in the industry:

1. It was suggested that an impartial three-member board be appointed by the President of the United States with authority to investigate complaints of violations of the iron and steel code and to mediate and conciliate in disputes arising between employers and employees under the code. The board, moreover, was to have power to arrange conferences with any employer when such a request was made by representatives of employees selected under Section 7 (a) of the National Industrial Recovery Act. The Board was to offer its services to arbitrate any dispute arising under the code if such dispute were voluntarily submitted for arbitration

by both parties. The Board was to hear and immediately determine charges of discrimination or discharge arising under Section 7 (a).

2. In order that workers employed in the steel mills might exercise the right of organization, free of interference, intimidation, or coercion by employers, and of bargaining collectively through representatives of their own choosing, the board appointed by the President was to be given authority to hold elections to determine the will of the majority of workers.

3. The Amalgamated asked that grievances and complaints regarding wages, hours, and other conditions of employment be settled through negotiations between management and the representatives selected by the workers. Questions not settled directly were to be submitted to the Board for final determination. Under these conditions the union was willing to cancel the strike order, so that all disputes could be settled.[4]

President Roosevelt informed the committee in a public statement subsequently issued that he had discussed the issue in dispute with the Secretary of Labor and representatives of the industry and that he had empowered the Secretary to take whatever action appeared advisable.[5] At the end of June 1934, President Roosevelt appointed the National Steel Labor Relations Board to investigate the issues in dispute and to hold elections to determine representatives for collective bargaining.

A strike had been avoided but the industry had not yet reached a point where it was willing to recognize an outside union, and an effort was made in June 1934 to establish a system similar to the one prevailing in the automobile industry. When reports of rising strike sentiment in the steel industry were noted by the administration, Green was called to the White House and certain proposals were made to him. Green went to Pittsburgh and appealed to the delegates to refrain from striking and to place their trust in the President and the Board he had set up. "Our organization," he said, "could never live under that, [proportional representation] negotiating with company unions, negotiating with independents. If they [the companies] were willing to make a concession they would make it to the company union and we could never live under it any more than we could live under the automobile settlement."[6]

The Amalgamated Association in the meantime faced a rebellion of its members who were dissatisfied with the progress in organizing the industry and the energy exhibited by the officers in recruiting new members. The insurgents called a meeting in Pittsburgh, Pennsylvania, for February 3, 1935, and Tighe countered by suspending the charters of twenty-two locals which sent delegates. Seventy-four other locals were suspended for nonpayment of per capita tax. In a letter to Green, Tighe explained: "In our desire to get them into the organization we laid down the bars and allowed them to do as they pleased, and they finally began to believe they owned the organization."[7]

The insurgents organized the National Emergency Committee of the Amalgamated Association of Iron, Steel, and Tin Workers, with Clarence Irwin, chairman, L. A. Morris, secretary-treasurer, and Melvin Moore, organizer. The insurgent movement was led by left-wingers, and many of the locals sought to stimulate greater aggressiveness in organizing and hoped to encourage more resourcefulness and imaginative activity. Several locals appealed to Green, who disavowed the responsibility of the A. F. of L. for the action of the international officers of the Amalgamated. Green argued that he had no authority.

to order, require or compel the officers and members of an international union to do thus and so or to carry a demand which we might make upon them to change their administrative affairs. Notwithstanding this fact, I have been doing all I can to heal the breach, to compose the differences and to bring about a settlement of the differences which exist. I hold that the internal strife which prevails in the Amalgamated Association of Iron, Steel and Tin Workers must be eliminated, differences settled, solidarity and unity established by an aggressive satisfactory organizing campaign which could be launched and caried on among those employed in the steel industries of the nation.[8]

Green did, however, appoint James Wilson to "restore harmony and solidarity in the Amalgamated Association of Iron, Steel and Tin Workers' organization." In informing Tighe of Wilson's appointment, Green expressed the conviction that "the family members and associates of the Amalgamated Association of Iron, Steel and Tin Workers, must become reconciled before it is possible to originate and carry forward an organizing campaign among those employed in the steel manufacturing industry as ordered by the San Francisco Convention of the American Federation of Labor."[9]

At first the International Executive Board of the Amalgamated rejected Green's peace efforts on the ground that the Board was duly elected by the membership of the union and "fully qualified and competent by the knowledge and experience they have acquired to deal with all questions that affect the Association welfare, without interference from outside sources, irrespective of what the good intentions of the sources may be." The Board was not unwilling to listen to Wilson at its convention, but they said that any attempt on his part to apply the principles of mediation "would be considered interference with the prerogatives of the International Executive Board, in the administration of our organization's affairs."[10] Green continued to plead for the elimination of "internal strife . . . as a primary requirement in any plan of organization which may be formulated and launched among the steel workers. Please impress this upon the mind and judgment of President Tighe and his associates, offering a fair basis of settlement, and appeal to President Tighe and his associates and all concerned to accept it."[11]

The Emergency Committee asked to meet the Executive Council in order to present its views. Reluctant to encourage secession, the Council wanted to avoid any suspicion that it sympathized with the insurgents. Consequently, Green again pleaded with Tighe to meet with the Committee and argued that "the interest of the steel workers calls for a settlement of the internal dissension which to say the least is deplorable."[12] Tighe finally agreed, after persistent prodding from Green who was convinced "that some understanding must be reached with these groups before it will be possible to unite the steelworkers in order to launch and carry forward a successful organizing campaign." Green was aware that some of the insurgent leaders were Communists, but he believed that "if the division which exists and [the] basic cause of the split [are] removed and solidarity again established, these leaders will lose much of the force of the argument they now offer to many steel workers who honestly think they are the victims of discrimination and persecution."[13]

Finally the Executive Board of the Amalgamated Association rescinded the suspension of the lodges which had sent delegates to the rump meeting at Pittsburgh. Tighe asked Wilson to mediate the dispute over back per capita which he claimed the suspended locals owed to the international union. Speaking through the National Emergency Committee, the suspended locals were willing to reach an agreement on per capita and urged Tighe to concentrate the efforts of the union upon an organization campaign in the industry.[14] The agreement between the Amalgamated Association and the National Emergency Committee called for obedience to the laws and rules of the international union, reinstatement of all suspended locals by October 1, 1935, and the payment of all per capita taxes and initiation fees.[15]

At the same time that the dispute was going on within the Amalgamated Association, there were serious differences within the Executive Council about the methods to be employed in organizing the steel industry. In reporting on the differences within the Amalgamated Association, Green told the Council that organizing the steel industry was a "huge, gigantic task—the biggest . . . we ever faced. The Amalgamated we know is not functioning, weak and inefficient, losing ground in my judgment all the time and we must meet the situation just as it is, not in a theoretical way but in a practical way. There are a lot of young men there wishing to be organized, enthusiastic. Perhaps we can organize a staff and carry it along and we will have to supply the money and place someone in charge, and press into service a staff to carry on the organizing work."[16]

Tobin, concurring with Green's view, said that "while an international union has rights in its jurisdiction, the mandate of the convention to organize must be taken into consideration." Tobin believed that the A. F. of L. would have to take the campaign over completely and direct it if it were to be successful. To a question asked by Hutcheson on whether the steel industry was to be organized in locals of the Amalgamated Association or into federal labor unions, Green replied that he would interpret the mandate of the convention "to mean that this Council was to determine how the steel workers shall be organized without regard to the Amalgamated."[17]

Wharton protested at this point against ignoring the rights of the craft unions, and Lewis responded that he had

arrived at the judgment that you cannot organize the steel industry in this country without putting the workers in one organization. If you believe otherwise you may as well save your efforts, your trouble and your money. The form of organization in the railroad industry which was the most remarkable character of cooperation ever manifested in the American Federation of Labor, had been brought about on a gradual basis starting with the most skilled men in the industry. You cannot do that in the steel industry. There is just one way to organize the workers in the steel industry if they can be organized and that is into one union. Unless the American Federation of Labor can arrange its affairs to do that we might as well save our money. . . . You have to utilize the services of these young men in the steel industry. They have no training, no background in trade unionism, no experience in the labor movement. . . . The steel workers were originally comprised of the skilled men and they refused to take in common labor in the plants. They were afraid of dragging down the skilled men to the status of common labor. The officers of the Amalgamated have been trained in that school. The world had gone by and left it sitting there, and the world will not go back. By the same token they have discredited themselves among the men in the steel industry and cannot win them back. I do not know the cost. I only know it should be done whether we win or lose.

Lewis called attention to the opposition to unionism shown by the steel industry over the years, and he regarded it as unreasonable to expect the industry to deal with fifteen or twenty separate unions. He believed that an organization campaign would encounter severe opposition. "If that is true," he said, "that the Machinists, Electrical Workers, Blacksmiths, and all the rest of the metal trades are going to insist that they continue their jurisdiction and have the right to take these men into their organization, in my judgment we might as well save our effort because we cannot organize the men on that basis." Lewis urged the setting up of a new international, with or without the approval of the Amalgamated.[18] Hutcheson did not think that as officers of international unions the members of the Executive Council should set up a dual international union in the steel industry. At Tobin's suggestion, Wharton, Tobin, and Lewis were appointed to plan a program for organizing the industry.

The committee met with the officers of the Amalgamated Association, but Tighe and the others would not consent to having another union chartered. Hutcheson again warned against interfering with an independent, autonomous union "even if it were in bad straits." Green was

satisfied . . . [that] the officers of the Amalgamated cannot organize these workers with their own resources or with the set-up as is, with the National Organization based upon a philosophy upon which it rests or upon pursuing the policy it is following. It may have been all right when the puddler and roller were factors but the mechanical devices have made him a less factor than years ago. The puddler has completely gone. The change has been taking place but the Amalgamated has been standing committed to its old traditional policy. You cannot organize a great industry that way.[19]

At the end of the discussion on February 12, Rickert proposed: "That the President be instructed to inaugurate a joint organizing campaign of all unions in the steel industry; that he endeavor to secure the cooperation, financial and moral, of all existing organizations in and out of this industry in this campaign and that to him be left and delegated the planning and directing of this campaign."[20] This proposal was adopted.

At the October meeting of the Executive Council, Secretary Leonard of the Amalgamated Association announced that with the help of James Wilson the difficulties facing the union had been straightened out and "there is nothing in the way now to carry out the instructions of the San Francisco Convention. We are ready. As to how you are going to do it, I do not know."[21]

Leonard said that about 150,000 steelworkers signed cards soon after the enactment of the National Industrial Recovery Act, but that the "newly organized group in our organization ran wild."[22] He claimed that the Amalgamated Association had between 25,000 and 30,000 members. Green assured Leonard that his union was not being blamed for failure to organize the steel industry. He declared

it is alleged that the Steel Corporations are no more afraid of your organization than they are of the League of Nations, but the American Federation of Labor is charged directly with failure to organize the Steel Workers of the country. You are out of the picture. . . . Are you willing to step aside and let the American Federation of Labor take charge so as to relieve itself of the charge of failure? . . . Are you ready to step aside and let us take charge and try to organize the Steel Workers?[23]

After some discussion it was agreed that the Amalgamated Association would submit a program for organizing the steel industry to the Executive Council.

When the plan for organizing the steel industry was submitted by the

Amalgamated Association, it called for the A. F. of L. to undertake the campaign in the steel industry, but the workers were to be organized into the lodges of the Amalgamated Association. Two types of membership were to be offered, one with and one without death benefits.[24] Dues were arranged on the basis of earnings in the industry.

The Executive Council found the plan unsatisfactory and directed President Green to prepare another and submit it to the affiliated internationals in accordance with the action of the 1935 convention. He was also directed to estimate the cost of the campaign which was to be directly supervised by the president of the A. F. of L. Another condition was that participating organizations were to agree to a uniform initiation fee not to exceed three dollars. "The jurisdiction of affiliated organization [was] to be recognized. Joint councils [were] to be set up in each locality as part of the organizing campaign in conjunction with the cooperation of State and Central Bodies, all to be under the central control of designated campaign chairman and President of the American Federation of Labor."[25]

On March 2, 1936 Green addressed a letter to the heads of all affiliated national and international unions in which he submitted the following preliminary plan for organizing the steel industry:

First: That a fund be created through the contributions of national and international unions affiliated with the American Federation of Labor, said fund to be placed at the disposal of the American Federation of Labor to be used for the sole purpose of carrying on an organizing campaign in the iron and steel industry; the Secretary-Treasurer of the American Federation of Labor to be custodian of the fund, and a full accounting of all receipts and expenditures to be made by the Secretary-Treasurer to all national and international unions.

Second: It is estimated that a fund of at least Seven Hundred Fifty Thousand Dollars ($750,000) is required to meet the preliminary needs for organizing requirements in the different steel manufacturing centers, for the employment of trained organizers, for the printing, publication, and distribution of literature, and for the establishment of a central as well as regional headquarters.

Third: That a competent representative of the American Federation of Labor be placed in charge of the organizing campaign, said representative to work under the direct supervision and instructions of the President of the American Federation of Labor.

Fourth: That the organizing campaign be carried on in accordance with an agreement which may be reached with the Amalgamated Association of Iron, Steel, and Tin Workers, and in full cooperation with that organization.

Fifth: That a conference of the representatives of organizations interested in and directly affected by an organization campaign which might be launched in the steel industry be held at the earliest possible date for the purpose of developing cooperation and understanding.

Sixth: That the organizing campaign in the steel industry be launched and carried forward in conformity with the organization plan adopted by the San Francisco 1934 Convention and reaffirmed by the Atlantic City Convention which was held in October 1935; all national and international unions to cooperate fully with the officers of the American Federation of Labor and the Executive Council in all the efforts which may be put forth to make the organizing campaign a complete success.

Green requested that he be immediately advised of the amounts of money each national and international union was willing to contribute.

The returns were far from generous. Of the 110 unions canvassed for funds, only thirty-eight replied; twenty-one of these referred the appeal to their executive boards; ten claimed they were unable to give financial aid; one stood ready to help if all unions of the A. F. of L. would support the drive to organize the steel industry; and five pledged $8,625 for the campaign.[26] The discussion on organizing the steel industry had shifted in the meantime from a dispute of unions of the A. F. of L. seeking a program and direction from the Executive Council to an argument between the Federation officers and the leaders of the newly organized Committee for Industrial Organization. John L. Lewis and Charles P. Howard, respectively chairman and secretary of the newly organized group, presented a program for organizing the steel industry to President Green. Offering organizers and $500,000 toward a fund of $1,500,000, Lewis and Howard called for "leadership . . . to inspire confidence of success. There must be placed in charge a responsible, energetic person, with a genuine understanding of the steelworkers' problems, who will work in conjunction with an advisory committee representative of the unions supporting the drive."[27]

The Lewis-Howard proposals were submitted to the Executive Council, which doubted the ability of the unions comprising the Committee for Industrial Organization to raise the sum their officers pledged. Tobin was opposed to industrial unionism, and he pointed to the action of the A. F. of L. convention as inhibiting any action by the Council which would wipe out the rights of unions to their jurisdictions in the steel industry. Even more, Tobin felt "there isn't a chance in the world at this time to organize the steelworkers. I make this statement after thirty-five years of following the history of that organization. It may be that if the Wagner Bill is sustained in the courts and other labor legislation is sustained, we may be able to get a foothold, but only after labor legislation allowing the workers to organize, is it possible to make any successful drive on organization."[28]

Several other members of the Council thought that the Lewis-Howard letter should not be answered. William Mahon was convinced that the steelworkers could not be organized. He was willing, however, to accept the money offered by the Committee and to send out an appeal for added donations to the A. F. of L. affiliates. He suggested that Lewis and Howard be put in charge of the drive in the steel industry.[29]

Members of the Executive Council continued to assume that they could determine the type of organization campaign to be conducted and the kind of union to be established in the steel industry, but they were underestimating the daring, resourcefulness, and generosity of the unions of the Committee for Industrial Organization, especially the United Mine Workers of America, the Amalgamated Clothing Workers of America, and the International Ladies' Garment Workers of America. These unions stood ready to undertake the herculean task and challenge the open-shop citadel of American industry. The last attempt of the A. F. of L. to win the Amalgamated Association over to its plan of campaign was made in the letter dispatched by President Green to the delegates attending the convention of the Amalgamated Association at Cannonsburg, Pennsylvania, on May 8, 1936.

1. In conformity with the decisions of the San Francisco and Atlantic City Conventions, the Executive Council must exercise the right to manage, promote and conduct the campaign, and as hereinafter outlined. There can be no division in administration and conflict in authority recognized in the conduct and administration of the organizing campaign.

2. The character of the campaign and the administrative policy pursued shall and must be in accordance with the organization policy of the American Federation of Labor as expressed and decided upon at the Atlantic City Convention of the American Federation of Labor. While it is the purpose of the Executive Council to apply the broadest and most comprehensive industrial policy possible, due regard and proper respect for the jurisdictional rights of all national and international unions will be observed in the execution of an organizing campaign.

3. The Executive Council will accept contributions from national and international unions directly affiliated with the American Federation of Labor for the purpose of carrying on an organizing campaign, but said contributions must be made unconditionally. The Executive Council cannot carry out the instructions of the Atlantic City Convention to "manage, promote and conduct" this campaign of organization by accepting conditional contributions from any source whatsoever, and which the Executive Council deems in conflict with the instructions and intent of the Convention action and with the organization policies of the American Federation of Labor.

4. The organizing campaign will be launched and carried forward by the Executive Council of the American Federation of Labor in cooperation with the Amalgamated Association of Iron, Steel, and Tin Workers and the representatives of other organizations interested, affected and involved. The Executive Council will use such funds and assign such organizers as may be made available. All details in connection with the organizing campaign will be arranged through conference and agreement by the representatives of all the or-

ganizations who may be called upon to "cooperate in the organizing campaign and who may be directly interested."[30]

The convention rejected the proposal of the A. F. of L. and instead tentatively accepted the offer of the Committee for Industrial Organization. Meeting in Washington on June 3, the Amalgamated Association and Lewis, acting as chairman of the Committee for Industrial Organization, agreed to the setting up of the Steel Workers' Organizing Committee. Lewis agreed to contribute up to $500,000 for the drive in the steel industry.[31] On July 7 Green issued a statement decrying the action of the Committee for Industrial Organization in thwarting "the purpose of the American Federation of Labor to inaugurate an organizing campaign in the steel industry, behind which the American Federation of Labor could have mobilized the united support and pooled resources of organized labor."[32]

It is, of course, obvious that President Green could not have mobilized the resources of the affiliates; he had tried and failed. In contrast, the Steel Workers' Organizing Committee started its campaign by renting the thirty-sixth floor of an important office building in Pittsburgh, Pennsylvania, at a rent of $1,000 a month. In addition, the Committee engaged a publicity staff, an attorney, three full-time district directors, and over 200 organizers. It was a massive campaign and on a scale Lewis had advocated.[33] In less than five months, the SWOC succeeded in organizing 148 lodges and thousands of members. It demonstrated the efficiency of the new organizing methods and the courage and imaginativeness of Lewis and his co-workers. It also meant that the Federation was not playing a significant role in the steel industry.

REFERENCES

1. Statement in files of A. F. of L.

2. Minutes of Executive Council, October 12, 1935.

3. Louis Lorwin and Arthur Wubnig, Labor Relations Boards (Washington, D. C.: The Brookings Institution, 1935), pp. 332-336; Carroll R. Daugherty, Melvin G. Chatzeau, and Samuel Stratton, *The Economics of the Iron and Steel Industry* (New York: McGraw-Hill Book Company, Inc., 1937), vol. 2, pp. 1034-1063.

4. Michael Tighe, Louis Leonard, Thomas B. Gillis, Edward W. Miller, and Michael Green to President Franklin D. Roosevelt, June 19, 1935.

5. Statement of President Franklin D. Roosevelt issued to the press on June 19, 1935, in the files of the American Federation of Labor.

6. Minutes of Executive Council, February 4, 1935.

7. Tighe to Green, April 25, 1935; May 4, 1935. On the latter date a full list of the locals suspended for non-payment of per capita tax was sent to Green.

8. Joseph J. Clair to Green, April 13, 1935; quotation in Green to Clair, April 29, 1935; Tighe to Green, May 8, 1935.

9. Green to Tighe, April 15, 1935.

10. Tighe to Green, April 16, 1935.

11. Green to Wilson, April 18, 1935.

12. Tighe to Green, July 2, 1935; July 19, 1935.

13. Green to Tighe, July 19, 1935.

14. Tighe to James Wilson, September 12, 1935; Clarence Irwin, L. A. Morris, and others to Tighe, August 22, 1935; Clarence Irwin to Green, August 22, 1935.

15. James A. Wilson to Clarence Irwin, September 30, 1935.

16. Minutes of Executive Council, February 11, 1935.

17. Both questions in *Ibid*.

18. Quotations since last footnote are from *Ibid*.

19. Minutes of Executive Council, February 12, 1935.

20. *Ibid*.

21. Minutes of Executive Council, October 20, 1935.

22. *Ibid*.

23. *Ibid*.

24. *Suggested Plan to Organize the Steel Industry Submitted to Executive Council of the American Federation of Labor by the International Executive Board, Amalgamated Association of Iron, Steel and Tin Workers of America,* October 20, 1935.

25. Minutes of Executive Council, May 5, 1936.

26. Information in the archives of the A. F. of L. Minutes of Executive Council, May 5, 1936.

27. John L. Lewis and Charles P. Howard to Green, February 22, 1936.

28. Tobin to Green, February 26, 1936.

29. William D. Mahon to Green, February 29, 1936.

30. Green to the Officers and Delegates in Attendance at the Convention of the Amalgamated Association of Iron, Steel, and Tin Workers, May 8, 1936.

31. *Amalgamated Journal*, June 4, 1935; *United Mine Workers Journal*, July 1, 1935.

32. Statement issued on July 7, 1936, in files of A. F. of L.

33. A complete list of officers and organizers for the SWOC as well as the amounts paid for rent and salaries of organizers is in the A. F. of L. files. See Walter Galenson, "The Unionization of the American Steel Industry," *International Review of Social History,* Vol. I, 1956.

# X

## The National Labor Relations Act

SECTION 7 (a) of the National Industrial Recovery Act exercised a favorable influence upon union membership. Many organizations increased their staffs and their memberships, and thousands of workers were recruited into the union ranks. Employers sought to counter the activity of organized labor by discriminating against those who had affiliated with a labor group and also by setting up company unions. In the view of Senator Robert Wagner, the company unions, which "multiplied with amazing rapidity," made "a sham of equal bargaining power by restricting employee cooperation to a single employer unit at a time when business men [were] allowed to band together in large groups. [They deprived] workers of the wider cooperation which [was] necessary, not only to uphold their own end of the labor bargain but to stabilize and standardize wage levels, to cope with the sweatshop and the exploiter, and to exercise their proper voice in economic affairs."

Pointing to the inability of the company union worker to select an outside representative to bargain for him, Senator Wagner argued that such a limitation placed the worker with his scant knowledge of business conditions or even of the labor market under a disadvantage in negotiations. "No one," he said, "would suggest that employers should not be allowed to employ outside lawyers, financial experts, or advisors. . . . Only representatives who are not subservient to the employer with whom they deal can act freely in the interest of the employees."[1]

The Labor Disputes Act, the bill introduced by Senator Wagner in 1934, sought to protect the right of workers to join organizations of their own choosing and to engage in any concerted activities, either in labor organizations or otherwise, for the purpose of bargaining collectively or for mutual aid or protection. This bill also made illegal a number of employer practices, such as discrimination against workers for joining a union.

Testifying on behalf of the measure, Green assured the Senate Committee that the A. F. of L. stood "wholeheartedly and unreservedly behind Senator Wagner in support of this bill."[2] Green also charged that employers were evading the requirement of Section 7 (a) of the National Industrial Recovery Act by coercing their employees and by formation of company unions.

John Frey, speaking as president of the Metal Trades Department, urged the enactment of the bill and protested the ability of employers to inhibit organization by forming company unions and by using other methods of coercion.[3] John L. Lewis came to the hearings and assailed the industries which denied by subterfuge the right of their workers to form unions uncontrolled by employers. In Lewis's opinion, "this . . . offensive of industry to gain control of American labor through the imposition of company unions is only akin to the efforts of gangsters in some of our large cities 'to muscle in' on labor unions and get control of those labor unions for their own selfish benefits."[4]

Speaking for industry, James A. Emery of the National Association of Manufacturers, opposed the measure which he regarded as

invalid in law and unsound in policy. . . . It is not an exercise of the commerce power of Congress but a deliberate and indefensible invasion of the right to regulate and even compel local employment relations, which the Supreme Court, without exception, has declared are exclusively a subject for State and not Federal control; but, assuming the bill were within the commerce power, the administrative body established, the authority proposed, the manner of its exercise are arbitrary, destructive of the fundamental rights of the parties, and vest in an administrative body the determination of questions of fact and law, without judicial review, that may be adjudicated only by a court.[5]

The Labor Disputes Act was also attacked by Communist-dominated unions. E. P. Cush, president of the Steel and Metal Workers' Industrial Union, an organization that belonged to the Communist Trade Union Unity League, argued that "the worker has no right under this bill."[6] Henry I. Harriman, president of the United States Chamber of Commerce, was another opponent. In general, industry groups spoke out against the act.

Charles H. Hook, the president of the American Roller Company and a leading spokesman for open-shop industry, went further and suggested that

it would be tremendously advantageous to . . . [the recovery] program if Mr. Wagner could be induced to resign from the Labor Board, because of the widespread feeling on the part of industry that he is unfairly prejudiced against industry and industrial management generally. . . . A change in personnel of the Labor Board would have a tremendously helpful influence in securing the attention, careful thought and cooperation on the part of thousands of industrialists who, I am afraid, are either lukewarm or openly hostile, because they are mad at the Labor Board, and when you analyze their hostility you invariably find it is directed to the Senator himself.[7]

Colonel W. D. Anderson of the Cotton Manufacturers' Association urged Roosevelt to disapprove of the Labor Disputes Act and to allow

existing machinery an opportunity to operate. Anderson believed that
Roosevelt had "done more for the working-man than any one who [had]
ever held the high office of President and in return . . . you have every
right to call in the leaders of labor and insist that they cooperate in your
recovery program by throwing the weight of their influence toward a
peaceful composition of all labor disputes arising throughout the country
in which they have an official influence."[8]

Leaders of the automobile industry expressed their dislike of the act
through the National Automobile Chamber of Commerce. To them the
bill was

unfair to both worker and employer. It takes from the worker certain essential
rights [of which] he is now assured. It is bound to increase industrial strife.
. . . It will put into the hands of agitators a new weapon with which to coerce
men into joining outside labor unions. It will encourage coercive methods on
the part of labor. It condemns coercive action by employers, but says nothing
about coercion of employees by labor organizations. Gives immunity to organized labor. It gives labor a monopoly of labor representation in all American industry. Rights of minority groups would be practically destroyed.[9]

The flood of mail decrying the bill which reached the Secretary of
Labor was called to the attention of President Roosevelt by Secretary
Marvin McIntire who believed that the President should know the mag-
nitude of opposition to this proposal.[10]

When the Labor Disputes Act was not approved by Congress, legislation having the same general aim but modified to take account of criticism
which had been made of the earlier measure was introduced in the spring
of 1935. Green, on behalf of the A. F. of L., urged Congress "that nothing
be permitted to stand in the way of the adoption of the . . . Bill." In no
other way, could

Congress make it clear to millions of workers that it intends to fulfill the promises it gave to the workers of this country. . . . They have suffered discharges
and want and humiliation, believing that the government was behind them in
the struggle. . . . But there is growing in the masses of American people a
bitter resentment at the position in which they find themselves and a deep
conviction that only their own economic strength will avail them in their
struggle against the injustices and inequalities under which they work.[11]

In testifying before the Senate on the same bill, Green charged that
employers had resorted to subterfuge and evasion of Section 7 (a) which
guaranteed workers the right to organize under the NIRA, and that they
had by discrimination and coercion sought to thwart the will of Congress.[12] Lewis, before the same committee, sharply attacked Donald
Richberg for his statement that proportional representation met the legal
requirements of collective bargaining.[13] In Lewis's opinion, such representation was actually a means of evading the law.

James A. Emery and Walter Harnischfeger, counsel and president respectively of the National Association of Manufacturers, assailed the bill on several grounds. Harnischfeger saw "no universal demand or necessity for such one-sided legislation at present. . . . It seeks to impose Federal regulation and control over a matter that is reserved to and properly being exercised by the States." He predicted that the bill would "'provoke and encourage labor disputes, rather than diminish them."[14] Emery repeated the argument he had presented on the earlier bill. He regarded it as unsound in law and policy because it sought to regulate local "employments in the guise of regulating commerce,"[15] and he insisted that the provisions of the bill would deny due process, violate the prohibition of unreasonable search and seizure and the principle of the separation of powers by branches of the Federal government inasmuch as they allow the executive to judge and punish and impose damages.

Walter Lippmann, in writing on the bill, had no fear that its enactment would produce a labor dictatorship, but rather that it would cause "interminable and inconclusive litigation and dispute."[16]

Opposition from the American Civil Liberties Union was of a different order. Its board of directors had little hope that a Federal agency "intervening in the conflicts between employers and employees, [could] be expected to fairly determine the issues of labor's rights."[17] While regretting its inability to support legislation favored by organized labor, the Civil Liberties Union announced that only militant unions could support the right to strike. It also opposed the legislation because it allowed a government board to act on its own initiative, because it failed to protect workers against discrimination on the grounds of race, sex, color, or political conviction, and because it held the threat of compulsory arbitration.

Senator Wagner was not impressed. He informed the Civil Liberties Union that whether "we liked it or not, government in every country is going to be forced to play a more important role in economic life and for that reason it seems to me more useful to attempt to direct the nature of the role than merely to state a truism that government is likely to be influenced by forces in society that happen to be strongest. Certainly these forces cannot be checked by governmental self-limitation." Senator Wagner also refused to accept the view of the Civil Liberties Union that government action over a reasonably long period served "to check the struggles that labor must carry on by extra-governmental means," nor did he believe, as the letter suggested, that "it could ever be proved that Section 7 (a) . . . lulled [labor] into a sense of security."[18]

In contrast, the A. F. of L., which knew directly the devices and stratagems that employers could use to prevent their workers from organizing for collective bargaining, looked upon the bill as one of the most important pieces of legislation in the history of the labor movement. To mobilize sentiment, Green summoned a meeting of representatives of international unions and central bodies for Washington on April 29, 1935. Almost 500 delegates came to the conference and made their position clear:

The right of labor to organization, to majority representation, and to collective action and collective bargaining, can no longer be dependent upon the provisions of any code of fair competition. Our experience during the last two years has made it imperative that Labor's right to organize, to apply the principle of majority representation, to collective action and collective bargaining, must be definitely declared by Congress instead of being left as it has been to the constructions, interpretations, and evasions which we have experienced under the administration of NRA.[19]

The delegates thought that the enactment of the Wagner-Connery Act transcended in importance any other measure then before Congress. "This measure," their resolution stated, "is intended to give to Labor the effective use of its right to organization. The provisions of this bill are intended to restate Labor's Bill of Rights and to make them effective as applied under modern conditions of industry. It is not designed to meet the present national emergency only; it is intended for all time."[20] Despite the furious opposition from many sections of the business community and the press, the Committee on Education and Labor of the United States Senate concluded "that the compelling force of . . . experience, demonstrating that the Government's promise in Section 7 (a) stands largely unfulfilled, makes unacceptable any further temporizing measures. In the committee's judgment the present bill is a logical development of a philosophy and a consistent policy manifest in many acts of Congress dealing over a period of years with labor relations."[21]

While the bill was under consideration, concern over the lack of protection to craft units was shown by Daniel Tobin, the president of the Teamsters' Union. Other members of the A. F. of L. Executive Council were also concerned with the interpretation that might be placed on this bill in the future. Vice President Thomas Rickert expressed the hope that something might be done to make clear the meaning of craft unionism "by inserting . . . a few words stating that each trade or craft, as now understood to obtain in many industries, shall have the right to say who shall represent them."[22]

When Senator Wagner conferred with the members of the Council, it was suggested that the sections governing the right of craft unions to be represented be clarified. John L. Lewis opposed altering particular parts of the bill. Many members of the Council were fearful that the interpretation placed on the bill would favor industrial or vertical unionism. Tobin informed Green that many members of the Executive Council would rather have the bill defeated than allow a government labor board to promote industrial organizations at the expense of the craft unions.[23]

Tobin approached Senator Wagner directly. The latter wrote that he was aware of the situation and could understand the apprehension of some of the members of the Executive Council. It was a difficult provision of the bill to draw and gave all of us more trouble than any other provision. . . . Representatives of the American Federation of Labor aided in the drafting of the bill and also were present at all conferences where proposed amendments were discussed. The power to fix the unit had to be lodged somewhere. Of course, we did not think of giving it to the employer and the difficulty of giving it to the employees is that many thought it would simply continue the company union because the employer has sufficient economic power over the workers to compel the fixation of a unit satisfactory to the employer. Therefore, there was no alternative but leaving it to the Board.[24]

Tobin's fears that the craft organizations might not find their definition of the bargaining unit acceptable by the Board were not allayed by the speech of J. Warren Madden, chairman of the National Labor Relations Board, to the A. F. of L. convention of 1935. Madden had assured the delegates that the Board "would be fair and reasonable in concrete questions of craft versus industrial representation in particular plants. . . . We shall not be pro-craft union or pro-industrial union."[25]

Tobin inquired of Senator Wagner whether Madden's statement indicated that the Board would have the power to decide which unions should "have jurisdiction over certain work after the American Federation of Labor has rendered decisions on jurisdictional lines at convention after convention."[26] Wagner assured Tobin that the National Labor Relations Board would not decide questions of jurisdiction and that his bill had not intended that the Board be given such power.[27] When Tobin remained unsatisfied, Wagner reassured him: "The National Labor Relations Board has no power to deal with jurisdictional disputes between labor organizations. These are matters that can be considered and determined only by the American Federation of Labor. . . . Any other policy would be in contravention of the statute."[28]

Although the division within the labor movement which was to follow the formation of the Committee for Industrial Organization, and although the subsequent burdens for deciding bargaining units placed upon the Board could not at the time be envisaged, Tobin's fears seem justified by developments. In fact, it had been suggested to Senator Wagner that in representation elections the Board be given power to decide whether "the unit appropriate for collective bargaining shall be the employer unit, craft unit, plant unit, or other unit";[29] but the particular amendment was never submitted to the committee handling the legislation.

Before the enactment of the bill, a new difficulty arose when the House of Representatives passed the Ramspeck amendment which "provided

that no unit should include the employees of more than one employer."
The A. F. of L. protested the proposal and used its influence to exclude
it from the bill. Although some members of the conference committee of
the House and Senate did not believe that the Ramspeck amendment
was significant, the A. F. of L. wanted it struck from the bill and in the
end it was.[30]

There was some question as to whether or not Roosevelt favored the
Wagner legislation. Raymond Moley has written that Roosevelt initially
had no intention of supporting the Wagner bill, but that early in June
he changed his mind because of his need for the support of Senator Wag-
ner after the Supreme Court's invalidation of the National Industrial
Recovery Act.[31] A different view was expressed by Congressman William
Connery, the chairman of the House Labor Committee. According to
Connery, President Roosevelt "wanted the [labor] Board to be inde-
pendent and with great powers, but in the Labor Department. . . . The
President [however] would sign the bill with the Board either in the
Department or out."[32]

The A. F. of L. tenaciously fought against the adoption of the principle
of majority rule favored by Donald Richberg and others and helped to
hold off efforts to emasculate the effectiveness of the legislation. Separate
bills were passed by the Senate and House, and on June 27, 1935 both
Houses approved the bill agreed to in conference.

When he signed the bill on July 5, President Roosevlt said:

This Act defines, as a part of our substantive law, the right of self-organization
of employees in industry for the purpose of collective bargaining, and provides
methods by which the Government can safeguard that legal right. It establishes a National Labor Relations Board to hear and determine cases in which
it is charged that this legal method is abridged or denied, and to hold fair
elections to ascertain who are the chosen representatives of employees.

A better relationship between labor and management is the high purpose of
this Act. By assuring the employees the right of collective bargaining it fosters
the development of the employment contract on a sound and equitable basis.
By providing an orderly procedure for determining who is entitled to represent
the employees, it aims to remove one of the chief causes of wasteful economic
strife. By preventing practices which tend to destroy the independence of
labor, it seeks, for every worker within its scope, that freedom of choice and
action which is justly his.

The National Labor Relations Board will be an independent quasi-judicial
body. It should be clearly understood that it will not act as mediator or conciliator in labor disputes. The function of mediation remains, under this Act,
the duty of the Secretary of Labor and of the Conciliation Service of the Department of Labor. It is important that the judicial function and the mediation
function should not be confused. Compromise, the essence of mediation, has
no place in the interpretation and enforcement of the law.[33]

Frank Duffy, a member of the Executive Council and secretary of the Carpenters' Union, questioned Green's enthusiasm for the law. Duffy hoped that Green's "anticipations may be fully realized," yet he had his doubts, especially when he recalled the Supreme Court's emasculation of the Clayton Act. Green refused to share Duffy's apprehension and pointed to the opposition of the Communist Party, the American Civil Liberties Union, the United States Chamber of Commerce, and the National Association of Manufacturers as proof of the desirability of the legislation.[34]

Green submitted a list of names of those who in his view possessed the necessary qualifications for membership on the National Labor Relations Board. Among the eleven names suggested were Harry A. Millis, Edwin S. Smith, George W. Taylor, Otto S. Beyer, and Carter Goodrich. Secretary of Labor Perkins recommended Father Francis J. Hass, Donald Wakefield Smith, John A. Lapp, Edward Berman, Thomas Woodward, and Mercer Evans. Roosevelt wanted to appoint Donald Wakefield Smith, whose candidacy was supported by Senator Joseph Guffey, a leading administration man and a powerful political figure. Only one name on the lists submitted by Green and Perkins, Edwin S. Smith, was appointed. He was to become the highly controversial member of the Board, one whose removal the A. F. of L. sought almost from the beginning. The names of neither Chairman J. Warren Madden nor John Carmody, the third member, were on the lists submitted.[35]

The Executive Council expressed its satisfaction at the passage of the law and the establishment of a board to administer it. Reporting to the convention of 1935, the Council noted that certain of the more important principles established by the National Labor Relations Board functioning under the National Recovery Administration had been written into the new law.

The right of majority representation is specifically included and employers have the affirmative duty to bargain collectively with duly chosen representatives of their employees. The company union is outlawed and the union shop is specifically legalized. . . . Under the National Labor Relations Act, we have every reason to believe that new goals in the field of Labor relations will be achieved. The one outstanding question in connection with this legislation is to what extent will the National Labor Relations Board be permitted to protect the right to organize and bargain collectively under the commerce clause of the constitution.[36]

The uncertainty of the A. F. of L. with regard to the ability of the National Labor Relations Act to survive the scrutiny of the Supreme Court was shared by high officials in the Roosevelt Administration. After the resignation of John Carmody, one of the first members of the National

Labor Relations Board, President Roosevelt's secretary Steve Early wrote in a memorandum "that there seems to be a general opinion prevailing on the part of Miss Perkins and others that the Supreme Court will soon decide against the National Labor Relations Act, and that there is little, if any urgency or need for the appointment to this Board."[37]

In its report to the convention of 1936, the Executive Council approved the Board's activities and found that its record "gives undisputable evidence of the Board's ability to prevent unfair labor practices outlawed by the Act."[38] The Council also recognized that the very existence of the law and the administrative machinery designed to enforce it made it easier to gain arrangements satisfactory to the workers in cases involving violations of the statute. The convention directed the Council to continue to study the work of the Board and to note immediately what might "develop in the provisions of the law with particular reference to the right of labor to organize."[39]

Protests from labor, however, soon began to be heard. Dissatisfaction with the activities of the Board was expressed by the Metal Trades Department and its president, John Frey, who questioned whether "the right of voluntary trade union association and the structure of our American trade union movement [could] be modified, reshaped and restricted by governmental influence and authority."[40]

The Federation's hope when it supported the National Labor Relations Act was that the agency set up under this statute would aid its unions in overcoming the company-dominated organizations. Unexpectedly, the C.I.O. had been established, and its organizations were now challenging those of the A. F. of L. in a number of industries. In February 1937 the unions of the Metal Trades Department appealed to the Council for assistance.

The A. F. of L. objected to the setting aside of collective-bargaining agreements by the National Labor Relations Board on the ground that such agreements were collusively made in violation of the provisions of the Act. On March 25, 1937 at a conference of unions in the Metal Trades Department, Frey protested the procedure followed by the Board in selecting the bargaining unit in a number of the mass-production industries. The conference directed attention to the verbal or written contracts held by unions of skilled workers with some employers in the mass-production industries and challenged the right of a government body to annul them.

In many of the industries these skilled workers are in a minority, perhaps a small one [Frey said]. The outnumbering majority [are] so-called mass production or semi-skilled workers. It is obvious that if a vote of all the employees were taken on the question of establishing one organization as the sole body to represent all of the employees, that the semi-skilled or production workers could easily prove a majority in favor of the organization they desired. A vote taken on such a basis and under such circumstances would be a denial of the rights of a minority, the very minority who had first established trade union organization, a minority having a prior right to consideration.[41]

Chairman Madden answered that where the question had arisen concerning unions affiliated with the A. F. of L., the Board had "sought to have the question of appropriate bargaining units agreed upon by the unions themselves, or when this could not be done, [had] as a matter of policy waived jurisdiction in hope that the matter would be settled by the Federation itself."[42]

However, Madden continued, in instances where there was no parent body to decide this type of conflict, and different unions sought representation but with "different ideas on bargaining units, the Board [seemed] plainly to have the responsibility of decision. It is equally plain that the Board should be guided by the wishes of the employees, ascertained in such a way as to make their choice a free one. As to just how these general principles would work out in any particular case which might come before the Board, neither I nor the Board can speak with finality except in the decision of our cases."[43]

The Board found the problem of deciding the bargaining unit unexpectedly difficult because of the emergence of the C.I.O. as an independent entity. Another thorny point was the status of contracts between affiliates of the Federation and employers which the Board might regard as collusive arrangements entered to frustrate, in particular instances, the assumed desire of the workers to join a union of the C.I.O. The A. F. of L. was especially aroused by the cancellation of contracts entered into between employers and its affiliates. The making of such contracts was not altogether new, and the Federation regarded the Board's action as an interference with the legitimate activity of the trade unions. When the Electrical Workers' Union had secured a closed-shop contract at a time when a C.I.O. union was also seeking to organize the workers in a plant, the Board set the contract aside on the ground that the company had violated the National Labor Relations Act because the A. F. of L. organization did not represent the free choice of the majority. The Federation saw the action of the Board as a serious threat to the existence of its affiliates and an unwarranted interference with a contract between a legitimate union and an employer. The Federation also objected to the practice of the Board's regional representatives of engaging in conciliation and mediation.[44]

At the convention of 1937, G. M. Bugniazet of the Electrical Workers and the Executive Council was given the floor to make a detailed indictment of the Board and its practices. He charged that the Board had set itself up as the final arbiter of jurisdictional disputes, had acted as a propaganda medium for dual unions, permitted elections to be held in a partisan atmosphere, conducted hearings in partisan surroundings, had selected regional directors favorable or affiliated with the dual movements, set aside proper contracts of A. F. of L. unions, and had consistently violated the letter and spirit of the Wagner Act.[45] The recommendation that the Council seek a remedy for the conduct of the Board was unanimously adopted.

On August 19, 1938 Green conferred with President Roosevelt and complained that the law was not being properly administered. He told the President that the attorney for the A. F. of L. had not been able to find a single instance in which a contract of a C.I.O. union had either been set aside or modified by the Board.[46] The Council thereupon informed President Roosevelt that the Board had written "its biased economic ideas into its decisions. It has established a principle which organized labor has opposed for over fifty years, dictating by governmental decree the form of organization a group of workers shall select."[47] The Council also indicated its intention to oppose the reappointment of Donald Wakefield Smith, whose term had expired.

Roosevelt did not take kindly to the Federation's strictures on Smith. He informed the Council that the reference to Smith's bias

standing by itself means nothing, and as a mere expression of opinion does not accord with the opinion of thousands of people who know Mr. Smith and have appeared before him in connection with his official duties. It is an interesting fact that complaints relating to decisions of the National Labor Relations Board have come from employers and employees representing almost every organization of capital and labor which happens to have lost their case before the Board. There are just as many complaints from labor organizations not affiliated with the American Federation of Labor as from organizations affiliated.[48]

Notwithstanding the President's words, the Council reiterated its disapproval of the reappointment of Donald Wakefield Smith, and Secretary McIntire had a "discouraging report to make" on him.[49]

The Council's report to the convention of 1938 did not relax its criticism. In a detailed review of the Board's policies, the Council accused the members of "flagrant bias and prejudice . . . which attempt to undermine and destroy the American Federation of Labor unions."[50] More specifically, the Council charged the Board with thwarting the intent of Congress in determining what should constitute an appropriate unit for collective bargaining and also with assuming powers contrary to the interests of the A. F. of L. unions. The report reviewed the evidence of the Board's favoritism for the C.I.O. and its attempts to undermine existing relations between employers and A. F. of L. unions.[51]

Much of the criticism was directed at Edwin S. Smith and Donald

Wakefield Smith. Although the Council favored retention of the major provisions of the Wagner Act, it believed that "proper amendments are necessary to curtail the unlawful assumption of broad powers by the Board, also to curtail unlimited discretion in construing and administering the Act, and to make specific the jurisdictional limits of the Board."[52]

The resolutions committee, in considering several proposals on the administration of the National Labor Relations Act, declared that decisions had been unduly delayed, elections fairly won had been annulled, and contracts lawfully made by A. F. of L. unions had been set aside. It recommended, therefore, that the unit rule be changed to conform to the one in effect under the Railway Labor Act so that it would be obligatory to grant a craft or class the right to select its bargaining representative by majority vote. The committee also recommended that the power of the Board to invalidate contracts be curtailed; intervention by interested parties should be a matter of right and not discretion; better qualified examiners should be selected; records should be open to examination by all interested parties; and representation elections should be held within thirty days after the filing of a petition and all cases be decided in forty-five days.[53] In addition, the committee supported the Council's opposition to the reappointment of Donald Wakefield Smith and directed the President of the A. F. of L. "to leave no stone unturned or . . . avenue unexplored for the purpose of preventing . . . [his] confirmation."[54] Largely as a result of the opposition of the A. F. of L. to Smith, William L. Leiserson was chosen to fill the vacancy.

The A. F. of L. had to be careful that its criticism of the Board was not interpreted as an attack upon the basic purposes of the Act. In testifying before the House Committee on Labor, Green accused the Board of partisanship for the C.I.O. The A. F. of L., therefore, felt justified, Green said, despite the great benefits that had accrued to its unions, in asking for a reorganization of this agency. In addition, Green asked that an employer should be allowed to express an opinion, as long as such expressions were not accompanied by threats or acts of discrimination. His most vehement attack was delivered against the rulings of the Board on the bargaining unit in cases of representation elections. Green explained that the A. F. of L. had initially been opposed to giving the Board blanket power to decide the unit of bargaining and had favored a proposal that would have allowed the Board such power only when employers and their employees could not agree "as to what constitutes the bargaining unit." Green contended that it had never been contemplated that the power to decide the units of bargaining carried with it the power to determine the form of organization that the trade union movement was to assume. The A. F. of L. wanted an amendment which would compel the Board to grant workers of a particular skill or class a separate bargaining unit. Green's position, however, was not supported by the facts.[55] It may have been an error for Congress to have granted the power to decide the unit of bargaining to the Board, but Senator Wagner believed that it was necessary to allow the Board to make such decisions.

As a result of A. F. of L. pressure, changes which were designed to meet some of the criticism of administrative procedure were introduced. The Council's report to the 1939 convention expressed general satisfaction with the formal changes in rules and regulations of the Board and the decision to require elections by secret ballot whenever requested by a labor organization which was a party to the proceeding. The A. F. of L. continued, however, to demand that the Board be enlarged to five members and that its power to fix the bargaining unit be curtailed. It was unsuccessful in its efforts. In December 1939 the House of Representatives began an investigation of the National Labor Relations Board, and the outcome of this was the submission of a series of amendments known as the Smith amendments. Virtually all were opposed by the A. F. of L. because they would have seriously weakened the effectiveness of the Act as a means for protecting the workers' right to organize and to bargain collectively.[56] Green's opposition to the Smith Committee drew a sharp rebuke from William Hutcheson, head of the Carpenters' Union, who charged that the National Labor Relations Board was a New Deal agency and an exponent of the policies of the C.I.O. Hutcheson characterized Green for his opposition to the Smith amendments as "a traitor to those people who are trying to help you."[57]

The Federation went on with its efforts to have its own amendments adopted by Congress. On the whole, it succeeded only in having its point of view given more sympathetic consideration by the Board. The A. F. of L. influenced President Roosevelt's decision not to reappoint Donald Wakefield Smith, and it opposed the selection of Chairman J. Warren Madden. The strongest opposition was directed toward the reappointment of Edwin S. Smith, who was regarded as highly biased against the A. F. of L. In fact, when Chairman Madden's reappointment was being considered by the Administration, "Secretary [Perkins] . . . told Mr. Smith that if he himself resigned, she thought Madden would be reappointed."[58]

Thus the Council opposed the reappointment of Edwin S. Smith and held him to have been "largely responsible for the bias, unfairness and prejudice which until recently characterized many of the labor Board's decisions and permeated its administrative setup."[59] The Council, while arguing that there was still room for improvement, conceded in its report to the 1941 convention, that "the present administration and application of the Act by Chairman Millis and Board Member Leiserson is fair and impartial and constitutes a vast improvement over the previous administration."[60]

Nevertheless, the Federation pressed for changes to limit the Board's authority in deciding the bargaining unit so that greater recognition would be given to the wishes of skilled workers in the crafts. Although it annually demanded that the Board mend its ways and that it give greater recognition to the wishes of the craft unions and avoid reconstructing the labor movement, many leaders of labor remembered, as did Daniel Tobin, that "that law, the Wagner Act, has been responsible for the growth of organized labor in our country."[61]

Although it failed to have its major recommendations adopted by Congress, the Federation did succeed in having passed the Frey amendment which prohibited the use of funds appropriated for the National Labor Relations Board "in any way in connection with a complaint case arising over an agreement between Management and Labor which has been in existence for three months or longer without complaint being filed." The rider also required that posting of notice of the agreement and its accessibility for inspection by interested persons be allowed. The Council believed that the Frey amendment effectively stopped the raids of C.I.O. unions.

### ESPIONAGE

The A. F. of L. and other organizations of labor had suffered over the years from the infiltration of spies into the unions and from the use of professional strikebreakers during labor disputes. Normally, the worker who remained on the job during a strike or lockout, the so-called "hunger strikebreaker," was a different type from the professional for whom strikebreaking was a way of life. Aggressive and violent, the professional sometimes fomented violence and created fear and loathing among strikers.

The 1914 A. F. of L. convention had called upon Congress and state legislatures to pass laws prohibiting labor espionage and the importation of strikebreakers from one state to another. In 1915 Gompers had submitted a lengthy report to the convention outlining in detail the activities of private detective agencies, their methods of recruiting and operation. He had charged that "appealing letters and craftily worded circulars [were] addressed to employers. . . . They endeavor to persuade employers that their 'expert detective agencies' can discover leaks in business—waste of material—inefficient management—irregular personal conduct and habits of trusted employees. . . . They undertake to ferret out the active spirits in the shops and factories . . . or who in an unguarded moment might talk too freely concerning the rights of a citizen. Of course, such men are instantly spotted for discharge."[62]

These agencies, according to Gompers, had worked upon the "sensibilities of many innocent, honest workingmen whose services they secure, and by craftiness and stealth have seduced men to betray their fellow workingmen." They have "secured the services of many innocent men and not infrequently, men who have records of faithfulness and honor among their associates. After they [the detective agencies] secured control over these poor fellows, they made their lives miserable by insisting upon daily reports from the shop in which they are sent to work among fellow workers."[63]

During the negotiations between the street railway company and the union in Pittsburgh, Pennsylvania, it was discovered that some high-ranking local labor men were on the payroll of detective agencies and were reporting the activities of their unions to the employer. A vice president of the Firemen's and Oilers' Union and editor of its journal was on the payroll of several companies which were kept informed of union activity. The Molders', Electricians', the Operating Engineers', and the Street Car Men's Unions were infiltrated with spies.[64]

Parallel and complementary to the spies were the professional strikebreakers who provoked violence and disorder during labor disputes. In 1925 and 1933 the A. F. of L. called for Federal legislation which would prevent interstate transportation of strikebreakers.[65] In 1935 the A. F. of L. again called for Congress to investigate the activities of private detective agencies. The convention unanimously approved the resolution.[66]

Upon evidence given by President William Green and other officers of labor unions, the Senate authorized a subcommittee of the Committee on Education and Labor to "investigate violations of the rights of free speech and assembly and interference with rights of labor to organize and bargain collectively."[67] The committee revealed a widespread network of private detective agencies which battened on labor strife and frequently promoted it as a means for increasing their business. Use of deception to entrap workers into betraying their unions, which Gompers had described to the convention of 1915, was now fully revealed through the testimony of the leaders of industry. The use of armed guards and arsenals by private industry and the promotion of violence against union members were also shown. Violation of other laws was revealed. Even though the Byrnes law, which went into effect in June 1936, made it a felony to recruit men for service as strikebreakers across state lines, it was the opinion of the subcommittee that the detective agencies were evading the intent of the statute. For three years the subcommittee of

Senators Robert La Follette and Elbert D. Thomas delved into operations of these agencies and revealed their questionable practices and their support by many business organizations. The revelations of espionage and oppression did much to discredit the more militant antiunion employer and improved the standing of organized labor before the public.

## REFERENCES

1. The quotations from Senator Wagner are taken from the *Congressional Record,* March 1, 1934, p. 3525. See Irving Bernstein, *The New Deal Collective Bargaining Policy* (Berkeley: University of California Press, 1950).

2. "To Create a National Labor Board," *Hearings before the Committee on Education and Labor, United States Senate, 73rd Congress, 2d Session on S. 2926* (Washington, D. C.: Government Printing Office, 1934), Part I, p. 68.

3. *Ibid.,* pp. 166–173.

4. *Ibid.,* p. 143.

5. *Ibid.,* Part 2, p. 341.

6. *Ibid.,* p. 489.

7. Charles H. Hook to General Hugh S. Johnson, March 8, 1934, in Official File 716, Box 1, of Franklin Delano Roosevelt Library.

8. W. D. Anderson to President F. D. Roosevelt, June 8, 1934, in Official File 716, Box 2, Franklin Delano Roosevelt Library.

9. Telegram from National Automobile Chamber of Commerce to President Franklin D. Roosevelt, signed by executive committee of Alfred Sloan, Alvan Macauly, Roy G. Chapin, G. W. Nash, July 7, 1934, Official File 716, Box 13, Franklin Delano Roosevelt Library.

10. Memorandum from Marvin McIntire to President Roosevelt, July 8, 1934, Official File 716, Box 1, Franklin Delano Roosevelt Library.

11. Statement of William Green before the Committee on Labor, House of Representatives, on the Connery Labor Disputes Bill, March 20, 1935, in files of A. F. of L.

12. "National Labor Board," *Hearings before the Committee on Education and Labor, United States Senate, 74th Congress, 1st Session, on S. 1958* (Washington, D. C.: Government Printing Office, 1935), p. 101.

13. *Ibid.,* Part II, pp. 194, 196.

14. *Ibid.,* Part III, p. 238.

15. *Ibid.,* Part III, p. 244.

16. *New York Herald Tribune,* March 28, 1935.

17. Roger N. Baldwin and Arthur Garfield Hays to Senator Robert Wagner, April 1, 1935, in the Wagner Papers of Georgetown University.

18. Wagner to Roger N. Baldwin, April 5, 1935, in Wagner Papers, Georgetown University.

19. *Resolution Adopted by Conference of Representatives of National and International Unions, State and City Central Bodies,* held at Washington, D. C. on April 29, 1935.

20. *Ibid.*

21. "National Labor Relations Board," *Senate Report No. 573, 74th Congress, 1st Session, Report to accompany S. 1958.*

22. Tobin to Green, June 17, 1935.

23. *Ibid.*

24. Robert F. Wagner to Tobin, June 14, 1935, in answer to Tobin to Wagner, June 10, 1935.

25. *Report of the Proceedings of the Fifty-fifth Annual Convention of the American Federation of Labor,* 1935, p. 360.

26. Tobin to Wagner, November 13, 1935, in Wagner Papers, Georgetown University.

27. Wagner to Tobin, November 13, 1935, in Wagner Papers, Georgetown University.

28. Tobin to Wagner, December 13, 1935; Wagner to Tobin, December 20, 1935, in Wagner Papers, Georgetown University.

29. Harold M. Stephens to Wagner, June 4, 1935. Justice Stephens was an assistant attorney general and the amendment was drawn at the request of Donald Richberg.

30. Memorandum to President Green from W. C. Roberts, Chairman of Legislative Committee of A. F. of L., June 24, 1935.

31. Raymond Moley, *After Seven Years* (New York: Harper and Brothers, 1939), p. 304.

32. Memorandum to Green from William Husing, A. F. of L. legislative agent, May 23, 1935.

33. *Public Papers and Addresses of Franklin D. Roosevelt* (New York: Random House, 1938) vol. 4, pp. 294–295.

34. Duffy to Green, July 15, 1935; Green to Duffy, July 20, 1935.

35. Official File 716A, Box 15, Franklin Delano Roosevelt Library.

36. *Report of the Proceedings of the Fifty-fifth Annual Convention of the American Federation of Labor,* 1935, p. 52.

37. Official File 416, Box 4, Franklin Delano Roosevelt Library.

38. *Report of the Proceedings of the Fifty-sixth Annual Convention of the American Federation of Labor,* 1936, p. 154.

39. *Ibid.,* p. 436.

40. Frey to unions in Metal Trades Department, March 9, 1937.

41. John P. Frey to J. Warren Madden, March 25, 1937.

42. J. Warren Madden to Frey, April 1, 1937; Frey to Madden, March 25, 1937.

43. Madden to Frey, April 1, 1937.

44. *Report of the Proceedings of the Fifty-seventh Annual Convention of the American Federation of Labor,* 1937, pp. 484–490.

45. *Ibid.,* pp. 490–500.

46. Minutes of Executive Council, August 22, 1938.

47. Letter to President Roosevelt in the Minutes of Executive Council, August 23, 1938.

48. President Franklin D. Roosevelt to Green, August 25, 1938, Official File 716, Box 5, Franklin Delano Roosevelt Library.

49. Memorandum from Marvin McIntire to President Roosevelt, August 25, 1938, Official File 716, Box 6, Franklin Delano Roosevelt Library.

50. *Report of the Proceedings of the Fifty-eighth Convention of the American Federation of Labor*, 1938, p. 135.

51. *Ibid.*, p. 136.

52. *Ibid.*, p. 139

53. *Ibid.*, pp. 344–345.

54. *Ibid.*, p. 352.

55. *Statement of William Green, President of the American Federation of Labor before the Committee on Labor of the House of Representatives,* June 14, 1939, in archives of A. F. of L.

56. *Analysis Prepared by William Green, President of the American Federation of Labor Amendments to the National Labor Relations Act, Proposed by the Smith Committee,* no date, in files of A. F. of L.

57. Hutcheson to Green, April 6, 1940.

58. Memorandum in Franklin D. Roosevelt Papers, August 8, 1940, Official File 716-A, Box 15, Franklin Delano Roosevelt Library.

59. *American Federation of Labor Weekly News, August 5, 1941.*

60. *Report of the Proceedings of the Sixty-first Annual Convention of the American Federation of Labor*, 1941, p. 117.

61. *Report of the Proceedings of the Sixty-second Annual Convention of the American Federation of Labor*, 1942, p. 490.

62. *Report of the Proceedings of the Thirty-fifth Annual Convention of the American Federation of Labor*, 1915, p. 81.

63. *Ibid.*, p. 81.

64. Minutes of Executive Council, February 10, 1925.

65. *Report of the Proceedings of the Forty-fifth Annual Convention of the American Federation of Labor*, 1925, pp. 55, 171; *Ibid., Fifty-third Annual Convention of the American Federation of Labor*, 1933, pp. 505–506.

66. *Report of the Proceedings of the Fifty-fifth Annual Convention of the American Federation of Labor*, 1935, pp. 603–608.

67. *Violations of Free Speech and Rights of Labor: Preliminary Report Pursuant to S. 266, 74th Congress, Subcommittee Print Report No. 46, 1st Session.*

# XI

## The Committee for Industrial Organization

### COMPLAINTS FROM CRAFT UNIONS

The Executive Council's policies in organizing the mass-production industries did not satisfy the newly established Federal labor unions, many of which had been temporarily organized on an industrial basis. Opposition to these policies was also expressed by several Council members who demanded that workers in the mass-production industries be granted industrial union charters and that a more aggressive organizing policy in this industrial area be followed. On the other hand, leaders of the craft unions, especially those in the Metal Trades Department, were seriously concerned with the "apparent belief of leading officers of the A. F. of L. that the industrial form of organization should replace [the] craft structure."[1] The craft unionists had actually wanted to take steps against any encroachment upon their jurisdictions at the 1933 convention. Although John Frey opposed action at the time, he and others were prepared at the 1934 convention to force the issue; but at the last moment the opposition agreed to a report from the committee of which Frey was secretary "which was reasonably acceptable to [his] group." Events since then have made it apparent that the understanding reached at the convention of 1934 was not acceptable to the advocates of industrial organization, who, Frey believed, wished to change the structure of the trade union movement.[2]

Frey's views were strongly supported by the Metal Trades Department. In a statement to the 1935 convention of his Department, Frey propounded his contract theory of affiliation under which a certificate of affiliation or charter granted to a union by the A. F. of L. constituted a contract between the A. F. of L. and the affiliate which could only be broken by the consent of the two parties. The argument was simply an adaptation to the A. F. of L. of the doctrine elaborated by the United States Supreme Court in the Dartmouth College case. Frey charged, moreover, that an "effort [was] now being made by others to compel us to abandon the form of organization which we have had from the beginning, and which has proven satisfactory to us. We are bringing no issue into the Convention of the American Federation of Labor, but apparently an issue is being forced upon us."[3] At the suggestion of Arthur

Wharton, a vote was taken to endorse the speech, which to the delegates was a defense of the "principles of craft autonomy." The endorsement was unanimously approved.

## THE CONVENTION OF 1935

Twenty-one resolutions on industrial unionism were submitted to the A. F. of L. convention of 1935. For the first time in many years, a minority report on an important issue, signed by six of the seventeen members of the resolutions committee, was presented. The majority report, signed by Matthew Woll and John Frey, among others, stated that those who had introduced the resolutions on industrial unionism "either misunderstood the Declaration adopted last year by the San Francisco Convention, or [desired] that the policy established in that Declaration should be set aside and existing International Unions merged into industrial organizations organized for the several industries."[4] It recalled the reaffirmation of the rights and jurisdictions of the national and international unions of the A. F. of L. by the 1934 convention, and argued that the A. F. of L. had entered into a contract with these organizations. According to the majority the "contract called for loyalty to the purposes and policies of the American Federation of Labor. In return the National and International Unions were guaranteed two specific things: first jurisdiction over all workmen doing the work of the specific craft or occupation covered by the organization; second, guaranteeing to the National or International Unions complete autonomy over all its internal affairs."[5]

In contrast, the minority report, signed by John L. Lewis, Charles P. Howard, David Dubinsky, and three other members, emphasized the changes in industrial methods and the obligation of the Federation to "organize the unorganized workers in the industrial field. The time has arrived," the minority report said, "when common sense demands [that] the organization policies of the American Federation of Labor must be molded to meet present-day needs. In the great mass-production industries and those in which the workers are composite mechanics, specialized and engaged upon classes of work which do not fully qualify them for craft union membership, industrial organization is the only solution. Continuous employment, economic security and the ability to protect the individual worker depends upon organization upon industrial lines."[6]

The ill feeling which had surrounded the discussion in the resolutions committee was manifest from the outset. Howard charged that pressure had been used upon a member of the resolutions committee and as a result the member had refused to sign the minority report. Moreover, Howard believed that the Council had failed to apply properly the decisions of the 1934 convention on this issue. He pointed to the enactment of the Wagner Act and the protection of the right to organize by the

government as significant changes in the political situation which should
be helpful in a campaign to organize the workers in the mass-production
industries. Howard charged that the assertion of jurisdictional rights
by the craft unions in the mass-production industries interfered with the
carrying out of an effective organization program.[7]

Woll centered his criticism on the following clause in the minority
report:

The Executive Council of the American Federation of Labor is expressly directed and instructed to issue unrestricted charters to organizations formed in
accordance with the policy herein enunciated. The Executive Council is also
instructed to enter upon an aggressive organization campaign in those industries in which the great mass of workers are not now organized, issue unrestricted charters to workers organized into independent unions, company-dominated unions and those organizations now affiliated with associations not
recognized by the American Federation of Labor as bona fide unions.[8]

Woll objected to the removal of the Executive Council's discretion in
judging the character and form of organzation to be allowed to affiliate.
He felt that the Council had the authority to determine the kind of organizations to be chartered in the mass-production industries and in the
miscellaneous trades, and he argued that appeals from Council decisions
could be made to the convention. He believed that it would be dangerous
to lay down specific rules which would fail to give the Council any
discretion in the matter of charters issued to prospective affiliates or the
area and workers that were to be organized by a given union.

Lewis, in his turn, scornfully attacked the organizing record of the
A. F. of L. during the past year. Like Woll, he thought that the practical
compromise, which he believed had been reached at the 1934 convention,
had been ignored by the Executive Council. The six days "and almost
six nights" that had been spent by the resolutions committee during the
1934 convention in evolving a compromise had made possible, Lewis
said, the organization of the mass-production industries while protecting
the basic rights of the craft unions. Claiming that the interpretation of
the 1934 resolution on industrial unionism by the Executive Council was
a breach of faith, he said he was "convinced that the Executive Council
[was] not going to issue any charters for industrial unions in any industry. The majority members of the Council say that that is their understanding and interpretation of the resolution passed at San Francisco
[Convention of 1934]. . . . My assurances to the convention last year that
I believed the Executive Council would fairly exercise its authority as
between the lines of demarcation of these unions is now withdrawn.
I do not believe it will."[9]

Frey, who offered the principal argument against the minority report, pointed to the differences of opinion among committee members about the meaning of the resolution passed at the 1934 convention on the same question. He argued that it was difficult to define either an industry or a craft, and he questioned whether workers who were within the jurisdiction of older organized craft unions should be absorbed in the newly established industrial organizations. On the whole, Frey seemed satisfied with the progress made, and to him the long years in which the Federation had functioned was a sign that new methods were not needed. Denying that the industrial unions in the Federation had a better record of organization or accomplishments for their members than the craft associates, he repeated his argument that a charter or a certificate of affiliation was a contract between the union and the A. F. of L. and should not lightly be set aside by one of the parties.[10] Wharton, agreeing with Frey, doubted that the workers in the mass-production industries were eager to affiliate with unions, as some of the speakers had claimed. Nothing, in Wharton's opinion, was preventing the workers from organizing: "the doors of this organization are open. We are begging and working, endeavoring to bring men and women into the movement. Why don't they come in?"[11] He reminded the convention that the Machinists' Union had grown from 100,000 to over 300,000 during World War I, but that the great majority of these workers had left the union in spite of the efforts made to protect and defend their interests. In the end, the majority report was accepted by a vote of 18,024 to 10,933.[12]

The general question of the chartering of industrial unions in the mass-production industries was settled, but the Mine, Mill, and Smelter Workers' Union appealed to the convention to allow it to exercise the jurisdiction which it claimed had been granted at the time of its affiliation with the A. F. of L. in 1911, under the name of Western Federation of Miners. The name of the Union had been changed with the permission of the Federation, because workers eligible for membership and working in the eastern part of the United States would not join a western organization. Lewis proposed that the Mine, Mill, and Smelter Workers be given the jurisdiction which had been promised by Gompers at the 1911 convention and that the craft unions which had signed the Anaconda Agreement of 1934 surrender their jurisdiction in the metalliferous mining and smelting industry when the Anaconda contract expired. The Executive Council had already rejected a similar proposal made by Lewis. The discussion narrowed down to whether jurisdiction had been granted to the Mine, Mill, and Smelter Workers over all those employed in and around the metalliferous mines, or whether the craft unions had chartered locals in this industry before the Western Federation of Miners had affiliated. In the end, the claim of the craft unions was again upheld and the right of the Mine, Mill, and Smelter Workers to control all employees in the metalliferous mines and smelters was denied by a vote of 18,464 to 10,897, with 385 not voting.[13]

Throughout the sessions the sharp differences of opinion engendered debates of a high intellectual order, and before adjournment the convention was to witness a dramatic clash between two of the leading personalities in the labor movement. When the resolutions committee recommended nonconcurrence in a resolution proposing industrial organization in the rubber industry, and the subject was opened for debate, William Hutcheson objected on the ground that the issue had already been resolved. After some discussion between a delegate from the Rubber Workers' Union and Hutcheson, who insisted that the resolution merely reintroduced the question of industrial unionism in another form, Lewis intervened by raising a point of order. He insisted that the resolution sponsored by the Rubber Workers' Union dealt with a specific matter. "It does not deal entirely with the question of industrial unionism as decided by this convention. It deals with a problem in Akron, Ohio, and elsewhere, and certainly in my judgment this organization and these delegates who introduce a resolution here have a right to tell this convention their own particular problems in relation to it. This thing of raising points of order all the time on minor delegates is rather small potatoes."[14]

The reference to small potatoes seemed to anger Hutcheson, one of the tallest and largest men at the convention. He retorted that if Lewis had given more "consideration to the questions before this convention and not to attempting, in a dramatic way, to impress the delegates with his sincerity, we would not have had to raise the point of order at this late date[;] we would have had more time to devote to the questions before the convention."[15] There was a quiet exchange of oaths and Lewis struck Hutcheson. The men tangled and fell to the floor. This was more than a clash between physically and politically powerful labor leaders; it was also a sign that the differences had reached a point where they would not be easily conciliated.[16]

The clash between Hutcheson and Lewis took place after the election for the Executive Council had been held. Only Woll of the sitting members was opposed; his rival was a left-wing leader of a Federal labor union. He polled only 264 votes, out of almost 29,000.[17] A strong movement to run Felix H. Knight against Lewis was squelched by Green when he threatened to decline the nomination for president if the metal trades' unions insisted on following their plan. When George L. Berry refused to stand for office, Philip Murray of the United Mine Workers of America nominated Charles P. Howard in opposition to William D. Mahon for the vacancy. Sidney Hillman, who seconded the nomination of Howard, based his support upon the need to have a representative of the minority. This, of course, had reference to the proponents of industrial unionism on the Council. Howard was defeated by 17,370 to 11,693 votes.[18]

### FORMATION OF THE COMMITTEE FOR INDUSTRIAL ORGANIZATION

On November 9, three weeks after the adjournment of the convention, "an informal meeting of the representatives of National and International Unions concerned with the organization of unorganized workers in mass-production and other industries was held in the headquarters of the United Mine Workers of America, Tower Building, Washington."[19] Lewis reviewed the purpose of the meeting and recalled the "questions discussed informally after the adjournment of the American Federation of Labor convention at Atlantic City."[20] Lewis was named temporary chairman and Howard was temporary secretary of the meeting. "After extended discussion of organization problems in mass-production and other corporate controlled industries, a motion was adopted by unanimous vote to make the temporary organization permanent, the organization to be known as the Committee for Industrial Organization."[21]

Lewis was named permanent chairman, Howard permanent secretary. The other members of the Committee were Sidney Hillman of the Amalgamated Clothing Workers of America; David Dubinsky, International Ladies' Garment Workers' Union; Thomas F. McMahon, United Textile Workers; Harvey C. Fremming, Oil Field, Gas, and Refinery Workers of America; Max Zaritsky, Cap and Millinery Department, United Hatters, Cap and Millinery Workers' International Union; and Thomas H. Brown, International Union of Mine, Mill, and Smelter Workers. Invitations were extended to other unions to join the Committee.

The purpose of the Committee was declared to be encouragement and promotion of organization of the unorganized workers in mass production and other industries upon an industrial basis, as outlined in the minority report of the Resolutions' Committee submitted to the convention of the American Federation of Labor at Atlantic City; to foster recognition and acceptance of collective bargaining in such industries; to counsel and advise unorganized and newly organized groups of workers; to bring them under the banner and in affiliation with the American Federation of Labor.[22]

The committee decided to set up a permanent office in Washington and selected John Brophy, a coal miner and a one-time candidate for president of the United Mine Workers of America against Lewis, as director. The representatives of several of the organizations present pledged contributions and gave assurances that financial support for the Committee would be forthcoming from organizations not represented at the initial meeting. "The attitude of members of the Committee as unanimously expressed was that its work would be to make organization efforts more effective, avoid injury to established National and International and Federal Labor Unions, and to stimulate and modernize the activities of the American Federation of Labor to meet the requirements of workers under modern conditions."[23]

Frank Duffy, the secretary of the Carpenters' Union, immediately called Green's attention to the formation of the Committee. In thanking Duffy, Green wrote that the movement "must be regarded as quite significant."[24] Without explanation Lewis submitted his resignation as a vice president of the A. F. of L. in a two-line letter to Green. He told Max Zaritsky that he "felt that further membership would avail nothing in the form of constructive action from the Executive Council."[25] Green was obviously irked at his resignation and informed Lewis that he had worked to assure his reelection to the Executive Council. According to Green, sufficient votes had been pledged to his opponent to assure Lewis's defeat, but his own action had rendered Lewis a service and was also designed "to promote harmony, cooperation, and solidarity within the American Federation of Labor."[26]

## REFERENCES

1. Frey to W. A. Appleton, March 21, 1935, in Folder 7, Frey Papers, Library of Congress.

2. *Ibid.*

3. *Report of Proceedings of the Metal Trades Department of the American Federation of Labor*, 1935, p. 99.

4. *Report of Proceedings of the Fifty-fifth Annual Convention of the American Federation of Labor*, 1935, pp. 521–522.

5. *Ibid.*, p. 521.

6. *Ibid.*, pp. 523–524.

7. *Ibid.*, pp. 524–528.

8. *Ibid.*, p. 524.

9. *Ibid.*, p. 538.

10. *Ibid.*, pp. 552–558.

11. *Ibid.*, p. 570.

12. *Ibid.*, pp. 574–575.

13. *Ibid.*, pp. 614–615.

14. *Ibid.*, p. 727.

15. *Ibid.*

16. *New York Times*, October 20, 1935.

17. *Report of Proceedings of the Fifty-fifth Annual Convention of the American Federation of Labor*, 1935, pp. 703–704.

18. *Ibid.*, p. 711.

19. Minutes of Meeting of Committee for Industrial Organization, Washington, D. C., November 9, 1935 (typewritten manuscript).

20. *Ibid.*

21. *Ibid.*

22. *Ibid.*

23. *Ibid.*

24. Duffy to Green, November 14, 1935; quote in Green to Duffy, November 19, 1935.

25. Lewis to Green, November 23, 1935; Lewis to Max Zaritsky, November 25, 1935.

26. Green to Lewis, November 25, 1935.

# XII

## The Road to Suspension

On November 23 Green addressed the heads of the unions of the Committee for Industrial Organization and said that officers of national and international unions would view with "apprehension and deep concern" the formation by subordinate local unions of an organization pledged to change the policies of their international union. Similarly, "when organizations within organizations are formed for the achievement and realization of some declared purpose," according to Green, "no one can accurately prophesy or predict where such a movement will lead. It could and may be diverted from its original purpose."[1] Green alluded to the fixed rule that differences over policies were decided by majority vote at regular conventions, and once a decision had been made, "it becomes the duty of the Officers and Members of the American Federation of Labor to comply with it and they should be permitted to do this free from the interference and opposition of those who constitute the minority. Those who disagree with the action of the majority are accorded the right to urge the acceptance of their point of view at succeeding conventions." Green expressed a feeling of "apprehension over the grave consequences which might follow from the formation of an organization within the American Federation of Labor even though it might be claimed that said organization is formed for the achievement of a laudable purpose. My conscience and my judgment lead me to advise against it and emphasize most vigorously the danger of division and discord which may follow."[2]

Green's letter brought replies from the officers of the unions to which it was addressed. Lewis offered to have Green elected to replace him as chairman of the Committee if Green "would return to [his] father's house."[3] Howard, on the other hand, wrote a courteous and reasoned reply in which he explained the basis for his association with the Committee for Industrial Organization. Noting that he would "bow to no one in [his] loyalty to the American Federation of Labor," Howard said that he considered "organization of the unorganized millions of wage workers as being so essential that it overshadows almost every other consideration."[4]

Howard did not agree with Green's outline of the rights of minorities.

148

In Howard's mind, where "the question is one of internal policy a labor organization is no different from any other democratic body. It is not unethical or improper for a minority to endeavor to have its proposals adopted by the majority through proper discussion of the issues and by an effort to convert those whose interests are most affected—the rank and file of the workers." Howard regarded the limitation Green sought to impose upon minorities as one that presumed "that only the officers and delegates are to be considered and that the members of National and International Unions, who support the Federation, as well as the millions of unorganized to whom we would make appeal, should have no direct interest or influence in making the fundamental policies of the American Federation of Labor." Nor would Howard accept Green's view that after the adoption of a decision by a majority at a convention "the rights and privileges of the minority are confined to urging 'acceptance of their point of view at succeeding conventions.'" Such an attitude, Howard said, would prevent minorities from carrying on educational campaigns essential to the making of proper decisions.

Howard, moreover, denied that the Committee constituted a menace to the success of the A. F. of L. program, and he declared that the Committee's purpose was to work for the recognition and acceptance of collective bargaining in industries where it did not then exist. He denied categorically any intent by the Committee to raid the membership of any A. F. of L. unions, to infringe upon any union's "rightful jurisdiction," to influence any union to change its form of organization from craft to industrial, to take any "action that will invite or promote organization that in any way can be considered dual to the American Federation of Labor."[5]

After some hesitation Green replied to Howard and said that he had not sought to deal with the merits of the different forms of organization but rather to call attention to the danger of discord and division if the Committee for Industrial Organization were allowed to conduct its activities.[6]

Howard was on safe ground when he asked for toleration of an organized minority and the rights of such minorities to present their point of view and to seek to convince the majority. Such a practice had always been a part of the traditions of Howard's International Typographical Union, manifesting itself in the recognition of political parties which had the right to compete for office in the union through support of slates of candidates. The Federation, moreover, had allowed its national and international affiliates to combine to promote objectives not always accepted by the Federation. Zaritsky, in his letter to Green, reminded him of the formation of the Conference for Progressive Political Action whose purpose was to reverse the nonpartisan political policy of the A. F. of L.[7]

A far more important example of Federation unions combining to achieve a purpose not approved by the parent organization was the forming of a number of building trades' unions in the National Building Trades Council and the Structural Building Trades Alliance. In fact, these organizations sometimes encouraged dual building trades' organizations, and although Gompers had been concerned with their activity, no steps had ever been taken by the Federation to compel the withdrawal of its affiliates from these bodies. Historically, an affiliated international could follow any policies it chose, and organizations whose jurisdictions were infringed upon could file complaints with the Executive Council at the convention. Neither law nor custom had granted the Federation any right to interfere with the internal affairs of affiliates.

In spite of Green's objections, the Committee for Industrial Organization continued its preparations for the massive organizing drives upon which it was to embark. In his report on January 9, 1936 to the members of the Committee, Director John Brophy outlined the plans and progress of the new organization. The report reflected considerable activity in laying the groundwork for the drive which was soon to come.[8] During this period the United Mine Workers of America had met in convention, and William Green, who had been its secretary-treasurer prior to his election to the presidency of the A. F. of L., appeared before the delegates. He defended the right of skilled workers to organize together so as "to force from unwilling, reluctant employers the highest wage and the most satisfactory conditions possible . . .; he can do this if he can associate with his fellow skilled workers and his key men serving in key positions in industry."[9] Conceding that there was a sharp difference of opinion on the meaning of the resolution on industrial unionism enacted by the 1934 convention, Green insisted that the charter granted to the automobile workers' union gave it jurisdiction over 98 per cent of the workers in the industry. Only one delegate supported Green's views.[10]

The Committee for Industrial Organization was inevitably a major topic for the Executive Council at its first meeting after the launching of this organization. At the Council's Miami meeting in January 1936, Green reviewed the history of the Committee's background and its declared aims. In his report, he alluded to the letter in which Lewis had asked Green to resign his presidency and take over the leadership of the C.I.O. He asked Dubinsky, a member of the Executive Council and the Committee, whether he had been consulted about the letter. Dubinsky answered that "Mr. Lewis did not consult with me or anyone about his resignation nor did he consult with me about the letter addressed to President Green. . . . As chairman of the Committee he took it upon himself to make that offer to you. This letter did not meet with the approval of myself or with the approval of the entire Board."[11]

Green did not think it was proper for a minority to organize after it had been fairly defeated. When the question of suspending the unions that had joined together in the C.I.O. was raised, the members of the Executive Council expressed different opinions. Green spoke out against division. He said that he had carefully studied the Federation's constitution and found that the Executive Council did not have the power to suspend an affiliated union; only the convention itself could order a charter revoked, and then a two-thirds vote was required. He reminded the members that Gompers had ruled that there was a difference between suspension and revocation of a charter and that a charter could be suspended by a majority vote of the convention. There was no precedent, he concluded, for the Executive Council to suspend a union.[12]

On the following day Charles P. Howard appeared. He disclaimed any "hidden motive," denied that he was motivated by personal ambition or intended to "do anything other than advance the interests of the trade union movement as expressed by [his] organization and . . . the American Federation of Labor."[13] Howard admitted that if the policy of organizing on industrial lines were successfully carried out, it might have an effect upon existing unions.

But, if the purpose of the trade union [he argued] is to improve the economic condition of its members . . . it is not an unworthy motive to attempt in accordance with our law to amend or alter the form of organization. In no paragraph of the [C.I.O.'s] declaration is there advocated any unethical or coercive method. A proper understanding of that declaration should indicate to any man of open mind . . . that we are referring to unorganized workers and we are attempting to educate them to understand the type of organization that would be the most effective form for the protection of their interests.[14]

Howard wanted to strengthen the position of every union affiliated with the A. F. of L., and he could not conceive how the organization of millions of workers into the A. F. of L. could injure the trade-union movement. He granted that industrial organizations might create jurisdictional disputes, but he did not find that possibility alarming, and he asked, "when in the life of the American Federation of Labor have there not been jurisdictional disputes?"[15]

Several members of the Executive Council challenged Howard, and questioned the right, especially of a minority, to set up an organization to carry on activities in defiance of the expressed will of the majority. Green asked Howard, "If you could be convinced that the activities of this Committee would lead to bitterness, discord, hate, and injury to the American Federation of Labor, would you be willing to continue it?" President Howard replied, "No, I would lay down my life to prevent that."[16]

Two proposals were submitted. Green called for the appointment of a committee to transmit to the unions affiliated with the C.I.O. the Council's view that the organization was harmful and divisive and that it should be dissolved. The committee would report back to the Council at its regular meeting in May. Woll offered a different proposal. He suggested the appointment of three members of the Council to interview the international officers of the unions affiliated with the C.I.O., but not the C.I.O. itself, in an attempt to convince them of the danger their activities held for the labor movement. The union leaders were to be asked to withdraw from the C.I.O. Failing in their mission, the committee was to recommend further action to the Council.

Dubinsky argued for the acceptance of Woll's proposal and asked the Council to avoid making any declaration on the subject. He based his views on the closeness of the vote on the Executive Board of the C.I.O., which Dubinsky attributed to

the letter of President Lewis to President Green, asking that he give up the Presidency of the American Federation of Labor. . . . The purpose of this Committee as declared in its declaration is to promote and encourage the organization of workers in mass production and unorganized industries and . . . its functions will be educational and advisory. We considered it a duty on the part of our organization to join this Committee. But we saw developments and when I spoke to President Green I said it might develop into something else and we do not want to be a party to it. At this stage of the game you have no evidence based upon pamphlets or anything else. You may prove or disprove that [it] is a disloyal act to the American Federation of Labor . . . it is the right of each individual organization, and we said, "We have joined the Committee for Industrial Organization to give it support as long as it adheres to the purpose originally outlined by the Committee."

Dubinsky emphasized that the International Ladies' Garment Workers' Union, which he headed, was opposed to dual unions. He made it clear that although he and his union wanted changes in organization tactics, they wanted these to take place within the A. F. of L. framework. "You are asking," he told the Council, "this Committee be dissolved without first establishing facts by an investigation that the Committee is violating the rules of the American Federation of Labor."[17]

Harrison, Weber, and Bugniazet were appointed as a committee to confer with representatives of the C.I.O. unions and they drafted the following statement. Bates, Duffy, Hutcheson, Rickert, and Wharton objected because the "document was not strong enough";[18] Dubinsky opposed the statement in principle.

All available facts and information, correspondence, printed publications, and pamphlets relating to the organization, policies and procedure of the Committee for Industrial Organization were examined and considered, and without forming a definite opinion regarding the character, purpose and objective of the Committee for Industrial Organization, the members of the Executive Council nevertheless find that there is the growing conviction among an ever increasing number of affiliated unions and those outside of the labor movement that the activities of this committee constitute a challenge of the supremacy of the American Federation of Labor and will ultimately become dual in purpose and character to the American Federation of Labor.

The Executive Council, while freely recognizing the right of officers and members of organizations affiliated with the American Federation of Labor to entertain and express their own opinions regarding organization and administrative policies which should be pursued, insists that policies adopted at conventions of the American Federation of Labor should be respected, observed, and carried out. Any other procedure must inevitably lead to internal strife, discord, and division within the ranks of organized labor.

It is the opinion of the Executive Council that the Committee for Industrial Organization should be immediately dissolved, that it should cease to function as assembled reports, facts, and information indicate, and that the officers of the several organizations which constitute the Committee for Industrial Organization cooperate fully with the Executive Council in the application and execution of the organization policies adopted by an overwhelming majority of the duly accredited delegates who were in attendance at the convention of the American Federation of Labor held in Atlantic City, New Jersey, from October 7 to 19, 1935.

In order to achieve this purpose and to prevent confusion, division, and discord within the ranks of organized labor, the Executive Council authorized a committee of its members to meet and confer with representatives of the organizations which make up the Committee for Industrial Organization and to present to them the recommendations and the point of view entertained and expressed by members of the Executive Council who attended the Miami meeting.

The Executive Council directs that conferences as herein referred to be held at the earliest date possible and that said committee report the results of the conferences together with such recommendations as it may decide to offer to the next meeting of the Executive Council.

The Council sent a statement to state federations of labor, city central bodies, and Federal labor unions urging these groups to support the decisions of the conventions and to avoid the division and discord which threatened to drive apart the forces of organized labor.[19]

The members of the C.I.O. quickly replied to the Executive Council's order. Their letter was signed by all the original members except Thomas H. Brown of the Mine, Mill, and Smelter Workers, and although expressing a willingness to meet with the Council's Committee, challenged their statement.[20]

The Executive Council did not, according to your communication, find that the C.I.O. had taken any actions contrary to the constitution of the A. F. of L.

or which went beyond our rights as representatives of over one-third of the members of the A. F. of L. The Executive Council expressed fears that the C.I.O. might become dual, [though] quoting no evidence to support these fears. We wish to emphasize again that we are trying to remove the roots of dualism by making it possible for the millions of mass-production workers now outside the A. F. of L. to enter on the only basis they will accept—industrial unions.

The A. F. of L. convention last fall instructed the Executive Council to extend A. F. of L. organization in autos, steel, and other mass-production industries, and it is precisely to this end that our efforts are directed. Many A. F. of L. affiliates in these industries testify that our activities have been of great value to them. We are forced to the conclusion that many of those who are trying to brand us falsely as dualists are themselves none too eager to see the unions in the mass-production industries grow in influence.

In the instructions of the Executive Council to state federations of labor, city central bodies, and directly chartered federal labor unions, transmitted in President Green's letter of February 7th, there is an implication that the C.I.O. is attempting to usurp the functions of the A. F. of L. This is absolutely contrary to facts. These instructions likewise forbid these bodies to "give allegiance, assistance or support" to the C.I.O. We have not attempted to secure "allegiance, assistance or support" from such bodies since our efforts are directed towards increasing sentiment for industrial unionism in mass-production industries, not to build any organization within the A. F. of L. As we understand it, these instructions in no way affect the right of these directly affiliated bodies to go on record for industrial unionism, nor to seek aid from or spread the literature of our Committee. Any attempt by the Executive Council to prevent such activities would be completely undemocratic and contrary to the policies of the labor movement.

In a separate letter, Lewis assured Green that "the members of the Committee for Industrial Organization will be very glad to confer with the Committee of the Executive Council."[21]

The Executive Council's committee waited until May 19, four months later, before suggesting to Lewis that it wanted to meet with representatives of the C.I.O. On less than one day's notice, "an effort was made to reach all members of the C.I.O."[22] Present at the meeting were Harrison, Bugniazet, and Weber for the A. F. of L., and Lewis, Murray, McMahon, MacCabe, and Brophy representing the C.I.O. Harrison explained that his committee had been instructed by the Council to urge the members of the C.I.O. to abandon their activity and go along with the policies agreed to by the majority at the 1935 convention. On behalf of the Executive Council, he declared that the C.I.O. had "delegated to itself functions reserved to the A. F. of L. and that certain of its actions had obstructed organizing progress by other affiliated unions." Harrison further stated that he saw no point in discussing the merits of the question at dispute.

The proposal was that the C.I.O. should be abandoned and "then we can get together and see if we can't find some solution." Harrison stated that it was his own individual judgment that if the C.I.O. did dissolve there was opportunity to find some common ground."[23]

Lewis asked Harrison whether "the Executive Council would identify a number of industries in which industrial unions could be set up?" Harrison replied that he did not know but offered to make an inquiry. Lewis and several others stated that they stood on the letter of February 20 in which they had asked that industrial organization in the mass-production industries be initiated, and they pointed to the good results in organizing that had followed from the activities of the C.I.O. Lewis then announced that the United Mine Workers would "not comply with your fiat issued without previous consultation with us."[24]

Harrison reported to the Executive Council that Lewis had again denied that he or the C.I.O. "had any purpose to interfere with or obstruct the ordinary functions of the American Federation of Labor and . . . [they] intended to carry on their activities through . . . the Committee for Industrial Organization."[25] According to Harrison, Lewis had been willing to discuss "a basis of understanding between the C.I.O. and the A. F. of L.; but the subcommittee had advised him that they were not there for that purpose." They had maintained that Lewis and the other representatives had to abandon the C.I.O. and return to the councils of the A. F. of L. for a solution to the problem.[26]

Green had been prepared for rejection, for neither the Executive Council nor Harrison's committee had been authorized to devise any program or suggest any plan to settle the differences which had arisen. There is no evidence that the members of the C.I.O. wanted to secede from the A. F. of L. Lewis had told the Harrison committee that his union and the other unions of the C.I.O. regarded themselves as members of the A. F. of L. and wanted to stay in it but that the A. F. of L. had to negotiate and suggest a program upon which the mass-production industries, especially the steel industry, could be organized. Green, instead of seeking some methods for solving the crisis, sought the advice of his lawyer, Charlton Ogburn, on how the C.I.O. unions might be legally suspended.

It is difficult to follow the reasoning of the majority of the members of the Executive Council. The A. F. of L. was confronted with the most serious crisis in its history: the formation of a joint organizing effort by several large and powerful unions. Certainly such a challenge called for more than the issuance of orders to dissolve. Yet the president of the A. F. of L. could think of nothing better in this time of crisis than to find a legal loophole by which the unions of the C.I.O. might be thrown out of the Federation. One member, George Harrison, objected to the Council's attitude, and although he lamented its formation, he insisted that the unions were within their rights in establishing the C.I.O.[27]

In commenting on the legal aspects of the problem which Green called to his attention, Charlton Ogburn stated that Article IX, Section 8 of the A. F. of L. constitution ("The Executive Council shall have power to make the rule to govern matters not in conflict with this Constitution, or the constitution of affiliated unions . . .") gave the Council "broad authority . . . to make rules for governing the Federation in its relation to the affiliated unions." Ogburn also said that a clause in Article IV, Section 5 ("No organization or person that has seceded or that has been suspended . . .") "shows that the Constitution certainly contemplates the *suspension* of affiliated organizations."[28]

Ogburn went on to say that power to suspend was not reserved to the convention and that the general authority given to the Executive Council in Article IX could be exercised by the Executive Council. Ogburn's advice was not only pernicious, it was wrong from any reading of the clause he quoted. A proper reading clearly indicates that this clause merely regulated representation, as does the whole of Article IV, which is headed "Representation." Ogburn's interpretation was a perversion of the constitution, and Harrison so informed the Council. The lawyer advised that the Executive Council adopt rules under which the Council would declare that its certificate of affiliation was a contract between the A. F. of L. and the affiliate and that violations of the orders of the Executive Council constituted a breach of contract, making the union subject to expulsion.

This was careless advice given by one who knew little of the customs and history of the A. F. of L.; its solicitation can only be explained as a paralysis of intelligence.

In the meantime, the Executive Council's committee wrote to the C.I.O. unions that it was[29]

necessary to point out that conventions of the American Federation of Labor are supreme in their authority to enact laws, formulate policies, and require strict adherence thereto, not only from all those who participate in the deliberations of these conventions, but, in addition, from all who are affiliated with the American Federation of Labor. All actions of American Federation of Labor conventions deliberately taken by majority vote are binding upon the membership of the American Federation of Labor. To follow any other course or to work at cross purposes with convention actions can only result in friction within the organized labor movement and will ultimately lead to division and discord.

Charters issued to international organizations by the American Federation of Labor specifically provide that the organizations to which they are issued "conform to the constitution, laws, rules, and regulations of the American Federation of Labor." Compliance with this provision, therefore, calls for the most strict and loyal adherence to decisions arrived at in democratic fashion at conventions of the American Federation of Labor.

In order to avoid chaos and provide for orderly procedure all fundamental questions affecting the American Federation of Labor as such, which includes organization policies, must be decided upon at conventions of the American Federation of Labor. The creation of a rival organization within the American Federation of Labor constitutes a menace to its success as well as to the establishment of unity and solidarity within its ranks. No organization commanding respect or worthy of existence can tolerate a dual movement within its field of jurisdiction.

Organizations of such kind and character can only be interpreted as an attempt to establish minority rule and to impose the will of a minority upon the officers and members of the American Federation of Labor, contrary to decisions arrived at in conventions by majority vote.

We regard the Committee for Industrial Organization as a rival and dual organization within the family of organized labor. Its activities justify such a conclusion. It advocates the pursuit of organizing policies in opposition to those formulated and adopted at conventions of the American Federation of Labor. It advises organizations and members affiliated with the American Federation of Labor to disregard decisions and instructions of conventions of the American Federation of Labor.

For this and other valid reasons we call upon the Committee for Industrial Organization to dissolve immediately and to recognize the convention of the American Federation of Labor as the sole authority within the American Federation of Labor to formulate and originate organization and administrative policies and to act on all fundamental policies of the American Federation of Labor. We are confident that such action is necessary if the unity of the labor movement is to be preserved and the solidarity and prestige of the American Federation of Labor maintained.

Howard sent a reasoned and lengthy reply repudiating the statement that the Committee for Industrial Organization is a "rival and dual organization within the family of organized labor." In the minds of reasoning men the Committee for Industrial Organization is not an "organization" in the same sense as is the American Federation of Labor. It has not attempted to exercise any of the powers or authority usually recognized as residing in the A. F. of L. . . . The work of the committee is education and its purpose is to assist and inspire the unorganized. . . . In no instance has a provision of the Constitution of the American Federation of Labor been violated by the Committee. In the absence of such violation I challenge the authority of the Executive Council to pass judgment or attempt to apply a penalty.[30]

Howard reminded the Council of the formation of other committees to promote organization and of the fact that such activities had never been regarded as unethical or illegal. He thought that the interest of the workers "transcends every other consideration—even sacrosanct jurisdictional claims which have never existed in reality. Any legal and ethical policy that will promote organization is justified. Any policy that interferes with and prevents organization cannot be justified and will not prevail."[31]

The Executive Board of the International Ladies' Garment Workers' Union disclaimed any intention of forming a dual movement and concentrated its criticism upon the conduct of the Harrison committee. The Board noted that Harrison's committee had called only one meeting during the four months of its existence—and that was on such short notice that many representatives were unable to attend.[32] The Ladies' Garment Workers' Union announced that it would continue to give support to the C.I.O. "as long as it adheres to the purposes originally outlined by it." The Board yielded to no one in "loyalty to the American Federation of Labor and the supreme right of its conventions to enact laws and formulate policies for the organized labor movement." The members of the Board were convinced, however, that it was "the inherent right of our Union, as well as of any other union affiliated with the American Federation of Labor, to advocate individually or jointly a change in organizing methods or in the form of organization and to promote our advocacy in a democratic fraternal manner, and at the same time preserve the unity of forces in the American labor movement."[33]

Max Zaritsky took the position that the C.I.O. was not a dual or rival movement to the A. F. of L. and informed the Harrison committee that he had joined the C.I.O. not as an officer of the United Hatters and Cap and Millinery Workers' Union, but as the representative of the Cap and Millinery Department of that union. The reason for Zaritsky's ambiguous position was that the two unions which had for many years operated in the hat manufacturing industry, the United Hatters and the Cap and Millinery Workers' Union, had merged two years previously, and the unions were still maintaining separate departments.[34]

Following the refusal of the C.I.O. unions to withdraw from the C.I.O., Green invited the leaders of the C.I.O. unions to meet with the Executive Council, so that the Council might "learn . . . the reasons for your refusal to comply with the request . . . to terminate the affiliation of your International Union with the Committee for Industrial Organization and to then consider and determine what further action it should take in the premises."[35]

In answering the information submitted to him by Green, William D. Mahon, a member of the Executive Council, criticised the C.I.O. unions for forming an organization, but he charged that the Executive Council was not "wholly blameless."

At the Atlantic City Convention [Mahon wrote] I was of the opinion that the Council had carried out the instructions of the San Francisco convention and I felt, of course, that those who were attacking the Council were absolutely wrong, and I was under that impression until I attended the Executive Council meeting . . . [in] January. At that meeting I found out that your Council had not carried out fully the instructions of the San Francisco convention. . . . I have always felt that organized labor must follow the industrial trend and develop with it. I believe in craft unions in the various crafts and appreciate what the craft unions have done for the trade union movement of America. . . . However, when we come to the great industries, like the automobile and the one in which my organization is engaged in, there must be a certain amount of industrial organization in order to protect the workers.

Mahon was doubtful of the success of an organizing drive in the steel industry and warned Green against interfering with it. He advised that consideration of the formation of the C.I.O. be allowed to wait until the next convention. "It is but a short time," he urged. "No one would be injured by doing that, and it would give an opportunity to all to express themselves."[36]

At the same time, other members of the Executive Council were demanding that the unions be called to answer charges. Frank Duffy advocated summoning the C.I.O. union leaders and allowing them to withdraw "from the Committee for Industrial Organization or take the consequences." Duffy's position was based on the argument that the C.I.O. was "opposed to the action of the . . . convention on the question of industrial unionism. They, therefore, are opposed to the will of the majority. They are now doing what the convention told them they could not do."[37]

Considering the frequent refusal of the Carpenters' Union to accept the decisions of the A. F. of L. convention on jurisdictional differences involving its organization, Duffy's view of the obligation to obey a convention verdict is an interesting if not accurate description of its customs and laws. Hutcheson limited himself to requesting that the C.I.O. be summoned to declare whether "they will or will not comply with the requests of the Executive Council."[38] Bates felt that the C.I.O. organizations should be served "with a Bill of Complaint setting forth violations of the rules and mandates of the American Federation of Labor and also of violation of the charter rights as granted to them at the time of their affiliation with the American Federation of Labor with instructions to appear before the Executive Council at its next meeting to make answer to the charges."[39] Woll, on the other hand, merely acknowledged the letters sent to him by Green, and Rickert wanted to avoid action until the meeting of the Council.[40]

Lewis deputized John Brophy to reply to Green's invitation, and

Brophy wrote that he hoped that the Council would follow "the usual union practice of putting such charges in writing so that we may be informed in advance of what specifically you wish to discuss."[41] Hillman supported the stand of his union's Executive Board which had already defined its position on the C.I.O. He, therefore, did not believe that his presence at the Council meeting on July 8 would serve any purpose.[42] Dubinsky was also in full accord with his union's statement "that the Harrison subcommittee did not follow out the specific instructions of the Executive Council . . . to meet and confer with the representatives of international unions comprising the Committee for Industrial Organization prior to making any recommendations in its report to the Executive Council. By failing to do so, it is evident that the Harrison subcommittee did not even make an attempt at conciliation."[43]

Howard wrote that his organization, the International Typographical Union, had not affiliated with the C.I.O. and that he was serving as an individual. He recognized that it was difficult to separate "in the public mind personal and official acts where he [was] the chief executive and official spokesman for an organization." Yet, as his union had not taken official action, Howard could not appear as its head, as Green wanted him to, and as a member of the C.I.O.[44]

### REFERENCES

1. Green to Lewis, November 23, 1935. The same letter was sent to the heads of other unions affiliated with the Committee.
2. *Ibid.*
3. Lewis to Green, December 7, 1935.
4. Howard to Green, December 2, 1935. Next quotations are from this letter.
5. All quotations following last footnote are from *Ibid.*
6. Green to Howard, December 12, 1935.
7. Zaritsky to Green, December 6, 1935.
8. Report of Director (Committee for Industrial Organization), January 9, 1936.
9. *American Federation of Labor Weekly News,* February 8, 1936.
10. *United Mine Workers Journal,* February 15, 1936.
11. Minutes of Executive Council, January 20, 1936.
12. *Ibid.*
13. Minutes of Executive Council, January 21, 1936.
14. *Ibid.*
15. *Ibid.*
16. *Ibid.*
17. Minutes of Executive Council, January 22, 1936.
18. *Ibid.*
19. Circular letter to Secretaries of State Federations of Labor, City Central

Labor Unions and Directly Affiliated Local and Federal Labor Unions, from William Green and Frank Morrison, February 7, 1936.

20. John L. Lewis, Charles P. Howard, Sidney Hillman, David Dubinsky, H. C. Fremming, Thomas F. McMahon, and Max Zaritsky to William Green, February 21, 1936.

21. Lewis to Green, February 13, 1936.

22. Summary of Meeting between C.I.O. and Subcommittee of the A. F. of L. Executive Council, May 19, 1936.

23. *Ibid.*

24. *Ibid.*

25. Minutes of Executive Council, May 19, 1936.

26. *Ibid.*

27. *Ibid.*

28. Charlton Ogburn to Green, May 1, 1936.

29. Harrison, Bugniazet, and Weber to Lewis, May 20, 1936. Similar letters were sent to the heads of other C.I.O. unions.

30. Charles P. Howard to Harrison, June 1, 1936.

31. *Ibid.*

32. *Ibid.*

33. David Dubinsky on behalf of General Executive Board to George Harrison, June 1, 1936.

34. Max Zaritsky to Green, July 8, 1936.

35. Green to Lewis, June 20, 1936. Similar letters were sent to all other heads of C.I.O. unions.

36. Mahon to Green, July 11, 1936.

37. Duffy to Green, June 15, 1936; G. M. Bugniazet to Green, July 16, 1936.

38. William L. Hutcheson to Green, June 18, 1936.

39. Harry Bates, June 15, 1936.

40. Woll to Green, July 15, 1936; Rickert to Green, July 15, 1936.

41. John Brophy to Green, June 23, 1936.

42. Sidney Hillman to Green, July 6, 1936.

43. Dubinsky to Green, June 30, 1936.

44. Howard to Green, June 26, 1936 and June 1, 1936; Green to Howard, June 30, 1936.

# XIII

## Charges

JOHN FREY appeared at the meeting of the Executive Council on July 9 and discussed the debate on the industrial union resolution at the 1935 convention and the formation of the C.I.O. According to Frey, "Mr. John L. Lewis, Mr. Charles P. Howard, and Mr. David Dubinsky [were] foremost in bringing the C.I.O. into existence." He referred to their membership on the resolutions committee of the A. F. of L. convention and their disregard of the decisions made there. He reviewed the agreement made between the Amalgamated Association of Iron, Steel, and Tin Workers and the C.I.O. to initiate a campaign of organization in that industry; and he charged that the C.I.O. had given assistance to dual organizations of shipyard workers, radio workers, and others, and that the activities of the C.I.O. had "materially affected the organization work carried on by the International Unions affiliated with the Metal Trades Department." "While there is no evidence," he said, "that the C.I.O. has any working agreement with the Communist Party in the United States, there is a mass of authentic evidence indicating that the Communist Party has ceased all of its other activities for the time being, and is doing all within its power to assist the C.I.O." Frey argued that the final authority in the A. F. of L. on questions of jurisdiction was "the Executive Council and the conventions of the A. F. of L. The C.I.O. has set itself up as a dual authority, and is now engaged in an effort to determine questions of jurisdiction and to make decisions which are in direct conflict with those of the Executive Council and conventions of the A. F. of L."[1]

Frey requested that the Council prevail upon the C.I.O. unions to disband and cease their attacks upon the A. F. of L. and its affiliates: "Should the Executive Council, A. F. of L., fail in its efforts for immediate action, the Metal Trades Department earnestly requests the Executive Council to immediately suspend such National and International Unions as may refuse to immediately withdraw from the C.I.O."[2] To Frey the activities of the C.I.O. constituted "an insurrection against both the authority of the Executive Council and the American Federation of Labor."[3]

At the same meeting Daniel Tobin questioned the Council's "right to suspend a charter because we believe there is a violation of the laws of the American Federation of Labor. There have been instances where I asked this Council to suspend a charter and the Council has taken the position it has not the right to suspend a charter."[4] Hutcheson wanted the Council "to take definite action," but he thought that the legal formalities should be observed. Tobin and Weber also discussed the legality of suspension by the Council. In Green's opinion the C.I.O. unions had already separated themselves from the A. F. of L., and as long as the unions were given their day in court, he believed the Council could suspend them. Harrison then addressed himself to the essential issues and in a long and forceful argument, reminiscent of Gompers, attacked the whole proceedings contemplated by the majority of the Council.

The issue of suspension revealed much about the customs and practices of the A. F. of L.; especially interesting was the position of the Carpenters' Union leaders who held that the decision of a convention had to be obeyed by the constituent unions. At the 1915 convention, the Carpenters' Union had been charged with refusing to obey the decision of the previous A. F. of L. convention, which had awarded millwrights' work to the machinists. The adjustment committee had then recommended that "the Carpenters and Joiners shall stand suspended until such time as this decision is complied with."[5]

Gompers, rising to oppose the recommendation, had pointed to his consistent opposition to expulsions of unions and had stated that he "was among the first, perhaps the first, to enter a protest against the revocation of charters of international unions, and insofar as it has been given to me to express myself by voice and vote . . . have pursued the course consistently." He had then described the A. F. of L. "as a voluntary federation, [in which] there are no powers which the American Federation of Labor can exercise except those powers conceded to the Federation by our international unions." Discussing the practical problems of enforcement, Gompers had said, "Suppose the recommendation of the committee is adopted, and we suspend the Brotherhood of Carpenters from the American Federation of Labor. . . . What are you going to do? The position of the Carpenters, in my judgment, as to their claims of jurisdiction, in many of the particulars read from their own journal, are unwarranted, untenable and I would go as far as any other delegate to this convention . . . to try to the very best of our ability and power to bring the Carpenters to their senses, so that they may recede from their unwarranted position."

Gompers conceded that the actions of the Carpenters and also other organizations had caused "pain and anguish . . . and [had] done grave and great injustice to other organizations; but [he asked the delegates] to bear in mind the exceptionally influential position now occupied by them among the toilers of our country and before the conscience and the judgment of the people of America and the whole civilized world. . . . Will it in any way affect the limitation of the Carpenters in the endeavor to enforce this clause."[6] Gompers had pleaded for the use of persuasion, conciliation, and patience rather than suspension.

Harrison was a part of the same tradition. He disclaimed any support or sympathy for the C.I.O. or any desire to support its program or the conduct of some of its affiliates. Having listened to the charges, he now expressed his desire to carry out his responsibility as a Council member.

I do not [he said] understand that this Council has any authority to suspend a union. I cannot find it in the constitution. For that reason as a member of the Council I shall not vote to suspend any union notwithstanding any advice the counsel of the Federation may give because I can get as many opinions as I want to hire attorneys. I have consulted the three attorneys of the Brotherhood of Railway Clerks, all judges of the Supreme Court of Ohio [;] they tell me there is no such authority in the constitution of the American Federation of Labor for this Council to suspend a union except in a mandate of the convention. They may be wrong. I don't ask you to accept their views but their views are as important as any other to the contrary. There is no precedent for the suggested power which I do not think is vested in me and I can not square that with my conscience, and I emphasize I shall not exercise the power which I do not think rests within me. I think organizations have a right to band together in furtherance of their interests. We have Departments of the American Federation of Labor and there is the Railway Labor Executives Association which embraces unions not affiliated with the American Federation of Labor as well as those that are affiliated, all for the purpose of serving our common needs in a particular field. I think they have the right to band together to serve their needs. If any of them transgresses upon the jurisdiction of any other organization, the constitution provides a guide to meet the situation. The injured union has the right to file a complaint, seek a conference with the organization against which it has a grievance, failing in that, bring it to the Executive Council for determination and from here to the convention for the application of the judgment of the sovereign body of this institution which is the convention.[7]

Harrison denied that charges had been submitted within the meaning of the customs and practices of the A. F. of L. He had heard Frey's statement, but he did not believe that it contained any charges within the jurisdiction of the A. F. of L. According to Harrison,

Frey simply reports that an insurrection is taking place among these organizations in the Committee for Industrial Organization. I respectfully submit these comments for your most serious consideration. He is charging nobody with anything except to say there is insurrection in the American Federation of Labor by organizations in the Committee for Industrial Organization. Any fair reading or any fair perusal of that document would be so held. I do not say this with any thought of defending these organizations but I am trying to intelligently and sincerely discharge the responsibility that rests upon me, because certainly I would not want to vote on a document of that kind as charges and then be reversed.[8]

Harrison went on to say that the Council had made no official effort to devise a solution to the differences, although some unofficial approaches to the opposition had been made. He explicitly stated that the C.I.O. had "a right to espouse the cause of industrial unionism within the limits of the constitution. If any organization has transgressed on the jurisdiction of any other union there is an established method of procedure. . . . I think we should proceed in the established way if we have any unions that have committed an offense under the constitution of the American Federation of Labor."[9]

Constitutionally Harrison was on sound ground. Indeed, there is something ludicrous about the members of the Executive Council exhibiting anger at the defiance of their decisions. In 1934 a majority of building trades had defied the Council and gone into court to have its decisions reversed. John Coefield, one of the members of the Council and the president of the Plumbers' Union, had rightfully argued then that the Building Trades Department had been established over the opposition of the A. F. of L. and had been accepted by the Federation only because no other alternative presented itself. The differences in this case had been settled, but by negotiation and compromise, which the Council at this stage refused to undertake. The Federation's policy had always been to settle issues on a practical basis and to show no haste in resolving controversies that concerned autonomous unions. The essence of voluntarism, as expressed by Gompers and others on numerous occasions, was that the Federation had only the power granted to it by the affiliates. Moreover, by 1936 the C.I.O. unions had done very little to interfere with the jurisdictions of other unions. Certainly the traditional method was to file complaints. The charge of insurrection was baseless and frivolous, and as Harrison reminded the Council, there never had been such an offense in the lexicon of the Federation. Instead of grabbing hold of Harrison's argument as a means of getting the Federation out of a blind alley, Green parried the arguments and drew a distinction between the departments and the Railway Labor Executives Association and the C.I.O. The only difference actually was that the older organizations had forced recognition from the A. F. of L., and the C.I.O. was a new effort of a group of unions to launch an organization drive by common effort.

At this point, Rickert, who felt a deep hatred of the C.I.O., proposed that the "President be directed to charge that the Committee for Industrial Organization and its activities are contrary to the action of the last convention of the American Federation of Labor . . . [and] is dual in character to the American Federation of Labor."[10] Harrison, making a final move to find a basis of accommodation, met with Lewis on July 14. He reported to the Council that "President Lewis said he would agree to dissolve the Committee for Industrial Organization providing the American Federation of Labor would agree to the organization of steel, rubber, automobile, and other mass production industries on an industrial basis. . . . That statement was not made by President Lewis in the nature of an offer, but in the course of the discussion."[11] Instead of embracing Harrison's recommendation and exploring the possibility of a reasonable compromise, the Executive Council ignored it and with unseemly haste voted "that the charges be accepted, the parties be notified that the charges have been filed and they be asked to meet with the Executive Council and make answer to these charges on a date when the Council reconvenes."[12]

Although Harrison voted against the charges, he made no further effort to halt the unprecedented and "illegal" move for summoning the C.I.O. unions, which had now grown to twelve. Evidently the task of finding a compromise was hopeless. The Federation's willingness to take summary action against unions with about one-third the total membership on questionable grounds shows a failure of leadership that has no equal in the history of American labor. As the president of the Federation and the man who might at this stage have prevented the action by threatening to resign, Green must bear the chief blame. He was abetted, however, by Wharton, Hutcheson, Coefield, Tracy, and Rickert, who were anxious to drive the recalcitrant unions outside the ranks.

In summing up the charges against the C.I.O., John Frey affirmed that "the final authority in the American Federation of Labor on questions of jurisdiction is the Executive Council and the conventions of the American Federation of Labor"; the C.I.O., he said, had set itself up as a dual movement, which was "fomenting insurrection within the American Federation of Labor." He concluded by charging that the Committee was "acting in violation of and in opposition to the decision of the Atlantic City convention of the American Federation of Labor and that its acts constitute rebellion against the administrative organization policies adopted by majority vote of the duly accredited delegates in attendance at said convention."[13]

In spite of the questionable basis of its authority and the lack of substance in the charges, the Executive Council accepted them and directed Green to transmit them to the twelve C.I.O. unions. (The eight original unions had been joined by the Amalgamated Association of Iron, Steel, and Tin Workers, and the Automobile, Rubber, and Flat Glass Workers' Unions.) The C.I.O. organizations were asked to appear for trial on August 3, 1936, and the following rules, devised by the Federation's attorney, Charleton Ogburn, were promulgated:

If any national or international union, chartered by the American Federation of Labor, violates any provisions of the Constitution or laws of the American Federation of Labor, or any resolution of the Convention or any proper order of the Executive Council of the American Federation of Labor, so that there is a breach of the contractual obligation assumed by said union in its charter from the American Federation of Labor, and if notice of said breach of its obligations or of any violation of the laws and orders of the American Federation of Labor or of its Executive Council by said union comes to the attention of the Executive Council, the Council shall notify the said union of the information showing it is in default and shall request said union to appear at a given date before the Executive Council then and there to submit evidence it desires in refutation of said charges. The Council shall also hear evidence in support of said charges.

After said hearing—or if said union defaults in its appearance after notice and opportunity to be heard—the Executive Council shall then in executive session determine what step shall be taken, if the said union is held guilty of having breached its contractual obligation in its charter from the American Federation of Labor and the laws and orders of the American Federation of Labor and of its Executive Council. In the event the Council finds said union guilty, the Council may take any of the following steps: (a) forgive said breach with or without conditions to be fulfilled by said union; (b) suspend said union from the American Federation of Labor and from enjoying the benefits from said membership for a definite or for an indefinite time; (c) penalize said union for said breach in any other way; or (d) if the actions of said union have been so serious that all relations between it and the American Federation of Labor should be severed, revoke its charter, but only upon instructions from a Convention of the American Federation of Labor passed by a two-thirds vote ordering the revocation of said charter.[14]

At the meeting on July 20 in Washington, the C.I.O. unions unanimously decided to reject the ultimatum. The leaders of the C.I.O. informed the Executive Council in a letter that the proceedings contemplated were completely unwarranted by the A. F. of L. constitution. The letter argued that the Federation constitution defined expulsion of an affiliate by a two-thirds vote of the convention, and that suspension would automatically disqualify the unions affected from having any "delegate representation in the convention, and in this case [was] intended to have the effect of an expulsion." Claiming that the Council had no power to adopt a rule to suspend, the letter called attention to the fact that the rules adopted by the Council under Article 9, Section 8, of the constitution related to administrative affairs, and that the section forbade the adoption of any rule in conflict with the constitution.

The amendment requiring a two-thirds roll call vote of a convention to terminate an affiliation of national or international union was adopted in 1907. Since then the convention has ordered many suspensions, but the Executive Council, through all these years, has never pretended to exercise the power until the present case, where it assumes to sit in judgment of over 40 per cent of the A. F. of L. membership. The Council . . . is without authority to dismember the Federation. The C.I.O. declines to submit to its jurisdiction. The vague charges of dualism, rebellion, and fomenting insurrection, are wholly based upon the work of the C.I.O. in organizing the labor of certain mass production industries into industrial unions. The heads of certain craft unions dominating the Council, violently oppose this effort. They fear the inclusion of these unions as a jeopardy to their own dead-hand control of the Federation. Satisfied now, as they have been for years, they regard the labor movement in America as having culminated. They are mistaken; it has just begun, and if it cannot continue within the Federation it will be because of the desperate course of the Council itself.[15]

In reply to the charge that the C.I.O. was seeking to damage the efforts of the A. F. of L. to organize the steel industry and was infringing upon the jurisdictions of various other unions, the letter described the charter originally granted to the Amalgamated Association as industrial in character and in accord with the San Francisco resolution. It pointed out that the C.I.O. had not opposed craft organizations except in the mass-production industries.

In a special letter to his members, Lewis reviewed calmly the issues confronting the United Mine Workers of America in the attempt of the Executive Council to bring the officers of the C.I.O. to trial. He argued that the craft form of organization had proved impracticable in mass-production industries. He explained the reasons for his resignation as a member of the Executive Council of the A. F. of L., and described the formation of the C.I.O. and the growth of this organization until it had about 40 per cent of the total A. F. of L. membership. He informed his members that the officers of their union had been summoned for trial with the other officers of the C.I.O., and that "the members of the Committee for Industrial Organization will not appear for trial before the Executive Council of the American Federation of Labor. They do not admit the jurisdiction of the executive council. They believe that only the convention of the American Federation of Labor has power to deal with such charges; that only the convention has power to suspend or expel national and international unions who are members of the American Federation of Labor." He assured his members that those who favored industrial unionism

have never desired to infringe upon the jurisdiction of these craft organizations, in those industries which are already well organized. We do maintain, however[,] that such organizations should for the sake of the welfare of the workers, yield their jurisdiction in industries totally unorganized, and in which they have few members, to suitable national or international industrial unions. We maintain that there is room in the American Federation of Labor both for craft unions and for industrial unions; but the craft unions fear that supreme control will be wrested from their hands if they permit the entrance of millions of new members, organized industrially. . . . To sum up: The Committee for Industrial Organization believes that its acts are in accordance with the mandate of the convention of the American Federation of Labor, and with the wishes of the members of that body. We are fulfilling the instructions of the convention, which the executive council has flouted. We believe that the unorganized workers of this country can only organize effectively through industrial unions.[16]

The position of the Executive Council remained unchanged, and most of its members began to prepare for the trial of the C.I.O. unions, even though their counsel, Charlton Ogburn, now expressed doubt as to the efficacy of suspending the recalcitrant organizations. In his opinion, the "courts if appealed to by the 'C.I.O.' unions, would not permit suspension to be used as a subterfuge to evade the requirement of a two-thirds majority of the Convention for expulsion through depriving the suspended 'C.I.O.' unions of a vote on the question of their own expulsion."[17]

Upon learning of the contemplated trial of the C.I.O. unions, Howard wired a protest against such action. In his view, no "authority to suspend or expel national and international unions [had been] delegated to Executive Council by constitution of Federation. No charges have been filed and no evidence presented that laws of Federation have been violated. . . . It should be apparent the rightful jurisdiction of every national and international union can be fully protected by proper orderly procedure. It is your duty as President to prevent the Executive Council from exceeding the authority specifically delegated to it by the Constitution."[18] In a letter Howard advised the Council that the International Typographical Union had never joined with the C.I.O., and he denied that the Executive Council had any authority to interfere with his right to affiliate.[19]

Green notified the members of the Council of the refusal of the C.I.O. officers to appear for trial, and Wharton was convinced that the C.I.O. organizations had decided upon a course to pursue. In contrast, George Harrison continued to warn against the contemplated action. He believed in "the desirability of developing some mutually satisfactory basis of disposing of the pending controversy with the C.I.O., and [he urged] that every possible effort be exerted in that direction. Further, [he doubted] the authority of the Executive Council to suspend an affiliated union without a direct mandate from the convention."[20] Unfortunately, Harrison had more important business than being present at the suspension of almost half the A. F. of L. membership on charges which he questioned by a tribunal which he believed lacked authority to take such action; he claimed inability to be present at the trial.

In the meantime, the Wisconsin Federation of Labor proposed a compromise under which all charges against the unions affiliated with the C.I.O. would be dismissed, the Federation would participate wholeheartedly in the drive with the C.I.O. to organize the mass-production industries, and a committee made up of representatives of craft unions and industrial unions affiliated with the A. F. of L., representatives from state federations of labor, city central bodies, and Federal labor unions, would be appointed by Green to consider the problem of structure as it affected the trade unions and report to the A. F. of L. convention.[21]

## REFERENCES

1. John P. Frey to members of the Executive Council of the American Federation of Labor, July 9, 1936.
2. *Ibid.*
3. Minutes of Executive Council, July 9, 1936.
4. *Ibid.*
5. *Report of Proceedings of the Thirty-fifth Annual Convention of the American Federation of Labor,* 1915, p. 404.
6. *Ibid.*
7. Minutes of Executive Council, July 14, 1936.
8. *Ibid.*
9. *Ibid.*
10. *Ibid.*
11. Minutes of Executive Council, July 15, 1936.
12. *Ibid.*
13. John P. Frey to the Members of the Executive Council of the American Federation of Labor, July 15, 1936.
14. Green to Lewis, July 16, 1936. Similar letters were sent to the heads of other C.I.O. unions.
15. The letter addressed to the Council was signed by John L. Lewis on behalf of the Committee for Industrial Organization, Philip Murray for the United Mine Workers of America, Charles P. Howard for the International Typographical Union, Sidney Hillman for the Amalgamated Clothing Workers of America, Luigi Antonini as Acting President of the International Ladies' Garment Workers' Union, Thomas F. McMahon for the United Textile Workers of America, H. C. Fremming for the Oil Field, Gas, and Refinery Workers of America, Max Zaritsky for the Cap and Millinery Department of the United Hatters, Cap and Millinery Workers' International Union, Thomas H. Brown for the Mine, Mill, and Smelter Workers, Glen McCabe for the Flat Glass Workers of America, Michael Tighe for the Amalgamated Association of Iron, Steel, and Tin Workers of America, Homer Martin for United Automobile Workers of America, and Sherman Dalrymple of the United Rubber Workers of America.
16. Statement to the Members of the United Mine Workers of America by John L. Lewis, *United Mine Workers Journal,* August 1, 1936.

17. Charlton Ogburn to Green, July 22, 1936.
18. Howard to Green, July 11, 1936 (telegram).
19. Howard to Green, July 25, 1936.
20. Harrison to Green, July 31, 1936.
21. *The New York Times,* August 1, 1936.

# XIV

## Trial

BUT the Council was not amenable to compromise; the trial of the absent unions started on schedule on August 3. All members of the Council except Harrison, Weber, and Dubinsky were present. Weber was ill; Dubinsky was absent but arrived before the sessions had ended. Henry Ohl, the president of the Wisconsin Federation of Labor, asked permission to address the Council, and Coefield objected to giving him an opportunity to discuss the question. Green requested that permission be given, and on the motion of Tobin, Ohl was allowed to appear. Ohl repeated the proposals that had earlier been made by the Wisconsin Federation of Labor. Green questioned the right of the C.I.O. unions to intervene in organizing the steel industry, and he alluded to the instructions given by the San Francisco convention that the Council undertake such a campaign. According to Green, the "convention which is the supreme authority, did not instruct any other group. Now as the convention instructed the Council, how could it now surrender its right to originate, manage, and promote a campaign in the steel industry."[1]

Green's argument seems to be almost frivolous, for the refusal to accept the dicta of conventions had never been regarded by the Council or the affiliates as an offense warranting expulsion or suspension of unions. Moreover, Green was aware of the feeble response the A. F. of L. unions had made to his request for financial aid for the campaign of organization in steel. He appears to have been completely lacking in the rudimentary realization of the possible consequence of his action. When Ohl asked that the C.I.O. unions be drawn into the campaigns in the steel and other mass-production industries, Green wanted assurance from Ohl, which he could not give, that the C.I.O. would dissolve. Ohl reminded the Council of the short time before the next convention and of the harmful effects that expulsions of unions might have on the workers of the country. Green then asked if the C.I.O. unions would "not abide by the decision of the Atlantic City convention . . . what assurance have we that they will abide by the decision of the Tampa convention?"[2]

When Tobin and other members of the Council sharply heckled Ohl, Green did intervene with the statement that Ohl was only seeking to preserve the unity of the A. F. of L. Hutcheson, offended by Ohl's argu-

172

ment, wanted to know if there had been introduced at the convention of the Wisconsin Federation of Labor "any resolutions . . . to get the Committee for Industrial Organization to comply with the laws, rules and actions of the American Federation of Labor?"[3] Hutcheson charged that Ohl was asking the Council to retreat while he would allow the C.I.O. to continue. Ohl denied that such was the case; he said that it was imperative to avoid a split.

When the actual trial began, Frey presented the main case and Vice President Edward Bieretz of the International Brotherhood of Electrical Workers presented charges of the infringement of the jurisdiction of his union by organizations supported by the C.I.O. Frey's charges, when they were not general in character, resolved themselves into a claim that the jurisdiction of certain unions had been invaded by organizations affiliated with or supported by the C.I.O. He cited interference with the members of craft unions by a local union of rubber workers, and the statement by an officer of the Firestone local of the Rubber Workers that "we have an industrial union with Machinists, Engineers, and craftsmen in our organization and we intend to keep them, and we will see the Building Trades in hell before we give them up."[4]

Frey also reported statements by the head of the United Rubber Workers, Sherman Dalrymple, that his organization intended to accept craftsmen into its ranks; he described the invasion of the craft jurisdictions by the Mine, Mill, and Smelter Workers, as well as the continual interference with the organizing efforts of the International Association of Machinists by the United Automobile Workers. The Auto Workers, according to Frey, had "issued charters of affiliation to workers in jobbing and contract shops, an area which is specifically excluded from the jurisdiction of the organization in its own charter. The United Auto Workers have accepted tool and diemakers into the organization, a group of workers which are also specifically excluded from membership by its own charter."[5]

Complaints brought up during the trial by the International Brotherhood of Electrical Workers were of another variety. Through Edward Bieretz, a vice president, it charged that the

Committee for Industrial Organization abetted and unduly influenced the National Radio and Allied Trades to reject the proposal of affiliation with the International Brotherhood of Electrical Workers; that the Committee has taken this action arbitrarily; that this action is open defiance of the order of the Executive Council of the American Federation of Labor made at Miami, in January, this year [1936], which granted an orderly way by which the radio manufacturing union could achieve all of its major demands.[6]

The International Brotherhood of Electrical Workers argued that it had chartered unions in the electrical manufacturing industry as early as

1902 in General Electric Company plants in Schenectady, New York; and others had been chartered in Chicago in 1912, and in Lynn, Massachusetts in 1917.

In conclusion Frey accused the C.I.O. of forcing its "plan of organization upon members of other organizations affiliated with the American Federation of Labor," and of "deliberately violating the jurisdictional rights of other International Unions affiliated with the American Federation of Labor." Frey said that the C.I.O. was "attempting to apply their intention to organize labor along so-called industrial or vertical lines by compelling members of other trade unions to become members of the so-called industrial or vertical unions which they [were] endeavoring to force upon the trade union movement by applying dictatorial methods."[7] The setting up of the C.I.O. was analogous, in Frey's mind, to a minority group within an international union setting up a separate organization "for the purpose of enforcing policies which were in open opposition, and in violation to those which have been lawfully adopted by the majority."[8]

The analogy is not valid, for no subordinate group within a national or international union is autonomous or independent of the rules governing the organization. It is a part of a large whole. In contrast, the unions in the C.I.O. were autonomous and free to pursue their own policies within the framework of the Federation. Moreover, encroachments upon the jurisdictions of other unions had never been regarded as serious offenses, and the policies of procrastination and conciliation through conferences had always been used.

Dubinsky arrived on August 5, at the beginning of the Executive Council's discussion of the charge. After explaining his absence—he had attended a meeting of the British Garment Workers' Union—Dubinsky announced that he supported the position of Acting President Antonini, who had aligned himself with other unions in the C.I.O. in rejecting the charges, a position which had the full approval of the General Executive Board of the International Ladies' Garment Workers' Union. Turning to a discussion of the issues, Dubinsky made his position clear:

The evidence that has been submitted was one-sided, but assuming it is accurate, assuming it is so, I question the advisability of proceeding with a policy or plans that are contemplated by this Executive Council. I viewed this question and I am sure that every member of the Executive Council views it as I do, that the situation is quite serious for the American labor movement if you persist in suspending . . . these unions. . . . I see a definite split in the American labor movement; I see a great responsibility that some of you may not imagine. In my judgment better results can be obtained[;] a serious split could be avoided if this Council would not act drastically at this moment and if the matter would be referred to the next convention. I have sufficient experience in the trade union movement; I was confronted with difficult situations, [when we] were the battle ground of Communists in the labor movement. We defeated that element in our union and avoided serious consequences for the entire labor movement.[9]

Dubinsky further argued that action on the part of the Council at this time would lead to a division in the labor movement. He assured the Council that if a suspension were avoided the I.L.G.W. and several other organizations now affiliated to the C.I.O. would withdraw from it. Dubinsky was willing to accept the verdict of the majority of the next convention if the suspension of the unions in the C.I.O. were canceled. He pleaded that the convention would be held in three months and asked the Council to show just a little more patience.[10]

At the conclusion of Dubinsky's statement, Hutcheson asked him whether the Council had been patient. When Dubinsky answered that there was room for more patience, Hutcheson said that the C.I.O. unions had been asked to disassociate from that organization the previous January. "Vice President Dubinsky," said Hutcheson, "pleads now for further time. You can do it in November. If you can do it in November, why not do it in August."[11] Dubinsky pointed out that there was a question of the authority of the Council to act, but there would be no argument as to the authority of the convention. Asked by Wharton and Coefield if he had attended C.I.O. meetings, Dubinsky informed them that he had attended several. The questioning then shifted to the matter of whether or not the C.I.O. unions intended to establish a rival to the Federation. Dubinsky answered: "In my judgment, no. On the other hand, if there is a suspension of these unions, definitely, yes." Green asked if the formation of such an independent organizaiton were based upon "the contingency that the American Federation of Labor and the Executive Council will no longer tolerate the existence of such an organization within the American Federation of Labor."

Dubinsky argued that he did not share Green's view on this matter, but he emphasized the fact that the suspension of twelve unions by the A. F. of L. constituted a split, and that a suspension of that magnitude was basically different from the suspending of two or three unions. "When these unions, including our organization," answered Dubinsky, "are suspended, as is contemplated here, if the I.L.G.W. is to be suspended"—and he claimed the Executive Council had no right or authority to suspend—he believed, he said, that his union would, under these circumstances, "join the other camp."[12]

Green then asked whether an independent movement would be started by the C.I.O. unions if the Council did not postpone action. Dubinsky answered yes, it would be: "Right. If these twelve unions find themselves out, suspended, my information is they are going to form an independent union and my information goes further. It will not only be these twelve unions but several other unions that will resent the authority of the Council. They will probably find themselves in the other camp." Tobin intervened at this point, and although he stressed the seriousness of the step contemplated by the Council, he also emphasized the havoc being caused by the C.I.O. unions. Dubinsky asked: "If I gave you assurance that [the C.I.O. unions] will comply with the decision, even to disbanding the C.I.O., would you consider referring it to the convention?"[13] Dubinsky offered to bring signed statements from the presidents of five unions stating that they would comply with a convention decision.

Instead of a direct answer to this question, Wharton offered the following argument:

There has been delay and toleration on the part of the Council but what has been done . . . while the Council was being tolerant? The evidence shows a carefully drafted plan, carefully executed. They have gone out and interfered with the legitimate organizations affiliated with the American Federation of Labor. They have used every means . . . to defeat the purposes of the American Federation of Labor, disregard the actions and decisions, disregard of every right that organizations affiliated with the American Federation of Labor reasonably believe would be protected by the affiliated unions. No evidence was submitted to this Council that there was the slightest willingness on their part to discontinue their activities pending the consideration of the matter in the convention of the American Federation of Labor. With this plea of Vice President Dubinsky has he uttered any belief that the group will discontinue the activities it is guilty of? They ask us to have patience and tolerance. It seems to me that a time comes in the life of men when if they are going to perform their duty they have to stand up and be counted and be recognized as being in favor of the democratic rules of the American Federation of Labor and if we cannot stand up and be counted in the interest of laws we adopt for our government, then I think it is time for that man to cease to sit on a body that has been elected to carry out the policies of the American Federation of Labor, to protect affiliated organizations and to maintain the solidarity of the movement. Certainly no one on this Council can be charged with having been guilty of one single act that brought about this C.I.O. All organizations have experienced disappointment as well as success, but this is the first time in the history of our movement we have found a powerful group in the organization banding together for the express purpose of disregarding the decision of the American Federation of Labor and setting up what any man must conclude is a dual organization within the American Federation of Labor and for the purpose of setting aside the will of the majority.[14]

The Council voted to convict the C.I.O. and ten of its affiliates. Dubinsky voted "no" on the ground that he had not heard the evidence and because the Council had no such power. Wharton voted to convict, but he objected to exclusion of the International Typographical Union from the list of unions to be suspended.

SUSPENSION

The following findings were announced by the Council:

1. The Committee for Industrial Organization is a dual organization functioning within the American Federation of Labor as such and in its administrative activities it is clearly competing as a rival organization with the American Federation of Labor.

Despite the fact that the final authority in the American Federation of Labor on questions of jurisdiction is the Executive Council and the conventions of the American Federation of Labor, the Committee for Industrial Organization has set itself up as a dual authority, and is now engaged in an effort to determine questions of jurisdiction and to make decisions which are in direct conflict with those of the Executive Council and conventions of the American Federation of Labor.

2. The organizations which participated in the formation of the Committee for Industrial Organization and those which now hold membership therein, are engaged in fostering, maintaining and supporting this dual movement and of fomenting insurrection within the American Federation of Labor.

3. Each of the organizations herein named which holds membership in the Committee for Industrial Organization has thus violated the contract which it entered into with the American Federation of Labor when it was granted a certificate of affiliation, as follows:

"Provided, that the said Union do conform to the Constitution, Laws, Rules and Regulations of American Federation of Labor, and in default thereof, or any part, this Certificate of Affiliation may be suspended or revoked according to the laws of this Federation."

4. The Committee for Industrial Organization and the unions comprising it are by the organization campaigns now being conducted, acting in derogation of the charter rights of national and international unions which are loyal to the American Federation of Labor, and the acts of said Committee and of the unions comprising it constitute rebellion against the administrative organization policies adopted by majority vote of the duly accredited delegates in attendance at the two latest conventions of the American Federation of Labor, specifically with regard to the organization of mass production industries as expressed in the majority report of the Resolution Committee adopted by the Atlantic City Convention, 1935, and in the declaration of organization policy unanimously adopted at the San Francisco convention, 1934, for the organization of mass production industries (as contained in the Report of said Convention on page 586) a resolution and policy strongly endorsed and supported by Delegate John L. Lewis of the United Mine Workers in his speech on the floor of the convention in favor of said resolution, in which he stated that the resolution was not in conflict with the constitutional provision that:

No charter shall be granted by the American Federation of Labor to any National, International, Trade, or Federal Labor Union without a positive and clear definition of the trade jurisdiction claimed by the applicant and the charter shall not be granted if the jurisdiction claimed is a trespass on the jurisdiction of existing affiliated unions, without the written consent of such unions.

WHEREFORE, pursuant to its inherent and constitutional authority and upon the aforementioned findings of fact, the Executive Council orders and directs that each union affiliated with the so-called Committee for Industrial Organization withdraw from and sever relations with said Committee for Industrial Organization and so announce said withdrawal as its choice between the American Federation of Labor and the said Committee for Industrial Organization on or before September 5th, 1936. Any union so announcing its withdrawal from the Committee for Industrial Organization or any organization substituted therefore, by a communication to that effect addressed to the President of the American Federation of Labor on or before September 5th, 1936, and adhering to said withdrawal, shall not thereafter be affected by this order but will be forgiven its breach of its contractual obligation as expressed in its charter, and said contract will remain in full force and effect. Any union now affiliated with the Committee for Industrial Organization not announcing its withdrawal therefrom on or before September 5th, 1936, shall thereupon by this order automatically stand suspended from the American Federation of Labor and from enjoying all and any privileges and benefits of membership and affiliation with the American Federation of Labor.

The unions ordered suspended effective September 5th, 1936, unless prior to that date they withdraw from the Committee for Industrial Organization, are:

United Mine Workers of America
Amalgamated Clothing Workers of America
Oil Field, Gas Well, and Refinery Workers of America
International Union, Mine, Mill, and Smelter Workers
International Ladies' Garment Workers
United Textile Workers of America
Federation of Flat Glass Workers
Amalgamated Association of Iron, Steel, and Tin Workers
International Union, United Automobile Workers of America
United Rubber Workers of America

Green asked the head of the United Hatters, Cap and Millinery Workers whether it was possible for a department in his union to remain affiliated with the C.I.O.[15] It was explained to the A. F. of L. that the United Hatters, Cap and Millinery Workers consisted of two autonomous departments, and under its rules it was permissible for each department to make any decision it saw fit affecting the membership of the department and determining its policies. At this writing, Green was told, only the Cap and Millinery Department of the International Union was affiliated with the Committee for Industrial Organization. Consequently, the United Hatters, Cap and Millinery Workers' International Union, as an International union, was not accordingly affiliated with the Committee.[16] No further action was taken against the United Hatters.

The decision of the Executive Council led to the resignation of Dubinsky, whose union, like the others in the C.I.O., had voted not to comply
with the order of the Executive Council. Dubinsky's resignation from the
Executive Council was challenged by Arthur Wharton; he thought that
Dubinsky should be suspended[17] rather than be allowed to resign.[18]

The Federation was also now faced with the possibility of the C.I.O.
unions challenging the dubious legality of the suspension. Howard was
opposed "to abdicating our rights in [the] Federation because of [the]
Council's illegal decision."[19] The suspensions were described by Lewis as

an act of incredible and crass stupidity . . . dictated by personal selfishness
and frantic fear. . . . The Executive Council would not trust the judgment of
a convention of the Federation which meets in November. It hastened to prejudice the action of the convention by stripping the defendant unions of their
voting privileges. The constitution of the Federation contains no warrant for
the exercise of such arbitrary power. It amounts to an appalling blunder which
Mr. Green and his confederates may continuously rue. We will not disband
the Committee for Industrial Organization. The decision of the Executive Council will not change the policy of the C.I.O. nor will it have any effect upon
the organizing activities of the Committee.

In Dubinsky's view, the suspensions were "high-handed and undemocratic . . . calculated obviously to disenfranchise in advance a large
minority of unions from taking part in the next convention of the American Federation of Labor."[20] There were also protests against the suspensions from forty-one city central labor unions, the most important being
the Chicago Federation of Labor, which had unanimously warned against
the ultimatum issued by the Executive Council. Other important city
central bodies which protested were those in Philidelphia and Erie,
Pennsylvania, San Francisco, Columbus, Ohio, Jersey City, New Jersey,
Birmingham, Alabama, and Akron, Ohio. Protests were also received
from ninety-one local unions, four of them federal labor locals, and the
remainder affiliated with thirty-three international unions. Of the protesting locals, ten were affiliated with the Ladies' Garment Workers' Union;
nine were with the Machinists' Union; seven with the Hotel and Restaurant Employees' Union; five with the International Typographical Union;
and the remainder were scattered among a number of unions.[21]

The state federations of labor were almost equally divided on supporting the Council or the C.I.O.[22] Ten state federations of labor either
endorsed industrial unionism, protested the suspension of the C.I.O.
unions, or suggested a compromise which would have allowed industrial
organization in the mass-production industries. On the other hand, thirteen state federations supported directed or indirectly the position of the
Executive Council. In these organizations, resolutions endorsing industrial
unionism or the C.I.O. were either tabled or defeated.[23]

On September 5, 1936 Green advised the affiliates that the C.I.O. unions had refused to accept the orders of the Executive Council. He advised that "no action be taken by city central bodies and state federations of labor against local unions chartered by these organizations referred to and which are affiliated with city central bodies and state federations of labor for the present at least. Let the status quo be maintained."[24]

REFERENCES

1. *Proceedings of the Executive Council in the Matter of Charges Filed by the Metal Trades Department against the Committee for Industrial Organization and National and International Unions Holding Membership Thereon* (typed), p. 6.

2. *Ibid.*, p. 25.

3. *Ibid.*, p. 43.

4. *Ibid.*, p. 189.

5. *Ibid.*, p. 206.

6. *Ibid.*, p. 249.

7. *Ibid.*, p. 207.

8. *Ibid.*, p. 316.

9. Minutes of Executive Council, August 5, 1936.

10. *Ibid.*

11. *Ibid.*

12. *Ibid.*

13. *Ibid.*

14. *Ibid.*

15. Green to Michael Greene, August 7, 1936.

16. M. F. Greene and M. Zaritsky to Green, August 20, 1936.

17. Dubinsky to Green, September 1, 1936.

18. Wharton to Green, September 4, 1936.

19. Brophy sent Howard's telegram to Brophy to all C.I.O. unions. Quote is from telegram, August 26, 1936.

20. *The New York Times*, August 6, 1936.

21. In archives of A. F. of L.

22. These were in Alabama, California, Kentucky, Georgia, Pennsylvania, Tennessee, Virginia, West Virginia, Wisconsin, and Minnesota.

23. The state federations of labor of the following states were in the latter group: Idaho, Illinois, Maryland, Massachusetts, Mississippi, New Jersey, North Carolina, North Dakota, Ohio, Oklahoma, South Carolina, Washington, Vermont.

24. Green to the Officers of National and International Unions, State Federations of Labor, City Central Bodies, and Directly Affiliated Trade and Federal Labor Unions, and American Federation of Labor Organizers, September 5, 1936.

# *XV*

## In Search of a Peace Formula

HAVING suspended the unions of the C.I.O. without affecting in the least their attitudes or activities, the officers of the Federation faced a dilemma as to what new steps to take. Some officers in C.I.O. unions wanted to avoid a division within the labor movement, and they looked upon separation from the A. F. of L. as a serious emotional wrench. The United Hatters, Cap and Millinery Workers' International Union was internally divided. The union had only recently been formed out of an amalgamation of the men's and women's hat makers' unions. The United Hatters, which operated mainly in the men's hat division, was an old-fashioned union whose officers were personally and ideologically close to the A. F. of L. officers. The women's division, however, was a one-time socialist union which had always regarded itself as part of the needle trades. Zaritsky, who was a founding member of the C.I.O., very likely knew that he could not carry the men's division out with him from the A. F. of L., even if he were willing to allow his union to be suspended. He thereupon took the rather ambiguous position that only the Cap and Millinery department was a member of the C.I.O. and that the International had not joined the Committee. The Executive Council accepted that fiction, although there was some grumbling among the die-hards. A month after the suspensions had gone into effect, Zaritsky decided to attempt a larger role. Under his inspiration the convention of the United Hatters, Cap and Millinery Workers' International Union issued a "Declaration and Resolution on the Committee for Industrial Organization."

After dealing with the necessity for new methods of organization in the mass-production industries and the recognition of that need by the 1934 convention, the statement contended that Zaritsky had joined the C.I.O. "to bring the problem of the organization of the mass-production industries to the fore." The apprehension and bitterness which had been generated by the formation of the C.I.O. were deprecated, as there was "nothing in the purposes of the Committee to justify the fears that have been expressed, or to account for the bitterness which the controversy . . . engendered." The resolution deplored the injection of personalities into the discussion and the questioning of motives of the leaders in the campaign to organize the mass-production unions. The attention of the

Executive Council was called to its grave responsibility for avoiding a permanent rift within the labor movement.

To say that charter rights conferred fifty-five years ago and never exercised, constitute a contract which can never be broken without the consent of the parties, regardless of the consequences, will not be an extenuating circumstance when judgment is finally passed on the Council's action. To say that such rights conferred by such charters are to prevail against every need and interest of both organized and unorganized workers is to carry to an extreme the already extreme Doctrines. . . . No franchise remains in force in a vacuum. The grant of jurisdiction implies its exercise. Neglect of its privileges must render such franchises worthless.

The Declaration requested that the Executive Council allow the suspended organization full representation at the A. F. of L. convention on November 16, 1936, where the issues in dispute could be argued and decided; and it further suggested that pending the decision of the convention, subcommittees of the C.I.O. and the A. F. of L. meet and seek to work out an acceptable formula to the parties involved.[1]

Green notified Zaritsky that

The Executive Council of the American Federation of Labor interprets the resolution unanimously adopted by those in attendance at the Convention of the Hatters, Cap and Millinery Workers' International Union on the 8th day of October, as an expression of a sincere desire for peace within the family of Organized Labor and the establishment of solidarity within the American Federation of Labor.

The Executive Council sincerely desires to heal the breach within the American Federation of Labor for which it is in no way responsible. It will willingly supplement every previous appeal made for the removal of the cause for internal strife and division within the family of Organized Labor, by participating in conferences for the purpose of exploring the possibilities of reconciliation and of terminating the split within the American Federation of Labor which has been so unjustifiably created.

Without commitments or stipulations, a committee of the Executive Council is prepared to meet with a committee representing organizations holding membership with the Committee for Industrial Organization for the purpose of jointly exploring the possibilities of reconciliation and of seeking a formula which might be applied to the solution of differences.

In making this reply to the resolution adopted by the Hatters, Cap and Millinery Workers' International Union Convention the Executive Council is inspired by a keen sense of obligation to all the membership of Organized Labor and of its responsibilities and duties to exercise every effort possible to preserve both solidarity and unity of action within the Organized Labor Movement.[2]

Woll, Harrison, and Felix Knight were appointed to meet with representatives of the C.I.O. Zaritsky was assured by them "that if any one or more or all of the organizations involved will respond in like manner as has the American Federation of Labor, our Committee will be pleased to enter into conference without delay."[3]

Dubinsky asked Lewis to call a meeting of the C.I.O. to consider the letter of the committee appointed by the A. F. of L. in response to the Hatters' resolution.[4] The Acting President of the Mine, Mill, and Smelter Workers went even further. He endorsed the resolution of the Hatters' Union on peace between the A. F. of L. and the C.I.O. and expressed a readiness "to meet in a committee to try to iron out the situation between the C.I.O. and A. F. of L."[5] The officers of the Oil Field, Gas, and Refinery Workers said that they would meet the A. F. of L. committee only if the C.I.O. unions were allowed full representation at the next convention of the A. F. of L.[6]

At this point Lewis announced that no peace conferences could be held until the suspensions were rescinded; but he scheduled a meeting of the C.I.O. at Pittsburgh on November 9. to discuss the proposals of the Woll-Harrison-Knight committee. Zaritsky and Dubinsky were both disappointed at the dilatory tactics being pursued, and Zaritsky felt that the holding of a meeting of the C.I.O. unions on November 9, which was only one week before the convention of the A. F. of L. was scheduled to begin, left little time for negotiations which might settle the differences between the two groups. Anxious to avoid a permanent rift in the labor movement, he wanted an earlier meeting to explore whatever proposals the A. F. of L. committee might make.[7] Lewis advanced the date of the C.I.O. meeting to November 7. Instead of delegating a conference committee, the C.I.O. authorized its chairman to confer with the A. F. of L. president. Green replied immediately to the invitation that had been sent by Howard. Green was willing to meet Lewis but made it clear to Howard that he lacked authority to change the procedure outlined by the Executive Council. Lewis thereupon canceled the conference, which he said would now be "futile."[8]

The appointment of the peace committee was in itself an admission of a blunder by the Executive Council. Less than six weeks after the suspension of ten unions, the Council appointed a committee to seek an accommodation with the suspended organizations. Had the Council not been blinded by hatred and prejudice, it would have listened to the advice and warnings of Harrison and Dubinsky and avoided the step of suspension. Once having suspended these organizations, however, the Council discovered that it lacked any means of influencing them. The suspensions had given free reign to those who felt that affiliation with the A. F. of L. was undesirable for personal or organizational reasons and weakened the position of moderates such as Dubinsky and Zaritsky in the C.I.O.

Howard called Zaritsky's attention to the refusal of the A. F. of L. to accept per capita payments from the suspended organizations over several months, and noted that if they were now required to pay the arrears it might be a considerable burden on some of them. Howard thought that it would be hardly fair to these organizations to be required to pay these large sums unless they were assured of representation in the convention and were given further assurance that the constitution of the American Federation of Labor would be complied with in the matter of suspending or expelling national and internation unions.

The most important phase of this question so far as I was concerned is the precedent established by the Executive Council whereby it can suspend National and International Unions, thereby evading the provision of the constitution which requires a two-thirds roll-call vote of a regular convention to apply such a penalty. . . . While I am desirous of seeing harmonious relations re-established in the American Federation of Labor, I realize the suspended International Unions are at a distinct disadvantage in any peace negotiations until such time as the illegal action of the Executive Council has been rescinded. . . . When all phases of the question are considered it must be apparent that the suspended organizations are at a disadvantage if they should enter a peace conference without the Executive Council first having rescinded its illegal action in suspending National and International Unions.[9]

Rescinding the suspension as a preliminary condition was also requested by the head of the United Rubber Workers of America; he believed that the Executive Council had used suspension to compel the C.I.O. unions to forego the organization of the mass-production industries.[10] Nor was Michael Tighe, the president of the Amalgamated Association of Iron, Steel, and Tin Workers, more favorable to Zaritsky's proposal. He called attention to the plans of the C.I.O. to organize the steel industry. For Tighe, "the organization of the steel industry transcended all other questions. I . . . decided, and so ordered, that every effort should be given to the Steel Workers Organizing Committee, and every assistance rendered which would allow them to accomplish their worthy object."[11]

The delegates to the C.I.O. meeting at Pittsburgh on November 7 refused to appoint a committee to confer with the A. F. of L. In the meantime. Lewis showed his contempt for the action of the Executive Council by having charges filed against President William Green, who was also a member of the United Mine Workers of America. Green was informed that the International Executive Board would assemble in Washington on November 16, 1936 to review complaints that he had participated in "a conspiracy to suspend the United Mine Workers of America from membership in the American Federation of Labor contrary to the laws of said Federation." Green was also charged with failure to conform to the policies of the Miners' Union, with continuing "association and fraternization with avowed enemies of the United Mine Workers of America subsequent to its ejection by aforesaid Federation" and with distortion and misrepresentation of aims and objectives of the Miners' Union. He was summoned to appear for trial on November 18, 1936 in Washington, D. C.[12]

The Executive Board decided that Green had begun working against his own union in January 1936, that he had engaged in a "reprehensible enterprise," and that he had joined the enemies of his own organization. The Board ordered that Green "CEASE and DESIST from his present acts and associations."[13] Of course Green denied the charges and pointed to his obligation to preside over the A. F. of L. convention which was in session on the date of his trial before the Executive Board.

George Berry, the president of the Printing Pressmen's Union, seeking to reconcile the two factions, proposed arbitration of the differences. Berry believed that the suspension of the ten unions was illegal and was tantamount to expulsion.[14] To Green's invitation that the ten suspended return and confer, Lewis replied that "if they want us in Tampa and want to lift the suspension order we can go down to Tampa as peers of the gentlemen there[;] that will be another matter."[15]

The ten suspended unions sent no delegations to the A. F. of L. convention which assembled in Tampa on November 16, 1936. Max Zaritsky represented his union as a delegate, although he had been a founder of the C.I.O. The C.I.O. was given attention in the report of the Executive Council and in twenty resolutions: three from state federations of labor, nine from central labor unions, five from federal unions, two from international unions, one from a department of the A. F. of L.[16] Under a special order of business, Woll, on behalf of the majority of the resolutions committee, recommended the following:

1. That this convention approve of all actions taken, decisions reached and rulings made by the Executive Council, as hereinbefore noted and referred to. We specifically recommend approval of the suspensions noted, and all actions and decisions and rules relating thereto. Lest there be fear that this recommendation may be interpreted to mean permanent suspension or complete severance, let it be understood that the suspension noted shall remain in effect until the present breach be healed and adjusted under such terms and conditions as the Executive Council may deem best in each particular case or in all cases combined.

2. That the Special Committee [Woll, Harrison, and Knight] appointed to discover a basis of settlement be continued with the full faith and confidence of the convention.

3. In the event that by action of the suspended unions they make the present relationship beyond bearing and create a situation that demands a more drastic

procedure, the Executive Council be authorized and empowered to call a special convention of the American Federation of Labor, at such time and place it may deem best, to take such further steps and actions as the emergency of the situation may demand. We counsel this procedure and delegation of authority in the sincere desire to avoid any possible future and permanent severance unless such permanent separation comes as the choice of those who would permanently divide and bring warfare instead of peace and unity into the ranks of labor.[17]

The Executive Council's right to suspend was questioned by Zaritsky, who took umbrage at Woll's reference in his statement to the convention of "organizations composed largely of Jewish workers." Subsequently both Woll and Frey issued denials that the reference was designed to slur Jewish trade unionists. The issues were discussed by a number of speakers, with Frey, Coefield, and Woll offering the main arguments in defense of the Executive Council's action. At 12:35 A.M. the vote was completed, and the recommendations of the resolutions committee were upheld by 21,679 to 2,043, with the following international unions casting negative votes: Teachers, Bakery, Brewery, Brick and Clay, Elevator Constructors, Hatters, American Newspaper Guild, Paper Makers, Sleeping Car Porters, Pulp and Sulphite Workers, and Typographical Union.[18] The large unions supported the Council, and the representatives of the city central labor bodies, in the main, opposed suspension. If the 11,000 votes of the excluded unions had been added to the 2,043 cast against suspension, the Executive Council would have fallen slightly short of the two-thirds majority needed to suspend. Moreover, if representatives of the suspended unions had been present to argue their case, it is reasonable to assume that some unions which voted to support the Executive Council would have voted the other way. A good example is the Printing Pressmen's Union, whose president, George Berry, denounced the suspensions as illegal but voted to uphold the action of the Council.

Suspension forced neither surrender nor a change in plans of the ousted unions. In fact, the C.I.O., as distinct from its unions, began early in 1937 to broaden its activities. The *C.I.O. Organizers Bulletin* of May 19, 1937 announced that the organization was entering a second phase of its activities and that it had begun to organize the miscellaneous industries. It was still concentrating, however, upon "organizing the unorganized rather than on reorganizing the organized." It was not to be successful in the third stage which Lewis was subsequently to embark upon: an attempt to reorganize the building construction trades. The United Mine Workers of America carried the fight against Green a step further, when its Policy Committee, at its meeting on February 15, 1937, called upon the International Executive Board to expel Green from membership for making" gratuitous, insulting, anti-union, strike-breaking statements." The charge drew a rejoinder from the Executive Council declaring its confidence in President Green and pointing to the innumerable times John L. Lewis had placed him in nomination for his office at the A. F. of L. conventions.[19]

Although the attack upon Green could be interpreted as spiteful harassment, the Council did not appear to have any plan of procedure. At the February 1937 meeting of the Council, Green was instructed to advise central bodies not to aid the C.I.O.[20] On the motion of Rickert, Green was given power to disaffiliate C.I.O. unions from A. F. of L. central bodies whenever he regarded such step as advisable. In conformance with the instructions of the Council, Green called upon the organizers and members of A. F. of L. unions to renew their pledges of loyalty to the Federation.[21]

In the meantime, the C.I.O. continued to expand its activity. It announced in March 1937 that organization campaigns would be undertaken in the oil and textile industries. It also announced that thereafter the C.I.O. would charter city and state branches which would parallel similar organizations sponsored by the A. F. of L. The heads of the Federation were hopeful for the restoration of unity, but a number of affiliates adjusted their structural organization to meet the challenge of the C.I.O. The Carpenters' Union announced that it would organize the lumber and sawmill workers on an industrial basis; the International Brotherhood of Electrical Workers was ready to recruit the workers in the electrical manufacturing industry to its ranks regardless of skill or occupation; and the Machinists' Union was willing to absorb all automotive workers into its organization. The expanded plans of the A. F. of L. unions were obviously a reaction to the spectacular successes achieved by the C.I.O. in the automotive industry, where the United Auto Workers were able to win, with Lewis's assistance in the negotiations, a contract in the plants of General Motors Corporation. The contract of the Steel Workers Organizing Committee with the United States Steel Corporation attracted wide interest among unorganized as well as organized workers. In the report of Director John Brophy to the C.I.O. meeting on March 9, 1937, recommendations were made for widely extending the activity of the Committee. Very likely the C.I.O. organizing efforts would have been more constrained if the group had remained a part of the A. F. of L. To counter the expanding efforts of the C.I.O., the metal trades' unions met in Washington on April 8, 1937 to discuss the problems raised by the organizing drives; but they were unable to devise a plan.

Green and Lewis conferred on April 16 and 18. Green proposed that the international unions which had organized the C.I.O. reaffiliate with the A. F. of L. without stipulations or conditions, that a committee representing both sides be appointed for the purpose of dealing with the problems that had developed, and that this committee report to the next convention of the A. F. of L., to be held in October 1937. Lewis refused to agree to this proposal, and his suggestion that the A. F. of L. join the C.I.O. in a body was quickly rejected by Green.[22]

At the meeting of the Executive Council in the latter part of April, Green considered the activities of the C.I.O. and the widespread encroachments upon the jurisdictions of the affiliates:

The country seems to be filled with C.I.O. organizers. Every town and every city, small and great, seems to be filled with organizers employed, appointed and assigned to work for and by the C.I.O. I am amazed at the reports I get from our people in all towns and cities . . . advising they have ten or twelve, or five or six C.I.O. organizers active. . . . Because of these activities there has come a general demand that the Council proceed to take action as decided upon at the . . . [1936] convention. . . . The demand from many sources is that we proceed to call a special convention . . . for the purpose of taking further drastic action.[23]

It was finally agreed to call a special conference at Cincinnati on May 24. Several members of the Council regretted the failure of the A. F. of L. to carry on campaigns comparable to the ones of the rival organization. Green replied that the "one trouble is we have not had the finances to develop a publicity organization such as the C.I.O. has developed, not only here in Washington but in Detroit, Pittsburgh, and other places. Our foes are heavily financed and we are limited."[24]

The C.I.O. demonstrated that, at least in some industries, organization campaigns would have to be conducted on a scale different from those of the past. Yet the Council could not agree at this meeting on the size of an assessment to be levied. When Rickert suggested an assessment of 1 cent per member per month for five months, Coefield moved an amendment that it be ½ a cent for six months. The issue was thereupon postponed until the next meeting of the Council to be held after the conference.[25]

### REFERENCES

1. Declaration and Resolution on Committee for Industrial Organization adopted at convention of United Hatters, Cap and Millinery Workers' International Union on October 8, 1936.

2. Green to Zaritsky, October 13, 1936.

3. Matthew Woll, George M. Harrison, and Felix H. Knight to Zaritsky, October 15, 1936.

4. David Dubinsky to Lewis, October 16, 1936.

5. Dan Orlich to Zaritsky, October 19, 1936.

6. E. C. Conarty to Zaritsky, October 22, 1936.

7. Zaritsky to Lewis, October 19, 1936.

8. Howard to Green, November 7, 1936; Green to Howard, November 7, 1936; Lewis to Green, November 8, 1936.

9. Howard to Zaritsky, October 24, 1936, from the files of the United Hatters, Cap and Millinery Workers' International Union.

10. S. H. Dalrymple to Zaritsky, October 31, 1936.

11. Michael Tighe to Zaritsky, October 21, 1936.

12. Office of the Clerk of the International Executive Board of the United Mine Workers of America to William Green.

13. The Case of William Green: Adopted by the International Executive Board, United Mine Workers of America, Washington, D. C., November 18, 1936, by Walter Smethurst, Clerk of the International Executive Board. Smethurst to Green, November, 1936.

14. *The New York Times*, November 17, 1936.

15. *Ibid.*

16. Two members of the resolutions committee, A. A. Myrup of the Bakery Workers' Union and J. C. Lewis of the Iowa Federation of Labor did not concur in the report.

17. *Report of Proceedings of the Fifty-sixth Annual Convention of the American Federation of Labor,* 1936, pp. 502–503.

18. *Ibid.,* pp. 552–553.

19. To all National and International Unions, State Federations of Labor, City Central Bodies, Metal Trades Department, Building Trades Department, and Union Label Trades Department and All Local Unions Affiliated with the National and International Organizations, and Directly Affiliated with the A. F. of L., from Frank Morrison, February 25, 1937.

20. Minutes of Executive Council, February 19, 1937.

21. To the Officers and Members of All Organizations Affiliated with the American Federation of Labor, February 24, 1937.

22. Minutes of Executive Council, May 25, 1937.

23. Minutes of Executive Council, April 20, 1937.

24. Minutes of Executive Council, April 22, 1937.

25. *Ibid.*

# XVI

## Peace Proposals and Counterattack

In the call for a conference on May 24, the Executive Council described the change in the character of the C.I.O. and the new problems facing the Federation and its unions as a consequence. No longer was the A. F. of L. required to deal

with a group of International Unions, formerly associated with the A. F. of L. . . . who have banded themselves into a group solely for education or mutually protective purposes. Today, instead of a conference, we find these disloyal International Unions in a compact dominated not by a democratic spirit, form or procedure but inspired and directed by the arbitrary dictation of one or more individuals bent upon the destruction of the A. F. of L. and of any individual and organization that fails to submit to their will. . . . The C.I.O. in substance and in fact is no longer a conference—it is a body dual to and destructive of the American Federation of Labor.[1]

The evidence presented was the statement issued by the C.I.O. on March 9, 1937, in which its willingness to charter international unions and city central bodies and state federations of labor had been announced.

In the invitation to the national and international unions, Green warned that

grave questions affecting the rights, jurisdiction and the administrative policies of national and international unions have arisen out of the conflict which has divided the family of labor. The policy which national and international unions, as well as the American Federation of Labor[,] should follow in dealing with developments which have taken place since the adjournment of the Tampa Convention of the American Federation of Labor, should be formulated and definitely understood by the representatives of national and international unions, all of whom are vitally affected. The situation as it exists now needs to be examined, analyzed and carefully considered. Ways and means should be formulated in order to deal with it promptly and successfully.[2]

The following proposals were recommended for adoption to the conference:

First, that the National and International Unions represented in the conference do hereby pledge themselves to consider a resolution at the forthcoming convention of the American Federation of Labor, levying an assessment of one cent (1¢) per member per month effective June 1, and pending formal ratification of the resolution by the convention, the affiliated unions do hereby agree to advance voluntarily the amount of the assessment contemplated by the resolution.

Second, that all National and International Unions affiliated with the American Federation of Labor should expand and carry forward without limit aggressive organizing campaigns within their respective jurisdictions. So far as possible these special organizing campaigns to be coordinated so that the organizing staff of the National and International Unions, as well as of the American Federation of Labor, may effectually carry forward systematic organizing work.

Third, that because of the exigencies of the situation and for the purpose of maintaining the supremacy of the American Federation of Labor in the field of labor in states, cities and municipalities, all National and International Unions call upon and require duly chartered local organizations to become affiliated with State Federations of Labor and City Central Bodies.

Fourth, that the Conference recommend to the Executive Council that all local unions chartered by National and International Unions holding membership in the Committee for Industrial Organization be dissociated from membership in State Federations of Labor and City Central Bodies directly chartered by the American Federation of Labor; this action to be taken in conformity with Section 1, Article XI of the Constitution of the American Federation of Labor.[3]

Almost all international unions sent representatives to the Cincinnati meetings, and the recommendations of the Council were approved. Most unions paid the voluntary assessment and the funds of the Federation were appreciably increased, enabling it to undertake more extensive organizing campaigns. In its report to the 1937 convention, the Council reported that its organizing work had been carried forward and that the joint coordinated drives of the A. F. of L. and its affiliates had netted the Federation during the year almost one million "dues-paying members, men and women who show their determination to become organized through the payment of initiation fees and assessments."[4] The convention voted to continue the assessment that had been recommended at the special conference.

Opposition to the special meeting was expressed by the Executive Council of the International Typographical Union which informed the A. F. of L. that it would "not consider itself bound by any action of such a meeting."[5] Some members of the Executive Council favored ousting the International Typographical Union, especially after its convention had supported Howard's refusal to pay the assessment. Duffy of the Carpenters' Union wanted the Typographical Union suspended, but Green opposed this suggestion on the ground that Howard's activity in the C.I.O was arousing opposition within his own organization, and suspension would rob his opponents of an important issue. Green was also afraid that if the International Typographical Union were suspended, "President Howard would take [the Council] into court and it would result in endless litigation to restrain the Executive Council from suspending the International Typographical Union."[6] Duffy's proposal to suspend that union was rejected by a vote of 9 to 1.

Subsequently the question of Howard's right to be delegate to an A. F. of L. convention while serving as secretary of the C.I.O. was raised by the Carpenters' Union. Delegates from this union protested the seating of Howard at the 1937 convention. Howard challenged the right of the A. F. of L. to deny him a seat at its convention as long as he presented credentials from a "duly accredited and affiliated organization." After a long debate the convention voted to deny Howard a seat, by a vote of 25,376 to 1,245, but gave representation to the International Typographical Union.[7] Howard was defeated for reelection in his union in 1938.

The refusal of the International Typographical Union to pay an assessment of 1 cent per member per month, which had been approved by the A. F. of L. convention of 1937, raised another difficulty. In January 1938 a letter signed by Green and Morrison called attention to the requirement that assessments must be paid if a union was to retain its affiliation with the A. F. of L. Before the 1938 convention, sentiment existed in the Executive Council to refuse to seat the delegates from the Typographical Union unless that organization agreed to pay the assessment. After President Claude Baker assured Green that he would do all in his power to have his union agree to this payment, the Council recommended that the delegates be seated. Nevertheless, the membership of the Typographical Union, on a referendum vote, rejected the payment of this assessment, and at its 1939 convention voted that "continued affiliation [with the A. F. of L.] cannot be dependent upon the International Typographical Union paying said assessment."[8] As a result the Typographical Union was denied affiliation, and although an arrangement for reaffiliation in 1941 was worked out by committees of this union and the A. F. of L. Executive Council, the members, on the advice of Secretary Randolph and Vice President Jack Gill, rejected the agreement by a substantial majority. It was not until June 1944 that the membership of the Typographical Union by a vote of 29,295 to 23,260 decided to reaffiliate with the A. F. of L.[9]

While preparations were going on for the conference of international unions, Green again sought the advice of the Federation's attorney, Charlton Ogburn, on the right of this meeting to revoke the charters of the suspended unions. Ogburn told Green that a court would probably hold that revocation had to be ordered by a regular convention. Ogburn advised against taking the risk of losing in court, especially when the regular convention would meet in six months.[10] It is rather surprising that Ogburn, who had advised that the C.I.O. unions should be suspended even though the convention was to be held only three months later, now saw reason for waiting six months for revocation of charters. The 1937 convention authorized by a vote of 25,616 to 1,227 the revocation of the charters in the event the Executive Council believed it was necessary to protect the Federation.[11]

### PEACE CONFERENCE

During the A. F. of L. convention in 1937, Harvey Fremming, who had temporarily replaced the ailing Charles Howard as secretary of the C.I.O., wired a request on behalf of his organization for a meeting of a committee to be made up of 100 representatives from each organization. While expressing a willingness to meet, the A. F. of L. pointed to the existence of its standing committee ready to confer without strings or commitments. After an exchange of four letters, Philip Murray on behalf of the C.I.O. wired: "Our Committee will meet your Committee October 25 with or without commitments as you prefer, if you decide to cease quibbling and attend conference."[12]

As agreed upon, committees from the two organizations met in Washington on October 25. Frey submitted a brief memorandum on unity in which he stressed the need to eliminate dual organizations that had been established as a result of the issuance of C.I.O. charters, and he pointed not only to the setting up of organizations dual to A. F. of L. unions on a national basis, but to the 368 local unions in jurisdictions in which A. F. of L. unions functioned and to the establishing of central bodies in various cities.[13]

On December 13, 1937 Frey issued a more detailed memorandum, analyzing the situation as he saw it. Although his appraisal of the weakness of the C.I.O. was evidently wishful thinking, he argued that the A. F. of L.

delegates were encouraged . . . that instead of losing ground there had been a material increase in membership. There had been grave apprehension immediately after the adjournment of the Atlantic City Convention [in 1935]. Unquestionably there were doubts in the minds of many delegates at Tampa [in 1936]. But in Denver [in 1937] there was confidence in the virility of their International Unions, confidence in the A. F. of L. . . . . I am thoroughly convinced that any agreement with the C.I.O. reached by the representatives of the A. F. of L. which weakened this confidence, or opened the way for internal dissensions within the A. F. of L., would do far more damage than good."[14]

Hutcheson was no more enthusiastic than Frey about unity. On November 8 he pointedly informed Green that the consensus of opinion of members of our Board was that if any arrangements were made whereby the organizations comprising the C.I.O. were readmitted to the American Federation of Labor as far as the Brotherhood of Carpenters was concerned we might as well sever our affiliation and no longer be a part of the American labor movement through affiliation with the American Federation of Labor and I trust in the negotiations that you will put forth every effort and see that the committee representing the Executive Council does not commit themselves to any understanding that would bring about the above referred to situation.[15]

Hutcheson's concern was the result of the differences that had arisen between his union and the C.I.O. in the logging industry. The Carpenters' Union had been given jurisdiction over logging and sawmill workers and had established some organization in this industry on the West Coast. Many lumbermen were dissatisfied, however, with the relations of their locals to the Carpenters' Union and the kind of membership that had been offered to them. The C.I.O. responded to this dissatisfaction by setting up the International Woodworkers of America which sought to recruit members in competition with the Carpenters' Union. Green tried to allay the fears of the leaders of the Carpenters' Union by assuring them that

there could be no affiliation of the organizations formed by the Committee for Industrial Organizations in the lumber and logging industry except through a return of these organizations to the United Brotherhood of Carpenters and Joiners of America. . . . You may rest absolutely assured that no organization of the International Woodworkers of America will be taken into the American Federation of Labor. These woodworking unions who left your organization must return through your international union if they are ever to become a part of the American Federation of Labor. . . . The same situation prevails in the Electrical Workers' organization. There can be no consideration of any plan of affiliation of the dual electrical workers union except through absorption in and affiliation with the International Electrical Workers of America.[15a]

In answer to Hutcheson's warning not to "permit political pressure to be used in endeavoring to force or bring about an understanding between the committee of the American Federation of Labor and the C.I.O.," Green replied that "there would be no yielding to any political pressure of any kind no matter from what source it comes. Regardless of my views on political matters, I place the interests and welfare of organized labor above and beyond it all."[16] Tobin also showed concern about the possible terms of agreement. On December 1 he wired Green requesting that "no promises or commitments of any kind be made until Executive Council is informed of everything transpiring. International Brotherhood of Teamsters and United Brotherhood of Carpenters, two organizations most seriously involved in this controversy, will not be bound by any promise made in behalf of said organizations until they are fully consulted and have given their consent."[17] The secretary-treasurer of the Carpenters' Union was present when Tobin was dictating his telegram to Green and he approved of its contents. This meant that Tobin's position was shared by the second largest union in the A. F. of L., the United Brotherhood of Carpenters and Joiners of America.

Obviously the A. F. of L. committee was operating under serious difficulties; nevertheless, it continued to seek a basis of agreement. Woll, Harrison, and Bugniazet represented the A. F. of L.; and Murray, Howard, Hillman, Dubinsky, Joseph Curran, Harvey Fremming, James Carey, Michael Quill, Abraham Flaxer, Homer Martin, and Sherman Dalrymple represented the C.I.O. Harrison spoke for the A. F. of L. and Murray for the C.I.O. The first day was spent in discussing procedure, and on the second day the C.I.O. representatives offered the following proposals:

1. The A. F. of L. should declare as one of its basic policies that the organization of the workers in the mass production, marine, public utilities, services and basic fabricating industries be effectuated only on an industrial basis.

2. There shall be created within the American Federation of Labor a department to be known as the Committee for Industrial Organization. All the national and international unions and local industrial unions now affiliated with the C.I.O. shall be affiliated with such new department. This department shall be completely autonomous, operating under its own departmental constitution and shall be directed by its own properly elected officers. This department shall have the complete and sole jurisdiction in regard to (a) the organization of the workers in the industries described in '1' above, and (b) any matters affecting the organization and their members.

3. There shall be called at such time and at such place as may be agreed upon between the American Federation of Labor and the Committee for Industrial Organization a national convention which shall be attended by all national and international unions and local industrial unions affiliated with the American Federation of Labor and the C.I.O. This convention shall be called for the purpose of approving the foregoing agreement and for working out the necessary rules and regulations to effectuate the same and to guarantee the the fulfillment of the program.[18]

The conference discussed the C.I.O. proposals for two days, and on October 27 the A. F. of L. Committee countered with the following recommendations:

1. All national and international unions chartered by the American Federation of Labor now holding membership in the Committee for Industrial Organization are to return and resume active affiliation with the American Federation of Labor. Immediately upon resumption of such affiliation with the American Federation of Labor these organizations will be accorded all rights and privileges enjoyed by them prior to the formation of the Committee for Industrial

Organization and as is provided in the Constitution and Laws of the American Federation of Labor.

2. In respect to other organizations affiliated with the Committee for Industrial Organization: Conferences shall be held immediately between representatives of organizations chartered by the American Federation of Labor and organizations chartered by the Committee for Industrial Organizations and which may be in conflict with each other, for the purpose of bringing about an adjustment to bring the membership into the American Federation of Labor upon terms and conditions mutually agreeable.

3. Organizations and administrative policies not mutually agreed to shall be referred to the next convention of the American Federation of Labor for final decision. In the meantime an aggressive organizing campaign shall be continued and carried forward among unorganized workers along both Industrial and Craft Lines as circumstances and conditions may warrant.

4. The foregoing contemplates the establishment of one united solidified labor movement in America and the termination of division and discord now existing within the ranks of labor. Therefore, the Committee for Industrial Organization shall be immediately dissolved.[19]

Philip Murray, speaking for the C.I.O., found the A. F. of L. proposals unacceptable because they required that the international unions chartered by the A. F. of L. could return

with the distinct understanding that these . . . organizations desert and betray the . . . new national and international unions that have, since November 1936, affiliated themselves with the Committee for Industrial Organization. The proposal suggests abject surrender, dissolution of the Committee for Industrial Organization, which if accepted would have the immediate effect of millions of workers now affiliated with the Committee for Industrial Organization relinquishing their membership in any kind of a labor union, and creating the kind of situation that would render it impossible for any legitimate labor organization to ever reorganize them.[20]

No agreement was reached on the A. F. of L. proposals. Intermittent conferences continued until December 21, 1937. On December 29 Murray submitted a memorandum to the A. F. of L. committee summarizing the situation[21] which showed that the A. F. of L. committee agreed to recognize thirty-two C.I.O. unions.

An agreement was worked out in the end which was temporarily accepted by the C.I.O. committee. There were no obstacles in the road to the return of the twelve original unions which had been suspended, but since the C.I.O. had established twenty additional unions, it was agreed that it would be necessary to consider the position of these twenty unions separately in order to remove the conflict between them and the A. F. of L. unions in the same field. It was therefore agreed:

a. The twelve original A. F. of L. unions would not apply nor be admitted to the A. F. of L. until all matters affecting the twenty new C.I.O. unions were adjusted so that the interests of all would be cared for concurrently.

b. A joint conference committee equally representative of the A. F. of L. and the C.I.O. unions would be established for each of these twenty new C.I.O. and dual or conflicting unions to resolve the conflict or to work out a mutually acceptable understanding.

c. When these conflicts (b) were adjusted, then the membership of the C.I.O. unions would be admitted into the A. F. of L. concurrently with the original A. F. of L. unions.

d. If all other matters were adjusted the A. F. of L. Committee would consider recommending the amending of the Constitution of the A. F. of L. to provide that the Executive Council of the A. F. of L. could only suspend an affiliated International or National Union or revoke its charter on direct authority of a convention of the A. F. of L.

It was also agreed that a special convention of the A. F. of L. would be held within a reasonable time after the adjustment of all issues in dispute and that all organizations would be entitled to representation with all rights and privileges of other A. F. of L. unions. Certain industries would be specified where the industrial form of organization would apply. After an agreement had been reached, it was decided to withhold any public announcement of the contents until Philip Murray, who had been absent from the final session, could be informed. Upon learning of the arrangements, Murray asked to consult with the principals in the C.I.O., obviously meaning Lewis.

At the reconvening of the conference, Murray insisted that the entire controversy be submitted to a subcommittee. After requesting that the agreement reached be carried out, the A. F. of L. committee agreed to a conference through a subcommittee, and Lewis, Murray, Green, and Harrison met as representatives of the two groups. At this meeting, Lewis vetoed the agreement and suggested that the A. F. of L. charter the thirty-two C.I.O. unions and take up all conflicting issues in conference "with the understanding that when these unions were admitted to the A. F. of L. they could not later be suspended if the points of conflict were not adjusted."[22]

The subcommittee would not accept these proposals, arguing that their acceptance would introduce dual unionism into the A. F. of L. According to the A. F. of L. subcommittee,

acceptance of the C.I.O. proposal would not have terminated, but would have enlarged the conflict now raging and would have transferred the war within the Federation itself. In addition, acceptance of the C.I.O. proposal would hereafter have subjected every organization in the American Federation of Labor to constant attack within as well as without the fold. There would not and could not be any public good in a settlement of that nature. In addition to the conflict within the ranks of labor, employers everywhere would be caught between conflicting unions and conflicting forces, although both would be chartered and recognized by the American Federation of Labor. We could not possibly subject the public as well as labor to such an inconceivable relationship.[23]

A controversy on the responsibility for the failure of the peace negotiations ensued. The C.I.O. claimed that the A.F. of L. had surreptitiously sought to have the ten original and well-established C.I.O. unions desert the affiliates which had been formed after the establishment of the C.I.O. This charge was emphatically denied by Woll, and, according to the Murray memorandum, many of these unions would have been absorbed by the A. F. of L. if the agreement had been accepted by both parties.

Technically at least, it can be argued that Lewis wrecked the peace plans, yet it seems from the vantage point of history that his conduct was reasonable and understandable. The Federation had slightly more than a year before suspended these unions, and in spite of the suspensions the C.I.O. had been able to launch organizing drives on an unprecedented scale. Lewis had won a complete victory, at least at the conference table, by the Federation's willingness to take back the twelve unions it had cavalierly suspended, but Lewis may have suspected that a return to his old allegiance might hamper the enthusiasm and energies of the new movement. Moreover, it was difficult to visualize the possibility of failure by a leader whose legions had just stormed the citadels of mass-production industry. In addition, Lewis evidently underestimated the tenacity and vigor of the A. F. of L. unions, once they decided to organize. He also failed to recognize the limitations his own movement would be subjected to by the opposition of industry, by the competition of A. F. of L. unions, and by the political and administrative problems which the mushrooming organizations would generate.

For the A. F. of L., the refusal of the C.I.O. to accept honorable and generous terms meant that a permanent rival to its hegemony over the labor movement was in the field. Of course, it is by no means certain that the acceptance of the peace terms by Lewis and the C.I.O. would have been followed by a tranquil absorption of the recently created unions, or even that the terms would have received the approval of the powerful chieftains of the A. F. of L. who were not directly consulted on terms. Strong forces were opposed to any concessions to the C.I.O. on jurisdiction, and they might have torpedoed the agreement had it been accepted. Only one of the three members of the A. F. of L. subcommittee, Bugniazet, represented a union with an important stake in the industries being invaded by the C.I.O. unions. Nevertheless, Lewis, by refusing to accept what appeared to be favorable terms, had to bear the public stigma for destroying unity in the labor movement.

It is possible, had unity been achieved at this point, that the American labor movement might have avoided some of the problems which it faced as a consequence of the division. Lewis had by that time achieved his major goals; he had demonstrated that workers with government protection could be organized and retained in industrial unions in the mass-production industries, and he had shown that the old "chipping-away" technique of slow organizing was not an effective method for achieving permanent results in the mass-production industries. He had also proved that campaigns to organize large business units had to be financed and carried out on a much more extensive scale than had been customary with the older unions.

Exclusion from the A. F. of L., on the other hand, separated him from a large reservoir of trained and experienced trade unionists who might have been utilized in the organizing campaigns and forced him to rely in too large a measure upon Communist functionaries who "seized" control of many newly formed unions and used them for their own political ends. Lewis was to discover that these auxiliaries would not easily surrender their positions nor would they blindly follow his leadership when his aims conflicted with their own political objectives.

A. F. OF L. MEMBERSHIP 1933–1939

(*in thousands*)

| Year | Membership | Year | Membership |
|------|-----------|------|-----------|
| 1933 | 2,126 | 1937 | 2,860 |
| 1934 | 2,608 | 1938 | 3,623 |
| 1935 | 3,045 | 1939 | 4,000 |
| 1936 | 3,422 | | |

Another effect of the separation of the C.I.O. from the A. F. of L. was a diffusion of effort by invasion of organized industries and areas. The most extreme instance of this was Lewis's effort to launch an organizing campaign in the building-construction industry. This was a colossal failure and the attempt to duplicate existing organizations was not only a perversion of the original purpose of the C.I.O. but a serious drain on its trained personnel and finances. Other examples of duplication in the service, paper, office work, government, and even in the metal and machinery trades can be found. Some of the campaigns were devised as harassing operations against the A. F. of L., but they spent the money and human resources which the C.I.O. did not have in inexhaustible measure. Unity in 1937 might have enabled the C.I.O. to concentrate upon its initially chosen area, the mass-production industries.

By the end of 1937 the Federation had recovered from its initial shock. The loss of 982,343 members as a result of the suspension of the C.I.O.

unions in 1936 had been more than made up by 1938. In fact, membership which had steadily risen from 1933, except for the losses of the C.I.O. defection, moved steadily and strongly upward; by 1939 it was above 4 million.

During the same period, the C.I.O. was expanding at a rate unprecedented in American labor history. But, as Frey pointed out, the A. F. of L. unions in the fall of 1937 were no longer discouraged. Their own membership gains, coupled with the defeat inflicted upon the Steel Workers Organizing Committee in the spring of 1937 by the "Little Steel" companies, destroyed the aura of invincibility which had surrounded the C.I.O. since its inception. The Federation took steps to strengthen its own internal forces and began campaigns to eliminate the influence of the C.I.O. on its members. This unpublicized campaign, begun in 1936, went into high gear with the revocation of the charters of the C.I.O. organizations.

### COUNTERATTACK

Upon the receipt of information that a central labor union had endorsed the position of the C.I.O., Green's practice was to write to the international presidents of A. F. of L. unions whose local organizations might be affiliated with that central body and request that they communicate with their locals and inform them of the position the international had taken on this issue. For example, when the Janesville, Wisconsin, Central Labor Union endorsed the organization of the mass-production workers into industrial unions, Green advised the heads of twenty international unions having locals in Janesville "to take the matter up with your local for the purpose of insuring its full support of the legal, official organization policy of the American Federation of Labor."[24] As a rule the internationals followed Green's recommendation.

When the Central Labor Union of Great Falls donated $25 to a C.I.O. union, Hutcheson instructed a local of his organization (the Carpenters' Union) to cease paying per capita to that body since the Brotherhood would not "permit locals of our Brotherhood to remain affiliated with a central body that will not only recognize, but permit speakers of the C.I.O. and their affiliated organizations to appear before them."[25] The head of the Musicians' Union, Joseph Weber, learned through Green that a local of his organization was favorable to the C.I.O. Green wrote that the Federation's "efforts to place the Rochester Central Trades and Labor Council upon a sound and enduring American Federation of Labor basis have been considerably hampered and hindered by delegates to the Council."[26] Weber wrote his local officer that "it is understood you will have to vote with the A. F. of L."[27] As a result of the pressure of his international union, a business agent of the International Brotherhood of Electrical Workers, after an investigation by a vice president of his union, revised his views on the C.I.O.[28]

The effort to limit the influence of the C.I.O. to the areas where the mass-production industries were concentrated and where its shock tactics could be effective went on through the first years of the C.I.O. campaigns. The major burden fell upon Green, who sent out hundreds of letters to the heads of unions whose locals might have expressed themselves favorable to the C.I.O. or might have belonged to central bodies favorable to such views. Usually, the heads of the internationals communicated with their locals and either urged or ordered, depending upon the climate of the particular union, cooperation with the A. F. of L. In response to information that a local union of Bricklayers in Utah had joined a council made up of A. F. of L. and C.I.O. unions, President Bates of the Bricklayers' Union wrote: "We have notified our subordinate union to immediately disconnect itself from this Council, if they are part of this movement. We have also notified Don R. Evans, a member of our subordinate union No. 1 Utah, to cease and desist from further activity in the furtherance of this dual movement."[29]

Harrison reported that a member of his local union had resigned from this dual body. The presidents of the Barbers, Theatrical Stage Employees, and Machinists also directed their local officers to withdraw from this Council.[30] Tobin informed an officer of his union that "under no circumstances can this International Union or any of its locals, participate in any way, or give encouragement in any way, to the setting up of any dual organization to the American Federation of Labor, or any of its branches. I order you to withdraw your name immediately from this undertaking."[31]

In addition, the A. F. of L. revoked the charter of city centrals and state federations of labor which insisted upon maintaining friendly relations with the C.I.O. or its unions. Officers of central bodies favorable to the C.I.O. were removed. In West Virginia, Green demanded the ousting of all C.I.O. locals from membership of the West Virginia Federation of Labor, and John B. Easton, its president, answered that if all the locals of C.I.O. unions were "expelled, the Federation would be so weak that it would be of no material benefit to the workers of the State."[32] Nevertheless, Green told him that as the head of a subordinate organization chartered by the Federation it was his duty to conform to the rules and interests of the A. F. of L. The State Federation was, after a trial upon charges made by Green against it, reorganized.[33] Similar action was taken against the Kentucky and Pennsylvania Federations of Labor. Charters of central labor unions which favored C.I.O. unions in any way or allowed affiliates of the C.I.O. to be members were revoked after a trial.

The action of the A. F. of L. isolated the C.I.O. from the support of the general labor movement, except in areas where unions such as the United Mine Workers of America were the predominant organization. Its shock tactics were admirably suited to the organization of the mass-production industries where employers, as the La Follette Committee (investigating "oppressive labor practices" by employers) demonstrated, could by the use of labor spies and armed guards and disruptive tactics within the unions frustrate organization.[34] In local communities with diverse and many industries, these tactics could not be as effective. First, the workers did not all face the same problems either on the economic or organizational planes. Consequently, special appeals had to be directed toward various groups.

Second, the hostility or even the indifference of the local labor movement inevitably hampered the C.I.O. campaigns on this level. In addition, the revived activity of the A. F. of L. unions inevitably intensified opposition to the invasion of the C.I.O. when it began building unions dual to existing local organizations. As a result, the C.I.O. failed in the first years of its existence and throughout its independent history to penetrate in any great measure the industries where the A. F. of L. unions had heretofore been active and had established viable and effective unions. The strength of the A. F. of L. was in the diffusion of its membership geographically and industrially. Although none of the A. F. of L. unions engaged in organizing campaigns as extensive or dramatic as those of the C.I.O., the efforts of many organizations, each operating in a limited area, finally made themselves felt. The A. F. of L. grew larger than ever in its history, and, because its membership was spread through many industries and firms, its unions could regard their gains as permanent accretions of strength.

REFERENCES

1. Statement of Executive Council, Minutes of Executive Council, April 22, 1937.

2. Green to Presidents and Secretaries of National and International Unions, April 30, 1937.

3. To Representatives of National and International Unions Affiliated With the American Federation of Labor in Attendance at this Conference, May 24, 1937.

4. *Report of Proceedings of the Fifty-seventh Annual Convention of the American Federation of Labor,* 1937, p. 110.

5. Woodruff Randolph to Frank Morrison, May 22, 1937.

6. Minutes of Executive Council, May 23, 1937.

7. *Report of Proceedings of the Fifty-seventh Annual Convention of the American Federation of Labor,* 1937, pp. 457–458.

8. *Report of Proceedings of the Fifty-ninth Annual Convention of the American Federation of Labor*, 1939, p. 357.

9. Randolph to Green, June 7, 1944.

10. Charlton Ogburn to Green, April 21, 1937.

11. *American Federation Weekly News Service*, October 16, 1937.

12. Quote is from Murray to Morrison, October 16, 1937. Other letters were from Fremming to Morrison, October 12, 1937; Morrison to Fremming, October 14, 1937; Fremming to Morrison, October 15, 1937; Morrison to Fremming, October 15, 1937.

13. Memorandum by John Frey on Essential Conditions for Unity, October 21, 1937.

14. Frey to Committee Representing the A. F. of L. in Conference with Committee Representing C.I.O., December 13, 1937.

15. Hutcheson to Green, November 8, 1937.

15a. Green to Hutcheson, November 12, 1937.

16. Hutcheson's quote is from his letter of November 8, and Green's from the letter of November 12.

17. Tobin to Green, December 1, 1937.

18. Press release by the American Federation of Labor, October 25, 1937.

19. Press release by the A. F. of L., October 27, 1937.

20. Statement of Philip Murray, October 27, 1937. There is some discrepancy in the numbers of unions in the C.I.O. because two of the original unions were not suspended at the same time.

21. In files of the A. F. of L.

22. *Report of Proceedings of the Fifty-eighth Annual Convention of the American Federation of Labor*, 1938, pp. 89–91.

23. Release by A. F. of L., December 21, 1937.

24. Letter to Secretaries of Automobile Workers, Bakery, Barbers, Bricklayers, Railway Carmen, Carpenters, Cigarmakers, Post Office Clerks, Railway Clerks, Electrical Workers, Letter Carriers, Machinists, Meat Cutters, Sheet Metal Workers, Musicians, Painters, Plumbers, State Employees, Teamsters, February 28, 1936.

25. Hutcheson to Green, December 17, 1937.

26. Green to Weber, April 1, 1938.

27. Weber to Leonard Campbell, April 25, 1938.

28. Daniel Tracy to Green, October 24, 1938.

29. Bates to Green, March 11, 1941.

30. W. C. Birthright to Green, March 14, 1941; Louis Krouse to Green, March 14, 1941; Harvey Brown to Green, March 17, 1941.

31. Tobin to Fulmer H. Latter, March 11, 1941.

32. John B. Easton to Green, August 16, 1937.

33. Green to Easton, August 4, 1937.

34. *Hearings before a Subcommittee of the Committee on Education and Labor, United States Senate 76th Congress, 1st Session on S. 1970* (Washington: Government Printing Office, 1939).

# *XVII*

## Defense

IN peacetime the A. F. of L. opposed military conscription and in general pursued a pacifist policy. It took note of a movement for a military draft by registering its opposition to authorizing the President of the United States to muster workers into the armed services when there was no war.[1] The elevation of Hitler to power in Germany, the suppression of the German trade union movement, and the inauguration of the Nazi racial policies were watched by the Federation leaders with growing concern. In a statement issued in 1933, Green said that "American labor is becoming convinced that something more than protest is needed in dealing with the Nazis. We are being forced to the conclusion that a boycott is the only thing that will bring home to the German tyrants the abhorrence in which their rule is held by the rest of the world."[2]

In its report to the 1933 convention, the Executive Council voiced "profound regret and indignation" at the brutal suppression of the German labor movement, which "has been equalled only by the ruthless persecution of the Jewish people. Persecution of this kind," the Council said, "arouses intense feeling among the membership of organized labor. . . . We abhor racial persecution and we protest vigorously against the persecution of the Jewish people of Germany." The Council recommended that the Federation join with other public-spirited groups in boycotting German goods and services "until the German government recognizes the right of the working people of Germany to organize into bona fide, independent trade unions of their own choosing, and until Germany ceases its repressive policy of persecution of Jewish people."[3]

In the discussion of the proposal on the convention floor, Green assailed the conduct of the Nazi government and declared he could not "as a responsible leader . . . allow this case to come up without registering not only my judgment, but attempting to convey to you my feelings." He pleaded for unanimous adoption of the report of the resolutions committee so "that in ringing and clear tones, [it] will carry across the sea, so those in charge of the persecution of our German friends, your brothers, your sisters, and families who are suffering, will know and understand what we say. . . . Such a declaration will encourage and hearten and strengthen the morale and the purpose and the determination of our German trade unionists abroad to fight for the re-establishment of the trade union in Germany."⁴ The proposal was unanimously adopted.

Carrying out the instructions of the convention, Green requested the friends and organizations of labor to boycott German-made goods. John J. Fitzpatrick, Joseph P. Ryan, and Selma Borchardt were appointed to a committee that was to aid in carrying it out. In reporting to the 1934 convention, the Executive Council recognized the right of the German people to govern themselves and to adopt their own policies without interference from any other nation. It was not, they said, the intent of the A. F. of L. to fight any political order in Germany or any program of the German people. The Federation was "asking only that the annihilation of German trade unions shall cease and the persecution of German working people and of Jewish people merely because they are Jews, be terminated."⁵

After the committee directing the boycott on behalf of the A. F. of L. had reported that some measure of success had been attained, the delegates voted its continuation. Green promised that he would do all in his power to make the boycott a success. The convention also voted to support the "Chest for Liberation of Workers of Europe," which was established to seek financial aid for European trade unionists.⁶

Green invited a group of trade union leaders, among them John L. Lewis, Matthew Woll, David Dubinsky, Arthur Wharton, and Charles P. Howard, to be members of the Chest for Liberation of Workers of Europe. William English Walling was appointed Executive Director. In a circular letter to all city central labor unions and state federations of labor, Green called attention to the consideration given by the convention to the persecution of trade unionists and racial minorities in Germany and to the convention's endorsement of the Chest for Liberation of Workers of Europe. It was an appeal to American trade unionists for "financial support and contributions . . . and ultimately to unite all American wage earners not only as a voice of protest of that which is going on abroad, but likewise to serve as legions against similar tendencies and practices taking foot in our country."⁷

When he was attacked for his criticism of Nazi Germany, Green replied that the "American Federation of Labor will not remain silent when a tyrant like Hitler destroys a splendid organized labor movement in Germany similar to the organized labor movement in America, drives their leaders either out of Germany or places them in detention camps for the commission of no crime, takes the property these unions have accumulated over a period of years and forbids the existence of free trade unions."⁸ Walter Citrine, Gerhart Seger, and Julius Deutsch toured the United States under the auspices of this group. In the first year $46,000 was collected, and most of this was sent to Europe to be used in Germany and Italy in aid of fascist victims.[9]

The 1935 convention authorized the continuation of the boycott against German goods and services, urged all American sport organizations not to participate in the German Olympic games in Berlin, and asked for all possible support for the labor Chest for Liberation of Workers of Europe.[10] The 1936 convention reaffirmed the action, and the Federation continued to oppose Hitler's government and its persecution of trade unionists, socialists, racial minorities, and Catholics. In November 1938 Green spoke out against the intensified persecution of minorities in Germany. He denounced

the atrocities perpetrated upon helpless Jewish people residing in Germany . . . unparalleled during any period in the world's history. . . . We protest the brutal iniquities perpetrated upon a helpless race. We call upon the men and women of Labor in America, with all their friends, to assist in the mobilization of the moral strength of the world in opposition to the indefinable and inhuman policy pursued by the German government. . . . Labor cannot remain silent or passive. . . . I am calling upon the men and women of labor in a way I have never called upon you before, to boycott German goods and German service . . . because of the amazing and shocking treatment which is being accorded Jewish people and members of the Catholic faith in Germany and because the Fifty-eighth Annual Convention of the American Federation of Labor . . . urged "intensification of our efforts in behalf of the persecuted and oppressed minorities in Germany."[11]

Although the Federation was quick to denounce Hitler, it opposed any action by the United States government which might take this country into war. Green insisted that the United States was devoted to peace and would "never again . . . become involved in a European conflict."[12] He called for the strengthening of the recently enacted neutrality legislation that was designed to protect the United States against foreign entanglements. The Federation drew a line between its own action against a government and the conduct of the United States in foreign affairs. It was against any acts by the American government which might lead to accentuating international differences and increasing the probability of involvement in war. Consequently, the Executive Council refused to approve a request from Walter M. Citrine, the Secretary of the British Trades Union Congress, that the A. F. of L. use its influence on the United States government to impose an embargo upon Japanese goods after Japan invaded China. The Federation was willing to continue the boycott against Japanese goods ordered by the 1938 convention; nevertheless, it did not want to advocate a policy that might lead to open hostilities. The Council, Green told Citrine, was "reluctant to make representations to United States Government . . . but will consult with Government officials regarding any policy of cooperation with any other government which [the government] may formulate and carry into effect."[13]

When the war in Europe began in 1939, the A. F. of L. was completely opposed to the involvement of the United States. Favoring United States mediation of the conflict, the convention delegates demanded that "our government shall pursue a judicious policy, exercising care and caution and a firm determination to avoid involvement in European conflicts or in European wars."[14]

The Executive Council saw the so-called phony war phase as a temporary one, and in a statement in February 1940 it warned that war might soon break out with renewed fury. But again the Council called upon the American government to pursue a policy of "strict neutrality and peace," and enunciated the following statements of policy: (1) The United States should maintain strict neutrality and keep out of the European war; (2) the A. F. of L. condemned Soviet imperialism and the attack upon Finland; (3) the Federation denounced the Nazi-Soviet dismemberment of Poland; (4) it extended sympathy to the victims of racial and religious persecution in Europe; and (5) the Federation called upon the United States government to give every possible aid to Finland so that it could resist Soviet aggression without endangering our neutrality.[15]

After representatives of German labor met with the Executive Council, the Federation leaders appealed to all members to render every possible aid so that the representatives of free German labor would be able to carry on their work of restoring "democracy and democratic government to the German people. They are performing an honorable work and deserve a full measure of support."[16] At the same time George Meany appealed to President Roosevelt to help a group of German trade union leaders in Copenhagen, Denmark, who were in danger from the overrunning of their country by the Nazis. In a letter to General Edward M. Watson, one of Roosevelt's assistants, Meany requested him to "convey this information to the President as soon as possible with the urgent plea on behalf of the American Federation of Labor that he request the American Legation to use its good offices on behalf of these former members of the trade union movement in Germany."[17]

The invasion of Holland and Belgium in the spring of 1940 was condemned, but the Executive Council still did not change its conviction that the American government should remain out of the European war. The Council declared:

We in America are devoted to the cause of freedom and democracy. We are shocked by what is going on in Europe. But we do not see how the cause of democracy could be furthered by our involvement in a foreign war. The opposite is true. Democracy and freedom on this earth would be jeopardized if the United States were to go to war. Our function as a nation should be and must be to safeguard and maintain peace and democracy in the Western Continent by maintaining strict neutrality regardless of our sympathy and feelings toward the victims of totalitarian aggression in Europe.[18]

The A. F. of L. endorsed the efforts of the government "in assisting Great Britain and her allies to withstand the aggression of the totalitarian powers . . . thus defending the principles and ideals of human rights, freedom and democracy."[19] However, the Council attacked the bills offered in Congress which aimed to place restraints upon labor organizations. According to the Council the war was one of "machines and men who make them. . . . Efficiency and regularity in production are essential for the establishment of our own adequate defense. We understand, too, that it is essential for the preservation of American democracy that Great Britain win the war and that for her to do so America must supply her with materials, machines and weapons."[20]

After Hitler's successful invasion of the Low Countries and the request by President Roosevelt that the United States initiate an expanded defense program, the Federation wanted Congress to appropriate at once the funds needed. At the same time the Council warned against emotional attempts to suspend labor legislation. Such suspension, the Council said, might have a deleterious effect on war production.[21]

At the same session the Executive Council adopted a confidential statement in which it acknowledged the possibility of the United States becoming a participant in the war. In that event, the Council believed there would immediately arise the question of regulation and control over some civilian liberties and activities which were enjoyed without restriction in time of peace. The Federation approved of the National Defense Act and authorized President Green to cooperate with the Federal government in carrying out its provisions.

In connection with such cooperation the committee should at all times have in mind that civilian war-time agencies should be representative of labor, management and the public; that such civilian agencies as are established, should at all times have in their personnel representatives of labor and of management who have been approved by those they represent. Furthermore, should a crisis arise which requires national planning because of a national emergency, that the American Federation of Labor should place itself in a position before such crisis develops, as will assure its recognition and its participation in all governmental planning agencies having to do with civilian activities. It is further recommended that upon the appointment of such a committee, the President of the American Federation of Labor shall notify the Assistant Secretary of War of the committee's desire to be consulted in connection with all questions affecting civilians and civilian activities during a period of national emergency and of its instructions by the Executive Council to give every cooperation possible. This action of the Executive Council is to remain as an instruction to the President of the American Federation of Labor, to be kept confidential, for publicity at this time would create public fears, or might also operate to prevent the Assistant Secretary of War from fully carrying out his responsibilities under the National Defense Act.[22]

In harmony with the program described by the A. F. of L., the presidents of the unions in the Metal Trades Department announced their readiness to help in the training of an adequate supply of skilled workers for defense industries. The heads of these unions acknowledged that in the near future it might be necessary to institute programs of training and retraining for some jobs in defense industries. The declaration pledged the unions to give every assistance to place skilled workmen where they were required for national emergency production, to protect the right of labor to organize voluntarily into trade unions, to bargain collectively with employers, and to make use of the basic rights of American citizens. In the national emergency, these unions, conscious of their responsibility to contribute their support to the nation's defense, promised to protect and to perpetuate "those institutions of freedom which are now menaced by totalitarian powers."[23]

### MANPOWER

As Hitler's armies overran neutral and belligerent nations and stopped at the English Channel, the American government became more concerned with the state of its defense. In October 1940 Sidney Hillman was appointed chairman of the Labor Advisory Committee of the National Defense Commission. Green had not been informed of the pending appointment, and some members of the A. F. of L. wanted to register their disapproval. On further consideration, Green decided that it would be better if the A. F. of L. raised no question of the appointment. Hillman assured Green that he wanted to be fair and to do a good job. When Green demanded that the Federation be recognized as the predominating organization, Hillman replied that he thoroughly understood the A. F. of L. position. Hillman "stated that as evidence of his position he had advised Mr. Denny Lewis that they would have nothing to do with the building trades organization in the first place and had requested that the C.I.O. stay out of that field."[24]

Hillman's friendly attitude toward the A. F. of L. unions in the building trades did not influence the resident members of the Executive Council. They refused to appoint any one to work with him. Hillman, consequently, went over their heads and was able to gain the cooperation of the building trades' unions. At a second meeting of the resident members of the Executive Council, Daniel Tracy, the president of the Electrical Workers' Union, announced that he was "going along with Hillman," and several other A. F. of L. leaders, among them Harry Bates of the Bricklayers' Union, suggested a cooperative policy.[25] Hillman followed the policy he had explained to Green, and on July 22, 1941 he signed on behalf of the Office of Production Management, a "Memorandum of Agreement between the Representatives of Government Agencies Engaged in Defense Construction and the Building and Construction Trades Department of the American Federation of Labor." The memorandum laid down the labor policy that would be followed by the United States government on defense construction projects.[26]

The policy of dealing exclusively with the A. F. of L. building trades faced a serious challenge when the Currier Lumber Company of Detroit signed a closed-shop agreement with the C.I.O. United Construction Workers Organizing Committee for work on a housing contract for the Federal Works Agency. The A. F. of L. building trades' unions regarded the contract between this company, which had operated as a nonunion lumber concern, and the C.I.O. construction union as a threat to its position. Both the A. F. of L. and the Building and Construction Trades Department protested, and Sidney Hillman, in spite of his close association with the C.I.O., ordered cancellation of the agreement with the C.I.O. union. Both A. D. Lewis, who headed the Construction Workers Organizing Committee, and his brother, John L. Lewis, assailed Hillman's decision and Thurman Arnold announced that his antitrust division in the United States Department of Justice would look into the order. Hillman stood his ground and denounced the Currier agreement before the Truman Committee investigating defense operations.

Murray, who headed the C.I.O. at the time, requested President Roosevelt to direct the Office of Production Management "to set aside the . . . discriminatory stabilization agreement and thereafter proceed on a basis which would afford equality of treatment for the C.I.O., its affiliated unions, and members, on construction jobs."[27] Hillman, receiving some support from the A. F. of L. unions in the building trades, was invited to address the convention of the Building and Construction Trades Department over the objection of William Hutcheson, who opposed the invitation because of Hillman's membership in the C.I.O. John Coyne of the Building Trades Department defended Hillman's conduct in matters affecting the interests of the building trades' unions.

Toward the end of 1940, both the A. F. of L. and the C.I.O. proposed plans for strengthening the defense program. Murray suggested an industry-council plan which called for the establishment by the President of the United States of a council composed of equal representatives of labor, industry, and government in each major defense industry. Murray's plan would have given to industry councils powers to ascertain the labor needs of each industry and the production facilities by which they could be met. Over the industry councils, Murray advocated a National Defense Board composed of equal representatives of labor and industry with the President of the United States as chairman. This Board would be given over-all power to determine national policies relating to national defense.[28]

In contrast, the Federation's plan concentrated upon gaining representation for labor in defense agencies. At its meeting in May 1941 the Council submitted the following recommendations for making the administration of the defense establishment more efficient:

1. Labor was to be given representation through its unions so as to advise in the formation of basic principles and plans for defense production and the setting up of production plans and agencies.

2. In agencies where labor policies were formulated, labor should be represented through its unions.

3. Through adequate union representation, labor was to be allowed to participate in determining emergency controls and the allocation of skilled labor and in the regulating of apprenticeships and other forms of training.

4. Labor standards embodied in legislation were to be safeguarded, and the social insurance rights of workers in defense industries protected.[29]

The Executive Council's position was subsequently ratified by the convention. The A. F. of L. avowed that "grave injustice was done to its membership and to the principle of representation when the most representative organization of workers within this country was not given representation on the Defense Commission and the organization was not asked to name representatives to the committee advisory to the labor member of the Commission. The least that can be done to right this injustice is to make this principle and rule the guide in reorganization of the defense agencies."[30]

The members of the Executive Council increasingly feared that the needs of defense and the frequent labor disputes might stimulate the movement for compulsory arbitration or other types of government regulation of employment. Hutcheson suggested that a program of dispute-settlement similar to the one in effect during World War I be adopted. He thought that the action of the executive board of the Carpenters' Union in limiting initiation fees to a maximum of $50 was an example of cooperation with the defense effort. Secretary-Treasurer Meany favored a statement opposing compulsory work legislation and a plea to national and international unions to avoid work stoppages.[31] The Council then

reaffirmed its opposition to any development, system, or regulation with reference to National Defense in particular or stabilization in general which in any way may challenge or replace or weaken voluntary collective bargaining in the determining of wages and other conditions of work. We insist that all production for National Defense and for any other purpose must be done by free labor and not by labor working under dictation or compulsion.

Management and labor alone, cooperating with one another in our industrial plants produce the articles required for National Defense and for general consumption. Governmental committees, Boards, or other Federal Agencies may be of valuable assistance. However, such bodies or agencies do not and can not perform the actual work connected with production. That is a task performed by management and labor. Management and labor must therefore be given a clear and unrestricted field to cooperate and this cooperation can be established in its fullest measure through the method of voluntary collective bargaining. The Executive Council views with apprehension the efforts made in the name of stabilization to limit or restrict the field of collective bargaining and in its place set up governmental authorities to determine the rules, regulations, and the conditions which bear equally upon management and labor and to the extent to which they are applied interfere with free labor and free enterprise and thereby impair the possibilities of genuine cooperation in our industrial life.[32]

On March 19, 1941 President Roosevelt appointed a tripartite National Mediation Board; two labor members were selected from both the C.I.O. and A. F. of L. George Meany and George M. Harrison represented the Federation; Philip Murray and Thomas Kennedy represented the United Mine Workers of America and the C.I.O. The functions of the Board were to help in the settlement of labor disputes which threatened to interfere with the defense effort by assisting the parties to negotiate agreements, to afford means for voluntary arbitration, and to designate arbitrators when requested by the parties in a dispute. The Board was also to aid the parties in devising methods for settling future disputes when they arose; the United States Secretary of Labor was authorized to certify to the Board disputes which threatened to obstruct defense production.[33]

The A. F. of L. was critical of the performance of the War Production Board in its use of labor. At the 1942 convention, the delegates discussed unemployment and the lack of resources which had arisen as a result of the curtailment of civilian production. The Federation suggested that the Federal government ought to share in the cost of transporting workers and their families to the centers where they might be fruitfully employed.[34] Nor were the delegates satisfied with the role that had been given to labor in the war effort. Consequently, the Federation demanded that labor be included in the higher levels of operation and policy making. "The participation of the American Federation of Labor at this point should reinforce the operating work of Labor in the lower levels of the War Production Board. . . . It would entirely remove the distrust which the workingmen and workingwomen of this country now feel in relation to the various decisions and changes which are being made frequently without a voice by Labor on important matters which bring about an entire change in their method of living."[35] The A. F. of L. opposed the overextension of the hours of labor and offered the testimony of British labor leaders to prove that an undue prolongation of the work day was harmful to war production and to the work force.

As the war continued, some government quarters favored a labor draft. Immediately the A. F. of L. turned down the proposal and advocated instead better planning of labor needs so as to improve the utilization of the existing supply of labor. The Federation conceded that manpower was still being wasted through ineffective usage, high turnover, and restrictive practices; but it argued that large unused manpower resources, especially employable women, existed, and no reason for compulsion at this stage could be found.[36] At the same time, Green attacked President Roosevelt's request for a National Service bill which would have authorized the government to draft labor on strike. During a conference with President Roosevelt, Green made it clear that the A. F. of L. would denounce any measure for labor conscription.[37] Writing to members of Congress, Green said that the "American Federation of Labor has been unwilling to extend approval to compulsory service legislation because we are thoroughly convinced that the substitution of involuntary servitude for willing and voluntary cooperation is bound to be disastrous in its effects."[38]

Green was certain that National Service legislation, in the light of British experience, would not prevent strikes, would not solve manpower difficulties, but would undermine the basic concepts of democracy. Green's letter was followed by one from the Executive Council which affirmed that while the A. F. of L. was willing to submit to controls and regimentation as a means of serving the war effort, it would "never surrender the basic freedom of American workers."[39] The Council appealed to Congress to defeat the labor draft. Senator Harry Truman agreed with the Council members. He believed, however, that if the "National Service Law had been set up at the same time the Military Draft Act was passed there would have been a good reason for it and it would have been a successful arrangement. Now it would cause widespread dissatisfaction and will accomplish nothing."[40] The legislation was not enacted.

## THE BATTLE OF BRITAIN

Conquest of Belgium, Holland, Norway, and France by the armies of Hitler made England the last battleground of freedom in Europe. The 1940 convention recognized the seriousness of the Battle of Britain:

the fate of the last democratic nation of Europe is of importance to every other democratic country throughout the world. If Great Britain wins the battle of Britain, democracy wins. If Great Britain is defeated, then America and democracy are increasingly menaced and our peaceful pursuit of life is seriously threatened. . . . [Great Britain] stands as the last outpost in the Old World in defense of democracy and the democratic form of government. Figuratively speaking, she stands as the first line of defense against totalitarian aggression in the Western Hemisphere. We hope and pray Great Britain will win. Our sympathies go out to the people, the men and women who make up the British Trades Union Congress, and to all who are fighting a heroic battle against tremendous odds. We favor the extension of all help and assistance possible to Great Britain in her hour of need, on the part of our Government, short of war itself.[41]

In harmony with the convention's position, Green strongly endorsed Lend-Lease to England, and said it was "a necessary and indispensable instrumentality of the national defense of the United States." However, Green wanted the power given to the President under this legislation to be limited to two years and he also requested that in carrying out the Lend-Lease program, the Federal labor laws would apply to all activities.[42] Green's words were seconded by the Executive Council which, conscious as it was of the triumphs of the European dictators, refused to be pessimistic about the ultimate victory of freedom and democracy. The Council rejected the

defeatist counsel . . . [of] misguided spokesmen [who] try to tell us that an eventual totalitarian triumph is inevitable and that we should resign ourselves to it. We repudiate assertions that the United States of America can live and maintain her democracy in a world dominated by totalitarianism. We urge that our national policy of extending every possible aid to Great Britain and other democracies in their struggle against the totalitarian nations be not abandoned, but redoubled in quantity and speed.[43]

The Federation favored speeding up defense preparations and extending every possible aid to the English in their struggle for survival, but it insisted that the power given to the President of the United States in peacetime be strictly circumscribed. It was not in favor of the sections of the Selective Service and Training Act which gave the President power to seize and operate plants manufacturing arms and equipment and articles which might be required for the national defense. The Federation argued that the right to own and manage property was a fundamental American right, one which should not be impaired except in case of war. Moreover, Green feared that the adoption of such legislation might encourage employers to resist reasonable demands of their workers in the hope that the government would intervene and impose unfavorable terms of employment upon them. The bill, nevertheless, was enacted.[44]

The Nazi attack on the Soviet Union in June 1941 did not confront the Executive Council with a dilemma in spite of its historic opposition to that regime. In the report to the 1941 convention, the Council noted that Soviet Russia was now an ally of the democracies, but it was apprehensive that some people might interpret the changed position of the Soviet Union as a sign that she was now a defender of freedom. The Council repudiated this view and said that the Soviet government was not the willing ally of the free world. Forced into the war by the unexpected attack of Hitler, the Soviet Union was now the foe of Nazi Germany. "Practical consideration," the report said, "make it expedient that we extend such assistance as we can to help Soviet Russia fight the Nazi war machine." The Council again recommended and the convention endorsed the "pledge of support and cooperation with our Government in the completion of its national defense program, and in its policy of extending full and complete aid to Great Britain and her allies."[45]

In informing the unions of the establishment of the National Defense Mediation Board, Green asked prompt cooperation with it as well as with other defense agencies. In a letter addressed to national unions and central bodies, he reviewed the A. F. of L.'s support of the defense program and Lend-Lease legislation. He saw the need to

measure up to the requirements of the situation, maintaining the high standard of efficiency, loyalty and devotion . . . set by those who formed and established the American Federation of Labor. Every hour or day lost in service or production halts the defense program and serves to delay the date of its completion. . . . Seek a settlement of differences which arise through mediation, conciliation, and arbitration. By pursuing such a policy the working men and women of America will be making less sacrifice than the workers in those countries which have been invaded by the armies of the dictators. By giving service, by avoiding strikes, by making such sacrifices as the exigencies of the situation require now, you may avoid making greater sacrifices later on.[46]

After President Roosevelt declared an unlimited emergency, the Executive Council reaffirmed its no-strike policy. Unions were told "to exhaust every opportunity of conciliation and mediation before adopting the final resort to strike . . . to refrain for any reason whatsoever from calling a strike interfering with national defense production until full opportunity has first been given to the Conciliation Service of the Department of Labor and to the National Defense Mediation Board to bring about a peaceful settlement of the dispute."[47] The Federation announced that it would take disciplinary action against any local union under its jurisdiction which violated the declaration, and called upon its national and international unions to take such action as was provided in their constitutions against affiliated locals which failed to comply with the policy.

In June 1941 the A. F. of L. created the Federation Committee for National Defense to provide an organized channel through which the unions might aid in the national defense. Woll was chairman, and the members were the presidents of the trade departments of the A. F. of L., and George Lynch of the Pattern Makers' League of North America and

Edward J. Brown of the Electrical Workers' Union. Robert J. Watt was appointed secretary. Concentrating on the problems of labor which had come about with the changes in the peacetime economy by the shifts in labor and industry, the committee sought to prevent needless dislocation in the economy and to aid in the absorption of the unemployed.[48]

The Committee issued a series of bulletins advising local union officers on the methods of procuring defense contracts and other information useful in planning their activities. Local defense committees were advised to get information on subcontracting, farming out, and provisions for utilization of smaller factories and plants. Organized workers were asked to "do everything in their power to assist in finding substitutes for articles under priority."[49]

The Federation Committee on National Defense sought to increase the interest of the A. F. of L. membership in the work of the government defense agencies; it also acted to protect the rights and positions of union members and at the same time to help expedite the defense program. In dealing with critical shortages of higher skilled labor, the committee took account of the efforts of the Employment Service in providing shifts of workers to where they were needed without unnecessary transfers from their homes. A survey of industries was favored so that machine tools and jigs could be made available for defense industries and existing plants might receive defense orders. The Committee requested Green to make representations to the proper authorities for action.[50]

At its 1941 convention, the Federation gave its full support to the national defense program and at the same time asked that there be no abrogation of labor's legislative or economic gains.[51]

### REFERENCES

1. *Report of the Proceedings of the Forty-ninth Annual Convention of the American Federation of Labor,* 1929, p. 82.

2. *American Federation of Labor Weekly News Service,* September 30, 1933.

3. *Report of the Proceedings of the Fifty-third Annual Convention of the American Federation of Labor,* 1933, p. 142.

4. *Ibid.,* pp. 470–471.

5. *Report of the Proceedings of the Fifty-fourth Annual Convention of the American Federation of Labor,* 1934, p. 174.

6. *Ibid.,* pp. 385–390, 570–571.

7. Green to city central labor unions and state federations, February 28, 1935. A similar letter was sent to all international unions.

8. Green to William Willsbyly, January 7, 1935.

9. *Report of the Proceedings of the Fifty-fifth Annual Convention of the American Federation of Labor*, 1935, pp. 385–390.

10. *Ibid.*, p. 600; *Report of the Proceedings of the Fifty-sixth Annual Convention of the American Federation of Labor*, 1936, p. 592.

11. Green to National and International Unions, State Federations of Labor, Central Labor Unions, and Directly Affiliated Unions, November 18, 1938.

12. *American Federation of Labor Weekly News Service*, September 26, 1936.

13. Quote in cablegram from Green to Citrine, January 25, 1938; Minutes of Executive Council, January 25, 1938.

14. *American Federation of Labor Weekly News Service*, October 21, 1939.

15. Statement of Executive Council, February 2, 1940, in A. F. of L. files.

16. To the officers of National and International Unions, State Federations of Labor, and Central Labor Unions from Green and Meany, February 28, 1940.

17. George Meany to General Edward M. Watson, April 11, 1940.

18. Statement of the Executive Council, May 15, 1940.

19. Minutes of Executive Council, February 11, 1940.

20. *Ibid.*

21. Minutes of Executive Council, May 5, 1940.

22. Minutes of Executive Council, May 8, 1940.

23. Statement of Metal Trades Department, June 20, 1940.

24. Minutes of Executive Council, October 2, 1940.

25. *Ibid.*

26. John P. Coyne to Presidents of all National and International Unions, affiliated with the Building and Construction Trades Department and to all local Building and Construction Trades Councils, July 23, 1941.

27. Philip Murray to President Roosevelt, December 3, 1941; Memorandum to Sidney Hillman from President Roosevelt, December 5, 1941, in Official File 2546, Box 2, Franklin Delano Roosevelt Library.

28. Philip Murray, *Plan for Strengthening National Defense Program*, December 18, 1940, (no place or publisher) in Official File 172, Box 1, Franklin Delano Roosevelt Library.

29. Minutes of Executive Council, May 17, 1940.

30. *Report of the Proceedings of the Sixtieth Annual Convention of the American Federation of Labor*, 1940, p. 210.

31. Minutes of Executive Council, February 10, 1941.

32. Minutes of Executive Council, February 19, 1941.

33. Executive Order 1747, Establishment of National Defense Mediation Board, March 19, 1941.

34. *Report of the Proceedings of the Sixty-second Annual Convention of the American Federation of Labor*, 1942, p. 193.

35. Minutes of Executive Council, January 27, 1943.

36. *American Federation of Labor Weekly News*, November 9, 1943.

37. *Ibid.*, January 18, 1944.

38. Green to members of the United States Senate and House of Representatives, January 13, 1944.

39. Green and Meany to members of the United States Senate and House of Representatives, January 19, 1944.

40. Harry S. Truman to Green, January 21, 1944.

41. *Report of the Proceedings of the Sixtieth Annual Convention of the American Federation of Labor*, 1940, p. 202.

42. *American Federation of Labor Weekly News Service*, January 28, 1941.

43. *Ibid.*

44. Green to Congressmen and Senators of the United States, July 28, 1941.

45. *Report of the Proceedings of the Sixty-first Annual Convention of the American Federation of Labor*, 1941, p. 198.

46. Green to the Officers of National and International Unions, State Federations of Labor, City Central Bodies, and Federal Labor Unions, April 17, 1941.

47. Minutes of Executive Council, May 28, 1941.

48. Statement of President Green in appointing A. F. of L. Committee on National Defense, June 30, 1941.

49. *American Federation of Labor Committee on National Defense Bulletin*, No. 1.

50. *Sixth Meeting of the American Federation of Labor National Defense Committee*, September 17, 1941.

51. *Report of the Proceedings of the Sixty-first Annual Convention of the American Federation of Labor*, 1941, pp. 109–110.

# XVIII

## World War II

### AFTER PEARL HARBOR

Immediately after the attack on Pearl Harbor, Green called the Executive Council into session. Declaring that Japan and her allies must be defeated at all costs, the Council drew up a five-point program which was subsequently adopted by a conference of representatives of national and international unions:

1. Workers employed in war and defense industries were to relinquish voluntarily the exercise of the right to strike during the continuation of the existing state of war except where mediation, conciliation, and arbitration were refused by the employer.

2. A National War Labor Board, similar to the one which functioned during World War I, was to be created by the President of the United States for the purpose of dealing promptly with grievances, differences, and complaints which might arise between employers and employees.

3. Through such agency, mediation, conciliation, and voluntary arbitration were to be substituted for strikes and lockouts in all defense industries.

4. The mediation and conciliation of the government would be strengthened so that it might be more quickly available for the settlement of disputes.

5. Due regard for the health, safety, and welfare of workers must be shown in request for overtime work. In all situations, the standard forty-hour work week was to be maintained and overtime pay be provided for extra work hours.[1]

Soon thereafter, President Roosevelt called a meeting of representatives of labor and industry; the C.I.O. and A. F. of L. were invited to send delegates. For the President, the "first essential objective of the conference [was] to reach a unanimous agreement to prevent the interruption of production."

The Federation offered a plan whereby all disputes would be subjected to the decision of the National War Labor Board which the President was to appoint. The employer representative sought a formula whereby the board to be appointed would not order the acceptance of the union security provisions on firms unwilling to accept them voluntarily. A second proposal by the C.I.O. was found unacceptable, and the two labor federations then submitted a three-point joint proposal drafted by Secretary-Treasurer George Meany. It was agreed (1) that there would be no strikes or lockouts in defense industries; (2) a War Labor Board would be established by the President to settle all unresolved disputes; and (3) all grievances would be submitted to the Board appointed by the President. Efforts made by the employer representatives to exclude grievances arising out of difference on union security arrangments failed when President Roosevelt refused to modify point three and the Board was authorized to consider these as well as other issues. The War Labor Board was established by Executive Order on January 12, 1942, and Green recommended George Meany and Daniel Tobin to be the A. F. of L. members of this Board.[2]

The National War Labor Board was created in the office of Emergency Management; it consisted of twelve special commissioners appointed by the President, four of whom represented the public, four represented employees, and four, the employers. There was also a provision for appointing four alternate members representing employers and four alternates representing employees. The function of the Board was to adjust and settle labor disputes which might interrupt work that contributed to the effective prosecution of the war. Once the Board accepted jurisdiction, it had to determine finally the dispute, and for that purpose it was authorized to use mediation, voluntary arbitration, or arbitration under the rules established by the Board. The Board superseded the National Defense Mediation Board, which had been set up in March 1941. At this time, Green appointed a committee made up of Bates, E. J. Brown, and Hutcheson to confer with the Secretaries of War, Navy, and Labor on regulations to govern the performance of overtime work. It was tentatively agreed that employees would be allowed to work only six days a week.

As war production expanded, control of price and wage increases became necessary to carry out the government's program of inflation control. In a letter to President Roosevelt on April 22, 1942, Green opposed a rigid wage freeze or the repeal of collective-bargaining procedures. He described the harmful effects of inflation upon wage earners, and offered a program "whose application will enable us to avert price inflation and to maintain the necessary standards of living for all productive workers upon whose health, physical stamina, morale, and sustained ability to produce the winning of the war in such large measure depends."

Green suggested (1) immediate rationing of all scarce goods and extension of the rationing system to commodities in which scarcities were threatened; (2) enforcement of fair retail price ceilings on such basic necessities as clothing and food, and effective enforcement of rent controls; (3) allocation of critical raw materials within industry and placement of price ceilings upon commodities which showed evidence of inflationary price rises; (4) a comprehensive program of progressive taxation on personal and corporate income, which would make it impossible to earn excess profits from war effort; (5) expansion of the campaign for voluntary savings-bond purchases; (6) upward revision of social-security taxes to make possible extended and higher social-security benefits at the end of the war; and (7) the submission of all wage-policy differences which could not be settled by direct negotiation to the National War Labor Board for final determination.[3] Green defended his program with the argument that the inflationary rise in prices had not been caused by wage increases. Reminding the President of the tremendous rise in corporate profits, Green said that if the American worker was to maintain his morale and turn out the volume of goods needed for the winning of the war, he must be assured an adequate supply of consumer goods.

At the President's request, Anna Rosenberg, his labor advisor, answered Green. The President's letter of April 22 reviewed the various steps that had been taken by the Federal government to stabilize prices and wages. Roosevelt promised Green that his message to Congress would contain a request for an upward revision of social security taxes to increase benefits and to act as an anti-inflationary device. The President recognized the value of collective bargaining in the setting of wages and other terms of employment, but he asked whether it were possible to control prices without regulating wages. Putting a limit on wages, Roosevelt said, "does not mean a freezing of wages. It means that some bounds or limits may be put on wage increases, but that those wages which are below standard will be permitted, in fact, urged, to come up to recognized minimums and standards."[4] Finally President Roosevelt told Green that he was not at the time recommending a wage freeze, but he said the time had come to recognize that wage increases would hurt workers more than any other group in society.

COMBINED LABOR WAR BOARD

In January 1942 President Roosevelt asked the A. F. of L. and the C.I.O. to form a Combined Labor War Board to discuss "all matters concerning Labor's participation in the war."[5] Roosevelt thought that the Board should be small in number and that it should meet with him periodically for discussion of issues affecting the war. Green, Meany, and Tobin were chosen by the A. F. of L. with Bugniazet, Bates, and Knight as alternates. Murray, R. J. Thomas, and Julius Emspak represented the C.I.O. The A. F. of L. did not approve the appointment of Emspak, who had been a leader of the Communist block in the C.I.O., to the Combined Labor War Board because that Board might be given access to confidential war information. There was, nevertheless, reluctance to challenge the recommendations of the C.I.O. The Federation refrained from making a formal protest, but Dubinsky, Green, and Meany discussed the question with President Roosevelt. Evidently the President felt that he could not determine the representatives who would be recommended to him, and no steps were taken to relieve Emspak.

Evidently Roosevelt wanted the three largest unions in the C.I.O. represented, but Murray, who at the time was bitterly opposed to John L. Lewis, would not accept that suggestion. In a memorandum to the President, Wayne Coy head of the Office of Emergency Management said that Murray did not want to select representatives from the three largest C.I.O. unions because it would mean appointing delegates from the Miners', Steel Workers', and Auto Workers' Unions,

and that it would not be possible to select representatives of those unions without including John L. Lewis. . . . He states emphatically that if the Mine Workers select their own representative they will select John L. Lewis. In view of his very strong feeling about the matter, I suggest that he talk with you by telephone tomorrow morning. . . . I think you may want to discuss this matter with Tom Kennedy when you see him in the morning. Maybe— just maybe—it might be aranged for Kennedy to represent the Mine Workers, but I doubt it very much. My best guess is that Kennedy will tell you that the Mine Workers will be represented by Lewis. I believe he would make such a statement even though he agreed with you that he would support Murray's position on the proposition of the committee which you discussed with Murray.[6]

Lewis did not become a member of the Combined Labor War Board; undoubtedly Murray's opposition to his appointment was the chief reason for the failure to invite him. In view of the importance of the union which Lewis headed in the war effort, it is unfortunate that he was not drawn into an important executive or advisory post. Ernest Bevin demonstrated in England that men like Lewis can make important contributions in the time of crisis.[7] The railroad unions thought that they should be represented, and after a visit from a committee of the railway labor organizations, Alvanley Johnston was added to the Board. The Combined War Labor Board considered a number of issues such as the no-strike policy, manpower, and representation of the workers on government agencies.[8] Although eight meetings were held during 1943, the Board never became an important formulator of policy in the labor area.

### WAGE AND PRICE CONTROL

After the promulgation of the Little Steel Formula by the War Labor Board in July 1942—a formula that limited wage increases to 15 per cent above the hourly wage rates prevailing in January 1941—Green wrote to President Roosevelt that "developments of the past week have convinced me that as the spokesman for the American Federation of Labor whose membership have proven their loyalty through over sixty years of trial and in two world wars, I must speak plainly against the proposed invasion of Labor's basic rights. It is not necessary to freeze wages and suspend collective bargaining in order to prevent inflation."[9]

Green submitted a detailed anti-inflation program which included wage adjustment "through the process of collective bargaining between labor and management," and the use of voluntary wage stabilization agreements. He also suggested the appointment of a tripartite wage commission which would be given the power to unify and coordinate wage policies of all government agencies. Future wage increases, he said, should be paid in war bonds which could be cashed only after the end of the war. In addition, he asked for the enactment of a progam of progressive taxation designed to prevent profiteering in wartime, increased contributions for an extended social security program, effective control of prices at retail, wholesale, and manufacturers' levels, control of rents, and rationing of scarce commodities. Labor was willing, according to Green, to accept stabilization of wages if this were accompanied by control of profits. Moreover, wage "stabilization must not preclude correction of substandard rates, elimination of inequalities, nor adjustment of rates to compensate for increased skill and output."[10]

On October 2, 1942 President Roosevelt signed the anti-inflation bill, and under its authority he established the Office of Economic Stabilization and appointed Justice James F. Byrnes as the Director. Under the legislation, the President was authorized to stabilize the cost of living, and wages and salaries were not to be increased or decreased without the approval of the War Labor Board. The War Labor Board, however, was prohibited from approving increases in wage rates above those prevailing on September 15, 1942, unless such increases were necessary to correct maladjustments or inequalities or to aid in the effective prosecution of the war. The efforts to freeze wages disturbed several members of the Executive Council. Hutcheson, for one, felt that if established conditions were not recognized during the war, workers had a right to strike.[11]

The Executive Council spent considerable time discussing wage and price control. George Harrison approved of controls in general, but he doubted the fairness of the policies followed by the War Labor Board. Citing the official figures published by the United States Bureau of Labor Statistics, which showed a rise in the cost of living since January 1941 of 18 per cent, Harrison argued that foods, especially those used by working people, had risen over 40 per cent. "Vice President Harrison stated [that] that, however, that is only half of the story. The other half is that we are only getting about half the value we used to get for the money we pay.

The product is diluted and we are not getting what we used to get, and employers are using Government control of wages as an excuse for not . . . raising wages." Harrison's criticism of the cost-of-living index of the United States Bureau of Labor Statistics marked the first time that the validity of the index for the cost-of-living had been challenged. For some time the index was to be a matter of contention and later the center of the attack, when the unions decided on a campaign to weaken the application of the Little Steel Formula to wage changes. Harrison wanted employers to be given the right to raise wages 15 per cent without the approval of the War Labor Board, and he thought that increases up to 18 per cent should be allowed.[12]

Following this meeting, Green and Murray requested President Roosevelt either to relax wage controls or revise the Little Steel Formula so that larger percentage increases would be permitted.[13] Following its claim that larger percentage wage increases ought to be granted, the A. F. of L. filed a petition with the War Labor Board on March 16, 1943, asking for the relaxation of the Little Steel Formula so that the 15 per cent increase in straight time hourly rates would be replaced by what the Federation regarded as a more realistic percentage. The petition, although it was supported by the C.I.O., was rejected by the Board by a vote of 8 to 4. The Board did agree unanimously to proceed with the development of a wage policy which would recognize the existence of inequalities, substandard wages, and the need to devise standards which would aid in the more effective prosecution of the war. The Board also observed that rising food prices jeopardized the continued application of the Little Steel Formula and recommended subsidies as a means of holding down retail prices.

The uphill struggle against inflation led the government to try to strengthen its price and wage regulations. On April 8, 1943 President Roosevelt issued the Hold the Line Order in which he said "We cannot tolerate further increases in prices affecting the cost of living or further increases in general wages or salary rates except where clearly necessary to correct substandard living conditions. The only way to hold the line is to stop trying to find justification for not holding it here or not holding it there." The President asked that all items affecting the cost of living be brought under control and that no further price increases be sanctioned unless imperatively required. Adjustments in price relationships of different commodities were to be allowed only if they did not affect the general cost of living. Nor were price increases to be used to stimulate increases in production. Prices of commodities entering the cost of living which had risen above the levels prevailing on September 1, 1942 were to be rolled back. Specific directions were also given for the control of wages. There were to be no further increases in wage rates or salary scales beyond the Little Steel Formula, except where they were clearly necessary to correct substandards of living. Reclassifications and promotions were not to be permitted to affect the general level of production costs or to justify price increases or to forestall price reductions.[14]

Green immediately informed President Roosevelt that the Executive Order was not clear, and that workers were apprehensive that the "door has been closed to the correction of economic injustice and the correction of wage inequalities." Green insisted that individual increases in wages must be allowed and reclassification of workers permitted even if such changes meant wage increases for persons and groups, as long as such increases were necessary for justice and equity. Green also objected to the freezing of wages for workers whose cases were already under consideration by the War Labor Board or arbitration tribunals.[15]

Following Green's letter, the Federation members on the National War Labor Board defined their attitude on the President's Executive Order. As a first step they voted for the Directive Order in the Universal Atlas Cement Company case, decided on April 13, 1943. They were in full agreement with the public and industry members of the Board that a literal reading of Executive Order 9328 so limited the powers and jurisdiction of the War Labor Board that no other directive order on wages than the one issued was possible. Nevertheless, the Federation members believed that Executive Order 9328 was "neither sound in construction nor workable in practice. To the contrary . . . a literal interpretation and application of the order will work manifest injustices upon American labor and industry and be detrimental to the war effort."[16]

The statement made it clear that the A. F. of L. members of the War Labor Board would continue to cooperate and would urge union members to cooperate in the successful prosecution of the war. They intended to accept the verdict of the majority, but reserved the right to dissent in any opinion which was contrary to their own views. Moreover, they regarded it as "most unfair" and contrary to the war effort for an Executive Order to freeze wage inequities which were a manifest injustice in the wage structure. The principles embodied in Executive Order 9328 were rejected because they destroyed the power of the Board to grant wage increases so as to eliminate gross inequities and to aid in the more effective prosecution of the war. Objection to the effect of the President's order on the several commissions, such as the Trucking Commission, who were at the time seeking to stabilize wages either on a national or regional level, was also stated. Finally, the Federation members deplored the consequences of the President's order in the 17,000 cases of wage inequities that were being considered by the War Labor Board, because wage increases could not be made even in cases where evidence of gross inequities was presented.

As a result of the criticisms, Executive Order 9328 was modified on May 12, but the Executive Council did not think the changes went far enough. At its meeting in May 1943 the Council endorsed the position taken by the A. F. of L. members of the National War Labor Board.[17] In the meantime, dissatisfaction with the program of wage regulation had manifested itself among some organized labor groups. Serious work suspensions took place in the bituminous coal mining industry, and William H. Davis, the chairman of the National War Labor Board, proposed "sanctions through which to secure compliance by labor unions with orders of the National War Labor Board." Secretary of the Interior Ickes, who had managed the mines when they were taken over by the government, was consulted on this matter by Davis and the Attorney General.[18] Ickes believed that the Davis proposal was a much more severe sanction against unions than plant seizures were against employers.[19] He was especially concerned with the proposal that "there shall be withheld from any union that refuses to comply with an order of the Board all those benefits which accrue to the union under the terms and conditions laid down in the Board's order."[20]

In a letter to Davis, Ickes voiced his disagreement with the plan. The remedy, he said, did not reflect a

sound public policy and it imposes a much greater penalty upon a recalcitrant labor union than is imposed upon a disobedient employer. . . . With few exceptions, when the Government takes over a plant or a mine on account of a labor dispute, no damage is done to the owner except, possibly, to his feelings and prestige. He continues to collect all the profits of operation; executive management typically is retained and continues to receive the salaries; and operations continue under Government "supervision." Indeed, the company profits because, if the Government had not taken the plant, there would have been no operations and no profits. In addition, the companies retain and can assert a legal claim against the Government for any damages that they may suffer as a result of the Government "operation."

On the other hand, the moneys denied to a disobedient labor union by the refusal of the check-off will not be recaptured. They will be paid out to the employees, and the possibility of successful assertion of a legal claim against the Government is exceedingly remote, in fact, negligible.

Ickes feared that the denial of the closed shop in the South would greatly damage the union, and that some large-scale operators would welcome an opportunity to war on the United Mine Workers of America. In addition, he told Davis, there were dangers of the disruption of coal production. Instead of the drastic Executive remedy, Ickes suggested the possibility of enforcing penalties for refusing to accept orders of the War

Labor Board; the latter to be enforced through the courts, which was in harmony with traditional procedures.

President Roosevelt was worried about the language of the suggested law. An Executive Order authorizing the Stabilization Director to take certain action in connection with the enforcement of the directives of the National War Labor Board was actually drawn. It would have withheld privileges from unions failing to comply with orders of the Board, "but when the check-off is denied, dues received from the check-off shall be held in escrow for the benefit of the union to be delivered to it upon compliance by it."[21] Undoubtedly, Ickes' objections helped to forestall the imposition of severe penalties on unions that failed to accept the decision of the War Labor Board.

There was considerable dissatisfaction with the wage policies that had been decreed, and there was even severer criticism of the Economic Stabilization Office than of the Labor War Board. At "every meeting . . . [of] the Combined Labor War Board with the President," Green said, "we had this issue over control of food prices or opposition to the control by these people over wage awards made by the War Labor Board. We have never modified our position on that. We think the Board should be free to decide and its decisions should be final."[22] Green was convinced that because of labor's opposition the President had modified Executive Order 9328, but the Council was far from content. Meany believed that the attitude of some of the public members of the Board was unfair, and he suggested that an effort be made to convince the President of the desirability of returning the power to set wages, without further review, to the War Labor Board. The A. F. of L. members of the Board were especially vexed with the decisions of the Director of Economic Stabilization, Judge Fred Vinson.[23] Neither Meany nor Woll believed that the Federation should withdraw from the Board, and although they were critical of its decisions, they thought that the issues should be reported factually, with a minimum of criticism, to the convention.

In considering the report, the convention protested government fixed wage formulas which supplanted "wage policies hammered out by democratically organized bodies which have been voluntarily created." The convention was critical of the setting aside of the decisions of the War Labor Board by the Economic Stabilizer. Charging that some of the government edicts designed to fight inflation were inequitable, the delegates did not think it was in the interest of the country for the judgment of one man, the economic stabilizer, to supersede the decisions of the War Labor Board. They reminded the country of the A. F. of L.'s continuous efforts to assure victory, to its long espousal of voluntary arbitration, and they warned that the Federation "cannot and will not . . . after hostilities have ceased, agree to the continued existence in any form whatsoever of the National War Board, and will not countenance domination by the Government in any form or character of its right to bargain collectively, fairly, and freely."[24]

The leaders of the A. F. of L. were more and more disturbed by the wage policies of government agencies. Their efforts to control inflation were only partially successful, and the Federation leadership felt that the more stringent wage controls being attempted by the War Labor Board and the stabilization authorities were unfair and placed inequitable burdens upon labor. In particular, they insisted that the cost-of-living index of the Bureau of Labor Statistics did not accurately reflect changes in the workers' living costs.

In transmitting the 1943 convention's resolutions dealing with wage control, Green asked the President "to initiate action which will restore the National War Labor Board to its former position, return to the Board its power to adjudicate finally all labor disputes by democratic processes, and remove from its back the ever-increasing load of superagencies."[25] President Roosevelt told Green that he wanted the War Labor Board to maintain its independence in adjudication of labor disputes, and that no superagency was authorized to veto its decisions. The President claimed that he had "entrusted to the Economic Stabilization Director only that minimum control that is necessary to carry out the responsibilities imposed upon me with respect to the stabilization of the cost of living. I am sure that the Economic Stabilization Director is most eager to preserve the strength and standing of the National War Labor Board and will gladly cooperate with you to that end."[26]

The criticism of the cost-of-living index, coupled with the demands of organized labor for a change in the Little Steel Formula, led President Roosevelt to appoint a committee to examine the question as to whether or not the index truly reflected changes in living costs. Meany and R. J. Thomas of the C.I.O. were the labor members of the panel, which was headed by William H. Davis, chairman of the War Labor Board. Meany and Thomas filed a report at the end of the hearings which charged that the Bureau of Labor Statistics index, which then was about 124.5, understated the rise in the cost of living by more than twenty points. In the end Chairman Davis appointed a committee of experts to examine the question, and the committee concluded that the index understated the actual rise in the cost of living by about 5½ per cent.[27]

On February 9, 1944 the A. F. of L. members of the War Labor Board again petitioned for a revision of the Little Steel Formula. In a statement signed by Meany, Woll, Robert Watt, and James Bronlow, the A. F. of L. members attacked the assumption of the War Labor Board that the cost of living had risen only 15 per cent. Instead of this figure, they claimed that the actual rise had been 43 per cent. Stating that workers could not rely upon price control since it functioned to preserve their standard of living, the petition requested increases in wage rates which would adequately compensate for the widening disparity between wage rates and prices. The A. F. of L. called on the War Labor Board to request President Roosevelt to modify Executive Order 9328, which limited wage increases, to offset maladjustments to the Little Steel Formula as defined by the National War Labor Board, and to allow employers to apply the adjustment principle as modified without obtaining approval of the War Labor Board. The petition was rejected with the proviso that it would be reconsidered in the future if events warranted.[28]

In April the A. F. of L. members of the War Labor Board once again petitioned for a modification of the Little Steel Formula, and a panel was appointed by the War Labor Board to hear its plea. Meany argued that (1) the Little Steel Formula was based on maintaining the peacetime standards of living; (2) that stabilization of the cost of living would be achieved; and (3) that the policy of controlling inflation had not been realized.

Meany said that wage stabilization had not been accompanied by adequate taxes upon high incomes, whereas the taxation of workers had been steadily increased. He claimed that the cost of living of the workers had not been stabilized, that farm prices had been allowed to rise, and that rationing of scarce commodities had not been effective because of black markets. The only point of the President's anti-inflation program which Meany thought had succeeded was the stabilization of wages; consequently the failure of the other parts of the program meant that the workers' peacetime standards of living had deteriorated by about 25 per cent since 1941. The A. F. of L. maintained that "the inequity which had arisen from the application of the Little Steel Formula should be eliminated immediately by President Roosevelt."[29]

Although most members of the Executive Council were critical of the War Labor Board, they considered the support of that body a matter "of supreme importance." When it was attacked after the refusal of the Montgomery-Ward management to obey the dicta of the Board, the Council came to its defense and "declared that regardless of the material facts or of the issues involved in the controversy with the Montgomery-Ward Company, the Executive Council is primarily concerned in upholding the power and authority of the National War Labor Board. This is the issue which transcends all other considerations in the Montgomery-Ward case." The statement referred to the many unfavorable decisions which organized labor had accepted from the Board in accordance with democratic procedures and the necessity to support the war effort.[30]

Nevertheless, the Federation came back in August 1944 with the demand that the Little Steel Formula be relaxed. Subsequently, when the petition was rejected by the War Labor Board, the Council directed President Green to appoint a committee from its members to call on President Roosevelt to present to him the case for a revision of the wage policy followed in the decisions of this agency.[31] The A. F. of L. continued to seek a change in the policy of the government. In March 1945 it appealed to President Roosevelt to allow an 11 per cent increase in wage rates above the Little Steel Formula justified by the cost of living.[32] This request was not approved. At its meeting in July 1945 the Executive Council, forecasting the abolition of the War Labor Board, asked for an interim adjustment of the government's wage policy to facilitate the reconversion of the war economy to a peacetime basis. The Council again suggested an upward revision of wages that would take account of the increased cost of living. It was also necessary, the Council said, to raise wages to offset the loss of overtime pay and incentive bonuses and reduced wages that had followed the downgrading of the labor force. The Council also recommended the restoration of free collective bargaining to permit voluntary wage increases without the approval of the War Labor Board. In addition, the Council asked for the return of the power of the Board to decide upon policy and for the elimination of the Director of Economic Stabilization as its tutelary authority.[33]

In October the Council, called for the abolition of the Board and spoke out against "Government by Emergency" in peacetime. The Council was convinced that "the way to establish and maintain industrial peace and stability is to remove government control of wages immediately."[34] It was imperative, according to the Council, to abolish government controls, restore normal collective bargaining, and allow wages to rise to their "proper" levels. These policies were urged upon President Truman. After the surrender of Japan, wage controls were relaxed and wage increases which did not affect price ceilings could be made by employers without the permission of the War Labor Board. By Presidential direction, the War Labor Board was terminated at the end of 1945, and the wage regulation program was transferred to the National Wage Stabilization Board, established by President Truman in January 1946. Six members, two representing labor, two industry, and two the public, administered wage policy under the Director of Economic Stabilization. The Federation was unenthusiastic about these changes and continued to seek liberalization of wage policies and a return to unimpeded collective bargaining.

Notwithstanding its constant criticism of some policies of the National War Labor Board, the Federation commented favorably, however, upon the volume and quality of work the Board performed during its tenure. The revised program allowed for wage increases in any amount by an employer, except in agriculture and in the building-construction industry where wartime wage controls continued. In other industries, approval of a wage increase was only significant if such increases were used as a basis for a request for price relief from the Office of Price Administration. The latter agency would consider the effect of wage increases upon prices of only that part of the increase approved by the Board. Two new standards were added to those applied by the War Labor Board for approval of voluntary increases: (1) increases necessary to bring the rates of the applicant up to the prevailing rates in the industry or the area; and (2) increases necessary to bring rates up to a point where the average earnings of the employees in an appropriate bargaining unit would be 33 per cent above the average earnings of January 1941.

As in the past, the Federation was ready to accept government regulation of wages only to maintain minimum standards. The desire to go back to free collective bargaining between workers and employers was voiced by the 1946 convention. The convention authorized the Federation officers to take "positive steps . . . to free [it] from the remnants of Federal regulation which was necessary only in time of war."[35] The ending of wage control won wide approval in all ranks of the A. F. of L.

REFERENCES

1. Minutes of Executive Council, December 16, 1941.
2. Green to Frances Perkins, January 2, 1942.
3. Green to the President, April 16, 1942.
4. President Franklin D. Roosevelt to Green, April 22, 1942.
5. Roosevelt to Green, January 1, 1942.
6. Memorandum from Wayne Coy to President Roosevelt, January 22, 1942. Official File 4747, Box 1, Franklin Delano Roosevelt Library. Information on opposition to Emspak came from Dubinsky and Meany.
7. Memorandum for General Watson, April 1, 1943, in Official File 4747, Box 1, Franklin Delano Roosevelt Library.
8. *Report of the Proceedings of the Sixty-second Annual Convention of the American Federation of Labor*, 1942, p. 186; *Report of the Proceedings of the Sixty-third Annual Convention of the American Federation of Labor*, 1943, p. 117.
9. Green to Franklin Delano Roosevelt, July 20, 1942, Official File 142, Box 1, Franklin Delano Roosevelt Library.
10. *American Federation of Labor Weekly News*, July 21, 1942.
11. Minutes of Executive Council, January 17, 1943.
12. *Ibid.*
13. *American Federation of Labor Weekly News Service*, February 9, 1943.
14. Executive Order 9328, April 8, 1943.
15. Green to Honorable Franklin D. Roosevelt, April 14, 1943.
16. Statement of American Federation of Labor members of the National War Labor Board, April 13, 1943, in files of A. F. of L.

17. Minutes of Executive Council, May 21, 1943.

18. Harold L. Ickes to the President, July 28, 1943, Official File 4710, Box 2, Franklin Delano Roosevelt Library.

19. *Ibid.*

20. Harold L. Ickes to Honorable William H. Davis, July 27, 1943, Official File 4710, Box 2, Franklin Delano Roosevelt Library.

21. Memorandum in Official File 4710, Box 2, Franklin Delano Roosevelt Library.

22. Statement of Green to the Executive Council, August 14, 1943.

23. *Ibid.*

24. *Report of the Proceedings of the Sixty-third Convention of the American Federation of Labor,* 1943, p. 505.

25. Green to President Franklin D. Roosevelt, December 18, 1943.

26. President Franklin Roosevelt to Green, December 28, 1943.

27. George Meany and R. J. Thomas, *Cost of Living,* a 104-page statement of the labor point of view.

28. *American Federation of Labor Weekly News Service,* April 4, 1944.

29. *Statement of Mr. George Meany, Secretary-Treasurer, American Federation of Labor, to the Special Panel of the National War Labor Board on the Little Steel Formula,* April 4, 1944.

30. Minutes of Executive Council, May 3, 1944.

31. Minutes of Executive Council, August 23, 1944; *American Federation of Labor Weekly News Service,* October 17, 1944.

32. *American Federation of Labor Weekly News Service,* March 6, 1944.

33. Minutes of Executive Council, August 9, 1945.

34. Minutes of Executive Council, October 15, 1945.

35. *Report of the Proceedings of the Sixty-fifth Convention of the American Federation of Labor,* 1946, p. 485.

# XIX

## International Federation of Trade Unions

SOME A. F. of L. leaders had always worked for closer ties with European labor groups, but to obtain these closer ties was not the dominant view; there were many isolationists in the Federation who regarded foreign labor leaders with suspicion. Nevertheless, the 1924 convention expressed a hope that the A. F. of L. would soon find it possible to rejoin the International Federation of Trade Unions. The International Federation was quite anxious to win the support of the Federation, and its secretary, J. Oudegeest, assured Green that "we recognize that this principle of autonomy is . . . basic in your trade union movement. We should like to add that it is a basic principle of the International Trade Union Movement. We have attempted to express that principle . . . in our constitution."[1] In spite of these assurances, the Council refused to take action; it did, however, direct Green to continue his correspondence with Oudegeest.[2]

The convention approved continuing the negotiations, and Green for a time maintained friendly exchanges. What disturbed the leaders of the A. F. of L. at this time was the International Federation's endorsement of socialization of the means of production and distribution. Green made it clear to Oudegeest that the trade union movements of all countries were agreed on the principle objectives and that all members earnestly desired the betterment of mankind. The American trade union movement, Green wrote, was anxious to do its part in the effort to realize these objectives.[3]

The President of the A. F. of L. questioned, however, that part of the International Federation's program which called for the socialization of raw materials. To Oudegeest's assurance that such a declaration was not binding upon affiliates, Green answered that it would place the Federation in a difficult position with respect to the American public.

The delegates to the 1926 convention reaffirmed the hope that "ultimately the organized labor movement of the world will be in full accord on the question of trade union principles and activities." The delegates looked ahead "with pleasure to the time when organized labor will be fully united and affiliated to the International Federation of Trade Unions, in which the fundamental principles and . . . philosophy of trade unions

will be fully adhered to."⁴ But the fear that the I.F.T.U. might commit
the Federation to policies it could not support was still uppermost in the
minds of the leadership. In a letter to Oudegeest which ended serious
negotiations for almost ten years, Green objected to the cost of affiliating
and said that "the voting rules of the International Federation of Trade
Unions which [enabled] a minority of the membership affiliated to develop and declare the policies of [the] organization, prevented the
American Federation from becoming affiliated."⁵

### INTERNATIONAL LABOR OFFICE (ILO)

Since the United States government had not joined the International
Labor Organization, no American groups were represented at its conferences during the first sixteen years of its existence. A resolution authorizing the Federation to appoint an unofficial observer was referred by the
1931 convention to the Executive Council. The Federation was itself in
an isolationist mood and it was no more anxious than many Americans
to be involved in foreign alliances.⁶ A few years later the government's
attitude changed, and the United States sent official observers to the
seventeenth session of the International Labor Office held in 1934.
Hugh Frayne, an organizer for the A. F. of L., joined three other
Americans at the conference.⁷ A joint resolution providing for the membership of the United States in the International Labor Organization,
enacted on June 19, 1934, authorized the President to accept membership
in the ILO on behalf of the United States. In accepting this membership,
the President, the resolution stated, did not assume on behalf of the
United States any obligations under the covenant of the League of Nations. The first United States labor representative, John L. Lewis, was
selected at the recommendation of the A. F. of L.⁸ James Wilson, a former
president of the Pattern Makers' League of North America and a member
of the A. F. of L. Executive Council, served on the governing body of
the International Labor Office; he was succeeded by Robert J. Watt, who
held that office from 1937 until his death in 1947.

In 1944 President Roosevelt sought to have the A. F. of L. share representation with the C.I.O. at the International Labor Organization conference in Philadelphia that began on April 20, 1944. When he and Secretary
of Labor Perkins asked Green to agree to the division of appointments,
Green placed the question before the Executive Council. Green emphasized the point that the A. F. of L. was still the most representative labor
organization in the United States, and as one of the creators of the ILO,
the Federation was conscious of its responsibility for the ILO's development and success. He reminded the President that the idea of labor
being represented at peace negotiations had originated in the mind of
Samuel Gompers during World War I. Questioning the fairness of asking

the Federation to share its vote, Green told the President that "the American Federation of Labor cannot agree to share representation with any other labor organization at meetings of the International Labor Organization."[9]

## INTERNATIONAL COOPERATION

Many leaders of the A. F. of L. were not anxious to establish relations with European labor, and others believed that the A. F. of L. should not completely divorce itself from foreign labor movements. Following the practice of earlier conventions, delegates to the 1929 convention had looked ahead to eventual cooperation between European and American labor. The predominant sentiment, however, was for "no entangling alliances."[10] Walter Citrine, the secretary of the British Trades Union Congress and President of the I.F.T.U., made an effort to have the Federation represented at a conference of trade unionists on overcoming the economic crisis at Berlin in 1932. Green doubted the wisdom of sending a delegate, and all members of the Executive Council, except G. M. Bougniazet, voted not to participate.[11] Bougniazet believed that if the Federation could spare the time and money, it should help and learn from the European trade unionists.[12] The 1934 convention considered a resolution to instruct the Council to initiate negotiations with the I.F.T.U. with a view to eventual affiliation. The issue was referred to the Council with a request for a report to the next convention.[13]

The Council's report to the 1935 convention contained a favorable summary of the work of the International Federation and the committee considering this section of the Council's report stated:

A new situation now confronts the trade union movement the world over. The growth of dictatorships has been a powerful threat to the free trade union movement everywhere. One of the first actions taken by the Nazis, for example, was to liquidate the labor movement as the most effective method of suppressing opposition and mass protest. A similar procedure has been followed in other countries where dictatorships have been set up. Unless there can be created some effective vehicle for international labor solidarity, the trade union movement may be seriously weakened in those countries adjoining these dictatorships and over which they exercise such profound economic influence.[14]

The report also recognized the threat of war "'which becomes a more serious menace with the growth of dictatorship. The power of International organized labor is perhaps the most effective instrument to stand athwart the path of such dictatorships and their imperialistic plans.'"[15] Since the I.F.T.U. cooperated closely with the ILO, the committee believed that its delegations would be more effective if the A. F. of L. were associated with the International Federation. The committee was convinced that the time had arrived for reexamining the basis upon which

the reaffiliation of the A. F. of L. with the I.F.T.U. might be brought
about. The convention directed President Green to begin discussions to
find a basis of accommodation which would enable the A. F. of L. once
again to become a member of the world family of labor.

Negotiations were begun in December 1935, and Walter Schevenels,
secretary of the I.F.T.U., wrote to Green that the obstacles which had led
the A. F. of L. to isolate itself from European labor had now been
removed.[16] The British were undoubtedly anxious for the affiliation of the
A. F. of L. with the I.F.T.U., since sentiment for a united front was
increasing on the Continent and among English labor groups. In fact, the
British Trades Union Congress in 1936 had passed a resolution asking for
the establishment of "united trade union relations within the ambit of the
I.F.T.U. as a means towards international trade union unity."[17]

At its London congress in July 1936, the I.F.T.U. enacted a resolution
directing its Executive Committee to open negotiations with the unaffiliated national centers, including the Soviet Union. An invitation to begin
discussions was sent to the Soviet trade unions in October 1936; they did
not reply until August 1937. In the meantime, Walter Schevenels and
Walter Citrine, the two chief officers of the I.F.T.U., arrived in Washington in October 1936 and requested the Executive Council to send a delegate to the meeting of the I.F.T.U. to be held in Warsaw in August 1937.
The Council accepted, but when Matthew Woll arrived at Warsaw, he
found that his admission as a delegate was challenged by Camille Mertens
of Belgium and Léon Jouhaux of France. Annoyed, Woll told the delegates
that he had come at the invitation of the I.F.T.U. and if there was a belief
that he did not represent the largest federation of labor in the United
States, his invitation should have been canceled. The British delegates
supported Woll's admission, but Mertens and Jouhaux, who were joined
by the delegate from Mexico, insisted upon exclusion. It was finally
agreed, after several hours of debate behind closed doors, that Woll
would be recognized and a statement urging unification of the American
labor movement would be issued. According to Woll, "Sidney Hillman
and John L. Lewis . . . used every method they could in trying to block
affiliation of the American Federation of Labor with the International
Federation of Trade Unions." While the discussions were being carried
on, the secretary of the Clothing Workers' Secretariat phoned David Dubinsky from Warsaw and asked him what would be his attitude in
connection with the affiliation of the American Federation of Labor with
the International Federation of Trade Unions; Dubinsky replied that there
was only one decision they could reach, that they accept the American
Federation of Labor into membership, that there was no other organized
body, that "the C.I.O. is only a committee and they [the International

Federation of Trade Unions], would make a fatal mistake if they did not accept the American Federation of Labor."[18]

Dubinsky's attitude in this matter as well as that of others clearly shows that his concept of the C.I.O.'s role did not undergo much change; he always regarded that organization as a temporary one, needed to prod the Federation into a more aggressive organizing role in the mass-production industries. In this instance, his views were crucial, although the British strongly supported the necessity for accepting the affiliation of the A. F. of L.

Dramatic events were now shaking Europe. The revelation of Hitler's hostile intentions and the rise of a fascist threat in France had brought on a change in the Moscow line. The "united front from below" was now replaced by the demand for a popular front to be made up of men of good will ready to oppose fascist expansion by war. When the Soviet unions in August 1937 invited an I.F.T.U. delegation to visit Moscow and discuss affiliation, Schevenels, Jouhaux, and Assistant Secretary Stolz journeyed to the Soviet capital. Before they left for Russia, it had been clearly laid down by the Executive of the International Federation of Trade Unions that its purpose was to discuss the questions of affiliation and affiliation only. They were not to consider any question of a United Front or any other matter. It was pointed out to the members of the delegation that in the course of their investigation, they should endeavor to secure information as to whether the unions of the U. S. S. R. did, in fact, conform to another resolution passed by the London Congress in 1936. This second resolution laid down the necessity for trade union liberty as "an indispensable condition for an effective representation of the interests of the working class." It also affirmed "that the free decision of the Trade Unions cannot be replaced by an organization which people are compelled to join, and by means of which the Trade Unions are made helpless tools of the State, or even of the employers, as in the case in Germany, Italy, and Austria."[19]

Citrine's position on trade unionism as expressed by his letter to Green appears to be close to the one held by the A. F. of L. They agreed that unions had to be free to make their own decisions and remain independent of government control and that only unions conforming to these tests could be recognized in a federation of trade unions. The delegates to Moscow, obviously influenced by Jouhaux, whose French Federation of Labor had recently merged with a Communist labor group in his own country, paid little attention to the limits placed upon their mission. Not only did they forget the conditions for affiliation formulated by the I.F.T.U., but they accepted a nine-point program laid down by the Soviet unions as a condition for their affiliation, including support for a united front, the appointment of three general secretaries by the I.F.T.U., one of whom would represent the Soviet unions, and assurances that none of the funds contributed by Soviet unions would be used for propaganda against the Soviet Union or its organizations of labor. Citrine regarded the situation created by the Moscow delegates as "most embarrassing,"[20] for they apparently had "ignored the question of the relations between the Russian Trade Unions and their government, and [had] accepted the Russian conditions without any protest, actually signing the Minutes, thus going quite beyond their mandate."[21] The Executive Committee of the I.F.T.U. rejected the agreement which Jouhaux and Mertens had negotiated with the Soviet trade unions.

When the Executive Council of the A. F. of L. learned of the movement for affiliating the Soviet unions to the I.F.T.U., its members objected strongly to such a step. The Council refused to consider the Russian organizations as true trade unions, "in the sense which the term bears in every democratic country, and which it has always borne until the rise of dictatorships since the World War. They have no more freedom of action than have the official organizations commonly known as the 'labor front' in Italy, Germany, and Austria. Like these, they are in effect only a part of the administrative machinery of the dictatorial regime. . . . Free trade unions and governmentally controlled 'labor fronts' are as incompatible as are democracy and dictatorship in the state. The attempt to combine them in one world federation can result only in confusion, internal strife, and disaster. The American Federation of Labor will take no part in such a suicidal venture."[22]

At the meeting of the General Council of the International Federation, there was considerable support for allowing the Soviet unions to join. Hitler's occupation of Austria and the menacing declarations pouring from the German propaganda offices were warnings of the impending danger to all the labor movements in Europe, and many trade unionists believed that they could not afford to reject assistance from any source. There was in addition a widely held belief that the Communist dictatorship was more humane than the fascist, and in certain left-wing socialist circles, there was the feeling that communists and socialists were ideological brothers. Consequently, the proposal to accept Soviet terms received much support in spite of the two decades of bitter attack by the Communist organizations on the I.F.T.U. The French, Mexican, Norwegian, and Spanish delegations were willing to accept the Soviet terms. The delegates from Holland, Poland, Belgium, Switzerland, United States, Czechoslovakia, Denmark, and Great Britain registered their opposition. The American delegates opposed acceptance on several grounds. Others regarded the attempt of Soviet unions to restrain criticism of their government, then in the midst of Stalin's bloody purges, as highly objectionable. The Soviet terms were finally rejected.

Although the rejection of Soviet affiliation was approved by the General Council of the British Trades Union Congress, the Council's position was sharply attacked at the 70th Congress where the issue was discussed. In fact, George Hicks, who defended the position of the General Council, pitched his argument on an apologetic note. Hicks recalled the establishment of the Anglo-Russian Trade Union Committee in 1924 and the "declarations made by the Russian trade unions against the British T.U.C. were not only unjust, unfriendly, and unhelpful, but were also untrue." The declarations had called out so much resentment that the Trades Union Congress decided to disband the Anglo-Russian Committee.[23] Hicks also gave a résumé of the aims and the propaganda of the Red Labor Union International, whose chief task throughout the 1920's and most of the 1930's had been the destruction of the trade union movements not under Communist control. Nevertheless, the desire for unity against the fascist threat, coupled with a naïve faith in the basic goodness of the Soviet unions, compelled the General Council to agree to try again to have the Soviet unions admitted to the I.F.T.U. But this was not a sufficient concession to Communist sentiment; Arthur Horner, a delegate from the Mine Workers' Federation and a member of Great Britain's Communist Party, moved that this part of the report be referred back. His proposal was rejected by a vote of 2,619,000 to 1,493,000. Undoubtedly, the promise made by Citrine that another resolution endorsing unity would be submitted helped the General Council ward off the assault.

In a separate resolution, this Congress, while "regretting the absence of any satisfactory result of the negotiations between the I.F.T.U. and the Russian Trade Union Movement, reaffirmed the desire and policy of the British Trade Union Movement to establish complete unity and common action by Trade Union Organizations."[24]

On May 2, 1939 Citrine informed the A. F. of L. that the General Council of the British Trades Union Congress had decided to place on the I.F.T.U.'s agenda the question of the affiliation of the Central Council of Trade Unions of the U. S. S. R. The British wanted another invitation extended to the Soviet unions, asking them to affiliate on the basis of the statutes and rules of the I.F.T.U.[25] Green could not understand the reason for the change of attitude by the British Trades Union Congress, for he knew of no change in the principles and policies of the Soviet unions that justified modifying the earlier stand.

In his letter to Citrine, Green reviewed the stipulations that had been affixed to the A. F. of L.'s affiliation with the I.F.T.U. The American Federation of Labor had assumed that it would not be required to associate with national trade union centers which were not free, that all affiliates would be treated equally, and that the autonomy of all affiliated organizations would be recognized. Green found it

difficult . . . to understand how the Russian trade unions can possibly conform to the statutes of the International Federation of Trade Unions and be admitted only on the terms and conditions that apply to other centers. Certainly, under no circumstances, can the Russian trade unions comply with the same terms and conditions as govern free national trade union centers. If violence of interpretation is therefore to govern both in regard to the Statutes of the International Federation of Trade Unions and terms and conditions which apply to all other centers, then by the same token and decision, the German and Italian trade union centers and the alleged trade union centers of all other national socialist governments, whether communist, fascist, or nazi, are automatically eligible to membership. Once we admit into affiliation one governmentally directed, controlled and dictated labor organization, we will have no standard of measurement or justified reason for excluding others. Fundamentally, there is involved in the proposal of the British Trades Union Congress a change in the structure of the International Federation of Trade Unions, predicated on the basis of expediency . . . as may be manifested from time to time and made to conform to changed national situations quite without regard as to form and character of trade union organizations involved.

To this we cannot consent, much as we sympathize with the political and military situation confronting the British workers and British people generally, as well as the peoples and workers of the affiliated national trade union centers. It is our judgment that to alter the form and character of the International Federation of Trade Unions upon such predications will spell not only the early but definite dissolution of the International Federation of Trade Union itself.[26]

The British delegation, having been instructed by their own movement, had no choice but to present such a proposal to the I.F.T.U. Congress in Zurich in July 1939. On behalf of the British Trades Union Congress, George Hicks moved the adoption of the following resolution: "That it be an instruction to the Executive Committee of the I.F.T.U. to extend a further invitation to the Russian Trade Unions to affiliate on the basis of the Statutes and Rules of the I.F.T.U." Pointing to the increase in the political dangers as a result of the increased expansion in the armaments of fascist nations, Hicks said that all workers favored unity; and since the British Trades Union Congress had pressed its government to conclude the Anglo-French-Russian pact, labor had an obligation to unify its ranks. The Norwegian delegate, while agreeing with the British resolution, presented another which stressed the necessity of international trade union unity for a successful struggle for peace and freedom. The French delegate, Racamond, favored the affiliation of the Soviet unions and challenged the assertions that there was no freedom of association in Russia and that its trade unions were dependent upon the state. Robert Watt of the A. F. of L. repeated the arguments which Green had already presented in his letter. Great Britain, France, Norway, and Mexico cast thirty-seven votes for affiliation; and Belgium, Denmark, Finland, Holland, Luxembourg, Histadtut, Poland, Sweden, Switzerland, and the United States cast forty-six votes against the proposal.[27]

The British Trades Union Congress met again after the signing of the Hitler-Stalin pact, and the mood of this meeting was quite different from the one in the preceding year. The demands for inviting the Soviet unions were temporarily muffled. William Green was elected a vice president of the I.F.T.U.; in the election he received thirteen out of fourteen votes cast; the delegate from Argentina voted for Lombardo Toledano, a Mexican fellow traveler. At the beginning of World War II, the I.F.T.U. was compelled to transfer its headquarters to Paris and then, as France was overrun, to London. The A. F. of L. now agreed to pay full affiliation fees in order to aid the I.F.T.U. to continue its work.

After the attack on the Soviet Union had been launched by Hitler, there was an understandable softening of anti-Soviet feeling and a general admiration for the heroism of the Russian people who were bearing the terrible blows of Hitler's armies. Again the issue of cooperating with the Soviet trade unions was raised by the British. The Trades Union Congress in 1941, mindful of labor's pledge to support Soviet Russia in every possible way, offered "organized collaboration" with the Russian trade union movement. The delegates endorsed

the proposal of the General Council for the establishment of an Anglo-Russian Trade Union Council composed of an equal number of representatives of the All-Union Council of Trade Unions of the U. S. S. R. and of the British T.U.C. General Council, and providing for regular meetings alternately in Russia and Great Britain for the exchange of views and information upon the problems with which the Trade Union Movement in each country is called upon to deal, and affording opportunity for joint counsel and co-operation on matters of common concern, on the definite understanding that there shall be no interference on questions of internal policy and organization which must remain the exclusive responsibility of each body.[28]

Following the adoption of the resolution, Citrine approached Nicholas Shvernik, the secretary of the All-Union Council of Trade Unions of the U. S. S. R., and found that the British proposal was welcomed by the Russians. The Anglo-Soviet Trade Union Committee was established and held its first meeting in the Soviet Union during October 1941. The following eight-point agreement was reached, covering and endorsing

1. The joining together of the Trade Unions of Great Britain and of the Soviet Union for the organization of mutual assistance in the war against Hitlerite Germany.

2. Every possible support to the Governments of the U. S. S. R. and of Great Britain in their common war for the smashing defeat of Hitlerite Germany.

3. Strengthening of the industrial efforts of both countries with the aim of the maximum increase in the production of tanks, airplanes, guns, ammunition, and other arms.

4. Assistance in rendering the utmost help in arms to the Soviet Union by Great Britain.

5. To make use of all means of agitation and propaganda—the Press, Broadcasting, Cinema, workers' meetings, etc.—in the fight against Hitlerism.

6. All possible support to the people of the countries under the occupation of Hitlerite Germany, which are fighting for deliverance from the Hitler oppression for their independence and re-establishment of their democratic liberties.

7. Organization of mutual assistance of the Trade Unions of Great Britain and the Soviet Trade Unions and mutual information.

8. Strengthening of personal contact between the representatives of the Trade Union movements of the U. S. S. R. and Great Britain through the All-Union Central Council of Trade Unions of the U. S. S. R. and the British Trades Union Congress.[29]

At the next meeting of the Anglo-Soviet Trade Union Committee in England, the British suggestion that the Committee be broadened to include American representatives, "was cordially welcomed by the Soviet delegates and unanimously adopted."[30] Citrine was deputized to meet with the A. F. of L. Executive Council and present this proposal.

Citrine conferred with the A. F. of L. Executive Council in Washington on May 20, 1942. He assured the members of the Council that he had devised the proposal for setting up the Anglo-Soviet Trade Union Committee as a means of aiding the war effort, and that it had not been prompted by the British government. Stressing the advisory nature of the Committee, he strongly urged the A. F. of L. to become part of it. If the Federation were to join, Citrine said, all Committee recommendations would have to be ratified by the respective appointing bodies before becoming operative. When some Council members questioned one of the functions outlined by Citrine—postwar collaboration with Russia—he agreed that the Committee's role would be limited to the war period. At pains to show that the present collaboration did not mean endorsement of Communism, Citrine pleaded for a fuller collaboration after Green, speaking for the Council, said that the A. F. of L. could not join the Committee but might collaborate in an Anglo-American Trade Union Committee. The Federation's opposition to collaborating with the Soviet trade unions was not governed by whim, prejudice, or political changes, but by the deeply held conviction that they were not genuine labor organizations but instruments of the Soviet government.[31]

Green, replying to this appeal, agreed that if the Council members "were living in Great Britain, they would look at the matter in about the same way as Brother Citrine outlined it." But there was a different situation prevailing in the United States, and Green was ready to work toward closer cooperation with the British trades unions only. At Hutcheson's suggestion, Woll, Harrison, and Bugniazet were appointed to prepare a statement which stressed the points made by Green in his discussions before the Council. The statement also recognized the possibility of the Anglo-American Trade Union Committee acting as a liaison between the Federation and the Soviet unions on any matter of direct concern to the parties. A meeting for September was scheduled.[32]

In the meantime, Robert Watt, the A. F. of L. representative to the ILO, had been called to the American Embassy in London during April 1942, and had been requested to approve of the participation of the Soviet unions in the ILO. Refusing to grant such approval on his own responsibility, Watt advised Ambassador John Winant that this was a matter of Federation policy which only Green could change. Sometime later, Green reported to the Council that Mr. Isadore Lubin of the Department of Labor had called him and asked him to send a cablegram to Watt "urging him in the name of the A. F. of L. to unite with the representatives of other countries in favor of affiliation of the Soviet Government with the ILO." When Green asked Lubin who favored the proposal, he was told that the "matter was favored by our Government." Green refused to change the A. F. of L. position.[33]

Citrine told the next British Trades Union Congress that the A. F. of L. had "consistently asserted that there are no legitimate trade unions in the Soviet Union, and on those grounds had always opposed the admission of the All-Union Central Council of Trade Unions of the U. S. S. R." Citrine also informed the General Council of the British Trades Union Congress that if "they wished to continue their friendship with the American Federation of Labor it appeared clear that they could not negotiate with the C.I.O. without the agreement of the former body. If they did that they would antagonize the American Federation of Labor, and instead of promoting the cause of unity would do just the reverse."[34]

The railway brotherhoods and the C.I.O., having learned of the plan to set up an Anglo-American Trade Union Committee, insisted upon their right to representation in discussions between American and British labor leaders. Officers of the five railroad-operating crafts wired Citrine that "developments during the last few years and the present situation particularly emphasize the necessity for the closest kind of cooperation between workers of the world who are interested in preserving democracy . . . and the opportunity to express their views and assert their power and influence in shaping the national and international policies of their respective nations."[35] When Green received the cable, he angrily told the brotherhoods that the Federation had had friendly relations with the Trades Union Congress for more than fifty years, and that he could not recall "where one of the Railroad Brotherhoods, or all of them collectively, ever interested themselves in this Anglo-American relationship."[36] In the meantime, Philip Murray, the president of the C.I.O., protested to Citrine the exclusion of his organization by the Trades Union Congress from the plans for an Anglo-American Trade Union Committee.[37]

The refusal of the A. F. of L. to allow the C.I.O. and the railway brotherhoods to participate in a labor committee dealing with the war effort impressed the English as a stubborn and, because of the importance of the C.I.O. unions in steel, tank, and aircraft production, an unreasonable position. While the C.I.O. had fewer members than the A. F. of L., no one could have misjudged the relative importance of the industries the two organizations controlled in the war effort.

Notwithstanding the objections of the A. F. of L., the British Trades Union Congress could not easily ignore the requests for recognition by the railroad unions and the C.I.O. In August 1942 Citrine wrote Green that the General Council was anxious to include the railway unions and the C.I.O. in the Anglo-American Trade Union Committee. The General Council, he said, recognized the "difficulties which now stand in the way and made this appeal most earnestly. . . . [It was] confident if this course is adopted out of respect to the wishes of the Trades Union Congress, your action will be deeply appreciated not only by members of the British Trades Union Movement, but by all those conscious of the need for promoting the closest collaboration between British and American labour which the present war situation renders imperative."[38] For a time the second meeting between the British delegation and the Executive Council scheduled for September was postponed.

A committee of five from the British Trades Union Congress arrived in the United States in January 1943. Citrine repeated that he had originally hoped to get the trade union movements of the United States, England, and the Soviet Union to cooperate in the war effort. He regretted the stated attitude of the A. F. of L. in this matter, and he was also disappointed by the continued refusal of the A. F. of L. to allow the C.I.O. and the railroad brotherhoods to join the Anglo-American Trade Union Committee. When the General Council of the British Trades Union Congress had wired the A. F. of L. on August 12, 1942, making the request that the C.I.O. and railroad unions be admitted, the A. F. of L. had not replied. According to Citrine, the British government "then took a hand. . . . The Prime Minister was the first person to intervene in this. He put it to me that they had advices from Washington and he said if we went on with the committee meetings we would very greatly jeopardize

Anglo-American relations. . . . I expressed resentment pointedly to our Prime Minister. He asked me would I see our Foreign Secretary, Mr. Anthony Eden, about it. He showed me a long telegram from the British Embassy . . . in Washington which said that if the projected meetings were held . . . it would have a very serious effect upon Anglo-American relations. It would react unfavorably on war production."[39] Citrine's fears were baseless and it is doubtful whether his argument really reflected the views of the British government.

The General Council had also been informed, Citrine said, that a meeting in September might have undesirable political repercussions.

Hutcheson explained that the C.I.O. was not regarded as being on a par with the A. F. of L. and although the relations between the railroad unions and the A. F. of L. were friendly, the A. F. of L. would not agree to giving parity to either group on a committee dealing with the British Trades Union Congress. Citrine told the Council members of the difficulties he and other officers of the Trades Union Congress faced within their own ranks over this question.

Citrine gave some details of the pressure being exerted by the British government and he indicated that the United States government was also involved. The British felt that

there should be some way out. If you can sit side by side in committees under your President or under your Government departments with C.I.O. representatives, it should be possible to find an arrangement whereby we can sit side by side in this international phase of the war effort. We had hoped you would listen to our appeal just as much as you would listen to your Government. We do hope that you will, even at this stage, when perhaps it has become more difficult . . . try to see if it is not possible to find a way whereby we can be associated, through this committee, or the expansion of it by your inviting the C.I.O. or by any means that may suggest themselves to you by getting together, and so remove us from what has become an embarrassing position to us.[40]

Tobin declared that the A. F. of L. had been surprised at the original request to meet with the Soviet unions and that the meetings with the British were really a "matter of courtesy and for our respect and reverence for the British trade union movement and their officials whom we have known for many years."[41] He did not see what a conference could accomplish now, because labor was already doing everything possible to aid the war effort. Sharply assailing the C.I.O.'s early attitude toward Great Britain and the war, Green entered the discussion and charged that the group which then controlled the C.I.O. had denounced the British for conducting an imperialist war and had demanded that the United States abstain from any support of the English when they stood alone and beleaguered. In denouncing those who controlled C.I.O. policy, Green attacked Curran, Bridges, and Quill; but he said that his criticisms

did not apply to Phil Murray. "He was a miner. . . . I am not saying this
against Murray because he always had been different."[42]

As for the pressures of the British and American governments, Green
was convinced that the C.I.O. had approached the White House and the
British Embassy "and there exercised their influence to prevent that
meeting, because the White House called me in. . . . They got to the
British Embassy and pointed out it was going to create turmoil and strife
and injure the war effort and hurt production in the factories. . . ."[43]
Green was correct in his conjecture that someone from the outside had
approached the White House, but it was Citrine and not the C.I.O.
leaders. Undoubtedly Citrine was motivated by the highest motives; the
leaders of British trade unionism were in a difficult position because of
pressures within the Trades Union Congress. In a meeting with Murray
and several other members of the C.I.O., Citrine had explained that the
A. F. of L. would not agree to the inclusion of the C.I.O. in the Anglo-
American Trade Union Committee. In an effort to persuade the Federation to relent, Citrine had talked to the Ambassador in London, John
Winant, and had been told the matter had been discussed with President
Roosevelt. When Citrine was in the United States, he "had talked with
the President and [Roosevelt] said he would have a talk with the C.I.O.
and A. F. of L. and see whether it was not possible to get them together."[44] Citrine strongly emphasized that it was important to keep his
meeting with President Roosevelt confidential and that he "would regard
it as a very great breach if it were mentioned that he had been seen
either by the President or Mr. Winant."[45]

When Citrine repeated the charges made by Green against the C.I.O.,
Murray showed his anger and defended his record of support of the
British from the beginning of the war. Of course, Green had pointedly
excluded Murray from the charges of opposing the British war effort on
the ground that it was an imperialist struggle. His attack had been directed at other C.I.O. leaders and it certainly would not have been easily
denied by them. In the end, Murray said that the British could do whatever they wished, for he was tired of the whole matter.

The A. F. of L.'s stand in excluding the C.I.O. from participation in
international affairs might appear as an unwise one. It seemed to place
the leaders of the British Trades Union Congress in an untenable position
with respect to the demands by large sections of their movement that
the C.I.O. should not be ignored; some claim it also gave impetus to
plans for postwar collaboration with the Soviet trade unions, plans which
might have been resisted had the C.I.O. been allowed to join the Anglo-
American Trade Union Committee. The major reasons for the obduracy
of the A. F. of L. was the influence of the Communists at the time in the
C.I.O. Controlling ten or eleven unions and with powerful minorities in

a number of others, the A. F. of L. believed that concessions to the C.I.O., such as allowing it to affiliate with the Anglo-American Trade Union Committee, would not affect the international views of Lee Pressman and other Communists and fellow travelers in the C.I.O. Allowing the C.I.O. to affiliate would simply have meant, the A. F. of L. was convinced, giving the Communists an opportunity, through the C.I.O., to disrupt and poison the relations between the A. F. of L. and the Trades Union Congress.

The Federation considered the matter of sufficient importance to issue a detailed statement. While recognizing the difference in the problems confronting the British and the American labor movements, the A. F. of L. found no reason to cooperate with the Soviet trade unions. The Federation did recognize, however, that the Soviet Union was an ally in a common effort to defeat the Axis powers. "Unwillingness to recognize the Soviet trade unions other than as governmental agencies and . . . refusal to cooperate with them by reason of the fact that they are unlike our free trade unions had in no way, and will in no way, detract or lessen our zeal in rendering every possible aid, support, and help to the Russian government and its people who are so valiantly contributing their manhood and womanhood, of their wealth and effort in the titanic struggle now taking place."[46]

The Federation regretted the disappointment of the British labor movement over the unwillingness of the A. F. of L. to include in the delegation to the Anglo-American Trade Union Committee representatives of the C.I.O. and railroad brotherhoods. The Federation maintained, nevertheless, that it alone could decide a matter which governed the relation between organizations of labor in the United States. But the Federation was willing to review its decision.

The Executive Council's position was discussed and later endorsed at the 1943 convention.[47] Meanwhile the British labor movement was enthusiastically cooperating with the Soviet organizations, and sentiment for the expansion of the Anglo-Soviet committee to include other countries was widespread, although not at the time shared by the British leadership.[48] The Anglo-American committee did not become a very fruitful organization, mainly limiting itself to reviewing the action of the respective governments on common issues and reciting the particular problems confronting the two movements. Since conditions in Britain and the United States were in most instances basically different, neither group could offer much aid to the other. The periodic meeting, however, certainly did not harm the labor movements of the two countries.

Although it was not ready to modify its traditional policy of noncooperation with labor organizations under government control, the Federation increasingly recognized the importance of foreign policy to the labor movement, and its activity in the field slowly increased. In common with most Americans, the Federation leadership was in the 1920's essentially isolationist, and it recommended the avoidance of foreign entanglements. This attitude was reflected in the reluctance to cooperate with the labor movements of other countries. The long-term fraternal relations with the British Trades Union Congress was a special case—the result of the respect for the British labor movement which always existed in some parts of the Federation. The A. F. of L. had refused in 1929 to send a delegate to the Congress of the German trade unions.

Immediately before World War II, however, some of the hesitancy about cooperating with foreign labor groups lessened. The Federation raised thousands of dollars through the Labor War Chest to help relieve European trade unionists who had fled the Hitler terror. Although this work was conducted on a modest scale, it was a sign of a changing attitude. During this period, Woll reported that $25,000 had been sent to support the underground work being carried on by the International Transport Workers.[49] In the main, however, the Federation's attitude continued to be a passive one.

One reflection of the greater importance attached to international relations by the A. F. of L. leadership was the appointment of a permanent international relations committee upon which Secretary Meany, President Green, and Vice President Woll were to serve. This was a preliminary step in the development of an active policy in the field of foreign relations. The evolution was hastened by the steps taken by the General Council of the British Trades Union Congress to convene a conference of representatives of organized workers of all countries in London during June 1944. In addition to exploring new methods for promoting the war effort, the conference planned to discuss labor representation at the peace conference, postwar reconstruction, and the revival of the international trade union movement. The General Council was convinced that

if the Trade Union Movement is to be rebuilt, it must be attempted on the broadest possible basis. That basis can only be achieved if all bona-fide Trade Union Movements are invited to come together to see how it may be possible to rise above their domestic and national difficulties in the task of rebuilding the International Movement. The General Council feels very strongly that this is a supreme testing time in the history of the Trade Union Movement. . . . Unless the Trade Unions, representing the working classes, find it possible to sit together in conference, to commune on our common international problems, and to try to find a constructive policy to rebuild our great International Movement, the prospects of humanity are dark indeed.[50]

In Green's mind, the job of calling an international conference of trade unions belonged to the International Federation of Trade Unions to which both the A. F. of L. and Trades Union Congress belonged; it was not a task, Green thought, which should rightfully be exercised by a labor movement of a single country. "It would seem," Green advised Citrine, "quite appropriate and proper that all organizations affiliated with the International Federation of Trade Unions should have been consulted upon the question as to whether an international conference of trade union representatives should be convened, and if after consultation it was deemed advisable to call such a conference, that the International Federation of Trade Unions be authorized to call such a conference."

At its meeting in January 1944, the Executive Council endorsed Green's opinion and questioned the propriety of the action of the British Trades Union Congress in sponsoring an international conference without consulting the member organizations of the I.F.T.U. While admitting the need for a meeting of representatives of the trade union movements of the different countries, the Council feared that

the proposed London conference would defeat the ends it seeks to accomplish because it lacks the proper sponsorship, because it is untimely, and because the proposed representation at the conference invites discord and division rather than harmony and unity. The delegates of some nations invited to attend cannot truly represent free and democratic labor because no free and democratic movement now exists in those countries. . . . Many delegations from some nations would not be able to speak authoritatively in behalf of the workers in their countries because those countries are still under the heel of the enemy. Representatives of neutral countries which are nevertheless under Axis influence, if not actual control, also have been invited and the Executive Council fails to see how they could contribute to democratic solutions of labor's postwar problems.[51]

The President of the I.F.T.U. defended the action of the British. In his review of the question raised by Green, he said that the International Federation had supported the British invitation and that preliminary consultations had taken place between the General Secretaries of the British T.U.C. and the I.F.T.U. Moreover, the I.F.T.U. leaders had believed that fewer difficulties would be encountered if the British called such a conference.[52]

At first the Russians wanted the conference sponsored by the All-Union Central Council of Soviet Unions, the British Trades Union Congress, and the Congress of Industrial Organizations, but subsequently they agreed to allowing the Trades Union Congress to exercise that office.[53]

In the meantime, Schevenels explained to Green the reasons for the change in attitude by the I.F.T.U. He did not underestimate the problem of government control over trade unions, but he wanted the issue discussed at a later stage. "Though you may retort," Schevenels advised Green, "that the Russian delegates at such a conference are not free agents and do not genuinely represent their fellow workers, the fact remains that these representatives will voice the policy that will actually be upheld by and on behalf of 35 million industrial workers in Soviet Russia."[54]

Schevenels thought it would be helpful in the future if the labor movements of different countries exchanged views at this time, irrespective of their differing social structures. On the motion of George Meany, the A. F. of L. refused to attend the London conference.[55]

The General Council of the I.F.T.U. met in London in February 1945, with the reorganization of the Federation one of the questions on the agenda. Watt spoke out against inviting the Russian trade unions to confer with representatives of free labor. "You might as well invite the Government of Russia itself," he told the conference.[56] Will Lawther, representing the Mine Workers International Secretariat, accused Watt of not being aware "that time marches on." Lawther noted that the A. F. of L. did not have a single representative in the American Congress; the British miners had sent two of its members to Parliament seventy years ago. Watt's criticism of the Soviet unions was out of place, according to Lawther.[57]

The A. F. of L. Executive Council directed a committee—Harry Bates, Meany, and Green—to find out from President Roosevelt whether the American and British governments were participating in these conferences. Roosevelt replied "in the negative. . . . He knew nothing about it, had had nothing to do with it, and was not participating in it in any way, and . . . he did not know whether the British government was interested in the matter or not."[58]

The London conference took place, in spite of the A. F. of L.'s refusal to attend. Sidney Hillman, one of the C.I.O.'s vice presidents, played an important role at the conference in the launching of the World Federation of Trade Unions.[59] Citrine was sorry that the A. F. of L. had not sent a delegate to London, but he sent a verbatim report of the proceedings to Green so that the Executive Council would be fully informed.[60]

The Executive Council took special notice of the "sarcastic address" of Sidney Hillman in which he had charged that the A. F. of L. had isolated itself from world affairs. The Council was also disturbed by the support the new movement was receiving from the British Trades Union Congress "which must now decide whether to maintain its cooperative and fraternal relationship with other member organizations of the I.F.T.U. or to play second fiddle in Mr. Hillman's new Communist front."[61]

The A. F. of L. sought to salvage the International Federation of Trade Unions, but it was alone in this endeavor. It also continued in its refusal to allow the C.I.O. to join the I.F.T.U. Green, taking note of some of the proposals before the London conference, asked what attitude the representatives of the C.I.O. who are attending the London conference will assume toward the proposal which is being urged by Russian Communists that German labor must be made slave labor and through such action substitute involuntary servitude and slavery for freedom and liberty. The proposal to make German labor slave labor when the war is ended is economically unsound, indefensible from a social point of view, and contrary to the principles which the United Nations are seeking to establish when the war ends. Hitler and those responsible for the war must be punished, but the people throughout the world, including labor everywhere, must be made free and must be guaranteed the right to enjoy the blessings and benefits of freedom, liberty and democracy.[62]

At the same time Green was critical of Schevenels and Citrine, who had been active promoters of the London meeting of world labor. He suggested a later meeting of the I.F.T.U. to be held in the United States or Canada. Some members of the Executive Council were ready to withdraw from the I.F.T.U.; Tobin suggested that this step be taken after the Federation had paid its back membership fees. Meany said that the I.F.T.U. had been operating since 1938 without authority from its affiliates, and that an Emergency Council had been conducting its business. To Green's request for a meeting of the I.F.T.U., its secretary, Schevenels, replied that the World Trade Union Conference held in London from February 6 to 17, 1945, had made it necessary for the International Federation to reexamine its position. Schevenels argued that although it was "true to say that this World Conference has no power to determine the future of the I.F.T.U., it is not possible to ignore the fact that with the exception of only one organization [the A. F. of L.], all the affiliates were represented at the Conference and formally assented to the declaration."[63] Schevenels also told Green that the delegates to the London conference had favored setting up an international trade union organization "of the world irrespective of considerations of race, nationality, religion, or political opinion," and that the I.F.T.U. would be liquidated if agreement were reached by the promoters of the new world labor organization. The Federation rejected the invitation and expressed its opposition to destroying the I.F.T.U.[64]

The Federation was now standing alone in the international arena; it would not join a labor federation containing Communist unions. When Louis Saillant, a French Communist, became secretary of the newly formed World Federation of Trade Unions instead of Walter Schevenels, who had been the candidate of the British Trades Union Congress and who had occupied the post in the I.F.T.U., the Federation called public attention to these facts.[65] The C.I.O. joined the W.F.T.U. after playing an important role in its formation. In October 1945 Citrine informed the

A. F. of L. of the desire of the British Trades Union Congress to form a joint committee with the C.I.O., and he invited the A. F. of L. to become a member. Meany, who had been a fraternal delegate to the British Trades Union Congress, had informed Citrine that if the C.I.O. sent a fraternal delegate to the British Trades Union Congress, the A. F. of L. would feel obliged to discontinue its relations with the British Trades Union Congress—an association which had been in effect since 1894. On the motion of Harrison, Citrine was told that the A. F. of L. desired "to continue unaltered our long-standing relations with the British Trades Union Congress."[66]

The British Trades Union Congress and the C.I.O. were soon to rediscover that it was not possible for a free trade union movement to cooperate with one in a totalitarian country. That experienced labor leaders could completely forget the lessons of the past and succumb to the lure of "unity" must be set down to the bewitching effect the remarkable heroism of the Russian people had on the thinking of certain elements in the labor movements of different countries. Citrine was well acquainted with Communist tactics; he knew the experiences of British labor when it had collaborated with Soviet unions in the 1920's, and yet he allowed himself to lead a movement for creating a powerful propaganda and executive arm for world Communism. Many people not associated with the labor movement, influenced by the heroism of the Russian people and the feats of the Soviet armies during the war, had the same illusions, although these were more excusable. Such feelings were bound to become intensified among European socialist and labor groups where the views had always existed among a small minority. The Federation refused to be stampeded from its historic position; it was not pride or stubbornness, but rather experience and an evaluation of the Soviet unions and their labor satellites in other countries, including France and Italy, which determined Federation policy.

In reply to the criticism of the London *Economist* that there was "no inherent reason visible to the outside, why the American Federation of Labor and the Russians should not sit side by side in the new organization," Green presented in detail the position of the A. F. of L. He drew a distinction between the collaboration between governments and between trade unions, one which the A. F. of L. had always underlined.

States [said Green] are organizations of power, not ideological or political associations. Their policy is determined in the first place not by ideals or programs, but by geographic, economic, strategic, and even military considerations. . . . No one expects a state to be oriented in its foreign policy or its trade policy solely by moral and ideological motives. "We can trade even with cannibals," declared the British Statesman, David Lloyd George, in 1921. But would the British missionaries associate themselves with cannibals in their humanitarian endeavors? Such a moral attitude would be entirely impossible for a labor union organization. International cooperation among trade unions and other labor organizations can be based only on a certain community of moral principles, ideals, and methods.[67]

Green argued that the trade unions in free countries were based upon different concepts and methods from those in the Soviet Union. Collaboration with the Soviet trade unions could only be brought about, in his opinion, by the free trade unions betraying their democratic and humanitarian principles and by abdicating as free and independent labor bodies. Green forecast that the "result of closer collaboration with the Soviet trade unions would be that the world body of organized labor would lose its freedom to criticize the Soviet Union and the Communist dictatorship. While opposition to and criticism of the so-called 'capitalistic' countries and governments would meet with the approval of the Soviet delegates, every word of disapproval or the slightest criticism of the policy or of the methods of the Russian dictatorship would be vetoed by the delegates of the Soviet trade unions. Thus the world labor federation would practically be transformed in the political field into a 'yes organization' of the Soviet government and consequently of world Communism."

Green believed that the free trade unions faced a struggle for survival. With the "immensely increased prestige of Soviet Russia, [with] ample funds and [with] the world-wide and well-organized network of open and camouflaged Communist cells and groups, the Communist parties [Green said] will try to exploit the economic difficulties of the working men and of the independent workers and farmers." He concluded that the

international organization which the World Trade Union Conference in London has proposed to establish would unquestionably be of great assistance to the Communists in carrying out their plans.

Any attempt to improve the standard of living of all workers on an international basis would face the difficulty that the Russian trade unions would never or could never assume responsibility for putting the decisions of the World Federation into effect on the territory of the U. S. S. R. Even the prevention of unfair competition by cheap labor would be acceptable to the Soviet delegates only on condition that Russia be exempted from these decisions with regard to the products of Russian prison labor and also with regard to underpaid Russian free labor. All other decisions of world labor regarding the living conditions of workers, their conditions of work, the collective bargaining rights, their right to strike, etc., would be only partially acceptable to the Russian Communists who would represent the trade unions in the World Federation.[68]

Green repeated the A. F. of L.'s desire to cooperate to rebuild the international labor movement, but never, he declared, would the Federation join with labor organizations which were not free to make their decisions unhampered by government fiat.

## REFERENCES

1. J. Oudegeest to Green, September 25, 1925.
2. Minutes of Executive Council, October 16, 1925.
3. Green to Oudegeest, October 26, 1925.
4. *Report of the Proceedings of the Forty-sixth Annual Convention of the American Federation of Labor,* 1926, p. 360.
5. Green to Oudegeest, April 27, 1937.
6. W. N. Castle to Green, April 4, 1932.
7. Official File 499, Box 1, Franklin Delano Roosevelt Library.
8. *Report of the Proceedings of the Fifty-fourth Annual Convention of the American Federation of Labor,* 1934, pp. 724–725.
9. Green to Franklin D. Roosevelt, March 13, 1944.
10. *Report of the Proceedings of the Forty-ninth Annual Convention of the American Federation of Labor,* 1929, pp. 3–4.
11. Walter Citrine to Green, cablegram, November 11, 1931.
12. Green to Executive Council, November 19, 1931; Vote Book of the Executive Council, November 27, 1931.
13. *Report of the Proceedings of the Fifty-fourth Annual Convention of the American Federation of Labor,* 1934, pp. 573–574.
14. *Report of the Proceedings of the Fifty-fifth Annual Convention of the American Federation of Labor,* 1935, pp. 717–718.
15. *Ibid.,* p. 718.
16. Green to Walter Schevenels, December 20, 1935; Shevenels to Green, December 22, 1935; Minutes of Executive Council, May 5, and May 11, 1936.
17. *Report of Proceedings at 70th Annual Trades Union Congress,* 1938, p. 190.
18. Minutes of Executive Council, August 31, 1937.
19. Citrine to Green, December 14, 1938, in response to Green's request for information on the rumors that the Soviet unions would join the I.F.T.U.
20. Citrine to Green, January 14, 1938, answering a request for information in Green to Citrine, December 3, 1938.
21. Citrine to Green, January 21, 1939.
22. Minutes of Executive Council, February 2, 1938.
23. *Report of Proceedings at the 70th Annual Trades Union Congress,* 1938, p. 307.
24. *Ibid.*
25. Citrine to Affiliated National Centers, May 2, 1939.
26. Green to Citrine, June 16, 1939.
27. "Eighth International Trade Union Congress," *The International Trade Union Movement,* June-July 1939, pp. 197–206; Memorandum from Robert J. Watt to William Green, undated.

28. British Trades Union Congress, *Report of Proceedings at the 73rd Annual Trades Union Congress,* 1941, p. 243.

29. Walter Citrine to Green, March 20, 1942.

30. *Ibid.*

31. Minutes of Executive Council, May 20, 1942.

32. Declaration Adopted by the Executive Council of the American Federation of Labor, Minutes of Executive Council, May 22, 1942.

33. Minutes of Executive Council, May 18, 1942.

34. British Trades Union Congress, *Report of the Proceedings of the 74th Trades Union Congress,* 1942, p. 239.

35. Alvanley Johnston, D. R. Robertson, H. W. Fraser, A. F. Whitney, and T. C. Cashen to Green, August 6, 1942.

36. Green to A. F. Whitney, September 22, 1942.

37. Philip Murray to Citrine, August 6, 1942.

38. Citrine to Green, August 12, 1942.

39. Minutes of Executive Council, January 27, 1943.

40. *Ibid.*

41. *Ibid.*

42. *Ibid.*

43. *Ibid.*

44. Conference between British Trades Union Delegation and Congress of Industrial Organizations, at Washington on February 16, 1943.

45. *Ibid.*

46. Minutes of Executive Council, January 27, 1943.

47. *Report of the Proceedings of the Sixty-third Annual Convention of the American Federation of Labor,* 1943, p. 503.

48. British Trades Union Congress, *Report of Proceedings at the 75th Annual Trades Union Congress,* 1943, pp. 278–280.

49. Minutes of Executive Council, January 27, 1944.

50. Citrine to Green, November 2, 1943.

51. Minutes of Executive Council, January 25, 1944.

52. International Federation of Trade Unions, *Report on Activities, 1943–1944* (Issued in March 1944 in London).

53. Emergency Trade Union Council Summary of Meeting held in London, Transport House, September 14, 1944.

54. Schevenels to Green, January 14, 1944.

55. Minutes of Executive Council, November 19, 1944.

56. I.F.T.U. General Council Meeting held in Transport House, London, on February 1 and 2, 1945, p. 11.

57. *Ibid.,* p. 13.

58. Minutes of Executive Council, February 7, 1945.

59. See John P. Windmuller, *American Labor and the International Labor Movement 1940 to 1953* (Ithaca, New York: The Institute of International Industrial and Labor Relations, 1954).

60. Citrine to Green, March 21, 1945.

61. Minutes of Executive Council, February 13, 1945.

62. Statement of William Green, February 10, 1945, in files of A. F. of L.

63. Schevenels to Green, July 4, 1945.

64. Minutes of Executive Council, August 9, 1945.

65. Minutes of Executive Council, October 18, 1945.

66. Minutes of Executive Council, October 19, 1945; Citrine to Green, October 16, 1945.

67. William Green, "The American Federation of Labor and World Labor Unity," *The American Federationist*, August 1945.

68. *Ibid.*

# XX

## Postwar Economic and Political Programs

IN December 1942 President Green appointed a postwar planning committee of seven members with Matthew Woll as chairman. The committee was charged with (1) the development of a plan for labor representation at the peace conference following the end of the war; (2) the formulation of specific proposals for incorporation in the peace treaty; (3) the formulation of a broad program of postwar reconstruction to prevent a serious depression; and (4) the discovery of a means of expanding the social and economic security of the people of the United States and other countries.[1]

In its report to the 1944 convention, the Executive Council presented a detailed statement which had been elaborated by the postwar planning committee. The statement called for a lasting peace based upon the Four Freedoms promulgated in the Atlantic Charter of January 1941. The first step in a more extensive plan to assure permanent peace and prosperity to the people of the world was the allied victory on the world's battlefields. Consequently, the committee held that military programs had to be associated with far-reaching economic plans for the advancement of all the nations and for the raising of the standard of living of all peoples. This was a foreshadowing of the Marshall Plan. Emphasizing that freedom of thought should be safeguarded in all parts of the world, the Federation's committee pointed to the performance of the American economy during the war. "The world-wide depression of the previous decade, and the world-wide war which followed have proved," the report said, "that we are members one of another. Poverty, unemployment, and widespread economic insecurity are not endurable in the midst of potential plenty. To organize the economic life of the world so that these possibilities are made actual is the aim of organized labor."[2]

The Federation endorsed the establishment of an international organization for the settlement of differences between nations by peaceful methods rather than by war, and urged that the wartime alliance be transformed into an organization of united nations. The United Nations Relief and Rehabilitation Administration (UNRRA) was praised for its attempts to relieve hunger and suffering.

On the domestic scene the committee visualized an economy that would provide work with adequate pay for every worker. Using the productive output of the war as the index of what the American economy could accomplish, the report asked for a revised concept of the ultimate possibilities in the field of production. "Future productive capacity," the report declared, "can provide better homes, better food and clothing, more adequate medical care, finer communities and richer educational and cultural communities for all."[3] For the maintenance of a stable democracy, the report demanded jobs for all in the postwar period and the assurance that the demobilized servicemen would be able to find employment when they returned to their normal work. Cooperation of all functional groups for the achievement of higher production goals was needed, the committee said.

Although it endorsed the private enterprise system, the committee warned that "the free enterprise system . . . must be committed to the progressive raising of the national income and the maintenance of full employment. . . . We want free enterprise, but we also want an economy which will provide ample support for the health, educational, recreational, and similar public services so essential to the welfare of the working people in our industrial society. Finally we want a program of economic enterprise which will not be repressive, but will support the free exercise of civil and political liberties."[4]

Testifying before a Congressional committee on behalf of the postwar planning group of the A. F. of L., Matthew Woll recommended that the demobilization of the armed and defense forces should be accompanied by the reconversion of industry. The government, Woll advised, should integrate its discharge program with the employment situation and offer its help in the resettlement problem which many defense workers faced. The A. F. of L. thought that an Office of War Mobilization and Adjustment, similar to the one proposed in a bill introduced by Senator Harry Kilgore, would minimize the harmful economic effects of the shift from wartime to peacetime production.[5]

On May 1, 1944 the A. F. of L., the C.I.O., and the Railway Labor Executives Association came out jointly against any "piecemeal legislation to handle the problems of reconversion, with priority given to property legislation."[6] Representatives of the three groups recommended (1) an integrated program of reconversion; (2) a special unemployment compensation in the transition period from war to peace; (3) the establishment of an Office of War Mobilization and Adjustment to coordinate all government activities during the reconversion period; (4) the creation of a National Production-Employment Board made up of representatives of industry, labor, agriculture, and the public; and (5) the provision of adequate incentives to small business in reconverting to peace.[7]

At its meeting in February 1945 the Executive Council proposed that definite steps be undertaken to enlist labor, industry, and agriculture in a common program for achieving maximum peacetime production and full employment in private industry. As a prerequisite the Council suggested that organized industry announce its acceptance of free collective bargaining with the nation's trade unions. The Council also suggested the establishment of a public works program which could be carried on by local and state, as well as the Federal government, an increase in the hourly wage rate, and the abolition of all controls over industry and agriculture.[8]

In March 1945 the A. F. of L. was invited by President Roosevelt to participate in a meeting with the C.I.O., the United States Chamber of Commerce, and the National Association of Manufacturers. Because he feared the bad effect a refusal would have on public opinion, Green accepted the invitation.[9]

The conference participants drew up a code of principles that all the groups, except the National Association of Manufacturers, accepted. This "New Charter for Labor and Management," as it was called, sought to lay the groundwork for continuing the labor-management cooperation which had been achieved during the war. To this end, the groups acknowledged the following seven points as a basis of their continuing partnerships:

1. Increased prosperity for all involves the highest degree of production and employment at wages assuring a steadily advancing standard of living. Improved productive efficiency and technological advancement must, therefore, be constantly encouraged.

2. The rights of private property and free choice of action, under a system of private competitive capitalism, must continue to be the foundation of our nation's peaceful and prosperous expanding economy. Free competition and free men are the strength of our free society.

3. The inherent right and responsibility of management to direct the operations of an enterprise shall be recognized and preserved. So that enterprise may develop and expand and earn a reasonable profit, management must be free as well from unnecessary governmental interference or burdensome restrictions.

4. The fundamental rights of labor to organize and to engage in collective bargaining with management shall be recognized and preserved, free from legislative enactments which would interfere with or discourage these objectives. Through the acceptance of collective bargaining agreements, differences between management and labor can be disposed of between the parties through peaceful means, thereby discouraging avoidable strife through strikes and lockouts.

5. The independence and dignity of the individual and the enjoyment of his democratic rights are inherent in our free American society. Our purpose

is to cooperate in building an economic system for the nation which will protect the individual against the hazards of unemployment, old-age, and physical impairments beyond his control.

6. An expanding economy at home will be stimulated by a vastly increased foreign trade. Arrangements must therefore be perfected to afford the devestated or undeveloped nations reasonable assistance to encourage the rebuilding and development of sound economic systems. International trade cannot expand through subsidized competition among the nations for a diminishing market but can be achieved only through expanding world markets and the elimination of any arbitrary and unreasonable practices.

7. An enduring peace must be secured. This calls for the establishment of an international security organization, with full participation by all the United Nations, capable of preventing aggression and assuring lasting peace.

We in management and labor agree that our primary duty is to win complete victory over Nazism and Japanese militarism. We also agree that we have a common joint duty, in cooperation with other elements of our national life and with government, to prepare and work for a prosperous and sustained peace. In this spirit we agree to create a national committee composed of representatives of business and labor organizations. This committee will seek to promote an understanding and sympathetic acceptance of this code of principles and will propose such national policies as will advance the best interests of our nation.[10]

When the Executive Council reviewed the report, several members critized Green's action. Hutcheson objected to the Federation's president signing a report with the representatives of the C.I.O., although he was not unwilling to agree with the representatives of the Chamber of Commerce. President Green said "that it would be almost impossible to make it a practicable workable thing if it was accepted by the C.I.O. and industry alone, or by the A. F. of L. and industry alone, because as much as we might desire it, the situation involves the reality of the fact that the C.I.O. does represent the workers in a large number of big industries, like steel, etc."[11] A motion proposing that the Federation meet with representatives of the employers but that no collaboration be carried on with the C.I.O. was carried; Meany and Vice President Doherty opposed. Tobin, who had criticised the signing of the statement, then proposed that "in matters of this kind that may come up in the future, the President of this American Federation of Labor shall sign no document or agree to any national policy in behalf of this Council until it is first submitted to the Council for consideration."[12]

### Labor-Management Conference

In July 1945 Senator Arthur Vandenberg called for a labor-management conference "to lay the groundwork for peace and justice on the home front." Simultaneously, the same possibility was being considered by President Truman, who called a conference at which representatives of the A. F. of L., the C.I.O., the Chamber of Commerce, and the National Association of Manufacturers participated, with Secretary of Labor Lewis Schwellenbach in attendance. Following the preliminary meeting, committees were set up to prepare an agenda for the conference which was scheduled to begin on November 5.[13] At the Executive Council meeting on October 23, the Federation offered several simple principles: (1) that the conference subscribe to the full recognition and complete practice of collective bargaining between labor and management in industry; (2) that both parties recognize their obligation to make and maintain collective labor agreements; and (3) that the parties operating under such agreements have the duty to establish machinery for prompt and expeditious settlement of grievances which arise under the collective-bargaining contract.[14]

A delegation of eight members of the Executive Council, led by Green and Meany, was appointed; both the C.I.O. and the United Mine Workers of America were represented by their own members. Called to order by Judge Walter P. Stacy, who had been selected as chairman, the conference was opened by President Truman on November 5. A dispute over the make-up of the Executive Committee soon developed. Philip Murray charged "a veritable blitz was under way in the meeting to make Mr. Lewis a member of the Executive Committee." Lewis did not "like Mr. Murray's unique and despicable German terminology," and in the end Lewis was made a member of the Executive Committee. The conference appointed committees to deal with (1) collective bargaining, (2) management's right to manage, (3) representation and jurisdiction, (4) conciliation service, (5) initial collective-bargaining agreements, and (6) collective-bargaining agreements. Each group was equally represented on committees.

The committee on collective bargaining wanted to discover the extent to which industrial disputes could be minimized when collective bargaining was fully recognized by management and also what other measures would limit disputes. Neither the subcommittee nor the conference was able to agree on the nature of this problem. Nor were the parties able to settle upon the "extent to which industrial disputes could be minimized by full and genuine acceptance by organized labor of the inherent right and responsibilities of management to direct the operation of an enterprise."[15] The subcommittee and the entire conference agreed on the desirability of strengthening the government's conciliation service.

The Executive Council believed that the conference deliberations were concerned largely with long-run problems, and that short-run questions, inevitably tied to reconversion, would have required the participation of the Federal government. What was needed "to promote better industrial relations," the A. F. of L. said, was "honest effort by management and unions to bargain collectively for their mutual benefit supplemented by genuine efforts to work together for better and greater production so that there may be more for all. Cooperation, which is the spirit of partnership, constitutes grounds for increasing the proportional share going to workers, but if increased share is earned, justice requires compensation."[16]

The conference between management and labor, as far as the Federation was concerned, was not the kind that could solve the important problems confronting the country. Because of the autonomy of each union and the special problems generated by the environments in which the separate unions operated, a general conference could only set the public tone; it could not bind the affiliates. While engaged in these conferences, the A. F. of L. leaders remained seriously worried that haphazard cancellation of war contracts might materially injure the industrial life of many communities. They, therefore, requested that when cutbacks or cancellations of contracts were made, some means be found at the same time to cushion the impact so that the welfare of the community, industry, and labor might not be seriously damaged.

During this period the Federation favored the extension of price control without weakening amendments. Green opposed an amendment which was designed to remove from price control any item whose current production equaled the production rate for the fiscal year 1940–1941, and another that required that any commodity price had to be set to cover the current "cost of producing and processing and distributing" plus a reasonable profit. He argued that higher consumer demand at that time, as well as high cost of new production, negated these proposals. Green also spoke out against the ending of meat subsidies.

The only outcome of these amendments, he said, would be substantial price increases and further weakening of the price control laws.[17]

Soon after the end of the war, the Federation asked American unions to participate in the framing and upholding of world peace, and called upon the United States government to allow the labor movement to make constructive contributions to that end. While it regarded the opportunity to shape opinion and to influence government during these peace conferences as necessary and highly beneficial, the A. F. of L. announced that it would "decline to commit itself to or associate itself with any manifest or any other form of presentation which may be issued on behalf of a so-called World Trade Union Congress and resents and repudiates any attempt having been made or which may be made by any such international group or gathering to speak on behalf of organized labor. We do not intend that any foreign labor group or gathering has the right or authority to speak in behalf of American labor."[18]

UNITED NATIONS

A resolution before the Executive Council, proposed by Vice President Hutcheson in 1945, stated that the "deep-grounded determination of the American people that total war, with its horrors, shall not again return, justifies the fullest exploration by our nation of the possibilities of an international organization of nations which shall underwrite an enduring peace."[19] The Council submitted its suggestions for amending the Dumbarton Oaks proposals, which outlined the plan for the United Nations, to the San Francisco conference. The Federation thought that a declaration of the basic freedoms necessary for human progress and lasting peace should preface the Dumbarton Oaks agreement. Freedom of worship, of speech and press, of assembly and association, of privacy, and freedom from involuntary servitude except for punishment of crime, along with the right of accused individuals to a fair public trial and to speedy determination of criminal charges: these were the rights which the A. F. of L. wanted to have incorporated in the United Nations charter. In addition, the A. F. of L. wanted to include two other statements: the Atlantic Charter in which the signatory nations had declared that they sought no aggrandizement, territorial or other, and that they would seek no changes in territory which did not accord with the wishes of the people affected; and the principles of justice formulated by the Pan-American Juridical Commission, which affirmed that no state could claim to be exempt "from the observance of the moral law on the ground of political, economic or racial supremacy, or of a particular national culture which it believed to be inherently superior to that of other States."

The Federation encouraged member nations to include in their staffs functional groups representing labor, agriculture, and business. The Federation also asked that these functional groups be represented on the proposed Economic and Social Council. Finally, it recommended that the International Labor Organization be included as an agent of the United Nations Organization.[20]

The right of the A. F. of L. to representation and to participation in an advisory capacity on the United Nation's Social and Economic Council was challenged by the Soviet block with the argument that labor was already represented by the World Federation of Trade Unions, a Communist-dominated group which Sidney Hillman and the C.I.O. had helped to establish. At the Paris Congress of the World Federation of Trade Unions in September 1945, a resolution was passed that the World Federation of Trade Unions, "as the representative of World Labor . . . has the inalienable right to participate in the work of the United Nations Organization. It directs the Executive Committee to take all necessary steps to ensure the participation of the W.F.T.U. in the work of the Social and Economic Council, in an advisory capacity, pursuant to Article 71, of the . . . Charter of the United Nations Organization."

When proposals to give advisory status to a Communist-controlled international labor front came before the United Nations Assembly, Green wired every delegate, requesting recognition for labor groups not affiliated with the World Federation of Trade Unions. The Communist block immmediately insisted that the views of American and other free labor groups would be without difficulty presented by the World Federation. After a "long and hard fight, the A. F. of L. was allowed the same status as the World Federation of Trade Unions," and American labor was saved the ignominy of being represented in the United Nations by the spokesman for the Soviet block.[21] Woll and Dubinsky were appointed as representatives of the A. F. of L.

The recognition of the A. F. of L. in the United Nations was an important victory, for in 1945 it was the only national labor federation which could argue the democratic governments' point of view. The World Federation of Trade Unions was an auxillary of the Soviet block, and the democratic labor movements were powerless to affect its basic policies. The value of the A. F. of L.'s representation on the Economic and Social Council was soon confirmed. In March 1947 the World Federation of Trade Unions submitted to the Council a draft resolution on trade union rights that carefully avoided  such issues as the right to strike, slave labor, and the need to abolish forced labor—all of which might have embarrassed the Soviet Union and its satellites. The representatives of the W.F.T.U. even tried to by-pass the International Labor Office where issues affecting the interests of labor were customarily considered. Of even greater service was the insistence of the A. F. of L. consultants to the United Nations that the existence of slave labor be investigated.

## SLAVE LABOR

In August 1946 the Executive Council said that the aim of the trade union movement was to win greater freedom so that economic as well as political freedom would be enjoyed by men. Warning that the world was again confronted by a "formidable conspiracy against human freedom—determined to annihilate institutions which guarantee personal freedom and to impose totalitarian or Communist control over other peoples," the Executive Council demanded that the United Nations take "an uncompromising position" against forced labor.[22] The statement charged that forced labor in the Soviet Union exceeded the entire labor force of New York, New Jersey, Pennsylvania, Connecticut, Rhode Island, Vermont, Massachusetts, and New Hampshire, and that a large number of commodities exported by the Soviet Union were produced by slave labor. The Executive Council asked the United States government to urge the

United Nations to bar the products produced by prison and forced labor from the world's export trade.

In 1947 the A. F. of L. representatives moved to bring the slave-labor question before the Council of the United Nations. The A. F. of L. convention of 1947 had denounced the violations of the Geneva convention of 1929 and the "deliberate flouting of the Nuremberg verdict against slave labor." The convention requested the Economic and Social Council of the United Nations to direct the International Labor Organization (1) "to make a thoroughgoing survey of the extent of forced labor in all member nations of the United Nations; (2) to recommend a positive program for eliminating this tragic and inhuman evil; and (3) to foster human rights, and humane standards, and decent conditions of employment as free men." The Executive Council was empowered to make every effort to have the United Nations consider the proposal.[23]

The A. F. of L. consultants brought the convention proposal before the Economic and Social Council on November 29, 1947. The Council decided, after hearing it, to place the question of forced labor on the agenda for February 1948. The matter was continually postponed—sometimes with the approval of the delegates from the United States—and it was not until 1949 that the question was even considered. Matthew Woll made known his disappointment tō Secretary of State George C. Marshall at the "attitude of the United States' representative on the Council in supporting postponement of the consideration of the issue of forced labor. This attitude," Woll said, "is in sharp contrast to our professed belief in the basic human rights."[24]

According to Toni Sender, the assistant to the A. F. of L. consultants, the Soviet delegates, concerned about these efforts to bring the question before the bar of public opinion, had inspired the World Federation of Trade Unions to seek an investigation of death penalties which had been ordered against Greek trade union leaders, although the penalties had subsequently been lifted.[25]

Two years later the evasions and diversions of the Soviet block were defeated when the Economic and Social Council adopted the resolution sponsored by the American Office and the United Nations Secretariat to investigate slave labor. The Soviet Union, White Russia, and Poland voted against the proposal. The A. F. of L. representatives, documenting their charges with affidavits of former inmates of Soviet concentration camps, showed the spread of this system of human slavery beyond the Soviet borders into the satellite countries. In June 1951 the Economic and Social Council finally adopted a resolution asking for the cooperation of the International Labor Organization in establishing a committee and appointed the Secretary-General of the United Nations and the Director-General of the International Labor Office to an *ad hoc* committee on Forced Labor.

The *ad hoc* committee listened to testimony from various groups and acknowledged the role of the A. F. of L. in drawing attention to the problems of forced labor.[26] The investigating committee concluded that it "would . . . seem established that the work of prisoners, particularly in corrective labour camps and colonies, is used in the Soviet Union for essential tasks in the interests of the national economy, and that the part it plays is of considerable significance."[27] The evidence accumulated by the committee showed that for the most part political offenders were employed in the corrective labor camps. "Soviet legislation makes provision for various measures which involve a compulsion to work or place restrictions on the freedom of employment; these measures seem to be applied on a large scale in the interests of the national economy and, considered as a whole, they lead, in the Committee's view, to a system of forced or compulsory labor constituting an important element in the economy of the country."[28]

The A. F. of L., in another phase of its attack on slave labor, published a map of slave-labor camps in English and other languages. *Sklaven arbeit in Russland* became so popular in Germany and Austria that the Soviet occupation authorities raided a Vienna print shop and confiscated thousands of booklets that pinpointed the locations of the slave-labor camps on a map. Undoubtedly the publicity given to slave labor helped to check the spread of this system beyond the Iron Curtain; the whole affair demonstrated the importance of a free labor movement in international affairs. Had the A. F. of L. been a member of the World Federation of Trade Unions, it could not have undertaken this campaign against a great evil.

DISPLACED PERSONS

The A. F. of L. continued its policy of opposing free immigration to the United States, but it favored a temporary waiving of quota restrictions in order to offer a sanctuary to the displaced refugees of Europe. Green, testifying in 1947 on behalf of more generous entry rights for displaced persons, denied that their entry would adversely affect the job opportunities of American workers.[28a] The following year the A. F. of L. supported the annual admission of 100,000 displaced persons over a four-year period. President Green favored the elimination of preference in favor of farmers and people from some sections of Eastern Europe.[28b]

In 1950 the A. F. of L. again endorsed a bill to permit the entry of displaced persons and opposed an amendment which would prohibit further admissions of displaced persons whenever unemployment in the United States reached 4 million workers. The Executive Council felt this was a device to vitiate the spirit and purpose of the bill.[28c] The A. F. of L. also approved subsequent legislation to liberalize the rules for the entry of displaced persons, some of whom would compete with Americans on the labor market. This showed that the A. F. of L. was ready to set aside its long-held views in order to aid a humanitarian purpose. It opposed unlimited immigration because the free flow of labor competed with American workers and thereby helped to reduce wages. And although the A. F. of L. was cognizant of the possible effect of the increased labor supply, it believed the interests of humanity transcended the immediate danger to the workers of the United States.

### VETERANS

To lighten the financial burden on returned veterans, the Federation asked its affiliates to reduce as much as possible the fees for joining. The Executive Council directed the affiliated city central unions to set up employment registries and recommended to the international unions that arrangements be worked out with employers to allow for training and employment of veterans. The Federation was also in favor of counting service time for seniority purposes, and of assisting veterans in every possible way in their education and training.[29]

In connection with the economic problems of veterans and the rest of the community, the A. F. of L. had developed a series of suggestions for the maintenance of a high and increasing standard of living. To achieve this ideal, the Executive Council suggested a program of rural and urban housing development to smooth the transition from a wartime to a peacetime economy, and it consistently opposed international cartels and uncontrolled international trade. The Council wanted to have the domestic controls necessitated by the war abolished as soon as practicable.[30]

### CONTROL OF LEGISLATION FOR LABOR

Before and during the war, some of the practices of labor organizations came under attack. Critics condemned the restrictive policies of the unions, the use of the strike weapon during the war, and finally the unions' behavior in the management of their internal affairs and their members' conduct on the job. The first serious attack came from Thurman Arnold, Assistant Attorney General in charge of the Antitrust Division of the United States Department of Justice, with the charge that in the building-construction industry there existed a "series of restraints, protective tariffs, and aggressive combinations which had practically stopped progress."[31] Carrying his criticism further, Arnold said that the building trades' unions had interferred with the introduction of cheaper materials and technical improvements, thereby compelling employers to hire additional workers.[32]

Under Arnold's leadership, the antitrust division obtained indictments and injunctions against several unions and their members. Arnold used the criterion of "unreasonable restraints" as a basis of proceeding against the labor organizations. These were defined as (1) unreasonable restraints designed to prevent the use of cheaper material, improved equipment, or more efficient methods; (2) unreasonable restraints designed to compel the hiring of useless and unnecessary labor; (3) unreasonable restraints designed to enforce systems of graft and extortion; (4) unreasonable restraints designed to enforce illegally fixed prices; and (5) unreasonable restraints resulting from jurisdictional strikes."[33]

The A. F. of L. took the position that if unions had violated the criminal statutes, they should be prosecuted—but not under the antitrust laws or by injunctions. Anyway, arguing that it had always stood for improved methods of production, as long as new methods were safe and genuine and were not a disguise for the speed-up, the Federation asked whether changes leading to technological unemployment were not a proper subject for collective bargaining rather than judicial determination.

On the question of whether a union ought to be allowed to determine the number of workers hired for a particular job and be subjected to the charge of compelling the hiring of "useless and unnecessary" labor, the Federation wanted to know how such a question could be defined and who was prepared to state that the hiring of certain labor was useless and unnecessary. According to the A. F. of L., permitting judges to determine this question would mean "that one of the most complex problems, and the most crucial to our economy, a problem which must be dealt with in a setting of vast unemployment afflicting a major portion of our entire population, is no longer a proper matter for negotiation between labor and management. This also means that when such bargaining occurs between labor and employers and even when it takes the form of written contracts, such bargaining is to be dealt with by the Government as a plain conspiracy of restraint of trade. . . ."

As for the prosecution of graft and extortion under the Sherman law, the A. F. of L. denied that Arnold's approach was either proper or necessary as long as there were criminal statutes. The Federation made the same observation with regard to the price-fixing restraints charged to unions. Drawing a distinction between conspiracies to raise or fix prices and the activity of labor unions engaging in collective bargaining for mutual aid, the Federation insisted that the bargaining activity could not be regarded as a conspiracy. And finally, the Federation said that the claim that jurisdictional disputes are subject to the antitrust law was not proper in either law or custom.[34] In the light of these views, Green protested the prosecution of William Hutcheson to President Roosevelt. Hutcheson expressed his gratitude to Green and the Executive Council for this intercession and then made it clear that he did not want Judge

Joseph Padway, the A. F. of L. attorney, to have anything to do with any matter involving the Carpenters' Union.[35]

The campaign of Thurman Arnold ran aground when the Supreme Court refused to rule that the Carpenters' Union boycott against the Anheuser Busch Company, following a jurisdictional dispute with the International Association of Machinists, violated the Sherman Act. The Department of Justice had appealed the dismissal by the District Court of the indictments against William Hutcheson and several other officers of the Carpenters' Union.[36] In a majority decision written by Justice Felix Frankfurter, the Supreme Court found that, while the action of boycotting the beer products of the company in interstate commerce constituted violation of the Sherman law, Section 20 of the Clayton Act amended the Sherman law so that certain conduct carried on for the purpose of extending the union no longer fell under the prohibitions of the Sherman law. Reviewing previous Supreme Court decisions which had put a different construction upon this section of the Clayton Act, Justice Frankfurter said that Congress had by Section 4 of the Norris-La Guardia Act allowed a union to engage in activities against an employer as long as these were nonviolent, nonlibelous and nonfraudulent.

The quashing of the indictment in the Hutcheson case did not end Thurman Arnold's campaign. He continued his war on monopolistic practices which had no connection with wages, hours, health, safety, or the right of collective bargaining. The Federation continued to deny that the kind of distinction made by Arnold was valid.

Can it be seriously asserted [the Executive Council asked] that when a labor union seeks to maintain for its employees all the work available, or when it resists the introduction of cheaper materials and machinery which would displace employees, or when it attempts to keep as many of its members on given jobs as it can that under these circumstances a labor union is not acting "in its self-interest"? And if it is acting in its self-interest—as most certainly it is—then regardless of whether the Anti-Trust Division considers the end of its activities wise or unwise, right or wrong, selfish or unselfish, the union may, under the express language of the Clayton Act, as now interpreted by the Hutcheson case, engage in strikes, picketing, lawful assembly, persuasion, boycotts, and the like.[37]

## Smith-Connally Act

Although the effort to restrict organized labor through the antimonopoly laws had failed, Congress did enact the War Labor Disputes (Smith-Connally) Act which sought to control strikes and lockouts in war industries. The President of the United States was empowered to take over a plant engaged in war work whenever there was an interference with its activity. As long as the government possessed an industry, application for changes in wages and working conditions could be made to the War Labor Board, and workers were free to leave their employment as individuals; but unions and their officers were forbidden to call strikes or to pay strike benefits. In cases where work stoppages were likely to occur, the law required that the War Labor Board and the National Labor Relations Board be notified. Production was to continue uninterrupted for thirty days, after which time the National Labor Relations Board was to take a vote on whether or not the employees desired to strike. A strike could be called after the vote; if it were called before, the Federal government or any injured person could sue to recover damages for losses.

The A. F. of L. saw the bill as a "hodgepodge of anti-labor measures, many of which have no relationship whatsoever to the war effort. . . . It is a bitter reward for the contributions that labor has made to the present war effort. . . . No greater or more unmerited blow to the morale of millions of patriotic American workers can be conceived than that inflicted by the present bill."[38] In a message to President Roosevelt, Green described the bill as fascist legislation which strikes "at the very heart of democratic processes and is violative of the fundamental principles upon which our . . . government rests."[39]

During the last years of the war, the A. F. of L. objected to a number of bills that were introduced in Congress; with the exception of the Hobbs Anti-Racketeer Bill, these were defeated. The postwar strikes and the excesses charged against some labor organizations increased public sentiment for greater government regulation of union activities. Green was convinced that the corrective legislation introduced by Senator Case was one of the worst antilabor bills enacted by Congress; it would, Green said, impose a limitation upon the right to strike. The Case bill required that employers in industries affecting interstate commerce were to give notice of proposed changes in contract terms of employment and exert reasonable efforts to come to an agreement. The bill also provided for the final adjustment of grievances on questions involving interpretations of agreements. An employer violating the provisions was guilty of an unfair labor act, and an employee failing to comply with an agreement lost his status as an employee unless rehired. A new Federal mediation board was set up, and the bill included regulations for the management of welfare funds. The bill passed both houses of Congress and was vetoed by President Truman; the vote in the House of Representatives to override the veto failed to gain a two-thirds majority.

### THE TAFT-HARTLEY ACT

The passage of the Case bill by substantial majorities in both houses of Congress was a warning that there was a move toward greater control over the activities of organized labor. But because of the autonomy of each affiliated union, there was little that the A. F. of L. could do to impose more stringent standards of conduct upon the unions, even if it had wanted to. Moreover, there were many unions functioning outside the Federation, and a number of them were located in industries where serious labor tension existed.

A number of bills regulating labor were enacted by the 80th Congress in 1947. After the bill sponsored by Congressman Fred Hartley had passed the House of Representatives, the Executive Council met and condemned its provisions, charging that the measure revived government by injunction, made some legal strikes illegal, prohibited foremen from belonging to unions, provided for the abolition of the closed-shop agreement, and introduced a number of other changes which threatened the safety of the labor movement.[40] The Executive Council authorized the levying of a voluntary assessment of 15 cents a member to conduct an intensive radio and newspaper campaign against the antilabor legislation. Green, Meany, and Vice Presidents Woll, Harrison, and Dubinsky were authorized to direct the campaign which started with a fund of nearly one million dollars. With the cooperation of union leaders in the theatrical and radio industries, a radio campaign was launched with full-page advertisements in 212 leading newspapers. Assisted by the Entertainment Unions Committee, the A. F. of L. broadcast a program every afternoon for seven weeks. In addition, a fifteen-minute program, scheduled every Tuesday evening, was carried by 229 stations for six weeks. This program was rebroadcast every Sunday afternoon over 406 stations of a national network. The A. F. of L. spent $850,631.32 on this campaign.[41]

But this extensive campaign was of no avail; the Taft-Hartley Act was passed over President Truman's veto in 1947. The enactment of the Taft-Hartley Act marked a reverse in the direction of Federal labor legislation. Heretofore, the passage of labor laws by the Federal government had usually meant an enlargement of labor's rights and prerogatives; certainly this was the purpose and outcome of the Wagner Act. In contrast, the Taft-Hartley Act sought "to equalize existing laws" and it balanced the unfair labor practices of employers by a group of prohibited acts by employees defined as "unfair labor practices." It outlawed the closed-shop and permitted the union shop only after a vote of all workers in the bargaining unit. It restored the use of labor injunctions, although only the government was allowed, under the provisions, to apply for such orders in the Federal courts in cases of illegal strikes or boycotts. Jurisdictional strikes and secondary boycotts were placed under the ban, and the law allowed for intervention in the affairs of the union by the government on the theory that workers needed protection against their union officers as well as against employers. Unions were required to file their constitutions, by-laws, and financial reports with the Secretary of Labor, and suits against unions for violation of contracts were allowed. One of the less harmful, but more objectionable features of the law was the requirement that union officers had to sign an affidavit that they were not members of a Communist organization or in sympathy with such an organization as a condition for utilizing the services of the National Labor Relations Board. The law also prohibited labor organizations from making any contribution or expenditure in connection with national elections or primaries. Objections were also raised by the A. F. of L. to the separation of the Conciliation Service from the Department of Labor and its establishment as an independent agency.

Immediately after the enactment of the Taft-Hartley Act, the Executive Committee summoned a meeting of representatives of national and international unions. They carefully considered the details of the new law and then drafted a protest which charged that the law had created "confusion and uncertainty" and that it was "a strike and strife-provoking Act." The conference pledged its unfailing opposition:

1. Because we believe many of the provisions of the Taft-Hartley Bill are unconstitutional, we will challenge the validity of said sections in the courts. In doing so, we shall avail ourselves of the opportunity to appeal in accordance with court procedure to the Supreme Court of the United States. We shall exhaust every legal recourse at our command in the efforts we put forth to test the validity of this act.

2. The repeal of this notorious legislation shall be our fixed objective. We shall never be reconciled to the acceptance of this legislation. We shall oppose it—fight it at every step and every opportunity—until we succeed in our efforts to bring about its repeal. Our action in this respect will be based upon the fact that we regard the Taft-Hartley Bill as a slave measure, un-American, vicious and destructive of labor's constitutional rights.

3. We will organize, unite and concentrate our efforts toward bringing about the defeat of every member of Congress for reelection who voted in favor of final enactment of the Taft-Hartley Bill.

4. To protect our organizations against possible suits for damages and other vexations and destructive litigation under this law, it is recommended that no-strike provisions be omitted from all future agreements, written or oral.

5. In order that the workers of the Nation may be accorded a full and complete opportunity to vote in national elections, we recommend that our organizations set aside this day as a holiday to be devoted solely to election purposes.

6. We recommend that the Executive Council of the American Federation of Labor give full and complete consideration to the declarations of this conference and in addition, prepare for the consideration of the next convention of the American Federation of Labor a program giving full effect to these purposes.

The requirement that union officers sign a non-Communist affidavit as a condition for utilizing the services of the National Labor Relations Board led to a division in the Executive Council and to the disaffiliation of the United Mine Workers of America from the A. F. of L. for a second time. The general counsel of the National Labor Relations Board had ruled that in accordance with the Taft-Hartley law, the members of the Executive Council, as vice presidents of the A. F. of L., would be required to sign the non-Communist affidavit, if the federal labor unions and other affiliates were to be granted the right to utilize the services of the Board. The question came before the Council at its September meeting. Hutcheson, while he regarded the Tafe-Hartley law as obnoxious and the ruling of the general counsel as unfair, believed that the interests of the membership required that the non-Communist affidavit be signed. John L. Lewis took a contrary view. He said that the A. F. of L. should fight the law without compromise "until it is repealed without agreeing to qualifying amendments." For Lewis the law was "a hateful, despicable Act contrary to our concept of American privileges, and it makes second-class citizens out of every man around the Council table and every man he represents."[42]

Dubinsky wanted to apply practical standards to the decision—to sign or not to sign. He argued that there was danger that unless the Federation officers were willing to sign the non-Communist affidavit, the independent and company unions would have an advantage. In October the officers of the Building and Metal Trades Departments met with the Council and requested that the non-Communist affidavit be signed. Lewis again objected to the signing as a humiliating action. He was especially critical of the Council's procedure which allowed those in favor of signing to be heard and denied the opportunity to those who were opposed. After an angry discussion, the Executive Council, with Lewis dissenting, approved this counteraction in the form of an amendment to the Constitution to be submitted to the next convention.

There shall be constituted an Executive Council consisting of thirteen (13) members who shall be elected by the convention on the last day of the session unless otherwise determined by the convention. These thirten (13) members of the Executive Council shall be designated and elected as the First Executive Council Member, the Second Executive Council Member, and so forth.

All Executive Council Members shall be members of a local organization connected with the American Federation of Labor. The term of the present Executive Council shall expire when their successors have been duly elected; the newly elected Council Members shall function as such until December 31st following the next convention. The President and Secretary-Treasurer shall also be members of the Executive Council by virtue of their office.

John L. Lewis thought that this attempt to amend the constitution was a shameful humiliation for the A. F. of L., and he carried his fight against signing the non-Communist affidavit to the convention floor. He urged resistance to the law in a dramatic denunciation. Tobin refused to agree that the signing of the non-Communist affidavit was "surrendering our honor." He recognized the evils in the bill and the harm that it might inflict upon organized labor, but he did not believe the issue should be raised even though he did not like the singling out of union officers for discriminatory treatment. Meany said that the purpose of changing the Executive Council membership from two permanent officers and thirteen vice presidents to two permanent officers—the president and the secretary-treasurer—was to remove the requirement that the vice presidents sign the non-Communist affidavit. He thought that the Federal labor unions should be given an opportunity to use the services of the National Labor Relations Board, which they could not on the basis of the ruling of the general counsel unless all officers signed the non-Communist affidavit. The other thirteen members of the Council would not be listed as officers of the Federation and would not have to sign the affidavit. Although it was this change which Lewis had sharply attacked, Meany saw no difficulty in observing it. Obviously irritated by Lewis's posturing, Meany brought up the former's relations with some of the Communists active in the C.I.O.

Dubinsky looked upon the requirement as a stupid one, but he did not want to fight on this issue. He pleaded with the convention to support the changes recommended by the Executive Council so that the right of the federal labor unions to avail themselves of the privileges under the National Labor Relations Act would be protected.[43] In the end, the convention adopted the proposal. Lewis refused to stand for reelection and later left the A. F. of L.

One of the results of the Taft-Hartley campaign was the decision to embark upon a more extensive public relations program. Owen and Chappell, a New York advertising agency, was retained to work up an extensive educational and public relations program. The A. F. of L. also sponsored a radio program over a national network. These steps were a recognition of the need for greater information and knowledge of labor's activities and its role in American society.

### References

1. *American Federation of Labor Weekly News Service,* December 28, 1942.
2. *Report of the Proceedings of the Sixty-fourth Annual Convention of the American Federation of Labor,* 1944, p. 259.
3. *Ibid.,* p. 264.
4. *Ibid.,* p. 265.
5. Matthew Woll, Machinery for Reconversion: Statement by Matthew

Woll before the Subcommittee of the Untied States Senate Military Affairs Committee, April 4, 1944.

6. William Green, Philip Murray, and Julius Luhrsen to United States Senators, May 1, 1944.

7. Green to State Federations of Labor and City Central Labor Unions, August 1, 1944.

8. *American Federation of Labor Weekly News,* February 13, 1945.

9. President Franklin D. Roosevelt to Green, March 28, 1945.

10. Minutes of Executive Council, May 4, 1945.

11. *Ibid.*

12. *Ibid.*

13. Minutes of Executive Council, August 9, 1945.

14. Minutes of Executive Council, October 23, 1945.

15. "The President's National Labor-Management Conference," *United States Department of Labor, Division of Labor Standards,* Bulletin No. 77 (Washington, D. C.: 1946), p. 6; quote from Murray and Lewis in *General Plenary Sessions,* II, p. 23.

16. *Report of the Proceedings of the Sixty-fifth Convention of the American Federation of Labor,* 1946, p. 108.

17. Statement of William Green before the Senate Committee on Banking and Currency, April 29, 1945, in files of the A. F. of L.

18. *American Federation of Labor Weekly News Service,* February 5, 1946.

19. Minutes of Executive Council, May 8, 1945.

20. American Federation of Labor, Views and Suggestions to the San Francisco Conference for Amending the Dumbarton Oaks Proposals, May 2, 1945.

21. Quote is from Senator Tom Connally to Green, February 12, 1946.

22. Minutes of Executive Council, August 15, 1946.

23. *Report of the Proceedings of the Sixty-seventh Annual Convention of the American Federation of Labor,* 1947.

24. Matthew Woll to George Marshall, March 2, 1948.

25. Memorandum from Toni Sender to Woll and Dubinsky, no date, in files of A. F. of L.

26. *Report of the Ad Hoc Committee on Forced Labour* (Geneva: International Labour Office, 1953), pp. 12–13.

27. *Ibid.,* p. 91.

28. *Ibid.,* p. 98.

28a. Statement of William Green, President of the American Federation of Labor before the Judiciary Committee of the House of Representatives of the United States, 80th Congress, June 13, 1947.

28b. William Green to Honorable John C. Stennis, April 14, 1948.

28c. Minutes of Executive Council, February 7, 1950.

29. Minutes of Executive Council, August 13, 1945.

30. Minutes of Executive Council, May 8, 1945.

31. Thurman Arnold, *Restraint of Trade in the Building Industry: An Address delivered on June 21, 1939,* in Library of United States Department of Justice.

32. Thurman Arnold, *Anti-Trust Laws and Labor: An Address before the American Labor Club of New York City, January 27, 1940,* in Library of United States Department of Justice.

33. Thurman Arnold to Central Labor Union of Indianapolis, November 20, 1939, in *Report of the Proceedings of the Sixtieth Annual Convention of the American Federation of Labor,* 1940, p. 148.

34. *Ibid.,* p. 150.

35. Minutes of Executive Council, February 14, 1941.

36. United States *v.* Hutcheson, 312 U. S. 219 (1941).

37. Minutes of Executive Council, February 28, 1941.

38. Analysis of and Comments on Smith-Connally Bill S. 796 by the American Federation of Labor, June 1, 1943.

39. *American Federation of Labor Weekly News Service,* June 15, 1943.

40. Green and Meany to the Officers of National and International Unions, State Federations of Labor, City Central Bodies, and Directly Affiliated Local Unions, April 29, 1947.

41. *Report of the Proceedings of the Sixty-sixth Convention of the American Federation of Labor,* 1947, p. 260.

42. Minutes of Executive Council, September 18, 1947.

43. *Report of the Proceedings of Sixty-sixth Convention of the American Federation of Labor,* 1947, pp. 482–505.

# XXI

## Wages and Hours and Social Security

### WAGES AND HOURS

The A. F. of L. supported the adoption of wage and hour standards on Federal government jobs and sponsored bills that required payment of prevailing pay rates. The Federation regarded it "as a glaring inconsistency . . . for government officials to preach of the economic advantages of high wages and then permit the government in its capacity of a builder to undermine and destroy prevailing wage standards in any given community."[1] Supporting the legislation with a statement, Green urged Congress to enact the Bacon-Davis bill, which sought to compel prevailing rates on the construction, alteration, or repair of public buildings of the United States or the District of Columbia.

The A. F. of L. had consistently argued that the government should be a model employer, and in its support of wage and hour legislation, the Federation drew a distinction between government as an employer and government as a regulator of economic activity. Government as an employer was to set an example and maintain the model conditions of the labor market. This attitude did not contradict the Federation's insistence upon limiting the influence of government in the private sector of the economy.[2]

Notwithstanding President Hoover's approval of the prevailing wage principle, different government departments had awarded work to contractors who paid wages below the prevailing rates. Green denounced such practices, claiming that it was "unfair for contractors engaged in the performance of government work to take advantage of the unemployment situation to depress wages and to lower standards."[3]

In the meantime, the United States Comptroller General had announced that government contracts had to be awarded to the lowest bidder. For this reason, the Federation was extremely anxious for enactment of the Bacon-Davis bill, which had been introduced in Congress at its request. Largely as a result of its efforts, the Bacon-Davis bill was enacted. It required that contracts of $5,000, to which the United States or the District of Columbia was a party involving the employment of workers in the construction or repair of public buildings—should contain a clause that the contractor would pay at least the prevailing rate of wages paid for similar work in the community.

The same principle was involved in the Walsh-Healey (Public Contracts) Act. As a matter of fact, the sponsorship of this legislation, which provided for the maintenance of minimum labor standards in the performance of Federal government contracts by suppliers of materials, reflected the expanded activity of the government. As long as the government's economic role was limited largely to the construction of various kinds of public works, the A. F. of L. confined itself to seeking legislation that required the payment of prevailing rates on public works. Government economic activity expanded greatly in the 1930's and inevitably the Federal government increased its purchases of supplies and materials. The Federation thereupon sought expanded protection of standards so that government contracts might not. be allocated to low bidders able to maintain their competitive position through the payment of substandard wages.

A different issue was involved in general legislation governing wages and hours. When William Hutcheson learned that a bill to regulate wages and hours might be introduced in Congress, he registered his opposition with Green to this type of legislation. He was assured that the Federation had always opposed conferring such power upon Congress.[4] The Black-Connery bill, regulating wages and hours of workers in industries in interstate commerce, was introduced in Congress in May 1937. The international unions in the Building Trades Department and the Metal Trades Department opposed the measure as it had been written. They feared that it would "materially interfere with and modify the Walsh-Healey Bill, which has been of such great protection to labor standards."[5]

The Executive Council was also opposed to this legislation, although George Harrison argued for it because he believed "the main question is [that] something has to be done by legislation on . . . wages and hours."[6] Another Council member, Joseph Weber, a musician, feared that regulation of wages and hours by law might adversely affect collective bargaining. On the other hand, Green favored such a law in general and urged its approval. He called attention to the charge that ". . . the American Federation of Labor has been accused of being the aristocracy of labor, of caring for no one except the skilled worker, the man who is at the top, and that we have never been interested in the submerged."[7] The issue was again debated at the meeting of the Executive Council in October 1937. Frey appeared and announced that the enactment of the Black-Connery bill would interfere with collective bargaining. His views were supported by J. W. Williams, the head of the Building Trades Department. Harrison again stated his support of the legislation. Daniel

Tracy, a member of the Electricians' Union and also of the Executive Council, opposed the specific bill which authorized the appointment of Federal boards with power to fix wages; he said, however, that "there are many underpaid workers . . . who probably could be taken care of by such a law but these industries would have to be carefully defined and then minimum rates and maximum hours set up within these particular industries."[8]

At the convention of 1937, the Building Trades Department and the Metal Trades Department jointly supported a resolution which opposed the creation of a governmental agency with power to replace collective bargaining of wage earners and their employers. It also pointed out the failure of those who had drafted the wage and hour legislation to consult the officers of the A. F. of L. during its preparation. The convention took no position on the bill or its desirability, but it did approve of "establishing a point below which wages could not be paid and hours of labor beyond which wage earners could not be employed."[9] The officers of the A. F. of L. were instructed to consult with the heads of the Building Trades Department and other trades departments before taking action on this bill.

Green called the officers of the trade departments together on November 20, 1937 to discuss the pending legislation on this issue and to report on his discussion with President Roosevelt. Green had told the President of the view that wage and hour legislation must not be used to interfere with collective bargaining, that *minima* must not become *maxima*, and that the labor movement was strongly opposed to giving power over economic affairs involving labor to any boards, especially in light of the Federation's experience with the National Labor Relations Board. I. M. Ornburn, president of the Union Label Trades Department, favored endorsement of a bill which would eliminate child labor and set minimum wages and maximum hours; but he resolutely opposed giving power to a government board to interfere with standards. Bert Jewell, president of the Railway Employees Department, expressing the view taken by the executives of the railway employees' unions, offered to support any position taken by the Federation, providing railway employees were exempted from the provisions of the bill.

In response to the request of Congresswoman Mary T. Norton, chairman of the House Committee on Labor, Green submitted a detailed explanation of the Federation's position. He pointed to the 1937 convention's approval of the principle of placing a floor upon wages and a ceiling on the number of hours that would be worked. Nevertheless, he insisted that the experience of the A. F. of L. with the administration of the National Labor Relations Board had demonstrated "that it is no longer safe to permit a Government board of that kind to make the many determinations necessary in the administration of the Fair Labor Standards Bill as now written."[10]

The Federation's objection was no longer based upon its earlier opposition to government regulation of wages and hours of men workers, but rather to the wide grant of authority for setting wages and hours that the original bill gave to a Federal board. The bill allowed an administrator to establish pay in substandard and sweated industries at any figure below 40 cents an hour, and a work week at 40, 45, 50, and 54 hours or more. The bill also allowed the administrator to grant geographical differentials in minimum wages and maximum hours. It was these features which the Federation most strongly opposed. Seeing no need for granting wide and discretionary authority to a governmental board, the Federation believed that a floor on wages and a ceiling upon hours could be attained by a direct and simple measure. There was also some belief that the enactment of the original bill would reenforce existing geographical differences in wages and hours. "Working people," Green said, "are opposed to having fixed upon them by law such a 'hodge-podge' of wage and hour differentials by some administrator who might be influenced by political and other considerations."[11]

The Executive Council approved a simple bill, whose clear provisions promised to eliminate "the possibility of escaping or twisting out . . . [of them] by any manner of interpretation. The law . . . uniform through the nation . . . requires no administrative board or machinery to make it effective."[12] The most serious concern of the Federation was the grant of authority given to administrators who the A. F. of L. feared could interfere with the collective bargaining of unions and their employers. It wanted the simplest and most direct approach to the need for placing a floor upon wages and a ceiling on the hours. The Federation advocated a single enforcement officer rather than an administrator with power to set wages and hours.[13]

The Federation also objected to the subsequent amendments introduced in April 1938. The recommended bill provided for neither minimum wages nor maximum hours. Instead, it set up a series "of arbitrary wage scales with a ceiling of 40 cents per hour; it [provided] for a series of arbitrary maximum hour work-week schedules within the range of 40 to 48 hours per week."[14] Green contended that the bill did not carry out the intention of President Roosevelt and did not serve any benefical economic purpose.

Largely as a result of the Federation's criticism, the bill was revised. Green announced that the Federation favored the revised measure because it embodied the three fundamental requirements held essential by the Federation: a specific and universal floor for wages, a specific and universal ceiling for hours, and provision for enforcement through a cooperative arrangement between the Department of Labor and the Department of Justice.[15]

The Federation's approval of this legislation was attacked by George L. Berry, president of the International Printing Pressmen and Assistants' Union of North America. Berry believed that a "minimum wage established by Federal law will prove detrimental to the interests of organized workers in America."[16]

Green defended his position on the ground that since the administration had consistently urged upon Congress the enactment of legislation regulating wages and hours, the A. F. of L. was obligated, in order to protect the economic interests of labor, to seek the most effective and least objectionable measure possible. He emphasized that the law supported by the Federation was simple in character and gave no authority to a government board to fix rates of pay. When the bill, to go into effect on October 24, 1938, was finally enacted, Green declared that it was far from perfect, but that nevertheless it went a long way toward meeting the objections to the original proposal. He found that the administration provided, however, was cumbersome and undesirable, and that the allowing of differentials within industries and classifications was objectionable.[17]

In appraising the attitude of the Federation, one must recognize its historic antigovernmental position, as well as the trade unionists' belief that wage and hour problems could best be met through collective bargaining.

### SOCIAL SECURITY

The Federation had modified its traditional opposition to unemployment insurance in 1932, when it found that the ravages of unemployment and the failure of industry to provide for the millions of idle workers left the A. F. of L. no alternative but to endorse a system of compensation for the unemployed. Earlier, the Federation had endorsed workmen's compensation laws and the complete abrogation of the common law defenses. It strove through the years for the extension of coverage to all workers and for adequate benefits for those injured in industry and for occupational illnesses. A government program of old-age benefits was also endorsed.[18] In 1929 the convention had directed the officers to draft a model bill to be recommended to the states and to inaugurate a campaign for enactment of such a measure. John Frey, objecting to this proposal, had insisted that the considerations which could be raised in support of old-age security also applied to unemployment and health insurance. He feared that the adoption of old-age insurance would mean that labor would be placing itself "in the position of wards of the state, admitting the problems that affect us in sickness, unemployment and old age are so far beyond our capacity as trade unionists to deal with that we must have a state sick insurance to protect us." The convention was not persuaded by his argument.[19]

In spite of the efforts of the Federation and other groups to promote programs of unemployment and old-age insurance, these programs were scarcely begun before the Federal government entered this arena in 1935. A number of states had adopted old-age pension systems which allowed meager benefits to those who could meet the severe qualification requirements. The appointment of the Committee on Economic Security by President Roosevelt in 1934 had given the initial impulse to the Federal-state programs for offsetting the wage losses of unemployed and older workers. The A. F. of L., in general, supported the proposals and recommended changes aimed to improve the suggested plan. Green advocated positive action so that the government might "provide a reasonable amount of economic security to those millions of our population who are, even in the best of times, always on the edge of want and destitution."[20]

The Federation, however, did not approve of the latitude allowed to the states. The administration's program failed

to provide for the leadership and guidance of the Federal Government, which alone is qualified to assume the leadership essential in a measure so important as unemployment insurance. . . . It leaves to the states almost complete freedom of action in the adoption of unemployment insurance laws. There are no standards set for the state laws to follow. Each state is free to determine the waiting period to be imposed, the amount of benefit which shall be paid, the length of time benefits shall continue, the wage earning group which shall be included under the act, the type of funds which shall be set up, and the manner in which such funds shall be administered.[21]

The Federation feared that some states might not pass unemployment-insurance laws and that the tax rate levied would not yield enough revenue to provide benefits adequate in amount or duration. The following amendents to the sections of the measure dealing with unemployment were proposed:

1. Direct representation of labor on the Social Insurance Board.
2. Substitution of the grant-in-aid or subsidy plan for the tax offset plan.
3. No employee contributions to be permitted.
4. Increase of the tax on payrolls to 5 per cent.
5. Only pooled funds to be recognized as proper, and neither company reserves nor company accounts to be permitted.
6. Benefits to equal at least 50 per cent of a normal weekly wage, for a duration of twenty-six weeks in each calendar year.

In the provisions dealing with old-age assistance, the A. F. of L. recommended an increase of constributions by both employers and workers to the contributory old-age insurance program and a lowering of the eligibility age to sixty years. It vigorously assailed the amendment proposed by Senator Champ Clark which would have exempted industries having pension plans from paying the tax for old-age benefits. Green charged "that the management of many industries discharge employees when they approach the retirement age. . . . Another great objection to private pension plans is that [they tend] to discourage the employment of older men. . . . There is no hope for them except through the enactment of the National Security bill."[22] The determined opposition of the Federation to this amendment had much to do with its defeat. When the states enacted unemployment-compensation laws, so as to gain the advantage of the tax offset provision of the Social Security Act with regard to the tax on employers' payrolls, Green told the central bodies affiliated with the Federation that they had the responsibility for protecting the rights of wage earners under the law and that workers could not be required, as a condition for obtaining benefits, to sacrifice any privileges granted to them under the National Labor Relations Act.[23]

In the spring of 1938 Green suggested that central bodies study the administration of the state unemployment-compensation laws so that the method of operation could be ascertained and the rights of labor protected.[24] Local officers were especially urged to watch carefully the principles involved in decisions denying compensation to unemployed workers. To keep abreast of current developments in the field of social security, as well as to recommend improvements in all programs then operating, the Federation appointed a committee on social insurance. The recommendations of this committee—G. M. Bugniazet and Frey served under Woll's chairmanship—in January 1939 called for the liberalization of benefits by including dependents' allowances and opposed the reduction of the tax rates through systems of merit rating.[25] The report called attention to the inadequate payments under many state laws and asked for a "Federal unemployment compensation law with a single pooled fund to replace the . . . Federal-State structure of many funds and different types."[26]

The Federation supported improvements in benefits for the aged, and in May 1939 the Executive Council protested "any reduction of the Federal 3 per cent tax for unemployment compensation or any arrangement for offset credit to states based wholly upon the amount of their state unemployment compensation funds. . . . The 3 per cent tax rate should not be lowered until unemployment compensation adequately provides for workers who have lost their jobs and pays adequate benefits for an adequate period of time. Congress must adopt adequate standards upon which credits may be allowed."[27]

Following the views of the Council, the 1941 convention recommended that Congress amend the Social Security Act in order to establish a pooled fund out of which payments to those eligible for unemployment compensation, as well as old-age and survivors' insurance benefits, temporary and permanent disability insurance payments, and payments for medical and hospital care, could be met. In addition, the A. F. of L. wanted coverage extended to all workers not yet under the system. The 1942 convention declared that the "American Federation of Labor believes a Federal system with adequate standards of benefits and a single pooled fund is essential. It would be far safer and less expensive in unused reserves as well as in administrative cost than 51 separate systems. . . . Employment is a national problem. Unemployment is also national in scope." Workers called into military service or transferred to defense jobs should be protected, the delegates said, so that they would not undergo any loss of benefits.[28] In a letter to Chairman Doughton of the House Ways and Means Committee, Green wrote of "the importance of creating an adequate national system of unemployment compensation."[29]

The Federation wanted the limitation upon coverage to eight or more workers eliminated from the statute, the experience rating abolished, and old-age insurance extended to domestic and farm workers, public employees not already covered, lay employees of religious, educational, and charitable organizations, fishermen in boats of less than 10 tons, and self-employed persons. Higher benefits and supplementary allowances for dependents were also advocated, as well as benefits to workers permanently disabled.[30] It is obvious from the views of the Federation that, beginning in the early 1930's the A. F. of L. was one of the more important groups seeking to expand the coverage of the social security system and to obtain adequate scales of benefits from the Federal government.

Increasingly, as the officers of the A. F. of L. saw the field of social security becoming one of their major concerns, they recognized the need for a qualified and full-time staff to advise them in this area. Consequently, in the fall of 1944 Nelson H. Cruikshank was appointed Director of Social Insurance Activities. At the same time, the Federation's Social Security Committee was enlarged to nine members, with Woll continuing as chairman. This committee met twice a year, and between meetings all issues affecting social security issues were cleared by Cruikshank and his staff with this committee. It was the first time the Federation had ever appointed a standing policy committee with a corresponding staff, a procedure subsequently followed in other areas and one that was adopted by the merged Federation. The Committee always maintained close relationships with the legislative department of the A. F. of L., and the briefs and arguments on questions of social security presented to Congress were jointly prepared. The staff of the Social Security Committee was responsible for technical details.

The 1944 convention directed that legislation be prepared for submission to Congress providing for a comprehensive system of contributory social insurance and social security which would attain the following objectives:

1. A national system of unemployment insurance for workers engaged by all private employers, with provisions for inclusion at their request of the self-employed and the employees of various governmental units.

2. Extension of old-age and survivors' insurance to all employees of private firms, and the right to elect coverage by the self-employed and those employed by state governments, their instrumentalities, and political subdivisions not otherwise covered.

3. Complete protection of the social security rights of men and women in military service without regard to any veterans' benefits they might receive.

4. A national system of health insurance providing health services for all workers and their families.

5. Unification of the public assistance program and provision for a system of grants-in-aid by the Federal government adjusted to the relative financial needs of the states in order to enable them to provide more equal assistance to all needy persons.[31]

As World War II was ending, the Federation urged the enactment of provisions to provide for supplementary unemployment insurance, and pleaded that Congress allow the Federal government, in view of the inadequacies of many state programs, to take the lead in establishing an adequate unemployment-compensation system. Green emphasized the fact that American workers did not put their main hope for security in unemployment-compensation benefits. Instead, they placed "their reliance first on the prospect of steady, productive jobs under good conditions at high wages. They are convinced, however, that it is necessary and proper that their government provide unemployment insurance so that income will not stop completely in case something happens to their jobs."[32]

At its meeting in August 1947, the Executive Council reported to the convention that the major gap in the social security program was the failure to provide for the costs of medical care. The Council pointed out that dependency frequently arose as a result of the workers' inability to meet serious medical costs. Repudiating any desire to socialize the practice of medicine, the Council said, however, that it was entirely feasible to "spread the risk of the cost of illness by application of the compulsory insurance principle so that no worker need to labor under the constant fear of disastrously high doctors' and hospital bills."[33]

The 1947 convention approved a comprehensive program to provide and meet the costs of medical care through social insurance. "Such a program must preserve the individual rights of both patients and physicians. The program should include provision for an extensive program for the construction of hospitals and health centers, the training of medical personnel, and development of research."[34]

In 1949 the Federation again urged upon Congress the necessity for improving the social insurance system, which was described as "the primary defense against loss of income to working people." Calling attention to the legislative history of the Social Security Act, Federation leaders held that it revealed the intention of Congress eventually to substitute social insurance programs for relief.[35]

More specifically, the Social Security Committee of the A. F. of L. called for the adoption of the following four major objectives:

1. Extension and liberalization of the existing Federal old-age and survivors' insurance program by extending coverage to some 25,000,000 more persons and doubling the average benefits.

2. Extension, simplification, and liberalization of the existing unemployment insurance and employment service programs by replacing the state systems by one under Federal management and control.

3. Extension of the Federal insurance system so as to cover wage loss due to sickness or disability.

4. The development of a comprehensive health program, including health insurance for 125,000,000 persons with free choice of doctor, decentralized administration by utilizing state and local agencies, and full use of existing voluntary plans providing medical service.[36]

While endorsing the improvements in social insurance voted by Congress, the Executive Council in January 1950 called for wider coverage, increased benefits, and the avoidance of any needs test in unemployment compensation.[37] On behalf of the A. F. of L., Green strongly recommended the inclusion of disability insurance benefits in the program. In answer to the charge that it would be difficult to administer such a program, he directed attention to twenty other Federally operated retirement systems, including the Railroad Retirement system and the Civil Service Retirement system, which included disability benefits and which had been successfully administered over the years.

The Federation also argued that unless benefits provided under public programs were substantially increased, social security would continue to be a point of controversy in labor-management relations. Broadening of coverage so as to include workers then excluded and increasing the taxable wage base were also recommended.[38]

In 1950 Congress adopted legislation greatly liberalizing the social security program, and many of the improved benefit provisions followed the recommendations of the A. F. of L., although in most respects the law did not go as far as the Federation had requested. The A. F. of L., consequently, continued to advocate improvement of the existing programs and the establishment of a health insurance program. In May 1952 the Committee on the Nation's Health, which supported a government health insurance program, appealed to the Federation for funds to carry on its work. Hutcheson, a member of the Executive Council, opposed the request on the ground that a program of health insurance had been rejected by the Carpenters' Union's convention. "Harrison suggested a contribution be made to the committee in the same amount as we have contributed before. He said that the labor movement is behind a program to do something for those unfortunates who cannot get adequate care. . . . Secretary Meany stated that support of this program by the A. F. of L. is completely consistent with the principles of the A. F. of L.; we have fought for better education, safety legislation[,] and the principles . . . are entirely in line with our welfare plans." The Council, with Hutcheson dissenting, voted $10,000 in support of the Committee.[39]

At its meeting in February 1953, the Executive Council took notice of the attacks then being made upon the social security programs. In answer to the opponents' charge that the program was inadequate, the Council argued that the answer was not abolition of but an improvement in benefit levels. It again called upon Congress to extend coverage and raise the benefits under the old-age and survivors' insurance program. Merit rating in unemployment compensation was again criticised, and recommendations were made that unemployment-compensation benefits be so arranged that they would represent a greater percentage of wage loss. On health insurance, the Council took note of the opposition to such a program by the American Medical Association, but it refused "to be intimidated by the opposition. . . . Our demand for the enactment of health insurance is based on our knowledge of the needs of American wage earners—the fact that the greatest barrier to securing adequate diagnostic and curative medical service is the inability of individuals to pay for it. The 'voluntary' plans, with the exception of a few, where consumers share in their control, are completely inadequate."[40]

In the last quarter of a century, the A. F. of L. persistently fought for a broad, humane, and adequate system of employment insurance so that the unemployed, the aged, disabled, and the ill would receive some of the benefits that the great productivity of the American economy makes possible for those unable to obtain or continue in remunerative employment.

### REFERENCES

1. *Report of the Proceedings of the Fifty-first Annual Convention of the American Federation of Labor,* 1931, p. 232.

2. Green to President Hoover, January 14, 1931; Green to Secretary of Labor W. B. Doak, January 15, 1931.

3. Statement by Green, January 14, 1931.

4. William Hutcheson to Green, February 8, 1937; Green to Hutcheson, February 15, 1937.

5. Release issued by the Building Trades Department and the Metal Trades Department, July 30, 1937.

6. Minutes of Executive Council, August 28, 1937.

7. *Ibid.*

8. Minutes of Executive Council, October 3, 1937.

9. *Report of the Proceedings of the Fifty-seventh Annual Convention of the American Federation of Labor,* 1937, pp. 501–502.

10. Green to Mary T. Norton, November 22, 1937, in answer to Norton to Green, November 17, 1937.

11. To National and International Unions, State Federations of Labor, City Central Bodies, and Directly Affiliated Local Trade and Federal Labor Unions, December 21, 1937.

12. *American Federation of Labor Weekly News,* December 11, 1937. Quote is from Minutes of Executive Council, December 3, 1937.

13. William C. Hushing to Congressman John C. Dockweiler, December 13, 1937. Hushing was A. F. of L. legislative representative.

14. Green to Congresswoman Mary T. Norton, April 1, 1938.

15. Green to all organized labor, April 28, 1938.

16. George L. Berry to Green, May 16, 1938.

17. To National and International Unions, State Federations of Labor, City Central Bodies, and Directly Chartered Trade and Federal Labor Unions, June 15, 1938.

18. *Report of the Proceedings of Thirtieth Annual Convention of the American Federation of Labor,* 1910, pp. 262–263.

19. *Report of the Proceedings of the Forty-ninth Annual Convention of the American Federation of Labor,* 1929, p. 259.

20. *Hearings before the Ways and Means Committee House of Representatives 74th Congress, 1st Session on H. R. 4120,* 1935, p. 385.

21. Statement issued to Secretaries of all State Federations of Labor in May 1935.

22. Green to Senator Robert M. La Follette, June 19, 1935.

23. To State Branches and City Central Bodies, May 24, 1937.

24. To Selected State Federations of Labor from Green, March 24, 1938.

25. Social Security Committee, January 27, 1939.

26. Green to Secretaries of all State Federations of Labor and Central Labor Unions, March 10, 1939.

27. Minutes of Executive Council, May 17, 1939.

28. *Report of the Proceedings of the Sixty-first Annual Convention of the American Federation of Labor,* 1941, p. 119.

29. Green to Robert L. Doughton, January 26, 1942.

30. Green to State Federations of Labor and City Central Bodies, December 3, 1942.

31. *Report of the Proceedings of the Sixty-fourth Annual Convention of the American Federation of Labor*, 1944, p. 597.

32. *Statement by William Green, President of American Federation of Labor in Support of Senate Bill 1274 Submitted to the Committee on Finance, United States Senate*, August 29, 1945.

33. *Report of the Proceedings of the Sixty-sixth Convention of the American Federation of Labor*, 1947, pp. 180–181.

34. *Ibid.*, p. 451.

35. Statement by the American Federation of Labor Submitted to the Committee on Ways and Means, U.S. House of Representatives, March 18, 1949, in archives of A. F. of L.

36. *American Federation of Labor Weekly News Service*, January 18, 1949.

37. Minutes of Executive Council, January 30, 1950.

38. Memorandum in Support of Proposed Amendments to H. R. 6000 by the American Federation of Labor, May 26, 1950.

39. Minutes of Executive Council, May 19, 1952.

40. Statement by the Executive Council of the American Federation of Labor on Social Security, February, 1953.

# XXII

## Taxation, Housing, and Education

### TAXATION

Throughout its history the A. F. of L. has opposed sales taxation and supported personal and corporation income taxes as a means for providing government revenue. At the 1921 convention, taking note of the pressures for the enactment of a general sales tax by Congress, the Federation went on record against the imposition of such a levy and demanded "that the highest rate of taxation levied during the war [World War I] upon the incomes and excess profits be retained until the full money cost of the war has been paid, and . . . that the government promptly levy a rapidly progressive tax upon large estates and a moderate tax upon the value of land and other natural resources speculatively held in order that the national debt may be promptly retired."[1]

Increasing sentiment for a Federal sales tax compelled the Federation throughout the 1920's to fight enactment of such a measure. In 1924 it described Senator Reed Smoot, a Republican leader, "as the arch reactionary of the Senate, whose only concern for the wage earners appears to lie in looking for opportunities to further exploit them."[2] In the following year the Convention commended the Executive Council "for its vigilance and vigor in . . . repelling another attack on the part of these tax dodgers who would shift upon the wage-earners through a sales tax, the major burdens of taxation."[3]

When Congressional interest in a sales tax increased, the Federation again urged its members in 1929 and again in 1931 to fight against this proposal. The turnover tax introduced by Senator David Reed in 1931 drew a sharp attack. In a public statement, the Federation recalled the unanimous rejection of the sales tax by its conventions of 1921, 1922, 1923, 1924, and 1929, and charged that such a scheme "is a conspiracy of the well-to-do to relieve themselves from taxation and place the burden on the poor."[4] The convention which met in October 1931 reaffirmed the historic policy of the A. F. of L. in opposing the sales tax then being promoted in Congress. The Executive Council noted in its report to the 1932 convention the "determined efforts . . . during the last session of Congress to enact sales tax legislation. . . . The American Federation of Labor has consistently opposed sales tax legislation because it represents an attempt to transfer the burden of taxation from wealth and from those who are able to bear it, to the masses of the people and to those who are least able to bear the burden of taxation."[5]

The Federation did not concern itself with tax matters for the next several years, and in 1938 the Executive Council noted the desire of businessmen for repeal of the undivided profits and capital gains taxes. As "a step toward the restoration of public confidence . . . of those who allege they are inspired by fear and distrust, the Executive Council of the American Federation of Labor suggests that Congress repeal or modify the undivided profits and capital gains taxes. . . . Such action on the part of Congress would answer the demand of business for some concrete evidence on the part of government to supply a form of relief which they assert is so urgently needed."[6]

With the onset of World War II, the Federation again became concerned with government taxation policy. Expressing itself as chiefly interested in a fair distribution of the tax burden, the A. F. of L. advocated a program to meet the war emergency. In accordance with traditional policy, a general sales tax was opposed, because such a tax was said to fall inequitably upon the working population. Unqualified opposition to a manufacturers' sales tax was also expressed, since such a tax was believed to have a cumulative upward effect on the cost of living and was, consequently, strongly inflationary. The corporation income tax was approved, but the Federation advised the exercise of care so as not to interfere with capital accumulation needed to expand production. Although a corporate excess profits tax was favored, the A. F. of L. wanted the provision which exempted certain types of corporations struck from the bill. Liberal depletion allowances to oil companies were opposed, and the limiting of individual income after taxes to a maximum of $25,000 a year, as suggested by President Roosevelt, was not favored. In the view of the A. F. of L., such an arbitrary limit upon income would lead businessmen "to restrict their activities, reduce their war work, and decrease their employment of labor."[7]

Finally, the A. F. of L. declared that if rates of taxation were to be raised sharply above those prevailing in 1942, it would be desirable that provision be made for the return in cash of some part of that tax. Also favored was the withholding system of imposing the personal income tax. Green, in approving of this procedure, advised Congressman Robert L. Doughton, chairman of the House Ways and Means Committee, that in "the transition year substantial relief should be given to all taxpayers to avoid the hardship of a double tax."[8] Green suggested the cancellation of the normal tax and first surtax bracket on 1942 income for all taxpayers.

In the following year the Federation protested the failure of the Ways and Means Committee to recommend the A. F. of L. bill for raising contributions of workers and employers for social insurance. Green noted that the Ways and Means Committee had made the income tax on wage earners more burdensome by eliminating the exemption on earned income.[9] When President Roosevelt vetoed the tax measure passed by Congress, Green urged Congress to support it.[10]

After the war, the A. F. of L. opposed an immediate tax cut, observing that the welfare of the nation and continued high production should not be sacrificed for the sake of a tax reduction. The statement of Green pointed to the need "for a broad program of Federal aid to education. The American Federation of Labor is committed to the support of such a program." The A. F. of L. also favored improved social security financing and a Federal housing program which called for additional revenue.[11]

Subsequently, Arthur Elder, testifying on behalf of the A. F. of L., advocated that modification of the Federal tax structure should be made with the following objectives in mind:

1. The proposed taxes should be adequate to provide for necessary services and to maintain the Federal credit.

2. The proposed taxes should be equitable, increasing progressively as individual income increases with due regard for the necessity of exempting the incomes of those below minimum-subsistence levels.

3. The proposed taxes should operate so as to keep the buying power of consumers at the highest possible level, so that production and employment may be maintained.

4. The proposed taxes should not combine with other economic measures to depress or retard the development of any area or to place it at an economic disadvantage in relation to other areas.

These objectives would be attained, according to the Federation, by reliance upon the personal income tax to provide the bulk of national revenue, by lowering tax rates or increasing the exemptions for those in the lower income groups, and by full taxation of capital gains and full deductions to be permitted on capital losses. In addition, the statement called for repeal of excise taxes—except those on liquor, tobacco, and gasoline—retention of existing provisions penalizing unreasonable accumulation of earnings, and a restudy of estate and gift taxes with a view to closing loopholes for tax avoidance through the creation of trusts, gifts, and powers of appointment.[12]

When the country faced the need for increased defense expenditures in 1950, the Federation opposed an increase in corporation tax revenue. It had been suggested that the normal rate be raised from 21 per cent to 25 per cent so that a 45 per cent rate would apply to corporate income in excess of $25,000 annually. The Federation feared that such changes in the corporate tax rate would stimulate price increases and encourage sentiment for price control and a demand for rationing of goods in short supply. In addition, the proposal was opposed on the ground that a flat-rate increase in corporation tax rates would be unfair to new industries established in the high-cost period which had prevailed since the end of World War II. Consequently, the A. F. of L. advocated an excess profits tax if possible, without recourse to increases in normal or surtax rates.[13]

In January 1951 the Federation again criticized the financing of defense expenditures by government deficits. In proposing a program to raise 16 billion dollars of additional revenue, the Federation advised greater reliance on income and corporate taxes and less on excise taxes. Estate and gift taxes could, according to the A. F. of L., bear a greater share of the national burden.[14]

HOUSING

The A. F. of L. pioneered in the campaign for more active participation by the Federal government in the promotion of better housing for workers. A resolution enacted by the convention of 1914 called upon the Federal government to provide loans for the building of sanitary homes by municipal and private builders. It was hoped that Federal legislation would stimulate action by other divisions of government.[15] Bills were introduced in Congress, but the A. F. of L. was not at first successful in developing government-sponsored housing programs. Resolutions approving government support of low-cost housing were endorsed at a number of conventions, but beginning in 1922, the A. F. of L. showed little interest in the general problem. In fact the Federation doubted the advisability, in the late 1920's and early 1930's, of government subsidies for low-cost housing.[16] A minor change in policy was apparent in 1934. A resolution advocating a long-range program of slum clearance and low-cost housing, to be supported by government aid, was referred to the Executive Council for further study.[17]

A change in policy took place in 1935 with the adoption of a resolution sponsored by J. W. Williams, head of the Building Trades Department. The resolution endorsed the "Slum Clearance and Low Rent Housing Program which has for its purpose provisions that will furnish employment to those engaged in the building and construction industry."[18] At least equally important was the authorization then of a standing housing committee to provide information and develop projects and housing legislation.[19] Harry C. Bates, head of the Bricklayers' Union, was appointed chairman, with John Coefield of the Plumbers' Union and M. J. Colleran of the Operative Plasterers' organization, as the two other members. Boris Shishkin, an economist of the A. F. of L., was attached to the housing committee. The A. F. of L. committee cooperated with the Labor Housing Committee, made up of labor union officers and others interested in promoting a program of low-cost housing. The joint program was approved by the unions in the Building and Construction Trades Department, and legislation to effectuate this purpose was sponsored by the A. F. of L.

The joint program evolved by the A. F. of L. was introduced by Senator Robert Wagner and Congressman Henry Ellenbogen. The bill provided for Federal loans and subsidies to local agencies for the construction of low-income housing. It was hoped that this legislation would provide for improved housing and would also stimulate a revival of activity in the durable goods industries. The bill passed the Senate but was not enacted in the House.[20]

The appointment of the housing committee and the approval of government participation in the development of better housing and slum clearance marked a change in the attitude on these questions by the A. F. of L. It was one of the signs of shift from a policy of nonintervention by government to one in which government intervention was actively supported. The importance of such shifts in specific areas has been frequently overlooked because the Federation has never concerned itself with elaborating general principles. In 1937 the A. F. of L. supported the Wagner-Steagall bill to provide housing accommodations for millions of workers and their families. Under the proposed measure, the Federal government was to set up a Federal Housing Authority authorized to issue 1 billion dollars of government bonds, the proceeds of which were to be used for loans to state and local housing authorities for the construction of low-rent housing. This bill was to help provide low-cost housing to those unable to pay high rents for satisfactory quarters, but it was also advocated as a device for alleviating unemployment.[21]

In a letter to Chairman Henry B. Steagall of the House Committee on Banking and Currency, Green set forth the following reasons for the enactment of the bill:

1. The latest reports show that the country is plunging headlong toward the greatest housing crisis in the entire experience of our nation. Already, sky-rocketing rents in many localities are wiping out every gain made by the workers through increases in their earnings. In large metropolitan cities, in medium size towns, and in rural communities throughout the country, vacancies disappear so rapidly that families in low-income brackets are faced with 100 per cent occupancy and are forced to double up in crowded quarters. Thus the workers find themselves compelled to live in dilapidated and deadly city slums and in blighted, unproductive and unlivable rural areas. For these men and women workers and for their children the Wagner-Steagall Housing Bill opens the way out of this hopelessness, a way which cannot fail to lead them to clean, healthy and sanitary modern homes.

2. That one-third of the people of America are ill-housed has now become a recognized fact. It is for this third of our nation that private enterprise cannot provide modern homes without government aid. The Wagner-Steagall

Housing Bill recognizes housing as a national public responsibility and establishes the principle that public aid must be given where ordinary private enterprise cannot do the job.

3. The housing program contemplated by this bill will provide jobs for building trades mechanics and laborers who are now without work and will help reduce unemployment in hundreds of industries on which the construction of housing depends.

4. The bill sets up a permanent independent United States Housing Authority with a five-man board to be appointed by the President with the advice and consent of the Senate, whose sole duty shall be to assist in the provision of modern planned low-rent housing projects and who will devote their full time and attention to this pressing and special problem.

5. This bill contains ample provision to initiate a housing program in rural areas. A firm foundation for a rural housing program can be laid under the provisions of this bill and the United States Housing Authority will then be in a position to develop a comprehensive program of rural housing based on a careful first-hand study of facts.

6. The Wagner-Steagall Bill guarantees labor standards, including prevailing wage rates and proper working conditions as a condition of all aid or construction by the United States Housing Authority.[22]

The Wagner-Steagall bill was enacted, and Harry Bates believed that with its passage, the "Federal Government assumed a permanent responsibility for the housing conditions of that vast mass of our people whose housing needs would not be met by the operations of ordinary private enterprise."[23] Bates called upon labor to assume greater responsibility for the promotion of an adequate housing program and to develop the imagination and understanding to assure the success of the first giant step by the Federal government.

The convention of 1938 directed the officers to draw up amendments to extend the Wagner-Steagall Act. Bills introduced at the request of the Federation increased the authorization of the United States Housing Authority for financing the construction loans for low-rent housing and slum-clearance projects by $800,000,000. The amendments were not adopted by the House, and with the launching of the defense program, the A. F. of L. became primarily concerned with a program for providing adequate housing for workers on defense projects.

In addition to sponsoring aid to construction, the Building and Construction Trades Departments sought to help mobilize workers for building projects.

The international presidents of the nineteen unions affiliated with the Building and Construction Trades Department surveyed their membership in January 1941 and found "that there were available for employment on the defense program 370,000 skilled workmen. The varied activities of the defense program in many localities throughout the 48 states were far removed from the centers of population. The Building and Construction Trades Department in order to more effectively serve the government in their efforts have furnished the needs for men in the various skills from time to time and in every instance have supplied an adequate number of skilled workmen."[24]

In addition, an attempt was made to settle jurisdictional differences during the war without resort to strikes. On March 31 the executive council of the Building and Construction Trades Department, meeting in special session, voluntarily pledged that there would not be any stoppage of work because of jurisdictional disputes on any project essential to speedy completion of the national defense program; it pledged its membership to do "everything within their power to help the government of the United States to build the strongest possible national defense."

To translate the program into action, the officers of the Building and Construction Trades Department conferred with the representatives of the agencies of the Federal government responsible for defense construction. On July 22, 1941 a stabilization agreement between these government agencies and the Building and Construction Trades Department was concluded and put into effect.

Article 3 of the agreement provided: "The Building and Construction Trades Department of the American Federation of Labor agrees that there shall be no stoppage of work on account of jurisdictional disputes, or for any other causes. All grievances and disputes shall be settled by conciliation and arbitration."

The agreement also established a procedure for predetermination of wages to be paid construction workers and provided that "wage rates paid at the start on a project shall continue until the completion of the project." The agreement also provided for uniform standards of overtime, uniform shifts, and other procedures essential to harmonious relationships between labor and employers on defense building construction. A Board of Review was created under the agreement to adjust all disputes arising on defense projects.[25]

In 1946 the A. F. of L. presented a comprehensive housing program to Congress. It called for the following:

1. Federal aid to municipalities for a long-term redevelopment program designed to replan and rebuild our cities and towns for sound and stable growth.

2. Resumption and expansion of slum-clearance and rehousing programs by the local housing authorities, under improved U.S. Housing Act, to provide decent homes to families of low income whom private enterprise cannot reach.

3. Enlargement of market for rental housing for families of moderate

income through FHA insurance of yield on private investment in projects built for moderate rents.

4. Improvement of housing on the farm and provision of low-cost rural housing to farm families, on lease but for eventual ownership.

5. Orderly disposition of permanent war housing, authorizing local housing authorities to acquire such housing, and giving occupancy preference to servicemen and veterans.

6. Assurance that fair labor standards be maintained on postwar housing construction envisaged in the program.

7. Creation of a permanent statutory National Housing Agency.

The Federation also sought the adoption of the prevailing wage principle on projects sponsored by the Federal government.[26]

The postwar housing program had the double aim of promoting decent homes for low-income families and aiding in the maintenance of high employment levels through expanded investment.

The A. F. of L. favored the housing legislation sponsored by Senators Robert Taft, Allen Ellender, and Robert Wagner—bills which called for an annual construction of low-cost housing units for the next seven years. For five years the A. F. of L. sponsored such legislation. In 1949 its aim was realized when Congress authorized a six-year building of 810,000 low-rent public program for low-income families. The Executive Council believed that the legislation was the result largely of the "efforts of the Housing Committee of the American Federation of Labor."[27]

Now the Federation also turned its attention to measures that would aid in the construction of middle-income housing and supported legislation for encouraging construction of homes for middle-income families at rents and prices they could afford.[28]

EDUCATION

From the beginning of its history, the A. F. of L. supported free public education. The first convention of the Federation of Organized Trades and Labor Unions of the United States and Canada declared in favor of "legislative enactments that will enforce by compulsion the education of children."[29]

Subsequently, the Federation favored the establishment of classes in which boys and girls between the ages of fourteen and sixteen would be taught trades. However, the Federation insisted that courses of instruction also include subjects such as English, mathematics, physics, history, and chemistry.[30]

The convention of 1915 reiterated its belief that industrial or vocational education should be part of the public school curriculum. It held that children "must be educated not only to adapt [themselves] to [their] particular calling . . . but that they should be educated for leadership as well."[31] The convention favored administration of industrial education by the same officers who administered general education and asked that the pending Federal legislation for granting aid to state vocational programs be amended to provide for single control over the educational system rather than for seperate administrative bodies for general and vocational education. The A. F. of L. endorsed the Industrial Education and Trade Training (Smith-Hughes) Act under which the Federal government made funds for vocational training available through grants-in-aid to the states.[32]

At the same time the A. F. of L. urged its affiliated bodies to use their influence so that their respective states would qualify to receive Federal aid under the Federal law. It called attention to the need for safeguards so that Federal funds would be used to advance the training and not as a means for exploiting new entrants into the labor market. The chief safeguard against perversion of the purposes of the law, in view of the A. F. of L., was equal representation of labor upon boards of vocational education.[33]

From the beginning of its history, the Federation supported the issuance of free textbooks to all children by the school system. The A. F. of L. also favored the establishment of part-time classes for the education of minors engaged in regular employment. In 1920 the A. F. of L. set up a permanent committee to consider and report on educational matters to the Executive Council and conventions.

Interference with the school system or the teacher by private or public groups was always opposed, and in 1922 the convention advocated the repeal of legislation such as the Lusk law in New York State which sought to supervise the teacher and teaching. The A. F. of L. found that the "practical result of such laws was to endanger the independence of teachers in dealing with social problems."[34] The A. F. of L. also objected to unwarranted inquiries into the personal affairs of teachers in matters of "sex, race, creed, and other extraneous considerations," and declared that the "basis for the selection of teachers should be their preparation and training."[35]

With the onset of the Great Depression and the curtailment in the building of schools and hiring of needed teachers by many school districts, the Federation called attention to the "thousands of pupils . . . being housed in dilapidated portable buildings. . . . Teachers' salaries . . . cut 50 per cent. Many cities and counties have paid them in depreciated non-marketable commercial paper or not at all. . . . Those who through so-called Taxpayers' Leagues or Economy Leagues are bemoaning the taxes are loud in their demands that the social services of the community be cut. We cannot simply sit by and watch the passing of the free public school. . . . Federal aid in education is not federal control."[36]

The A. F. of L. advocated the raising of the salaries of teachers and increased appropriations for educational institutions from the kindergarten to the state- and city-supported universities. In 1938 the convention approved a program which called for well-planned education for all children and youth, safe and sanitary school buildings, suitable equipment, including textbooks, student aid so as to permit able young people to remain in school at least to the age of eighteen years, a plan for the protection of the physical and mental health of school children, school districts large enough to permit the raising of adequate tax funds, participation of teachers in the development of an educational program, and support of urban as well as rural schools.[37]

The A. F. of L. showed concern at the disclosure that many of those drafted for military service were unable to read or write. It believed that Federal intervention in this area was justified and it advocated an emergency program of Federal aid to the states to guarantee minimum salaries to teachers of at least $1,500 a year. In 1943 two bills were introduced in Congress at the request of the A. F. of L., one required emergency financial aid to the states for the support of their public schools; the other called for a study of the long-range problem of developing a program of Federal-state-local financing of school aid.[38] The following year the A. F. of L. called for the equalization of educational opportunities through Federal grants to the states. At the same time, it was the view of the A. F. of L. that Federal involvement in the selection of books, curricula, or methods of instruction should be avoided. In making appropriations, the Federal government was urged to require that a fixed proportion be set aside for salaries. Federal funds were to supplement and not supplant state funds. The A. F. of L. insisted that Federal aid to education must assure that those in need of aid would receive it.

Federal aid to education, for the A. F. of L., meant the following:

1. Assistance to states to enable them to pay adequate salaries to teachers.

2. Aid for the establishment of services to protect child health and welfare.

3. Scholarships to the needy youth so as to enable them to continue their studies.

4. Support of a school building program by Federal funds, and assistance in the development of an adult education program by the states and communities.

A number of safeguards for this program were included. Minority groups were to be assured of their equitable share of Federal funds;

states and their political subdivisions would be required to maintain at least their existing level of expenditures for education and salaries for teachers; a fixed sum of the Federal grant was to be allocated for payment of teachers' salaries; funds were to be distributed to states on the basis of relative need, and would be required to be distributed to every part of the state in need. In addition, states were to be required to publish their plans for expending Federal grants and to report subsequently on the methods used to carry out the program. A Federal audit of receipts and expenditures was also suggested.[39]

### WORKERS' EDUCATION BUREAU

Workers' Education as distinct from general or vocational education is designed to acquaint the worker, and more particularly the union member, with the history, practices, and problems of the labor movement. As in other educational institutions, the curricula of the labor institutes and classes have changed over time and have adapted themselves, at least in part, to the changing needs of the organizations of labor. Labor education in the United States was to a large degree initiated by unions with socialist or progressive leadership who hoped that their members would become better, more informed, and loyal members as a result of their training.

The New York United Labor Education Committee, established in 1918, sponsored a conference in the spring of 1921 which organized the Workers' Education Bureau. The Bureau was to promote and assist educational work by labor unions.[40] In 1924 a cooperative agreement between the Bureau and the A. F. of L. was devised whereby the general purpose of the Bureau remained unaltered. Dual and seceding unions were denied representation and three members of the A. F. of L. were placed on the Executive Board of the Bureau. The Bureau continued its activity, issued printed material, and helped to arrange labor institutes. Eventually it became a functional department of the A. F. of L.

### REFERENCES

1. *Report of the Proceedings of the Forty-first Annual Convention of the American Federation of Labor,* 1921, p. 314.

2. *Report of the Proceedings of the Forty-third Annual Convention of the American Federation of Labor,* 1923, p. 357.

3. *Report of the Procedings of the Forty-fourth Annual Convention of the American Federation of Labor,* 1924, p. 187.

4. Statement issued on September 18, 1931.

5. *Report of the Proceedings of the Fifty-second Annual Convention of the American Federation of Labor,* 1932, p. 123.

6. Minutes of Executive Council, January 24, 1938.

7. Statement of the American Federation of Labor to the Finance Committee of the Senate of the United States, August 11, 1942.

8. Green to Robert L. Doughton, March 11, 1942.

9. Green to Congressman Robert L. Doughton, November 1, 1943.

10. Green to Members of Congress, February 23, 1944.

11. Statement by William Green, President of the American Federation of Labor before the Senate Finance Committee of the 80th Congress Considering H. R. 1 and Senate Substitute for H. R. 1, Providing for a Reduction in Individual Income Tax Payments.

12. Statement of Arthur A. Elder of the American Federation of Labor before the House Ways and Means Committee on General Tax Revision, July 10, 1947, in A. F. of L. files.

13. Statement on Proposed Amendment to Revenue Act of 1950 (H. R. 8920) in the Light of Proposed Increase in Federal Expenditures by American Federation of Labor, July 31, 1950, in files of A. F. of L.

14. Minutes of Executive Council, January 25, 1951.

15. *Report of the Proceedings of the Thirty-fourth Annual Convention of the American Federation of Labor*, 1914, p. 355; Timothy L. McDonnell, *The Wagner Housing Act* (Chicago: Loyola University, 1957), pp. 11–15.

16. McDonnell, *op. cit.*, p. 68.

17. *Report of the Proceedings of the Fifty-fourth Annual Convention of the American Federation of Labor*, 1934, p. 414.

18. *Report of the Proceedings of the Fifty-fifth Annual Convention of the American Federation of Labor*, 1935, p. 612.

19. *Ibid.*, pp. 613–614.

20. *Report of the Proceedings of the Fifty-sixth Annual Convention of the American Federation of Labor*, 1936, p. 178.

21. *American Federation of Labor Weekly News Service*, April 17, 1937.

22. Green to Henry B. Steagall, August 3, 1937.

23. *Report of the Proceedings of the Fifty-seventh Annual Convention of the American Federation of Labor*, 1937, p. 607.

24. Memorandum of Agreement of the Building and Construction Trades Department, January 7, 1941, in files of A. F. of L.

25. Memorandum of Agreement between the Representatives of Government Agencies Engaged in Defense Construction and the Building and Construction Trades Department of the American Federation of Labor, July 22, 1941, in files of A. F. of L.

26. Statement of William Green, April 30, 1946.

27. *Report of the Proceedings of the Sixty-seventh Convention of the American Federation of Labor*, 1948, p. 163.

28. Minutes of Executive Council, May 21, 1953.

29. *Report of Proceedings of First Annual Session of the Federation of Organized Trades and Labor Unions of the United States and Canada*, 1881, p. 3.

30. *Report of the Proceedings of the Twenty-ninth Annual Convention of the American Federation of Labor*, 1909, pp. 275–276.

31. *Report of the Proceedings of the Thirty-fifth Annual Convention of the American Federation of Labor*, 1915, p. 323.

32. *Report of the Proceedings of the Thirty-sixth Annual Convention of the American Federation of Labor*, 1916, p. 192; *ibid., Thirty-seventh Convention,* 1917, p. 119.

33. *Report of the Proceedings of the Thirty-seventh Annual Convention of the American Federation of Labor*, 1917, pp. 413–414.

34. *Report of the Proceedings of the Forty-second Annual Convention of the American Federation of Labor*, 1922, p. 306.

35. *Report of the Proceedings of the Fifty-first Annual Convention of the American Federation of Labor*, 1931, p. 349.

36. *Report of the Proceedings of the Fifty-third Annual Convention of American Federation of Labor*, 1933, pp. 302–303.

37. *Report of the Proceedings of the Fifty-eighth Annual Convention of the American Federation of Labor*, 1938, pp. 487–488.

38. *Report of the Proceedings of the Sixty-third Annual Convention of the American Federation of Labor*, 1943, p. 107.

39. *Report of the Proceedings of the Sixty-eighth Convention of the American Federation of Labor*, 1949, p. 107.

# XXIII

## Political Action

IN the presidential campaign of 1928, the Federation returned in fact as well as in theory to its nonpartisan political policy. In 1924 the A. F. of L. had embraced the third-term candidacy of Senator Robert La Follette as a desperate measure when neither political party showed any sympathy for its demands. But Federation leaders were relieved when the railway brotherhoods withdrew from the independent political venture after the 1924 presidential campaign, thereby leaving its promotion to the traditional exponents of independent political action. In 1927 the Executive Council appointed a National Non-Partisan Political Committee.

In a letter to organized labor, William Green and Frank Morrison urged all union members to stand by the friends of labor and aid in their election, irrespective of the party ticket on which they ran. The letter reaffirmed the nonpartisanship policy of the 1927 convention and the duty of wage earners to support the candidate and platform which would in the end be of greatest benefit to labor. "The experience of 1924," the letter said, "should be a warning to both parties. Neither platform that year appealed to Labor. Representatives of the American Federation of Labor appeared before the Resolutions Committees of both conventions and urged that certain declarations be made in their platforms. Both parties ignored the plea of labor."[1]

The Federation submitted to the Republican and Democratic party conventions a series of recommendations with the request that they be incorporated in the platforms of the conventions.[2] The A. F. of L. delegation urged an amendment of the Sherman Act which would exempt labor from this statute and permit it to develop along normal lines with industry and agriculture.

The statement asked endorsement of legislation which would prevent judges in equity courts from misusing injunctions in labor disputes and for the approval of labor's right to organize. In addition, laws were requested to aid in the abolition of child labor and the limitation of competition by goods produced in prisons with those manufactured by free labor. The Federation also presented a program for dealing with unemployment "in a practical and constructive way. . . . This can be done through the appropriation of funds by the Congress of the United States to be made available for use in the construction of public buildings, in making public improvements, in the building of highways, in carrying forward the project of flood control, and building various other government projects during periods of wide and extended unemployment. On the other hand, the Government should refrain from launching a public construction program when men and women·are generally employed in private industry."[3]

The labor recommendations included provisions for wounded American veterans, general improvement in workman's compensation laws, and adequate protection against abridgments of personal freedoms and the threats of compulsory service and labor. Labor also favored the five-day week and the amendment of the Volstead Act to permit the manufacture and sale of beer containing more than 2.75 per cent alcohol.

After the adjournment of the Democratic and Republican conventions, Treasurer Daniel Tobin favored endorsing Alfred E. Smith for the presidency; he resigned when his suggestion was rejected. Instead, the Non-Partisan Political Committee distributed the records of the candidates for congressional office, the criteria to be used in supporting or opposing candidates, as well as the declarations made by the parties and presidential candidates on issues vital to labor.[4]

The same policy was followed in the campaign of 1932 when a Non-Partisan Political Campaign Committee of five members of the Executive Council was appointed. The Council in a statement to the membership said that the interests of labor "have been protected and conserved through a strict adherence to a non-partisan political policy. This procedure requires that the platforms of the political parties must be compared and the records of candidates for office must be carefully studied and scrutinized. . . . The wisdom of such action is clearly apparent when it is considered that the American Federation of Labor is composed of men and women who entertain different political opinions."[5]

The recommendations submitted to the conventions for approval were largely the same as had been presented in 1928. Discussing the 1932 campaign with the Executive Council, Green reported that he had "endeavored . . . to maintain a non-partisan policy in this campaign. In carrying out this matter we prepared a pamphlet entitled 'Labor Planks in the Political Platforms of the Republican and Democratic Parties and the Records of Candidates for President and Vice-President.' We endeavored to compile it as carefully as we could. We distributed a large number of copies of the pamphlet. . . . I have always kept this in mind as far as possible—the officers and members of the Non-Partisan Committee should follow a strictly non-partisan political policy, and that fact has impressed me because after all our movement is above and beyond any political campaign, political policy, and political consideration."[6]

A number of resolutions endorsing a labor party were introduced at the 1935 convention, and although the issue brought on some debate, in the end the policy of nonpartisanship was reaffirmed.[7] On April 25, 1936, the Federation announced, in accordance with the customary procedure, the policy of nonpartisanship for the presidential campaign of 1936. The Non-Partisan Political Campaign Committee, after "painstaking preparation and careful study," submitted a series of labor planks to both parties.[8] Unemployment, in the opinion of the A. F. of L., constituted "the vital, outstanding problem of the nation. It constitutes a challenge to our political, social and economic order. There can be no return to prosperity and social tranquility throughout the country until we find a solution for this serious and vexing problem. As a partial remedy, we urge a declaration in favor of a well-planned, systematic, public works relief program. We hold that public relief works should be well planned and systematically arranged so that during periods of unemployment, either national or local in character, the unemployed may be permitted to work on public projects until they are accorded an opportunity to return to private employment."[9]

The statement favored a census of the unemployed to gauge the magnitude of involuntary idleness; it advocated a shorter work week, higher wages, vocational training and education, and social security and pensions as other means to relieve idleness and those in need. The statement emphasized the necessity of maintaining inviolate treaties entered into between the United States and foreign countries. "Inasmuch," it observed, "as recognition was extended to Soviet Russia on condition precedent to the effect that the Soviet Government would restrain and refrain in any way from incurring or supporting Communist propaganda or activities of any kind or form in this country or permit the formation or activity on its territory of any group or organization having as one of its aims the preparation for the overthrow of our government by force, we hold that the Soviet Government should be required to meet this condition upon which official recognition was based."[10]

In 1938 the A. F. of L. asked its affiliated organizations to renew their support of the nonpartisan policy. It advised against affiliating with Labor's Non-Partisan League, which had been organized in 1936 to mobilize labor support for the reelection of President Franklin D. Roosevelt. George Berry, president of the Printing Pressmen's Union, had been named chairman of the League, and many other officials of A. F. of L. unions took an active part in the League's campaign. Early in 1937 Berry was appointed United States Senator from Tennessee, and John L. Lewis, then heading the C.I.O., became the League's chairman; Sidney Hillman was selected as its vice chairman.

The officers of the A. F. of L. believed that the character and activities of Labor's Non-Partisan League underwent a change with the withdrawal of Berry and the assumption of leadership by Lewis and Hillman. In their opinion, the League was attempting to become an independent political party, and the Federation was especially perturbed when the League put its own candidates into the political arena. In addition, the Federation did not favor certain radical elements which had become active in the League; in fact, it was viewed as nothing more than a mouthpiece of the C.I.O. As a result of these changes in the character of Labor's Non-Partisan League, the Executive Council made the following recommendations:

1. That all state federations of labor, city central bodies and local organizations affiliated with the American Federation of Labor withdraw from association with Labor's Non-Partisan League.

2. That all organizations affiliated with the American Federation of Labor and their individual members cease contributing to the financial support of Labor's Non-Partisan League.

3. That co-ordinated efforts be undertaken by the officers of the American Federation of Labor and all its affiliated bodies to examine carefully into the qualifications of all candidates for public office nominated or indorsed by Labor's Non-Partisan League and any subsidiary groups, to the end that effective opposition may be marshalled against any such candidates found lacking the proper qualifications for public office.

4. That all State Federations of Labor and City Central Bodies form American Federation of Labor Non-Partisan Committees, separate and apart from any association with the so-called "Labor's Non-Partisan League," for the express purpose of carrying out the non-partisan political policy of the American Federation of Labor; the officers of these American Federation of Labor Non-Partisan Political Committees to be men whose membership in and devotion and loyalty to the American Federation of Labor are publicly known.

5. That all Non-Partisan Political Committees formed in accordance with these recommendations cooperate with the officers of the American Federation of Labor in the support of labor's friends who are candidates for office, without regard to political party affiliation, and the defeat of those who are out of sympathy with and in opposition to the legislative and economic policies of the American Federation of Labor.

6. That the Non-Partisan Political Committees of State Federations of Labor and City Central Bodies endorse and support candidates for Congress and the United States Senate whose public records show that they are friendly and sympathetic to labor, without regard to political party affiliation, and who are approved and endorsed because of said records by the American Federation of Labor.

It is the opinion of the Executive Council that the recommendations herein made should be carried out by all organizations affiliated wtih the American Federation of Labor, without change or modification. Let your non-partisan political policy be truly and without compromise the American Federation of Labor Non-Partisan Political Policy as formulated and adopted by conventions of the American Federation of Labor, which after all is the highest tribunal within the American Federation of Labor.[11]

The 1938 convention considered a resolution submitted by the delegation from the Hotel and Restaurant Workers' Union directing the officers of the Federation to rescind their order to withdraw support from Labor's Non-Partisan League. The resolution was criticized by George Meany, representing the New York State Federation of Labor.[12]

In February 1939 the Executive Council took further action against Labor's Non-Partisan League when it approved Woll's motion that the League was "no longer a labor organization but purely a political organization."[13] In a letter to affiliates and central bodies, Green stated that the A. F. of L. followed a nonpartisan political policy and formulated nonpartisan policies. Requesting all labor groups to dissociate themselves from the League, he warned central bodies, state federations of labor, and federal labor unions that failure to carry out the instructions of the Executive Council in this matter would subject them to revocation of their charters for failure to obey the rules and principles of the Federation.[14]

At its May sessions the Council approved a program containing a series of planks to be presented to the platform committees of the party conventions. These planks included one approving the investigations of activities subversive to the American form of government supported and financed by communist and fascist groups. The Federation also sought to incorporate in the platforms an endorsement of labor's right to participate in the defense program by appointment of its representatives to defense agencies, acceptance of the principle of the shorter work-week, protection of the right to organize and to bargain collectively, and continued aid to the unemployed. The parties were asked to oppose any curtailment of the rights of free speech, free press, and free assembly and to embody in their platforms a strong declaration in favor "of the preservation of these rights to the end that they may continue unabridged by any agency of the government." Finally, the labor statement suggested improvements in the social security system and new legislation for the protection of wages and working standards.[15]

At its meeting on September 30, 1940, the Executive Council reaffirmed its stand that "the best interests of its entire membership have been protected and conserved through a strict adherence to a non-partisan political policy. This procedure requires that the platforms of the political parties must be compared and the records of candidates for office must be carefully studied and scrutinized."[16]

The A. F. of L. followed the same policy of nonpartisanship in the Congressional campaign of 1942. In August 1943 Sidney Hillman suggested that the Federation cooperate with the C.I.O. in its political activity. When the proposal was submitted to the Executive Council, it decided not to join with "any other group in the formulation of a political policy."[17]

In preparation for the presidential campaign of 1944, the Council announced in February that a nonpartisan committee would function for the A. F. of L. to acquaint the affiliates with the records of congressional candidates. Directly affiliated unions were requested to adhere to the historic policy of the Federation, and "under no circumstances must State Federations of Labor, City Central Labor Unions or our directly affiliated unions collaborate with representatives of dual organizations or allow the representatives of dual organizations to participate in the formation and execution of the non-partisan policy of the American Federation of Labor."[18] Green also asked all affiliates not to allow the prestige of the A. F. of L. to be exploited by "dual, rival, rebel movements," meaning, of course, the C.I.O. Political Action Committee. George Berry, president of the Printing Pressmen's Union, taking exception to Green's statement, doubted "the authority of the Executive Council of the A. F. of L. to direct International Unions to proceed on its political basis. That is the responsibility of the International Unions as they elect, and beyond that the question as to what party they may wish to join and the parties they support seems to me to be one to be determined by the individual, and we shall not interfere with that prerogative."[19] Berry was on sound ground, although it had never been regarded as beyond the Executive Council's authority to endorse and disapprove of candidates as long as the international unions reserved the privilege of following or rejecting the Council's advice.

In spite of Berry's objections, the A. F. of L. submitted a series of proposals to the conventions of the two parties and asked for their inclusion in the 1944 platforms. On behalf of its members, the Federation expressed "the hope that one of the objectives reached at the conclusion of the war . . . will be the end of wars and the substitution thereof of national and individual security." To achieve these objectives, the Federation advised the setting up of an international organization able to safeguard peace and to enforce it if necessary. To deal with domestic problems, the A. F. of L. asked for approval of the elimination of wartime restrictions on manpower and wages, full employment and high wages by public works if the objective could not be achieved through private investment, fair and reasonable tax exemptions for the low-income groups, equal educational opportunity for all, enactment of a sound and comprehensive system of social security, repeal of the Smith-Connally Act, and the amendment of the National Labor Relations Act to make it more responsive to skilled workers' wishes for separate representation.[20]

Although the A. F. of L. officially followed a nonpartisan political policy, many of its officers were delegates to the Democratic Party's convention and a few to the Republican Party's. The A. F. of L. took some satisfaction in the defeat of Henry Wallace for renomination as Vice President and in the success of his replacement, Harry Truman. According to the Federation leaders, the fifty delegates from unions affiliated with the A. F. of L. thereby achieved their principal objective. "Because of the non-partisan policy of the A. F. of L., Federation leaders could not commit themselves to endorsement of any particular ticket and therefore their activities at the convention were conducted with a minimum of publicity. Nevertheless, they made no secret of their hostility to Wallace, whose record showed repeated acts of discrimination against the A. F. of L. and whose allegiances were obviously to the left-wing element in the C.I.O."[21]

In the congressional elections of 1946, there was no change in Federation policy. Records of congressmen and senators were sent to the central bodies, and again the nonpartisan policy was recommended.[22] Playing host to the leaders of the two major parties, Green said that voting a straight party ticket did not make for good government. He explained that the "nonpartisan political policy of the American Federation of Labor is based on the principle that the workers should elect the friends of labor and defeat its enemies regardless of their political affiliation."[23]

## REFERENCES

1. Green and Morrison to all organized labor, February 11, 1928.

2. Statements submitted to the National Republican Party Convention in Kansas City, Missouri, June 12, 1928, and to the Democratic National Convention in Houston, Texas, June 26, 1928.

3. *Ibid.*

4. *Report of the Proceedings of the Forty-eighth Annual Convention of the American Federation of Labor*, 1928, pp. 75–76.

5. Minutes of Executive Council, July 15, 1932.

6. *Ibid.*

7. *Report of the Proceedings of the Fifty-fifth Annual Convention of the American Federation of Labor*, 1935, pp. 758–776.

8. Labor Planks Submitted by the American Federation of Labor to the Republican National Convention, Cleveland, Ohio, June 9, 1936. The same proposals were submitted to the Democratic National Convention in Philadelphia.

9. *Ibid.*

10. *Ibid.*

11. By the direction of the Executive Council of the American Federation of Labor, William Green, President, March 21, 1938.

12. *Report of the Proceedings of the Fifty-eighth Annual Convention of the American Federation of Labor*, 1938, pp. 403–411.

13. Minutes of Executive Council, February 14, 1939.

14. Green to National and International Unions, State Federations of Labor, City Central Bodies, and Directly Affiliated Local Unions, March 1, 1939.

15. Minutes of Executive Council, May 6, 1940.

16. Minutes of Executive Council, September 30, 1940.

17. Minutes of Executive Council, August 9, 12, 1943.

18. Green to the Officers of National and International Unions, State Federations of Labor, City Central Bodies, and Directly Affiliated Unions, February 23, 1944.

19. George L. Berry to Green, March 17, 1944.

20. *Proposals Submitted to the Resolutions Committee of the Republican National Convention in June 1944*, by William Green. The same proposals were presented to the resolutions committee of the Democratic National Convention.

21. *American Federation Weekly News Service*, July 25, 1944.

22. Green to Officers of State Federations of Labor and Central Labor Unions, September 16, 1946.

23. *American Federation of Labor Weekly News Service*, October 29, 1946.

# XXIV

## League for Political Education

THE enactment of the Taft-Hartley law greatly increased the political activity of the A. F. of L. Although the policy of nonpartisanship was retained, the creation of a permanent political organization and the greatly expanded level and range of its activity really marked a new departure in the political program of the A. F. of L. In its report to the 1947 convention, the Executive Council recommended that a Labor's League for Political Education be set up to promote the economic and political philosophies of the Federation. The League would be authorized to prepare and disseminate information among the workers of the country to acquaint them with A. F. of L. policies, to make known the views of candidates for public office, particularly on questions affecting organized labor, and to raise money and employ a staff to carry out their tasks.[1] Accordingly, after the adjournment of the convention, the Executive Council called into special session the presidents of the international unions and appointed George Harrison, Matthew Woll, and Charles Mac-Gowan of the Executive Board to prepare the plan.[2] The union presidents met in conference on December 5, 1947 to "adopt plans designed to make vital and effective the political purposes formulated and adopted at the 66th Annual Convention of the American Federation of Labor."[3]

The committee's, or the Harrison, report was submitted to the international officers at the opening of the meeting. After charging the United States Congress with "having placed unwarrantable and highly destructive limitations and restrictions upon the rights of wage earners to voluntary organization and their effective functioning in the industrial as well as the legislative and political fields," the report called upon labor, both organized and unorganized, to challenge the assault "upon the rights and liberties of the workers of America," and to "galvanize the workers of America, their friends and sympathizers into concrete action along definite and public-spirited channels."[4] To carry out these aims, the report recommended the establishment of a National Committee made up of the members of the Executive Council of the A. F. of L. and the presidents of all the national and international unions affiliated with the Federation. A chairman and a secretary-treasurer were to be elected, and an Administrative Committee made up of the Executive Council of the A. F. of L.

and fifteen representatives of national and international unions was to be chosen by the National Committee. The National Committee was also to appoint a national director and staff.

Labor's League for Political Education would compile the records of candidates for public office and circulate them among members of unions and sympathizers with the labor movement. Speeches, special features, cartoons, recordings for use on radio, and short announcements were to be prepared by the staff and circulated among state and local labor political groups. The Administrative Committee, with the advice of state federations of labor and city central bodies, would recommend endorsement of congressional candidates. The League was also directed "to bring about the largest possible registration of union members, their friends, associates and sympathizers and [to get] out the votes."[5] The Administrative Committee was to make the Taft-Hartley law one of the principal issues in the forthcoming presidential campaign and was to determine the congressional and senatorial districts in which labor's efforts were to be concentrated.

A special finance committee would be appointed to raise funds by voluntary contributions. The report also suggested that the national and international unions try to raise $1 in voluntary contributions from each member, and use 50 per cent of the contribution to finance their own political activity, and send the remainder to the League. The League was authorized to use these funds to finance its activities and the political campaigns in various areas.

President Green told the meeting of international officers that their task was to decide the steps to be taken by the A. F. of L. in the presidential campaign of 1948. The presidents were also to devise means and methods to carry out the plans which they adopted. During the discussion of the Harrison report, Daniel Tobin made it clear that the Council wanted all representatives to suggest any changes in program and policy that might more effectively carry out the purposes of the campaign they were embarking upon. Commending the work of the Harrison committee in preparing the report, Tobin said that "regardless of the results obtained by this League in the 1948 election campaign, its activities will be of great value to the workers in the future."[6] A committee of eight was appointed to examine the report and bring back recommendations for action; a nominating committee of five was also appointed to recommend nominees for the Administrative Committee. Subsequently, the report was unanimously accepted, and fifteen officers of international unions were elected to the Administrative Committee.

At the conclusion of the conference, Secretary-Treasurer Meany described the actions taken as marking "a new departure . . . but by no means a departure from the old political philosophy of the A. F. of L. of 'defeating your enemies and rewarding your friends.' . . . That policy is just as valid today as when it was initiated many years ago by Samuel Gompers and those associated with him in the founding of the Federation. . . . What has happened here today is that we are starting something to attempt to give effect to that philosophy in line with present condition."[7] Meany said that the A. F. of L. faced a practical situation and that it was no longer sufficient to send central labor unions and local unions the voting records of congressmen or state representatives. The Federation had to make the members of organized labor "politically conscious; develop them politically in their own self-interest, not for the purpose of attempting to run the country but for the purpose of protecting ourselves."[8]

The Administrative Committee appointed committees on finance, organization, and the selection of a director for the League. The organization committee recommended that four departments be created—finance, public relations, organization, and political direction—and that the committee on finance allocate to the four departments the money that would be required to carry out their particular functions. The Administrative Committee also voted to appoint an executive committee made up of a chairman, William Green, a secretary-treasurer, George Meany, and as many additional members as were deemed advisable.

Woll, who was chairman of the committee on organization, said that the purpose of the program was to distribute authority rather than to concentrate it. The organization committee suggested that the department of finance, of which David Dubinsky was chosen chairman, determine the level of financial contributions to be sought, conduct campaigns for their collection, and perform the duties usually conducted by a finance department. The department of public relations, Matthew Woll, chairman, was to explain the purposes of the League, establish publicity and speakers' bureaus, and prepare speeches and publicity material. The department of organization under Herman Winter would organize state leagues, assist them in forming subbranches and develop cooperation between the labor movement and the League. It would also aid in organizing union members in district and ward political groups and help these activities financially. This department had the responsibility for helping to register voters and for seeking a large registration of voters in the primaries and elections. The department of political direction, George M. Harrison, chairman, would assemble the records of public officeholders and those seeking public office and endorse candidates in the primaries and elections on the basis of their records and statements.[9]

A number of persons were considered for the position of director. Former Senator James Mead had support because of his favorable labor record and political experience, but since he was about to receive a political appointment, he was unavailable. Former Senator Robert M. La Follette, Jr. could have had the post, but he did not wish to reenter active politics. Former Senator Matthew Neely of West Virginia was a candidate for reelection and consequently could not be considered, although he had supporters. Former Senator Burton K. Wheeler finally accepted the appointment subject to a conference with the Administrative Committee to determine exactly what his duties would be. Some members were worried about Wheeler's record, but MacGowan said that the "Administrative Committee is going to make policy, and with all due respect to Burton K. Wheeler if he is not going to follow out a policy fixed by this group here, he makes himself unavailable." Hugo Ernst, president of the Hotel and Restaurant Workers' Union and a member of the Administrative Committee, was "absolutely opposed" to the appointment of Senator Wheeler. In his opinion, "the history of Senator Wheeler in the recent past is one that makes him absolutely unfit to do this job in a manner . . . we as members of the A. F. of L. would like to have it done."[10] Ernst thought it would be very unsafe to entrust Senator Wheeler with such grave responsibilities because of the fact that "Mr. Wheeler would be swayed by his personal likes and dislikes against persons with whom he differed rather than to be guided by the objectives of this committee."[11]

In the discusions with George Harrison, Wheeler tentatively accepted the position at a salary of $20,000 a year. He was assured that he would have complete freedom subject "to policy determinations by the Administrative Committee and the Chairman of the League."[12] While the discussion was going on, Wheeler announced that he could devote only part time to the job and withdrew. Meany was angered by Wheeler's action, for Wheeler had told Harrison that he "had to have a month to clean up certain existing law cases and then he was free and would devote his full time to the job; that he had no reservations in so far as our position on the Marshall Plan was concerned. Meany reported that Mr. Harrison contends that Senator Wheeler is not telling the truth if he says Mr. Harrison misunderstood him."[13]

Pending his appointment as director at the next meeting, Joseph Keenan, secretary of the Chicago Federation of Labor, was hired and directed to begin organizing a staff for the League.

Under Section 313 of the Federal Corrupt Practices Act of 1925, as amended by Section 304 of the Taft-Hartley Act, labor unions were forbidden to make expenditures from union funds in connection with elections, including primary elections, political conventions, and caucuses. Consequently, the unions could not directly support financially any political activities. Union members, however, were not prohibited from freely and voluntarily making contributions for political purposes. Unions were also allowed to contribute and spend their monies in a general educational campaign to enlighten their memberships and the electorate on issues which concerned their well-being and self-interest, as long as there were no exhortation to vote against or for a particular candidate. To meet legal requirements, the League had to set up two funds: a political fund to be raised by voluntary contributions, and an educational fund to which unions could contribute.

The Executive Committee sent out requests for contributions, and at first the returns were slow. At the outset, some unions refused to participate in the program; others undertook their own projects. In May Joseph D. Keenan, who had been serving as assistant to the executive officers of the League, was appointed director. He announced that the first big job was to conduct registration drives among union members. Keenan claimed that the surveys made by the League showed that union members had often lost their voting rights by failure to register and that the League would seek to remedy this shortcoming.[14]

In the meantime, the A. F. of L. went on record as "completely and unanimously opposed to the presidential candidacy of Henry Wallace." The Federation made this announcement so that members of organized labor would not be misled by the "false liberalism of Mr. Wallace and his so-called third party organization." The A. F. of L. charged that Wallace had been taken over "lock, stock and barrel" by the Communists. It said that the "strategy behind the Wallace campaign is devious, but transparent. The Communists, of course, have no hopes of electing him. Their purpose is to confuse the workers of America and split the liberal vote. The object of this strategy is to bring about the election of an arch-reactionary with isolationist leanings. This would play into the hands of Soviet Russia's expansionist policies. It would also bring about a state of affairs in this country which would promote the revolutionary aims of the Communists. Oppression and depression provide converts to their cause."[15]

As in the past the Federation presented a list of proposals to the national party conventions. The principal demand was for the repeal of the Taft-Hartley law on the ground that it "undermined the constitutional, civil, and economic rights of workers," engendered suspicion, aroused resentment, and created industrial unrest. The Federation also charged that the Act encouraged delay, interfered with proper union activity by outlawing the secondary boycott, and interfered with collective bargaining.[16]

As a means of curbing inflation, the Federation suggested that the government consult cooperating committees of businessmen, labor, agricultural, and other groups to develop a joint program to check inflation. A plan of voluntary allocation of scarce materials and utilization of monetary and fiscal policies which would check the "abnormal increase in money supply and bank credit" was advocated, and broad programs of Federal aid to education and public housing were proposed. The Federation favored a revision of the tax law with emphasis on the reduction of excise taxes; and it also called for extensive improvements in social security, including extension of coverage, substantial increases in benefits, and the establishment of a comprehensive program of medical care insurance. Amendment of Fair Labor Standards Act, providing for a minimum wage of $1 an hour, was held necessary, since many workers were not able to raise their standards through collective bargaining.

Although they were anxious to have their proposals embodied in the party platforms, the A. F. of L. leaders sought to avoid too close involvement in old-line politics. When James Roosevelt, on the eve of the Democratic Convention in 1948, asked Green to join a caucus in the convention city, Philadelphia, to draft a candidate, presumably Dwight Eisenhower, "of such stature that the prosperity of our nation and a lasting peace for the world will become secure," Green refused to allow the use of his name for that purpose.[17] He said that he was not a delegate to the convention, and he was not in accord with the "purpose and plan outlined in the telegram."[18] The Executive Council discussed the policy to be pursued in the presidential campaign, and Green wanted to adhere to the traditional policy of no endorsement. Harry Bates, president of the Bricklayers' Union, thought that if the Executive Council could not endorse a candidate for president in the name of the A. F. of L., Labor's League for Political Education should follow the same policy. George Harrison agreed that it would be wise to delete the endorsement of Harry Truman for reelection in the League's report.[19]

In the summer, the League set up in every state a Labor League for Political Education. The Department of Public Relations issued the *1948 Campaign News Service* and sent it to all affiliates. The service was started in the second week of July, immediately after the Supreme Court removed the prohibition on political advocacy by the labor press. Special cover designs for the months of August, September, and October were mailed to all international union journals, and an instruction manual for local political workers, *Blueprint for Victory*, was distributed to affiliates.[20]

The Department of Political Direction sent out lists of candidates running in the primaries. Some were endorsed by Labor's League for Political Education; in other instances the endorsement of the Railway Labor's Political League was accepted. The mailings gave the dates on which the primaries of different states were to be held, and emphasized the need of concentrating support on behalf of labor's friends. The League's Department of Political Direction avoided to a large degree districts where it had little chance to influence the electorate, as well as states in which antilabor senators and congressmen were strongly entrenched. The greatest effort was concentrated in areas where the chances of success were deemed favorable. The department focused on the selection of senators because of their six-year terms and because it was believed that the labor vote could frequently have more influence on a state basis than in a single district.[21]

Labor's League for Political Education raised somewhat less than $115,000 for its educational fund and over $360,210 for its political activities. The political fund, built by voluntary contributions, was used for financing the work of the several departments, for aiding state and local groups, and for assisting candidates endorsed by organized labor. The amounts contributed to any single state or indvidual candidate could not be decisive. The largest amount donated to a state was over $18,000 to Illinois; this included the total advances made to all candidates and groups in the state in the 1948 campaign. The highest amount for an individual candidate was given to Senator James Murray in his campaign for reelection in Montana. No contributions were made in those states where the League did not believe they would be effective. The Southern states received almost no financial contributions from the League.[22]

After the campaign, the Department of Political Direction found the results of the 1948 elections "very gratifying" and a vindication of labor's position on many of the principal issues of the election. The League thought that organized labor deserved a large share of the credit for getting out the urban vote and for publicizing important issues.[23] The Administrative Committee believed that Labor's League for Political Education should be continued on a permanent basis and should be active on national, state, and local levels. The committee recognized that even more important than the financing of campaigns and candidates had been the ability of the League to mobilize volunteer workers in every one of the nation's 110,000 precincts. It recommended that the League concentrate its main efforts between campaigns upon supplying information to the membership of trade unions and to the public at large on the principal issues before Congress, those which would have a significant effect upon the welfare of large numbers of citizens. The League was also directed to seek the cooperation of other groups engaged in the promotion of legislation in the general interest of the community. Between December 1, 1948 and February 1, 1950, the Committee wanted the League's activity to be financed solely by contributions from the A. F. of L. and the national and international unions. It asked that each cooperating union contribute an amount equal to 10 cents per member for the fourteen-month period.[24]

The educational work of the League was to be carried on in accordance with A. F. of L. legislative policy, and the League was not allowed to lobby in Congress or before the state legislatures. A drive for voluntary contributions would be undertaken so as to have adequate funds available in advance of primary elections. Voluntary contributions were to be held in a separate account and reserved for exclusive use in political campaigns.

Although the leaders of the political effort were not unmindful of the limitations of the Labor League's work, they were not discouraged. From many points of view, the 1948 campaign had yielded favorable results, and the Federation through the League had played an important role in influencing the outcome. At the outset the League had been regarded as a temporary organization, and not all Federation officers had been enthusiastic about the new venture. The defeat of Thomas Dewey, however, convinced a number of the more hesitant leaders that the Federation should continue on the political path. Harrison thought the League was "one of the greatest inspirations brought to the American Federation of Labor for a great many years."[25] The Administrative Committee decided to recommend to the National Committee that the League be placed on a permanent basis.[26]

One of the A. F. of L.'s major political objectives continued to be the repeal of the Taft-Hartley Act and the reenactment of the Wagner Act with the amendments suggested by the President in his message to Congress on January 5, 1949. The Truman proposals prohibited jurisdictional strikes and unjustifiable secondary boycotts, as well as strikes over interpretation of contracts and strikes in industries vital to the public. Although the A. F. of L. put forth every effort to have the bill reported out, it was evident by March 1949 that the legislation could not be enacted in the form presented.

Upon learning that Speaker Rayburn had requested Secretary of Labor Tobin to present additional amendments, Green called Executive Council members Harrison, MacGowan, and Daniel Tracy. Together with Green and Meany, they agreed to amendments guaranteeing employers free speech, applying the non-Communist affidavit to employers and workers, requiring bargaining in good faith, public listing of information on salaries of union and corporation officers, and procedures to be followed in emergency disputes—those which endangered health and safety. This last provision allowed for the appointment of a board to decide proper compensation for the use of a plant and also for the scales of wages and salaries to be in effect during government occupancy which was to be limited to fifty-five days. Although the Federation was not happy about the five additional amendments, it was willing to accept them as the price for the repeal of the Taft-Hartley Act and its replacement by the Wagner Act.

A coalition under the leadership of Senator Taft, however, retained, according to William C. Hushing, chairman of the A. F. of L. legislative committee, virtually all the most objectionable features of the Taft-Hartley law. The Taft amendment, Hushing said, "provided for the use of injunctions both to curb various union unfair labor practices and to curb so-called national emergency strikes, the prohibition of closed shop agreements, the prohibition on secondary boycotts and the provision for damage suits against labor organizations. In one very vital respect, that involving the use of injunctions in national emergency disputes, the Taft amendment is even more objectionable than the Taft-Hartley provisions, for the reason that under the Taft amendment the President can obtain an injunction at any time, while under the Taft-Hartley Act he can do so only after the Presidential Board has inquired into the dispute and has issued a report."[27]

On June 29, 1949 Green told Senator Scott Lucas, majority leader in the Senate, that a meeting of representatives of the A. F. of L., state federations of labor, city central unions, national and international unions, the national legislative council, the national legislative committee, and Labor's League for Political Education believed that the Taft substitute and the Thomas bill, as amended, designed to modify the Taft-Hartley bill, should be defeated.[28] The Taft substitute for the bill reported from the Senate Labor and Public Welfare Committee by Senator Elbert Thomas of Utah was adopted by a vote of 44 to 49. The Federation used its influence to kill the amendments, and no agreement was ever reached on the proposals. Thus the most favorable opportunity for the enactment of amendments favorable to organized labor was lost.

Even though the main purpose of Labor's League for Political Education, the repeal of the Taft-Hartley Act, had not been achieved, the Federation believed that the League had justified itself, if only by the greater political awareness it had encouraged among organized workers. In the fund-raising campaign for political education, launched in December 1948, the A. F. of L. had asked the internationals to donate 10 cents per member to the educational fund. In the drive which ended in January 1950, the League collected for this purpose $600,832. Only one union, the Building Service Employees, refused to contribute; the Carpenters' Union donated $100,000. In the 1950 campaign $506,037.79 was collected. In May 1951 the Executive Council abandoned the raising of educational funds by special voluntary assessment, and assumed responsibility for financing this activity.

Political activity, which was the responsibility of Labor's League for Political Education, continued to be dependent upon voluntary donations. In 1950 requests for voluntary contributions of $2 per member were asked from all members of A. F. of L. unions, and the League raised $592,222.40. It was estimated that only some 300,000—400,000 members, or 5 per cent, contributed to this fund.[29] Although the activity of the League was curtailed between national election campaigns, it continued to function. The *League Reporter*, which was issued once a week during campaigns, was published twice a month in other periods. Every national union officer, labor editor, state federation of labor, and city central body received this newspaper; in 1951 it had a circulation of 86,000.[30]

Eighty unions were participating in fund raising in 1952, and the League again circulated the records of congressmen on legislation and organized support or opposition to candidates in the primaries and in the presidential election. At the meeting of the Executive Council in August 1952, Harrison and Meany discussed the dissatisfaction with the treatment of the labor delegation at the Republican National Convention. They agreed that the presidential candidates should be invited to address the convention in New York, an unusual procedure.[31] On September 22, 1952 President Maurice A. Hutcheson and Secretary Albert E. Fischer of the Carpenters' Union registered their organization's views on the political policies that should be pursued by the A. F. of L. Their statement endorsed the heightened political interest manifested by the Executive Council, and declared that it was "the unalterable and unanimous opinion" of the General Executive Board of the United Brotherhood of Carpenters and Joiners of America that the traditional nonpartisan policy of the Federation should be continued. Recalling the harmful effects of bringing partisan politics into the trade union movement in the 1890's, the statement warned that a

repetition of that uphappy chapter in Federation history must not be written in 1952. Therefore, for the following reasons, the General Executive Board of the United Brotherhood of Carpenters and Joiners of America is vigorously opposed to any abandonment of the traditional non-partisan policy of the last forty years:

1. To endorse one presidential nominee or party would be to violate Section 8 of Article 3 which specifically prohibits partisanship on the part of the Federation.

2. To endorse one candidate is tantamount to endorsing the party he represents. Unfortunately anti-labor sentiment is not confined to one party. There are opponents of labor in both parties. An implied blanket endorsement of one party could well hurt Congressional candidates friendly to labor and help candidates who are unfriendly, thereby nullifying the sound policy laid down by those two immortals, Gompers and McGuire, and putting into power another unfriendly Congress.

3. History has proved that partisan politics are a grave danger to organized labor. Nothing can more quickly divide, disrupt and weaken the labor movement than partisan politics. On the other hand, a policy of rewarding labor's political friends and punishing labor's enemies, without concern for party

labels, serves only to nurture, enhance and strengthen the solidarity and economic strength of the labor movement.

4. Furthermore, as affiliation with the American Federation of Labor is on a voluntary basis, the question of endorsement of any candidate should be left to each individual organization to determine the course they wish to take and by doing so the American Federation of Labor would then preserve its traditional policies.[32]

The policies recommended by the Carpenters' Union were rejected.

The invitation to the two presidential candidates to address the convention of 1952 was another significant change in policy. The custom of the A. F. of L. had been to hold its conventions in presidential election years after the political campaign had ended. This policy was designed to prevent partisan speeches or demands by delegates which would allow the convention hall to become a forum for political debate. Only once in the history of the A. F. of L., in 1924, had it explicitly endorsed a candidate, Robert M. La Follette. In 1952 both candidates addressed the convention and outlined their policies. Following the speeches the Executive Council submitted a supplemental report which stated "that the economic welfare and future well-being of America's workers will be determined more than ever before in history, by legislation. This changing order, this break with past tradition, is none of our doing. It was forced upon us by the reactionaries. While publicly decrying the invasion of private libetry by government, the reactionaries have aggressively mobilized to undermine and destroy the freedom of labor by restrictive legislation at the Federal and State levels."[33]

The Council presented an indictment of the Taft-Hartley law which in its view symbolized "the legislative club big business holds over the heads of labor." The Council believed that the A. F. of L. had a responsibility to its membership to "state frankly and sincerely where we stand in this election. Political neutrality would be an evasion of the responsibility. Our enemies do not practice political neutrality. If we hope to cope with them successfully, we must survey the facts and the issues and take our stand."[34]

In detail the declaration examined the views of the conventions of the two parties on the issues held to be crucial by the Executive Council. When it requested a replacement of the Taft-Hartley law by one fairer to labor and protecting the interests of management and the public, the Council learned that its request was approved in the platform of the Democratic Party, whereas the Republican platform "praised and favored the retention of the Taft-Hartley Act." The Council also noted the Republicans' rejection of a workable method of price and rent control, and the Democrats' approval of these measures. Similar differences were found between the parties in their readiness to accept the Federation's views on the need for the development of a public low-rent housing program, higher social security payments and the extension of coverage, and the establishment of a health insurance program. Nor did the Council find the Republican Party's views on aid to education, civil rights' protection, and taxation acceptable. The differences between the parties on domestic issues were summarized as follows: "The Democratic Party's platform is responsive to the needs and desires of the workers and liberal-minded people of our country. The Republican Party's platform is responsive to the demands of the ultra-conservative, anti-union elements in the nation."[35]

While paying tribute to the patriotism of General Eisenhower and voicing their respect and admiration for his military achievements, the Council held that Adlai E. Stevenson, who favored the repeal of the Taft-Hartley law, espoused a positive program. Therefore, the Council advised and urged the members of the A. F. of L. to support his candidacy for the presidency of the United States. In making this recommendation, the Council emphasized that "the affiliated unions of the American Federation of Labor and each and every one of their members are free to make their own individual political decisions without any compulsion on our part. It is not our intention or desire to endorse any political party or to enter into partisan politics."[36]

One of the remarkable features of the proposal to change an historic policy was its failure to generate debate. George Meany, reporting for the Council, moved the adoption of the supplementary report and the motion was seconded by Executive Council member Charles MacGowan; the Chair called for a vote and then announced its unanimous approval.[37] Not all delegates, of course, approved the attitudes expressed in the Supplemental Report: delegates from the Carpenters' Union and the Building Service Employees' Union were not in favor of the new policy. The president of the latter organization, William L. McFetridge, was a member of the Executive Council, and although he did not publicly oppose the change of policy, he subsequently supported Eisenhower. In addition, there were individual delegates, some of them influential—for example, Richard Gray, president of the Building and Construction Trades Department—who opposed the abandonment of the nonpartisan policy and favored the election of General Eisenhower. Their failure to debate the Council's recommendations was not due to fear of voicing a contrary view; it was influenced rather by the limited support their opposition would find within the convention. It demonstrated that two decades of the New Deal and Fair Deal had greatly increased the political consciousness of the American labor movement and had eliminated divergencies in outlook which had existed over the years.

A suggestion for endorsing a specific old-party candidate would have in the period before the 1930's encountered objections from the proponents of independent political action, as well as from those who opposed the endorsed candidate. The Federation leadership would have been hesitant to deviate from the traditional course, even if it had been inclined toward such a move. Acceptance of the Executive Council's recommendations demonstrated that the leaders of American labor had in the main reached similar political conclusions, and although the traditional policy of not endorsing third parties or third-party candidates was still in force, the willingness to endorse a presidential candidate by name marked a sharp turn in policy. In one sense, this was the inevitable completion of the step the A. F. of L. had taken when it organized a permanent political adjunct, Labor's League for Political Education.

## REFERENCES

1. *Report of the Proceedings of the Sixty-fifth Convention of the American Federation of Labor*, 1946, p. 407.

2. Minutes of Executive Council, October 17, 1947.

3. Green and Meany to the Presidents of National and International Unions, November 3, 1947.

4. *Recommendations of the Executive Council of the American Federation of Labor to the Conference of International Presidents*, December 5, 1947.

5. *Ibid.*

6. *Conference of Officers of National and International Unions*, Washington, D. C., December 5, 1947, p. 8 (typed).

7. *Ibid.*, p. 13.

8. *Ibid.*, p. 14.

9. *Ibid.*, pp. 4–5.

10. *Minutes of the Meeting of the Administrative Committee, Labor's League for Political Education*, February 4–5, 1948, p. 10.

11. *Ibid.*, p. 11.

12. Memorandum to President Green from George Harrison, dictated to Irving Bucklin, February 2, 1947.

13. *Minutes of the Administrative Committee, Labor's League for Political Education*, February 4–5, 1947, p. 16.

14. *Ibid.*, May 11, 1948.

15. *American Federation of Labor Weekly News Service*, January 30, 1948.

16. *Proposals Submitted to the Resolutions Committee of the Republican National Convention, by William Green, President of the American Federation of Labor*, June 18, 1948. The same proposals were submitted to the Democratic National Convention.

17. James Roosevelt to Green, July 2, 1948.

18. Green to James Roosevelt, July 3, 1948.

19. Minutes of Executive Council, August 24, 1948; *Meeting of Administrative Committee, Labor's League for Political Education*, August 25, 1948.

20. Department of Public Relations, Labor's League for Political Education, *Report of the Administrative Committee*, July 22, 1948.

21. Labor's League for Political Education, *Report of Department of Political Direction*, August 25, 1943.

22. Labor's League for Political Education, *State Allocations*, November 15, 1948; *Statement on Receipts and Expenses as of December 13, 1948.*

23. Department of Political Direction (Labor's League for Political Education) *Report to the Administrative Committee*, November 15, 1948.

24. *Recommendations of the Administrative Committee to the National Committee of Labor's League for Political Education*, November 17, 1948.

25. *Minutes of the Administrative Committee, Labor's League for Political Education*, November 15, 1948.

26. *Ibid.*, February 1, 1949.

27. *Minutes Joint Meeting of Labor's League for Political Education and the National Legislative Council of the American Federation of Labor*, July 19–20, pp. 8–9.

28. Green to Honorable Scott Lucas, June 29, 1949, in files of A. F. of L.

29. *Minutes of the Administrative Committee of Labor's League for Political Education*, January 15, 1951; *Ibid.* September 17, 1951; *Minutes of Executive Council*, May 9, 1950.

30. *Minutes of the National Committee of Labor's League for Political Education*, September 21, 1951, p. 4.

31. *Minutes of Executive Council*, September 14, 1952.

32. Maurice A. Hutcheson and Albert E. Fischer to Green, September 22, 1952, in Minutes of Executive Council, September 22, 1952.

33. *Report of the Proceedings of the Seventy-first Convention of the American Federation of Labor*, 1952, p. 508.

34. *Ibid.*, p. 509.

35. *Ibid.*, p. 310.

36. *Ibid.*, p. 511.

37. *Ibid.*, p. 512.

# XXV

## The Legislative Committee

UNDER the constitution of the A. F. of L., the president was responsible for carrying out the political program approved by the Executive Council and the conventions. He was also "the court of last resort to decide upon policies to be followed on legislation that has not been acted upon by the American Federation of Labor or its Executive Council."[1] To protect the interests of labor before Congress and the Executive branch of the Federal government, the National Legislative Committee, headed by a chairman, was appointed and placed under the direction of the president. The Legislative Committee, one of the more important and least publicized agencies of the labor movement, has been of tremendous influence in national lawmaking. This Committee was given the job of reading and analyzing every bill and joint resolution introduced in Congress. Any bill which affected labor directly or indirectly was to be followed through committees and both branches in an effort to defeat or aid in the passage of the proposal. In carrying out this part of their duties, the members and staff of the Legislative Committee would have to interview dozens of congressmen to convince them that a bill deserved to be enacted or defeated. At one time or another the Legislative Committee would, during a session, appear before virtually every congressional committee. Primarily, the Legislative Committe was most concerned with bills pending before the House Committee on Education and Labor, the Senate Committee on Labor and Welfare, the two Appropriations Committees, the two Post Office Committees, the Armed Service Committees, the Judiciary Committees, the Ways and Means and Finance Committees, the Interstate and Foreign Commerce Committees, and the Public Works Committees.

The Legislative Committee was responsible for maintaining a "complete file of bills, committee reports, committee calendars and all related material to keep close touch with the progress or lack of progress of a given bill or resolution."[2] It also kept track of the records of members of Congress and carefully examined the *Congressional Record* for information that was of value to labor. The Legislative Committee was charged with setting forth the views of the A. F. of L. on all legislation referred to it by the conventions. Each member of the Legislative Committee was assigned special bills which he had to follow through all stages, from the drafting, consideration by the subcommittee, full committee of the House and Senate, and floor discussion until a conclusion was readied on the bills entrusted to his care.

A number of national and international unions have over the years maintained legislative agents in Washington, but the chief burden for labor's legislative program rested upon the A. F. of L. The Federation's Legislative Committee acquired the greater experience, knowledge of the legislative process, and acquaintance with congressmen and their aids. Unless there existed a decision of an A. F. of L. convention to the contrary, the Legislative Committee supported the requests of labor groups before Congress and aided them in securing a hearing for their point of view and in assembling information and exhibits to present their cases adequately.

Specifically, at the adjournment of a convention, the Legislative Committee was given a list of legislation pending in Congress endorsed or opposed by the convention. After the 1926 convention, the Legislative Committee received a list of fifty-one bills which were either endorsed or opposed by the convention. An examination of the Committee's instructions for this legislation will reveal more clearly the functions of this group.

The convention approved the reenactment of the Pitman Act authorizing the Federal government to purchase silver bullion to replace the worn-out silver dollars. The Legislative Committee, acting in accordance with this decision, was to present the view of the A. F. of L., and Charles Moyer, head of the Mine, Mill, and Smelter Workers, was asked "for the arguments of the metalliferous miners."[3] On the tariff question, the instructions were "to prevent repeal of the section . . . which provides for repairs of American ships in American ports."[4] The Executive Council, following its instructions, asked the Legislative Committee to petition Congress to enact legislation to place the Virgin Islands "under a civil government, release them from the control of the navy department and grant them the rights of American citizenship."[5]

The Committee was also told "to continue vigorous opposition to the elaborate system of espionage on aliens provided in the Aswell bill or any other bill that may be introduced in Congress." The action of the convention on trademarks, sales taxes, Sunday blue laws, convict labor, child labor, and education was passed on by President Green to the Legislative Committee. The Committee regularly reported to the Federation president the status of bills in which labor had either a direct or indirect interest, and the president gave this information to the Executive Council. On January 17, 1928 the Legislative Committee had reported that influences were being used to substitute a less desirable workmen's compen-

sation bill for the District of Columbia than the one supported by the
A. F. of L. When the Committee discovered that a congressman from
Indiana was in a strategic role to effect the outcome in committee, it sent
letters "to the officials of the State Federation of Labor of Indiana . . .
and the Secretaries of three Central Labor Unions in Mr. Hall's district
requesting them to send letters to Representative Hall urging him to
support the Fitzgerald Bill."[6]

In 1930 Bert Jewell, president of the Railway Employees Department,
suggested that the A. F. of L. call a conference of all the legislative representatives of labor organizations stationed in Washington and ask them
to meet regularly to coordinate their activities. Jewell also raised the
question whether in endorsing a senator or congressman for reelection,
it might not be desirable to judge the records not only on the support of
labor bills but on "bills which would affect more broadly the interests of
all citizens, the workers in particular, and which would give a greater
test to the attitude of each Congressman and Senator."[7] Jewell believed
that there were a "considerable number of Congressmen and Senators
who find it possible to support our strictly labor bills and gain our endorsement and support—yet support the vested interests of this country
in the securing of special privileges for them, which privileges are dis-
tinctly detrimental to the interests of the workers."[8] Jewell also thought
that roll calls on legislation other than the labor legislation might be a
more accurate guide to the record of legislators—records which could
be used to endorse or oppose them in elections. Green, while recognizing
the validity of Jewell's suggestion, did not think that the Federation
could, in fairness, offer to its members anything but the actual record
of each member of congress. He said that in preliminary discussions, the
view or the vote of a congressman might be different from his ultimate
position, and that registering any but the views upon the final vote on a
bill might lead to controversy and injustice.[9] As for organizing the legislative agents of the various unions, Green reminded Jewell of the unfortunate earlier experience when an attempt had been made to bring
together the Washington representatives of labor. "In many instances
attempts were made to formulate and develop the legislative policy of
Labor. Action was taken at these meetings upon labor measures either for
or against them without regard to the question as to whether or not the
organization which these Legislative Agents represented had considered
and acted upon said measures. Then supplementing all this there developed rivalries, personal dissension, jealousies and bickerings. It did not
seem that any good purpose could be further served through the holding
of such conferences."[10] Nevertheless, on December 20, 1932 the "Joint
Legislative Conference of the American Federation of Labor and the
Standard Railroad Labor Organizations" was formed. This group usually

considered legislation directly connected with government employment or affecting railroad employment.[11]

The Legislative Committee's job of keeping a record of congressmen's votes on labor legislation sometimes involved delicate problems, for congressmen, because of pressure from the President, from their party, or from some group at home, occasionally felt it necessary to vote against legislation favored by organized labor. For example, in 1935 the A. F. of L. sought to have an amendment enacted that required payment of the prevailing wage on all government jobs, including relief work. This amendment was introduced by Senator Patrick McCarren and was opposed by President Roosevelt. Senator Wagner informed President Green that "he had to go along with the President." Green told him it would not be held against him. Senators Wagner and LaFollette voted against the prevailing rate of wage amendment.[12] W. C. Roberts called Green's attention to a number of senators who had voted against the prevailing wage amendment and noted that "some of these Senators who voted against us will have to be supported when they are candidates."[13]

The Legislative Committee, although ready to aid an affiliated union or a central body on any matter before Congress, nevertheless always took cognizance of the wishes of the organizations directly involved. In 1946 the Sailors' Union of the Pacific presented a list of bills it regarded as favorable or unfavorable to the interests of American seamen, and a member of the Legislative Committee was assigned "to look after these bills."[14] On legislation affecting housing, the Legislative Committee took its direction from the A. F. of L. Housing Committee. The knowledge gained of legislative procedures over the years, and the close acquaintance with key legislators and committee chairmen made it possible for the Legislative Committee to remain informed on the prospects of certain bills and the strategy of those opposed to labor's position.

Quotations from the report of William Hushing, chairman of the Legislative Committee for almost a quarter of a century, indicate the important although frequently unknown and unheralded work of this committee. The A. F. of L. Housing Committee wanted certain amendments to the 1936 Housing bill, but its efforts had failed in the House. Hushing was able to gain an agreement from Speaker Bankhead "to have the amendments offered in the Senate as an amendment to the Relief Bill and the Speaker in due course conferred with Senator Wagner and advised me to the same. . . . Hushing conferred with Senator Wagner and he agreed to talk with Senator Barkley in regard to the feasibility of offering the amendment. The latter advised that Senator Barkley agreed, and that it would be necessary to have the Senate Committee on Education and Labor report favorably on the amendment. We, therefore, began working to that end . . . only the following knew of this proposal to attach the Housing Amendments to the Relief Bill: Speaker Bankhead, Senators Thomas, Barkley and Wagner."[15]

The tasks of the Legislative Committee often involved careful negotiations with individual members of Congress. Over the years it became a rule that the general views of congressmen toward labor were not allowed to determine whether or not the particular congressman would be interviewed on specific legislation, for experience had shown that even extreme antilabor legislators might be influenced to support or oppose a specific piece of legislation. Much of the importance of the Legislative Committee arose from its knowledge of the legislative process, the views of individual members of Congress, and the types of pressures to which they were likely to respond. When the A. F. of L. amendments on the Housing bill of 1940, Senate 591, were to be considered in the House of Representatives, Chairman Steagall of the House Banking and Currency Committee advised Hushing "confidentially that he was working to that end by endeavoring to swing over part of the farm vote, arguing to this faction that in order to secure some votes from the Metropolitan areas for the parity payments carried in the Agricultural Appropriation act that they should vote for the Housing" measure.[16]

The A. F. of L.'s influence increased as its support became valued by members of the Congress. In 1939 Senator Tom Connally sought the aid of the A. F. of L. in his campaign for reelection the following year. Hushing advised Green to talk to Connally so that he would be "better and more active in our behalf."[17] Hushing frequently advised Green of the desire of other congressmen and senators for endorsement of their reelection.[18]

In accordance with the decision of the 1941 convention the Legislative Committee supported legislation outlawing the requirement for the payment of a poll tax as a condition of voting in Federal elections. The A. F. of L. wanted Senator Hatch to incorporate the following amendment in his bill to enforce the rights of citizens in the nomination and election of senators and representatives:

It shall be unlawful for any person, whether or not acting under the authority of the laws of a State or subdivision thereof, to require the payment of a poll tax as prerequisite for voting or registering to vote at any election.

Senator Hatch sympathized with the amendment, but he could not see his way clear to sponsor it as a part of his bill, "because the inclusion of the amendment would arouse the united opposition of all Southern Senators to his Bill."[19] The Legislative Committee during this period also supported an antilynching bill. Hushing, in a memorandum to Green, argued that even though lynching had steadily declined, "legislation is needed. . . . From time to time statements have been issued by the

American Federation of Labor wholeheartedly supporting the legislation and the Legislative Committee has, of course, advised congressional committees and individual members of the attitude of the A. F. of L. toward the bill."[20]

The Legislative Council had to consider annually more than 100 separate topics upon which the Executive Council or the conventions had already taken a position. In 1948 Hushing reported that 136 subjects "in the form of resolutions, extracts from the Executive Council report, or from reports of Convention Committees were referred to the National Legislative Committee by the Convention, by the Executive Council, or by President Green. . . . Because Conventions or the Executive Council have laid down definite policies regarding most of these subjects, I have them under control. . . . However, the following subjects should be considered by the Executive Council and the resulting action conveyed as soon as posible to the Legislative Committee."[21]

Even if a general policy were not approved, the Legislative Committee had to be on guard to make sure that in bills setting up projects requiring employment of labor, the usual safeguards for workers would be incorporated. The railway unions were instrumental in the A. F. of L.'s failure to endorse the St. Lawrence Seaway. When it was evident that an agreement would be worked out between the Canadian and United States governments on this issue, Hushing wrote Meany that regardless "of whether your Committee or the A. F. of L. approves of the construction of the St. Lawrence Deep Waterway, amendments to the pending legislation protecting labor's interests should be prepared and presented to Congress. . . . Having considerable experience with our State Department diplomats, I realize the necessity of not permitting them to sit down to negotiate with those from other countries without ironclad instructions, regarding the interests of those we represent, if we expect to get any consideration."[22]

The Legislative Committee of the A. F. of L. could not always prevent the enactment of legislation unfavorable to organized labor, nor could it always convince Congress to accept the proposals it supported, for the legislative results were determined by the various pressures and by public sentiment at a particular time. Congress was, however, not likely to enact legislation dealing with a labor question unless the A. F. of L. Legislative Committee supported it. In other words, although the Committee could not determine the legislation that would be enacted, no positive legislation would normally be passed without its approval and support.

In 1948 the convention decided to establish the National Legislative Council, made up of the Legislative Committee of the A. F. of L. and the representatives of national and international unions desiring to participate in the Council's activities. The purpose of the Council was to aid in the work carried on by the Federation in the legislative field. The Council, to meet at least once a month during the time Congress was in session, was required to submit a report to the Executive Council. The president and secretary-treasurer of the A. F. of L. served respectively as chairman and secretary of the National Legislative Council.

### REFERENCES

1. Statement by W. C. Roberts, *Legislative Committee.* This typewritten statement was drawn up by W. C. Roberts in December 1923 and presented to the Executive Council. Roberts was chief of the Legislative Committee at the time.

2. *Legislative Achievements of the American Federation of Labor* (Washington, D. C.: American Federation of Labor, 1953), p. 3.

3. Instructions as to Legislation, 1926, in files of A. F. of L.

4. *Ibid.*

5. *Ibid.*

6. *Legislative Situation,* January 17, 1928.

7. B. M. Jewell to Green, November 12, 1930, in files of Legislative Committee of A. F. of L.

8. *Ibid.*

9. Green to B. M. Jewell, November 21, 1930.

10. *Ibid.*

11. Meeting of Legislative Conference of the A. F. of L., November 17, 1937.

12. Memorandum from W. C. Roberts to Green, September 11, 1935.

13. *Ibid.*

14. Memorandum from W. C. Hushing to Paul Scharrenberg, February 15, 1940.

15. Memorandum from W. C. Hushing, June 1, 1940.

16. Memorandum from W. C. Hushing to Harry Bates, April 1, 1940.

17. Memorandum from W. C. Hushing to Green, August 9, 1939.

18. Memorandum from W. C. Hushing to Green, June 22, 1944.

19. Memorandum of Paul Scharrenberg (Legislative Representative A. F. of L.) to Green, January 29, 1941.

20. Memorandum from W. C. Hushing to Green, September 11, 1940.

21. Memorandum from William C. Hushing to President Green, January 21, 1948.

22. Memorandum from W. C. Hushing to Secretary-Treasurer Meany, May 8, 1951.

# XXVI

## Korea

PRIOR to the outbreak of war, the A. F. of L. was aware of the danger facing the Korean government. In a letter to Secretary of State Dean Acheson a year before the attack upon North Korea, Matthew Woll, speaking for the A. F. of L., warned against the withdrawal of United States troops which was planned for July 1, 1949. In Woll's view, the Korean and Chinese problems were interrelated and inseparable, and he asked that at least 5,000 American soldiers—"a token force"—be retained in North Korea as a symbol of the determination of the United States government to safeguard Korean national independence.[1]

Acheson rejected the suggestion on the ground that the resolution of the United Nations General Assembly on December 12, 1948 provided for the withdrawal of troops by the occupying powers. Acheson also called attention to the efforts to strengthen the security forces of the Republic of Korea so that they might "serve effectively as a deterrent to external aggression and a guarantor of internal order in South Korea."[2] He was of the opinion that the withdrawal of American troops would strengthen rather than weaken the Korean Republic.

As soon as the invasion of North Korea was announced, the A. F. of L. supported the decision of the United States to resist the attack. At its meeting in August, the Executive Council denounced as "unwarrantable and unjustified [the] invasion of South Korea by Soviet Russia," and declared this action should not be regarded as an isolated incident. The Council feared that Communist aggressors might launch small-scale wars at a number of key points and advised that "our program and that of free democratic nationals of the world . . . must be sufficiently broad and inclusive to meet any and all of these contingencies."[3]

### WAGE STABILIZATION

Under the authority of the Defense Production Act of 1950, President Truman created in September 1950 the Economic Stabilization Agency with Allan Valentine as Administrator. Two major divisions were organized—the Price Stabilization Division and the Wage Stabilization Board—each of which was headed by a director. The Wage Stabilization Board was originally composed of three representatives each from labor, management, and the public. It had no authority, but it could make recommendations to the Economic Stabilization Administrator. Harry Bates of the Bricklayers' Union, Elmer Walker of the Machinists' Union, and Emil Rieve of the Textile Workers' Union, C.I.O., were the labor members. The 1950 convention recommended a program for the rolling back of prices to the levels that had existed prior to the outbreak of the Korean war. An increase in taxes was held necessary, but taxes should be levied "on a basis reflecting a genuine equality of sacrifice." An excess profits tax, the Council believed, would be an effective way to combat inflation and profiteering. In addition, the Council advocated the closing of tax loopholes and the enactment of a progressive schedule of income tax rates.

While wage controls were held inevitable, the Council believed that no attempt should be made to set wages at existing levels.[4] The convention of 1950 reiterated the traditional policy of the A. F. of L. that to "the fullest extent possible, we must rely upon the voluntary action of individuals and groups to accomplish this task.[5]

Despite its preference for voluntary action, the convention believed that the experience of the first several months of the Korean war justified a recommendation that price controls "be imposed as soon as possible." Freezing of wages was opposed because wages had remained, according to the convention, fairly stable in the immediate period following the outbreak of the Korean war. "Before any wage stabilization measures were undertaken, collective bargaining ought to be allowed," it was argued, "so as to bring wages to a pre-invasion level with prices. . . . We emphatically reject any rigid formulas which would tie changes in wages with changes in the cost of living. There must always be room for wage changes to correct interplant and interindustry inequities and for wage increases based on increased productivity."[6]

The convention also urged prompt action to control the distribution of raw materials and other goods in short supply. No need for imposing strict regulation of manpower existed at the time, it argued. The declarations of the convention were policy guides used by the Executive Council to formulate its attitude toward economic issues arising out of the Korean conflict. In the first stages, a widespread belief existed, in labor as well as in other circles, that the struggle would last only a short time and that no drastic changes in the civilian economy need be imposed to assure victory. Officers of the A. F. of L. met with Stuart Symington, chairman of the National Security Resources Board, who had been given authority by President Truman to coordinate the work of the several government agencies handling defense problems. Symington indicated that he was anxious to give labor representation in defense agencies. The American Federation of Labor joined with the Congress of Industrial Organizations, the International Association of Machinists (then outside the A. F. of L.)

and the Railway Labor Executives' Association in setting up the United Labor Policy Committee for the purpose of developing uniform policies on issues affecting labor. The Committee was formally organized on December 14, 1950. Green, Meany, Harrison, Daniel Tracy, and William C. Doherty represented the A. F. of L. Philip Murray, Walter Reuther, L. S. Buckmaster, and Jacob Potofsky were the C.I.O. members. George Leighty and A. E. Lyon were the Railway Labor Executives' Association members, and A. J. Hayes was the member from the International Association of Machinists. A subcommittee made up of George Harrison, Arthur J. Goldberg, the attorney for the C.I.O., and Elmer Walker was appointed to draft a statement of wage policy, and Murray and Green were authorized to seek a conference with President Truman.[7]

In the meantime, active intervention of the Chinese Communists drastically changed the optimistic atmosphere generally prevailing in the United States. Stronger action and harsher policies appeared imperative. On December 15, 1950 President Truman declared a national emergency, appointed Charles E. Wilson, president of the General Electric Company, as Director of the newly created Office of Defense Mobilization, and gave him authority to "direct" rather than "coordinate" the defense program. At the conference with President Truman on December 20, representatives of the United Labor Policy Committee presented labor's views on the principal issues.

The Committee declared it was "imperative that Labor be granted active participation and real leadership in every important agency in our mobilization effort." In view of increases in food prices and rents permitted by the government, the Committee believed that "compensatory wage adjustments" should be permitted. Objections were entered against allowing wage decisions made by a board representing industry, labor, and the public to be reviewed by a single administrator. "Wage stabilization must not become wage freezing," the committee declared. "Provision for the correction of substandard wages and the adjustment of inequities in existing wage rates within or between industries must be made." The "now well-recognized principle that wage earners should share in the benefits of industrial progress and increases in productivity which the nation must and will have from its industrial workers, should be specifically embodied in the wage stabilization policy. Any wage stabilization policy must recognize existing collective bargaining agreements which themselves assure stability."[8] An equitable tax, savings, and rationing program was, according to the Committee, the answer to the need for managing the excess purchasing power generated by the stepped-up spending by the government, and a program to encourage increases in the labor force by voluntary methods was recommended.

In January 1951 the Wage Stabilization Board called public hearings at which representative groups of workers and employers were asked to present their views. Representatives of the United Labor Policy Committee charged that the power of the Wage Stabilization Board "was unwisely limited. . . . Its submerged status and lack of authority" does not offer "an effective or real opportunity to the representatives of Americans who work for wages and salaries to get their views and problems before those persons having the power of decision in the field of wage stabilization."

The United Labor Policy Committee believed that in the discussions with the above officers it "had specific suggestions to offer—suggestions which [it] felt would contribute to the defense program." The representatives did not expect that every one of Labor's suggestions would be adopted and put into practice. They hoped, however, that a way would be found under which organized labor could make a genuine contribution to the defense program. They hoped that the responsible government officials would recognize that organized labor did have a contribution to make and that a successful defense program required teamwork from all the economic groups in the country. More specifically, the United Labor Policy Committee found that the Director of the Office of Defense Mobilization, Charles E. Wilson, carried over into government his private philosophy and viewpoint as a representative of "Big Business."[9]

Two principles were, in the opinion of the Committee, essential to effective wage control: "(1) No wage stabilization program will be imposed, or can succeed unless an over-all system of anti-inflation controls will be simultaneously imposed—on the basis of the principle of equality of sacrifice. (2) Wage stabilization must be a supplement to, not a substitute for, collective bargaining."

The statement argued that collective bargaining was itself a method of stabilizing wages. "Negotiated wages," the Committee declared, "unlike many prices which can change from day to day, eliminate uncontrolled fluctuations. Furthermore, collective bargaining itself develops realistic and stable procedures for determining work standards on the basis of firsthand experience of those most familiar with the facts of a particular situation."[10] The Committee insisted that no wage-stabilization program could succeed unless it was part of an over-all system of anti-inflation controls.

A detailed program for handling specific issues that might arise in the course of administering an anti-inflation program was presented: wage inequities existing on the date when the wage stabilization was inaugurated were to be recognized, and unions allowed to correct them; partial wage settlements, changing economic conditions, and changes in the status of union organization were to be noted. In addition, the Committee emphasized the necessity for allowing wage adjustments to compensate for increases in the cost of living, regardless of whether these adjustments were secured through existing contract provisions, collective-bargaining negotiations, or other means. Contractual provisions adjusting wages to the Consumers' Price Index should be allowed, in the opinion of the Committee, to serve as a basis for wage changes. The desirability of permitting such practices was especially important, it was claimed, for the unorganized workers, because, if workers who belonged to unions were denied cost-of-living adjustments, the unorganized would be deprived of the only means available to them—pressure in the labor market—to bring wages more nearly into line with prices. Because the Committee believed that there was little possibility under the Defense Production Act for controlling the cost of living, allowances for wage adjustments on the basis of changes in the cost of living was, in its view, a very important method for compensating labor for upward changes in price.[11]

The United Labor Policy Committee argued that provisions in existing contracts requiring future wage increases were arranged so as to spread out an increase in wage costs and such arrangements were integral parts of wage settlements. The Committee asked that industry-wide and inter-regional wage uniformity be promoted by the Board. Organized labor, the Board was informed, had always sought to reduce and eliminate what it regarded as unwarranted differences in wages, "which represent a carry-over from rates established under non-union or depressed economic contions."[12] A warning was issued against any attempt on the part of the Board to control the many details of wage administration within a plant; such functions were, the Committee claimed, beyond the ability of any government agency. Instead, the Board was advised to confine its activities to devising broad general checks against abuses.[13]

A crisis over wage-stabilization policy soon developed, and it centered around what has been described as the "catching-up problem." Wages and prices had been frozen on January 25, 1951 by the order of the Director of Economic Stabilization, Eric Johnston. The labor group argued that as a consequence of the wage freeze, many inequities had been frozen into the wage structure. Labor favored a policy under which workers whose wages had fallen behind would be allowed to catch up with the others. On February 15, 1951, when the Wage Stabilization Board issued Regulation No. 6 limiting wage increases to 10 per cent of wages prevailing on January 15, 1950, the labor members dissented and withdrew from the Board. The following day, the United Labor Policy Committee endorsed the withdrawal and recommended that the labor members submit their formal resignation to the President. Subsequently, a dissenting opinion was issued in which the labor members charged that Regulation No. 6 was harsh and inflexible in its application in that it had failed to make provision for handling cases involving hardships, inequities, and substandard payment. They also charged that the terms of some collective-bargaining agreements would inevitably be upset and that the cost-of-living formula devised by the Wage Stabilization Board was not an adequate basis for eliminating inequities. The labor members recommended that the Board be reconstituted with eighteen members, the wage-stabilization formula be modified, and that the reconstituted Board be given final authority to settle all labor disputes which might affect the defense effort.[14]

In conclusion, the labor members charged that in many decisions, "the considered recommendations of labor have been totally and arbitrarily disregarded. Our defense program cannot succeed without the full and wholehearted participation of every group in the country. So far it has succeeded only in disaffecting and disillusioning men and women who must do the real work and make the major sacrifices."[15]

Obviously the statement was a clear warning that the labor organizations would demand greater recognition in the defense agencies. On February 28 the United Labor Policy Committee unanimously decided that all labor representatives of the constituent organizations serving on existing defense agencies should resign immediately. The decision was taken after the Committee had explored exhaustively the situation and had failed to have the objectionable policies of the defense agencies modified. In the Committee's view, the price order issued amounted "to legalized robbery of every American consumer, together with a wage order which denies justice and fair play to every American who works for wages."[16] The Committee was convinced that there was no desire on the part of the head of the government defense establishment, Charles E. Wilson, to give labor a real voice in the formulation of policy. Consequently, labor had "arrived at the inescapable conclusion that such representation which already has been accorded to labor in defense agencies and such further representation as is now offered are merely for the purpose of window dressing. There is absolutely no desire on the part of Mobilization Director Charles E. Wilson to give labor a real voice in the formulation of defense policy."[17]

On March 21, 1951 the conference sponsored by the United Labor Policy Committee called for modifications in the Defense Production Act so that equality of sacrifice by all groups would be recognized. "Real" price control was advocated so that profit margins which inevitably resulted in higher prices would not be approved. A flexible wage-control program, housing and rent controls, and the financing of the defense program on a pay-as-you-go basis were advocated.[18]

In the end, the protests of the labor group led to significant changes. On March 1 Economic Stabilization Administrator Johnston issued Regulation No. 8 which modified the wage policy previously enunciated so as to permit cost-of-living wage increases negotiated prior to the wage freeze. Subsequently, wage changes which had been blocked by the wage freeze and were related to wage increases in other employer units or to negotiations in an industry were allowed. The newly formed National Advisory Board voted, with industry members dissenting, to recommend to President Truman the reestablishment of the Wage Stabilization Board. In line with this recommendation, President Truman, by Executive order, set up an eighteen-man tripartite board with power to assume jurisdiction in labor disputes which were not resolved by collective bargaining or by prior use of conciliation and mediation and which threatened an interruption of work affecting the national defense. Parties to a dispute would jointly submit such a dispute to a decision of the board, or disputes threatening the defense effort might be sent for adjudication of the board by the President. In the cases where the parties jointly submitted their dispute, the decision was binding; in the second type of case, the decision was only a recommendation. Subsequently, Harry C. Bates, Elmer E. Walker, and William C. Birthright were appointed A. F. of L. representatives on the board. The new board modified immediately a number of regulations dealing with wages and fringe benefits.

### DISSOLUTION OF UNITED LABOR POLICY COMMITTEE

On April 30 the United Labor Policy Committee voted for an immediate return of labor representatives to the war agencies. It was felt that the creation of the National Board on Mobilization Policy composed of sixteen members, with Wilson as chairman and Green and Meany representing the A. F. of L., had made it possible for representatives of labor as well as those of agriculture, business, and the general public to participate in the defense effort. Wilson agreed to a representative of labor serving on his top staff, and George M. Harrison of the Brotherhood of Railway Clerks was appointed as his special assistant.[19]

The appointment had only symbolic value, for the representatives of labor on the defense agencies could not, because of their union duties, devote much time to their governmental posts. The fears of Wilson that organized labor would attempt to dominate the policies of the defense agencies were baseless.

Throughout the dispute over economic and price policy, the Federation and its associated labor organizations staunchly supported the government's war effort. In a statement on May 17, 1951 the Executive Council charged that

the war in Korea is a war planned, plotted and prepared by the imperialist ruling class of Russia as an organic part of its drive to conquer all Asia and, thereby, hasten Soviet domination of the entire world. . . . In view of the global nature of the crisis precipitated by Russian aggression and the urgent need for strengthening the political, economic, and military forces of the free nations in Europe, Asia, and elsewhere, the present objective of the United Nations in the Korean conflict should be to halt and defeat this Soviet aggression, to restore the territorial integrity and protect the sovereignty of the Republic of Korea as founded and recognized by the UN, and to aid its people in achieving reconstruction and security against future aggression.[20]

The Council advocated the training and equipping of the troops on Formosa and a continuance of military aid to the Chinese National Government based there, so as to prevent its seizure by the Chinese Communists. "Under no circumstances or pretext whatsoever should our government in any way recognize or approve the admission of Communist China into the UN. Furthermore, our government should do all in its power to have other governments desist from recognizing it or seeking its admission into the UN." The Council opposed the use of American troops on the Chinese mainland, despite the sympathy expressed for the Chinese nationalists.[21]

When the United States government refused to agree to the forced repatriation of Korean prisoners held by the United Nations' forces, the A. F. of L. strongly approved this view. The A. F. of L. was "in the forefront of the forces rallying public sentiment against the policy advocated in some quarters that UN negotiations should make concessions to Communist insistence on the issue of forced repatriation of the prisoners of war. This rallying of public opinion was urgent because of the heavy pressure of 'neutralists,' appeasers, and short-sighted allied government representatives for a deal with the Communist aggressors over the question of repatriating by force the prisoners of war held by the UN in Korea."[22]

In the summer of 1951 a number of members of the Executive Council came to believe that the United Labor Policy Committee was a barrier to the achieving of organic unity between the A. F. of L. and C.I.O. Reports that many people outside the labor movement believed that the Committee was living evidence that the breach between the two federations had been healed irked some members of the Council. Other members felt that the emergency which had confronted the labor movement at the outbreak of the Korean conflict had been overcome and that the relationship to the C.I.O. should be reexamined. On the motion of Meany, the A. F. of L. Council voted to withdraw its members from the United Labor Policy Committee.[23]

In a statement explaining its action, the Federation explained that the Committee had been set up to meet the "immediate problems arising out of defense mobilization. . . . To a large extent it has accomplished its purpose. . . . From now on, basic improvement in defense policies must be sought by labor through legislation by Congress. It was never intended that the United Labor Policy Committee should serve as the joint legislative representative of its component organizations. In fact, that would be impossible."[24] Emphasizing that the United Labor Policy Committee was established on a temporary basis and that it could not be regarded as a substitute for organized unity, the statement announced that only "through a united labor movement, merged into a single organization, can the workers of America attain the power, the status and the consideration which is their due."[25]

President Philip Murray of the C.I.O. was of a different opinion. He was keenly disappointed at the decision of the A. F. of L., which has "scuttled a method of inter-union cooperation that has won the acclaim not only of union members, but of the general public." Murray did not believe that the national and international problems which had given rise to the United Labor Policy Committee had been solved. In fact, he argued that the country and the labor movement would have to deal in the years ahead with "a host of critical issues. Through the United Labor Committee," Murray declared, "the overwhelming majority of American labor had found a working method of extending their areas of agreement and of enjoying the benefits of united action. At no previous time have the A. F. of L. members of the committee indicated dissatisfaction with the committee's progress or with the overwhelming need for joint consideration of the great and complex problems arising from the national emergency."[26] Murray rejected the idea that the United Labor Policy Committee was incompatible with the organic unity of the two federations.[27]

The hesitancy of the C.I.O. to move in negotiating a merger was one cause of the withdrawal; internal politics in the Federation was another. Some irritation was also expressed at the C.I.O.'s opposition to some of the A. F. of L.'s proposals at the Conference of the International Confederation of Free Trade Unions at Milan in 1951. Some leaders of the A. F. of L. believed that continuance of the United Labor Policy Committee weakened the pressure from the membership of the C.I.O. for organic unity, which they believed would be hastened if the A. F. of L. refused to cooperate. The Federation saw no reason to cooperate with the C.I.O. in the solution of normal, everyday problems. When vital issues arose affecting the entire labor movement and requiring united action or close cooperation as one, the A. F. of L. was willing to overlook its historic abhorrence of another labor federation. Once the emergency was gone, there seemed to be no further reason to continue a relationship which some of the leaders found distasteful and the advantage of which virtually all doubted.

Under the 1952 amendments to the Defense Production Act, the Wage Stabilization Board was again reorganized. An eighteen tripartite board was authorized to make recommendations to the Economic Stabilization

Director on wage policy. The Board refused to allow the full increase negotiated for the bituminous coal miners by the United Mine Workers of America. John L. Lewis called a strike; President Truman intervened, reviewed the decision, and directed approval of the full increase. The order led to the resignation of Archibald Cox, chairman of the Board, and the industry members. Early in 1953 President Eisenhower terminated the Board's existence by an Executive order.

REFERENCES

1. Matthew Woll to Dean Acheson, June 24, 1949.
2. Acheson to Woll, July 13, 1949; in *Advisory and Review Section, Department of State, 740,001 19 Control (Korea—16/2449)*.
3. Minutes of Executive Council, August 10, 1950.
4. *Ibid.*
5. *Report of the Proceedings of the Seventieth Annual Convention of the American Federation of Labor*, 1950, p. 440.
6. *Ibid*, p. 442.
7. Minutes of the United Labor Policy Committee, December 14, 1950.
8. United Labor Policy Committee, Statement to the President of the United States, December 20, 1950.
9. Statement issued by the United Labor Policy Committee, February 16, 1951.
10. *Ibid.*, p. 5.
11. *Ibid.*, p. 10.
12. *Ibid.*, p. 15.
13. *Ibid.*, p. 16.
14. Minutes of United Labor Policy Committee, February 16, 1951.
15. Statement of United Labor Policy Committee, February 16, 1951.
16. United Labor Policy Committee, Statement of February 28, 1951.
17. *Ibid.*
18. United Labor Policy Committee, *Equal Sacrifice for the Defense of America* (Washington, D. C., 1951).
19. Statement of United Labor Policy Committee, April 30, 1951.
20. Minutes of Executive Council, May 17, 1951.
21. *Ibid.*
22. *Report of the Proceedings of the Seventy-frst Convention of the American Federation of Labor*, 1951, p. 119.
23. Minutes of Executive Council, August 10, 1951.
24. Statement of William Green to the United Labor Policy Committee presented on behalf of Secretary-Treasurer George Meany, Vice President George M. Harrison, Daniel W. Tracy, William C. Doherty, William L. McFetridge, and William C. Birthright.
25. *Ibid.*
26. Statement of C.I.O., President Murray, August 28, 1951.
27. *Ibid.*

# *XXVII*

## Foreign Policy and Activity

FOREIGN affairs and foreign policy, as they affected the country at large and specifically the labor movement, were increasingly important to the A. F. of L. Beginning in 1914 a committee on international relations was annually chosen to report on resolutions dealing with issues in this field. A step forward was taken in 1941 when, in response to the growing importance of foreign affairs, the convention approved a resolution, sponsored by the American Federation of Teachers, to set up a standing committee on international relations authorized to publish regularly material on questions dealing with the foreign policy of the United States or with the relations between the A. F. of L. and foreign labor movements.[1] In 1947 a Department of International Relations was established.

The standing committee published materials on international relations and focused more attention on subjects in this sphere than had been customary in the past. Its work was, however, limited. During 1943 Matthew Woll asked for an expanded and more active program in international affairs. Green was at first hesitant to allow the A. F. of L. to become more deeply involved in such activity.[2] Nevertheless, the Executive Council voted to create the International Labor Relations Committee and assigned Green, Secretary-Treasurer George Meany, Matthew Woll, Edward J. Brown of the Electrical Workers' Union, and Elmer E. Millman of the Maintenance of Ways Employees to serve on it. Robert Watt was made the secretary.[3]

The 1944 convention made an important decision when it endorsed the Free Trade Union Committee. This committee was to undertake a project to raise one million dollars to "assure prompt practical assistance to the workers of the liberated countries in Europe and Asia as well as to the workers of South and Central America in their efforts to organize free democratic trade unions." The fund was to be administered by a special committee appointed by the president of the A. F. of L.[4]

The formation of the Free Trade Union Committee was the most important step in the field of foreign relations that the A. F. of L. had taken in its history. It was a recognition by the Federation that passive cooperation among national labor centers which respected each other's autonomy,

342

even when they had serious differences on policy, was no longer sufficient. Gompers' international policies were wise and adequate for their time, but they were outdated in an age when an international Communist apparatus, supported by the resources of powerful governments and disciplined political parties, made it extremely difficult for free labor movements to function in many parts of the world.

Before World War I, the international trade union movement had recognized the right of each national center to shape its own rules and policies, and organizations with widely differing outlooks could live in the same International Federation of Trade Unions. The growth of Communism as a world force after World War I brought a new and alien element into the international labor movement. Communism was a world movement determined to undermine the position of the moderate reform political and labor movements and to substitute a centrally directed and controlled labor international for the free and autonomous organizations that had heretofore functioned in the Western world. In the stable period between the two world wars, the influence of the Communist apparatus on European labor was not decisive, and the older socialist and labor groups were able to retain their authority. With the destruction of the moderate labor movement in many countries, however, the Federation saw the need to support a labor movement devoted to freedom and democracy. It had to go slowly, however, to escape the suspicion of the isolationist groups within its own ranks. The Free Trade Union Committee was, therefore, decided upon as a relief organization; it was destined to make a major contribution in the struggle for a free trade union movement in Europe.

A. F. OF L. CONTRIBUTIONS TO THE FREE TRADE UNION COMMITTEE[5]

| 1947 | $ 6,200 |
|------|---------|
| 1948 | 24,965 |
| 1949 | 32,400 |
| 1950 | 19,135 |
| 1951 | 20,000 |
| 1952 | 15,000 |
| 1953 | 35,000 |
| 1954 | 35,000 |
| 1955 | 55,000 |

The Free Trade Union Committee selected Jay Lovestone as its secretary. Lovestone had been a founder of the American Communist Party, its national secretary, and then the leader of the Communist opposition. Gradually shedding his communistic views, he had become a dedicated believer in the merits of trade unionism and a prophet of the danger that

Communist totalitarianism presented to the free world. Industrious and energetic, Lovestone brought to the job an encyclopedic knowledge of the labor movements and the politics of the European and Asian countries.

Considering the meager resources that were devoted to international activity, the achievements of the A. F. of L. were very considerable in this field. The Free Trade Union Committee was supported by contributions from the A. F. of L., whose donations ranged from $6,200 in 1947 to $55,000 in 1955.

In addition, many unions made contributions on their own. The International Ladies' Garment Workers' Union furnished office space, light, local and long-distance telephone service, and all mailing arrangements without charge. This union also paid the salary of the executive secretary of the Committee.

With these contributions, the committee maintained representatives in Europe and in Asia, published monthly magazines in English, Italian, French, and German, as well as a number of pamphlets. The Committee also sent representatives to international labor congresses, distributed food parcels to several thousand people annually, prepared material on foreign relations and labor movements for the A. F. of L., and kept in touch with hundreds of exiles and foreign unionists all over the world. At a paltry expense, the Free Trade Union Committee helped to ward off the Communist threat to democratic trade unions, and it provided the intellectual capacity and the drive for a free world labor movement.

The necessity for a more active role was impressed upon the A. F. of L. by Joseph Keenan, Labor Advisor in the Office of Military Government in Germany. Keenan, a respected trade unionist, had been secretary of the Chicago Federation of Labor and a labor officer of the War Production Board. On a visit to the United States, Keenan addressed the Executive Council and sharply assailed the policies of the United States Occupation authorities in Germany. Keenan strongly advised the A. F. of L. to station in Europe a representative who would cooperate with the free trade unions emerging under the occupation and help them in dealing with the American occupation authorities. Keenan's report was sufficiently alarming to move Hutcheson and other members of the Council to ask Green to call on President Truman to advise him of the danger involved in the American policy in Germany.[6]

The rise of Hitler had led to the destruction of the German trade union movement, the largest trade union movement on the European continent. Its leaders killed, driven into exile or concentration camps, the German unions were replaced by the Nazi Labor Front. Once the destruction of the Nazi regime appeared imminent, the kind of government and labor movement that would be established in Germany had become a controversial matter. The A. F. of L. believed from the beginning that a vigorous labor movement was essential if a new Germany was to rise out of the ruins of the Nazi empire. There were many theorizers who wanted to pursue a policy of vengeance which would destroy once and for all Germany's capacity to wage war. The Federation had opposed such a policy on both political and humane grounds. It could not visualize Germany as the "economic desert" described and proposed in the Morgenthau Plan. Nor did it believe that the anti-Nazi, pre-Hitler labor movement was responsible for the misery and disasters brought upon Germany and the world by the Nazis.

Matthew Woll, the head of the A. F. of L. International Labor Relations Committee, reminded Green in 1945 of the refusal of the American Military Occupation authorities to allow German workers to form more than plant unions. German unions, Woll said, were

completely without resources and facilities with which to operate. They find it difficult to secure meeting rooms or even office space or equipment with which to carry on their activities. The funds and resources of the Nazi labor front are regarded by the AMG as properties of the National Socialist Party of Germany subject to confiscation. They fail to recognize that in 1933 when the Nazis destroyed the bona fide German labor movement, they confiscated about four and one-half million Reich marks together with buildings and other properties and resources worth considerably more. The policy was in sharp contrast to that followed in connection with Employer's Association, Chambers of Commerce, and other business groups which were allowed to function under the Nazis. The resources of the latter have remained in their hands because the AMG has not regarded them as properties of the National Socialist Party.

Thus all associations and groups other than labor which had been destroyed by the Nazis are able to function at this time with their resources intact, whereas labor, which suffered the greatest destruction and complete confiscation at the hands of the Nazis find it impossible, or almost impossible, to carry on any constructive work.[7]

Woll informed Green that the American Military Government authorities tended to regard German union officers as Communists, and he believed that this attitude should be brought to the attention of the State Department and the War Department, "with a strong expression of the desire of the American Federation of Labor to help facilitate and assure the development of free democratic trade unions of the future Germany."[8] The Federation appealed to the State Department and Keenan, who was still in Europe, was able to report in April 1946 that "the directives in force in the American zone if properly applied would give us everything we ask for in the developing of free democratic unions."[9]

Although the A. F. of L. could use its influence with the American Military Government to gain more favorable treatment for German trade unionists, it needed its own representatives on the scene if it was going to influence directly the European labor movement. At the time, the Federation had little experience in dealing with European labor movements. Although there had been friendly exchanges with the British Trades Union Congress for many years, contacts with the Continental labor movements had never been extensive. Like most American organizations, the A. F. of L. always had within its ranks large groups of members and influential leaders who wanted to remain free from the "bloody struggles" of Europe and to uphold a policy of "no entanglements in European affairs."

Yet the A. F. of L. recognized quite early in World War II that its task on the international field would never again be as parochial and limited as it had been in the past. Its great awareness of the danger of totalitarianism, its understanding of Communist manipulation and intrigue, and the deep conviction held by the leadership that only a free trade union movement could assure peaceful progress had induced the Federation to expand its international activity. In March 1946 Matthew Woll, chairman of the International Labor Relations Committee of the A. F. of L., demanded that the Federation be granted equal recognition with the World Federation of Trade Unions by the allied military governments in Germany, and that the A. F. of L. be given full freedom to work with the German trade unions in all the occupation zones. The affiliation of the British Trades Union Congress and the C.I.O. with the World Federation of Trade Unions left the A. F. of L. as the only influential free labor federation which could argue that it was not represented by the Communist W.F.T.U. Woll denied the right of the W.F.T.U. to speak "for the predominant groups of organized labor in America," and he demanded that the Allied Control Council in Berlin grant independent representation in Germany. In a statement, Woll said that

the interest of the A. F. of L. in the development of bona fide free trade unions as the bulwark of a peaceful and democratic Germany is not of recent origin or dictated by a desire to gain narrow organization advantage in the international labor movement. Even in the darkest hours of the war, even in the moments of the most bitter military struggle, the A. F. of L. was true to the solidarity of international labor and vigorously rejected every proposal for organizing slave labor battalions of German workers after Germany was defeated. Our record shows continuous support of truly democratic elements within Germany and resistance to all the totalitarian forces within Germany before the war, during the conflict, and since its conclusion.[10]

The suggestion that the Federation open a permanent office in Europe and issue monthly publications and other propaganda materials came from two sources almost simultaneously. Raphael Abramovich, the veteran Menshevik, editor of the *Sotsialistische Vestnik* (*Socialist Courier*) and lifelong enemy of dictatorship (he was Lenin's opponent in 1917), recommended the immediate establishment of a permanent office in Belgium or France, with Irving Brown as director. Abramovich saw signs that European labor was increasingly disenchanted with Communism, and that opposition to continued control by Communist functionaries was rising among Europe's workers. He wanted the A. F. of L. to come before the Economic and Social Council adequately prepared with research materials and proposals.[11]

Joseph Keenan came to the same conclusions and offered the same advice as Abramovich; he even suggested Irving Brown as one of the European representatives.[12] He also requested that food packages be sent to German trade unionists so that they would be able to carry on their work.

The Executive Council approved the appointment of Henry Rutz as its representative in Germany and authorized Irving Brown to open offices in Paris and Brussels to represent the A. F. of L. in Europe. Rutz, a veteran trade unionist, had been active in the Milwaukee Typographical Union and in the Wisconsin labor movement. An alumnus of the University of Wisconsin, he was an expert in workers' education and had been an officer in the Military Government of the United States Army. Rutz had also been a socialist, and being of German descent and a native of Milwaukee, he was thoroughly familiar with the German language. Irving Brown had long been an active trade unionist and a participant in the organizing drives of the 1930's; he was quite knowledgeable in radical and labor movements and was a firm and dedicated opponent of totalitarian Communism. At this time, the permanent international staff of the Federation was made up of only three men; but they did have the loyal aid and support of the Executive Council. Matthew Woll, David Dubinsky, George Meany, and George Harrison were the most active in foreign affairs and in the relations of the A. F. of L. to the labor movements of other countries.

Rutz had been authorized to use his office to "further cooperation between the American Federation of Labor and the trade union organizations of Europe, including Germany and Austria." He was responsible for coordinating the relief activities of the A. F. of L. and the labor organizations of Germany and Austria. Another office was contemplated for Stuttgart, Germany, and a travel itinerary was planned between Stuttgart, Frankfort, Berlin, Munich, Vienna, and other industrial centers in Germany and Austria.[13]

On the advice of General Lucius Clay, the State Department refused to authorize an A. F. of L. office in Germany. The General did not object to the A. F. of L. plan, but he did not want it formalized with the sanction of the State and War Departments. The General feared that the granting of such permission to the A. F. of L. "might lead to the W.F.T.U.

countering with permanent offices in each of the four zones."[14] Under the arrangement agreed to by General Clay, the A. F. of L. representative was allowed a military permit to travel through Germany and carry on his functions while theoretically working out of the A. F. of L.'s main European office in Geneva or Brussels. His travel permit was renewed at two-month intervals. General Clay believed that such an arrangement was necessary, at least until the foreign ministers met in Moscow in 1947.

The A. F. of L. office offered the first opposition that the Communist-dominated W.F.T.U. had encountered in Germany. The initial action taken by the A. F. of L. was to have the American Military Government officers withdraw their request for a weekly financial statement from the trade unions in Greater Hesse. There were other and more pressing problems. Among the occupation trainees of the United States element of the Allied Control Council were a group of Communist functionaries and fellow travelers led by George Wheeler, who later defected to Communist Czechoslovakia. Wheeler became chief of the Allocations Branch of the Manpower Division to which other fellow travelers also belonged. This group tried to prevent the formation of trade unions which the Communists could not dominate and encouraged shop committees which could be easily manipulated. In fact, one of Wheeler's associates drafted the procedure which would have prevented the recognition of trade unions by the American Military Government for two years, and the order was approved by the director of the Manpower Division in Germany, General Frank J. McSherry, over the protests of Rutz and Paul Porter, an AMG officer who later became Deputy Administrator for Economic Aid in Europe.

Although German socialist and trade union leaders understood the Communist problem and were hostile to its attempts to control the labor movement, they had to contend with the W.F.T.U. and its American allies who were making an intense effort to capture the German trade union movement. General McSherry had been warned by Rutz, Brown, and others that this group were not working for American interests, but instead of dismissing them, he permitted the group to rewrite the regulations governing the formation of trade unions which had been drawn up by Paul Porter, Lieutenant Charles Doerr, Rutz, and others before the General arrived in Germany. Under the rewritten rules, German trade unions were to be dissolved and shop committees organized in their place. The Communists knew that it would be easier to gain control of individual workers' councils than of trade unions, whose leaders, in many instances, had been trained during the Weimar Republic.[15]

Wheeler and his associates were continually hounding and threatening the socialist and employment office officials about presumed violations of government regulations. These administrators took a more lenient view of the conduct of Communist officials. Wheeler consistently fought against measures to help displaced persons from Poland and other satellites, whom he described as "criminals." This group did all in its power to remove German non-Communist trade union officers from their posts and even went so far as to try to court-martial American officers who were anti-Communists.[16] Until the intercession of the A. F. of L. brought about "a slow house cleaning" in the American occupation government, Irving Brown, Henry Rutz, David Saposs, a noted labor historian, and a few others were for a time the only opponents of the Communists who had infiltrated the AMG. Woll called the attention of the State Department to "the urgency of preventing Communists from infiltrating our government apparatus in Germany. The absolute necessity of our government not being fooled by any camouflage or bluff by the Communists when they pose as democrats in order to hide their real purpose."[17]

Shortly after their arrival, Henry Rutz and Irving Brown conferred with General Clay and demanded to know by "what authority the World Federation of Trade Unions had called four-zone meetings of German trade unions." Such meetings, they said, placed the trade unions under the pressure of the organizations in the Soviet zone. They wanted to know why the American Military Government had sanctioned these meetings and they asked for equal representation for the A. F. of L. with the W.F.T.U. at all meetings to which American-zone trade unionists were invited.[18] After a talk with General Clay, it was agreed that "future meetings of German trade union leaders of the four zones of occupation will be definitely German affairs." The W.F.T.U. would no longer be allowed to "sponsor nor will it provide the chairmanship. . . . The American Federation of Labor will hereafter be accorded the same privileges at these four zonal meetings as those accorded the W.F.T.U."[19]

One of the important issues confronting the emerging German labor movement was the relationship between the organizations formed in the different zones. Closer cooperation between the unions in the American and British zones would strengthen the democratic block. On the other hand, the merger of unions in the American zone with those in the Soviet zone would place the democratic organizations at a disadvantage by subjecting them to pressures from organizations controlled by the Soviet military occupation authorities. Rutz and Brown were instrumental in drawing up the regulations to govern mergers of the unions in different zones, thus preventing the use of pressure to achieve premature zonal mergers.[20]

From the beginning, the Soviet military had aided the Communist functionaries who were directing some of the unions. "The Russians tried by all means at their disposal to keep the Communist-inspired political leadership of the unions against the very obvious majority of the membership. The American Military Government was charged by the communists with being under the influence of the A. F. of L. and the democratic elections procedures insisted upon by the Military Governments of the Western zones were said to be designed to split the German labor movement in two."[21]

The A. F. of L. was carrying on a two-front activity on behalf of the German and Austrian labor movements. On one side, the few members of the Federation staff had to keep watch on the conduct of the American occupation authorities so that their decisions would not paralyze the democratic elements in German labor. On the other side, the staff had to stand up to W.F.T.U. representatives, Soviet occupation authorities, and concealed Communist functionaries who worked in the AMG. When the A. F. of L. representative charged in a speech in Hamburg that "the country which prides itself on being a Workers' Republic is at present the greatest and worst center of slavery in the world," the Deputy Political Advisor to the Chief of the Soviet Military Administration in Germany, N. Ivanov, protested to Sir William Strang, who was the political chief in the British Zone. Ivanov specifically complained against the broadcasting of the speech over the British-controlled radio. Sir William expressed regret at the broadcast, and at the same time drew Ivanov's attention to the "Soviet slander campaign against British and American Military Governments." Rutz was advised to "moderate his language."[21a]

Along with these demands on their time and energy, the Federation staff constantly prodded the State Department to acknowledge the desirability and necessity of supporting the democratic elements in German labor. In a letter to Secretary of State James F. Byrnes, President Green described the shortage of equipment which was seriously handicapping the German trade union movement. 

As you well know, [Green wrote] the end of the war did not mean an automatic full-scale revival of German trade unionism. Twelve years of Nazi domination had left its mark by decimating the number of union leaders, stifling any spirit of organization, and crushing any evidence of criticism. Moreover, the vast destruction caused by the war has meant that during the past year, the mind of the average German workers has been occupied more by thoughts of ensuring his daily existence than by any ideas of economic self-organization. Slowly, organization has taken hold. However, this organization has been severely restricted by lack of even the most rudimentary equipment necessary for union activity. Union activity of any sort depends on frequent personal and written contacts among local unions, individual organizers, and national unions. Without this interchange of information, ideas, personal contact, union activity cannot exist. I ask you to do everything in your power to make certain that sufficient equipment is made available to the German trade unions as promptly as possible.[22]

Green requested that some of the War Assets Administration properties—automobiles, printing presses, office furniture, and duplicating machines—might be made available to the German trade unions.

On behalf of the State Department, Undersecretary Dean Acheson replied that the State Department had "consistently subscribed to and actively supported the policy of encouraging the formation of democratic trade unions in Germany. . . . In this connection your suggestion as to the possibility of making available to German trade unions some of the surplus property still held by the United States in Germany is a helpful one."[23] General Clay offered more specific information on American aid being extended to German trade unionists. In his letter to Green, Clay spoke of his awareness that the "leaders of the American Federation of Labor are concerned in restoring property and rights to German trade union members."[24] He reviewed the action of the American occupation authorities and promised to help the trade unions resume their normal activities.

The Executive Council was increasingly critical of the Big Four policy of dividing occupied Germany into zones, for instead of concentrating on reorganizing Germany on a democratic basis, the occupation authorities had, it seemed to the Council, divided it into four zones "without regard for the economic needs and welfare of Europe. Instead of reorganizing Germany's industry and utilizing the skill of its workers for the purposes of peace and the economic reconstruction of the continent, destructive de-industrialization schemes have been launched in the industrial heart of Europe. Instead of aiding the restoration of free trade unions, half-hearted de-nazification schemes, forced merging of political parties, and the restriction of the right of free association in unions and political parties have become the established practices in the various zones of occupied Germany. Similar policies have been followed in Austria."[25]

The Council said that the American government and its allies had to direct their energies toward overcoming the difficulties inherent in existing international relations by (1) a loyal adherence by all countries to the principles of the Atlantic Charter; (2) the transformation of the United Nations Organization into an effective agency for preserving international peace; (3) the encouragement of former trade unionists to resume their activity and to assume the responsibility for aiding in the revival of free trade unions in their own countries; (4) the calling of a world peace conference at an early date; (5) the inclusion of the spokesmen of free trade unions in the deliberations affecting the peace and prosperity of the world; and (6) the support of an American program before the United Nations for overcoming the threat of famine in many parts of the world, and for a humane resettling of the displaced and uprooted population of the world.[26]

Anxious about the unfolding events in Germany, the Federation sent a mission to Germany in October 1946. William C. Doherty, a vice president of the A. F. of L., and Israel Feinberg, a vice president of the International Ladies' Garment Workers' Union, were members of this group. Anton Jakobs, an organizer of the Amalgamated Meat Cutters and Butcher Workmen of North America, went along as an interpreter. The commission was allowed to visit only the zones occupied by the United States and England. Aware of the need to revive German industry, at least enough to meet the nation's needs, the commission strongly condemned the philosophy of deindustrialization, which was the guide for American policy. According to the commission, deindustrialization meant "the slaughter of economic Germany. Its accomplice is the four-power zonal arrangement, which has torn Germany into four helpless pieces of civilization, each economically lifeless without the other, all spiritually and physically resigned to an outlook of uselessness. Each zonal border is more than a military line; it is an economic barrier, blocking the normal movement of essential goods and material through the nation. Consequently, each zone suffers from the loss of trade with neighboring zones."[27]

The Commission's report emphasized the desperate need to improve the living conditions of the German people, especially the food allowances, because the caloric intake allocated to each individual had been found insufficient even for seminormal activities. The commission thought that American occupation officials could lend more vigorous encouragement to the free trade union movement. Finally, the group advised the Federation to station qualified representatives in a number of areas of Germany.

The A. F. of L. convention of 1946 approved the action of their officers and accepted the fact that the A. F. of L., "as the strongest free trade union federation in the world . . . must now assume new and greater responsibilities for preserving and extending the ideas of genuine trade unionism."[28]

The convention reporter noted that there no longer existed an international rallying center for the free trade unions of the world; the International Federation of Trade Unions had been replaced by the W.F.T.U., which in "its brief period of existence . . . had clearly and unmistakenly proven itself as an agency to foster Russia's expansionist policy. It had vigorously and regularly defended Russia's imperialist interests. It had delayed and prevented the revival of bona fide trade unions in Germany and elsewhere."[29]

The views of the A. F. of L. were in sharp contrast with those voiced by a commission of the World Federation of Trade Unions, of which Sidney Hillman, the head of the Amalgamated Clothing Workers was a member. The report warned that the

German labor movement lacked the ability to prevent Hitler's seizure of power. Indeed even after the reverses suffered by the German war machine in 1943, the remnants of that labor movement lacked the vitality displayed by the working people of the occupied lands to strike a blow for their own freedom.

In view of these facts and of the terrible experience through which we have passed, we believe that it would be folly to rely wholly on the ability of the German workers to transform their land and their institutions as a guarantee that the world may be free of the menace which twice in our lifetime has plunged us into war.

Germany must, therefore, be deprived of the economic means to disturb world peace. This is the principle laid down at Potsdam. There the three powers declared:

In organizing the German economy, primary emphasis shall be given to the development of agriculture and peaceful domestic industries.

The prompt and complete implementation of the Potsdam decision including the removals which it contemplates is most essential . . . .

Finally, we wish to record our conviction that the interests of world peace and security require the prolonged military occupation of Germany. It is impossible to predict the number of years that must elapse before the allied armies can be safely withdrawn.

In our opinion, the period of occupation should and must be a long one. It is of the utmost importance that the Allied Armies remain until such time as the peaceful character of German economy, the re-educational policy of the German people, and the reshaping of the German political and social institutions give the positive guarantee that Germany shall never again have the will or the power to threaten their neighbors or to disturb the peace of the world.[30]

The general problems facing the international labor movement and the difficulties it ran into with the W.F.T.U. were behind the protest which Woll cabled to Ernest Bevin on January 7, 1947:

Shocked to learn of decision just made in Paris by World Federation of Trade Unions and its experts to introduce forced labor in Ruhr mines. In line with its traditional unconditional opposition to every form of involuntary servitude, American Federation of Labor vigorously condemns this decision as promoting rank slavery and worst evils of imperialism. We categorically deny that imposing forced labor on German miners will solve European coal crises. Instead of forced labor, American Federation of Labor proposes more food, rights and responsibilities for Ruhr miners, and immediate increased coal shipments from Soviet zone for needy population. Free labor proved its superiority over slave labor in war and if given decent conditions and standards will again prove its decisive superiority in peace over every type of forced work. World Federation of Trade Unions supervising enslavement of Ruhr miners does not change its despicable slave status. Such supervision only adds insult to injury and inflicts irreparable damage on democracy in Germany and on trade union movement which should be a bulwark of freedom and democracy in all countries. It is utterly repugnant to dignity of human life and democratic ideals that an organization claiming to be the world trade union center should after the defeat and destruction of Nazis seek to reintroduce their abominable forced labor policies. We cannot believe that present British government and trade union congress with their devotion to individual liberty and human freedom will countenance this outrageous forced labor scheme. American Federation of Labor strongly urges your support in its fight in United Nations Social and Economic Council against this dangerous measure which menaces labor's freedom and standards everywhere.[31]

The Executive Council at its meeting in January 1947 again discussed the needs of Germany and the policies that would lead to its political and economic reconstruction on a democratic basis. In a public statement the Council called the "Quadripartite control of Germany . . . a colossal failure." Advocating the unification of Germany, the Council asked the United States to grant a large measure of "material relief . . . to alleviate the misery bred by starvation and confusion."[32] An increase in food allowances was not only imperative on humanitarian grounds, the Council stated; it was essential for the carrying on of important political activities.

In March 1947 a serious situation was facing the German trade union leadership. Most of the duties, Rutz said, fell on a few experienced leaders who had to work more than twelve hours a day, sometimes on only 800 calories a day. It was imperative that there be no interruption in the distribution of food packages to German trade unionists and that more be sent if possible.

Notwithstanding the cooperation of some American occupation authorities, the A. F. of L. was running into many obstacles. At its meeting on April 9, 1947 the International Labor Relations Committee of the A. F. of L. considered the failure of the American representatives on the staff of the AMG to cooperate with A. F. of L. representatives. The committee delegated Woll to follow up this problem and help in any way possible.[33]

In the meantime, the occupation authorities in the French zone and the *Confederation Générale du Travail* were putting pressure on the German union leaders to take their unions into the Communist trade union auxiliary, the W.F.T.U. At this same time, Martin Plettl, who had been president of the German Clothing Workers' Union during the Weimar Republic, publicized the vigorous efforts of Soviet-controlled unions to enroll all German unions in the W.F.T.U.[34] The French military government went so far as to bar Rutz from the French zone. On behalf of the A. F. of L., Matthew Woll denounced the ruling of the French military authorities. In a cablegram to the Socialist Premier, Paul Ramadier, Woll questioned the explanation that Rutz had been denied entry because the A. F. of L.'s paper, *International Free Trade Union News,* had criticized leaders of the *Confederation Générale du Travail.*

The A. F. of L. has criticized and will continue to criticize any American, French or other organization with which it disagrees. We have not denied CGT right to criticize us and its Communist official Franchon has even threatened life of AFL European representative Irving Brown if he establishes office in Paris. Despite these slanders and threats against American labor by Franchon, Saillant and company, AFL has never tried to prevent them from touring American zone. We further protest against refusal of French military government to accept mail including AFL publication *Free Trade Union News* for residents of French zone. Such arbitrary prohibitions are typical of totalitarian dictatorships.[35]

There were equally difficult situations in the American zone. The German unions were anxious to publish materials presenting the democratic view and answering the charges emanating from the Soviet zone. Rutz went to see General Clay in March 1947 to protest the refusal of the American occupation authorities "to grant more print for the three semi-monthly publications in the three Lander of the United States zone. . . . Of equal importance to the official publications is the preparation of mimeographed material. In a country where print shops have been bombed and where every piece of printed matter must have prior Military Government approval, a mimeograph machine becomes indispensable. It is the best medium to supply a quick answer. . . ."[36]

He asked the International Labor Relations Committee to supply several mimeograph machines and 500 stencils to German trade unions in the American zone to ease the serious shortage until the American occupation authorities made more generous allocations.

The paper needs of the German unions were no better satisfied, and in June 1947 the A. F. of L. representative again protested to General Clay the unsatisfactory arrangements. Although General Clay was unable to increase the paper allotment of the trade unions, he agreed to exempt them from the 50 per cent reduction imposed upon all other publications. The failure to return a rest center seized by the Nazis from the national office workers' union to the labor organizations was also considered. After his meeting with General Clay, Rutz thought that the "sanitorium would be returned in time to work out a rest program for the overworked and underfed union leaders of the United States zone."[37]

It was also reported from this meeting that General Clay had reprimanded the Manpower Division Director for arranging the attendance of American Zone trade unions at a W.F.T.U. meeting in Prague. The A. F.

of L. declared that it would now insist that trade union leaders of Germany also be given permission to attend the conference of labor federations of the free countries scheduled for the summer of 1947.[38]

In a meeting with Secretary of State George Marshall in May 1947 the International Labor Relations Committee protested the policy of "forced repatriation" of refugees from the Soviet Union and its satellites. Marshall endorsed the traditional American policy of no coercion of people fleeing from political persecution and promised to discuss the matter with President Truman. The committee also "felt assured that something would be done about the . . . coercion that has been exercised by officials in some of our government agencies."[39]

During this period, the recovery of German industry was seriously threatened by the dismantling program which the allied powers had agreed upon. On July 11 a delegation representing the Federation of Bavarian Trade Unions pleaded for the cooperation of the A. F. of L. in an appeal to the AMG for a reexamination of the industrial dismantling program. The Bavarian unionists said that the dismantling of German industrial facilities had already led to bottlenecks in the machine-tool, agricultural-machinery, electrical manufacturing, and mining-machine industries, and the planned dismantling of German ball-bearing plants would even more seriously hamper the recovery of German industry. When Woll learned of the contemplated dismantling, he asked General Clay to do everything in his power to delay the dismantling of German industries.[40] Woll explained that the program was destroying a vital portion of the peaceful German economy and constituted a serious threat to the future welfare of German labor.

In a letter to President Truman, Green asked for reconsideration of the United States economic policy for Germany. Green was convinced that economic "chaos in Germany has blocked economic recovery for the other countries in Europe, for Germany was its industrial center."

The whole world wants to prevent German production facilities from producing war materials, but it also believes that scrupulous care should be used not to interfere with production facilities needed for civilian materials. The Directive by the Joint Chiefs of Staff, of April 1945, followed by the Potsdam Agreement for Germany, denied jobs to a nation of unemployed persons. . . . The Allied Council's decision on the postwar level for Germany's economy, in the spring of 1946, forms the basis for determining the production facilities to be dismantled and shipped as reparations. . . . The new level of industry announced by the United States and Britain last August was intended to lessen the restrictions which kept industrial workers unemployed, hungry, without proper shelter, fuel and clothing. But it has been grudgingly administered. Even last October, a new list of over six hundred (600) plants to be dismantled was made public with the admission that part of them were for nonmilitary production. Such looting of Germany has occasioned charges that other countries wanted to eliminate firms competing with other nations. . . . A limit to this dismantling policy would mean hope to a people that now faces starvation and suffering. It would eliminate the waste in dismantling and moving facilities. . . . Our trade unionists who have worked in Germany and Europe during the past year have urged more construction reparation policies and an end to the dismantling of production facilities not classed as war potential. These men, Joseph Keenan, formerly vice-chairman of the War Production Board, Major Henry Rutz, formerly in our Army of Occupation, and Irving Brown, formerly employed by the War Production Board during the war, have publicly urged steps for speedy resumption of industries so that Europe, including Germany, might become self-supporting.[41]

The A. F. of L. was the first important public group to protest the policy of dismantling German industry that had been agreed to at the Potsdam conference. The contribution of the A. F. of L. to a sounder and saner policy was recognized by Hans Boeckler, the first president of the German Federation of Labor.[42]

The appeal of the Bavarian unions was forwarded to General Clay who was asked to reconsider the question of dismantling German industry. "Bavarian union leaders," the General was told, "realized that Germany must pay reparations. In their judgment, however, Germany will be in a much better position to pay reparations if its mining machinery, its transportation and its agricultural machinery be kept in repair and in running order. The uncertainties of the immediate post-hostilities period during which the size and kind of reparations were decided were such that no one could have predicted accurately what effects the removal of bearing plants would have on a level of industry yet to be determined."[43]

General Clay sympathized with this view, but felt he was incapable of fully complying with the request because of the agreement to which the United States was a signatory. At a meeting of the bizonal control council, General Clay tried unsuccessfully to reopen the subject of dismantling German industry. In a letter, Clay said that he thought that "the United States was making a fetish of its agreement made at Potsdam during a period when no one could have predicted accurately the effects which the removal of certain industries would have on the future level of industry for all of Germany yet to be determined. Other nations have not lived up to their parts of the agreements. Why should the United States always be left holding the bag? I strongly urge the United States government to be asked to re-examine the whole reparations question."[44]

In November 1947 the A. F. of L.'s European representatives, Rutz and Irving Brown, submitted a tentative program to be followed in Austria and Germany during the following year. The W.F.T.U. had been allowed to establish an office in the Soviet sector of Berlin, and Rutz and Brown thought that the Federation might approach the State Department, or President Truman if necessary, for permission to open an office in the American sector. The two representatives requested a supply of thin paper which could be smuggled easily into the Soviet zone and be readily disposed of when necessary. The A. F. of L. would be able to use the underground channels established by the Socialist Party in return for the use of American paper, and Rutz recommended that at least 10,000 sheets of 9 x 12 paper be sent monthly to the A. F.of L. office so that the message of democratic unionism could be brought to the German workers in the Soviet zone.

A stepped-up CARE-package program was also requested. Shortly after the end of hostilities, the A. F. of L. had begun to send CARE packages to trade union officers in the American zone; but the gifts were never enough to take care of all the trade union officers. The International Ladies' Garment Workers' Union alone spent $60,000 in the first part of this program.[45] Trade union officers, as a rule, had no outside sources for getting more than the official ration and were consequently often hungry. It was also pointed out that Austrian trade union officers were handicapped by lack of gasoline, because all refineries in that country were in the Soviet zone. Communist trade union functionaries were plentifully supplied, and the democratic free trade union officers were not able to move about the country. Rutz asked to be allowed to spend $250 to purchase gasoline in Switzerland so that the Austrian trade union officers could carry on a campagin in the works council elections taking place in Austria in the fall of 1947.[46]

The work of the A. F. of L. in Europe was always restricted by the moderate funds appropriated for this purpose. When the Stuttgart office needed a full-time American secretary who could write press releases and could read the hundreds of trade union publications which came to the office, the International Relations Committee had to postpone approval of the hiring until additional funds were at hand.[47] The convention of 1947 endorsed the proposals of the International Ladies' Garment Workers' Union for more active participation of the A. F. of L. in promoting the reconstruction of the European labor movement on a democratic basis.[48]

In November 1947 Irving J. Brown described the importance the A. F. of L. had achieved as a world force in conflict with Communist apparatus in every part of the world. "Those who are fighting for free trade unionism," Brown said, "for democracy and against communist inroads in the trade union movement naturally gravitate towards the A. F. of L. for encouragement, support and assistance. Those who are in the other camp —the communist movement and their many allies—single out the A. F.

of L. as the main target, with daily and weekly attacks of a most scurrilous nature. Thus, in the fight between free trade unionism and totalitarianism, both friends and enemies have elevated us to the top rung in this international struggle both as a target for attack and support."[49]

Brown's memorandum to Meany outlined the development of the trade unions' international work in Europe during the period immediately following the end of World War II. The Federation had maintained relationships with trade unions where the Communists were in a minority and where the trade unions were controlled by Socialists and Christian Democrats—a type of activity common in Great Britain, Scandinavia, and the Benelux countries. Although most of the trade union centers of these countries were affiliated with the W.F.T.U., their ideological positions were largely in agreement with the A. F. of L., at least on trade union matters. Brown recommended intensified effort in the international trade secretariats with which many A. F. of L. unions were affiliated. He also urged the convening of a trade union conference of the sixteen involved countries to consider the Marshall Plan. If such a conference was to be successful, Brown was convinced that the cooperation of the British Trades Union Congress was imperative; he suggested that Foreign Secretary Ernest Bevin be approached so that his influence could be used to gain the cooperation of the British Trades Union Congress.[50]

Brown carefully emphasized the vital importance of French and Italian trade unions in the fight against Communist totalitarianism. In France and Italy, "where the communists have control of the trade unon apparatus, we are engaged in our most immediate and critical activity to advance free trade unionism. . . . Due to this communist hold of the trade unions, these countries are in danger of going communist. Such an eventuality means not only a defeat for free labor, but would push America off the continent. Therefore, the A. F. of L.'s past aid to the free trade union forces must not only be continued but stepped up."[51] The A. F. of L. had already helped to establish a Committee for Free Trade Unionism in the French railway union, an oppositional force in the miners' union, and an independent union of Postal and Telegraph Workers. Brown wanted more help for the French oppositional groups which were fighting Communist control. For the trade unionists who wanted to build organizations free of Communist rule, Brown reported that the support of the A. F. of L. was often the difference between life and death.

The Communists were at the time, Brown wrote, more strongly entrenched in the Italian trade union movement than they were in the French. A free trade union movement had not existed in Italy for a quarter of a century, and the nonpolitical tradition within the movement was much weaker than in France. Brown listed the multiple groups that were beginning to challenge Communist hegemony over the trade union movement of Italy, and he advised additional financial aid for these Italian groups.[52]

Brown reported that in Greece the A. F. of L. had helped to frustrate the W.F.T.U. in its attempt to dominate the trade union movement. No one, in Brown's view, could predict with much confidence how

long the non-communist Greek trade union forces will stick together. A lot will depend on how the A. F. of L. follows through in terms of personal contact of its representatives; constant advice and guidance to the inexperienced trade union leaders; and direct relationships with the State Department and the Greeks, to assist in developing policy . . . which will aid rather than hinder the new trade unions of Greece. A. F. of L. work in Greece has had its repercussions in Turkey and the Middle East, where the communists and the W.F.T.U. have begun to proselyte amongst the new and inexperienced trade unionists. . . . We should at least have our representative establish contact and relationships with trade unionists of Turkey, Iran and Egypt. This area is fast becoming an international arena for the East-West struggle now under way.[53]

In addition, Brown requested that the Brussels office be allowed to issue regularly mimeographed bulletins in French, German, and English for circulation among the key trade union personnel of the Continent. The A. F. of L. should, he said, promote exchanges of trade union delegations by international unions with their counterparts in European countries and should encourage a better understanding of American labor by translating relevant books into European languages. Finally, Brown requested the appointment of qualified labor or labor-endorsed personnel to aid the State Department in developing policies affecting foreign workers and foreign labor movements.

When the Information Control Division of the American Military Government asked for suggestions on improving propaganda for counteracting Communist newspaper and radio programs, the advice was to "leave the job to the Germans." If the occupying forces would provide the Germans with paper, mimeograph machines, gasoline, and radio facilities, he said, the Germans, who were well versed in the methods and slogans effective in central Europe would be able to counter the propaganda from the Soviet authorities and its German allies.[54]

Although "the positive policy" of the A. F. of L. was increasingly praised by European leaders like Kurt Schumacher, its small staff still had to struggle with the mighty Communist apparatus. The unwillingness of the American military authorities to aid the German trade union leadership was a constantly vexing problem. On January 20, 1948 Woll wrote to both Secretary of Defense James W. Forrestal and Secretary of State Marshall protesting the conduct of the American occupation authorities. Woll called their attention to the failure of American representatives to provide a minimum supply of paper to the bona fide free trade unions and other democratic forces in Germany dedicated to the struggle against Communist totalitarianism. The pleas of the A. F. of L. had been disregarded and the situation, according to Woll, had become extremely dangerous in the midst of the wave of Soviet propaganda flooding the Western zones. "We feel," Woll told Marshall and Forrestal, "that if the Russian dictatorship can find sufficient supplies of paper for its totalitarian propaganda in Germany, our democratic government should be able to find the necessary paper for pleading the cause of democracy. That is all the more urgent because the most effective way of counteracting Russian propaganda in Germany is not through our own military authorities, but by the genuine democratic German organizations themselves."[55]

Woll warned that the American Military Government, in reorganizing the German economy, was not giving

sufficient recognition to the constructive and responsible role that bona fide free trade unions can and must play in the restoration of a healthy economic life in Germany. This false policy on the part of the AMG plays right into the hands of Russia and its tireless and well-financed agents who boast of the important role assigned to the trade unions in the economic processes of the Soviet zone of Germany. We, of course, realize that the Russian unions are a fraud. But the AMG's mistake of omission is seized upon by the Soviet demogogues and lackeys to arouse German labor against America. It is essential that this error be corrected promptly. . . . The Communists failed in their maneuver to grab Germany through the Socialist Unity Party and through their recently so-called German People's Congress. They are now playing their trump card in attempting to capture the unions. We cannot warn too strongly against this menace.[56]

Forrestal requested immediate information from the Office of Military Government "to answer Mr. Woll's allegations."[57] The defense offered was that the trade unions were receiving their share of print paper which was in short supply, that two new trade union publications had been started recently in Berlin, and that new means were being sought to increase German paper production. The military authorities also said that the German unions could procure pamphlets and books from licensed publishers who were provided with print paper.[58] When the German unions continued to be hampered by inadequate material allowances, especially print paper, Rutz suggested approaching members of Congress on this issue so as to jar some additional printing materials out of the AMG. The pressure of the A. F. of L. eventually brought an increase in the allocation of printing paper to the trade unions.[59]

By 1948 the need for a currency reform in Germany became apparent and the German trade unions and the A. F. of L. were anxious about the effect of such a reform on the trade unions. Recalling that one of the first

acts of the Nazis had been to confiscate the treasuries of the trade unions
and that the reviving unions of Germany had been able with great effort
to build up modest reserves, Woll, speaking on behalf of the A. F. of L.,
pleaded that nothing should be done "directly or indirectly, through currency reform" which would wipe out the small treasuries of the trade
unions. Convinced that there were moral and political reasons for his
stand, he proposed to the State and Army Departments that "in any contemplated reform, the funds of the trade unions should be spared and
honored at their full value this time. In other words, any new marks that
will be issued should be exchanged for an equal number of old marks in
the possession of the trade unions on a specified date."[60] Woll tried to
impress upon the American government the opportunity it had for demonstrating to the German and the international labor movements a
thoughtful and humane consideration for trade union membership. He
emphasized that the bulk of the funds in the treasuries of the German
trade unions were monies allocated for pensions. The views of the A. F.
of L. were supported by the Department of Labor's Advisory Committee
on International Affairs, made up of Irving Brown, Arnold Steinbach, Rutz,
and Michael Ross of the C.I.O. In a report to the Secretary of Labor on
March 3, 1948, the committee recommended the return of property seized
by the Nazis to the German trade unions, increased allowances of news-
print and other facilities, and a series of other actions to strengthen the
trade unions of Germany. The committee was especially anxious that
German labor organizations be provided with the means to counteract
the propaganda barrage of the Soviet authorities and their followers.
Although Ross represented the C.I.O., he was from the beginning, sympathetic to the international viewpoint of the A. F. of L., and did much
to counteract the influence of Hillman in this area.[61] In the main, General
Clay approved of the suggestions made by Ross and the other com-
mitteemen.[62]

On April 13 Woll and Lovestone conferred with General G. L. Eberele,
assistant to the Chief of Civil Affairs in the War Department, and a
number of aides from the State Department on the revaluation of the
mark and the restitution of property to the trade unions seized by the
Nazis. In discussing the efforts to protect trade union funds from the
effect of revaluation of the mark, Lovestone asked that the matter be
kept confidential.[63] He was assured that General Clay had "reiterated
that every consideration will be given to possible means of protecting
the financial position of trade unions in the event of financial reform."[64]

In the meantime, the Allied General Control Council issued Directive
No. 50 under which the assets of the Nazi Labor Front were to be dis-
tributed among the Lander, or provincial governments. The International
Labor Relations Department and the Free Trade Union Committee of

the A. F. of L. immediately requested the return of these assets to the reviving German trade unions.

Woll informed Secretary of Defense Forrestal that

the American Federation of Labor is in full accord with the Trade Union Council of the United Zones and wholeheartedly supports their claims to these funds as made in their appeal . . . to the Allied Control Council. They are the only organizations which have a legal right to these funds. Millions of German workers from whom these funds were forcibly taken by the Nazi DAF are now members of the German trade unions. . . . The grave lack of office space and supplies, furniture, typewriters, mimeographs, and stencils has already rendered much too much harm to the program of these unions and, therefore, of democracy in Germany. . . . We strongly urge that Directive No. 50 be changed so as to classify all dues collected by the DAF as property of the German trade unions and the said assets as well as other properties . . . taken by the DAF from the free trade unions of Germany be returned in full to these organizations of labor.[65]

Undersecretary of the Army William H. Draper, Jr. replied to Woll that "there was very little disparity" between the views of the A. F. of L. and those of AMG. Draper said that Directive 50 would not interfere with the return of property to the trade unions, for it gave to the zone commander "a great deal of discretion in assigning property of former Nazi organizations to whatever use is deemed appropriate." Answering for Woll, Lovestone argued that the A. F. of L. believed it was

imperative to have a firm rule instead of a loose approach—based on improvisation and not on definite principle. We take the position that the bona fide trade unions are entitled to all the property and the assets stolen from them by the Nazis. We take the position that only through the application of this principle can the unions be assured of adequate office facilities and supplies with which to operate in rebuilding their organizations as powerful forces for democracy in Germany. . . . Mr. Woll and I have met with the Civil Affairs Division. We felt that our session was rather fruitful. But we are still looking forward to concrete results. The problem we raised there was the safeguarding of the German trade union treasuries against being wiped out by the forthcoming revaluation of the mark.[66]

In October 1948 the A. F. of L. representative asked for a reexamination of the planned dismantling of the Feinblechwalzwerk Bruckhausen in Duisburg, Hamburg, in the English zone. Even more disturbing was the attitude which General Clay had been revealing toward labor. A protest direct to President Truman was suggested. The A. F. of L. was especially incensed at General Clay's disapproval of a proposal to declare the Trade Union Federations the legal successors of their predecessors in the Weimar Republic, thereby allowing them to inherit the property of Hitler's labor front.[67] The 1948 convention, taking note of the complaints of the German trade unions that American occupation authorities were favoring industrialists who had been friends and supporters of the Hitler regime, demanded a change in this policy.[68] The convention charged that the American military authorities had not appreciated labor's role in building a democratic Germany; and the convention deplored "the belated and utterly inadequate restitution of property stolen from the trade unions by the Nazis . . . the disregard of the elementary interests of trade unions in revaluating the mark, and the policy of continued wage freezing while all price controls were lifted."[69]

General Clay did not regard the criticisms of the A. F. of L. convention as just; he insisted that the American military authorities had recognized the importance of trade unions and encouraged their growth. Conceding that there had been difficulty in returning some of the property the trade unions claimed, he attributed this to the complexities involved in separating trade union property from the property of other groups, and argued that such issues could only be decided by competent legal tribunals. Woll answered the General's letter in detail.[70]

Acknowledging the outstanding service rendered by General Clay in organizing the Berlin airlift, Woll extended the gratitude of labor for this magnificent achievement. An A. F. of L. delegation—Dubinsky, Harrison, and Lovestone—flew to Berlin in July 1948 to express American labor's solidarity with the resistance to the Soviets. He went on to discuss the importance of Germany for the future of the democratic world and the absolute need for the existence of an unfettered German labor movement if that country was to remain a bastion of freedom. Historically, Woll wrote, the free labor movement has been "one of the strongest and only consistent democratic force in Germany. . . . Any weakening of this movement, will in the long run, play into the hands of the Communists."[71] Woll criticised the occupation authorities' view that there could be no full restriction of property to the trade unions because the revived German trade unions were legal entities which did not exist in 1933. On the contrary, he argued, "the present German trade union movement is the only legitimate and only legal successor of all the bona fide trade union federations which existed in 1933 prior to their being outlawed by the Nazi dictatorship."[72] He insisted that the reconstituted bona fide trade unions would equitably distribute the restored property to their constituent unions.

The A. F. of L. also protested the appointment of ex-Nazis to important economic and political posts and the voiding by the American authorities of the decision to allow the trade unions a voice in the economy. While stressing the A. F. of L.'s adherence to a system of private property, Woll decried the efforts of anyone acting for the United States government "to impose any type of economy or economic policies on any country. . . . While it is the paramount duty of the AMG to promote and to help the establishment of a democratic Germany, it should refrain from trying in any shape, manner, or form to impose upon the German people any specific American political institutions or economic methods. We think that the aim of American policy should be the consolidation of democracy throughout the world."[73]

The A. F. of L. International Labor Relations Committee was critical of the AMG's policies toward German trade unions, but it applauded the courage and initiative that had broken the Berlin blockade. The Committee warned against any concession to Russian attempts to prevent the formation of a West German democratic government, or against any "move . . . to delay, devitalize or destroy the Atlantic Pact as an instrument for deterring, and if need be defeating, the Russian imperialist aggressors."[74]

A committee of Green, Meany, Woll, Doherty, and Lovestone visited the State Department on March 9, 1949 and asked for the integration of the Western Zones of Germany "into an independent German State and that great care be taken to avoid the assigning of 'friends and supporters of German militarism and nazism to posts of managerial responsibility in the Ruhr iron and steel operations.'" They proposed further that "bona fide German free trade unionists be accorded adequate representation in its [Ruhr iron and steel industry] management."[75]

Securing reasonable treatment for German trade unions and preventing the economic dismemberment of that country continued to be major tasks of the A. F. of L. throughout these years. On May 24, 1949 Green wired Dean Acheson that continued dismantling of German industry was "indefensible" and that "the key to democratic Europe was a busy, courageous Germany."[76] Acheson answered that Germany had an important place in European recovery, but he questioned the desirability of revising the reparations program which had been recently reexamined by American industrialists. Green insisted that the dismantling decision was so serious that it should be deferred.[77]

When authority over Germany was transferred from the military to civilian authorities, the A. F. of L. immediately wrote the High Commissioner for Germany, John J. McCloy, urging recognition of the importance of labor and trade unionism, and the appointment of a top labor advisor to his staff.[78]

Reviewing for McCloy its interest in a strong, democratic Germany, the A. F. of L. proposed "that there be constituted for the coal industry in the Ruhr a Board of Trustees like the one which has been constituted for the German Steel Industry. We further propose that the bona fide free trade unions be given representation in this Board of Trustees for the coal industry just as they have been accorded representation in the Board of Trustees named for the steel industry."[79]

In a letter to McCloy, Woll defended these proposals with the argument that the German trade unions were the most reliable element in German society for the promotion of democracy. If they were given a voice in the coal industry, there would be another incentive for efficient production which would contribute to an effective German economy and the economic health of Europe. In Woll's opinion there was

no other force in Germany . . . as well equipped ideologically and industrially as the free trade unions to facilitate and assure the wholehearted participation of the German productive forces in the reconstruction of democratic Europe on a continental scale. . . . We have given this particular proposal most careful and thorough-going consideration. In offering it to you and sincerely soliciting your support thereof, we are animated only by the highest ideals and interests of our national welfare and by the urgent need of fostering peace, reconstruction, and human liberty through encouraging and enlisting the fullest support of these aims by the bona fide trade unions and all other genuine democratic forces in Germany and on a world scale.[80]

Throughout this period the A. F. of L. presented the views of the German trade unions to the American authorities and defended them whenever possible. When the German trade unions opposed the Federal "Provisional" Civil Service Law in 1950, the Federation supported their stand and requested the High Commissioner of Germany to veto this proposal, thereby "keeping Military Government Law No. 15 in force."[81] The German trade unions were convinced that the recently enacted civil service law would have strengthened the position of the old bureaucracy —many of whom were friendly to the Nazis.

The importance of the activity of the A. F. of L. in Germany, although it was carried on with a small staff and little money, was acknowledged by George Reuter, a leading German trade unionist, who requested the Federation to support the demand of the German trade unions for the continuation of equal trade union representation on the Board of Directors of the plants in the Ruhr when the Ruhr was returned to the German government. Woll advised Reuter that it had always been the policy of the Federation to "support our allied and friendly trade unions in other lands in their undertakings whether or not we might find ourselves in accord with their point of view—in other words, that it was for the German trade unions to decide what they deemed best and that we would help as best we could."[82] In keeping with this policy, the International Labor Relations Committee unanimously approved the recommendation that the A. F. of L. support the German trade unions in this demand for equal union representation.[83]

A large amount of the effort of the A. F. of L. in central Europe was devoted to aiding German trade unions and other democratic forces in Germany, but the interests of Austrian labor were by no means neglected. In October 1951 Matthew Woll reviewed the relationship which had existed between the American occupation forces and the Austrian trade unions, a relationship which up to that time had been quite satisfactory. Until 1950 the functions of the Commanding General of the United States Forces in Austria and the functions of the High Commissioner were performed by Lieutenant General Keyes. Personnel policies, devised by the Labor Division functioning under Lieutenant General Keyes, were largely an adaptation of Austrian law and practice, and collective agreements were formulated in accordance with Army regulations and military necessity. Although this system was only partially satisfactory to the Austrian trade unions—which would have preferred full recognition of Austrian law, participation in collective agreements, and use of the Austrian labor court system—they did not object very strenuously, since they were provided with well-defined channels for discussion and negotiation of both individual and general problems.

In October 1950 the military occupation functions were separated from the Office of the High Commissioner, and the Labor Division was retained by the Office of the High Commissioner for Austria. The relationship between this office and the Austrian trade unions and the American High Commissioner's Office continued to be satisfactory. However, the United States Forces in Austria (USFA) did not establish a labor division after the separation, and it introduced changes in the working conditions of Austrian workers without consulting the trade unions. Woll wrote to the Secretary of the Defense, Robert A. Lovett, that the American Ambassador, who was also High Commissioner for Austria, had assured the A. F. of L. that he had "done all in his power to get the Army to realize the harmful effects of its policy."

But an Ambassador can only make suggestions—the Army will react only when ordered to from superiors in the Pentagon. Therefore, I urge that you be kind enough to request the USFA to reexamine its labor policy with a view of establishing regular contact with the Austrian Trade Union Federation for discussing and negotiating mutually satisfactory labor practice. . . . We of the American Federation of Labor . . . would appreciate prompt and favorable action by you in this vital matter. The Austrian trade unions have been in the forefront of the fight against every attempt of Communist infiltration and subversion. They are the very backbone of the democratic and anti-totalitarian forces. It is most timely and important that our government's policies in Austria particularly in relation to organized labor, should demonstrate in deed and reality the democratic way of life and also reveal to the working people of Austria our appreciation of their loyalty to the democratic cause and of our readiness and determination to treat them on the basis of equality in every way possible.[84]

Secretary of the Army Frank Pace did not agree with Woll's argument, and he suggested a meeting between Woll, the A. F. of L. Austrian representative, and the commanding general in Austria.[85] Pace told Woll that channels for the satisfactory resolution of problems arising out of the "employment of Austrian civilians in United States Army installations" existed, and that United States Forces Austria Civilian Personnel Office was the agency charged with responsibility in this area. Woll denied that the relationship between the Austrian trade unions and the American military in Austria was the same as had existed during the administration of Lieutenant General Keyes. Moreover, he insisted that the USFA Civilian Personnel Office did not have well-defined channels for discussion and negotiations on either individual or general problems. In fact, General Secretary Proksch of the Austrian Trade Union Federation had complained that the American authorities had denied Austrian workers wage increases and had even refused to negotiate with Austrian labor. Woll asked Secretary Pace to reconsider the proposals of the A. F. of L. for greater recognition of the Austrian trade unions and the granting of the wage increase.[86]

Pace denied that the Army in Austria was hostile to the trade unions or that it had refused to engage in conferences and discussions with the officers of the trade unions. He reminded Woll that civilians employed by the USFA were paid from appropriated funds which had to be administered within the framework of United States laws. "In paying employees from appropriated funds, the United States Government," he told Woll, "does not engage in negotiations and collective bargaining with its employees in the United States or any other area as a means of establishing wage and labor regulations. Accordingly, the USFA civilian personnel office does not have the authority to 'negotiate' wage or labor regulations with Austrian employees."[87] Woll was told that personal representatives of the commanding general were always available to "discuss impartially matters pertinent to labor based upon the concepts of equality, justice and fair play."

Rutz had met with Lieutenant General George P. Hayes, Commanding General, USFA, and discussed the complaints of the Austrian trade union leaders. In August 1952 Rutz wrote to Lieutenant General Hayes to remind him that the meeting with the Austrian trade union officers, which he had promised to hold, had not yet taken place. In view of the failure to rectify the complaints of the trade union leaders, Hayes was advised that a recommendation would be made that the A. F. of L. "request Secretary of Defense Lovett to institute an investigation as to the complaints made by one of America's best European friends—the Austrian Trade Union Federation—against the U.S. Army. I believe such an investigation will find that anti-labor officers . . . do not fit in the United States plan of selling modern democracy to Europe."[88] Hayes denied the charges that Army was antilabor. In November 1952 Matthew Woll protested the ignoring of the Austrian Trade Union Federation by the officers of the

Mutual Security Administration. The A. F. of L. was assured "that agreements for sharing our provisions under which wage earners and consumers will be assured of a fair share of increased productivity should be executed with the Unions."[89] It was also recommended that the head of the Mutual Security Mission in Austria meet with the trade unions and eliminate any misunderstanding that might have arisen. The situation in Austria improved after the A. F. of L.'s intervention.

In keeping with its policy of defending and supporting democratic labor movements and free governments, the Executive Council requested the American government and its British and French allies to demand the elimination of Article XVI from the projected Austrian peace treaty. The Federation charged that under the provisions of this clause the Soviet government could plant upon Austrian soil "teams of Soviet political police serving as inquisitors to hound and terrorize helpless men and women and even Austrian citizens friendly to refugees and displaced persons. Through their notorious secret police methods, the swarm of Soviet agents would seek to drive them back into Iron Curtain countries where they would be subjected to torture, slave labor and the firing squad. Article XVI should be unreservedly rejected as a violation of the fundamental human rights proclaimed in the Charter of the United Nations."[90]

The A. F. of L.'s interest in democratic Germany never slackened. In a discussion of American policy toward that country, Matthew Woll, speaking for the A. F. of L. International Labor Relations Committee, urged the United States to break with the obsolete and erroneous policies being utilized in German matters. As a result of our policies, Woll thought that "German democratic labor has become increasingly suspicious of the intentions and policies of the Western powers in regard to their country. . . ."[91] "This is all the more unfortunate," Woll said, "since German democratic labor has consistently demonstrated its fundamental solidarity with the West, its attachment to the cause of democracy and unswerving opposition to all forms of totalitarianism. . . . It is in this spirit and toward these ends that the activities of the German Trade Union Federation (D.G.B.) and the Social Democratic Party, which is generally considered the principal political expression of the labor movement, have been conducted."[92] The lack of a clear-cut and consistent policy "to restore full equality of rights to Germany" was "at the bottom of the repeated and unwarranted Allied interference with German political life."[93]

Woll warned the State Department that German labor's full economic cooperation was essential if the restoration of the economic health of the European community was to be achieved. He urged that German sovereignty be fully restored and that any clause giving the allied governments the right to withdraw some governmental powers, in certain emergencies, be avoided.

Independence from foreign rule [he said] is an absolute necessary prerequisite for the development of any healthy democratic nation. This applies to Germany as well as other countries. Actually, the fact that Germany has not yet been granted full equality of rights has become a costly obstacle to closer cooperation between the people of Western Germany and the democratic world. . . . Neither the problem of effective German participation in the defense of the free world nor that of cooperation by Germany in the economic integration of Europe can be dealt with in a constructive manner as long as negotiations with Germany are conducted on a basis implying second-class status for her.[94]

Woll pointed to the confidence of the A. F. of L. in the democratic character of the German labor movement and the complete support the German trade union movement had always received from the Federation. He criticised the decision of the Allied High Command to hand over the shares of new iron and steel corporations to the old owners of these industries, in spite of the pledge of the Allied Powers to leave "the question of the eventual ownership of the coal, iron and steel industries . . . to the determination of a representative, freely elected German government. This step was taken by the Occupation authorities though they knew very well that the German democratic labor movement had demanded that these industries be transferred to public ownership, a reform possible under Article 15 of the Basic Law of the German Federal Republic."[95] Woll emphasized that whether "one agrees or disagrees with the German democratic labor movement in such a demand is quite aside from the real issue at stake." In conclusion, Woll wanted the American government to support and seek approval from the other allied powers of a reunified democratic Germany.[96]

While taking issue with many of the points raised by Woll, the State Department thanked him for "the real interest and thoughtfulness which have gone into the letter.[97] Woll remained dissatisfied with the answer to his complaints, and he again described the necessity for full sovereignty for Germany rather than "so-called 'substantial equality' for Germany."[98]

"To continue," Woll wrote, "to deny the people of Germany full equality of rights because of the differences and difficulties arising from the Four Power Occupation is to continue the fallacies and folly of the Potsdam Declaration. . . . It would be unjust, unwise and unrealistic to adopt a position which is tantamount to telling the German people that they could not recover their sovereignty and obtain full equality with other nations as long as Stalin (one of the Four Occupying Powers) is willing not to withdraw his troops from the Eastern Zone."[99] Woll insisted that the Western powers should pursue a policy of unifying Germany on a democratic basis. And unless Germany was given full rights, the A. F. of L. was certain her freedom would remain only of "symbolic value."

The A. F. of L. also supported the position of the German trade unions on codetermination. In a letter to Walter Freitag, President of the *Deutscher Gewerkschaftsbund* (German Federation of Labor or D.G.B.), Secretary-Treasurer George Meany noted that the A. F. of L. approved the resolution supporting codetermination at the Milan meeting of the International Confederation of Free Trade Unions. The A. F. of L. did not seek codetermination in the United States, Meany explained, but said "we can readily understand the aim of your organization to utilize codetermination as a means of defeating the attempts of big industrial and financial magnates to resume their domineering and dominant position in the economic life of the German people. Furthermore, the American Federation of Labor realizes that the exercise of excessive powers by the biggest business groups which had financed and supported the Nazi party and the Hitler regime must be prevented in the interest of world peace and democracy."[100]

Meany cited the statements of the A. F. of L. International Labor Relations Committee over several years as proof of the desire of the A. F. of L. to support a democratic free trade union movement working out its problem in accordance with the needs of the German people and free institutions. The A. F. of L. practiced as well as preached, Meany said, the right of the workers of each country to solve their own problems in their own way within a context of freedom and democracy. The A. F. of L. delegate in Germany continued to act as an intermediary between the civilian and military officers of the United States and the German trade unions. In 1952 the A. F. of L. sought to have properties which had been requisitioned by the United States Army returned to the trade unions and also tried to have the violation of certain labor regulations curbed. Changes were eventually made which ended such abuses as the failure to hire through government employment offices, failure to pay social security benefits on time, providing substandard housing for itinerant workers, favoritism to contractors by avoiding selection on the basis of lowest bids, and discharge of a union officer who protested some of these practices. In each case, the charges which led to ultimate reform were presented by the A. F. of L. representative to the High Commissioner.[101] Gradually, German labor like the German nation became increasingly independent, developed its own resources, and was able to solve its own problems without aid from the outside. The work of the A. F. of L. within Germany slowly diminished in importance.

The A. F. of L., however, made one more contribution to the German trade union movement which needs to be mentioned. Unlike the pre-Hitler trade union movement, in which the German unions were divided on religious grounds, the German Federation of Labor (D.G.B.) sought to retain all trade unions and trade unionists within its ranks regardless of religious affiliation. Opposition to this policy existed from the beginning of the revived German labor movement among some Catholic religious and trade union leaders. While the first leader of the German Federation of Labor, Hans Boeckler, was alive, the movement was held in check, but with the election of Walter Freitag to the presidency of the German Federation of Labor, a new drive began to split German trade unions on religious lines. The group included right-wing politicians, Dutch and Belgian Christian union leaders, and the *Katolische Arbeiter Bund* (KAB)— Catholic Action groups. While the agitation for a separate Christian trade union movement was going on, the Western German bishops issued a statement for the guidance of their people.

The bishops' statement approved the formation of unions and the affiliation of Catholics with such organizations. It praised the work of Catholic Action groups which had "pointed out to its members . . . in the trade unions the increasingly perceptible dangerous tendencies and . . . warned the trade unions themselves emphatically about maintaining neutrality in world outlook and genuine tolerance." The statement, rather than encouraging a split in the trade unions, asked for more neutrality. In a press release the Executive Committee of the German Federation of Labor in December 1952 reaffirmed its support of the statement of the Roman Catholic bishops, and approved of the view that the trade unions had to maintain "neutrality" in social, political, and religious matters.

The A. F. of L., in view of its concern for the welfare of the German democratic trade union labor movement and the support it had given, was greatly disturbed that the possibility of a weakening split within German labor might develop. George Meany spoke out at the convention of 1953, the first A. F. of L. convention over which he presided, about the danger of a split to Germany and the free world. "The German labor movement," Meany declared, "must remain free. Germany can make a great contribution to world peace, but it can only make that contribution by following the lines that lead to peace, by the maintenance of freedom of all segments of the German economy, and particularly by the maintenance of freedom on behalf of the workers of that great country."[102]

Matthew Woll also decried any division within German labor on denominational grounds. Answering the claim of Auguste Cool, president of the Christian Trade Union Confederation of Belgium, that only Christian trade unions represented a barrier against Communism, Woll emphatically denied that

in order to be consistent and vigorous in their opposition to the Communist or any other brand of totalitarianism, the free trade unions must be denominational—to wit—Christian trade unions. This is not so. The A. F. of L. yields to no one in the world in the vigor, consistency, and militancy of its uncompromising hostility to Communism or any other form of tyranny. Nor has the

A. F. of L. ever given preference to one Communist coterie as against another Communist conspiracy, let us say to the Tito troupe as against the Stalin slave system. Nor have we limited our opposition to words or to a defensive policy. We have been actively on the offensive against Stalinism, Titoism, Peronism, Falangism, Nazism, Fascism and every military or other form of dictatorship. Yet the A. F. of L. is completely opposed to every form of denominational unionism."[103]

The unequivocal statement of Woll and the speech of President George Meany at the A. F. of L. convention, coming at a time when the executive board of the German Federation of Labor was on the defensive, had a significant influence in strengthening the determination of the leaders of the German Federation of Labor to resist vigorously the threatened schism on denominational lines. And it was not only because Meany and Woll were leaders of a great free trade union movement that their warnings were given special attention by German unions and religious leaders; it was widely felt that as practicing Catholics, Meany and Woll would not be biased against the Church. The leaders of the German labor movement deeply appreciated the support the A. F. of L. gave them in their struggle to maintain a united German labor movement.

## REFERENCES

1. *Report of the Proceedings of the Sixty-first Annual Convention of the American Federation of Labor*, 1941, p. 609.

2. Matthew Woll to William Green, November 12, 1943; November 26, 1943; Green to Woll, November 23, 1943.

3. Minutes of Executive Council, January 18, 1944.

4. *Report of the Proceedings of the Sixty-third Annual Convention of the American Federation of Labor*, 1943, p. 557.

5. Taken from the financial reports of the A. F. of L.

6. Minutes of Executive Council, August 14, 1945.

7. Woll to Green, December 12, 1945.

8. *Ibid.*

9. Joseph D. Keenan to Green, April 19, 1946.

10. *American Federation of Labor Weekly News Service*, March 12, 1946.

11. Memorandum from Harry Lang to Woll, July 14, 1946.

12. Minutes of Executive Council, August 16, 1946.

13. George Meany to Passport Division, United States Department of State, November 18, 1946.

14. Henry Rutz to George Meany, January 14, 1947.

15. Rutz to Jay Lovestone, April 26, 1950.

16. *Ibid.*

17. Matthew Woll to Secretary of State George C. Marshall, April 3, 1947. Advisory and Review Branch, Historical Division, State Department (862.008/4-347).

18. Rutz to Meany, December 24, 1946.

19. Rutz to Meany, January 14, 1947.

20. *Ibid.*

21. Rutz to Meany, February 27, 1947.

21a. Memorandum from the United States Political Advisor in Germany to the Secretary of State, June 26, 1947. Advisory and Review Branch, Historical Division, State Department (862.5043/6-2647).

22. Green to Secretary of State James F. Byrnes, June 11, 1946.

23. Undersecretary of State Dean Acheson to William Green, in *American Federation of Labor Weekly News Service,* July 9, 1946.

24. General Lucius Clay to William Green, July 23, 1946.

25. Special Bulletin of Labor League for Human Rights, August 1946.

26. *Ibid.*

27. Minutes of Executive Council, January 29, 1947.

28. *Report of the Proceedings of the Sixty-fifth Convention of the American Federation of Labor,* 1946, pp. 433–434.

29. *Ibid.,* p. 434.

30. *Report of the Commission of the World Federation of Trade Unions to Investigate Conditions in Germany.* The commission was authorized at the Paris Congress of the W.F.T.U. in September 1945. It assembled in Berlin on January 30, 1946 and returned to Paris on February 19. The report is undated.

31. Woll to Bevin, cable, January 7, 1947.

32. Minutes of Executive Council, January 14, 1947.

33. Meany to Rutz, April 14, 1947.

34. Martin Plettl to Robert Watt, February 24, 1947.

35. Quote from Woll to Paul Ramadier, May 21, 1947; Rutz to Meany, May 14, 1947.

36. Rutz to Woll, March 29, 1947.

37. Rutz to Meany, June 17, 1947.

38. *Ibid.*

39. Frank P. Fenton to Matthew Woll, May 16, 1947.

40. Woll to General Lucius Clay, cablegram, July 7, 1947; for quote, Rutz to Woll, July 19, 1947.

41. William Green to Honorable Harry S. Truman, November 27, 1947.

42. In a letter to Rutz, on July 26, 1949, Boeckler wrote: "Wir setzen unser bemühen um eine Milderung der Demontage fort und empfinden dabei besonders dankbar die Hilfe und Unterstutzung, die Amerikanische Gewerkschaften zuteil werden lassen. Die deutsche Arbeitnehmerschaft erkennt dankbar an, dass die Verantwortlichen Kollengen der A. F. of L. sich ernsthaft um eine Aenderung der Demontagefrage bemühen, und wir hoffen sehr, dass es den vereinten Anstrengungen gelingen wird, doch noch im letzen Augenblick eine Milderung zu erreichen."

43. Henry Rutz to General Lucius Clay, July 19, 1947.

44. Quote from General Clay's letter is in letter of Rutz to Meany, August 20, 1947.

45. Minutes of Meeting of International Labor Relations Committee, November 13, 1946.

46. Rutz to Meany, November 5, 1947.

47. *Ibid.*

48. *Report of the Proceedings of the Sixty-sixth Convention of the American Federation of Labor,* 1947, p. 464.

49. Memorandum from Irving J. Brown to George Meany, November 11, 1947.

50. *Ibid.*

51. *Ibid.*

52. *Ibid.*

53. *Ibid.*

54. Schumacher wrote "that the present W.F.T.U. constitutes a war-international. . . . One cannot with an international of hatred and destruction exercise the functions of an international of reconciliation and construction." Kurt Schumacher to William Green, January 2, 1948.

55. Woll to James W. Forrestal, January 20, 1948. The same letter was sent to Secretary of State Marshall.

56. *Ibid.*

57. Telegram from Secretary of Defense to OMGUS, February 12, 1948.

58. Cablegram from Office of Military Government United States to Department of Army, February 25, 1948, in files of A. F. of L.

59. Rutz to Meany, February 9, 1948.

60. Woll to Secretary of State Marshall, March 17, 1948. An identical letter was sent to Secretary of Defense Forrestal.

61. To the Honorable Secretary of National Defense from Lewis B. Schwellenbach, March 3, 1948.

62. Comments by General Clay on Trade Union Advisory Committee's Recommendations for Immediate Action to Strengthen Democratic Elements in German Trade Unions. MCIN57694, 19th March 1948, V-29561 from OMGUS.

63. Jay Lovestone to Rutz, April 16, 1948.

64. G. L. Eberle (Deputy Chief, Civilian Affairs Division of United States Army) to Lovestone, May 10, 1948.

65. Woll to Secretary of Defense James Forrestal, April 6, 1948.

66. Jay Lovestone to William H. Draper, May 6, 1948.

67. Rutz to Matthew Woll, October 16, 1948; Rutz to Lovestone, January 6, 1949.

68. *Report of the Proceedings of the Sixty-sixth Convention of the American Federation of Labor,* 1947, p. 483.

69. *Ibid.,* p. 486.

70. Lucius D. Clay to Matthew Woll, January 5, 1949.

71. Woll to General Lucius D. Clay, February 14, 1949.

72. *Ibid.*

73. *Ibid.*

74. Matthew Woll to Honorable Dean Acheson, April 29, 1949.

75. Memorandum submitted to Secretary of State Dean Acheson by International Labor Relations Committee, March 9, 1949.

76. Green to Dean Acheson, May 24, 1949.

77. Acheson to Green, May 30, 1949; Green to Acheson, June 1, 1949.

78. Matthew Woll to John J. McCloy, June 29, 1949.

79. Woll to McCloy, July 25, 1949.

80. *Ibid.*

81. Henry Rutz to John J. McCloy, March 14, 1950.

82. Woll to Rutz, December 15, 1950.

83. *Ibid.*

84. Matthew Woll to Secretary of Defense Robert A. Lovett, October 31, 1951.

85. Secretary of the Army Frank Pace to Woll, December 11, 1951.

86. Woll to Secretary Frank Pace, January 25, 1952; A. Proksch to Matthew Woll, January 11, 1952.

87. Secretary of the Army Pace to Woll, February 18, 1952.

88. Henry Rutz to Lieutenant General George P. Hayes, August 22, 1952; General Hayes to Rutz, August 27, 1952.

89. Henry Rutz to Jay Lovestone, November 10, 1952.

90. Minutes of Executive Council, May 4, 1952.

91. Matthew Woll to George C. Marshall, October 10, 1951.

92. *Ibid.*

93. *Ibid.*

94. *Ibid.*

95. *Ibid.*

96. *Ibid.*

97. Geoffrey P. Lewis (Acting Director, Bureau of German Affairs) to Woll, November 6, 1951.

98. Woll to Geoffrey P. Lewis, November 26, 1951.

99. *Ibid.*

100. George Meany to Walter Freitag, December 4, 1952. Codetermination has reference to granting the trade unions the right to elect members of the boards of directors of certain corporations.

101. *Report to the American Federation of Labor on Labor Activities in Germany and Austria*, 1952.

102. *Report of the Proceedings of the Seventy-second Convention of the American Federation of Labor*, 1953, p. 10.

103. *International Free Trade Union News*, July 1952.

# XXVIII

## Foreign Relations and Foreign Policy

### THE MARSHALL PLAN

The establishment of the World Federation of Trade Unions in 1945 meant that the A. F. of L. now faced a powerful rival, one that could be used by the Communist apparatus in uncommitted parts of the world, and which could use its trade union affiliates in the free world as proof that it was not a Communist instrumentality. From the outset the A. F. of L. was convinced that the W.F.T.U. could not continue to function as a unified whole. The emphasis of the *Information Bulletin,* a fortnightly published by the W.F.T.U., indicated that its criticism of institutions in the Western orbit was not balanced by analogous criticism of events and institutions within the Soviet Union's orbit.

In June 1946 Louis Saillant, the executive secretary of the W.F.T.U., recommended to the Executive Committee, meeting in Moscow, a blockade of Franco Spain by the joint action of the maritime unions affiliated with national centers belonging to the W.F.T.U. James Carey, representing the C.I.O., objected to any decision made by the W.F.T.U. which would require a strike by members of the C.I.O. Such decisions, he argued, were made by the membership of individual unions and were not within the province of the C.I.O., let alone that of the W.F.T.U. As a consequence, the Federation's Executive Committee dropped the proposal.[1]

For the sake of harmony the leaders of the W.F.T.U. could yield on an issue of this character, but the announcement by the United States government in June 1947 of a program to support economically—via the Marshall Plan—the economic recovery of Europe brought unbridgeable differences to the forefront. For several months the W.F.T.U. took no position on the Marshall Plan. On October 5, 1947 the Cominform— the newly resurrected old Comintern, the Communist International, made up of the Communist Parties of most countries, which had been disbanded by Stalin during the war—laid down the Communist Party line on the Marshall Plan. It was soon obvious that the pronouncement of the Cominform was accepted as a policy directive by the W.F.T.U. officers. At the Paris meeting of the W.F.T.U. Executive Bureau, the C.I.O. delegation tried to present its views on the Marshall Plan. The delegates from the Soviet Union, Giuseppe Di Vittorio, the Stalinist leader of the *Confederazione Generale del Lavoratori* (Italian Federation of Labor), and General Secretary Louis Saillant, a French Communist, objected to this protest; but in the end the statement was presented and it aroused vehement denunciations from those who controlled the W.F.T.U.[2]

The A. F. of L. appreciated the importance of the Marshall Plan as a means for enabling Europe to regain its economic well-being. President William Green endorsed the program soon after it was presented.[3] In response to a request from President Truman, he suggested that emergency relief should be extended as a separate policy for the "sole purpose of providing food and fuel to maintain life," and that the reconstruction program should provide for investment in capital in order to revive and facilitate production. The administration of the program, Green thought, "should be based upon an understanding that the Communist Parties of all countries are members of an international revolutionary party, organized for the purpose of establishing totalitarian governments controlled and directed from Moscow." Green favored the vesting of operating responsibility in a corporation formed for the purpose of administering the Marshall Plan rather than in existing government agencies. The corporation's directors should include representatives of industry, agriculture, and labor. He also advised against the use of any forced labor and said that "aid forthcoming under this proposal in the form of bank credits or materials should be invested in productive capacities. Any returns from the sale of aid materials should be used for the purpose of stabilizing currency or for additional productive facilities." In Green's view, the objective of the Marshall Plan was the "establishment of a European economy (including Germany) which would provide for adequate production facilities and which would serve all nations without discrimination and without wasteful and destructive competition due to uneconomic rivalries. Under either public or private ownership, free competitive enterprise should be the permanent objective sought, such objective to provide for the highest standard of living for the greatest number of citizens."[4]

Meeting with President Truman in December 1947, an A. F. of L. committee, including William Green, Matthew Woll, and George Harrison, endorsed the Marshall Plan. The committee recommended that aid be given to all countries

which are prepared to cooperate earnestly, energetically and sincerely in the mutual undertaking to secure European reconstruction on a continental basis. Any nation which has not yet accepted the Marshall Plan shall be considered eligible for aid as soon as it honestly breaks with all moves and schemes calculated to interfere with the execution of the European Recovery Program and agrees to cooperate wholeheartedly with the other nations on a collective basis. In this spirit, the A. F. of L. endorses the emergency aid program of $597,000,000 for France, Italy, and Austria. This emergency aid should be used primarily to overcome the great threat of hunger and destitution among the working populations of these countries.

The A. F. of L. committee reassurred the American people and European workers that the only purpose of the Marshall Plan was to end worldwide hunger and misery through an economic reconstruction of Europe.

The full benefits of the European Recovery Program could be applied, the A. F. of L. believed, only on a democratic basis. To the Federation this meant that:

labor must be adequately represented in the planning, administration, and execution of the European Recovery Program. . . . The A. F. of L. proposed that our government forcefully reiterate and firmly adhere to the policy that all nations whom we aid have the inviolable right to decide democratically their own political and economic relations. Our government cannot emphasize too strongly that it is not the purpose of American economic assistance to impose on any nation any particular political pattern or economy. It is not the purpose of American assistance as envisaged in the Marshall Plan to infringe in the least on national sovereignty or independence of any people. . . . The Federation believed that Germany's remaining industrial potential should be harnessed for the rebuilding of European recovery. There can be no reconstruction of Europe otherwise. Hence, all dismantling of German industrial plants should be discontinued forthwith. Immediate steps should also be taken to reconvert all remaining military plants of Germany into industrial units producing commodities needed by the people in the pursuits of peace and in aiding the reconstruction of the other countries. The reconversion shall be under the supervision and guidance of a committee of international experts, on which German labor and industry shall also be represented. In line with this policy, the establishment of an independently unified German central government should be hastened.[5]

The Federation also suggested the release of all war prisoners, the return of those who had been forced to repatriate to the countries they had fled, and an early declaration of the end of the war with Germany and Austria. The views of the Federation officers reflected the opinion of the convention, which had endorsed the Marshall Plan, although two of the seafaring unions objected to the proposal to give 500 American ships either by sale or transfer to countries participating in the Marshall Plan.[6]

Testifying before Congress, Green said that "economic rehabilitation of Europe is in the interest of all wage earners." Emphasizing Soviet opposition to the Marshall Plan, Green accused the Russian Communists of preparing to profit from the chaos that hunger and misery would foster in Europe. "We want," Green told the congressional committee, "to give the people of Europe aid that will sustain their courage and their faith in democracy. We hope our relations will be worthy of the Christian ideals of living which should guide our relations with our fellowmen and instill all nations with the will for peace."[7]

The opposition of the Soviet Union and labor centers in the Communist block to the Marshall Plan had serious repercussions within the trade unions of the free world. The leaders of the British Trades Union Congress were especially worried about the attitude of the Soviet Union leaders and their followers in other countries. In fact, Irving Brown reported late in 1946 that the British leaders were already disillusioned with the W.F.T.U., although they continued to hope for improvement in their relations with the W.F.T.U. since they were convinced that "they must show their own people and the world how much time and opportunity have gone to build a world labor organization with the Russians."[8]

A common interest in the success of the Marshall Plan provided a basis for united action by the trade unions of the free world, and the A. F. of L. leadership was anxious that the free trade unions be separated from their Communist allies in the W.F.T.U. The Federation tried to enlist the support of Ernest Bevin for its planned conference of Marshall Plan labor movements. Although Bevin was no longer an officer of the British Trades Union Congress, he still had great influence with British labor. It was thought imperative that the British Trades Union Congress act as one of the host organizations if the conference was to be successful. J. H. Oldenbroek, head of the International Federation of Transport Workers, believed that the A. F. of L. had

handled this Marshall Plan business in a masterly way. Though you had taken the initiative for calling a conference, you did not insist when it became clear that there were forces at work in Europe which pursued the same purpose. The A. F. of L. has still more endeared themselves to those European trade unionists who are in the W.F.T.U. without really belonging to it. It is these same trade unionists which have put the British Trades Union Congress "on the spot." . . . This attitude has largely influenced wavering T.U.C. leaders to embark on a full-scale attack against the Communists and fellow travelers in their own ranks. I admit this would have come anyway, but the process has been hastened because the T.U.C. felt they were losing their hold on the Western European trade union movements.[9]

There was some difficulty about the date of the conference. Oldenbroek and the Trades Union Congress were anxious to hold the conference as soon as possible, and they agreed upon March 8 and 9. This date conflicted with another meeting which the A. F. of L. officers wanted to attend, and Green requested that the conference be called after March 29 so that several members of the Executive Council might attend. Arthur Deakin, president of the Transport and General Workers' Union in England, as well as the W.F.T.U., and Evert Kupers of the Dutch Federation of Labor wanted the conference on the Marshall Plan scheduled before the meeting of the W.F.T.U. Executive Bureau in April 1948, so that the position of the free trade unions could be explained to the world. The A. F. of L. agreed to the earlier meeting, and appointed Frank Fenton, Director of Organization, and Irving Brown, its European representative, as delegates.[10]

The British Trades Union Congress, the Confederation of Free Trade Unions of Holland, the Belgium General Federation of Labor, and the General Confederation of Labor of Luxembourg issued the invitations. On behalf of the Conveners, Vincent Tewson, the general secretary of the British Trades Union Congress, announced that the purpose of the conference was to "discuss American Aid for the Reconstruction of Europe." The leaders of European labor promoting the conference pointed to the refusal of the W.F.T.U. to discuss the Marshall Plan immediately and to view "the need for early consultation between the national centers in the countries directly concerned and the necessity of National Centers having an opportunity to discuss the matter jointly before the United States Congress legislation was finally adopted."[11]

The conference, assembling at Transport House, London, on March 9, was welcomed by Miss Florence Hancock, chairman of the General Council of the Trades Union Congress. Delegates from twenty-six organizations in fifteen countries appointed forty-eight representatives, thirty-eight of whom were delegates, four observers, and six secretaries. Organizations under Communist influence, such as the French *Confederation Général du Travail,* the Italian *Confederazione Generale Italiana del Lavro,* and several others followed the Communist line and refused to send delegates, although representatives from the Christian, Republican, and Social Democratic parties in Italy were seated as observers.[12]

Both James Carey, who represented the C.I.O., and Frank Fenton, the A. F. of L. delegate, stressed the desire of the American government to aid Europe in rebuilding its war-shattered economy. Speaking on behalf of the A. F. of L. and the Railway Labor Executives' Association, Fenton said that it was the understanding of the organizations he represented that the European Recovery Program envisaged the determination of European economic needs by the European people themselves on a "joint, cooperative basis retaining their initiative and sovereignty," and that no "political conditions would be attached concerning internal economic methods and policies as long as democratic methods are adhered to and not eliminated."[13]

Both Arthur Deakin and Léon Jouhaux praised the European reconstruction program embodied in the Marshall Plan, and asked the national trade union centers of each country to approach their governments with the object of being associated with the administrative machinery of the program. Another conference was planned to devise methods of working with the program as soon as it was enacted. In a lengthy statement, adopted by the Conference, the participating trade union centers declared that the European Recovery Program offered the means by which they could "continue their historical task of improving the conditions of life and employment of the working people with prospects of positive results."[14] The statement examined the means by which Europe, with the help of the United States, could build a prosperous economy based upon peace and freedom.

The importance of the meeting of the trade union centers from Marshall Plan countries was not limited to the effect which such an organization might have on the administration of the European Recovery Program. Actually, this organization was the first open move to mobilize the trade union centers of the countries of the free world in opposition to the Communist-controlled W.F.T.U. The refusal of the W.F.T.U. to support the European Recovery Program and its denunciation of the program as a disguised attempt at domination of Europe by American imperialists revealed the character as well as the loyalties of its leaders.

The two most important free organizations allied with the W.F.T.U., the British Trades Union Congress and the C.I.O., were thus placed in a difficult position by the W.F.T.U.'s opposition. Recognizing this situation, Woll addressed a plea in June 1948 to the C.I.O. to withdraw from the W.F.T.U. Such a move, he said,

would render a great service not only to the early attainment of the unity of the American labor movement, but to the cause of democracy and peace everywhere. . . . It is only by virtue of the A. F. or L.'s being outside the W.F.T.U. that the voice of free labor, unmuffled and unhampered by alliances and pacts with agencies of totalitarian cliques and despots, has been heard clearly at a time when it is vitally urgent for labor to play a positive and constructive role. The American Federation of Labor has thus rendered a real service to the cause of democracy and trade unionism the world over.[15]

The second conference of trade unions on the European Recovery Program met in London in July 1948. Two members of the Executive Council, George Harrison and David Dubinsky, headed the United States delegation. Jay Lovestone was secretary of the American delegates. Irving Brown was an alternate. The C.I.O. delegation was David McDonald and Victor Reuter. Twenty-five organizations were represented by forty-five delegates. Evert Kupers, head of the Netherlands Federation of Labor, opened the conference and stressed the need for unity among the labor organizations of the free world. During the meeting, both Harrison and Dubinsky stressed the imperative need for European labor to support the Recovery Program.

A committee, to which George Harrison was appointed, presented a declaration, unanimously accepted by the conference, that "the [European] Recovery Program depends in large measure for its success upon the combined efforts of the millions of workers in all the countries concerned, including the United States, and . . . implies the effective representation and participation of our organized national movements and their international coordination in all administrative machinery."[15a] The conference emphasized that the purpose of the recovery program was to correct the distortions in the economies caused by the war, and that the funds should not be used for the repayment of old state debts or to establish the dominance of the old and discredited industrial groups, such as the Krupps. It called upon the labor movements to co-operate so that a more efficient economy could be built, one which would serve all the people of the Continent.

In September 1948 the A. F. of L. Executive Council reaffirmed its hope that free trade unions would leave the W.F.T.U. and welcomed the observation of Arthur Deakin, a leading British trade unionist, that the W.F.T.U. had been "captured by the Communists."[16] During this period the General Council of the British Trades Union Congress became increasingly concerned about the policies of the W.F.T.U. The Margate Congress approved the criticisms made by the General Council, and the future relationship between the Trades Union Congress and the W.F.T.U. was left in the hands of the General Council. On October 27, 1948 the differences between the two organizations came under discussion.

A report from the Council's representative at the recent Paris meetings of the W.F.T.U. Executive Bureau indicated that no basis of agreement had been found on proposals formulated by the General Council with the object of securing satisfactory arrangements regarding the . . . administrative activities of the W.F.T.U. Secretariat. Moreover, despite the effort of the British and other representatives to get the World Federation operating on a sound basis, fundamental differences on questions of both policy and organization have been revealed, and the Trades Union Congress representatives reported that as the time has gone on it has become more and more difficult to prevent the intrusion of political tactics when questions of Trade Union policy came before the W.F.T.U.[17]

Of course, the leaders of the British Trades Union Congress should have been aware that the possibilities of a free trade union movement working harmoniously with a Communist-controlled federation were virtually nonexistent. Many of the British leaders had embarked upon this venture with heavy hearts, yielding to the proposals of Walter Citrine that the Trades Union Congress join with the government-controlled unions of the Soviet block. Citrine himself was an experienced trade unionist and an extremely able administrator. He had hoped with the highest motives, that the trade unions of the free world would be able to work with Soviet groups and thereby advance the cause of peace and international understanding. The A. F. of L. never deluded itself with such a possibility. In spite of the obstacles placed in the way of real cooperation, the officers of the Trades Union Congress believed:

it might have been possible to register a measure of common agreement on many matters if confidence and good-will [had been] exerted within the various executive bodies of the W.F.T.U. That confidence and good-will, however, has been undermined by the way in which matters put forward for consideration are the subject of propaganda, if not before, then certainly after, any major questions are discussed. The stream of vilification and abuse which has been poured on the British T.U.C., American Labor, and the leaders of those national centers who are not prepared to become subservient to Communist doctrine and dictation is not restrained by any desire to overcome inherent difficulties. Any realization that international Trade Union unity depends on the good-will and good relations between the Trade Union Movements of the participating countries is completely absent in the tactics we have encountered. From all Communist-controlled national centers—and they speak with remarkable accord—propaganda is regarded either as a strategic barrage to facilitate a given line of tactics or, alternatively, to discredit any individual, movement, or government which does not wholeheartedly accept the point of view of the authorities.[18]

The Trades Union Congress still showed some reluctance to break completely with the W.F.T.U. British leaders feared that the withdrawal of the non-Communist trade union centers from the W.F.T.U. would lead to the "organization of a rival international . . . and international rivalries would become intensified." They suggested instead that the W.F.T.U. "should suspend its functions; that one representative from each of the five main contributing national centers be appointed as Trustees who shall hold the accumulated funds of the World Federation and meet in twelve months' time, or earlier, in order to discuss the conditions in which an attempt to revive an international Trade Union body may be made."[19]

The British proposals were submitted to the General Secretary of the W.F.T.U. and were discussed at the Paris meeting of the Executive Bureau which began on January 17, 1949. Vincent Tewson, presenting the British position, said that he would "abstain from bringing any passion into the debate." He could no longer, he said, as he had done up to the present, defend the organization and try to correct its failings. Repeated warnings had been given to the W.F.T.U., by Citrine to the Executive Committee at Moscow, then by some T.U.C. delegates to the

Prague session, and finally at the last meeting of the Executive Bureau. "But they had been misunderstood and misinterpreted. . . . Today, the T.U.C. representatives no longer asked the W.F.T.U. to abandon the path along which it was proceeding. It had arrived at an impasse."[20] Tewson cited the continued attacks upon the English trade unionists, and he argued that the people could not at one and the same time "declare themselves in agreement on the respecting of the autonomy of the Centers with which they were collaborating within the same organization and refuse to apply this principle in practice."[21]

Arthur Deakin, the presiding officer, supported Tewson's stand and warned that the W.F.T.U. "must completely, and not partially cease its activities."[22] Deakin, in explaining his position, noted that the Soviet Union had established a Cominform which transmitted Soviet policy to all the Communist groups in the world. However, the Trades Union Congress could only participate in the W.F.T.U., and that was the agreement made during its formation, on condition that a policy of noninterference in the internal affairs of the affiliated centers was followed. In the course of the discussion, Giuseppe Di Vittorio, the Communist head of the Italian Federation of Labor, denounced the C.I.O. representative and said that the Marshall Plan was "a political and military pact which was being used to enslave a certain number of countries to the world domination of capitalist interests."[23] After this outburst, Deakin deplored Di Vittorio's speech—"Which could be only completely repulsive to all those who gave value to the truth"—and assailed the charges against the T.U.C. and the C.I.O.[24]

After two days of argument, the Soviet block attempted to prevent a vote on the British proposals, and Deakin, James Carey, Evert Kupers, a leader of the Dutch Federation of Labor, and Assistant General Secretary Elmer Cope withdrew from the meeting. Walter Schevenels, who had been secretary of the International Federation of Trade Unions, remained, would not leave, and was thanked for his action by the Communist Louis Saillant, the general secretary of the W.F.T.U.[25]

The A. F. of L. subsequently opposed Schevenels as Secretary of the Trade Union Advisory Committee to the European Recovery Program on the ground that he "was unfit to hold office in the ranks of democratic world labor."[26]

The withdrawal of the C.I.O., the T.U.C., and the Netherlands Federation of Labor from the W.F.T.U. convinced the A. F. of L. that it was now possible for "freedom-loving workers to join hands on an international scale. The building of a truly international and really effective world organization," the Federation announced, "has always been close to the hearts of the eight million members of the American Federation of Labor. Such international labor cooperation must not be a pious phrase. Nor can it be the echo and replica of government policies. To be genuine, such international labor cooperation must be entirely independent of all political parties, governments, and employers."[27] The Federation warned that a world body of free labor must be carefully developed and must not be created by some "elaborately staged gathering."

William Green was in no haste to set up a new trade union international. The need for granting full representation on any international labor body to the C.I.O. was especially unacceptable to him. In anticipation of a meeting with British trade union officials, who were visiting the United States as members of an E.C.A. productivity team, Green, Meany, Woll, Dubinsky, and William C. Doherty met with a group of C.I.O. representatives in March 1949 and discussed the question of an international labor federation. The A. F. of L. leaders refused to meet jointly with the Briitsh labor members and the C.I.O. officers. In one of the conferences, the British officials, Tewson and Deakin, explained that no international federation would be approved by the British Trades Union Congress unless the C.I.O. were a full partner. The condition was accepted by the Executive Council, although Green still was reserved about the participation of the C.I.O. An agreement between the A. F. of L. and the C.I.O. on representatives and on consultations by the two federations was reached in a "friendly discussion" on April 28, 1949.

The Executive Council was now ready to make every effort to unify free world labor "on a sound and thoroughly democratic basis." In preparation for forming the new trade union international, the Executive Council insisted on "a complete break with the methods of big power politics and preliminary collective discussions among the free trade union movements of all countries—regardless of their size—and on thoroughgoing consideration of their proposals."[28] The A. F. of L. wanted something better and more aggressive than the old International Federation of Trade Unions. Consequently, the Federation proposed that preliminary conferences decide the sponsorship of the conference, the structure and functions of the organization, the type of staff to be recruited, the methods of financing the new federation, and the location of the central headquarters. It accepted, over William Green's protest, the full partnership of the C.I.O. in international trade union matters.

## THE INTERNATIONAL CONFEDERATION OF FREE TRADE UNIONS

In May 1949 Vincent Tewson invited the A. F. of L. to a conference to explore "the early formation of a new trade union international organization and to discuss the possible form and character of such a body." Each invited organization was asked to send one and not more than two delegates. The Executive Council unanimously approved the formation of a new international trade union federation and voted to have the

A. F. of L. affiliate with it as soon as it was organized.[29] George Meany, Irving Brown, and George Philip Delaney were sent to the preparatory meeting in Geneva.[30]

The preliminary conference met in Geneva on June 25 and 26 under the chairmanship of Arthur Deakin and acknowledged the "imperative need for an effective means of collaboration and consultation between the free and democratic trade union movements of the world and accordingly decided to appoint a Preparatory Committee from delegates assembled in this Conference."[31] The Committee was charged with the task of drafting a constitution and program for the international trade union organization. Embracing all free and democratic trade union organizations throughout the world, this organization would, with the cooperation of the International Trade Secretariats, make possible the convening of a fully representative trade union delegate conference for the purpose of establishing the new international body. The Preparatory Committee was specifically directed to devise a program which would ensure close

contact between the free and democratic trade union movements throughout the world; the provision of assistance in the establishment and development of trade union organizations in economically and socially underdeveloped countries; the furtherance of peace between the nations of the world; to seek association with such international organizations both Governmental and non-Governmental, as will further the aims of the international trade union organization in protecting and developing the interests of the peoples generally and guaranteeing fundamental human rights; to pay particular regard to the economic, social, and cultural interests of the population of war devastated countries and the rebuilding of their economies; to ensure full employment and to increase the standard of living of the peoples throughout the world, particularly through the development of backward countries and self-governing territories.[32]

Irving Brown was the A. F. of L. representative on the Preparatory Committee, and George Meany actively participated in the discussions with trade union leaders of other countries. Meany conferred with Léon Jouhaux, who submitted several proposals.[33] Jouhaux had no desire to interfere with the autonomy of the national trade union centers which would affiliate with the new International, yet he wanted some form of "limited discipline" written into its constitution that would at least act as a moral force to induce national trade union centers to comply with important decisions of the new International.[34] Jouhaux was particularly worried about the trade union centers which might in the course of time come under Communist influence.

The Preparatory Committee in London met from July 25–29 and worked on a draft constitution which the British Trades Union Congress had already prepared. The A. F. of L. delegate, Irving Brown, described the document as what the British termed a "positive" draft, rather than the anti-Communist statement which the Americans wanted. In the end Brown was more satisfied, although he still felt that the draft failed to speak out with sufficient clarity on a number of issues. For example, the British had objected to the wording, "trade unions free of domination from political parties, government, employer, or church," which the A. F. of L. delegate had suggested; the British substitute, "free from external domination," was adopted.

A more important dispute developed over the question of the relations that were to exist between the new international and the Christian trade unions. The A. F. of L. had always opposed denominational unions, but it was forced to recognize that these organizations existed and had substantial support in many European countries. Hopeful that unity between the confessional or denominational unions and the other non-Communist unions could eventually be achieved, the A. F. of L. believed that it would be an error to exclude them from membership at this time. The C.I.O. supported this opinion, but it was rejected by the Committee. The A. F. of L. insisted that the headquarters of the new federation be located in a small country and that the top offices be given to members who were not citizens of "great power" countries. The A. F. of L. wanted an international organization free from big-power domination. Vincent Tewson, Arthur Deakin, William Richter, Evert Kupers, J. H. Oldenbroek, Irving Brown, and Mike Ross were delegated to seek a solution of the differences. When the tentative constitution and by-laws were submitted for inspection, President Green suggested the following inclusion:

The International Federation of Free Trade Unions proclaims the right of all peoples to full national freedom and self-government and demands that conditions be created for the realization of this right at the earliest possible moment wherever it is not yet enjoyed. . . . As an organization fervently upholding the principles of democracy, it will champion the cause of human freedom, oppose totalitarianism in any form, tendency or shape, and combat directly or indirectly totalitarian aggression. It pledges solidarity with and support to all working people deprived of their rights as workers and human beings by totalitarian oppressive methods.

Green also proposed that the federation

contribute to the raising of the general standard of well-being by engaging and fostering educational and publicity work with the object of increasing the knowledge and understanding of national and international problems confronting the workers; to coordinate the defense of bona fide free trade unions against any international campaign aiming at the destruction of free trade unions, at the restriction or abolition of the rights and achievements of free labor and at the infiltration and subjugation of labor organizations by totalitarian or other anti-labor forces; to further the international exchange of experiences in regard to such problems as the structure of the trade union movement and its methods of organizational work.[35]

A delegation of ten, headed by Green and Meany, was sent to the London conference which was held November 28 to December 9, 1949 by the A. F. of L. The Federation again requested that the Christian trade unions be given full recognition and representation at the conference. The Preparatory Committee agreed to extend invitations to the Christian unions only if no objection was presented by the national trade union centers which ordinarily affiliated with the international trade union federation. The Belgian and Dutch trade union centers would not accept the admission of the Christian trade union centers in their countries, and their views were supported by the British. A compromise which allowed the Christian unions to send observers was finally devised.[36]

The A. F. of L. fought the establishment of denominational unions in the United States and bitterly assailed their activities in Canada. Although the Federation used all its persuasive power and influence to eliminate division within the European trade union movement, it could not overcome the traditional divisions and attitudes. Believing that this was the time for concessions—the A. F. of L. had yielded to recognizing the C.I.O. as an equal in the international area—the Federation leadership could not understand the unwillingness of European trade union leaders to allow the non-Communist Christian trade unions representation in the international federation. The Federation leadership attributed the adamant position of the Continental unions to the British support of their views.

Not all leaders of Christian trade unionism were anxious to enter the new international. In fact, the moderates who wanted to collaborate with nondenominational anti-Communist labor groups always faced strenuous opposition from those who wanted to have the Christian unions follow an independent course. Irving Brown decried the attitude of the intransigents within the Christian trade union movement, and urged Christian workers in Europe to become "an activating element in a single union, equally independent of the Church, the Government or of a Party."[37] When his statement was interpreted as an attack upon the Christian unions, Brown and Elmer Cope, the C.I.O. representative, clarified their views in a statement:

It should be clear to everyone that the new International Confederation of Free Trade Unions does not ask any national union or federation of unions to merge with any other national union or federation as a condition of membership. So long as they are free, non-Communist unions, whether neutral or Christian (Catholic, Protestant, or non-sectarian) in their institutional character, they are eligible for membership and are welcome. In affiliating with the International Confederation of Free Trade Unions, they will retain their own autonomy. This new International Confederation of Free Trade Unions is attempting to unite all free, non-Communist labor unions in the world for the welfare of labor and for peace and justice everywhere. It draws no religious lines.[38]

All evidence indicates that the A. F. of L. made every effort to bridge the gap that divided these organizations. Those who observed the success of the Communist Party in directing and redirecting its instrumentalities on the trade union field mistakenly believed that other organizations operated in the same fashion. The A. F. of L. used every means at its disposal to bring harmony into the ranks of non-Communist European labor. It felt, therefore, that the refusal to grant recognition to the Christian unions was both unfair and a tactical mistake, because it encouraged the isolationists and weakened the ability of European unions to serve the workers and resist the influence of the Communists.

The meeting in London established the International Confederation of Free Trade Unions. J. H. Oldenbroek, was elected general secretary. Green hoped that the new House of Labor would be "enduring and indestructible."[39] The Executive Council greeted the formation of the ICFTU

as an event of inestimable significance in the history of free labor. The International Confederation of Free Trade Unions provides an organization which can coordinate and assist on a world scale the efforts of the working people of all lands to protect and promote their economic interests, social security and well being. . . . As the most all-inclusive organization of free labor ever established, the I.C.F.T.U. can render signal service to mankind in defending and expanding human freedom and social justice. Through devotion to democratic ideals and the mighty cohesive force of vigorous international labor solidarity, the I.C.F.T.U. can play the decisive role in fostering and preserving world peace. . . . Despite the vast differences in historical background, experience, and tradition of the delegations at its London Foundation Congress, the I.C.F.T.U. was able to achieve a remarkable degree of unity of fundamental concepts and aims. . . . The American Federation of Labor is proud of the contribution made by the A. F. of L. towards the creation of the I.C.F.T.U. We heartily endorse the active part played by our delegation in helping the London Congress attain its fruitful outcome.[40]

The Executive Council noted the failure of Communism to win many adherents in countries where effective trade union movements had already existed and been permitted to exercise an influence. The Council pledged itself to fulfill its duties toward the new international labor federation "in a spirit of true international labor solidarity and boundless devotion to human freedom, social justice and lasting world peace."[41]

The Federation donated $15,000 for the purchase of office equipment, which was part of $25,000 donated to get the organization established. In the first year the A. F. of L. contributed $65,000.

The 1950 convention approved the Council's action in joining the ICFTU and commended the officers and representatives for the aid they had given in bringing this organization into being.[42] The Federation leadership, however, was not altogether satisfied with the performance of the organization in its first year. There was some disappointment over the ICFTU's lack of vigor in opposing Communist activity on the trade union front in many parts of the world and its failure to set up active regional organizations. Both A. F. of L. Vice Presidents Woll and Dubinsky, who at the time were consultant representatives of the ICFTU to the United Nations, were angry at the appointment of George Philip Delaney as an ICFTU consultant to the United Nations. They considered the appointment of another American without their approval as astounding and immediately submitted their resignations. Only the intervention of President Green, who convinced them that no reflection was intended, persuaded them to withdraw their resignations. Woll and Dubinsky secured the promise that they would be kept informed on all matters affecting the United Nations emanating from the ICFTU.[43]

The A. F. of L. selected a delegation, led by six members of the Executive Council, to attend the Milan congress of the ICFTU in July 1951. At the request of Oldenbroek, George Meany drew up a statement entitled, "The Aims of Free Trade Unionism and its Struggle against the Totalitarian Menace." It was, according to this statement, "utterly false to consider any type of totalitarianism as progressive or genuinely revolutionary in an historical sense."[44] In fact, said Meany, every brand of totalitarianism inevitably seeks the destruction of the free trade union movement and its replacement by gigantic company unions. The free trade union movement must unrelentingly expose the real character of totalitarianism, but it must also develop a positive program for the promotion of social justice and social security. "Free labor," the report concluded, "can have no more lofty ambition or nobler goals than its devotion to human freedom, social justice and lasting peace. Here is the road the ICFTU must take in building a world free from the fear of hunger, poverty, dictatorship and war."[45]

The A. F. of L. officers were pleased by the number of delegates who were willing to take clear-cut antitotalitarian positions, but they also feared that the good intentions proclaimed in the resolutions would not be carried out in the actual program of the ICFTU, especially in the Middle East and Asia. Nor were they enthusiastic about the election of Vincent Tewson to the presidency of the ICFTU. They respected Tewson for his direction of the British Trades Union Congress and for his knowledge and devotion to the trade union movement of the world, but American labor leaders doubted whether an organization headed by a British citizen was not under a handicap in seeking to convince the people of the colonies and those who had been colonials in the recent past to resist Communist totalitarianism and add their strength to the labor movement of the free world. There was also some feeling that Tewson's acceptance of the office violated the original agreement between the British and American trade union leaders to avoid big-power domination of the international federation. Although the British could claim that Tewson had been freely elected, the A. F. of L. leaders knew that as a practical matter the trade unions of the Continent would not oppose a British candidate. In contrast to the Continental labor leaders, the A. F. of L. officers were not dependent upon the good will of the British, and they felt no restraints in making their views known.[46]

The failure of the A. F. of L. to contribute to the $750,000 fund that the ICFTU set about raising to carry on its regional activity was another source of misunderstanding. The European leaders contrasted this failure with the A. F. of L.'s continuation of its independent international activities.[47] Woll requested the Executive Council to reconsider, at its August 1951 meeting, the financial request of the ICFTU, but no action was taken. In commenting publicly on the Milan meeting, the Executive Council extolled the progress made by that organization in the first year of its life, and called on the "democratic labor forces . . . through united action to offer a progressive program which can provide an attractive alternative for the great number of workers who have deserted the ranks of the Communist Party controlled unions of France and Italy."[48] The statement warned that the defense of the democratic way of life could not be carried on by armaments alone.

The leaders of the ICFTU came to the United States in June 1952 to attempt to eliminate existing differences. Tewson and Oldenbroek met with Dubinsky, Meany, Harrison, Green, and William Doherty. John Owen and Thomas Kennedy of the United Mine Workers of America were also present. Meany explained that the A. F. of L. in helping to organize ICFTU had surrendered a long-held policy of not sharing international representation with another American federation in order to promote harmony within the international labor movement. The A. F. of L. was still opposed, Meany said, to big-power domination of the ICFTU. Although the American Federation had opposed the admission of the Italian Union of Labor, Meany reported that his organization was willing to accept the decision of the majority. In conclusion, Meany defended the A. F. of L. policy on Cyprus, and made it clear that he wanted United States proposals to be considered rather than be rejected out of hand. Assuring the meeting that the

A. F. of L. would remain in the ICFTU, he asked that the A. F. of L. be consulted on policy.[49]

During the discussion Meany charged that the Australian Workers' Union, whose affiliation the A. F. of L. had supported, had been kept out of the ICFTU by trickery. Oldenbroek denied this charge. Meany also wanted the ICFTU to take a clear and more critical position on Yugoslavia. When he asked Tewson whether the ICFTU should not take a stand on Yugoslavia, Tewson answered "We don't like their system; their principles bar them from ICFTU affiliation. But we recognize it is an area of great pressure and don't want them to look and move away from the west. Not all is black or white. There is also gray. We don't want to repel them." Tewson said that the British Trades Union Congress had no ambition to control the ICFTU and he pleaded for understanding. Unless these differences could be settled, he knew that no free international labor federation could exist.

In a meeting which the British did not attend, Harrison reviewed the unsettled problems. He acknowledged the tremendous power wielded by the T.U.C., and said, "we must find some way to participate effectively and jointly with them. We must fight inside and not outside for our ideas." When the British returned to the discussion, Harrison tried to state the attitude of the A. F. of L. He said that the American Federation had joined the international federation as a partner and had found itself treated like an appendage. Because the European nations consistently followed the British, the T.U.C. had dominated the international federation. "In all frankness and friendliness," Harrison said, "we want to be considered and consulted in full partnership and not to come in to meetings to be voted down and slapped down. We believe we are not given the recognition we deserve. If you agree to cooperate and work with us and give us a feeling that our views are being considered, then our troubles are dissipated."[50]

When Tewson said that he could not consult with the A. F. of L. without arousing suspicion, Harrison retorted: "You are not kidding me. It is a practical proposition. You do consult with people when you want to." At the end of the meeting, Meany thought that the tensions had eased and that the A. F. of L. might now take its rightful place in the International.

FRANCE

The A. F. of L. had been effective in Germany because the German labor movement had been completely destroyed and its old leadership reduced by death and exile. With the passing of old leaders and the inexperience of the new, the trade unions had had to be reconstructed from the ground up. Finally, and perhaps most important, Germany was an occupied country and the United States was one of the occupying powers. Conditions in France were basically different from those prevailing in Germany. During the occupation, which had lasted only three years, some of the old trade union leaders had been in the forefront of the resistance to Hitler. Eventually the French Federation of Labor had been captured by the Communists, and in December 1945 Irving Brown reported that there was no "possibility of dealing directly with the C.G.T. or any of the leading national unions due to their Communist Party control."[51] United under the leadership of the Communist Benoit Franchon, the non-Communist organizations found they could no longer remain in the C.G.T. because of what a leading French syndicalist described as the "Molotov strikes."[52] During the summer of 1945 an opposition to the Communist control of the trade unions and to the use of these unions for political ends developed in a number of large unions. Léon Jouhaux and Robert Bothereau, who were determined to carry on the rebellion against Communist domination, appealed to David Dubinsky, who was visiting Europe, for financial aid. On behalf of his union, Dubinsky gave $5,000 to *La Force Ouvrière,* so that it might expand its activities. Dubinsky requested that the transaction be openly acknowledged and that a receipt be given him for this donation.[53]

Five thousand dollars was, of course, not adequate to get the movement started. Without resources, facing a powerful organization, the French trade unions had to turn to the A. F. of L. and the British Trades Union Congress for additional help. Dubinsky and George Harrison conferred with Léon Jouhaux in London and learned that $35,000 would take care of the needs of *La Force Ouvrière* through the remainder of 1948. Harrison and Dubinsky strongly advised that a loan be made—although it was not likely to be repaid—for it was important that the A. F. of L. support workers who were trying to rid themselves of Communist rule.[54] A loan of $25,000 was made by the Federation. Dubinsky was irritated at the time by the reluctance of the French leaders to acknowledge the A. F. of L. help.

The Federation continued to take an active interest in the work of *La Force Ouvrière,* and occasionally offered its advice. A trade union movement of a highly developed country, however, could not become a financial dependent of another nation; the burden of opposition fell upon the French leaders. Nevertheless, the A. F. of L.'s willingness to provide financial aid at a time when such assistance might have been decisive in the attempt of the French trade unions to free themselves of Communist control was an important contribution.

ITALY

The Italian trade union movement, like its German counterpart, had been totally destroyed by more than two decades of Fascist control. After the fall of Mussolini in July 1943, the corporative laws regulating labor and employer activity had been abolished, and a revival of trade unionism had begun. In February 1944 two labor conventions were held at Salerno, and the General Labor Federation (*Confederazione Generale del Lavro*), inspired by Socialists and Communists, and the Italian Federation of Labor (*Confederazione Italiana del Lavoratori*), in which Christian influence predominated, were organized. Secret conferences between the leaders of the two groups led to an agreement, the Pact of Rome, on June 4, 1944, to establish trade union unity. The three main currents in the Italian labor movement—Communist, Socialist, and Christian-Democratic—came together in one organization, the Italian General Federation of Labor (*Confederazione Generale Italiana del Lavro*) or the C.G.I.L. This agreement was approved at a national convention in January 1945. The organization, based upon internal democracy, was to be independent of all political parties. A Communist activist, Giuseppe Di Vittorio, was elected president of the organization. The belief that a Communist-led organization would maintain political neutrality can only be explained by the desire for unity generated by the common struggle against Mussolini's rule. It was soon obvious that the Italian Labor Federation was an instrument utilized by the Communists to advance their political interests, frequently at the expense of the workers.[55] The Socialist groups, not closely allied to the Communists, and the Christian Democrats increasingly felt that the unified federation was violating the basic principles of political neutrality.

The internal conflicts of the Italian Labor Federation were accentuated by Communist opposition to the Marshall Plan. The Italian Labor Federation, following the lead of Moscow, had opposed participation in the trade union conference called by the British Trades Union Congress and trade union movements of the Benelux countries to support the Marshall Plan. Giulio Pastore, a leader of the Christian group, insisted that participation of the representatives of the Italian workers in the trade union conference at London was imperative, if only to discover if aid for the reconstruction of Italy's economy might be promoted. Pastore was supported by the Republican trade unionists and those Socialists who were not close to Pietro Nenni, who favored collaboration with the Communists on both the political and trade union fronts. Over the objections of the Communist leadership of the Italian Federation of Labor, Pastore, G. Canini, and E. Parri attended the London conference in March 1948. Canini and Parri represented, respectively, the moderate Socialists and Republican trade union groups.

The readiness of the Italian labor minority to attend the Marshall Plan conference encouraged the opponents of Communist control to work more closely together. Subsequently, the antitotalitarian groups formed an alliance to oppose Communist rule of the trade union movement and denounced the intolerable acts of those in control of the Italian Federation of Labor.[56] The minority was soon confronted by a crisis which followed the shooting of Palmiro Togliatti, the leader of the Italian Communists, on July 14, 1948. A general strike was immediately called as a protest against the attempted assassination and soon took on the appearance of an armed attempt to seize state power. Pastore condemned the strike in the councils of the Labor Federation and issued a call for the workers to return to work. Soon thereafter, in July 1948, the National Council of the Christian Association of Italian Workers (*Associazioni Christiane Lavoratori Italiani*) announced that the general strike had violated the Pact of Rome on political neutrality and that a new organization based upon political neutrality would be established.[57]

In September 1948 the Christian Democrats formed the Free General Confederation of Italian Workers (*Libera Confederazione Generale Italiana del Lavro*) which was to be free of political and religious domination and devote itself to advancing the economic interests of the workers. The Socialists and Republicans, unwilling to be part of the Christian Confederation, established the Federation of Italian Labor (*Federazione Italiana del Lavro*) in June 1949. The Socialist and Christian groups met in 1949 and decided to merge the two organizations.[58] Some Socialists and Republicans regarded the fusion of the two organizations as an error because they believed that the Christian Democratic organization was Church-dominated; this group in turn organized in March 1950 the Italian Union of Labor (*Unione Italiana del Lavoro*). Finally, under the leadership of Giulio Pastore, the Italian Confederation of Workers' Unions (*Confederazione Italiana Sindicati Lavoratori*), C.I.S.L., was created in April 1950 to promote trade unions independent of political parties and free from the various ideological currents.

In discussing the problems and divisions of Italian trade unionism, Dr. Joseph La Palombara charged that "for many American officials and trade unionists who supported fusion of Italian non-communist labor, a social-democratic labor confederation was ideologically unpalatable."[59] Whatever truth this statement may contain with regard to American officials, it is not a correct estimate of the A. F. of L. policy. Throughout its history, the A. F. of L. has always taken the position that the ideological views of a national federation were the concern of the workers in that particular country and of no one else. A distinction was always drawn between the view of an international confederation to which the A. F. of L. might affiliate and a national federation in a particular country. As long as the national federation was independent of government or employer domination, the A. F. of L. believed that the policies it pursued in its own country were matters it had to decide for itself. The A. F. of L. could only help; it could not decide the type of organization that the Italian workers would set up. The failure of Italian labor to build an effective free trade union movement was certainly not the result of the deficiencies of American labor and the American government. The trips of Italian labor leaders to the United States may have served no good purpose, and the emphasis on productivity in the context of the Italian scene may have been misplaced, but the chief problems in Italy were native ones.

The A. F. of L. supported the Italian Confederation of Workers' Unions in the belief that only an aggressive and unified, free and democratic trade union movement could weaken the hold of the Communist-dominated labor federation upon the Italian worker. It thought that the Socialist labor center was too weak to form a barrier against Communist rule over the economic wing of the labor movement. The A. F. of L. fought the admittance of the *Unione Italiana del Lavoro* into the International Confederation of Free Trade Unions, and it supported to the degree its resources permitted the trade union federation headed by a Christian Democrat.[60]

### Greece

The A. F. of L. supported the free trade union movement in Greece. In December 1947 Woll wrote Premier Themistocles Sophoulis and condemned the "legislation denying workers' right to strike and providing court martial and death penalty for those daring to exercise this inalienable right vital to all forms of democratic society and fundamental human liberty."[60a]

Irving Brown was sent to Greece in 1948 to examine the situation, and he reported that the absence of a trade union movement since 1936 and the pitifully low wages of the majority of workers were the major problems. Brown believed that since the liberation in 1944, there had been a series of events which made it possible for the Communists to become a dominant group within the Greek trade union movement. Deplorable economic conditions, the reluctance of employers to recognize independent trade unions, and government control of certain non-Communist labor organizations made the situation serious. Brown advised against any cooperation with government-dominated unions; for,

"from the standpoint of the A. F. of L. . . . we stand not only against
the domination of the trade union movement by a single type of state
but of all states. Nor do I believe that it is our job to force unity between
extremely opposite groups nor assume that because a united labor
movement is the best thing that it must be achieved irrespective of
principle and the basis upon which such unity is consummated."[61]

Brown recommended that greater economic aid be dependent upon
the willingness of the Greek government to introduce a larger measure
of democracy. Loans granted for industrial reconstruction and economic
recovery should, Brown said, be sufficiently safeguarded so that they
would be used for real investment rather than for speculation. There
was an immediate need to improve living conditions and to write a
"bill of rights . . . guaranteeing workers' protection from persecution . . .
through a separate system of legal procedure . . . similar to a labor court
or our National Labor Relations Board."[62] Brown also advised that the
Greek government be asked to discontinue its intervention in the affairs
of the trade unions and that the forced deduction of dues by government
fiat be abolished.

American labor—specifically, the American Federation of Labor—[Brown re-
ported], has a basic responsibility to aid the Greek workers in attaining a real,
free trade union movement by aiding in the eventual creation of a united free
trade union movement, free of Communist Party political domination and of
government control or favoritism. Until such time as there is a really national
free trade union movement, we cannot declare ourselves in support of any
existing organization. This should not free us from the responsibility of impress-
ing upon our government the need for the recommendations made, assisting in
any way possible to see to it that the Greek government carries out the basic
reforms suggested and lending any aid possible to bring about unity and an
eventual national trade union organization, based upon the principles already
enunciated.[63]

### AFRICA

Reporting on Africa, Irving Brown said that there was a growing opposition to colonialism, which had to be taken into account. He thought
that some steps should be taken to develop an interest in trade unionism
among the African people.

The convention of 1951 urged a break with all colonialism in all parts
of the world. It called for just and equal treatment for Morocco and
Tunisia and urged that these nations should be aided to "become respected and effective partners of democratic France."[64] The 1951 convention was addressed by Farhat Hached, general secretary of the
Tunisian Federation of Labor, who was later assassinated by French
terrorists. Hached pleaded for support of free trade unionism, abolition

of all remnants of colonialism, and the improvement of the living conditions of the great masses. The A. F. of L. joined in a statement with the C.I.O. denouncing the "totalitarian colonialism now rampant in this French Protectorate (Tunisia). We are helping the Tunisian trade unionists because their struggle against brutal colonialism is as much ours as the struggle of the oppressed workers behind the Iron Curtain against communism. That is why we are particularly critical of our own Government and our State Department for demonstrating an unfortunate neutrality in a cause where our basic traditions should range America on the side of the exploited, and on the side of the victims of a brutal imperialist regime."[65] The joint statement was critical of the failure of the United States delegation at the United Nations Security Council to support the placing of the Tunisian complaints on the agenda. "The American labor movement," the statement concluded, "can only condemn such a policy of neutrality which is not neutrality at all, but, in reality, is an implied endorsement of the undemocratic practices of the French colonial government in Tunisia. Colonialism and Communism are both enemies of free trade unionism and democracy." The A. F. of L. and the C.I.O. asked the American government to support the demand of the Tunisian people for home rule.

In another statement, the Executive Council demanded home rule for Tunisia as part of the French Commonwealth and asked that negotiations begin with the democratic forces represented by Habib Bourguiba to prepare for full national independence.

Early in 1953 the A. F. of L. denounced the murder of Farhat Hached, the leader of the Tunisian Trade Union Federation. In a statement, the Council blamed "the French government's colonial policy. . . . This dastardly crime dealt a fatal blow to the hopes and prospects for a peaceful and just settlement of the crisis in Tunisia." The A. F. of L. condemned "this brutal political murder," and demanded an investigation by the United Nations.[66]

On August 22, 1953 Woll urged Secretary of State John Foster Dulles to instruct the United States delegation to the UN to "support proposals for placing on agenda [the] Moroccan crisis. Such American support will greatly encourage all forces for peace and freedom, enhance our nation's traditional role as champion of all peoples aspiring to national freedom and democracy, and promote effectiveness of the United Nations as instrument for understanding and peace among nations." The refusal of the American delegation to vote for a discussion of the events in Morocco was deeply regretted by Woll who charged such refusal with being "a stain on the American government. It is in utter contempt of anti-colonialist traditions of our country and contrary to the overwhelming opinion of the American people as expressed in the nation's press."[67]

The convention of 1953 urged the United States government to call upon France "to grant immediately self-government to Tunisia, Morocco and Indo-China and to establish with these sovereign states a relationship modeled after the British Commonwealth."[68] On December 10, 1953 Woll appealed to the French government through Ambassador Henri Bonnet to release the Moroccan and Tunisian labor leaders imprisoned by the French.[69]

### SPAIN

During the Spanish Civil War, the A. F. of L. had taken no stand. It opposed Franco as a dictator, however, and in 1945 advised that the Spanish government in exile be recognized. Declaring that the Spanish government in exile represented the "most inclusive constellation of genuine democratic elements," the Executive Council wanted the American government to accord "full diplomatic recognition and moral support to the Spanish Republican Government in Exile."[70]

In April 1946 Rafael Robeldo had been arrested and was awaiting trial before a military court in San Sebastian on the charge that he had money in his possession given to him by the Soviet government for underground work in Spain. Woll denied the charges and said that the funds had been donated by the Free Trade Union Committee for relief. Woll appealed to Secretary of State Dean Acheson to intervene on behalf of the prisoner.[71] In May 1947 Woll again appealed to the State Department to intervene with the Franco government on behalf of a trade unionist. Woll proposed that "our State Department should exercise all moral pressure to save the life of this outstanding trade union leader [Manuel Fernandez Peon] and fighter for democracy inside Spain. May we also suggest that our government would render a great service to humanity if it were to issue an appeal pleading for the abolition of the death penalty in all political cases."[72]

In 1948 the A. F. of L. opposed inclusion of Spain in the European Recovery Program and sharply criticized the amendment of Congressman O'Konsky to allow Spain to become a participant. Charging that this was a crass repudiation of American democratic policies, the A. F. of L. asked the Senate to throw out this amendment.[73]

In 1951 Woll again pleaded for the use of American influence to halt the terror in Spain. Secretary of State Acheson was urged "to have the representatives of our government in Madrid present a vigorous memorandum to the Spanish Dictator urging him in the interest of friendship with the American people to discontinue the persecution and terror against bona fide trade unionists and democrats in his country."[74]

During this time Secretary-Treasurer George Meany had intervened with the State Department to gain permission for the General Union of

Spanish Workers in Exile to circulate its journals in the international zone of Tangier. The administrator of the international zone of Tangier had forbidden the circulation of the *Monthly Bulletin of the General Union of Spanish Workers* at the request of the Franco government. Because the United States was a party to the 1945 agreement which had established the international administration in this area, Meany asked if "there is anything our State Department can do to protest to the Administrator of the International zone of Tangier, the decision to bar entry of a monthly publication of the Spanish General Trade Union, which is an affiliate of the I.C.F.T.U."[75]

When the United States government entered into a pact with Franco Spain, the A. F. of L. restated its objection to dealing with a regime based upon totalitarian principles. The Executive Council asked that the aid received from the United States by the Spanish government be used to improve the conditions of the Spanish people, and that the United States exert "the fullest pressure on the Franco regime to release unconditionally all those imprisoned because of their loyalty to bona fide free trade unions and devotion to political freedom. . . . The A. F. of L. reaffirms its wholehearted solidarity with the heroic free trade unionists of underground Spain and their courageous colleagues in exile. To these brave front-line fighters for freedom and human decency . . . we pledge our most energetic efforts to help hasten the day when the great Spanish nation will take its rightful place in the community of free people."[76]

### YUGOSLAVIA

The A. F. of L. welcomed Tito's resistance to the demands of the Soviet Union, but would not in the least endorse his despotic domestic regime.[77] "The people of Yugoslavia . . . have been subjected to and continue to be the victims of a ruthless so-called proletarian dictatorship under which they are denied all democratic rights. Under the Tito regime, the workers of Yugoslavia are denied every right to free trade union organization and all freedom of conscience and other basic democratic liberties. . . . We must not lose sight of the facts and must not hesitate to condemn the systematic annihilation of genuine democratic forces, the brutal denial of religious liberty, and savage persecution of churchmen, and the suppression of human rights by the present Belgrade regime."[77a]

### NORTH ATLANTIC PACT

In 1949 the Executive Council discussed the North Atlantic Pact, which was designed to defend the Western democracies against Soviet aggression. Vice President William Hutcheson wanted it made clear that any endorsement of the Pact by the Council should indicate that the United

States was not expected to furnish European countries with funds to rearm. He opposed the endorsement which was voted by the Council.[78] Calling upon the Senate to approve the North Atlantic Pact, "as an act of living solidarity and full partnership with all the forces of freedom," the Council's statement emphasized that "the American people have a spiritual and moral bond which binds them to all liberty-loving peoples. This community of sacred purpose underlies the basic necessities for our joining the Atlantic Alliance."[79] The A. F. of L. sought "inclusion of minimum labor standards in the bilateral agreement with other NATO countries and all procurement contracts negotiated by the U.S. Government. . . . We are particularly concerned over the danger of an administrative by-passing of these essential procedures in the interest of narrow short-run expedients in placing off-shore procurement without the necessary labor considerations." Meany recommended that the bilateral agreements with the NATO countries and the contracts-let include a requirement that contractors comply with local labor laws and regulations affecting hours, wages, social security, workmen's compensation, safety, and child labor. Wages, "including allowances and benefits in firms working on U.S. Contracts must be at least as high as the best for comparable work in the industry and area. The contract should include a commitment on the part of the contractor to conclude a collective bargaining agreement with the appropriate union or unions concerned."[80] Meany suggested that adequate sanctions be included in the contracts to assure compliance.

### AID TO BRITAIN

In keeping with its policy of supporting free democratic governments, the A. F. of L. in 1949 supported aid to Britain, so that country would be able to meet some of the economic difficulties which were the consequence of two world wars and the shift of economic power in the world. In a statement in the summer of 1949, Woll denied that the dollar crisis facing England was the fault of the British people, especially of its working people. "Elementary fairness and facts of history demand that the British government and the labor movement of Britain should not be held responsible for the deep-going dislocation and disruption brought on by two world wars, by the transfer of the world's economic center of gravity to the United States, and by the chaos-breeding consequences of the rise of Communist, Fascist and Nazi totalitarian dictatorships."[81]

As for the prejudice against England on the part of those who were still fighting the war against George III, Woll reminded the American people that the "courage and sacrifices of the British people in two world wars and their loyalty to our common principles today, to a very important extent were responsible for our democracy surviving." The statement pointed to the great reforms introduced in Britain on behalf of the ordinary man and woman, the great capacity of its industry and the vigor of its society, and the imperative need for aiding an ally in economic distress. The statement suggested immediate assistance by the International Monetary Fund, acceleration of stockpiling of strategic commodities needed for national defense, encouragement of joint Anglo-American productivity councils, and the setting up of a permanent European-American conference to deal with the economic imbalance between Europe and the United States.[82]

## POINT FOUR

The 1949 convention approved President Truman's Point Four program for economic aid to the underdeveloped countries.[83] In line with this approval, the Executive Council backed aid to the Republic of India to deal with its food difficulties, to develop public education, and to improve public health. The Council also asked the World Bank to advance funds to help speed the growth and improvement of India's agriculture.[84] Subsequently, the Council described the Asians' understandable fear that "evil practices of colonialism will continue," and called for the mobilizing of the material and moral resources of the American people to aid the newly formed free nations of Asia.[85]

In recent years the A. F. of L. has continued its demands for the development of an adequate program of support for the underdeveloped free nations. In May 1953 the Executive Council reviewed the need for a revitalized Point Four program to benefit the economic growth and living conditions of the Asians. The following year the Council called for adequate military and economic rearmament to discourage Communist aggression; "setting of definite time limits for granting independence to the colonial and semi-colonial peoples, as the United States did in the Philippine Islands;" rigid and permanent opposition to admitting Communist China into UN membership; and bilateral non-aggression mutual aid pacts between the United States and the Republics of Korea, Philippines, and National China until an adequate collective security system can be established.[86]

## JAPAN

The 1947 convention pledged support to the workers of Japan in their efforts to build a free and democratic trade union movement.[87] Earlier in 1947 Matthew Woll, as the chairman of the International Labor Relations Committee of the A. F. of L., sharply protested to the War and State Departments and to General Douglas MacArthur the permission granted Louis Saillant, head of the W.F.T.U., to affiliate Japanese trade unions with the W.F.T.U. Woll claimed that it was unfair and "injurious to the rising Japanese Trade Union movement to place it in a position of hearing only W.F.T.U. viewpoints without at the same time having the A. F. of L. present its case against affiliating with the W.F.T.U."[88] Woll said that Saillant's visit was a move to place Japanese trade unions under covert domination of the Soviet government, and that it constituted a threat to democracy in general and the United States in particular In 1948 the convention objected to the abridgment of the rights of government workers in Japan by the occupation authorities and asked for moderation in the restrictive policies imposed upon Japanese labor.[89] Richard Deverall represented the A. F. of L. Free Trade Union Committee in Japan.                    .

The Executive Council advocated, in May 1951, the restoration of full sovereignty to Japan and advised that the peace treaty between the United States and Japan be so formulated as to discourage the rise of militarism and monopolies similar to those existing before World War II by guaranteeing Japanese security against external aggression.[90] After the Japanese treaty had been signed, the Executive Council urged its ratification by the United States Senate and expressed the hope that social, agrarian, and labor reforms introduced during the American occupation would be continued.[91]

### CHINA AND ASIA

After the seizure of power by the Chinese Communists, the A. F. of L. showed the same inflexible opposition to their recognition as it had shown to diplomatic relations with Communist Russia. The convention of 1949 attributed the victory of the Chinese Communists to the financial and military aid of the Soviet government and urged the United States not to forsake the Nationalists maintaining themselves on the island of Formosa.[92]

The convention of 1951 approved "moral and material assistance to the developing democratic resistance movement on the Chinese mainland, to the furtherance of democratization of the constitutional regime on Formosa, and the strengthening of its Nationalist military forces thereon."[93]

In a detailed analysis of the rise of Communist China, the convention of 1953 recognized that while the "fatal blunders of the Chiang Kai-Shek regime . . . and the appalling poverty of the people have certainly facilitated the Communist rise to power, they were not the decisive factors which brought about the Mao Tse-tung victory. The Communists could never have seized power without Russian military support and direction."[94] The statement emphasized the fact that the Communist regime in China represented a more dangerous threat to the free world than the Soviet government. Recognition of the Mao Tse-tung regime or its admission to the United Nations was opposed in line with the doctrine elaborated by Secretary of State Henry L. Stimson, "that recognition be denied to any government *forcibly imposed on any people with the aid of a foreign power.*"[95]

The Executive Council opposed the recognition of Communist China and her entrance into the United Nations. The Council charged that the Chinese Communists had seized power with Soviet military and economic support, that Communist China had carried on an aggressive military campaign against the United Nations, and that it was a bloody repressive regime which warred upon its own people and was a threat to the people of Asia and to the rest of the world. There was no place in the United Nations for dictatorships, the A. F. of L. said, whether they be Communist China's or Falangist Spain's.[96]

While opposing recognition of Communist China, the A. F. of L. wanted the United States to "proclaim a policy of cooperation with all democratic groups in Asia. We should offer them economic aid and cooperation similar to what we have given Europe." The A. F. of L. pointed to its consistent support of "national freedom for all peoples" by the United States and especially its organized labor movement which had always viewed "with the warmest of sympathy and the keenest of interest the aspirations and efforts of the hundreds of millions of the common people of Asia for human freedom and national independence."[97] The A. F. of L. advocated policies to: not interfere with the people of Asia in their efforts to attain national freedom, support a mutual defense pact by the free governments of Asia, oppose diplomatic or commercial recognition to Communist China, support the democratic forces in China, and prepare, in cooperation with the democratic Asian authorities, "the application of President Truman's 'Point Four'."[98]

### INDIA

The Free Trade Union Committee sent a representative to the India National Trade Union Congress in 1949. Irving Brown spent an entire month in India during 1949 and sought to interest the Indian leaders in promoting a labor movement free of political domination.[99]

In a report, Irving Brown pointed to the late development of Indian trade unionism. Even though strikes had taken place over the years, these were desperate reactions to misery which left little permanent trade union organization. Brown described the efforts to create a trade union organization not dominated by political groups and the urgency of providing Indian workers with some means for improving their economic standards.[100] He urged that trade unions be supported and that the A. F. of L. emphasize the importance of Point Four for the future development of India and of a democratic trade union movement.

Brown urged that the Indian National Trade Union Congress and Hind Mazdoor Sabha should be welcomed as full affiliates of the projected free trade union federation. The A. F. of L. was advised to seek the establishment of and help promote a free trade union movement in India and to set up a bureau in that country to aid such a movement. An exchange of workers and trade union officers between the two countries was to be encouraged, and a cultural exchange between the people of the two countries was to be promoted. Finally, Brown advised that the Western world

just accept the fact [that] self-determination—the movement for economic and social justice and the desire for an end of European or white man's domination —characterizes the Asian world. Unless we break with the past in Indonesia, in Indo-China, in South Africa, and in our country, there will be no hope for maintaining what is left of Asia in the democratic camp. Racial discrimination and foreign domination of colonial peoples serve as the greatest arguments against Western democracy. . . . American foreign policy must more and more reflect the fact that the United States is in the forefront of the fight for the self-determination of colonial problems.[101]

## THE INTERNATIONAL ROLE OF THE A. F. OF L.

The active entry of the A. F. of L. into the arena of foreign policy has meant that millions of workers in the United States have become more aware of the importance of foreign policy to the welfare of the United States and the world. Through its educational activity among the organized workers, the A. F. of L. has helped to prevent a revival of isolationist sentiment among the masses of people. On the international scene it has shown a keen awareness of the basis of the struggle between the free and totalitarian nations, and it has emphasized in its activity that the stakes were not only economic but that the right of men to freedom was involved. It was the insistence of the A. F. of L. which forced the question of slave labor on the agenda of the United Nations and exposed the hollow pretensions and brutal practices of the Soviet Union. The contribution of the A. F. of L. was acknowledged by the investigating committee. The A. F. of L., on both humanitarian and political grounds, has fought for an end to all vestiges of colonialism and for generous assistance to the underdeveloped areas so that they might begin their task of raising the standard of living of their people.

## REFERENCES

1. World Federation of Trade Unions, *Session of the Executive Bureau,* Moscow, June 1946, pp. 4–12.

2. The views of the World Federation of Trade Unions on the Marshall Plan can be noted in the *Information Bulletin* in the last two months of 1947

and through 1948; World Federation of Trade Unions, *Sessions of the Executive Bureau held in Paris* November 18–24, 1947, pp. 51–52.

3. *American Federation of Labor Weekly News Service,* August 5, 1947.

4. William Green to Honorable Harry S. Truman, November 17, 1947.

5. *International Free Trade Union News,* January 1948.

6. Memorandum from W. C. Hushing to Green, January 8, 1948.

7. Statement of William Green, President of the American Federation of Labor, on the European Recovery Program, before the House Committee on Foreign Affairs, February 17, 1948, in files of A. F. of L.

8. Report by Irving Brown to the International Labor Relations Committee of the American Federation of Labor, December 4, 1946.

9. J. H. Oldenbroek to David Dubinsky, February 22, 1948.

10. Green to J. H. Oldenbroek, February 18, 1948; Oldenbroek to Green, February 19, 1948; Irving Brown to Louis Major, February 23, 1948.

11. Vincent Tewson, Evert Kupers, Louis Major, and Antoine Krier to William Green, February 25, 1948.

12. European Recovery Program, *Report of the International Trade Union Conference,* March 9 and 10, 1948, (London: Trades Union Congress, 1948), pp. 1–6.

13. *Ibid.,* p. 9.

14. *Ibid.,* p. 33.

15. *American Federation of Labor Weekly News Service,* June 22, 1948.

15a. *International Free Trade Union News,* October 1948.

16. *Ibid.,* September 14, 1948.

17. Statement was made by the Trades Union Congress Publicity Department, October 27, 1948.

18. *Ibid.*

19. *Ibid.*

20. Speech in *World Federation of Trade Unions, Session of the Executive Bureau, Paris,* January 17–22, 1949, p. 3.

21. *Ibid.,* p. 5.

22. *Ibid.,* p. 8.

23. *Ibid.,* p. 16.

24. *Ibid.,* p. 17.

25. *Ibid.,* p. 66.

26. Minutes of Executive Council, February 2, 1949.

27. Declaration of Matthew Woll, Chairman International Labor Relations Committee, on the Break-Up of the W.F.T.U., January 19, 1949. John P. Windmuller, *American Labor and the International Labor Movement 1940–53* (Ithaca, New York: The Institute of International and Labor Relations, 1953), deals with the developments in international labor.

28. *American Federation of Labor Weekly News Service,* April 8, 1949.

29. Minutes of Executive Council, May 16, 1949.

30. William Green to Vincent Tewson, May 19, 1949.

31. Preparatory International Trade Union Conference, Geneva, June 25–26, 1949.

32. *Ibid.*

33. Memorandum from George Meany to President William Green, July 19, 1949.

34. *Ibid.*

35. William Green to Vincent Tewson, September 19, 1949.

36. "Free Trade Unions Form the ICFTU," an undated mimeographed summary of events at the congress. See Louis Lorvin, *The International Labor Movement* (New York: Harper and Brothers, 1953), pp. 265–280, for details of the meeting.

37. *Le Figaro* (Paris), December 6, 1949.

38. Statement issued by Irving Brown and Elmer Cope, January 16, 1950.

39. *Free Trade Unions form the ICFTU.*

40. Minutes of Executive Council, January 31, 1950.

41. *Ibid.*, January 30, 1950; February 7, 1950; May 14, 1951.

42. *Report of the Proceedings of the Sixty-ninth Convention of the American Federation of Labor*, 1950, p. 505.

43. David Dubinsky to J. H. Oldenbroek, April 4, 1951; Matthew Woll and David Dubinsky to Oldenbroek, April 20, 1951; Green to Dubinsky, April 6, 1951.

44. Item 12 of the Agenda submitted in a letter from George Meany to Oldenbroek, June 1, 1951.

45. *Ibid.*

46. *Report on Second World Congress of the ICFTU*, October 2, 1951, in archives of the A. F. of L.

47. Irving Brown to William Green, August 2, 1951.

48. Minutes of Executive Council, August 10, 1951.

49. Notes on International Committee Meeting of the A. F. of L. held at A. F. of L. Building, Washington, D. C., June 18, 1952. Present were George Harrison, David Dubinsky, George Meany, W. McSorley, J. H. Oldenbroek, Vincent Tewson, William C. Doherty, William Green, Florence Thorne, Jay Lovestone, John Owen, and Thomas Kennedy. Notes taken by Lovestone.

50. *Ibid.*

51. Irving Brown reported this information to someone not fully identified in a letter dated December 3, 1945.

52. Pierre Monatte, *Trois Scissions Syndicales* (Paris: Les Editions Ouvrières, 1959), p. 7. "Quant à la troisième scissoin, celle de 1947, ne pourrait-on dire qu'elle est liée etroitement aux consequences de la seconde guerre mondiale puisequ'elle a été provoquée par les grèves Molotov de 1947, 48, lancées en travers de l'application du plan Marshall qui avait pour objet de ranimer l'économie des pays européens épuises par la guerre?

53. David Dubinsky to Robert Bothereau, August 30, 1947.

54. George M. Harrison to William Green, August 21, 1948; David Dubinsky to William Green, August 30, 1948.

55. A. Toldo, *Il Sindacalismo in Italia* (Milano: Centro Studi Sociali, 1953), pp. 79–85.

56. *Ibid.*, pp. 91–92.

57. Toldo, *op. cit.*, p. 98. Joseph La Palombara, *The Italian Labor Movement* (Ithaca, New York: Cornell University Press, 1957), pp. 22–24.

58. Toldo, *op. cit.*

59. La Palombara, *op. cit.,* p. 26.

60. Letters answering the A. F. of L. and C.I.O. request for unity were received from C.I.S.L. on July 21, 1952 and from the U.I.L. on June 12, 1952.

60a. Woll to Premier Themistocles Sophoulis, December 26, 1947, in Advisory and Review Branch, Historical Division, State Department (868–504/12–1647).

61. Irving Brown, "Report on Greece." Mimeographed and no date listed.

62. *Ibid.*

63. *Ibid.*

64. *Report of the Proceedings of the Seventieth Convention of the American Federation of Labor*, 1951, p. 463.

65. Joint statement of A. F. of L. and C.I.O. on Tunisian Question, April 15, 1952.

66. *International Free Trade Union News,* February 1953.

67. The letters addressed on August 22 and September 2, 1953 appeared in the *International Free Trade Union News,* October 1953.

68. *Ibid.,* December 1953.

69. *International Free Trade Union News,* February 1954.

70. *Special Bulletin of the Labor League for Human Rights of the American Federation of Labor,* October 1945.

71. Matthew Woll to Dean Acheson, April 26, 1946, Advisory and Review Section, Department of State (852.00/4–2446).

72. Woll to Honorable George C. Marshall, May 27, 1947, in Advisory and Review Section, Department of State (852.5043/5–2747).

73. Statement of Executive Council, March 31, 1948.

74. Woll to Honorable Dean Acheson, April 26, 1951.

75. George Meany to Cleon Swayze, June 5, 1951.

76. Statement of Executive Council, February 8, 1954.

77. *International Free Trade Union News,* July 1950.

77a. Declaration by the Executive Council on the Tito Regime, May 11, 1950.

78. Minutes of Executive Council, May 14, 1949.

79. Declaration by Matthew Woll, Chairman, International Labor Relations Committee, A. F. of L., April 14, 1949.

80. Meany to W. Averell Harriman, December 27, 1951.

81. *International Free Trade Union News,* November 1949.

82. *Ibid.*

83. *Report of the Proceedings of the Sixty-eighth Convention of the American Federation of Labor,* 1949, pp. 149, 157.

84. Minutes of the Executive Council, February 6, 1950.

85. Declaration on the International Crisis by the Executive Council of the A. F. of L., May 11, 1950.

86. Statement of the Executive Council, August 12, 1954.

87. *Report of the Proceedings of the Sixty-sixth Convention of the American Federation of Labor,* 1947, p. 685.

88. Woll to Secretary of War Robert Patterson, Acting Secretary of State Dean Acheson, and General Douglas MacArthur, March 13, 1947.

89. *Report of the Proceedings of the Sixty-seventh Convention of the American Federation of Labor*, 1948, pp. 489–490.

90. Minutes of Executive Council, May 17, 1951.

91. Minutes of Executive Council, January 30, 1952.

92. *Report of the Proceedings of the Sixty-eighth Convention of the American Federation of Labor*, 1949, pp. 436–437.

93. *Report of the Proceedings of the Seventieth Convention of the American Federation of Labor*, 1951, p. 466.

94. *Report of the Proceedings of the Seventy-second Convention of the American Federation of Labor*, 1953, p. 240.

95. *Ibid.*, p. 242. Italics in the original.

96. *Why Communist China Should not be Admitted to the United Nations* (New York: Free Trade Union Committee, American Federation of Labor, 1954).

97. *American Labor Looks at the World: IV* (New York: International Labor Relations Committee, American Federation of Labor, 1950) pp. 18–19.

98. *Ibid.*, p. 20.

99. *Report of the Proceedings of the Sixty-eighth Convention of the American Federation of Labor*, 1949, p. 126.

100. Irving Brown, "Labor in India," *International Free Trade Union News*, September 1949.

101. Brown, *op. cit.*, January 1950.

# XXIX

## Pan-America and the A. F. of L.

THE A. F. of L. officers were attacked within the ranks and from the outside for the friendship shown to the Mexican labor movement during the 1920's. Frank Duffy, who had reproved Gompers for his friendship with Mexican revolutionists, called the attention of the Executive Council to the Catholic-press attacks on the A. F. of L. for its defense of the Mexican labor movement. President William Green was aware that the policy of the Mexican government was "causing deep concern . . . to our members who profess the Catholic faith and he expressed apprehension lest the situation . . . threaten the friendly relations . . . between the labor movements of the two countries."[1] Notwithstanding their misgivings, the A. F. of L. leadership did not allow its views to be determined by religious considerations. When James Fitzpatrick, a delegate from the Waterbury, Connecticut, Central Labor Union, attacked the Mexican labor movement, he was called to task by Matthew Woll and Daniel Tobin, both of them practicing Roman Catholics. Tobin scolded Fitzpatrick for bringing the religious issue into a labor convention, and said, "we have no right . . . to tell the people of Mexico what they are going to do on their religious situation." Tobin described the efforts of the Executive Council "to obtain freedom of religion . . . in Mexico, as it has done in every instance wherever the question arises in any country of the world. But that is as far as we can go at the present time. . . . We have done a great deal for Mexico from a political standpoint, we are still working on it, and we are quite hopeful that we can help the situation, but we can't do it by heaping unnecessary abuse . . . on the working people of Mexico or the government of Mexico at this time."[2]

The A. F. of L. constantly found it difficult to maintain close relations with all the labor movements of the Latin-American countries. The rise and decline and shifts of organizations, the influences exerted by native governments, and the low level of unionization in many Latin-American countries made the permanent establishment of a Pan-American labor organization extremely difficult. In 1931 Green reported that national organizations had not been working and making contributions to the

Pan-American Federation of Labor; as a result, the organization had virtually gone out of existence.[3]

In the late 1930's Lombardo Toledano, a Mexican fellow traveler, tried to establish a Latin-American Federation with an anti-United States bias. The A. F. of L. regretted the growing division between the labor movements of North and South America. The Latin-American Labor Congress, held in Mexico City in September 1938, was attended by delegates from labor organizations in fourteen South American countries. The A. F. of L. believed that differences between the labor movements of North and South America were harmful, but it would not offer any public criticism.[4]

The Pan-American Federation of Labor, which the A. F. of L. helped to organize and had hoped to develop into a bridge between the North and South American labor movements, had ceased to exist. The labor movements of the South American countries were in many instances weak and without great resources. Nevertheless, the A. F. of L. officers did not want to lose all direct contact with Pan-American labor movements. In September 1942 Robert Watt of the A. F. of L. and Emil Rieve of the C.I.O. met in Santiago de Chile with labor representatives from Argentina and Chile to discuss the possibilities of calling an all-American labor conference. The revival of active interest in Latin-American labor was largely the work of George Meany who believed that the cooperation of the labor movements of the two continents would promote peace and the prosperity of the workers of all the North and South American countries. Following the visit of several delegations of Latin-American labor leaders in 1943, Meany sponsored the Spanish-language *Noticiario Obrero Norteamericano,* which has sought to build a bridge of understanding between the labor movements of the Western Hemisphere.

Privately, the Argentine delegation made it apparent that it wanted the American labor movement to call a conference. If American labor did not arrange such a meeting, the Argentines expected Lombardo Toledano to call a conference that would concern itself with political rather than economic problems.[5] Although the conference was never called, the A. F. of L. did not lose interest in Latin-American labor movements. The Federation responded to the appeal of the Bolivian Federation of Mine Workers when they asked for assistance in their negotiations of a new contract with the tin interests of their country. In the absence of President Green, Watt wrote the State Department asking the American "government to agree to such terms as will sustain and wherever possible improve the standards of living among working people. This is especially our hope in connection with contracts involving the production of tin." Watt had visited Bolivia with a group of Americans to inspect working conditions in the tin mines, which, he reported to the State Department, were deplorable. He asked that the United States seek to bring about an improvement.[6] In the same period the Free Trade Union Committee pledged A. F. of L. support to the Chilean Federation of Labor in its refusal to comply with the Chilean government's order dissolving the Nitrate Workers' Union. In a public statement the Free Trade Union Committee declared its solidarity with the workers of Chile in their struggle to maintain their rights of organization "in the face of such irresponsible governmental action and in an industry which [was] financed . . . by United States business interests and their representatives."[7]

The A. F. of L. through Matthew Woll, chairman of its International Committee, also announced in this period that the A. F. of L. could not collaborate with the Argentine Confederation of Labor which had fallen under the control of a Perónist henchman and had "degenerated into a political arm" of a dictator. According to Woll, by allowing itself to be used to advance the aims of Perón, the Argentine Federation of Labor had forfeited its status as a free democratic organization of labor.[8] Woll's estimate was subsequently verified by a labor mission which included three members of the Federation: Arnold Zander of the American Federation of State, County, and Municipal Employees; Michael Garriga, vice president of the Hotel and Restaurant Employees' Union; and William Munger of the United Hat, Cap, and Millinery Workers' Union.[9]

In 1947 several South American labor groups wrote to the A. F. of L. concerning their interest in attaining closer unity with the North American labor movement. Serafino Romualdi, who had been active in the International Ladies' Garment Workers' Union, was assigned by the A. F. of L. to work in South American affairs. Largely as a result of the efforts of Romualdi and Bernardo Ibanez, president of the Confederation of Labor of Chile, the labor organizations in several South American countries agreed to an Inter-American Labor Conference in 1948.[10] The conference planned for Lima, Peru, was sponsored by the Peruvian Confederation of Labor, the Chilean Confederation of Labor, the National Union of Workers' Syndicates of Panama, the National Union of Industrial Workers of Bolivia, and unions in Uruguay, Venezuela, Argentina, and Puerto Rico. In addition, a number of unions in Haiti, Colombia, Brazil, Ecuador, Costa Rica, and El Salvador agreed to send delegates. The A. F. of L. accepted an invitation to attend and assigned Phil Hannah, secretary of the Ohio Federation of Labor, James M. Duffy, president of the National Brotherhood of Operative Potters, and T. J. Lloyd of the Amalgamated Meat Cutters and Butcher Work-men of North America to its delegation. Romualdi accompanied the group.

When the delegates were appointed, Green observed that the A. F. of L. had been interested in developing "friendship and fraternity be-tween the free and democratic trade union movements of this country and those of our neighbors in North and South America."[11]

Before the Lima conference opened on January 9, 1948, the local Communists sought to organize a demonstration against "Yankee Im-perialism" and the Peruvian government was also hostile toward the meeting. Nevertheless, delegations from the following seventeen coun-tries opened the meeting on schedule: United States, Chile, Peru, Costa Rica, Colombia, Dutch Guiana, Mexico, Puerto Rico, El Salvador, Panama, Argentina, Bolivia, Brazil, Cuba, Dominican Republic, Vene-zuela, and Ecuador. The largest delegation—fifty-seven—was sent by Peru. The delegations from the Dominican Republic and Venezuela did not have power to make decisions, for they were fraternal delegates; the delegates from Ecuador were present as observers.

At the beginning of the conference, an Argentina delegate charged that the A. F. of L. delegation was financed by the State Department. At the demand of Serafino Romualdi, a committee was appointed to investigate the charges, and after a hearing, it condemned the charges. One of the more important results of the conference was the organiza-tion of the Inter-American Confederation of Workers; Bernard Ibanez was elected president. The Confederation was responsible for developing cooperation between and support of the organized labor movements of the Western Hemisphere.[12] The A. F. of L. Executive Council was pleased with the promise of closer relations between the workers of the North and South American continents and went on record as confident that the new Confederation would promote wider understanding and "greater good will in the Western Hemisphere because of the cooperation and the fraternity of the free labor movements of the member nations."[13]

The meeting of the Executive Committee in San Francisco in June 1948 requested the A. F. of L. to support the efforts of the Guatemalan workers employed by the United Fruit Company to improve their wages and working conditions, to cooperate with A. F. of L. representatives in an investigation of labor conditions in the Canal Zone, and to promote meetings between the National Farm Union of the United States and Mexican unions of farm workers in order to devise a common program of defense of mutual interests.

The A. F. of L. in 1948 protested the antilabor measures of the Peruvian government. It objected to the abolition of constitutional government and its replacement by a military dictatorship and asked that full civil rights be immediately restored to Peruvian citizens. President Green, on behalf of the A. F. of L., requested that the labor officials who had been arrested be given fair and public trials and that labor organizations from other American countries be allowed to participate in their defense. The A. F. of L. convention of 1948 reaffirmed its solidarity with Brother Arturo Sabroso Montoya, president of the Peruvian Confederation of Labor, and with other victimized labor leaders of Peru.[14] In December 1948 Vice Presidents Matthew Woll and David Dubinsky, the A. F. of L. consultants at the UN, submitted a detailed memorandum to Trygve Lie, Secretary General of the United Nations, reviewing the suppression of the rights of trade unions in Peru and requesting a discussion of the problem at a meeting of the Economic and Social Council.

In March 1949 President Green protested to the Venezuelan government its suppression of the Venezuelan Confederation of Labor. Green urged the military government of Venezuela to rescind its order dissolving the trade unions, to release the leaders who had been imprisoned, and to end the repression of trade union activities.[15]

The A. F. of L. Executive Council also sought improvements in the conditions of workers in the Canal Zone. After the report of the joint committee of the A. F. of L. and Inter-American Confederation of Workers had been made, the Council asked that improvements in housing for local-rate employees be introduced. It asked Congress to provide these workers with retirement and disability benefits, and to increase immediately the minimum wage for local-rate employees of the Panama Canal, Panama Railroad, and other government agencies up to the legal minimum paid in the United States. In addition, the Council proposed a gradual increase in all rates of pay until they reached the level prevailing in the United States. Finally, the Executive Council endorsed the extension of membership in the A. F. of L. unions to workers employed at local rates in the Canal Zone.[16]

In March 1950 the International Labor Relations Committee denounced the assassination of Louis Negreiros, Secretary of Organization of the Peruvian Confederation of Labor, by the secret police. The A. F. of L. strongly protested "against this latest crime committed by the Fascist-minded military dictatorship of Peru. We extend [our sympathy] to our brothers and sisters of Peru who are mourning with the family of Louis Negreiros, the death of such a valiant and courageous leader."[17]

This protest was not an isolated gesture; the A. F. of L. was always ready to help the Latin-American labor groups which often found themselves exposed to governmental persecution, suppression, and interference. When the Colombian government was dilatory in granting recognition to the Confederation of Labor of that country, President

Green addressed a letter to the Colombian Ambassador, Eduardo Zuleta-Angel, in Washington, explaining the difficult position of the Confederation because of the failure of his government to grant it legal recognition. President Green advised the government of Colombia to cease its hesitancy and grant recognition without delay. His appeal had some effect, for the Colombian government shortly afterward relaxed its ban.[18]

The A. F. of L. participated in the establishment of the Regional Organization for the Western Hemisphere of the International Confederation of Free Trade Unions. The founding conference was held in Mexico City, January 8–12, 1951, with fifty-five delegates, twenty-three substitutes, and eleven observers representing over 29 million trade unionists in twenty-seven countries.[19]

The A. F. of L. delegation was headed by Secretary-Treasurer George Meany and included Vice Presidents William F. McFetridge and William C. Doherty. The delegates discussed the cooperation of free trade unions against the Continental dictatorships which threatened the free labor movement and suggested an affirmative and aggressive program of economic development as a means of raising the standard of living in Latin America.[20]

The Executive Council directed special attention to the economic problems of Latin-American workers at its meeting in August 1951. Low living standards, the Council declared in a statement,

provide fertile ground for the growth of neo-Fascist totalitarian movements and give the Communists opportunity to renew their efforts to regain lost positions. We believe that the strengthening of the free labor movement offers the best guarantee that totalitarian forces will not prevail and, therefore, renew our pledge of active cooperation with the free trade unionists of Latin America in their endeavor to raise the standard of living of their respective peoples.

In this connection, the Executive Council strongly urges that the special prices above the world market levels which the United States Government is paying Latin America for materials which are needed for our defense stockpiling should be used primarily for better work and wage standards.

At the same time, we reaffirm our opposition to the granting of economic aid of any form to those Latin-American governments which have suppressed civil liberties and are denying the free exercise of trade union organization and action.[21]

In the same year the Executive Council, in response to an appeal from the Bolivian Confederation of Workers, requested the use of the offices of the Reconstruction Finance Corporation to permit a price for tin high enough to assure the Bolivian tin miners a decent wage and a continuation of social security benefits. Serafino Romualdi, stating the position of the Council, informed the State Department of the A. F. of L.'s concern with the impasse in the negotiations between Bolivia and the

United States which had led to the suspension of tin shipments and threatened to disrupt the Bolivian economy. The Federation feared that deteriorating economic conditions might seriously weaken the Bolivian government and lead to a resurgence of the totalitarian menace. The State Department assured the A. F. of L. that it was interested in a solution that would be satisfactory to both countries and was transmitting the views of the A. F. of L. to the Reconstruction Finance Corporation.[22]

On May 7, 1953 President George Meany wrote to the State Department recommending that the United States government resume the purchase of tin from Bolivia. Meany wanted the government to adopt a policy "that, compatible with our national requirements and interests, would allow the Bolivian Government to sell to the United States a sufficient amount of tin at a reasonable price, so that it can meet its normal expenditures and promote a program of welfare activities for the benefit of its people."[23]

In line with its general policy, the convention in 1953 objected to the United States extending economic or military aid to the Perónist dictatorship; and it requested the American government to ask for the transfer of the Tenth Pan-American Conference from Caracas, Venezuela, to another Latin-American city because of the suppression of the democratic trade unions in that country. As a move toward eliminating poverty from the Western Hemisphere, the convention also suggested that the United States sponsor an economic development program "akin to the Marshall Plan."[24]

The 1954 convention proposed a broad program of action for the United States in Latin America. It asked the United States to propose at the forthcoming Inter-American Economic Conference in Rio de Janeiro a concrete plan for fostering economic progress and eliminating poverty through joint development and use of natural resources and the industries of all the nations of the Americas. The convention supported closer economic collaboration with the Latin-American countries and an appropriation of at least 50 million dollars for technical aid to the Latin-American countries.[25]

The A. F. of L. submitted its program to the Inter-American Economic Conference held in Rio de Janeiro during November and December 1954. One of the points it emphasized was the need for stabilizing the prices of the principal raw materials exported by the Latin-American countries. The wide fluctuations in the prices of minerals and food products exported by these countries were, in the view of the A. F. of L., an obstacle to long-range planning and economic growth. The A. F. of L. asked the United States for greater direct aid for investment—modeled on the Marshall Plan—and for a fund to guarantee private investors against losses. The A. F. of L. program was not adopted.[26]

At its meeting in February 1955 the Executive Council urged the United States government to encourage the development of free labor unions and democratic forms in Chile, Colombia, Ecuador, and other Latin-American countries "where the totalitarians, Communist and Fascist, are again on the offensive. . . . Toward correcting the inadequacies and shortcomings of the United States policy at the recent Rio de Janeiro Inter-American Economic Conference, we reiterate our proposal that our government, as the representative of the most industrially developed and strongest democracy in the New World, extend adequate and generous material and technical assistance in the form of an Inter-American Marshall Plan, to our Latin-American neighbors with a view of evolving and executing a joint program for developing their natural resources, increasing their productivity, stabilizing the prices of their basic raw materials, and improving the purchasing power and living standards of the people."[27]

The A. F. of L. also participated in the attempt to devise a program for regularizing the movement of Mexican farm workers into the United States. The C.I.O. and the United Mine Workers of America were represented at the conference, and the Brotherhood of Maintenance of Ways Employees, which included many Mexican workers in its ranks, sent a special delegate. Representatives of the Inter-American Regional Organization of the I.C.F.T.U. were also present. The conference, meeting in Mexico City, issued a lengthy statement in which the problems arising out of the migration of Mexican workers into the United States were examined. The conferees agreed that the movement of Mexican workers, called *braceros*, to certain agricultural areas of the United States was beneficial to both countries, and that employers had been quick to take advantage of labor surpluses to exploit the migrants.

The delegates recommended that Mexican workers employed in the United States be allowed the right to organize into unions so that they might have protection against exploitation. More accurate labor requirements, it was believed, would make for fairer wages and would prevent surplus Mexican labor from competing with American workers. The conference suggested a stricter application of agreements in effect for importing labor and for new enforcement legislation in both countries. Organized labor of both countries, it was urged, should be allowed to participate in discussions of agreements. Finally, the labor unions of the United States and Mexico were advised to establish relations with their counterparts in the other countries for the purpose of facilitating an exchange of information concerning wages, hours, and working conditions.[28]

The Executive Council continued to be dissatisfied with the United States' failure to regulate the flow of Mexican migrant labor into the

Southwest. Speaking for the Executive Council, President Meany charged that the "Border Patrol was certifying the passage into the United States of Mexicans who came here illegally at a time when unemployment was rising among American workers in California, Texas, and the border states." This policy has been pursued, Meany said, to "create a surplus supply of labor for the corporate farms and big ranches of the Southwest so that wage standards can be depressed."[29] He recalled a number of measures long advocated by the A. F. of L. as a means of halting the illegal entry of the so-called wetbacks. These proposals included tighter supervision of entry by strengthening the border patrol, enactment of legislation which would make it an offense to hire wetbacks, and consultation with trade unions in the area before the United States Department of Labor certified the existence of a shortage of farm labor.[30]

At this time George Meany, acting at the request of the striking Honduran banana workers, appealed to the United Fruit Company to reach an honorable settlement with its striking workers. Similar appeals were made by the leaders of the C.I.O. and United Mine Workers of America.[31]

Each organization donated $1,000 to the strikers. The failure to reach an agreement led President Meany to request the United States government to put pressure on the recalcitrant employer who was providing grist for the Latin-American Communists' mill. Meany wired United States Ambassador Whiting Willauer in Tegucigalpa, Honduras: "While I appreciate the fact that the State Department cannot dictate to United Fruit Co. settlement of current Honduras strike, nevertheless AFL is most concerned over protraction of such conflict and over reports received from strike leaders that Company is unwilling to accept mediation proposals."[32] An agreement acceptable to the workers was reached in July 1954.

### REFERENCES

1. Minutes of Executive Council, August 26, 1926.
2. *Report of the Proceedings of the Forty-sixth Annual Convention of the American Federation of Labor,* 1926, pp. 364–365.
3. Minutes of Executive Council, January 14, 1931.
4. Matthew Woll, "Report on Mexican Labor Relations and Affairs," Minutes of Executive Council, January 11, 1939.
5. Memorandum from Robert J. Watt to President William Green, September 11, 1942.
6. Robert J. Watt to Honorable James F. Byrnes, August 17, 1945.
7. Special bulletin published by the Free Trade Union Committee of the League for Human Rights, American Federation of Labor, October 1945.
8. *American Federation of Labor Weekly News Service,* March 11, 1947.

9. *American Federation of Labor Weekly News Service,* March 28, 1947.

10. Memorandum from Serafino Romualdi to Matthew Woll, March 11, 1947.

11. *American Federation of Labor Weekly News Service,* November 25, 1947.

12. Report of the United States Delegation to the Lima, Peru Inter-American Trade Union Conference, January 10–13, 1948.

13. Minutes of Executive Council, February 3, 1948.

14. *Report of the Sixty-seventh Convention of the American Federation of Labor,* 1948, p. 493.

15. William Green to Military Government of Venezuela, March 1, 1949.

16. "Text of A. F. of L. Canal Zone Statement," *Inter-American Labor News,* March 1949.

17. Statement of A. F. of L. Labor Relations Committee, *International Labor News,* April 1950.

18. *Inter-American Labor News,* November 1950.

19. *Report of the Proceedings of the Seventieth Annual Convention of the American Federation of Labor,* 1951, p. 71.

20. *Inter-American Labor Bulletin,* February 1951.

21. *Report of the Proceedings of the Seventy-first Convention of the American Federation of Labor,* 1952, pp. 123–124.

22. Serafino Romualdi to Assistant Secretary of State Edward G. Miller, August 15, 1951; Acting Assistant Secretary of State Thomas C. Mann to Serafino Romualdi, August 27, 1951.

23. George Meany to Assistant Secretary of State John C. Cabot, May 13, 1953.

24. *Report of the Proceedings of the Seventy-second Convention of the American Federation of Labor,* 1953, p. 666.

25. *Report of the Proceedings of the Seventy-third Convention of the American Federation of Labor,* 1954, pp. 603–604.

26. Robert J. Alexander, "The American Labor Movement and the Rio Conference," *Inter-American Labor News,* January 1955.

27. *Report of the Proceedings of the Seventy-fourth Convention of the American Federation of Labor,* 1955, p. 283.

28. *Inter-American Labor Bulletin,* December 1953.

29. *Inter-American Labor Bulletin,* February 1954.

30. *Ibid.*

31. *Inter-American Labor Bulletin,* July 1954.

32. George Meany to Ambassador Whiting Willauer, July 8, 1954.

# XXX

## Communism and Corruption

THE response of the A. F. of L. to the efforts of the Communists to infiltrate the American labor movement was more direct and vigorous than its response to the infiltration by racketeers.

### RACKETEERING

Racketeering—the use of union office or power for personal profit—is not of recent origin. It has many manifestations: the embezzlement of funds, the acceptance of bribes by various union officers to overlook the violations of labor agreements, or of payments for calling off a strike or a campaign to organize a firm, the so-called strike or organization insurance, collusion between employers and union officers to create monopolies which are in the interest of employers and union officers rather than members of the union, and the acceptance of kickbacks and rebates for the placement of union health and welfare contracts.[1]

Almost from the beginning of its history, the A. F. of L. officers were aware of these dangers. Although they warned against allowing businessmen or other profit-seeking groups to use the labor movement for their personal ends, the Federation leadership did not devise any policy to meet this problem.

Frequently the charge of abuses related not only to corruption but to the regulations and restrictions which some unions imposed in the form of work rules and admission requirements. For example, the New York State Joint Legislative Committee on Housing, which investigated conditions in the building-construction industry between 1919 and 1922 exposed the cupidity and corruption of Robert P. Brindell, president of the Building Trades Council of New York City, and at the same time criticized the limitation of apprentices and other work rules. Inevitably union members tended to regard the problems raised by such criticism indifferently; they might consider the activities of a corrupt union officer as indefensible, but they would not condemn their own restrictive practices.[2] In testifying before the New York Legislative Committee, Samuel Gompers objected to any legal regulation. He denounced the abuses but argued against legal remedies. Education alone would encourage self-

421

restraint and self-regulation; these were the best and surest methods for eliminating abuses.³

New York State had no monopoly on labor abuses. In Illinois a legislative investigation exposed the tight control exercised by combinations of building contractors, material dealers, and labor unions over the allocation of jobs and materials. The largest part of the gains from the illicit combinations flowed into the pockets of employers, both in New York and Chicago, but the labor union performed a strategic function in the imposition of monopoly controls, since contractors who refused to join the collusive arrangements had their labor supply cut off. The A. F. of L. looked upon these matters as outside its province.

The general public, unacquainted with the constitutional theory of the A. F. of L., its customs, and lack of power, did not always absolve the general labor movement of responsibility for the wrongdoing of union officers. Even men like Father J. W. R. McGuire, who believed in trade unionism, were compelled to draw attention to the few faithless men who had betrayed the "high and holy cause of labor by dishonesty, by graft, by crime, yes, even by murder. And from time to time the argument is thrown into my teeth by those who know that I [Father McGuire] have always tried to uphold and defend the great labor movement, that there are men who are criminals even in official positions in the ranks of labor, and I have to hang my head in shame and acknowledge it."⁴ Father McGuire, a teacher in St. Viator's College, Bourbonville, Illinois, denounced labor racketeering before the 1930 convention and pleaded with the A. F. of L. to rid itself of the men who used the movement for selfish ends.⁵

In 1931 the Executive Council considered the published testimony that Theodore M. Brandle, a regional officer of the Structural Iron Workers' Union, had accepted a payment of $10,000 from the Iron League of New Jersey, an organization of employers. "No member of organized labor," the Council concluded, "can understand why it would be proper for a representative of organized labor [, who] because the position in which he is placed is bound to clash and differ strongly with employers over the settlement of wage and working conditions controversies, to accept payment for his services from the workers and at the same time accept a large payment from those employers who by force of circumstances he is compelled to oppose on many occasions, and after accepting such contributions divide it in a substantial way among a number of business agents of the organizations associated with him. Such action is unethical. It tends to reflect upon the good name, the standing and integrity of the organized labor movement."

Green told President Morrin of the Iron Workers' Union that "because the Executive Council is jealous of the good name of the American Federation of Labor, because it feels that the Council as well as the officers of the American Federation of Labor are duty bound to safeguard and protect the good name of the American Federation of Labor, I was directed to communicate with you and request you in the name of the Executive Council to take such action as may seem necessary as a result of the testimony given in the trial of Mr. Brandle in order to protect and safeguard the integrity, the good name and the standing of your own International Union, as well as the organized labor movement as represented by the American Federation of Labor."[6] Morrin was not eager to take immediate action

A year later Green again wrote to Morrin and informed him that the Executive Council was

clothed with the responsibility of protecting the standing, the integrity and the honor of the American Federation of Labor. It is compelled, by force of circumstances, to bring to the attention of an International Union facts and information when such facts and information reflect upon the good name and the standing of the American labor movement. . . . It must in justice to the men and women who make up our great labor movement, bring the matter forcibly to the attention of the proper officers for consideration and action. . . . On the other hand, the Executive Council makes no charges. It has no authority to make charges. Under the authority granted you and your associates when your International Union was granted a charter by the American Federation of Labor, you have the power to deal with this case . . . and neither the Executive Council nor any other International Union has any authority to do so.[7]

In the end the Iron Workers expelled Brandle and four associates.[8]

In the same year at the orders of the Executive Council, Green discussed with the president of the International Union of Operating Engineers the charges of corruption that had been made against several officers of that union. Among those so charged was Vice President Joseph Fay, who was to be convicted of extortion several years later.[9] John Possehl, president of the Engineers' Union, said that there was no widespread corruption in his union.

Serious abuses were shown to have existed at this time in the New York local of the International Alliance of Theatrical Stage Employees and Moving Picture Machine Operators of the United States and Canada. An investigation by Edward McGrady revealed that the president of Local 306 in New York, Sam Kaplan, was a manufacturer of moving-picture machine supplies and an employer of labor; that his salary had increased from about $11,000 a year to over $20,000 a year; that in addition his union made him annual presents of $10,000 and sometimes $20,000; and that he employed nonunion help and sold the goods manufactured under nonunion conditions to employers with whom he bar-

gained. Green, reviewing these facts for International President William
C. Elliott, said that "the Executive Council appreciates fully its lack of
authority to interfere in the internal affairs of a Local Union or of an
International or National Organization. It respects the jurisdictional
power and authority of National and International Organizations. On the
other hand, the Council is clothed with authority to administer and direct
the affairs of the American Federation of Labor between conventions
and to guard jealously the welfare of labor." In another letter Green
told Elliott that "the facts warrant decisive action on your part. Un-
pleasant as the duty may be, it seems that the duty cannot be evaded."[10]

Kaplan was convicted of income tax evasion and lost his office. Elliott
subsequently resigned the presidency of the International. He was succeeded by George E. Browne.

There was no public mention of the efforts of the A. F. of L. to stimulate more vigorous action against labor criminals. The 1932 convention
condemned racketeering and said that too "often legitimate trade union
activities are described as racketeering. . . . That there is room here and
there for improvement within the labor movement is not to be denied,
but the greater danger is from without."[11]

In the meantime, a serious threat to the unions in Illinois, especially
those located in and around Chicago, came with a gangster invasion. In
a statement on this threat, the Illinois Federation of Labor called for
defensive trade union action in the face of a menace which had reached
a stage that endangered "the future of some of the organizations."[12]
Several A. F. of L. officers conferred with the mayor of Chicago and
police officials about protection for the unions endangered by this
invasion.[13]

The conventions of both 1933 and 1934 spoke out against corrupt
elements in the labor movement and asked that they be purged by the
national and international organizations. In 1935 Thomas Dewey was
appointed to investigate racketeering in New York County. Matthew
Woll, David Dubinsky, and Joseph Weber conferred with him to determine what matters he regarded as within the scope of his investigation and to offer the cooperation of the A. F. of L. in rooting out criminal
elements from the labor movemeint. Dewey told them that he did not
regard the occasional violence arising in labor disputes as coming within
the area of his investigation. The committee reported to Dewey that
selfish elements had at times invaded labor organizations and used them
for selfish and improper purposes; they asked for a vigorous prosecution of such criminals.[14]

Although the 1935 convention did not specifically discuss the question,
it approved a resolution instructing the Executive Council to initiate a

campaign to wipe out racketeering and gangsterism in the labor move-ment.[15]

In the meantime, the election of George E. Browne as head of the International Alliance of Theatrical Stage Employees was the beginning of a scandal which was to shake the labor movement. Browne started his labor career as business agent of Local 2 in Chicago. In 1932 he ran a complete slate against the International Alliance's administration and was defeated by a vote of 608 to 236.[16] The rest of the Browne ticket did not fare any better. In 1934 at the next convention, Elliott refused to run for reelection, and it has been charged that the convention was dominated by criminals acting under the direction of the Capone gang.[17] In alliance with Willie Bioff and with the aid of leading Chicago gang-sters, Browne used his union to extort hundreds of thousands of dollars from the motion-picture industry. Browne's illicit activities were not publicly known, and in 1936 he was elected to the Executive Council.

The Building Service Employees' Union was another organization rotten at the top. With the aid of underworld allies, George Scalise, a professional thug, had become the union's international president in 1937. The Executive Council of the A. F. of L. was not happy about Scalise's elevation to the top post of an international union, but Scalise was able to convince the Council that he had long redeemed his youth-ful errors and now sought only to serve his members and the labor movement. There was not much the Council could do, in any event. As head of the union for three years, Scalise looted its treasury of hundreds of thousands of dollars and extorted thousands more from hapless land-lords and property owners who dealt with his organization in New York. A reckoning came to him in 1940. District Attorney Thomas E. Dewey secured sufficient evidence to bring him to trial and convict him of grand larceny, for which he was sentenced to a long term in prison.[18]

The revelations of graft in the highest quarters of the Building Service Employees and the reports that all was not well in the Stage Employees and Moving Picture Operators' Union prompted the International Ladies' Garment Workers' Union to seek A. F. of L. action. The Garment Workers' delegation requested the 1940 convention to authorize the Executive Council to order the removal by a national or international union of any officers convicted of moral turpitude or of using their official union positions for personal gain.

The Executive Council, aware of the mounting criticism among labor people and the general public, pointed to the relatively few malefactors in its ranks and argued that the national and international unions were autonomous organizations. In accordance "with the voluntary as well as the democratic procedure established and followed by the American

Federation of Labor . . . the American Federation of Labor could not confer upon these organizations full and complete power to administer their own affairs and at the same time reserve to itself the right to exercise dictatorial control."[19]

During this convention Joseph Fay's assault on David Dubinsky, when the latter refused to withdraw his union's resolution on racketeering, publicized the existence of widespread corruption. Fay, a vice president of the International Union of Operating Engineers, had been drinking and he became incensed at the proposal of the Ladies' Garment Workers.[20] The resolution, however, was not approved; instead, the convention suggested that all national and international unions adopt rules or amendments to their constitutions which would enable them to take necessary action against officers and members who had been found guilty of betraying the trust imposed on them or who had used the union or their official position for personal and illegal gain. However, "whenever the Executive Council has valid reason to believe that a trade union official is guilty of any such offense, and the National or International Union in question seemingly evades its responsibility, the Executive Council shall be authorized to apply all of its influence to secure such action as will correct the situation."[21]

The same convention reelected George E. Browne as twelfth vice president, although the International Ladies' Garment Workers' Union publicly refused to vote for him. Browne was soon to be indicted for extortion. He was convicted and served a sentence in prison.

Soon after the adjournment of the 1940 convention, the Executive Council had an occasion to act under the provision governing the "suppression" of racketeering. District Council No. 18 of Brooklyn, New York, complained to the Council that its efforts to remove Jake Wellner, who had been convicted of extortion and had served a sentence, were being frustrated by the National Executive Board of the Painters' Union which insisted that the District Council recognize Wellner as business agent or have its charter revoked. President L. P. Lindeloff claimed that Wellner had been wrongfully convicted and that he had worked for two years at his trade as a painter after his release from prison. The Executive Council decided to find out whether or not the Brotherhood of Painters, Decorators, and Paperhangers was trying to evade its responsibilities.[22]

When Matthew Woll inquired into the charges made by the District Council, he learned that Wellner had been tried and convicted by the District Council, removed from office, and prohibited from holding office for life. The verdict had been approved by the District Council by a vote of 15 to 5. After the General Executive Board of the Painters' International decided that the charges were unsubstantiated, the District Council appealed to the courts, which found the General Executive

Board had acted within its powers. Woll argued that the resolution under which the Executive Council acted only authorized the A. F. of L. to request information of or to advise an international union. "It was not," according to Woll "a mandatory order; neither does this provision delegate to the Federation the authority to become a reviewing body of wrongdoing . . . in appeals from local unions chartered directly by national and international unions which have exclusive jurisdiction and authority over local unions."[23]

Unsympathetic to the position of the District Council, Woll noted its right to appeal to the General Executive Board of the Painters' Union for redress. He stated firmly that the "Federation has no compulsory or disciplinary power. The power delegated to it is that of the use of its influence." Although he was distressed by the failure of the general public to appreciate the limitations imposed upon the A. F. of L., Woll believed that the Executive Council should limit itself to persuading unions to follow a policy consistent with the ideals of the labor movement.[24]

The 1941 convention approved the action taken to stimulate greater activity against wrongdoing by various affiliates; it went further and directed all central bodies to refuse to seat any union delegates convicted of serious crimes which reflected dishonor on the trade union movement.[25]

The restrained action of the A. F. of L. had almost no effect upon the multiple causes responsible for established and systematized racketeering. Corruption existed in highly competitive services and markets and was usually accompanied by patterns of irregular employment. On the docks of New York where virulent and widespread racketeering existed, it had its origin in the 1890's when the docks were unorganized and when employment was sought by thousands of newly arrived immigrant workers. Reports of kickbacks and extortion on the New York docks had long been common. Not until the investigations of the New York Crime Commission in 1952 was the extent of racketeering and the viciousness of some of the practices on the docks clearly known. Extortion, forced borrowing from loan sharks, favoritism in the allocation of jobs, kickbacks of wages, as well as payroll padding, nonenforcement of contract rules, and outright bribery were evident on a large scale. Dubinsky wrote to Meany that the disclosures before the New York State Crime Commission point up "very clearly the problem before the A. F. of L. to which our union called attention . . . in 1940 at the A. F. of L. convention. . . . This problem is more acute today than it ever was."[26]

Dubinsky was sensitive to the traditional restriction upon the right of the A. F. of L. to intervene in the affairs of affiliates, but he raised the question whether the resolution which had authorized the Executive Council to "apply all of its influence to secure such action as will correct the situation" might not be a vehicle for taking action. Meany replied, "it is my position that the Council has the power now to apply all of its influence in order to correct a situation such as the press reports indicate exists in the New York waterfront. . . I intend to bring this matter to the attention of the Executive Council at the forthcoming meeting."[27]

When the Council met on February 2, Meany requested that some action be taken on the New York longshore situation. Considering the problem from a trade union angle, Meany described the victimization of the longshoreman by the hiring or pier boss; and he stressed that it was the job of the A. F. of L. "to see that the Union protects its members. . . . We ought to tell the Union that it is not protecting its members and we would like to have them . . . [the officers of the International Longshoremen's Association] let us know within a reasonable time what they have done about it."[28]

At the direction of the Council, Meany wrote to the officers of the International Longshoremen's Association about the testimony before the New York Crime Commission which showed that the "workers of the Port of New York are being exploited . . . and that they are not receiving the protection which they have a right to expect as trade unionists and members of your organization. . . . Your relationship with the A. F. of L. demands that the democratic ideals, clean and wholesome free trade unionism must be immediately restored within your organization and all semblance of crime, dishonesty and racketeering be forthwith eliminated."[29] The long list of corrupt practices—the acceptance of gifts and bribes by local and international officers, the persistence of the shape-up and other objectionable job practices, the toleration of known criminals as officers, and the reign of crime and lawlessness—demanded, Meany said, immediate remedial action. Acknowledging that the A. F. of L. had no authority to undertake the clean-up job itself, Meany concluded: "We do feel, however, that your international union must forthwith take the necessary action to remove any and all of those representatives who may be participants in these unlawful activities."[30]

When the Longshoremen's officers raised the question of the autonomy of affiliates, Meany informed them that there was no intention of modifying the traditional position; nevertheless, he made it clear that autonomy was not absolute. "The exercise of autonomy by affiliated units in an organization such as ours presupposes the maintenance of minimum standards of trade union decency. No affiliate of the A. F. of L. has any right to expect to remain an affiliate 'on the grounds of organizational autonomy' if its conduct, as such, is to bring the entire movement into disrepute. Likewise, the cloak of organizational autonomy cannot be used to shield those who have forgotten that the prime purpose of a trade union is to protect and advance the welfare and interests of the individual members of that trade union."[31]

The Executive Council requested the International Longshoremen's Association to institute the following reforms: (1) the abolition of the shape-up method of employment, which required longshoremen to assemble before the piers so that the hiring bosses would select workers for jobs; (2) the removal from office and the elimination from the union of all union officers who accepted gifts and bribes from employers; (3) the removal from positions of authority in the I.L.A. of all union representatives with criminal records; and (4) the democratization of any local unions which did not abide by the recognized democratic procedures of the A. F. of L. The executive officers of the I.L.A. replied that they were willing to abolish the shape-up, install fair procedures in disciplining of members, and discuss the introduction of a requirement prohibiting persons with criminal records from holding office. They defended the I.L.A. and claimed that much of the information given before the Crime Commission had distorted the facts and that this was part of a studied campaign to destroy individuals who had served the labor movement well.[32] When the A. F. of L. Executive Council was unwilling to accept this statement of the I.L.A. as complying with the formal request, the I.L.A. officers asked for and received permisison to appear before the Council and present their case directly.[33]

On August 10, 1953 the Executive Councils of the two organizations met, and Vice President Harrison and President Meany insisted that the I.L.A. had to meet the terms laid down by the A. F. of L. Executive Council if it were to retain its affiliation. When the I.L.A. officers refused, the Executive Council recommended to the 1953 convention that the charter of the I.L.A. be revoked.[34] After the I.L.A. had been expelled, the convention directed that a new union of longshoremen be chartered. This action marked a new policy; heretofore the A. F. of L. had not invaded a jurisdiction which had been occupied by an expelled union. The Federation had always maintained that the reasons for expulsion would be eliminated and that the expelled union would rejoin the family of organized labor. In the present situation, however, the Executive Council believed it was obligated to rescue the New York longshoremen from the gangsters and criminals who had fastened upon them. The Federation embarked upon an extensive drive in behalf of the Brotherhood of Longshoremen, but it was unable to dislodge the I.L.A. from the control of the New York Port.

The expulsion of the I.L.A. represented a significant shift in A. F. of L. policy, for unions could no longer hide their corruption behind the principle of autonomy. Under the leadership of George Meany, the A. F. of L. had finally insisted that it could exact minimum standards as the price of affiliation. Since his views encountered little opposition from other members of the Executive Council, it is reasonable to suppose that if his predecessors had taken similar action they might have succeeded in preventing the worst abuses. At any rate, the A. F. of L.'s position was now clear; its affiliates had to maintain standards of conduct which would free the labor movement from suspicion of harboring and overlooking criminal activities.

### COMMUNISM

The A. F. of L. never faltered in its opposition to Communism and dictatorship. Objecting to Communism as an undemocratic movement threatening the liberties of mankind, the Federation fought the attempts of Communist organizations, open and disguised, to gain control of the economic organizations of labor. Throughout the 1920's the A. F. of L. conventions had rejected the frequently introduced resolutions suggesting the reopening of diplomatic relations between the United States and the Soviet Union.[35]

In 1926 a number of labor union officers requested that the American trade unions send a delegation to the Soviet Union. The chief promoter of the plan was Albert F. Coyle, the editor of *Locomotive Engineers Journal;* he had no standing in the A. F. of L., but he had been able to gain the support of several officers of the A. F. of L. unions. The leader of the delegation was Timothy Healy, president of the International Brotherhood of Stationary Firemen and Oilers. The movement was stimulated by a lecture tour of A. A. Purcell, an English labor leader who had served as president of the British Trades Union Congress, and who spoke in many sections of the United States in favor of closer relations with the Soviet Union. Coyle had asked Green to serve on the committee or to nominate someone in his place. Green was informed that the sponsors had "agreed that no Communists, Socialists, or even any of our Jewish brethren should be asked to make the trip with us, but only men of outstanding position and repute in the labor movement . . . in no way connected with any of the radical groups."[36] Green was not in favor of sending such a commission, for he believed that the report of such a group might be interpreted as the official view of the American labor movement. He was also suspicious of the sources from which this commission would be financed. The Executive Council, after considering the question, decided that no "good purpose could be served through such action. In fact, we seriously doubt the good faith of such a self-constituted Commission."[37] The Council recalled the rejection of a similar proposal by the A. F. of L. convention of 1925. When the proposal came indirectly before the 1926 convention, the delegates rejected the invitation.[38]

The A. F. of L. took a strong position against the recognition of the Soviet Union until such time as it would disavow "its declaration of world revolution as made through the Third International." Granting the right of the Russian people to "adopt the Soviet form of government and to administer their own political and governmental affairs free from interference by any other nation," the Executive Council nevertheless insisted that the Soviet Union "respect and recognize the right of all other nations to do likewise."[39] Because much as the A. F. of L. was opposed to Communism on philosophic and humanistic grounds, its primary objection was based upon the Soviet Union's interference in the affairs of other nations and its attempts to subvert and control the American labor movement.

In 1933 the A. F. of L. submitted a long brief containing evidence "of subversive activity on the part of Communists in the United States and of a direction of such activity from Moscow, where a group of international organizations, of which the Communist or Third International is but one, operate under the command of the one dictatorship."[40] Green warned that it was imperative that, as requisite to recognition of the Soviet government, "positive guarantees that subversive activities inspired and directed . . . by the Communist organization and its created auxiliaries in Russia shall cease in the United States and that none of the various agencies of International Communist propaganda will continue to function in the United States under the direction or with the assistance of the Soviet Government, or its immediate subsidiary organizations."[41] Green asked for an appointment with President Roosevelt in order to place the A. F. of L.'s case before him. Green's objections were formally met when Maxim Litvinoff, People's Commissar for Foreign Affairs, agreed to a stipulation that the Soviet Union would refrain from propagandizing in the United States.[42] Of course, the stipulation had no effect on the Communist auxiliaries operating in the United States, especially within the labor movement.[43]

In 1934 the Executive Council assailed the Communist infiltration of the labor movement and warned the unions to guard against subversion. The Council submitted a three-point program for combatting the Communists: (1) expulsion from the trade unions of those who had been shown to be associated with Communist organizations; (2) alertness on the part of the officers and members of unions to prevent the imposition of Communist doctrines through violence or deceit; and (3) deportation of alien Communists to their native lands.[44]

The next convention in 1935 amended the constitution so that "no organization officered or controlled by Communists or advocating the violent overthrow of our institutions, shall be allowed representation or recognition in any Central Labor Body or State Federation of Labor."[45]

Daniel Tobin, chairman of the convention's law committee, drew a distinction between a member holding radical ideas, which in itself could not be regarded as a cause for sanction, and one who was an adherent of the Communist Party. John L. Lewis interpreted the remarks of one of the delegates as a reflection upon his union, and he rose "to hurl the charges back into his teeth. The United Mine Workers," he declared, "has made some contributions in the mass-production industry, and we are going to continue that course, but we are not supporting any Communist organization."[46] The proposal was adopted, and it gave the central bodies the authority to expel any delegate whom they could prove was a member of the Communist Party.

The A. F. of L. supported the work of the House Un-American Activities Committee headed by Congressman Martin Dies. In 1939 the Executive Council asked for a continuation of this committee with sufficient appropriations to carry on its work.[47] In a circular letter to representatives and senators, Green reported that the 1939 A. F. of L. convention had endorsed this committee's work.[48]

During World War II, the A. F. of L. favored aid to the Soviet Union, but it did not modify its opposition to the activities of the Communists. Even during the war, the Federation officers retained their suspicion of the intentions of the Communists and of the Soviet government. In 1942 Green asked the State Department to help locate Henrich Erlich and Victor Alter, two Polish Socialists who had been arrested by the Soviet military forces in the fall of 1939. After being in prison for two years they had been sentenced to death in August 1941. They had been released in accordance with the Soviet-Polish pact, however, in September 1941 and invited to participate in the work of the Polish National Council in London. On December 16, 1941 the Polish Embassy informed American friends of the two Polish Socialists that they had again been arrested by the Soviet forces.[49] Erlich and Alter were subsequently executed by the Soviet government and their execution was deplored by Green and other leaders of American labor.

Immediately after World War II, the A. F. of L. exposed the aggressive policies being pursued by the Soviet Union. The Council charged the Soviet Union with trampling "on the high principles proclaimed by the United Nations, denying fundamental freedoms to the citizens of other countries and depriving them of self-determination."[50]

The A. F. of L. consistently looked upon the Communist movement as an instrument of the Soviet government. Testifying before the House Committee on Un-American Activities, Green denounced the "devious techniques and covert tactics" of the Communists.[51] The Federation did not, however, believe that the suppression of Communism or Communist propaganda could be achieved by outlawing the Party. In Green's opinion, legislation suppressing the Communist Party was

altogether alien to the spirit and letter of our Constitution to outlaw ideas. The Constitution of the United States holds inviolate the inalienable right of every American to believe what he will and to speak freely what he believes. Beliefs, be they political or religious or, as in the case of communism, a combination of both, may not be outlawed. Freedom of speech or of the press likewise may not be abridged by Congress. The very strength of democracy lies in its unswerving adherence to the rights of free speech, free inquiry, and free interchange of ideas. . . . To surrender one iota of our basic constitutional freedoms is to detract from the very strength that makes democracy unassailable and to confess of a weakness in the democratic order which does not in reality exist. Totalitarian methods have no place in a democracy. Americans must reject their use, no matter how laudable the ends to which such methods may be put.[52]

The A. F. of L. also opposed the bills introduced in 1948 by Senator Karl Mundt and Congressman Richard Nixon and in 1949 by Senators Karl Mundt, Olin D. Johnston, and Homer Ferguson which were designed to outlaw the Communist Party. Green strongly opposed the Mundt-Johnston bill which would have set up a Subversive Activities Control Board of three "with extraordinary powers over minority political parties and voluntary organizations of citizens."[53]

The A. F. of L. took the same view of a revised bill introduced by Senators Karl Mundt and Richard Nixon in 1950. The Federation again rejected legislation that gave wide powers to a Subversive Activities Control Board, believing it to be a dangerous power to place in the hands of any body of administrators. The A. F. of L. officers thought that the Communist danger could be more effectively met by education and the improvement of the economic position and the broadening of the rights of American citizens.[54]

In its constant watch over Communist activities through the years, the Federation learned to identify Communist propaganda, no matter how well disguised. When the Communist-inspired Stockholm peace appeal was launched, the Executive Council immediately labeled it "a rank fraud" and urged "every working man and working woman to spurn the peddlers of this spurious proposition."[55]

The Executive Council said that the peace petition was designed to weaken the democratic world. The Stockholm peace advocates did not oppose all aggression with all weapons, the Council noted, but only the weapon in which the United States held superiority. The Council warned that if the "fake peace maneuver were to succeed, were the United States to fall into the Russian bear-trap of banning atomic weapons—

while Russia rejects America's plan for their effective international inspection, control, and elimination—the possibility for Communist world domination by the Soviets would be enormously enhanced."[56]

Because the A. F. of L. regarded the International Trade Conference, scheduled for Moscow in April 1952, as a Communist maneuver to create doubt and disunion among the nations of the free world, Green rejected an invitation to send a delegate. In his reply he explained his conviction that every American businessman, banker, economist, and labor officer should boycott the meeting because it was a "transparent trick by the Soviet regime."[57]

In 1954 the A. F. of L. was asked to approve the merger of the Amalgamated Meat Cutters and Butcher Workmen of North America with the Fur and Leather Workers' Union, which had been under control of Communist functionaries over the years and had been expelled from the C.I.O. for following the Communist line. Patrick Gorman, secretary-treasurer of the Meat Cutters' Union, promised that the Fur and Leather Workers' Union would be completely dissolved and that its local officers would be required to sign non-Communist affidavits. Meany commented that the name, "American Federation of Labor belongs to all the unions of the A. F. of L. and if one union is going to lend the name A. F. of L. to a group that is under communist domination . . . the A. F. of L. has a great interest in it."[58] Meany informed Gorman that the Executive Council had refused to accept a Communist-dominated organization into the fold, and the Fur and Leather Workers' Union under the leadership of Ben Gold and his associates "have never failed . . . to follow the Communist propaganda line through all its twists and turns."[59] Meany wrote to the officers of the Meat Cutters' Union that the A. F. of L. would gladly accept the members of the Fur and Leather Workers' Union into its ranks, but it could not accept the leadership which had openly identified itself with the Communist Party. In their reply, the officers of the Meat Cutters' Union told Meany that they had been assured by President Abe Feinglass of the Fur and Leather Workers' Union that no Communist activities of any nature would be tolerated. They offered two proposals:

1. If the Federation cannot give its outright approval, then it should give its temporary approval, because of its faith in an International Union which, as you say, is "one of our oldest and honored affiliates," of the A. F. of L., and which the Council knows is thoroughly anti-Communist. It would agree, under the circumstances, that in approving or temporarily approving the absorption . . . it will watch closely and will ask the Amalgamated to expel the group or any offending segment thereof, if the Fur and Leather Workers engage in any subversive activities.

2. Inasmuch as there is no charge of Communist activity against the 45,000

leather workers, the Federation, in approving or temporarily approving, could insist upon the appointment of an observer of the New York activities of the Fur and Leather Workers' group, and could ask for the expulsion of the group if the provisions of the absorption agreemennt are abridged in any way by the Fur Workers' Group.[60]

Although the Executive Council would not approve the merger, it acknowledged that the Meat Cutters' Union, under the constitution of the A. F. of L., had complete autonomy to decide whether it wanted to absorb the Fur and Leather Workers' Union.[61]

In spite of the Executive Council's objections, the Amalgamated resolved to carry through its agreement to merge with the Fur and Leather Workers' Union, although the final decision would be made by the conventions of the two organizations. Insisting that they were doing everything possible to eliminate the influence of the Communists, the Meat Cutters' officers pointed to the requirement that all officers of the Fur and Leather Workers' Union sign non-Communist affidavits, the suppression of the *Fur and Leather Worker,* the closing down of White Lake Camp, and the transfer of all funds of the Fur and Leather Workers' Union to the Amalgamated.

At the same time Max Federman, who had been a leader of the fur workers affiliated with the A. F. of L., requested approval of the merger between the two unions. The Executive Council, after considerable discussion, agreed that it "could not . . . take the position that the Amalgamated Meat Cutters and Butcher Workmen of North America are not attempting to meet the requirements of the American Federation of Labor; but the Council cannot truthfully say that they had met the requirements of the A. F. of L., although they were moving in that direction."[62]

Vice President Dubinsky believed that the Amalgamated had performed a good job of cleaning out the Communists from the old New York locals of the Furrier's Union, and he agreed that the job could not be finished during the short period in which the merger had been in effect. In response to the repeated requests of the Amalgamated as well as in recognition of its efforts to eliminate Communists from official positions, the Executive Council finally approved the merger at its meeting in October 1955.[63]

The A. F. of L.'s policy toward Communism underwent no basic changes from the beginning of the Russian Revolution to the time of the A. F. of L.-C.I.O. union. It had no illusions about the Soviet Union; it resolutely opposed the sending of an American trade union delegation to the Soviet Union. The A. F. of L. thought that such an invitation was merely another means of lending "a cover of genuineness and international free trade union respectability to the State company unions."[64]

The Federation did not think it was necessary to visit the Soviet Union to see that its government denied the elementary democratic rights to its people; it would no more allow its officers to be a guest of the Soviet autocrats than of "Hitler, Mussolini, and Franco. . . . Everything we have said about the Nazi, Fascist and Falangist totalitarian regime[s] holds with equal force for the Krushchev regime."[65]

## REFERENCES

1. Philip Taft, "Corruption and Racketeering in the Labor Movement," *New York State School of Industrial and Labor Relations Bulletin No. 38*, February 1958, is an attempt to explain the reasons for the development and persistence of these practices.

2. State of New York, *Intermediate Report of the Joint Legislative Committee on Housing* (Albany: J. B. Lyon Company, Printers, 1922).

3. Mimeographed copies of Gomper's testimony were examined. A summary of his views can be found in *Legislative Document No. 48: Final Report of the Joint Committee on Housing* (Albany: J. B. Lyon Company, Printers, 1923), p. 57.

4. *Report of the Proceedings of the Forty-eighth Annual Convention of the American Federation of Labor*, 1928, p. 245.

5. *Report of the Proceedings of the Fiftieth Annual Convention of the American Federation of Labor*, 1930, pp. 187–188.

6. William Green to P. J. Morrin, June 19, 1931.

7. Green to Morrin, July 27, 1932.

8. Morrin to Green, June 23, 1932.

9. Minutes of Executive Council, July 20, 1932.

10. Green to William C. Elliott, July 27, 1932; August 22, 1932.

11. *Report of the Proceedings of the Fifty-second Annual Convention of the American Federation of Labor*, 1932, pp. 297–298.

12. "To Trade Unionists and All Other Interested Citizens in Illinois," from the Illinois Federation of Labor, R. G. Sonderston, president, and Victor O. Olander, secretary-treasurer, January 9, 1933.

13. *American Federation of Labor Weekly News Service*, May 20, 1933.

14. Minutes of Executive Council, August 5 and October 6, 1935.

15. *Report of the Proceedings of the Fifty-fifth Annual Convention of the American Federation of Labor*, 1935, p. 589.

16. *Proceedings of International Alliance Stage Employees and Moving Picture Operators of the United States and Canada, Thirty-first Convention*, 1932, pp. 147–418.

17. Malcolm Johnson, *Crime on the Labor Front* (New York: McGraw-Hill Book Company, Inc., 1950), pp. 19–20.

18. *Ibid.*, pp. 34–54.

19. *Report of the Proceedings of the Sixtieth Annual Convention of the American Federation of Labor*, 1940, p. 64.

20. *The New York Times,* November 21, 1940.

21. *Report of the Proceedings of the Sixtieth Annual Convention of the American Federation of Labor,* 1940, p. 505.

22. Minutes of Executive Council, February 13, 1941.

23. Report of Matthew Woll to Executive Council, May 27, 1941.

24. Matthew Woll to William Green, May 27, 1941.

25. *Report of the Proceedings of the Sixty-first Annual Convention of the American Federation of Labor,* 1941, p. 543.

26. David Dubinsky to George Meany, December 30, 1952.

27. Meany to Dubinsky, January 15, 1953.

28. Minutes of Executive Council, February 2, 1953.

29. George Meany to the Officers and Members of the International Longshoremen's Association, February 3, 1953.

30. *Ibid.*

31. *Ibid.*

32. To the Executive Council of the American Federation of Labor from the Executive Council of International Longshoremen's Association, May 15, 1953.

33. Meany to Joseph P. Ryan, May 26, 1953.

34. Minutes of Executive Council, September 21 and 23, 1953.

35. The attitude of the A. F. of L. can be noted in *Report of the Proceedings of the Forty-fifth Annual Convention of the American Federation of Labor,* 1925, pp. 333–334.

36. Albert F. Coyle to William Green, June 26, 1926.

37. Statement of Executive Council of the American Federation of Labor, June 28, 1926.

38. *Report of the Proceedings of the Forty-sixth Annual Convention of the American Federation of Labor,* 1926, pp. 262–279.

39. *American Federation of Labor Weekly News Service,* April 22, 1933.

40. Brief submitted to the Secretary of State by William Green, November 10, 1933.

41. *Ibid.*

42. Memorandum in Official File 142, Box 1, Franklin Delano Roosevelt Library.

43. *Congressional Record,* July 29, 1935, pp. 12, 466.

44. *American Federation of Labor Weekly News Service,* September 1, 1934

45. *Report of the Proceedings of the Fifty-fifth Annual Convention of the American Federation of Labor,* 1935, pp. 778–779.

46. *Ibid.,* p. 782.

47. *Report of the Proceedings of the Fifty-ninth Annual Convention of the American Federation of Labor,* 1939, pp. 410–411.

48. Circular letter to Congressmen and Senators from William Green, January 20, 1940.

49. Green to Assistant Secretary of State Breckenridge Long, January 12, 1942; Maxim Litvinoff to Green, February 23, 1943.

50. Minutes of Executive Council, May 17, 1946.

51. Statement of William Green before the Committee on Un-American Activities of the House of Representatives on H. R. 1884 and H. R. 2122 in files of A. F. of L., March 25, 1947.

52. *Ibid.*

53. *Report of the Proceedings of the Sixty-eighth Convention of the American Federation of Labor*, 1949, pp. 211–212.

54. Statement of George D. Riley, Member, Legislative Committee, American Federation of Labor, on H. R. 7595, House Un-American Activities, March 24, 1950.

55. Statement by the Executive Council of the American Federation of Labor, August 6, 1950.

56. *Ibid.*

57. Robert Chaberion to William Green, February 23, 1952; Green to Chaberion, March 10, 1952. Chaberion was secretary of the International Conference in Moscow.

58. Minutes of Executive Council, December 15, 1954.

59. George Meany to Patrick E. Gorman, December 20, 1954.

60. Patrick E. Gorman and Earl W. Jimerson to Meany, December 23, 1954.

61. Minutes of Executive Council, February 4, 1955.

62. Minutes of Executive Council, May 3, 1955.

63. Gorman and Jimerson to Meany, August 9, 1955; Minutes of Executive Council, August 9 and October 2, 1955.

64. Statement of the Executive Council of the American Federation of Labor, August 10, 1955.

65. *Ibid.*

# XXXI

## Negro Workers

ALTHOUGH the A. F. of L. was officially opposed to discrimination for reasons of race, creed, or color, discrimination against Negroes and other minority groups was tolerated in practice throughout the years. Only this much can be said for the federation's policy: the A. F. of L. had no power to compel international unions to obey its pronouncements against racial discrimination. Even directly chartered central bodies could not be forced to accept Negro delegates if they lived in sections of the country where strong prejudices existed. The Federation leadership had long since learned the limits of its power; it had become accustomed to avoiding the use of force against its affiliates whenever another —however unsatisfactory—solution offered itself.

In 1925 a representative of a federal local of Negro freight handlers requested the withdrawal of the jurisdiction of the Brotherhood of Railway Clerks because this union had refused to admit Negro workers. The same delegate, Albert C. Campbell,. an organizer for the A. F. of L., submitted a resolution calling upon the Federation to launch a drive to organize Negro workers and to request international unions to eliminate anti-Negro clauses from their constitutions. Reporting on this resolution, the resolutions committee explained that the A. F. of L. had always promoted a policy of organizing all workers irrespective of creed or color; it claimed that only a few of the 107 affiliated international unions excluded Negro workers from membership. Two A. F. of L. conventions had warned national and international unions that if they did not admit Negro workers, the A. F. of L. would organize and charter them directly. The resolutions committee said that this policy was being carried out.[1] The Committee must certainly have been aware that this arrangement did not meet the needs of the Negro workers, and that federal labor unions existing in a trade or calling in which an effective international functioned were likely to be neglected orphans rather than fully represented trade unionists. When a similar resolution was presented to the 1927 convention, the resolutions committee dismissed the subject by pointing to the action of earlier conventions.

In 1925 T. Arnold Hill, representing the Department of Industrial Relations of the National Urban League, and Rienzi B. Lemus, president of the Grand Council of Dining Car Employees, appeared before the Executive Council to discuss the organizing of Negro workers. The report from organizer Hugh Frayne in which he described the program of the National Trade Union Committee for Organizing Negro Workers was considered at this meeting. The National Trade Union Committee had suggested that a Negro organizer be employed to direct the work of enrolling Negroes. The Committee wanted the A. F. of L. to assist in the adjustment of racial problems within national and international unions; specifically, it requested that the Brotherhood of Dining Car Employees be allowed to affiliate with the A. F. of L. The Executive Council decided that the Brotherhood be asked to affiliate with the Hotel and Restaurant Employees' Union, and that the other question be turned over to President Green for action.[2]

In April 1928 A. Philip Randolph applied for a charter on behalf of the Brotherhood of Sleeping Car Porters. Randolph, a former editor of a Negro socialist magazine, *The Messenger,* had become convinced that labor organization on the economic plane was the most pressing need of the Negro worker. Without any help from the A. F. of L., Randolph's organization had become firmly established by 1927 when it sought to gain recognition from the Pullman Company. When it did not succeed, the Brotherhood applied for affiliation with the A. F. of L. Edward Flore, president of the Hotel and Restaurant Employees' Union, arguing that there were no Negro barriers in his union, objected to the granting of a charter.[3] Randolph maintained that a nonrailway organization could not effectively handle the problems of the Pullman porters; they were not hotel workers and only part of their duties could be classified as hotel work. Randolph also reminded the Executive Council that the porters had organized themselves without any outside aid. "The granting of an International Charter to the Brotherhood of Sleeping Car Porters," Randolph said, "will be so historical and epochal that it will tend to awaken and stimulate an interest among Negro workers and the Negro public in general in becoming part of the American labor movement."[4]

Although Green was sympathetic to Randolph's request, the Pullman porters were not given a charter at this time because of the objection of the Hotel and Restaurant Employees. When the Pullman porters threatened to strike in the summer of 1928, Green demonstrated his friendliness in a wire to Randolph:

Because of my belief in the economic welfare of all working people, I am taking the liberty of communicating with you regarding the impending strike of Pullman Porters and Maids. All thinking observing people know these groups of workers are suffering under the imposition of accumulated wrongs. The Pullman Company which exercises the right to organize its capital and corporation and which demands the right to be represented by officers and representatives of its own choosing denies the exercise of this right to its employed Porters and Maids who daily render faithful and efficient service. This arrogant and dominating attitude assumed by the Pullman Corporation is contrary to the American spirit of fair play and justice.[5]

Green reported to the Executive Council that he had informed the Hotel and Restaurant Employees that it "had not been able to organize these men . . . and that there were a lot of people, both inside and outside, who think the American Federation of Labor should help them to raise their standards."[6]

In February 1929 the A. F. of L. granted the Pullman porters a temporary charter as a federal labor union. At the convention in the same year, Randolph made clear that he intended to use his affiliation with the A. F. of L. to call attention to the need to organize the Negro workers and to gain for them equal treatment from the labor movement. He proposed, in a resolution, that the convention favor the program of educational work among Negro wage earners outlined by William Green. This proposal was sent to the Executive Council.[7]

After enactment of the National Industrial Recovery Act, Randolph asked the 1933 convention to authorize the employment of Negro organizers for a campaign among Negro workers. In discussing this resolution, Randolph described the size of the Negro labor force and its importance to the trade union movement. He emphasized the fact that his organization, the Brotherhood of Sleeping Car Porters, was making every effort to organize Negro workers, but that it was limited by lack of funds. Frank Duffy, chairman of the organization committee of the convention, approved the resolution, but he asked that it be referred to the Executive Council for action if funds were available.[8]

At the same convention, the Pullman Porters objected to their exclusion from the terms of the Emergency Transportation Act of 1933. At Randolph's request, Green approached the Coordinator of Transportation, Joseph B. Eastman, and was informed that the Pullman Porters did not come under the terms of that law. The Porters had started injunction proceedings against the Pullman Company, seeking to have it enjoined from discriminating against its employees who joined unions, and the A. F. of L. appealed for funds to aid the Porters in their suit. The Pullman Company had an agreement with a company union for its porters and maids and for a time refused to do business with the Brotherhood of Sleeping Car Porters.[9]

At the 1934 convention, Randolph brought the problem of discrimination by international unions against Negro workers to the floor. He asked the convention to undertake an inquiry to find out the "status of Negro workers in the National and International unions, Federal unions, and the general policy of the American Federation of Labor on the matter of organizing Negro workers, and report to the next convention its findings with recommendations as to the future policy in relation to Negro workers."[10] The organization committee, in considering this resolution, reviewed the official policy of the A. F. of L. and emphasized again the policy that the "American Federation of Labor . . . cannot interfere with the autonomy of National and International unions. The American Federation of Labor cannot say who are eligible or who are not eligible to membership in National and International unions. That is the right of the National or International union itself, of which it cannot be deprived." Mr. Duffy reminded the committee that Article IX, Section 6, of the A. F. of L. constitution provided that "separate charters may be issued to Central Unions, Local Unions, or Federal Labor Unions, composed exclusively of colored members, where, in the judgment of the Executive Council, it appears advisable and to the best interests of the trade union movement."[11] On these grounds the organization committee recommended nonconcurrence in the resolution.

Randolph argued that the resolutions annually enacted on this subject had not had any results. He had no expectations that the labor movement would get very far in organizing the Negro worker by the mere passage of resolutions. Instead, he believed that a committee should hold hearings in different parts of the country and on the basis of information developed in these hearings develop a program. William Hutcheson, while agreeing with the views of the convention committee, thought that there was merit in the resolution. He suggested that Green appoint a committee of five to investigate the condition of Negro workers and report to the next convention. Both Andrew Furuseth of the International Seamen's Union, and Frank Duffy, secretary of the United Brotherhood of Carpenters and Joiners of America, the union headed by Hutcheson, wanted the investigation, if it were made, to be conducted by members of the Executive Council. Hutcheson thought that the convention might wish to appoint a convention delegate who was not a member of the Council.[12]

On June 10, 1935 Green asked John E. Rooney of the Operative Plasterers' and Cement Finishers' International Association, John Brophy of the United Mine Workers of America, John W. Garvey of the Laborers' Union, Jerry L. Hanks of the Journeymen Barbers' Union, and T. C. Carroll of the Maintenance of Ways Employees to serve on this committee and report to the 1935 convention. Brophy was appointed chairman. Preliminary hearings were held on June 25, and a circular letter was distributed to international unions to find out whether they discriminated against Negroes or barred them from membership. The Committee of Five held hearings in the A. F. of L. Council Room on July 9 and 10, and Randolph presented evidence of the discrimination practiced by affiliated unions against Negro workers. When the hearings concluded, the committee reported that "the whole problem of the right relationship between white and Negro labor is one of education. By this is meant a full and free opportunity to discuss frankly the cause of differences and discriminatory practices within the unions against colored workers, with the object of finding solutions that lessen friction and produce more good-will among the races. This is, as we understand it, a function of our committee."[13] The committee asked the Executive Council for permission to hold regional hearings because some witnesses might not be able to afford the time and money to come to Washington. The regional meetings were not authorized.

The committee's report—which was not included in the Executive Council's report to the 1935 convention—asked that all international unions which barred Negroes from membership or discriminated against them through formation of separate locals or denied their Negro members representation at conventions or on committees, eliminate at their next convention these restrictions in order to conform with the principles and practices of the A. F. of L. The Committee believed that A. F. of L. charters should conform with the Federation's admission policies which granted the same rights to Negro workers as to other workers. "Separate Negro Federal Unions shall be discontinued by the A. F. of L. and such membership be transferred to mixed locals of the respective Internationals, where they may have an effective voice in determination of wages and other conditions." The committee also asked that a campaign of education on racial issues be conducted by the A. F. of L. and that the Committee of Five be continued.[14]

Part of the committee's report was made public by A. Philip Randolph during the discussion on his resolution opposing discrimination against Negro workers at the 1935 convention. John Brophy was incensed at the Executive Council's failure to include the committee's recommendations in its convention report. He wrote to Green that the committee "acted in good faith and in accordance with the definite instructions of the San Francisco convention, but the arbitrary action of the Executive Council and yourself in denying us the opportunity to report completely nullified the committee's work and completely nullified the mandate of the previous convention."[15] Brophy charged that his committee had been appointed only as a "face-saving device," and not as an honest attempt to solve the Negro problem in the labor movement. Another member of the committee, Thomas C. Carroll, praised Brophy's sincerity but noted that Brophy had been

rather insistent that the committee, in making the report, recommend that all National or International Unions that had any kind of a bar against colored workers . . . be directed to immediately eliminate them. The Committee members endeavored to show Brother Brophy that such a recommendation could not be made under the present law of the American Federation of Labor, that if such a recommendation was to be made, it would first be necessary to amend the constitution and by-laws of the A. F. of L. and take from its component organizations the self-autonomy guaranteed them in respect to their membership and it was, finally, more as a compromise measure that the other members of the committee who signed the majority report went along with Brother Brophy as far as we did.[16]

Another member of the committee, Jerry Hanks, was opposed to any action, because the Negro problem antedated the formation of the A. F. of L.[17]

The supplemental report of the Executive Council reviewed the factors which had led to the appointment of the Committee of Five and concluded that there were few national and international unions which denied membership to Negro workers. In most instances, special provisions had been made to organize Negro workers into federal labor unions directly chartered by the A. F. of L. Randolph attacked the Council's failure to publish the report that had been made by its own committee. He denounced the special federal labor unions set up for Negro workers as "racial unions" which had no justification, and he argued that Negro railway workers who were members of federal labor unions had no satisfactory method of influencing the demands that would be made upon the carriers. Under the existing law, the federal labor unions could not even present a grievance to management. He further charged that the "Federal form of organization that the American Federation of Labor provides for the Negro workers is virtually no organization at all."[18] Pleading for the Negroes' full rights as members of the A. F. of L., he insisted that the Federation should compel international unions to cease discriminating against the Negro workers.

John Frey sympathized with Randolph's views and explained that he himself had no prejudices against Negro workers; he had in fact brought them into his own organization, the International Molders' Union. Nevertheless, he was aware of the racial barriers which had to be met realistically at the present time and he hoped that education would in time solve the problem. Green stressed the autonomy of the internationals and also argued for education as the eventual remedy. George Harrison, whose union, the Brotherhood of Railway Clerks, had been criticized for barring Negroes, admitted that his union did not admit Negroes, but he said that their grievances were handled in the same manner as those of white workers. Harrison thought that "every worker ought to be organized, they all should be in the same organization, but it is a matter that will have to be worked out and I don't want this convention to pass a resolution or a motion that will say that my International Union will be expelled if we do not amend our constitution."[19]

Although Randolph's proposals were defeated, they did bring the problem into the open. Moreover, the debate on the floor of the convention was of a high order, with Randolph and several of his opponents stating the issues clearly. For the first time restricted unions were placed on the defensive, and even though the walls of prejudice did not immediately come tumbling down, the insistence upon equality in organization made a deep impression upon those present and compelled some leaders to adopt an apologetic attitude.

Resolutions opposing restrictions upon the membership of Negro workers were submitted to subsequent A. F. of L. conventions, but their fate was usually the same. Following the Federation's policy of organizing Negro workers whose membership was not accepted by other unions, Green sought the view of D. H. Robertson, head of the Brotherhood of Locomotive Firemen and Enginemen, on enrolling Negro firemen. Robertson answered that his union negotiated agreements for all locomotive firemen, regardless of organization, membership, or color. Committees from his union, he told Green, insisted that the same wages and working conditions be paid Negro firemen as were granted to white workers. Robertson wanted the A. F. of L. to refrain from organizing Negro firemen. "These men," he told Green, "are not promoted to positions of locomotive engineers, with the result that as time goes on they become the senior firemen and in order that there may be no discrimination against white men, agreements have been negotiated to limit the seniority of colored firemen."[20]

The constant prodding of the unions which discriminated against Negroes had an effect upon their admission policies. At no time had the Federation approved of such discrimination, but under its doctrine of "self-restraint" and the autonomy of the international unions, the exclusion of Negro workers continued over the years. While the A. F. of L. could not force a policy of equal treatment upon the national and international unions, the leaders of the Pullman Porters acknowledged that the "American Federation of Labor in its various conventions had condemned and declared against various racial and color discriminations in the trade unions which is slowly but surely bringing the Negro and white workers to realize that they have interests in common and that they should work and unite with each other and not fight each other." The resolution submitted by Randolph in 1939 called attention to the condemnation by President Green and the Executive Council of the lynching evil and the refusal of Constitution Hall in Washington to open its doors to a concert by the famed Negro vocalist, Marian Anderson. The resolution expressed the "sincere appreciation and profound gratitude for the fine and constructive spirit of the American Federation of Labor and its leadership in constantly going on record for the principle of equality among the workers and the high and noble ideals of democracy and the Brotherhood of Man without regard to race or color."[21]

In 1936 the Brotherhood of Sleeping Car Porters was given an international charter, and in 1940 the union sought to extend its jurisdiction over train porters. Two locals of Negro porters and trainmen, about 400 workers, were affiliated with the A. F. of L., and the Sleeping Car Porters wanted them in their union. The Council turned down the request on the ground that the work performed by brakemen-porters was different from the jobs of the Pullman porters.[22]

In 1941 the Brotherhood of Sleeping Car Porters again introduced a resolution calling for an investigation by a committee of the A. F. of L. of the discrimination practiced by trade unions. Randolph offered a long list of instances where Negro workers had been denied employment or entrance into unions. His denunciation provoked a heated debate and several presidents of internationals rose to defend their organizations against the charge of discrimination. Randolph held his ground and denied that he had charged "that the American Federation of Labor, as such, discriminates against Negroes. Now, everybody knows that . . . the Brotherhood of Sleeping Car Porters takes this position definitely in favor of the fact that the American Federation of Labor does not discriminate against Negroes; you accept Negroes in the federal unions."[23]

With the beginning of the defense effort in 1941, Negro labor leaders began to demand that Negro workers employed by firms holding government defense contracts be accorded equal rights to employment and promotion. Randolph threatened to lead a march on Washington to demand fair and equal treatment. In June 1941 President Roosevelt appointed a Committee on Fair Employment Practice to consider complaints of discrimination in the employment of workers in defense industries because of race, creed, or nationality. Green was a member of the Committee. It was a difficult task and some employers and unions were not happy about such pressure. For example, the president of the Seattle Boeing Aircraft Local of the International Association of Machinists begrudgingly accepted the order that his local stop discriminating against Negro workers. He regretted that, while organized labor was helping the war effort, other groups "should choose this time of National emergency to press for redress of all their grievances."[24]

President Roosevelt had emphasized in a letter to Green the necessity for abolishing discrimination in employment, and he later wrote "we must all be unremitting in our efforts to see that discrimination is stamped out wherever possible."[25]

At the 1943 convention several resolutions were introduced requesting the A. F. of L. to compel its internationals to eliminate restrictions on Negroes and other minority groups joining their unions. The resolutions committee again traced the historic policy of the A. F. of L. and declared that "national origin, race or color must in no manner or form restrict any American from a free opportunity to prepare himself to become a skilled mechanic, a craftsman, and take his place as such in any trade employment requiring the skill which he has acquired. The doors of our trade union movement must be open. This country must not maintain an industrial standard which discriminates against a wage earner because of his color."[26] The report also endorsed fair employment practice.

Randolph, paying tribute to the efforts of Chairman Woll and Secretary Frey of the Resolutions Committee, said, "the purpose of the report, the aim and objective of the report are all commendable, but we feel morally bound to discuss a very important phase of the trade union movement at this time in connection with Negro workers."[27] Randolph spoke of the practices of a number of international unions which had barred Negroes from membership or placed them in auxiliary locals in which they were denied a voice or vote in the organization. Charles MacGowan, head of the Boilermakers' Union, one of the organizations criticized by Randolph, described his own "long record in our convention of advocating the organization and the protection of the colored workers."[28] MacGowan admitted that his union's use of the auxiliary local for its Negro members might not be the answer to the demand for equal treatment, but he asked for understanding of the difficulties faced by his union and a recognition of the efforts that had been made by the officers toward establishing greater concern for the Negro craftsman.

Green extolled the A. F. of L. policy as being the "most advanced and progressive position taken upon this subject. . . . If any representative of the American Federation of Labor attempts to discriminate against the workers because of race, creed or color when we seek to organize them into Federal Labor Unions, he can no longer represent the American Federation of Labor."[29] Green deplored the criticism of the A. F. of L. and the antagonistic attitude of a number of Negro organizations toward it. Milton Webster of the Pullman Porters reminded the convention of the help given by his organization to other A. F. of L. affiliates in their efforts to organize Negro workers. He observed that although his union had not been "satisfied with everything that goes on in the American Federation of Labor . . . we don't expect anybody to pull any rabbits out of their hats . . . to try to wave a wand and solve these problems overnight."[30] He assured the delegates that the officers of the Pullman Porters were trying to help in the organizing of Negro workers into the A. F. of L. and were trying to eliminate the

barriers to organization of Negroes which had been set up by some of
the international unions.

At first the Fair Employment Practice Committee operated as an
independent agency; it was transferred to the War Manpower Commission in July 1942. Toward the end of 1942, several major cases were
scheduled for hearing, including one involving the southeastern railroads. The hearings were canceled by Chairman Paul McNutt of the
War Manpower Commission in January 1943 at the request of the
White House.[31]

On May 27, 1944 President Roosevelt established a new Committee
on Fair Employment Practice; his Executive Order reaffirmed the need
to end discrimination in all war plants, departments, and other agencies
of the Federal government, and in all labor organizations. Hushing
pointed to the traditional opposition of the A. F. of L. to discrimination
on the basis of race, creed, or color, but he questioned the desirability
of the government imposing such a policy upon freely constituted associations of workers. Green, from the beginning, supported legislation
for the permanent establishment of a Fair Employment Practice Committee, and he wrote to the state federations of labor and city central
bodies asking them to support such legislation.[32] Green testified on behalf
of the Anti-Discrimination bill sponsored by Senators Dennis Chavez and
Irving Ives, and in his testimony he deplored the disparity in the
average incomes of Negro and white families. He attributed the difference to the denial to many Negroes of employment opportunities in
higher grade jobs which they were qualified to perform, the barring of
many Negroes from training and job opportunities in which they could
acquire the skill and experience which could qualify them for better
jobs, and the lower rates paid to Negroes doing the same kind of work
as white workers.[33]

REFERENCES

1. *Report of the Forty-fifth Annual Convention of the American Federation
of Labor,* 1925, pp. 322–325.

2. Minutes of Executive Council, March 25, 1925.

3. Minutes of Executive Council, April 5, 1928.

4. Quote is from A. Philip Randolph to William Green, April 23, 1928, in
Minutes of Executive Council, April 23, 1928.

5. Green to Randolph, June 7, 1928.

6. Minutes of Executive Council, November 18, 1928.

7. *Report of Proceedings of the Forty-ninth Annual Convention of the
American Federation of Labor,* 1929, p. 217.

8. *Report of the Proceedings of the Fifty-third Annual Convention of the
American Federation of Labor,* 1923, pp. 268–269.

9. *Ibid.,* pp. 520–522. Joseph B. Eastman to William Green, November 21,

1933; Randolph to Green, December 6, 1933. Circular letter sent to national and international unions and state branches appealing for aid for pullman porters, January 6, 1933.

10. *Report of the Proceedings of the Fifty-fourth Annual Convention of the American Federation of Labor*, 1934, p. 330.

11. *Ibid.*, p. 331.

12. *Ibid.*, pp. 332–333.

13. John Rooney, John Brophy, T. C. Carroll, and John W. Garvey to William Green, July 30, 1935. Hanks did not sign the statement.

14. *Report to Executive Council*, signed by John E. Rooney, John Brophy, T. C. Carroll, and John W. Garvey.

15. John Brophy to Green, November 6, 1935.

16. T. C. Carroll to William Green, November 21, 1935.

17. Jerry L. Hanks to Green, December 4, 1935.

18. *Report of the Proceedings of the Fifty-fifth Annual Convention of the American Federation of Labor*, 1935, p. 810.

19. *Ibid.*, p. 818.

20. D. B. Robertson to Green, February 25, 1938.

21. *Report of the Proceedings of the Fifty-ninth Annual Convention of the American Federation of Labor*, 1939, p. 456.

22. Minutes of Executive Council, January 30, 1940.

23. *Report of the Proceedings of the Sixty-first Annual Convention of the American Federation of Labor*, 1941, pp. 490–491.

24. R. G. Cotton to Green, March 25, 1942.

25. President Franklin D. Roosevelt to Green, February 21, 1942; quote from Roosevelt to Green, April 24, 1942.

26. *Report of the Proceedings of the Sixty-third Annual Convention of the American Federation of Labor*, 1943, p. 421.

27. *Ibid.*, p. 422.

28. *Ibid.*, p. 432.

29. *Ibid.*, p. 443.

30. *Ibid.*, p. 445.

31. William C. Hushing to Honorable Dennis Chavez, September 7, 1943.

32. William Green to the Officers of State Federations of Labor, City Central Bodies, and Federal Labor Unions, November 14, 1945.

33. Statement of William Green before the Senate Committee on Labor and Public Welfare on S. 984, June 20, 1947, in files of A. F. of L.

# XXXII

## Membership, Income, Attitudes, and Problems

THE membership of the A. F. of L. remained fairly stable throughout the period between 1923 and 1930. In 1924, the year of Gompers'
death, members numbered 2,865,000 and by 1930, 2,961,000. The year-to-
year changes in this six-year period were usually less than 100,000, a fact
indicating that the Federation, on an over-all basis, was not gaining or
losing members, although slight changes often represented important
shifts in strength within the Federation. The effect of the depression
was very severe, and almost 850,000 members—almost 29 per cent—
were lost between 1930 and 1933. By 1933 membership was lower than
it had been since 1916. The Federation more than recouped its depression losses in the first three years of the New Deal. Its enrolled membership of 3,422,000 in 1936 had been exceeded in its history only by two
years—1920 and 1921. Membership dropped by over 561,000 in 1937
as a result of the suspension of the C.I.O. unions; the net losses experienced by the A. F. of L. in this year were appreciably below the membership of the suspended organizations, because many A. F. of L. unions
had substantial gains in enrollment. From 1937 through 1955, the A. F.
of L. gained steadily. In no single year, however, did it match the
spectacular membership increases of the C.I.O. unions in their first years
of existence. In only one year in the entire period did the Federation
gain as many as 900,000 new members, but it showed net losses only
in the three years 1948, 1949, and 1950; its highest membership was
attained in 1955.

Per capita tax payments were always the major source of income for
the A. F. of L. Their drop as a percent of total income between 1937
and 1940 was due to the assessment levied in those years. Paid subscrip-
tions to the *American Federationist*, payments into the defense fund,
and initiation fees of federal labor unions and directly chartered trade
unions were other important sources of income. Inevitably, as affiliated
membership increased, the ratio of per capita tax payments to total
payments tended to rise. The ratio of per capita tax income to total
income is greatly influenced by the number of workers in federal labor
unions. For example, in 1941, when per capita tax income constituted
slightly above 50 per cent of total income, the A. F. of L. received 19

per cent of its income from monies deposited in the defense fund of Federal labor unions and initiation fees paid by new recruits in these organizations.

The percentage of annual income devoted to organizing ranged from slightly more than 20 per cent to almost 66 per cent. On the basis of

INCOME, PER CAPITA TAX PAYMENTS, EXPENSES, AND
ORGANIZING EXPENSES 1925–1955*

| Year | Income† | Per Capita tax pay-ments† | Per cent of total income | Expenses† | Organizing expenses† | Per cent of total expenses |
|------|--------|-----------|-----------|-----------|-----------|-----------|
| 1925 | $ 509 | $ 372 | 73.0 | $ 533 | $ 132 | 24.8 |
| 1926 | 518 | 360 | 69.5 | 519 | 105 | 20.2 |
| 1927 | 524 | 343 | 65.5 | 485 | 114 | 23.5 |
| 1928 | 545 | 336 | 61.7 | 496 | 111 | 22.4 |
| 1929 | 609 | 432 | 70.9 | 575 | 125 | 21.7 |
| 1930 | 560 | 377 | 67.3 | 531 | 130 | 24.5 |
| 1931 | 569 | 357 | 62.7 | 561 | 139 | 24.8 |
| 1932 | 466 | 312 | 67.0 | 468 | 112 | 23.9 |
| 1933 | 457 | 273 | 59.0 | 424 | 100 | 23.4 |
| 1934 | 1070 | 385 | 36.0 | 906 | 323 | 35.6 |
| 1935 | 1032 | 454 | 44.0 | 975 | 338 | 34.7 |
| 1936 | 974 | 453 | 46.5 | 977 | 293 | 30.0 |
| 1937 | 1184 | 440 | 37.2 | 1167 | 457 | 39.2 |
| 1938 | 1844 | 580 | 31.5 | 1987 | 1174 | 59.1 |
| 1939 | 1800 | 583 | 32.4 | 1697 | 889 | 52.4 |
| 1940 | 1938 | 629 | 32.5 | 1768 | 953 | 53.9 |
| 1941 | 2126 | 1075 | 50.6 | 1835 | 1039 | 56.6 |
| 1942 | 2309 | 1283 | 55.6 | 2049 | 1270 | 62.0 |
| 1943 | 2422 | 1360 | 56.2 | 2010 | 1270 | 63.2 |
| 1944 | 2702 | 1543 | 57.1 | 2333 | 1534 | 65.8 |
| 1945 |  |  |  |  |  |  |
| 1946 | 2280 | 1458 | 64.0 | 2625 | 1453 | 55.4 |
| 1947 | 3847 | 1888 | 49.8 | 3847 | 1979 | 51.4 |
| 1948 | 3347 | 2498 | 74.6 | 2901 | 1601 | 55.2 |
| 1949 | 3571 | 2881 | 80.1 | 3258 | 1885 | 57.9 |
| 1950 | 3599 | 2935 | 81.2 | 3624 | 1877 | 56.8 |
| 1951 | 3811 | 3013 | 79.1 | 4060 | 1813 | 44.7 |
| 1952 | 3621 | 2499 | 82.8 | 3459 | 1373 | 39.7 |
| 1953 | 4983 | 4210 | 84.5 | 4575 | 1735 | 37.9 |
| 1954 | 5582 | 4735 | 84.8 | 5488 | 2568 | 46.8 |
| 1955 | 5712 | 5011 | 87.7 | 6163 | 1753 | 28.4 |

* Compiled from Convention Proceedings.     † In thousands.

expenditures in behalf of federal labor unions, it would appear that 40–50 per cent of all funds spent for organizing was used to promote and aid the directly affiliated unions and the remainder to help the national and international unions and central labor bodies.

The A. F. of L. never had large reserves. The founders and leaders of the A. F. of L. had envisaged only a limited role for the Federation. The international unions fought any increases in per capita with the argument that the A. F. of L. was not a financing institution.

The greater activity forced upon the Federation by the emergence of the C.I.O. and the realization that it would have to be more active in organizing compelled the Federation to find a permanent substitute for the assessment which it had levied in 1937. In 1941 a committee made up of Secretary-Treasurer George Meany and Vice Presidents Harrison and Bugniazet suggested a per capita tax of 1½ cents per member per month upon all members of national and international unions up to 300,000 members, and 1 cent per member per month upon all members in excess of 300,000. An added tax of 1 cent per member per month was to be imposed upon directly chartered unions. The differential rate to unions with over 300,000 members aroused some protest, and Daniel Tobin, who had been treasurer of the A. F. of L. for eleven years, stated the historic position that "the Federation is not a financial institution; it never was intended to have large amounts in its treasury, and the founders of the Federation so agreed. It was merely to take from the general membership each year enough to run the Federation for the coming year."[1]

Meany distinguished between the financial needs of the Federation and those of the international affiliates, and he acknowledged the international unions' need for ample financial resources. The recommendation of the committee was adopted.

In 1946 the per capita tax was again increased. International and national unions were required to pay 2 cents per member per month upon all members up to 200,000 and 1½ cents for members in excess of this number. A minority report, signed by two of the seventeen members of the Law Committee, opposed the lower tax upon the membership above 200,000, rather than the 300,000 mark then in effect. They believed that this change would adversely affect the income of the Federation. Meany supported the majority report and repeated the argument that the Federation should not try to build up a large surplus, that it should pay its way out of current income and avoid the accumulation of large surpluses. The increase in per capita was justified on the ground of higher costs of operation. In 1940 the A. F. of L. had spent $442 to keep an organizer in the field for one month; in 1945 the average cost per organizer per month had risen to $624. Again there was some objection to discrimination against smaller unions, but the argument of the committee was that, since the dividing line between the higher and lower per capita had been lowered from 300,000 to 200,000 members, the proposal was really less discriminatory than the existing provision. The plan of the majority was accepted.[2]

In 1951 the Executive Council had to ask for another increase because of increased expenditures in radio and publicity programs, greater activity in foreign relations, and the higher costs of goods and services purchased by the A. F. of L. The per capita tax on members of national and international unions was raised to 4 cents per month. As on previous occasions, the per capita tax of directly chartered locals was also raised. The request was granted without debate.[3]

### SECRETARY OF LABOR

After the election of Franklin D. Roosevelt to the presidency in 1932, the Executive Council tried to have Daniel Tobin appointed Secretary of Labor. Green, Matthew Woll, and Joseph Weber were appointed to call on the president-elect and urge the selection. Green recalled the differences which had arisen between the Federation and President Hoover after he had appointed William Doak as Secretary of Labor. Green believed that the appointment of Tobin would accord the kind of recognition the A. F. of L. deserved and he assured Roosevelt that the A. F. of L. was anxious to cooperate with the new administration. Roosevelt "responded by stating that he had cooperated with the American Federation of Labor for twenty years while engaged in public service, and that he was determined to work with and have the cooperation of the American Federation of Labor for the next four years, while he was serving as President." Green informed Tobin, "that this was a significant remark and while it was susceptible of numerous interpretations, I was of the actual opinion that it could be construed as favorable to your appointment."[4]

A large number of labor organizations and their officers endorsed Tobin's candidacy. When Frances Perkins was appointed Secretary of Labor, Green voiced his disappointment "over President-elect Roosevelt's selection of a Secretary of Labor. Labor has consistently contended that the Department of Labor should be what its name implies and that the Secretary of Labor should be a representative of Labor, one who understands Labor, Labor's problems, Labor's psychology, collective bargaining, industrial relations, and one who enjoys the confidence of Labor."[5]

George L. Berry, president of the Printing Pressmen's Union, thought that Green's statement was a serious error, and "not in harmony with the magnificent record Secretary Perkins has made in the work which has challenged her attention in New York State."[6]

### Reorganizing the Supreme Court

A proposal to endorse President Roosevelt's program to enlarge the Supreme Court aroused some opposition. Harrison wanted the Executive Council to endorse the "court packing"; he announced that he was with Roosevelt's program "all the way." Wharton seconded this view, but Frank Duffy and T. A. Rickert were in general opposed. In the end, Roosevelt's program was endorsed by a vote of 9 to 3, with two members not voting.[7]

### Advertising in the *American Federationist*

Some labor people were always critical of the policy which allowed corporations to advertise in the *American Federationist*. Although the labor policy of the advertiser might be antiunion, John Morrison, who had been in charge of soliciting advertisement for this journal since 1902, never questioned the material. After Morrison's death in 1938, the Executive Council found that no contract between the A. F. of L. and Morrison existed. Green reported that the Federation had lost $4,500 on advertisements in 1940 and $7,737 in 1939. In addition, Green referred to other undesirable aspects of this policy, especially the possible misrepresentation by solicitors and the misunderstanding by business of the significance of their purchase. Harry Bates's proposal that advertisements be discontinued beginning with the June 1940 issue was adopted.[8]

### National Union for Social Justice

The Executive Council rejected, for the Federation, the invitation of Father Charles Coughlin to cooperate with the National Union for Social Justice, which he had organized. Father Coughlin had asked Green to attend a mass meeting of his organization, and Green had sent an observer. When the issue was presented to the Council, there was some criticism of Green's action, and the A. F. of L. rejected the invitation after Hutcheson, Daniel Tobin, and Arthur Wharton criticized the Coughlin movement.[9] Father Coughlin was severely criticized for his use of nonunion building labor as well as for his views.

### Changes in the Executive Council

The Executive Council was expanded in 1934 to include fifteen vice presidents, the president, secretary, and treasurer, for a total of eighteen members. After the death of Treasurer Martin Ryan, the posts of secretary and treasurer were combined and Secretary-Treasurer Morrison served in this post until 1940, when he was succeeded by George Meany. Morrison had served in the two offices for forty-three years. In general, he held the same views as Gompers and the group which dominated the Executive Council. On some matters, however, he did not follow the leadership. He was less opposed to political activity and he did not have the strong philosophic bias against government intervention shared by many Federation leaders.

George Meany was born in New York City on August 16, 1894. The son of Michael Meany, the president of a plumbers' local union, he became a journeyman plumber in 1915 and joined the union of his trade. Seven years later he was elected business agent of his local. He became widely known in trade union circles of his native state, was elected president of the New York State Federation of Labor in 1934, and served in that office until he succeeded Morrison in 1940. Unlike his immediate predecessor, Meany is not a florid orator. His strong points are tenacity and courage in pursuing his purpose, a capacity for absorbing information, and a high ability for logical analysis. He is not easily diverted from a point under discussion, and in an argument he is likely to go directly "for the jugular."

Prior to the Council's enlargement in 1934, George Harrison, president of the Brotherhood of Railway Clerks, was appointed to succeed James Wilson, who resigned after his defeat for reelection as chief executive of the Pattern Makers' League of North America.

In 1936 William L. Hutcheson, who had been elected to the Executive Council when it was enlarged in 1934, resigned. Hutcheson was opposed to the policies of the Executive Council, especially those which touched upon New Deal legislation, and he did not care to have his name appended to certain statements. Majority decisions of the Council were always formally approved by all members.[10] Hutcheson returned to the Executive Council in 1940 as first vice president, replacing Frank Duffy, the secretary of his union. His election violated a custom which had been followed in almost every instance since the founding of the A. F. of L.: that is, that a new member of the Executive Council started at the bottom of the list (at this time as fifteenth vice president) and moved up the scale as vacancies occurred with deaths or retirements. Of course, it had always been permissible for a nominee to challenge a particular member, but those who were chosen without contest usually started at the bottom. It was the failure of the Council to give the second vice presidency, formerly held by a coal miner, John Mitchell, to U.M.W.A. President John P. White, which led him to reject a post on the Council in 1916. In only one other instance was the rule of succession violated: that was in 1900 when Gompers requested James O'Connell of the Machinists to waive his position in favor of John Mitchell.

Edward Flore of the Hotel and Restaurant Employees' Union defeated George E. Browne in 1941. Flore had the support of the administration against Browne who was subsequently convicted of extortion.[11]

In 1943 Edward J. Gainor of the Letter Carriers resigned, and Green wanted a replacement from the needle trades. Since the death of Thomas Rickert in 1941, those industries had not been represented. Green thought that "the promotion of the welfare of our movement, of our best interests would be served by the selection of David Dubinsky to fill this vacancy."[12] Tobin nominated Doherty of the Letter Carriers and Green nominated Dubinsky, who received only one vote, presumably Green's. After the death of Edward Flore in September 1945, a place was again open on the Council. Tobin wanted to postpone the decision about a replacement, but he was overruled and Dubinsky was chosen.[13]

In 1947, along with the withdrawal of John L. Lewis from the Executive Council, two veteran members resigned. G. M. Bugniazet, who had served since 1930, was replaced by Charles J. MacGowan of the Boiler Makers' Union. Felix H. Knight, who had been on the Council since 1935, retired and was succeeded by Herman Winter, a baker. In 1950 William L. McFetridge of Building Service replaced W. D. Mahon, a Carman, who had organized his union in the 1890's and who had been closely associated with Gompers and Green.

On November 21, 1952 William Green's career ended. Born in Coshocton, Ohio, he had served in the Ohio legislature, as a district officer of the United Mine Workers of America, and as a secretary-treasurer of the national union for almost eleven years. He was elected to the Executive Council in 1914 when John P. White, the president of his union, rejected the post because he did not want to begin at the bottom of the list of vice presidents. Green was sympathetic to the policies of the A. F. of L., but he was by no means a confirmed disciple of Gompers. He favored greater government intervention, health insurance, and a more active political role for the Federation. Yet, his first years as president of the A. F. of L. were devoid of progress; the movement was at a standstill by 1925.

Himself a believer in industrial unionism, Green was destined to lead the defense against the head of his own organization, John L. Lewis, who rallied the coal miners behind his program of industrial organization in mass-production industry. Upon Green fell the burden of resisting the challenge of the C.I.O. to the Federation's hegemony over the American labor movement. Eloquent, kindly, and considerate as he was, Green lacked the "iron core" necessary to resist the powerful men who surrounded him on the Executive Council. Men like Hutcheson and Tobin were able to intimidate him, and he frequently yielded to other strong men. Yet the A. F. of L. during his tenure was able to ward off the greatest challenge it had ever faced from a rival and attain the highest membership in its history.

Four days after his death, on November 25, the Executive Council met to choose a successor. Daniel Tobin, who had already retired from the presidency of his union, wanted to finish out Green's term. He tried to organize a caucus in the hope that lightning would strike him; he had apparently forgotten his unsentimental attitude toward the claims of James Duncan, who had hoped to complete Gompers' unexpired term. Tobin had argued then that sentiment had no place in the selection of a new president, that a choice had to be made on practical grounds. When he was nominated by McFetridge, Tobin paid tribute to the office and then withdrew in favor of George Meany. Meany was unanimously chosen to succeed Green. Tobin sought to have the selection of a secretary-treasurer postponed until the next meeting of the Executive Council, but he was overruled and William F. Schnitzler of the Bakers' Union was selected.[14]

### THE MINERS

After he had organized the C.I.O., John L. Lewis discovered that its views on many issues were not in harmony with his own. He withdrew from the C.I.O. and in May 1943 tried to reaffiliate with the A. F. of L. He sent along $60,000 with his request as payment of per capita taxes upon his membership. When the application was presented to the Executive Council, the members discussed the jurisdiction the coal miners were to exercise. Daniel Tobin reviewed the cause for the departure of the coal miners from the A. F. of L. and suggested the appointment of a committee to discuss the terms of reaffiliation with Lewis. Tobin wanted Lewis to define the jurisdiction which the United Mine Workers would claim. William Hutcheson believed that the monies for per capita taxes should be accepted and differences settled later. Hutcheson's view was based on his desire to reunify the labor movement, but several members, including Harvey Brown of the Machinists, believed that the affiliation of the United Mine Workers of America with the A. F. of L. would hinder rather than aid reunification. Finally, Tobin, Harrison, and Woll were appointed to meet with the officers of the United Mine Workers of America.[15]

The stumbling block to immediate reaffiliation of the Miners' Union was District 50 which had been established as a catch-all for organizing any and all industries. Several Executive Council members whose jurisdictions had been invaded by District 50 wanted some restrictions placed upon its activity as a condition for the Mine Workers' union reentering the A. F. of L. The Miners' representatives refused to agree to any restriction upon District 50 in advance, although they indicated that the possibility for some limitation of its organizing would be considered after the Mine Workers had rejoined the Federation. At the Executive Council meeting in August 1943, the terms upon which the United Mine Workers of America was to be readmitted were again discussed. Tobin and George Harrison wanted the matter referred to the next convention; Hutcheson favored immediate readmission. Hutcheson's views were rejected, and the matter was referred to the 1944 convention.[16]

The proposal to readmit the coal miners was debated at length by the convention. The Progressive Mine Workers of America, which had seceded from the United Mine Workers in the early 1930's and had affiliated with the A. F. of L. in 1938, naturally opposed readmission of Lewis's organization. Others were doubtful whether the Executive Council would guarantee protection to affiliates whose jurisdictions were being invaded by District 50. On the basis of precedent and expediency, Hutcheson and others pleaded for the readmission of the United Mine Workers of America. Immediate entry, however, was denied. Instead, the Executive Council was given broad authority to bring it about by negotiating an arrangement with them.[17] Tobin was appointed chairman of the negotiating committee.

Several meetings with Lewis and his associates failed to produce any results. The A. F. of L. committee wanted Lewis to divest himself of the members not employed in and around the coal mines. Lewis was obdurate in his insistence that his union had to be accepted as it then existed.[18] The Executive Council at its meeting on May 8 repeated its earlier view, and Lewis immediately withdrew his application for reaffiliation and publicly charged that the failure to accept his union on its own terms was motivated by "New Deal politicians who are opposed, for political reasons, to unity in the ranks of labor."[19] Green, who had sought to work out an acceptable formula with Lewis, drew the fire of several members of the Council. Tobin sharply attacked him, insisting that Lewis should have been told to confer with the committee appointed by the Council to negotiate with him. Green defended himself by arguing it had never been ruled that he was not allowed to "talk to Lewis."[20]

In 1945 negotiations for the readmission of the United Mine Workers of America to the A. F. of L. were resumed. In the end, it was agreed that the Miners' Union would reaffiliate, and that soon thereafter the president of the United Mine Workers would consider any complaints filed by unions affiliated with the A. F. of L.; failure to reach a settlement would place the complaint before the Executive Council.[21] Lewis assured Green that he would discuss any jurisdictional problems with A. F. of L. unions after his union was reaffiliated; he made it clear that his unions' "acceptance of a charter of reaffiliation with the American Federation of Labor was contingent upon being given its usual representation on the Executive Council."[22] The Council could not promise a reappointment and it appeared that the miners would not rejoin. At this point,

Harvey Brown of the Machinists' Union resigned from the Executive Council and his place was assigned to Lewis.[23]

At his return, Lewis explained his reaffiliation as "a constructive action . . . in the interest of the labor movement and of the country as a whole. . . . This reaffiliation marks an historic turning point in the annals of labor. The ancient questions which in the past divided the house of labor have been abated. The important questions of the future are largely economic and industrial in character. . . . Let it be known that labor in America is destined to play an increasingly greater part in our national economy."[24] Lewis also announced that the membership of William Green in the United Mine Workers of America had been maintained, and Green was given documents to attest his good standing in his old union.

Lewis's tenure in the A. F. of L. was destined to be very short. Deeply opposed to the signing of the non-Communist affidavit required by the Taft-Hartley Act as a condition for utilizing the services of the National Labor Relations Board, Lewis decided, when his views were rejected by the 1947 convention, to withdraw again. On December 12, 1947 he sent the following wire: "Green—A. F. of L. We disaffiliate. Lewis"[25]

REFERENCES

1. *Report of the Proceedings of the Sixty-first Annual Convention of the American Federation of Labor*, 1941, p. 368.

2. *Report of the Proceedings of the Sixty-fifth Convention of the American Federation of Labor*, 1946, pp. 563–582.

3. *Report of Proceedings of the Seventieth Convention of the American Federation of Labor*, 1951, p. 414.

4. Green to Daniel Tobin, January 24, 1933.

5. *American Federation of Labor Weekly News Service*, March 4, 1933.

6. George L. Berry to Green, March 3, 1933.

7. Minutes of Executive Council, February 17, 1937.

8. Minutes of Executive Council, May 15, 1940.

9. Minutes of Executive Council, April 30, 1935.

10. William L. Hutcheson to Green, October 7, 1936.

11. *Report of the Proceedings of the Sixtieth Annual Convention of the American Federation of Labor*, 1940, p. 630; *Report of the Proceedings of the Sixty-first Annual Convention of the American Federation of Labor*, 1941, p. 572.

12. Minutes of Executive Council, January 21, 1943.

13. Minutes of Executive Council, October 19, 1945.

14. Minutes of Executive Council, November 25, 1952.

15. Minutes of Executive Council, May 17, 19, 1943.

16. Minutes of Executive Council, August 10, 1943; Green to Lewis, August 11, 1943.

17. *Report of the Proceedings of the Sixty-third Annual Convention of the American Federation of Labor*, 1943, pp. 471–501.

18. Green to Tobin, March 28, 1944; Tobin to Lewis, April 13, 1944; Lewis to Tobin, April 17, 1944.

19. Lewis to Green, May 8, 1944.

20. Minutes of Executive Council, May 8, 1944.

21. Minutes of Executive Council, February 13, 1945.

22. Lewis to Green, February 10, 1945.

23. Minutes of Executive Council, January 25, 1946.

24. *American Federation of Labor Weekly News Service,* February 5, 1946.

25. Statement of Lewis in file of A. F. of L.

# XXXIII

## Jurisdictional Disputes

As in the past, jurisdictional disputes continued to be a problem, although the tactics of conciliation and discussion frequently had results. In some instances, the A. F. of L., in spite of great efforts, was unable to devise a satisfactory formula, and unions dissatisfied with the decisions withdrew. Two of the more recalcitrant disputes were in the brewery and building erection industries.

### BREWERY WORKERS AND TEAMSTERS AND OPERATING ENGINEERS

The controversy between the Brewery Workers' and Teamsters' Unions began with the formation of the International Brotherhood of Teamsters' Unions in 1901. The Brewery Workers' Union was suspended in 1907 when it refused to abide by the recommendations of several conventions, as well as those of an arbitrator appointed by the A. F. of L.; at the insistence of Gompers, the 1907 convention voted to restore the charter of this union. At its meeting in January 1908, the Executive Council decided that all employees of breweries could remain in the Brewery Workers' Union, but engineers, firemen, and teamsters employed in breweries could withdraw and join the respective unions of their crafts without prejudice or discrimination by the Brewery Workers' Union.

The United Brewery Workmen's Union was directed not to admit to membership any engineers, firemen, or teamsters; such craftsmen were to be referred to the respective organizations of these trades that were affiliated with the A. F. of L. The Council recognized the possibility that in some breweries the workers might have chosen to join the union of their craft instead of the Brewery Workers' organization. In such instances, the respective organizations were to appoint a committee which jointly with the Brewery Workers' Union would negotiate with the employers.

For a time the dispute was quiescent. In 1913 when the Teamsters' Union again demanded the transfer of drivers of beer trucks to its organization, the convention decided "that in handling and distributing the product of breweries, the teamsters are generally employed in such dual capacities as to make many of them also brewery workers; that brewery teamsters are nearly all organized into and holding voluntary

membership in the brewery workers' organization." The convention held
that the Brewery Workers' Union was not required to transfer its driver
members to any other organization.[1]

As a result of the Eighteenth amendment to the Federal constitution,
which prohibited the sale of alcoholic beverages in the United States,
the brewery industry underwent virtual extinction. By the time the
amendment was repealed in 1933 and the sale of alcoholic beverages
was resumed, the industry was greatly transformed. Daniel Tobin, president of the Teamsters' Union, regarded the 1913 decision as "dead,"
on the ground that there now existed a new industry. He also argued
that the decision of the 1913 convention had not reversed the one made
in 1906. Joseph Obergfell, president of the Brewery Workers' Union,
pointed to the ending of differences between the organizations after
1913 as proof that the decision of that year had been accepted by both
organizations.[2]

The Operating Engineers' Union again presented their claim to engineers employed in the breweries, and in this instance, the Brewery
Workers' officers also referred to the decision of the 1913 convention as
proof that they had a right to organize these workers. After hearing the
views of the several organizations, the Executive Council awarded jurisdiction over the truck drivers employed in delivering beer to the
Teamsters' Union.[3]

The Brewery Workers' Union refused to accept the decision. When
the Council's view was upheld by the 1933 convention, an effort was
made to find a formula which would be mutually acceptable. I. M.
Ornburn and Green, in an attempt to settle the dispute, suggested that
the collective-bargaining contracts of the crafts employed in the breweries
and the brewery workers expire simultaneously, that the separate organizations seek joint agreements, and that the president of the A. F. of L.
appoint a tribunal which would decide on the reasonableness of wage
demands to be submitted. Part-time craftsmen would retain their membership in the United Brewery Workers and all the organizations would
pool their economic strength.[4]

The agreement worked out by Green and Ornburn was to be submitted to a referendum vote of the membership of the Brewery Workers'
Union, with the understanding that the officers were to remain neutral.
Instead, Obergfell launched an attack upon the proposal and Green
charged that such an action was a breach of faith.[5] Even though the
agreement included a requirement that "pending acceptance of this
proposal all hostilities among organizations shall cease," Obergfell denied
that his attack upon an arrangement which he had accepted violated
the spirit of the agreement. Tobin demanded that the Brewery Workers'
Union be censured and denied affiliation in the A. F. of L. central bodies,

and he threatened to direct his organizations to withdraw from all central labor unions and state federations of labor.[6] The members of the Brewery Workers' Union rejected the agreement proposed by representatives of the A. F. of L. by an overwhelming vote of 24,181 to 170.

Green showed no surprise at the outcome in view of Obergfell's attack. In replying to Obergfell's argument that the members had a right to self-determination, Green said that the jurisdictional dispute in question was passed upon by a convention of the A. F. of L. "This supreme tribunal in the ranks of organized labor decided," Green reminded him, "that teamsters and chauffeurs even though employed by brewery manufacturing interests come under the jurisdiction of the International Brotherhood of Teamsters, Chauffeurs, Stablemen, and Helpers of America." Green asked Obergfell whether the Executive Council could in good conscience respect the will of a particular group of workers or was it obligated to obey instead the mandate of the highest court of the American labor movement.[7]

The Executive Council thereupon voted to suspend the Brewery Workers' Union if it was unwilling to accept the convention's decision. Tobin was willing to make one more attempt at an adjustment, and if no agreement could be reached by the unions involved, he wanted the Council to recommend to the convention the suspension of the Brewery Workers' Union.[8] The 1935 convention asked the Executive Council to try once again to work out a settlement between the two organizations.

No agreement was reached. The efforts of the Brewery Workers' Union to have firms recognizing the Teamsters' Union placed on the unfair list drew a rebuke from William Green, who told Obergfell that "it would be a reflection upon Union Labor and upon our honor as union men if a firm which complies with the decisions of the highest tribunal within the American Federation of Labor, and is willing to establish the closed shop . . . to pay satisfactory wages, should be punished . . . because it did so."[9] The Brewery Workers' Union went further; it sought an injunction in the United States District Court to restrain the A. F. of L. from enforcing the decision on the jurisdictional differences between the Brewery Workers' and the Teamsters' Union.[10] In arguing for their position, the Brewery Workers emphasized that their union was autonomous and that this principle was clearly stated in the certificate of affiliation granted to all its unions by the A. F. of L. The Federation countered with the argument that autonomy was not "a guarantee of complete freedom of activity . . . something separate and apart from any obligation devolving . . . through such affiliations."[11]

The A. F. of L. insisted that an affiliate was obligated to obey the rules and constitution of the Federation. The petition for an injunction was dismissed by Judge Bailey, and in March 1938 the Brewery Workers' Union filed an amended petition which was argued before Judge Goldsborough. In October 1939 Judge Goldsborough granted the injunction, basing his decision on the "contract of affiliation" which guaranteed to the Brewery Workers' Union "jurisdiction over beer drivers." Judge Goldsborough found that the A. F. of L. could not decide to give the Teamsters' Union control over beer drivers without violating the contractual rights of the other union.[12] On March 17, 1941 the United States Circuit Court of Appeals reversed this decision, declaring that the controversy between the two unions constituted a labor dispute as defined by the Norris-La Guardia Act, and that the A. F. of L. had acted within the "scope of its delegated constitutional power, and that no contractual or other rights of the Brewery Workers' Union had been violated by the A. F. of L.'s decision of 1933."[13]

In the meantime, the 1939 convention appointed a committee made up of James Maloney, William C. Birthright, and Harry Stevenson, heads respectively of the Glass Bottle Blowers', Barbers', and Molders' Unions, to seek a settlement of the differences. In a statement to the committee, Obergfell examined the controversy between the Brewery Workers' Union and the Teamsters' Union. He insisted that the dispute had culminated in the International Working Agreement between the Teamsters' and the Brewery Workers' Unions of February 15, 1915, under which drivers and stablemen employed in delivering the products of breweries and bottling plants were to come under the jurisdiction of the Brewery Workers' International Union. The 1915 convention had approved this agreement and no protest against it had been raised until May 1933. Obergfell expected the Teamsters' Union to accept and carry out the contract of 1915.[14] When the Teamsters' Union rejected his proposal, Obergfell suggested that the question of transferring the beer-wagon drivers to the Teamsters' Union should be decided by a referendum of the beer drivers themselves, and he asked that the president of the A. F. of L. be directed to appoint a committee to hold such an election. In the meantime, a truce of one year would be declared by the parties in the dispute, and the A. F. of L. would again try to find a basis of agreement.[15] This proposal was also rejected by the Teamsters' Union. The committee which had sought a settlement recommended that the Executive Council continue its efforts to find a solution acceptable to both parties, but the Executive Council believed that it could not continue after the Brewery Workers' Union had attacked through the courts the very basis of the A. F. of L.'s relationship to its affiliates.[16] After the United States Supreme Court had rejected an appeal, the 1941 convention by a vote of 30,202 to 1,765 (with 9,859 not voting) suspended the Brewery Workers' Union for failure to accept the decision on transferring beer-truck drivers to the Teamsters' Union.[17] Subsequently, the Brewery Workers affiliated with the C.I.O.

### PROHIBITION OF THE MANUFACTURE AND SALE OF ALCOHOLIC BEVERAGES

The employment of members of the Brewery Workers' Union was seriously affected by the passage of the Eighteenth amendment to the United States Constitution, which outlawed the manufacture and sale of alcoholic beverages, and by the Volstead Act which was passed to enforce the amendment. Naturally, the union was opposed to the amendment and the law. Gompers on behalf of the A. F. of L. protested the restrictions on the sale of beer and light wines when they were submitted to Congress.[18]

Gompers wrote to President Wilson in October 1919 to protest prohibition as an interference with the lives of individuals, and he asked that the people be given an opportunity to decide whether prohibition should be enforced or the sale of light wines and beer allowed.[19] The 1921 convention by unanimous vote requested that the Volstead Act be modified so as to permit the manufacture and sale of beer and light wines.[20]

The conventions of 1919, 1921, 1923, and 1927 overwhelmingly voted against the extreme enforcement of the Volstead Act and again requested that the law be modified to permit the sale of light wines and beer.[21]

The A. F. of L. did not advocate outright repeal of the Eighteenth amendment; it argued that the Volstead Act was an extreme, unwarranted, and unenforceable device for promoting temperance.[22] There was some opposition to the views of the leadership, but it was a minority view.

### CARPENTERS AND MACHINISTS

The jurisdictional controversy between the Carpenters' and Machinists' Unions was also a long-standing one. It began in 1912, when the International Association of Machinists directed its members not to install machinery produced in the plants of the York Manufacturing Company because that firm refused to recognize the Machinists' Union in its plant. The Carpenters' Union did not abide by that request; its members, in fact, used the opportunity to perform work that had heretofore been done by members of the Machinists' Union. The Machinists appealed to the A. F. of L. and the 1914 convention awarded them millwrights' work—the installation and erection of machinery. The convention decided that the "United Brotherhood of Carpenters and Joiners is fundamentally a craft composed of skilled workers in the erecting, forming, and assembling of wood materials and has never been recognized as a metal craft organization or granted jurisdiction over the making, repairing, erecting, assembling, or dismantling of machinery; therefore, be it Resolved, That the United Brotherhood of Carpenters and Joiners . . . is hereby instructed to discontinue the infringement complained of; and be it further Resolved, that the President and Executive Council of the American Federation of Labor stand instructed to render every possible assistance in enforcing the intent of the resolution."[23]

When the Carpenters' Union refused to accept the decision, the adjustment committee of the A. F. of L. convention recommended that "the Carpenters and Joiners shall stand suspended until such time as this decision is complied with."[24] When Gompers protested against suspension of an international union, the convention directed the two organizations to confer and devise a settlement. The 1917 convention considered the issue again and ordered the parties to continue their quest for an agreement. In the meantime, it reaffirmed the decision which had earlier awarded the building, assembling, erecting, dismantling, and repairing of machinery in machine shops, buildings, factories, or elsewhere to the Machinists' Union.

For a time the issue was in abeyance, but in 1930 the Machinists' Union again claimed the right to organize millwrights. Arthur Wharton and William Hutcheson, the presidents respectively of the Machinists' and Carpenters' Unions, accepted the appointment of a joint commission. The commission agreed that one organization should be awarded the work in dispute and that all workers performing this work should transfer to that organization. No agreement could be reached, however, on the union to which the disputed work was to be given. Wharton then appealed to Hutcheson directly for a settlement on the basis of the ultimate benefit that might accrue to organized labor. The Carpenters' Union, Wharton said, had at the time, a normal membership between 300,000 and 400,000, and the relatively few millwrights would not add much to the power of the Carpenters' organization. "They do not represent an essential link in the material power and influence of . . . the organization; neither are they necessary to extend . . . organization into the mills or shops where the materials erected by your craft are shaped, formed, or fabricated. These men are almost exclusively employed on the product of machine shops and power manufacturing plants. They are a vital link and . . . important in connection with our struggle to organize the machine and power manufacturing industry."[25]

On October 15, 1931 the Carpenters' and Machinists' Unions signed an agreement to promote harmonious relations between the members of the two organizations so that they might jointly improve the wages and conditions of their respective members. Disputes were to be settled on a local basis, and if an agreement could not be reached, the matter was to be submitted to the presidents of both international unions. In spite of the agreement, members of the Carpenters' Union continued to harass machinists who tried to perform millwrights' work.[26]

Wharton complained of these tactics, and in October 1932 a more detailed agreement was signed defining the work of each union. Hutcheson accepted the agreement, he claimed, because of the decision of the 1914 A. F. of L. convention. Nevertheless, under pressure from the Carpenter's Union, building trades' councils disaffiliated the locals of the International Association of Machinists. Wharton asked Green for a declaration of the rights of the Machinists' Union.[27] When the Executive Council finally instructed Green to inform central labor bodies that under the decision of the 1914 convention millwrights' work was within the jurisdiction of the Machinists' Union, Hutcheson threatened to withhold per capita taxes until such time as the Federation stopped advising its central bodies of these facts.[28]

In 1941 the Building and Construction Trades Department entered the struggle by telling contractors that millwrights affiliated with the Carpenters' Union were entitled to millwrights' work. According to A. F. of L. custom, a trades department had no authority to rule on jurisdictional disputes that came up between a union affiliated with and one unaffiliated with a department. The 1941 convention upheld that principle, but the decision did not prevent the Building and Construction Trades Department from aiding the Carpenters' Union in this dispute.[29]

When Harvey Brown, president of the Machinists' Union, took the matter to the Executive Council in an effort to have the convention decision enforced, Green would only say that the dispute should be settled by conference.[30]

The Machinists' delegation to the 1942 convention wanted to bring the dispute between their union and the Carpenters' organization and Building and Construction Trades Department to the floor. Their request was rejected on the ground that Section 12 of Article III of the A. F. of L. constitution prohibited consideration of a grievance which had been decided by a previous convention except at the recommendation of the Executive Council; there was also a rule that a grievance could not be considered unless the parties involved had held a conference and tried to reach an adjustment.[31]

Unable to procure their rights from the Executive Council, officers of the Machinists' Union placed the question of their withdrawal before their own membership, which overwhelmingly voted to withdraw from the A. F. of L.

In a letter to Green, Brown recalled that the International Association of Machinists had repeatedly requested that the officers of the A. F. of

L. instruct the leaders of the Building and Construction Department not to make decisions involving the Machinists' Union.[32] Since the Executive Council of the A. F. of L. had rejected these demands, the International Association of Machinists had been forced, Brown said, to consider withdrawal from the A. F. of L. Brown wrote to George Meany: "An impartial analysis of the manner in which the Council has handled our repeated appeals for justice can only lead to one conclusion; namely, that A. F. of L. convention decisions and rulings pertaining to the work jurisdiction of our union were totally disregarded and the merits of our contentions completely ignored when our case was decided. By their refusal to abide by A. F. of L. convention decisions and rulings affecting our jurisdiction and to grant us the relief asked for, they once more placed their stamp of approval on the practice whereby thousands of our members are compelled to pay tribute to other A. F. of L. unions for the right to work at our trade."

When the Executive Council failed to make any adjustment for the Machinists, their officers voted to withhold their per capita payments to the Federation. The withholding of per capita began in November 1944 and subsequently was endorsed by the Machinists' convention.[33] The Machinists said that they would not return until the A. F. of L. by written notice accorded them jurisdiction over the erection and repair of machinery voted by the 1944 convention. They also demanded that the president of the A. F. of L. write to the officers of the Building and Construction Trades Department directing them to cease interfering with the right of the Machinists' Union to negotiate with employers over the terms of employment on such jobs.

The disaffiliation of the Machinists' Union from the A. F. of L. created a series of problems for the unions of the Metal Trades Department with which the union was affiliated. The officers of the Metals Trades Department feared that unless some systematic plan were devised, a number of its international unions might feel free to allow machinists to enter their membership, and inevitably cause confusion and conflict. The Executive Council of the A. F. of L. was requested to charter locals of machinists in federal labor unions, and to issue such charters with the guarantee that the International Association of Machinists would be required, as a condition of reaffiliation with the A. F. of L., to allow such federal locals of machinists to rejoin the International without discrimination or discipline of any kind.[34]

In January 1946 the Metal Trades Department instructed its Metal Trades Council to suspend all locals of the International Association of Machinists. The Metal Trades Department advised that wherever possible, however, locals of the Machinists' Union were to be allowed to participate in negotiations with employers and then sign a separate agreement. The dissociation of the International Association of Machinists from the A. F. of L. and the Metal Trades Department was not to be used "to place any difficulty in the matter of joint negotiating agreements with employers."[35]

Efforts to have the Machinists' Union reaffiliate with the A. F. of L. began almost immediately. After several conferences between the officers of the Machinists' Union and members of the Executive Council, two complaints of the Machinists were met; the A. F. of L. withdrew the letter stating that the Operating Engineers' Union had jurisdiction over ships on trial runs, and the Building and Construction Trades Department was instructed not to interfere in jurisdictional controversies involving unions not affiliated with the Department.[36] The Machinists were told that it would be easier to settle their differences with the Carpenters' Union if they were inside the A. F. of L. The Machinists' officers issued a statement to the membership without recommending reaffiliation. When the A. F. of L. sent out a circular giving its side of the story, President Harvey Brown informed members of his union that he was opposed to reaffiliation on the present terms.[37]

President A. J. Hayes, who succeeded Brown, and a group of union officers met with the Executive Council in February 1950. Hutcheson assured the meeting that the Carpenters' Union was willing to try to work out jurisdictional differences with any organization "on a sane basis." In turn, President Hayes assured the conference that the Machinists would make every effort to find a reasonable solution.[38] The A. F. of L. Executive Council was ready to invite the Machinists to reaffiliate with the same rights and obligations they had held before their separation from the A. F. of L. The Machinists' committee wanted assurances that the president of the A. F. of L. would be authorized to notify employers that the decision of the Building and Construction Trades Department was rendered without authority and was, therefore, null and void. It was agreed that Green would have the right to quote the decision of the A. F. of L. convention of 1941 to that effect.[39]

Green was authorized to invite the International Association of Machinists, and in the invitation he repeated the decision of the 1941 convention: "in the event . . . a ruling or decision thus rendered by the Department affects the jurisdictional right of an organization not affiliated to such Department, and not having previously agreed to such arrangement or procedure, direct or indirect, that such ruling or decision shall not be binding on a non-affiliated organization to the Department. In other words, the Department possesses no authority to render a decision in jurisdictional disputes between an affiliated and non-affiliated union to the Department, unless by agreement of all the unions involved."[40]

After an exchange of letters in which the terms of agreement for

reaffiliation were clarified, President A. J. Hayes and Secretary-Treasurer
Eric Peterson decided to recommend to their membership reaffiliation
of the Machinists' Union.[41] When the reaffiliation of the Machinists'
Union was discussed at the meeting of the Executive Council, Hutcheson
stated that he wanted the jurisdiction of the Machinists' Union clarified
before it reaffiliated.[42] The Machinists reaffiliated with the A. F. of L.
on January 1, 1951, and the jurisdictional dispute between the Machinists' and Carpenters' Unions was soon renewed. The Machinists, despair-
ing of favorable action by the Executive Council, took several cases to
the National Labor Relations Board. The Council regretted the action
of the Machinists' Union and tried to prevent their bringing disputes
involving other A. F. of L. unions to a government agency for settlement.
Although he refused to agree that his conduct was improper, President
Hayes was willing to try again for a settlement.[43]

The long controversy was finally settled by an agreement between
the two organizations under which the Carpenters' Union retained the
right to install and dismantle machinery and the Machinists' Union
was given the other disputed work. The agreement was made easier
by the retirement of William Hutcheson, who had fought the Machinists'
claims for more than forty years. His successor, Maurice A. Hutcheson,
was also insistent upon protecting the jurisdictional rights of his organization, but he was less determined to avoid any concession to other
labor groups.

### Joint Plans for Settlement of Jurisdictional Disputes

In the meantime, the unions of the building trades had established in
1947 a joint plan for the settling of jurisdictional disputes throughout
the industry. A voluntary board with Professor John T. Dunlop, chairman, was appointed in 1947. In 1954 the Executive Council established
a special Committee on Jurisdictional Disputes to formulate procedures
for settling jurisdictional disputes within the A. F. of L. President Meany,
Secretary-Treasurer Schnitzler, and Vice Presidents Charles J. MacGowan,
William C. Birthright, Daniel Tracy, George M. Harrison, and A. J.
Hayes were appointed to bring in the report, which was presented to
a special conference of officers of international unions in Chicago, Illinois,
on May 13, 1954. The plan was accepted.

The American Federation of Labor Internal Disputes plan was designed to prevent raiding among affiliates and to provide a method for
adjusting jurisdictional disputes with the A. F. of L. Only those national
and international unions which subscribed to the plan were obligated
to accept the decisions made under this arrangement. Whenever a
dispute occurred over jurisdiction between unions signatory to the plan,
they were obligated to seek a settlement by direct conference and nego-

tiation; the parties could call upon the head of the A. F. of L. for assistance as conciliator and he could act himself or through an appointee. If the parties had failed to agree ten days after they had called upon the A. F. of L. for assistance, the dispute was to be submitted to arbitration and the decision made final and binding.[44]

### REFERENCES

1. *Report of the Proceedings of the Thirty-third Annual Convention of the American Federation of Labor,* 1913, p. 327.

2. Minutes of Executive Council, April 20, 1933.

3. Minutes of Executive Council, April 24, 1933.

4. William Green and I. M. Ornburn to Joseph Obergfell, February 21, 1934.

5. Green to Obergfell, March 26, 1934.

6. Daniel Tobin to Green, April 30, 1934.

7. Green to Obergfell, May 15, 1934.

8. Minutes of Executive Council, May 11, 1934; Tobin to Green, May 15, 1934.

9. Green to Obergfell, March 7, 1936.

10. *Report of the Proceedings of the Fifty-seventh Annual Convention of the American Federation of Labor,* 1937, pp. 537–548.

11. Quote is from A. F. of L. brief in Obergfell *v.* Green, submitted to U.S. District Court in District of Columbia, December 7, 1937.

12. Opinion of Justice Goldsborough, October 6, 1939.

13. Decision of Circuit Court of Appeals in Obergfell *v.* Green, quoted in circular letter by William Green and George Meany, May 29, 1940.

14. Joseph J. Hansen, A. J. Kugler, and Joseph Obergfell to the Committee of the American Federation of Labor appointed by President William Green, to endeavor to find a basis of accommodation in the controversy between the Teamsters and Brewery Workers, November 13, 1939.

15. Joseph Obergfell to the Committee of the American Federation of Labor appointed by President Green, to endeavor to find a basis of accommodation in the controversy between the Teamsters and Brewery Workers, January 12, 1940.

16. Report on Teamster and Brewery Workers' controversy signed by Harry Stevenson, chairman, James Maloney, and W. C. Birthright. Minutes of Executive Council, February 9, 1940.

17. *Report of the Proceedings of the Sixty-first Annual Convention of the American Federation of Labor,* 1941, pp. 631–647.

18. Samuel Gompers to Honorable Woodrow Wilson, December 14, 1917.

19. Samuel Gompers to Honorable Woodrow Wilson, October 20, 1919.

20. Statement issued by Executive Council, February 25, 1922.

21. William Green to George W. Wickersham, February 1, 1930.

22. Statement of W. C. Roberts, legislative agent of the A. F. of L., before the Wickersham Committee.

23. *Report of the Proceedings of the Thirty-fourth Annual Convention of the American Federation of Labor,* 1914, p. 417.

24. *Report of the Proceedings of the Thirty-fifth Annual Convention of the American Federation of Labor,* 1915, p. 404.

25. Arthur Wharton to William Hutcheson, June 3, 1930, in undated memorandum for William Green.

26. Tentative understanding between the Carpenters' and Machinists' Unions, signed October 15, 1931. Also William Hutcheson to Arthur Wharton, May 2, 16, 24, 1931; Wharton to Hutcheson, May 12, 21, 1931.

27. Wharton to Green, July 24, 1933.

28. Hutcheson to Green, March 9, 1938; Green to Hutcheson, March 23, 1938.

29. *Report of the Proceedings of the Sixty-first Annual Convention of the American Federation of Labor,* 1941, pp. 518–521.

30. Minutes of Executive Council, January 15, 17, 1942.

31. *Report of the Proceedings of the Sixty-second Annual Convention of the American Federation of Labor,* 1942, pp. 469–480.

32. Harvey Brown to Green, May 20, 1943.

33. Brown to Green, November 29, 1945, February 6, 1946; Green to Brown, December 31, 1946.

34. *Minutes of the Executive Council of the Metal Trades Department of the American Federation of Labor,* January 21, 1944.

35. Quote in John Frey to local Metal Trades Council, February 7, 1946.

36. Green to Harvey Brown, August 1, 1947; Green to Brown and other members of Machinists' Executive Council, August 7, 1947.

37. Minutes of Executive Council, April 21, 1947.

38. Minutes of Executive Council, February 6, 1950.

39. Minutes of Executive Council, February 7, 1950.

40. The letter was approved by the Executive Council and sent by Green to A. J. Hayes, April 7, 1950.

41. Green to A. J. Hayes, June 8, 23, 1950; A. J. Hayes and Eric Peterson to Green, July 13, 1950.

42. Minutes of Executive Council, August 9, 1950.

43. Maurice A. Hutcheson to Green, May 9, 1952; Green to A. J. Hayes, February 15, 1952; Hayes to Green, February 28, 1952.

44. *Report of the Proceedings of the Seventy-third Convention of the American Federation of Labor,* 1954, pp. 61–67.

# XXXIV

## In Search of a United Labor Movement

At no time did the A. F. of L. accept the division in the ranks of labor as permanent.[1] In February 1939 President Rosevelt, in letters to the two labor federations, stressed the need for labor unity so that the organized workers' movement would be better able to serve the interests of its members and the country. He reminded the leaders of the "great variety of opportunities to be of service which will come to a united labor movement," and he urged unification because "your membership ardently desires peace and unity for the better ordering of their responsible life in the trade unions and in their communities, and . . . because the Government of the United States and the people of America believe it to be a wise and almost necessary step for the further development of the cooperation between free men in a democratic society such as ours."[2]

Green accepted the President's appeal and appointed Harry C. Bates, Matthew Woll, and Daniel Tobin to a negotiating committee; he informed the President that "thinking men and women . . . realized from the beginning that there was no place . . . for the establishment . . . of competing rival labor organizations. . . . Time has developed new complications which will now make it more difficult to establish a basis of accommodation and compose differences."[3] He also said that the A. F. of L. regarded the preservation of its democratic principles of "transcendent importance. . . . The economic and political philosophy evolved by the American Federation of Labor . . . cannot be compromised."[4]

John L. Lewis, Philip Murray, and Sidney Hillman represented the C.I.O. Roosevelt, opening the conference on March 7, hoped that the meeting marked the beginning of negotiations in good faith for the settlement of differences. He asked that both sides enter the negotiations with "open minds and with a determination to explore every aspect of the problem together."[5] Acting on the premise that both sides wanted peace, the President told the committees that he had received telegrams and letters from at least one million workers urging peace in the labor movement.

The A. F. of L. delegation presented a six-point program for achieving unity: (1) unions which had originally left the A. F. of L. would not apply for readmission until all matters affecting the newly organized

C.I.O. unions were settled; (2) a joint conference committee, representing both groups equally, would be established to work out jurisdictional differences; (3) when differences had been adjusted, all the C.I.O. unions, that is, the original group in the A. F. of L. and the unions since established, would enter the A. F. of L. simultaneously; (4) as soon as all issues were settled, the Executive Council would recommend an amendment to the A. F. of L. constitution to provide that an international union could be suspended or expelled by the Executive Council only upon direct instructions of a convention; (5) within sixty to ninety days after the adjustment of matters in dispute, a special convention of the A. F. of L. would be called with each organization entitled to representation with full rights and privileges; and (6) the A. F. of L. would specify certain industries in which the industrial form of organization would be effective.[6]

The C.I.O. program was much wider in scope: (1) a convention would be called not later than June 1, 1939, at which the unions of the A. F. of L., C.I.O., and railroad brotherhoods would be represented; (2) the convention would establish the American Congress of Labor designed to supersede the existing federations; (3) neither John L. Lewis nor William Green was to be eligible for any office, and the permanent officers of the A. F. of L., Green and Frank Morrison, were to be retired; (4) the governing body of the merged federation would be equally composed of members from the A. F. of L. and C.I.O., with the railroad brotherhoods being given proportional representation; (5) the United States Department of Labor would be used as an aid in mediating differences between the two federations; and (6) the President of the United States would be requested to preside at the sessions "of the unified ranks of labor, when its constituent representatives assemble for the purpose of stating objectives, electing officers, and adopting a constitution."[7]

The conferees met several times in March and April 1939 and adjourned when Lewis had to begin negotiating with the anthracite coal operators for a new contract. The national administration was anxious that peace negotiations between the two labor federations be resumed whenever possible, and Secretary of Labor Perkins communicated with Matthew Woll to find out what the wishes of the leaders of the A. F. of L. and C.I.O. were in the matter.[8] Following the postponement of the conferences, President Roosevelt conferred with William Green three times in an effort to find a basis for the resumption of negotiations. Green wanted to renew the talks but Lewis was unwilling. In September 1939 Roosevelt wrote to Green and again urged peace between the two labor federations; Lewis, however, remained adamant. At its meeting in October 1940 the Executive Council, after reviewing the efforts of President Roosevelt to promote peace in the labor movement and the refusal of the C.I.O. to discuss terms, asked that the facts be made public by President Roosevelt.[9] Secretary of Labor Perkins drew up a statement which President Roosevelt could have issued, but she advised against its release. It stated that the committees from the A. F. of L. and C.I.O. had met and adjourned in all friendliness, and that they would meet again at the call of Lewis.[10]

To meet a threat of a dual movement, the Council recommended to the 1940 convention changes in the constitution which would not allow the suspension of a national union by a majority vote of delegates at a convention, "except in cases where two or more national and international unions unite and conspire to create and launch an organization for any purpose dual to the American Federation of Labor. In that event, if two or more organizations conspire to create or form a dual movement to the American Federation of Labor, charges may be legally and properly filed against said organizations, a hearing held upon said charges, and if found guilty, said organizations may be suspended from affiliation with the American Federation of Labor by the Executive Council subject to appeal to the next annual convention of the American Federation of Labor." David Dubinsky, who headed the delegation from his union which had voted to reaffiliate with the A. F. of L. during that year, wanted unions suspended by the Executive Council to be entitled to full representation at the convention which would consider the suspension, but his proposal was not approved. The proposal of the Council was adopted.[11]

Addressing by letter the 1940 convention, President Roosevelt again asked for a reopening of peace negotiations between the two federations. The A. F. of L. stated its willingness to resume the conferences that had been suspended in the spring of 1939. In the meantime, important leadership changes had taken place in the C.I.O. John L. Lewis had decided to support Wendell Wilkie in his bid for the presidency of the United States, and in his appeal on behalf of Wilkie, Lewis promised to resign as head of the C.I.O. if the workers did not follow his advice. The C.I.O. met in convention after the reelection of President Roosevelt, and Lewis carried out his promise and refused to stand for reelection. A movement to draft him did not get off the ground. Instead, Philip Murray, vice president of the United Mine Workers of America and a close associate of Lewis, was elected to the presidency of the C.I.O.

No effort to reach a settlement was made through 1940 and 1941. In January 1942 in a letter to Green, Lewis said that the strength of organized labor in the United States was divided into "two great houses," and that both the A. F. of L. and the C.I.O. had demonstrated their capacity for survival. It was obvious to Lewis that

if accouplement could be achieved, with unified and competent leadership, the results would be advantageous and in the public interest. . . . Labor imperatively requires coherency, in order to give maximum assistance to the nation in its war effort to defend American liberties and American institutions. . . . If labor can compose its major internal problem, then the Government will be aided in the operation of its war economy and the membership of labor appreciably benefited. Every material conviction, which will be shared by every thoughtful citizen, that the leadership of labor should now accept the responsibility of this task, and in all good faith devote themselves to its solution.[12]

Although Lewis's initiative could have been regarded as a violation of the prerogatives which belonged to Philip Murray, his invitation was welcomed by William Hutcheson, who had been chosen to replace Woll on the A. F. of L. committee to negotiate with the C.I.O. George Harrison's motion to enlarge the committee from three to five members was defeated by a vote of 4 to 5.[13] Harry Bates, Hutcheson, and Tobin, who comprised the A. F. of L. negotiating committee, stood ready to meet with a delegation from the C.I.O. Frank Duffy, secretary of the Carpenters' Union, wanted Green to ask President Roosevelt to call for conferences between the two organizations.[14] Green was hopeful that he would soon have an opportunity to discuss labor unity with President Roosevelt. The speed with which negotiations were being promoted did not satisfy Hutcheson, who now was anxious to have Lewis rejoin the A. F. of L. When he asked Green to give the matter his immediate attention, Green replied that he had suggested to President Roosevelt that he convene a meeting of representatives of the two organizations.[15]

President Roosevelt was not anxious, at this time, to call together the representatives of the two labor federations. The anxiety of Hutcheson, who was a Republican, to have Lewis reenter the A. F. of L. was in part a manifestation of his desire to block the pro-New Deal influences within the Federation and the Executive Council. The Combined Labor War Board, which met periodically with Roosevelt and which had representatives of both the A. F. of L. and the C.I.O. in its membership would in Roosevelt's view be the medium for a resumption of peace negotiations. Hutcheson wanted to know whether the periodic meetings with the President and representatives of the C.I.O. constituted a "Peace Committee." Green was finally forced to say that he did not believe President Roosevent had "given any consideration to the composition of peace committees which may represent the American Federation of Labor and the C.I.O. in peace negotiations. I base this opinion on the fact that at no time did the President ever suggest who the committee should be, how said committee should be constituted or how they should be selected as representatives of the American Federation of Labor and the C.I.O. in peace negotiations."[16] When the Executive Council considered the exchange of correspondence between Green and Hutcheson, as well as the failure of President Roosevelt to summon a peace conference between the two organizations, George Meany suggested that the A. F. of L. issue a statement indicating its long desire for unity of the labor movement.[17]

Following the adjournment of the Executive Council, Green proposed to Murray a meeting of committees representing both organizations to seek a basis for establishing peace and unity within the labor movement of the United States and Canada. A committee from the A. F. of L., he told Murray, stood ready to meet with a committee representing the C.I.O. for the purpose of "exploring the possibilities of labor peace and the establishment of unity and solidarity within the ranks of labor."[18]

Murray replied with a copy of the resolution of the C.I.O. Executive Board on this question, adopted on June 3. The resolution pointed to the need for labor unity as a means of promoting the war effort and requested the Combined Labor War Board to issue a call for a "Win the War" conference of the affiliates of the A. F. of L. and the C.I.O. The conference would discuss methods for increasing war production, for supporting candidates who backed President Roosevelt and the war effort, and for gaining increased labor participation in the administrative and executive branches of the government. For establishing labor unity, Murray proposed that the Executive Councils of the C.I.O. and the A. F. of L. jointly set up a United National Labor Council to develop a concrete program of labor unity. "Through this unity under the National Labor Council, an increasing mutual confidence will be developed between the several National and International unions of the C.I.O. and the A. F. of L. On this firm basis, discussions can then be encouraged by the United National Labor Council between A. F. of L. and C.I.O. unions having similar jurisdiction, looking toward organic unity."[19]

The A. F. of L. Executive Council believed that the C.I.O. had failed to answer directly its request for a resumption of peace negotiations. Green informed Murray that the Combined Labor War Board had been created for the purpose of promoting the war effort, and the A. F. of L. regarded that agency as adequate and effective for this purpose.[20] In August 1942 Murray suggested that the A. F. of L. and C.I.O. establish "a committee from both organizations, with an impartial arbitrator, to which shall be submitted all jurisdictional disputes which may arise between us. Pending a decision by such committee, there shall be no stoppage of work."[21] Murray believed that increased cooperation between the two federations would inevitably be a prelude to organic unity. Green immediately accepted the invitation and in a statement said that Murray's letter proposing a settlement of jurisdictional disputes constituted an official accepance by the C.I.O. of the A. F. of L.'s proposal that conferences be resumed to seek a basis "for establishing peace and unity in the labor movement."[22]

In the meantime, differences over jurisdiction were being raised by officers of both the A. F. of L. and the C.I.O. as a reason for proceeding slowly with negotiations. On August 12, Green sharply criticized Murray for attacking the A. F. of L. because of its toleration of jurisdictional raids. Green told Murray that the record shows "numerous stoppages are taking place at plants where C.I.O. organizations function. We are not advertising that fact to the public. In fact, we are bending every effort possible to prevent stoppages and to carry out the no-strike pledge made to the President of the United States. The enemies of organized labor are continually advertising stoppages of work, slight as they may be or extended as they may become. . . . I do not believe that any good purpose will be served, particularly now when attempts are being made to resume peace negotiations, by giving publicity to criticism of either the American Federation of Labor or the C.I.O. because of local stoppages."[23]

Because the Metal Trades Department of the A. F. of L. was fearful that its interests would be neglected by the negotiating committee, it asked for two members of unions affiliated with the Metal Trades Department to be appointed to the committee meeting with the C.I.O.[24] Early in December 1942, Stabilization Director James Byrnes called a meeting between the A. F. of L. and C.I.O. representatives of unions employed in the shipyards and other plants producing war goods. He hoped that an agreement might be reached to avoid jurisdictional disputes in the industries vital to war production. Van Bittner, Del Garst, and John Green represented the C.I.O., and William Masterson, Harvey Brown, and Charles MacGowan represented respectively the Plumbers', Machinists', and Boiler Makers' Unions. Brown took exception to a statement made by the "peace committee" that differences over jurisdiction would be submitted to a joint committee, and the failure of such a committee to reach an agreement would be followed by the appointment of an arbitrator by the President of the United States. Brown said he was not in favor of this kind of policy and that his union would not subscribe to it. MacGowan, on the other hand, believed that if the war effort was strongly supported, the action of the peace committee, which meant an armistice on jurisdictional warfare at least for the duration of the conflict, would have to be accepted. All the executives of the metal trades' unions of the A. F. of L. were united in wanting someone from their organizations on the peace committee.[25]

In spite of the objections of the Metal Trades Department, the following agreement was negotiated on December 2, 1942:

The A. F. of L. and C.I.O. committee, in an effort to make its maximum contribution to our country in the war and for the furtherance and protection of the conditions of the workers, . . . agreed upon the following:

We are convinced that if peace negotiations are to be successful and unity achieved, cooperation among our respective members and organizations must be encouraged and promoted. It is our belief that it would be extremely difficult to make satisfactory progress toward unity through these negotiations if in the meantime there is an absence of practical cooperation between the two organizations.

We agree to the establishment of a joint A. F. of L.-C.I.O. committee to hear and decide any disputed jurisdictional differences that may arise between the two above named organizations. If the joint committee fails to agree upon a complaint lodged with the committee, it shall select a disinterested arbiter to render a decision on the dispute in question. The arbiter's decision shall be final and binding on both parties. In the event an arbiter cannot be agreed upon by the committee within five days, the President of the United States shall be requested to name an arbiter. We recommend that this understanding shall remain in force until labor unity is effected. The agreement is subject to the approval of the Executive Councils of the two organizations.

The agreement was signed by Bates, Hutcheson, and Tobin for the A. F. of L., and Philip Murray, R. J. Thomas, and Julius Emspak for the C.I.O. An off-the-record understanding was that "no grant of authority shall be vested in an arbiter selected by the A. F. of L.-C.I.O. joint committee, or an arbiter named by the President of the United States to deal with any subject affecting the rights of a labor union or an individual worker under existing law."[26]

Several presidents of A. F. of L. affiliates complained of raiding by the C.I.O. Green defended the peace agreement as a necessary prelude to "unity within the labor movement. We cannot discuss peace while we are at war. An armistice must be declared. We believe this can be done through an agreement which will provide that neither side will engage in raiding tactics pending final action by the two committees representing the American Federation of Labor and the C.I.O. upon the question of organic unity."[27]

Continual raiding was the basic reason why the A. F. of L. leaders were convinced that the C.I.O. did not desire peace and unity. Testifying before the committee investigating military policies and procurement, headed by Senator Harry Truman, Green challenged the C.I.O. to end its encroachments upon existing unions. Green believed that where a union was established and held an agreement with a company, another organization of labor should not seek to displace it as a bargaining agent, irrespective of that particular union's affiliation.[28] The failure of the C.I.O. to stop its efforts to win over workers already belonging to A. F. of L. unions was, according to Vice President Harry Bates, the primary cause for the failure of the A. F. of L. to appoint a committee to settle jurisdictional disputes. Bates was sure that if a clear-cut, no-raiding policy were announced, the A. F. of L. would immediately appoint representatives to serve on the joint committee with members of the C.I.O. for the settling of jurisdictional disputes. He sought to have the C.I.O. agree to the following announcement: "It is the unanimous policy of the (joint) committee to pursue its object, namely labor unity, that there will be no raiding by the A. F. of L. where the C.I.O. has a contract or has won a representation election and in turn there will be no raiding by the C.I.O. where the A. F. of L. has a contract or has won a representation election."[29]

Following the C.I.O. rejection of the first proposal, the A. F. of L. delegation proposed that the "A. F. of L. and C.I.O. Peace Committee . . . agree that as a matter of policy . . . raiding between the organizations shall cease and the jurisdiction committee shall proceed to function as soon as possible." The C.I.O. countered by asking that the railway brotherhoods be included in the negotiations, but the A. F. of L. would "under no circumstances agree to such a proposal."[30] The A. F .of L. was willing to meet and try to work out a nonraiding agreement, but the Executive Council insisted that before any committee on jurisdiction met with the C.I.O. some agreement had to be reached on general policy.

Finally, the Executive Council reaffirmed the view expressed in the resolution submitted by Vice President George Harrison at its meeting in January 1943, "that to pursue the objectives that our committee sought it . . . [should] be the policy of the A. F. of L. not to undertake to raid C.I.O. unions where they hold bargaining rights and that we [should] pursue the same objective under this agreement in trying to prevent the C.I.O. from raiding the A. F. of L. unions where they hold bargaining rights, and that our committee [should] pursue the objective in further relations with the committee."[31]

Little effort was made to carry on serious negotiations until 1947. On December 5, 1946 Murray warned Green of the concerted attack upon labor being planned by large business. He believed that only by the united action of the A. F. of L., the C.I.O., and the railway brotherhoods could the labor movement achieve a common legislative and economic program and repel the onslaught directed against its interest and welfare.[32]

The Executive Council regarded Murray's warning as a different type of proposal from the one he had made in December 1944 when he called for cooperation of the two federations in legislative matters. Green had denounced that proposal as "phony" and as a "flat refusal on the part of the C.I.O. to accept the American Federation of Labor's appeal for resumption of conferences seeking a united labor movement in America."[33]

Dubinsky was critical of Murray's proposals, although he repeated that he had always favored organic unity. Dubinsky suspected that Murray's letter was the work of Communists within the C.I.O. He noted the Communist Party had just called for the "widest joint action of the C.I.O.,

A. F. of L., and the Railroad Brotherhoods everywhere at every level."[34] Green accepted Murray's invitation on the condition that the only aim of the conference would be to achieve a unified labor movement. William Green, George Meany, William L. Hutcheson, Daniel Tobin, and John L. Lewis, who had rejoined the A. F. of L. in 1946, were the A. F. of L. conferees. Philip Murray, Walter Reuther, Jacob Potofsky, Emil Rieve, and Albert J. Fitzgerald represented the C.I.O.

Early in the conference, the A. F. of L. offered the following proposals: (1) the national unions of the C.I.O. would reenter the A. F. of L. on the same basis that the United Mine Workers of America entered, that is, as they were organized with their full membership; (2) this "jointure would be complete and effective as of the date of the October Constitutional Convention of the A. F. of L., with full privileges and participation by the delegates from the now existing C.I.O. national unions; (3) the joint committee of ten would be continued for the purpose of adjusting details and making recommendations on all recurring matters of importance; and (4) the resources of the two organizations would be pooled so that they could be used more effectively in defense of the labor movement. The Federation's plan was rejected by the C.I.O. delegation, who offered a program of "functional unity to fight antilabor legislation, and deferred all concrete steps on the merger."[35]

After the enactment of the Taft-Hartley law, Murray, on behalf of the Executive Board of the C.I.O., again urged that the A. F. of L., the C.I.O., and the Railroad Brotherhoods formulate a joint program for the protection of the labor movement. Rejecting Murray's proposal, Green asked that the committees from the two federations meet once more to seek a formula for labor unity. Since no agreement could be reached on the scope of a joint meeting or of the organizations which were to be invited, no meeting was held.[36] Murray periodically made the same request for a common defense against the attacks of opponents of organized labor; and his suggestions were just as regularly rejected.[37] For Green, the A. F. of L. would not collaborate with the C.I.O. along "political or any other lines," except on the basis of organic unity.[38]

In the meantime, closer cooperation between sections of the A. F. of L. and C.I.O. was on the increase. Local groups affiliated with both federations were able to work out joint policies on some special or general problem. An important step toward labor unity on a national basis was the cooperation of the A. F. of L. and C.I.O. in the launching of the International Confederation of Free Trade Unions in November 1949. The ousting of the Communist unions from the C.I.O. in 1949 was also a favorable step toward unity. Moreover, to devise a basis for participation of both the A. F. of L. and C.I.O., discussions between representatives of the two federations were held in Washington on April 28, 1949, at which methods of representation on various executive bodies and committees of the ICFTU were agreed upon. On April 4, 1950 Murray asked the A. F. of L., the Railway Brotherhoods, the United Mine Workers of America, and several other unaffiliated unions to meet the challenge of the "reactionary forces" which were in his opinion then in the ascendancy. Murray thought that the ideal way to meet this threat was through organic unity, but until that was achieved, it would be necessary for organized labor to marshal its strength through the existing "organizational structure." Therefore, he called for the establishment of a joint standing committee which could provide the needed leadership.[39]

Before the meeting of the A. F. of L. Executive Council in May, Murray told Green, in a conference of the two, that steps ought to be taken "toward blending all unions into one organization." Murray wanted to include the United Mine Workers in the blend. At the Executive Council meeting, Woll, Meany, and Charles MacGowan drew up the reply which informed Murray that the A. F. of L. was ready to begin discussions on a program for uniting the two federations.[40] Tobin, MacGowan, and Daniel Tracy were appointed to meet the C.I.O. committee which was led by Murray and included eight other members.[41]

After the July 25 meeting, the committees issued a statement pledging both federations to cooperate in the international field and in the areas of domestic legislation and political action—an important step forward in the development of unity. On the following day, Allan Haywood of the C.I.O. and MacGowan of the A. F. of L. were appointed a subcommittee to summarize the discussions and agreements of the larger group. Haywood wanted Lewis to be invited to the negotiations, but MacGowan said the A. F. of L. Executive Council had limited the discussions to representatives of the A. F. of L. and C.I.O. MacGowan spoke to Murray on the organizations to be included, and Murray strongly urged that an invitation be extended to Lewis; MacGowan insisted he was bound by the orders of the Executive Council. Murray, because of his prior invitation to Lewis and other heads of unaffiliated unions, claimed that he was embarrassed by his inability to ask Lewis to attend the discussions of the negotiating committees. MacGowan said that the A. F. of L. as a federated body had no objection to meeting with the C.I.O., another federated body, but the A. F. of L. did not want to meet with individual international unions. At MacGowan's suggestion, the committee to negotiate with the C.I.O. was enlarged to nine members.[42]

For two years, unity negotiations were at a standstill. In September 1952 Lewis, seeking to initiate a new movement, asked the A. F. of L. convention to designate representatives for a meeting with a variety of labor organizations. Green was ready to appoint a committee in accordance with Lewis's suggestion. Vice President James Petrillo opposed any meeting with Lewis, and Meany recalled the Federation's earlier stand that it would not negotiate with single unions on this question. The Council supported Meany and Petrillo. The convention of 1952 expressed the willingness of the A. F. of L. to resume negotiations with the C.I.O.[43]

In November 1952 the A. F. of L. unity committee was reactivated. The deaths of Murray and Green placed the negotiations in the hands of their respective successors, Reuther and Meany. The first meeting was held in Washington on April 7, 1953. The A. F. of L. was represented by nine members of the Executive Council, and the C.I.O. sent eleven officers to the meeting. The conference appointed a subcommittee of three members from each federation to study the raiding problem and attempt to devise an agreement. Meany, Woll, and William F. Schnitzler represented the A. F. of L., and Reuther, James Carey, and David J. McDonald represented the C.I.O.

On May 4, 1953 the subcommittee studied the outcome of representation elections held by the National Labor Relations Board in 1951 and 1952 and found that the great majority of raids initiated by A. F. of L. or C.I.O. unions were unsuccessful and that the net result was only a change of affiliation in less than 2 per cent of the cases. In this survey of raiding, the committee showed that 1,245 elections had been held in 1951–1952 in which 366,470 employees were involved. In these elections the union which filed the petition was able to gain certification as the bargaining representative for approximately 62,000 employees, or 17 per cent of the number involved. Of the 62,000 employees, 35,000 were won from a C.I.O. union by a union affiliated with the A. F. of L., and 27,000 workers were gained by a C.I.O. union from an A. F. of L. union. The net change was about 8,000 employees, or 2 per cent of the workers involved. The full committee, on the basis of these facts, as well as its independent observations, was convinced that mutual raiding was unprofitable to the unions and harmful to the workers and the labor organizations. Therefore, the full committee concluded that it would be desirable for the unions of both federations to adopt a no-raiding policy:

(1) Both the American Federation of Labor and the Congress of Industrial Organization should adopt as a fundamental policy of both federations this principle: No union affiliated with either federation shall attempt to organize or to represent employees as to whom an established bargaining relationship exists between their employer and a union in the other federation.

(2) This fundamental policy should be incorporated into the "no raiding" agreement . . . entered into between the American Federation of Labor and its affiliates and the Congress of Industrial Organization and its affiliates.

(3) Each federation should urge that its affiliated unions subscribe and become parties to this "no-raiding" agreement.

Although the A. F. of L. could not compel its international unions to accept the proposal, the Joint Committee urged the unions to subscribe to the arrangement. Differences were to be settled in conference between the parties in a dispute, and an impartial umpire was authorized to settle all disputes that could not be settled by the parties themselves.[44]

The no-raiding agreement came before the Executive Council on August 11, 1953 and it ran into the opposition of Vice President William Hutcheson, who argued that the A. F. of L. should put its own house in order before it tried to work out friendly arrangements with the C.I.O. He seemed especially irked by the failure of the Council to settle a jurisdictional dispute in the building-construction industry where his union functioned. Meany reminded the Council of its endorsement of the no-raiding principle at its May meeting and said that only approval of the final form of the arrangement was necessary at the time. He emphasized that the agreement had to be approved by the convention and that only the unions accepting it were obligated to obey its provisions. Meany discussed the renewal of serious discussions with the C.I.O. on unifying the labor movement and said that the no-raiding agreement was the first and necessary step to achieve this goal. As for internal disputes—jurisdictional differences between unions in the A. F. of L.—Meany told Hutcheson that the agreement had nothing to do with them. He thought that the unity discussions would end if the no-raiding agreement was rejected by the Council.

Harrison suggested that the no-raiding agreement include railroad workers and federal employees who had not been included, and with these changes the agreement was adopted over Hutcheson's objections. After the adoption of the agreement, Vice President Doherty asked for a reconsideration of the motion, and on the next day, August 12, the agreement was again discussed. The members of the Council wanted Hutcheson to reconsider his opposition, so that the Council could report approval of the no-raiding agreement by a unanimous vote. Hutcheson refused to go along and announced that the president of the Carpenters' Union, Maurice Hutcheson, who had become president upon the retirement of his father, Vice President William Hutcheson, would not approve the agreement. Meany, insisting that the no-raiding agreement was a simple arrangement, said that it was based on the Federation's philosophy of voluntarism.[45]

On the afternoon of August 12, Meany received a letter from Maurice Hutcheson in which he referred to the Executive Council's failure to take action in the jurisdictional disputes which had arisen in the Building and Construction Trades Department. Such failure, Hutcheson said, indicated that the officers of the A. F. of L. were more concerned with "the affairs of the C.I.O. than they were with those of the Federation."[46] Although he did not explicitly object to the no-raiding agreement, Hutcheson doubted the wisdom of his organization continuing to pay per capita tax to the A. F. of L., and therefore announced the withdrawal of his union.

In announcing its withdrawal, the Carpenters' Union was following a long-time policy of threatening the A. F. of L. whenever decisions disapproved by the officers of the Carpenters' Union were made. Although such threats had always frightened William Green during his tenure as president of the Federation, Meany refused to be alarmed; instead he announced that a vacancy existed on the Executive Council and took steps to disaffiliate locals of the Carpenters' Union from A. F. of L. central bodies. Meany decided to call the bluff of the Carpenters' organization, which in the past had been able to have its way on virtually every issue. Harry Bates of the Bricklayers' Union, soon after the adjournment of the Council meeting, brought the heads of the A. F. of L. and the Carpenters' Union together. Meany, Schnitzler, Bates, Daniel Tracy, and W. C. Doherty conferred with President Hutcheson and several members of the executive board of his union. They agreed that more effort would be directed to settling disputes between A. F. of L. unions and that the Carpenters would rejoin the Federation.[47]

George Lynch, the president of the Pattern Makers' League of North America, led a committee from the Metal Trades Department before the Executive Council to protest the no-raiding pact. Lynch believed that the agreement represented a change in A. F. of L. policy, inasmuch as it would force unions to accept adjudication of their differences. Such a policy, Lynch held, violated the principle of voluntarism.[48] Lynch was advised to take his complaint to the convention. However, no objection to the agreement was made before the 1953 convention, and the delegates agreed that the arrangement was "the first and indispensable step toward the achievement of organic unity between the American Federation of Labor and the Congress of Industrial Organizations; that its terms and purposes are in the best interests of the American Federation of Labor, its affiliates and the labor movement as a whole."[49]

Both federations endorsed the no-raiding proposals, and the officers were directed to seek authorizations from the single unions accepting the agreement, as the no-raiding agreement was binding only upon those unions which endorsed it. On June 5, 1954 the meeting of the A. F. of L.–C.I.O. Unity Committee was told that sixty-five unions of the A. F. of L. and twenty-nine of the C.I.O. had signed the no-raiding pact. The Committee believed that the agreement was a step toward a united labor movement; that it represented a "cease-fire" arrangement. The Joint A. F. of L.–C.I.O. Unity Committee decided to spend the next two years examining the differences between the two federations and in working out the manifold problems standing in the way of unity. In accordance with the no-raiding agreement, David L. Cole was appointed as official umpire to decide all unresolved differences.

On October 15, 1954 the A. F. of L.–C.I.O. Unity Committee appointed a subcommittee made up of Meany, Schnitzler, and Bates for the A. F. of L., and Reuther, James B. Carey, and David J. McDonald of the C.I.O. Meetings were held in January and February 1955, at which Albert Woll and Arthur Goldberg, counsel respectively for the A. F. of L. and C.I.O., were present. At the meeting on February 9, the subcommittee arrived at an agreement in principle. The full committee met later in the day and agreed to accept the plan worked out by the subcommittee. The Merger Agreement was signed on February 9, 1955.

The Merger Agreement provided for the recognition of both craft and industrial unions, and the right "of each national and international union, federal labor union, local industrial union, and organizing committee holding a charter or certificate of affiliation" from either federation to enter the newly formed American Federation of Labor–Congress of Industrial Organizations. President George Meany and Secretary-Treasurer William F. Schnitzler were selected for the same posts in the merged organization, and membership on the Executive Council was allotted upon the basis of the respective membership of the two federations. The assets of the federations were pooled. The last convention of the A. F. of L. was held in New York on December 1 and 2, 1955, at which the merger was ratified. The A. F. of L. had completed seventy-five years of existence.

### REFERENCES

1. The various attempts at unity and its eventual consummation are dealt with in Arthur J. Goldberg, *AFL-CIO Labor United* (New York: McGraw-Hill Book Company, Inc., 1956).

2. Franklin D. Roosevelt to William Green, February 23, 1939.

3. William Green to President Franklin Roosevelt, February 24, 1939.

4. *Ibid.*

5. *The New York Times*, March 8, 1939.

6. *American Federation of Labor Weekly News Service*, March 18, 1939.

7. *The New York Times*, March 8, 1939.

8. Memorandum of a telephone conversation between Matthew Woll and Secretary of Labor Frances Perkins, April 10, 1939.

9. Statement by the Executive Council of the American Federation of Labor, February 8, 1940.

10. Memorandum from Secretary of Labor Perkins to President Roosevelt, Official File 142, Box 1, Franklin Delano Roosevelt Library.

11. *Report of the Proceedings of the Sixtieth Annual Convention of the American Federation of Labor*, 1940., pp. 447–460.

12. John L. Lewis to William Green, January 17, 1942.

13. Minutes of Executive Council, January 17, 1942.

14. Frank Duffy to Green, February 25, 1942; Green to Duffy, March 3, 1942, contains quote.

15. Hutcheson to Green, March 9, 1942; Green to Hutcheson, March 13, 1942.

16. Quote in Green to Hutcheson, March 28, 1942, in reply to letter of Hutcheson to Green, March 20, 1942.

17. Minutes of Executive Council, May 22, 1942.

18. Green to Murray, May 23, 1942.

19. Murray to Green, June 6, 1942.

20. Green to Murray, June 23, 1942.

21. Murray to Green, August 1, 1942.

22. Statement of William Green, August 4, 1942.

23. Green to Murray, August 12, 1942.

24. John Frey to William Green, December 4, 1942.

25. *Minutes of the Executive Council of the Metal Trades Department of the A. F. of L.*, December 7, 1942.

26. Agreement signed by Peace Committee representing A. F. of L. and C.I.O., December 2, 1942.

27. Green to William Schoenberg, March 1, 1943. Complaints of raiding by the C.I.O. were made at this time by (among others) Harry Stevenson, head of the Molders' Union, January 13, 1943; H. W. Brown, president of the Machinists' Union, February 13, 1943; and Edward Flore, president of Hotel and Restaurant Employees' Union, February 15, 1943.

28. *American Federation of Labor Weekly News Service*, March 30, 1943.

29. Minutes of Executive Council, May 21, 1943.

30. *Ibid.*

31. *Ibid.*

32. Philip Murray to William Green, December 5, 1946.

33. Statement of William Green, December 8, 1944.

34. David Dubinsky to William Green, December 10, 1946.

35. *American Federation of Labor Weekly News Service*, May 2, 1947.

36. Philip Murray to Green, July 2, 1946; Green to Murray, July 16, 1947.

37. Green to Murray, February 28, 1948; Murray to Green, December 15, 1948.

38. Minutes of Executive Council, October 2, 1949.

39. Murray to Green, April 4, 1950.

40. Minutes of Executive Council, May 8, 11, 1950; Green to Murray, May 8, 1950.

41. L. S. Buckmaster of the Rubber Workers' Union; James Carey, International Union of Electrical, Radio, and Machine Workers; Joseph Curran, National Maritime Union; Allan Haywood, Vice President and Director of Organization; Walter Reuther, United Automobile Workers; Emil Rieve, Textile Workers' Union of America; and Frank Rosenblum, Amalgamated Clothing Workers.

42. Memorandum on Meeting of Sub-Committee on Agenda—A. F. of L.-C.I.O. from Charles J. MacGowan to D. J. Tobin and Daniel Tracy, July 31, 1950.

43. John L. Lewis to Green, September 15, 1952; Green to Lewis, September 16, 1952; Minutes of Executive Council, September 24, 1952.

44. *Report of the Proceedings of the Seventy-second Convention of the American Federation of Labor,* 1953, pp. 82–89.

45. Minutes of Executive Council, August 11, 12, 1953.

46. M. A. Hutcheson to Meany, August 12, 1953.

47. Minutes of Executive Council, August 12, 13, 14, and September 20, 1953.

48. Minutes of Executive Council, September 20, 1953.

49. *Report of the Proceedings of the Seventy-second Convention of the American Federation of Labor,* 1953, p. 635.

# Index

490

498